DOMESDAY BOOK

Index of Subjects

History from the Sources

DOMESDAY BOOK

A Survey of the Counties of England

LIBER DE WINTONIA

Compiled by direction of

KING WILLIAM I

Winchester
1086

DOMESDAY BOOK

38

Index of Subjects

J. D. Foy

PHILLIMORE
Chichester
1992

1992

Published by

PHILLIMORE & CO. LTD.
Shopwyke Hall, Chichester, Sussex

© J. D. Foy, 1992

ISBN 0 85033 704 6

Printed and bound in Great Britain by
Bookcraft (Bath) Ltd.

Publisher's Note

Medieval cathedrals often took so long to build that their completion ceremonies looked back not only to the long-departed original architect but to one or two of his successors who also failed to survive until the 'topping out'. Dr. John Morris approached Phillimore, in 1969, with a proposal that the entire text of Domesday Book should be translated afresh into modern English to provide the first ever uniform English version, free from the inconsistencies and transliterations of the mainly Victorian translations that impeded research and comparative study. With the help of such scholars as Herbert Finberg, W. G. Hoskins, Vivian Galbraith and John Dodgson, the work was begun in 1970 but, seven years later, with only half a dozen counties completed, Dr. Morris tragically died at the early age of sixty. Professor Dodgson took over and saw the whole translation – and the rapidly growing apparatus of notes – through to completion, co-ordinating what had now become a team of around forty scholars engaged on the project. The county-by-county edition was finished in time for the Domesday Ninth Centenary celebrations of 1986, and Dodgson turned his attention to the 'cumulative' index and analysis that had been discussed since 1970 but could now begin in earnest with considerable input from Dr. John Palmer of the Hull University Domesday Project. John Dodgson died, sadly, in 1990 with the Persons and Places parts just completed in respect of his personal input. J. D. Foy, working independently, had by then finalised his great subject index in typescript.

The magnitude of their achievement earns increasing recognition with every year that passes and for decades to come historians and students will have cause to recall Morris's inspiration and Dodgson's industry. Like most pioneers they suffered from critics and detractors, ranging from the first question asked by the then chairman of Phillimore, in 1969, 'but surely anyone working on Domesday is able to cope with medieval calligraphy and abbreviated Latin?' to 'why are they wanting to change the translation on which I've based my lectures for the past 30 years?'. But they persisted and, in the end, prevailed. They made our greatest public record reliably and cheaply available for the first time since 1986 and, with their unique three-part Index, provided the first comprehensive apparatus to meet the needs of serious study and historical research. Their publisher is proud to have worked with them and to have seen their scholarly edifice constructed to stand as an enduring monument to their memory.

Introduction

The publication of the complete Domesday Book in parallel Latin text and English translation under the general editorship of Dr. John Morris, is the occasion for the issue of the present Index which attempts to provide comprehensive coverage of Great and Little Domesday. Some additional material supplied from the 'Satellites' is also indexed.

The referencing system adopted for the Morris Edition whereby every separate holding has an individual reference number, as well as the general consistency of translation, permits a precision of coverage not previously possible.

This Index (which can also be used by those without access to the Morris Edition, as will be explained below) has been compiled on the following principles:

1. To conform with the Indices of Persons and Places, entries are put in alphabetical order of Counties of which there is a table, with the County abbreviations used, at the beginning of this volume.

2. The text has been indexed strictly according to what it appears to say, without any attempt to supply an editorial gloss or to give the text a meaning which it does not literally express.

3. An endeavour has been made to index every item except pounds ('librae'), shillings ('solidi'), and pence ('denarii'). Hides, carucates and sulungs are only indexed when they appear in Counties other than those where they are the usual unit of measurement or assessment. Hundred and Wapentake rubrics are not indexed.

4. The English renderings used in the Morris Edition have been used throughout with only minor exceptions of which the most common are the use of 'TRE' ('in the time of King Edward') instead of 'before 1066', and the use of 'render' instead of 'payment' for the giving of objects, 'payment' being reserved for money.

5. Items which are found only in the Satellites are printed in italics in the reference number column of the Index. The entries themselves will be found either in small print in the translation of the Morris Edition (in the case of Exon Domesday) and/or in the notes and Appendices to the relevant volumes. 'Satellites' are the various associated texts (of which Exon [Exeter] Domesday is a prime example) which are generally considered to have had a contemporary, or near contemporary, relationship with Domesday.

The following points should be borne in mind:

Categories

A few general headings have been included to help identify items of related interest. These have been drawn in fairly wide terms and are as follows:

Agriculture
Animals
Commodities
Ecclesiastical matters
Historical events
Legal and social matters
Military matters
Narrative entries
Occupations
Persons – classes
Resources
Taxation
Transferability
Urban affairs
Weights and measures

Comparative information

Certain entries contain comparative information ('Plough' and 'Value' for example). These items are particularly capable of different interpretations (the number of oxen to a plough is crucial in some cases) but the analyses are substantially correct. The expression 'TRE' in these entries does not necessarily refer to King Edward's time in all cases: a later date can often be involved.

Where the number of ploughlands ('land for x ploughs') is compared with the number of hides, carucates or sulungs, the comparison is with the number of hides, or other assessment, in 1086 if that is given in the Domesday entry; otherwise with the number TRE. A hide is assumed to contain 120 acres and a plough team 8 oxen, assumptions which are almost certainly wrong in some cases. A carucate is assumed to contain 8 bovates.

No comparative data has been given for animals, although Essex, in particular, contains such information.

Narrative entries

There are a few entries which present an extended narrative of events and whilst the subject matter of such entries is included in the appropriate place or places, it has been thought useful to highlight a selection of such entries under this heading.

Persons and places

In general, matters are not indexed which occur in the Indices of Persons and Places. The main exceptions are Boroughs and Cities named as such; occupations (which include occupational names which may be doing duty as surnames); thanes and other classes of persons; family relationships (sons etc.); clergy below the office of Bishop or Abbot/Abbess; and the holdings of named women. In this last case it is often difficult, if not impossible, to be certain whether a personal name is masculine or feminine ('Goda' is an example) and the user must be prepared to disagree with some of the Indexer's identifications. When tracing every reference to a particular subject (burgesses or sheriff for example) account should be taken of sub-entries which are not invariably included in the opening general item of enumeration.

Shire

'Shire' ('scira/scyra') has been indexed as 'County' throughout, although under the head 'Shire' will be found every reference to the occurrence of that word in Domesday. In some contexts the meaning is probably 'County Court' but as Domesday does not differentiate in terminology between 'County' and 'County Court', the latter expression is not indexed here. Similarly with 'Hundred'.

Transferability

This details the headings covering the cases where landholders had the ability to depart from their lord and/or their land – an ability expressed in a great variety of formulae which have been followed in the Index.

TRE and 1086

Subject to the qualifications noted with regard to Comparative Information, unless an entry specifically refers to TRE or 1086 it should be assumed that the matter referred to may relate to either or both periods. Similarly 'King' may be either King Edward or King William or both.

Variants

There are a few cases where the Latin text may bear a meaning other than that given in the Morris Edition translation, or where the translation has departed from its usual rendering. In such cases the Index silently effects the change, or may index under all alternative meanings or forms. For example 'Quarter' ('ferlingus') in Sussex and Hampshire is rendered 'furlong' elsewhere and is indexed under both 'Quarter'and 'Furlong' for Sussex and Hampshire. Again 'town' ('villa') is indexed under both 'town' and 'village' ('villa').

Villagers' holdings

These have been noted, together with those of cottagers ('cotarii') and smallholders ('bordarii') only where the Domesday entry refers to a number of villagers ('villani') 'each' of whom holds a defined quantity of land.

Vocabulary

Some of the renderings of the Morris Edition, and hence of this Index, may be unfamiliar. For example 'revenue' ('firma') is used instead of the more familiar 'farm'; 'jurisdiction' ('soca') for 'soke'; 'patronage' ('commendatio') for 'commendation'; 'in lordship' ('in dominio') for 'in demesne', and a number of other cases, some of which have already been noted in this Introduction. This Index does nevertheless include many of the more traditional translations with a cross reference to the equivalent words used here. Reference to the Word List will also help.

Word List

A word list has been included which lists many of the Latin and Old English words used in Domesday with the English equivalents used in the Morris Edition. Minor variations in spelling have been ignored and verbs put in the infinitive form. The diphthong 'ae' of classical Latin has been replaced by the 'e' of medieval Latin, although Domesday Book often uses the classical form.

The List may be supplemented from pocket Latin/English dictionaries and, for the specialised medieval forms, from R.E. Latham's Revised Medieval Latin Word List.

The Index can also be used by those without access to the Morris Edition. For this purpose tables have been printed after the Word List which show the relationship between the referencing system used here and the folio referencing system used in other publications.

The compiler of this Index acknowledges his indebtedness to the Editors of the County Volumes of the Morris Edition which form the basis for this work, and to the late Professor J.McN. Dodgson who undertook the completion of that Edition following Dr. Morris' death. Thanks are also due to Dr. F.R. and Mrs. C.M. Thorn for their helpful comments and advice on the Word List. Needless to say any errors and infelicities contained herein are the responsibility of the present Indexer.

Finally an enormous debt is owed to my wife who bore the considerable burden of typesetting this work. Without her efforts it could not have appeared.

County Abbreviations

Bedfordshire	BDF	Lincolnshire	LIN
Berkshire	BRK	Middlessex	MDX
Buckinghamshire	BKM	Norfolk	NFK
Cambridgeshire	CAM	Northamptonshire	NTH
Cheshire	CHS	Nottinghamshire	NTT
Cornwall	CON	Oxfordshire	OXF
Derbyshire	DBY	Rutland	RUT
Devonshire	DEV	Shropshire	SHR
Dorsetshire	DOR	Somersetshire	SOM
Essex	ESS	Staffordshire	STS
Gloucestershire	GLS	Suffolk	SFK
Hampshire	HAM	Surrey	SRY
Herefordshire	HEF	Sussex	SSX
Hertfordshire	HRT	Warwickshire	WAR
Huntingdonshire	HUN	Wiltshire	WIL
Kent	KEN	Worcestershire	WOR
Leicestershire	LEC	Yorkshire	YKS

A

ABBESS (abbatissa)
Holding land HEF 1,14.
House of ESS B3s.
HAM 16,7.
See also: Man; Reeve.
ABBEY (abbatia)
Being built 1086 SHR C14. 3b,1.
Burgesses given to SHR C14.
Chief lord's daughter
in SOM 37,7.
Despoiled of land WOR 2,12-13; 42-44; 68-
69. 9,5c. 10,12.
11,1-2 .14,2. 26,15-
17.
Destruction of GLS 1,63.
Formation of SHR 3c,1.
King's hand, in SFK 21,2.
WOR 2,42-44.
Monastery, given to SHR 3b,1.
Payments to
1 corn load per hide WOR 9,7.
Martinmass, at WOR 9,7.
Penalty for late
payment WOR 9,7.
Site of (sedes) NFK 17,35.
Work (werke) of LIN 8,38.
See also: Altar; Chapter; Clothing; Crime/offence;
Custom; Customary due; Death duty; Division;
Forfeiture; free man; free woman; Freeman; Gift;
Grant; Grant and sell; Hall; Head; Jurisdiction;
Jurisdiction,full; Land; Man-at-arms; Manor;
Monastery; Monk; Ox; Patronage; Pledge; Priest;
Reeve; Remove; Restoration; Return; Revenue;
Sell; Separated; Service; Sheriff; Supplies; Taken
away; Tax; Tenure; Thane; Third/two thirds part;
Villager; Wapentake; Wife; Withdraw; Woman;
Writ.
ABBOT (abbas)
Evidence by NFK 8,8; 10.
House of ESS B3a.
Land
in hand of WIL 7,7.
for use of DEV 5,1; 4.
DOR 11,6; 12. 15,1.
SOM 10,2.
Manor house of GLS 12,3.
Officer of SFK 14,37.
See also: Adjudge; Aid; Annexation;
Appropriation; Command; Commendation;
Court; Crime/offence; Customary due; Death
duty; English; Fold; Forfeiture; free man;
Freeman; Gift; Hunting; Jurisdiction; Jurisdiction,
full; Man; Man-at-arms; Market; Monk; Outlaw;
Patronage; Plea; Pledge; Priest; Reeve; Re-

purchase; Revenue; Steward; Supplies; Tax;
Tenure; Thane; Tribute; Villager; Withdraw; Writ.
ABSTRACTED property (auferre) – See Taken
away.
ACCOUNTED (computare) – See Manor.
ACKNOWLEDGMENT
Payment for land WOR 2,71. 9,1b,e.
ACQUIRE (recipere)
free man for land SFK 34,2.
Land ESS 27,17.
NFK 52,3.
from King SFK 66,10.
wrongfully DEV 23,5.
ACRE (acra) BDF 3,6. 19,2. 21,1; 10.
24,12. 25,7. 29,1.
54,2.
BRK B2-3. 1,1-3; 5-11;
15-23; 25-28; 30-42; 44-45; 47. 2,1-2. 3,1.
4,1. 5,1. 7,1; 3; 6-14; 16-19; 21-28; 30; 32-
33; 36-39; 41-42; 44-47. 8,1. 10,1-2. 11,1.
12,1. 14,1. 15,2. 16,1-3. 17,1; 4-13. 18,1-
2. 20,1; 3. 21,3-11; 13-18; 20-22. 22,1-2;
4-5; 8; 10-12. 23,1; 3. 26,1-3. 27,1. 28,1-
3. 29,1. 30,1. 31,1; 5-6. 32,1. 33,1; 3-5; 7-
8. 34,1-4. 35,2. 36,2-5. 38,1; 3; 5-6. 39,1.
40,1-2. 41,1-4; 6. 42,1. 43,1-2. 44,2; 5.
45,1. 46,1; 3-4. 47,1. 48,1. 49,1-3. 50,1.
51,1. 52,1. 53,1. 54,1-4. 55,1-2; 4. 56,1.
57,1. 58,1-2. 61,1-2. 62,1. 63,2-5. 64,1.
65,1-3; 5; 8; 10-11; 13; 15; 20.
BKM 3a,1. 33,1.
CAM 1,2-4; 13. 2,3. 5,5-
7; 15; 22; 25-27; 36-37; 40; 49-50; 53-55;
57; 59-63. 7,4-5; 9. 8,1. 11,1. 12,5. 13,2.
14,17; 22; 38; 41; 48; 59; 62; 72; 75; 82.
17,2; 5. 18,1-3; 5. 22,4. 23,2. 25,8; 10.
26,3-5; 10; 18; 20; 39-40; 51-52; 55; 57.
28,1. 29,1; 3-4; 6; 8. 31,7. 32,1; 3; 14; 18;
21-22; 35; 38; 40-43. 39,1. 41,2-4; 13. 44,1.
CHS B5-6; 9. A4; 6-9;
12; 15-17. 1,1; 3; 7-8; 13-15; 18; 26; 33-34.
2,1; 3-4; 8-9; 12-13; 15; 17; 25; 27; 29-30.
3,1-2; 8. 5,1-2; 5-8; 11-13. 6,1. 7,1-2. 8,3;
8; 13-16; 26; 30-32; 34; 37-38; 42-44. 9,4-
5; 13; 16-20; 25-26. 11,1; 3. 12,4. 13,2; 4-
5. 14,1-6. 16,2. 17,1-5; 8-9; 11-12. 18,1-
4. 19,1. 20,12. 21,1. 24,2. 26,8-9; 11-12.
FD1,1. FD3,1. FD5,2-3. FD8,1-2. FT1,5-
6. FT3,1.
CON 1,1-9; 11-12; 14;
16. 2,1-2; 5; 8-10; 13. 3,1-6. 4,1-5; 7-17;
19-20; 23-28. 5,1,1-22. 5,2,2-15; 17-27;
29-31; 33. 5,3,1-2; 4-8; 10-19; 22-28. 5,4,2-
19. 5,5,1-16; 19-22. 5,6,1-10. 5,7,1-13.

1

5,8,1-10. 5,9,1-4. 5,10,1. 5,11,1-6. 5,12,1-3. 5,13,1-5; 7-12. 5,14,1-6. 5,15,1-6. 5,16,1-2. 5,17,1-4. 5,18,1. 5,19,1. 5,20,1-2. 5,21,1. 5,22,1. 5,23,1-5. 5,24,1-25. 5,25,1-3; 5. 5,26,1-4. 6,1. 7,1.

DBY 1,1; 8-9; 11-16; 18-22; 24-29; 31-32; 34-38. 2,1-3. 3,1; 3; 5; 7. 4,1-2. 5,1-5. 6,3-14; 16-18; 21; 24-28; 30-35; 37-40; 42; 44; 46-47; 49-60; 62; 64-66; 68-69; 71-79; 82-86; 88-99; 101. 7,1; 4; 6-7; 9; 13. 8,1-4. 9,1-6. 10,1-2; 4-8; 10-12; 15; 18-20; 22-27. 11,1-5. 12,1-5. 13,1-2. 14,1-6; 8. 15,1. 16,1-2; 6-8. 17,2; 5-6; 8-9; 11-12; 14-16; 18-20; 22. B2-4.

DEV 1,3-15; 17-20; 23-26; 28-72. 2,1-7; 9; 11-24. 3,4-31; 33; 35-70; 73-81; 83-99. 4,1. 5,1-14. 6,1-12. 7,1-4. 8,1. 9,1. 10,1-2. 11,1-3. 12,1. 13,1. 13a,2-3. 14,1-2. 15,3-5; 8-26; 29-34; 37; 39-44; 47-50; 52-68; 70-72; 73-79. 16,3-12; 14-27; 29-78; 80-125; 128; 133; 135-154; 156-173; 175-176. 17,3-14; 17; 20-24; 26-36; *37;* 38-79; 81-83; 85-92; 94-107. 18,1. 19,2; 4-15; 18-31; 33-35; 37-42; 44-46. 20,1; 3-8; 10; 13-17. 21,1-4; 6-10; 12-20. 22,1-2. 23,1-26. 24,1-32. 25,1-17; 20-25; 27-28. 27,1. 28,1-16. 29,1-6; 8-9. 30,1-3. 31,1-3. 32,1-4; *5;* 6-10. 33,1-2. 34,1-2; 4-8; 10; 12; 14-40; 42-44; 46; 48-55. 35,1; 3-23; 25-29. 36,1-8; 10; *12;* 13-26. 37,1. 38,1-2. 39,1-19; 21. 40,1-2; 4-7. 41,1-2. 42,1-23. 43,1-5. 44,1-2. 45,2. 46,1-2. 47,1-2; *3;* 4-8; 11-14. 48,1-12. 49,1-3; 5-7. 50,1-5. 51,1-3; 5-9; 11-16. 52,1-6; 8-10; 12-14; 16-29; 31-47; 51-53.

DOR 1,1-8; 10; 12-21; 23; 26-28; 30-31. 2,1-6. 3,1-8; 10-18. 4,1. 5,1. 6,1-4. 7,1. 8,1-3; 6. 9,1. 10,1; 3-4; 6. 11,1-6; 9-17. 12,1-5; 7-8; 10-12; 14-16. 13,1; 3-6; 8. 14,1. 15,1. 16,1-2. 17,1-2. 19,1-5; 7-10; 12-14. 20,1-2. 21,1. 23,1. 24,1; 5. 25,1. 26,1; 3-10; 12; 14-26; 28; 32-33; 35-37; 40-42; 44-47; 49-52; 54-56; 58-60; 62-64; 66-67; 69-71. 27,1-6; 8-11. 28,1-7. 29,1. 30,1-4. 31,1-2. 33,1-3; 5. 33,1-2; 4-6. 34,1-2; 4-11; 13-15. 35,1. 36,1-8; 10-11. 37,1-2; 4-9; 11-12; 14. 38,1-2. 39,1-2. 40,1-6; 8-9. 41,1-5. 42,1. 43,1. 44,1. 45,1. 46,1-2. 47,1-10; 12. 48,1. 49,1; 3-12; 14-16. 50,1; 3-4. 51,1. 52,1-2. 53,1-2. 54,1-14. 55,1-4; 6-9; 10; 14-17; 19-20; 22; 24-26; 29-34; 37-38; 40; 42. 55a,1. 56,1-2; 4; 8-9; 12-14; 17-21; 24; 27-31; 33-38; 42; 44-46; 48; 50-51; 53-55; 57-60; 62. 57,1; 3-4; 8-9; 11-15; 21. 58,1-3.

ESS 1,1-13a; 16-22; 24-25; 27-31. 2,1-3; 9. 3,1-2; 4; 6; 8-16. 4,1-3; 5-9; 12; 15-18. 5,1-8; 10-12. 6,1-3; 5; 7-9; 11; 14. 7,1. 8,1-11. 9,1-8; 10-11; 14. 10,1-5. 11,1-8. 12,1. 13,1-2. 14,1-7. 15,1-2. 16,1. 17,2. 18,1-5; 7-15; 17; 20-25; 27-

29; 31-34; 37-43. 19,1. 20,1-2; 6-20; 22-34; 36-53; 55-60; 63-65; 69-74; 76-80. 21,1-12. 22,1-21; 23. 23,1-41. 24,1; 4-7; 9-12; 14; 16-17; 19; 22-27; 30; 32; 34-37; 40-49; 51; 53-61; 64-67. 25,1-5; 7-26. 26,1-5. 27,1-3; 5; 7; 10-11; 13-18. 20,2-8; 11-17. 29,1-2. 30,1-4; 7; 49-51. 31,1. 32,1; 3-12; 16-27; 31-45. 33,1-7; 10-13; 15-23. 34,3-12; 14-16; 18-22; 24-25; 27-34; 36-37. 35,1-14. 36,1-12. 37,2-7; 9; 11-20. 38,1-8. 39,1-6; 8-9; 11-12. 40,1-9. 41,1-4; 6-12. 42,1; 3; 6-9. 43,1-6. 44,1-4. 45,1. 46,1-3. 47,1-3. 48,1-2. 49,1; 3; 6. 50,1. 51,2. 52,1; 3. 53,1. 54,1-2. 55,1. 56,1. 57,1-6. 58,1. 60,3. 61,1-2. 62,1-4. 63,2. 64,1. 65,1. 66,1-2. 67,1-2. 68,1-2; 5; 7-8. 69,1-3. 70,1-2. 71,1-4. 72,1-3. 73,1. 74,1. 75,1-2. 76,1. 77,1. 78,1. 81,1. 82,1. 83,1-2. 84,1-2. 86,1-2. 87,1. 88,1-2. 89,1-2. 90,3-4; 6-22; 24-77; 80-87. B1; 3a-d,t; 4-5; 7.

GLS 1,24-25; 27; 37; 41; 43-45. 2,9; 11-13. 3,2-5. 4,1. 5,1-2. 6,1-5; 8. 7,2. 8,1. 9,1. 10,1-2; 6; 8; 10; 12. 11,1-3; 7-8. 14,1-2. 15,1. 19,1-2. 20,1. 23,2. 25,1. 26,1-2; 4. 28,2. 30,3. 31,2; 10. 32,4; 11. 34,11. 35,1. 39,9; 12-13; 15-16; 21. 41,2; 5. 42,1-3. 43,2. 45,5. 46,2. 47,1. 50,1. 51,1. 52,3-5. 53,3; 5; 9; 11. 54,1-2. 55,1. 56,1-2. 58,1. 60,4-6. 63,3-4. 64,2-3. 66,4-6. 67,1; 3-6. 68,7; 9-10. 69,6-7. 74,1. 75,1. 78,5; 12-13; 15-16.

HAM 1,1-3; 8; 11-13; 15-22; 25-30; 35-37; 39; 41-47; W3-4; W8; W13-15; W19. 2,1-11; 13-15; 17-18; 20; 23; 25. 3,1-11; 13; 16-20; 24-26. 4,1. 5,1. 5a,1. 6,1; 3-9; 12-17. 7,1. 8,1. 9,2. 10,1. 14,1-6. 15,1-5. 16,1-5. 17,1-3. 18,1-3. 19,1. 20,1. 21,2-4; 6-9. 22,1. 23,1-8; 10; 12-20. 22-23; 25-26; 33-34; 36-38; 40; 42; 49; 51-59; 62; 64-68. 27,1-2. 28,6-9. 29,1-3; 5-6; 10-16. 30,1. 31,1. 32,1; 3-4. 35,1-3; 6-7; 9. 38,1. 39,1; 3. 42,1. 43,1-2; 4; 6. 44,1; 3-4. 45,1-2; 5-6; 8-9. 46,1. 47,3. 49,1. 50,1-2. 51,1-2. 52,1. 53,2. 55,1-2. 56,1-2. 58,1. 60,2. 61,1. 62,1-2. 63,1. 66,1. 68,1; 6-7; 9-11. 69,1-5; 7; 9; 11-12; 14; 16-17; 22; 27-29; 32; 35-39; 41-43; 45-47; 50-52. NF2,3. NF3,2-3; 5-6; 9-11; 13-15. NF4,1. NF6,1-2. NF7,1. NF8,1-2. NF9,2; 11-13; 16-20; 23-24; 26-27; 32-33; 36-40; 43; 45. NF10,3. IoW1,1-7; 10; 13-15. IoW2,1. IoW6,1-8; 10; 14-16; 19. IoW7,5; 7-8; 17-18; 21. IoW8,3; 6; 8-9; 11-12. IoW9,1-2; 5; 8; 11-12; 17-20; 23-24.

HEF 1,4; 7; 10a. 2,4; 6; 8; 11-17; 19-21; 23-36; 39-40; 42-46; 49-51. 9,14. 15,6-9. 19,1. 31,2; 7.

HRT 2,4. 4,24. 5,4; 9-10; 12; 22. 16,7. 17,5; 7; 9; 12. 20,8-9. 28,6. 29,1. 30,3. 31,3; 5. 32,2. 33,11; 17; 20.

34,7; 9-10; 13; 25. 35,3. 36,9; 11. 37,3-4;
6; 8; 11; 14; 17-18. 42,4; 11-12.
HUN B18. 1,1-2; 5-10.
2,1-8. 3,1. 4,1-4. 5,1-2. 6,1-9; 11-16; 18-
26. 7,1-7. 8,1-4. 9,1-4. 10,1. 11,1. 12,1.
13,1-5. 14,1. 15,1. 16,1. 17,1. 18,1. 19,1-
6; 8-9; 11; 13-15; 17-19; 23-25; 27-32.
20,1-9. 21,1. 22,1-2. 23,1. 24,1. 25,1-2.
26,1. 28,1. 29,1; 3; 5-6.
KEN M12-15. C3. P1;
17-18. 1,1-2; 4. 2,3-20; 22-23; 25-26; 28-
30; 32-33; 35-36; 41-42. 3,1-6; 8-9; 11-21.
4,1-3; 5-6; 8-14; 16. 5,1-2; 5-6; 8-20; 23-
24; 27; 29-33; 38-51; 53; 56-60; 63; 65-68;
70-80; 82-91; 93-106; 108; 110-111; 113-
114; 119; 122-124; 126-129; 138; 142; 144-
146; 158; 162-168; 170; 172; 175; 185; 190-
191; 207-209; 213-214. 6,1. 7,2-7; 9-14; 17;
19; 22; 27. 8,1. 9,1-5; 16-18; 22; 24-25; 28;
30-33; 36; 38; 42; 47; 49; 53. 10,1-2. 11,1-
2. 12,1-4. 13,1.
LEC 1,1-6; 8-10; 12. 2,1-
2; 4-6. 3,1-2; 6-9; 13-16. 5,1-3. 6,2; 5-6.
7,2. 8,1; 4-5. 9,1; 3. 10,7; 10; 15; 17. 11,1.
13,1-2; 4; 7-8; 13; 15-18; 20-24; 26; 28; 30;
32; 34; 38-41; 50; 53-58; 60-64; 66-67; 69;
72-73. 14,1-2; 4-7; 12-14; 16; 20; 22-24; 29;
31-33. 15,1-2; 7-13; 16. 16,3-4; 6-9. 17,1;
4-5; 14; 16; 18-19; 21; 23-26; 29; 32-33.
18,1-5. 19,1-3; 6; 9; 11; 13-15; 17-20. 20,1-
4. 23,1; 4-6. 24,1; 3. 25,1; 3-5. 27,2. 28,3-
5. 29,2-5; 10-11; 13-20. 30,1. 31,1. 32,1-
2. 33,1. 34,2. 35,1-2. 36,1-2. 37,1. 38,1.
39,2. 40,1-4; 6; 11-13; 15-19; 21-24; 26;
28-29; 31-36; 40. 41,2-3 42,1-3; 6-9. 43,1-
6; 9-11. 44,1; 3-6; 8-9; 12-13.
LIN C12; 14. S7-10; 12;
14-15. T2. 1,2-13; 17-32; 34; 36; 38; 40-42;
44; 48; 50; 52-53; 55-58; 60-61; 63; 65-70;
75; 77; 79-82; 84; 86; 88-97; 99-106. 2,1-7;
11-14; 16-23; 26-29; 32-42. 3,2-10; 12-18;
20-22; 24-27; 31-36; 38; 41-42; 44; 46-49;
51-54. 4,2-3; 5; 7-17; 20; 23-24; 26; 30-32;
34-36; 38-40; 42-47; 50-59; 61; 63-69; 71-
78; 80-81. 5,1. 6,1. 7,3-8; 10-11; 14; 16-
17; 19; 23-25; 27-28; 30-34; 36; 38-41; 43;
45-48; 50-54; 56-59. 8,1; 3-9; 11; 14-15;
17-20; 22-23; 25-28; 31; 33-34; 39. 10,1-3.
11,1; 3-6; 9. 12,1; 4-7; 11-12; 18-25; 28-
29; 34-40; 42-44; 47; 49-50; 52-53; 55-62;
64-68; 70-77; 79-82; 84-97. 13,1-10; 13-16;
18-24; 26-36; 38-42; 44-45. 14,1; 3-6; 9-20;
22-26; 31; 33; 36; 39; 41-60; 62-90; 92-96.
15,1-2. 16,1-2; 6-12; 14; 16-20; 22-23; 28;
30; 32-33; 36; 39; 41; 43-44; 46-47; 49.
17,1-3. 18,1-4; 7-17; 19-24; 26; 28-32. 19,1.
20,1. 21,1. 22,1; 3-5; 7-8; 10-14; 16-19; 22-
36; 38. 23,1. 24,1-2; 4-7; 10; 14; 16-20; 22;
24-27; 31-32; 36-40; 42-48; 50-51; 54; 56-
59; 61-68; 70-74; 76-77; 80-89; 92-93; 95-
100; 102-105. 25,6-9; 11-13; 15-20; 22; 24-

25. 26,3-4; 8-11; 13-14; 16; 20; 22-28; 31-
36; 38-41; 43-52. 27,1-3; 5; 7; 9-10; 14; 19-
20; 22-27; 30; 32; 34-35; 38-44; 47; 50-51;
53-62; 64. 28,1-3; 7; 11; 13-15; 17; 20-21;
23; 25-31; 41. 29,1; 3-12; 14-15; 18-21; 23-
24; 27-30; 32. 30,2-4; 6; 9-14; 17-20; 22;
26-29; 31-33; 36-37. 31,1-5; 7-12; 14-18.
32,1-3; 5-9; 11-12; 14-18; 20-22; 24; 26-27;
29; 31-32; 34. 33,1-2. 34,1-3; 6-10; 12-17;
19-25; 27. 35,1-4; 6-7; 9; 11-15; 17. 36,1;
4. 37,1-2; 5-7. 38,1-5; 7-13. 39,1-4. 40,2-
10; 12; 14; 16-17; 20-21; 23; 25-26. 41,2.
42,1-5; 7; 9-10; 13-17; 19. 43,1-5. 44,4-5;
7-8; 10-11; 16-18. 45,1; 3-4. 46,1-4. 47,1-
5; 7-10. 48,1; 4-6; 8-15. 49,1-2; 4. 50,1.
51,1-4; 6-12. 52,1-2. 53,1-2. 54,1-2. 55,2-
3. 56,1-6; 8; 10-11; 18-20. 57,1; 3-7; 10-16;
18-19; 21-33; 35; 37-38; 41-50; 55-56.
58,1-8. 59,1-5; 7-8; 10-11; 16-21. 60,1.
61,1; 3-4; 6; 8-10. 62,1-2. 63,1-3; 5-7; 15.
64,1; 3-7; 10; 12; 14-19. 65,5. 66,1-2. 67,1;
4-5; 7-10; 12-14; 16; 18; 20-26. 68,1-6; 9-
25; 27; 29-30; 32-35; 37; 40; 42-43; 45; 48.
CS8; 20; 24. CN4; 21. CK2; 8-9; 18; 22;
61.
MDX 1,1. 3,2-3; 6-8; 13-
14; 16; 24; 27; 30. 4,1; 5; 7. 5,1. 6,1. 7,4-
8. 8,3; 6. 9,2; 8-9. 10,1-2. 11,1-4. 13,1.
15,1. 16,1. 18,1-2. 19,1. 20,1. 22,1. 24,1.
25,1.
NFK 1,1-5; 7-30; 32-33;
40; 42-62; 64-65; 69-71; 73-77; 79-174; 177-
231; 234; 236-241. 2,1-4; 7-12. 3,1-2. 4,2-
4; 6-18; 20-57. 5,1-6. 6,1-7. 7,1-21. 8,1-4;
6-19; 21-22; 24-28; 30; 32-41; 44; 46-84;
86-88; 90-93; 96-115; 117; 119-128; 130-
136. 9,1-4; 6-83; 86-134; 136; 139-140;
142-173; 175-186; 188-226; 228-234. 10,1-
8; 10-11; 13-93. 10a,1. 11,1-5. 12,1; 3-25;
27-45. 13,1-7; 9-10; 12-16; 19-24. 14,1-43.
15,1-29. 16,1-5. 17,1-6; 8-39; 42-65. 18,1.
19,1-5; 7; 9-13; 15-18; 20-40. 20,1-2; 4-36.
21,1-37. 22,1-5; 8-16; 18-23. 23,1-2; 4-18.
24,1; 3-7. 25,1-13; 15-22; 24-28. 26,1-6.
27,2. 28,1-2. 29,1; 3-4; 6-11. 30,1-6. 31,1-
45. 32,1-7. 33,1-6. 34,1-4; 6-15; 17-20.
35,1-18. 36,1-7. 37,1-3. 38,1; 3-4. 39,1-2.
40,1. 41,1. 42,1. 43,1-4. 44,1. 45,1. 46,1.
47,2-7. 48,1-8. 49,1-8. 50,1-13. 51,1-6; 8-
10. 52,1-4. 53,1. 54,1. 55,1-2. 56,1-7; 9.
57,1-3. 58,1-3. 59,1. 61,1-4. 62,1-2. 63,1.
64,1-9. 65,1-17. 66,1-17; 20-108.
NTH 1,1; 2a-f; 3-5; 7; 10-
11; 13a,e; 14; 15a; 16-20; 23-24; 30; 32. 2,1-
3; 7; 10; 12. 4,1; 3-4; 7; 9; 11-14; 16-17;
21-23; 30-31; 33-36. 5,2-4. 6,1-2; 4-7; 9-
10a,c; 11-14; 16-17. 6a,5-6; 8-11; 13-15;
19-25; 27-29; 32-33. 8,13. 9,3-6. 10,1; 3.
11,1-6. 12,3. 14,6. 16,1. 18,1-5; 7; 9; 11;
13-14; 17; 19; 23-24; 27-29; 34-35; 37; 41-
43; 45-47; 49; 51; 53-61; 70-73; 77-84; 86;

23-25; 28; 30-35; 37-41; 43-59; 61-64; 66-70. 18,3-6; 8-9; 11. 19,1; 4-5. 20,1. 21,1. 22,1; 3-4; 17; 25-27. 23,1-3. 24,1-2. 25,1. 26,1. 27,3. 28,1; 3; 5-8; 10-19. 29,1; 3-5. 31,1; 3; 6-7; 9-12. 32,1. 33,1. 34,1. 35,1. 36,1-2. 37,1-5; 7; 9. 38,2. 39,1-4. 42,1; 3. 43,1. 44,1; 3; 5-9; 12; 14. WIL B5. 1,1-6; 8-9; 11-23a,e. 2,1-12. 3,1-5. 4,2-4. 5,1-7. 6,1-2. 7,1; 3-12; 14-16. 8,1-13. 10,1-5. 11,1. 12,1-4; 6. 13,1-14; 16-20. 14,1-2. 15,1-2. 16,1-4; 6-7. 17,1. 18,1-2. 19,1-2; 4. 20,1-6. 21,1-3. 22,1-6. 23,1-2; 4; 6-10. 24,1-7; 9-10; 12; 16; 18-23; 25; 27-38; 40-42. 25,1-5; 7-8; 10-15; 18-20; 22-28. 26,1-5; 7; 9-22. 27,1-3; 5-11; 13-27. 28,1; 3; 5; 7-8; 10-13. 29,1-2; 4-8. 30,1-2; 4-7. 31,1. 32,1-3; 5; 7; 9-13; 16-17. 33,1. 34,1. 35,1. 36,1-2. 37,1-2; 4-13; 15. 38,1. 39,1-2. 40,1. 41,1-5; 7-10. 42,1; 5-10. 43,1-2. 44,1. 45,1. 47,1-2. 48,1-6; 8-12. 49,1-3. 50,1-5. 51,1. 52,1. 53,1-2. 54,1. 55,1. 56,2-4; 6. 57,1. 58,1-2. 59,1-2. 62,1. 64,1. 65,1. 66,1-4; 6. 67,1-2; 5-9; 14-17; 20; 22-23; 25-27; 31-32; 34; 37; 39-40; 43-46; 48; 54; 59-64; 68; 72; 76-77; 80-81; 83; 85-90; 94; 98. 68,2-3; 10; 13; 15-16; 18-22; 24-30; 32. WOR 2,2-3; 5-7; 10-11; 13-15; 18-19; 21-23; 27-36; 38-42; 45-48; 52-53; 56; 58-68; 70; 72; 75-79; 85. 8,1; 3-9a,d-g; 10a; 11; 14-17; 19-20; 22-24; 26a. 9,3; 5a. 10,1; 3; 5-6; 8-11; 13-15. 15,11-12. 19,1; 13. 27,1. YKS C30-32. 1Y2; 4-5; 7; 11-13; 16; 18. 1N5; 9; 12-13; 15; 19; 38; 54; 66. 1W25. 2,1-2. 2B1-2; 9; 19. 2N2-4; 14; 21. 2W1-4; 6-8; 12. 2E23; 32-33; 38; 40. 3Y9; 15. 4N1-2. 5N1; 5-9; 17-18; 21-22; 26-27; 47-48; 53; 58-60; 63; 65; 67. 5E17; 59; 65. 5W1; 4-5; 8; 13; 15-16; 18. 6N1; 11-13; 15-17; 21; 27; 32-33; 36; 46; 49; 51; 56; 59; 102; 104-105; 113; 120; 122; 125; 136-137. 6W1-2; 5-6. 6E1. 7E2. 8E1; 5-8; 10; 22. 8W1. 8E3. 9W1-6; 8; 16-19; 23-24; 26-28; 31-32; 34; 37-40; 42-43; 45-46; 49-50; 56-57; 59-61; 64; 66-68; 74; 76; 79-80; 96; 98-99; 104; 108; 116; 119; 121; 125; 139. 10W3; 8; 15; 24-25; 28; 31; 38-39; 41. 11N4. 12W1; 5. 13W1-2; 6-7; 9-12; 14-18; 26; 28; 31; 33; 35. 13E13-14. 13N2; 4-5; 12; 14; 18. 14E1-2; 4-5; 7-9; 11-25; 27-30; 32-34; 36-40; 42-48; 50-53. 15E14. 16E3-4. 16N1. 16W6. 19W1; 3. 21E10-11. 21W6. 22W3. 23N4-5; 7; 13; 16; 20-21; 24-25; 28-29; 31-33. 23E10; 12; 14; 18-19. 24W4; 18. 25W1-2; 6; 9-10; 12; 15-16; 18-20; 22; 28-30. 26E1; 11. 28W33; 39-40. 29W6-7; 14; 25; 36. 29E5. 29N1; 8; 12. CW10. SN,Y5. SW,Sf1; 30. SW,An18.

fifth should belong
to church CHS 1,35.

See also: Sown; Tithe; Vineyard.
ADJOURNMENT (respectum) – See Plea; Possession; Postponement.
ADJUDGE (deratiocinare)

Claim	CAM	1,16.
	ESS	18,44. 90,29.
	LIN	12,84. 57,14.
		CW14.
	NFK	1,195.
	OXF	29,13.
	SFK	35,3.
	SRY	5,28. 19,25.
	WIL	24,42.
Dwelling to use of Abbot	SFK	38,3.
free man to King's use	SFK	32,16.

ADJUDGMENT

At King's command	SFK	20,1. 21,95.
By:-		
Bishop at King's command	ESS	3,7.
County	WOR	9,6a.
Hundred	NFK	1,192.
Hundred against party not appearing	SFK	39,3.
Sheriff	CAM	29,12.
thanes	WIL	24,42.
Wapentake	LIN	CS6.
free man in King's hand pending	SFK	76,16.
Of mode of trial	NFK	34,17.

See also: Judgment; King's hand; Prove; Thaneland.
ADMINISTRATION (ministerium)

Land in King's	BDF	57,1; 3; 11; 13.

See also:Queen.
ADULTERY (adulterium; legrewita) – See Crime/offence.
AETHELRED – See King.
AFFAIRS (res) – See Concerns.
AGREEMENT

(conventio; consilium)	HAM	29,3; 9.
	WIL	12,1.
Breach, land repossessed for	LIN	CK48.
Fishing rights,on	HUN	7,8.
Land concerning	SFK	67,5-6.
held by	ESS	B,3a.

AGRICULTURAL work

Remitted	WOR	2,4.

AGRICULTURE – See Arable; Burgess; Cultivation; Harrowing; Harvest; Haymaking; Plough; Ploughing; Ploughland; Reaping; Scything; Sheriff; Smallholder; Sown; Sowing; Villager.
AID (adjutorium)

Given to Abbot	SFK	14,167.

See also: Exactions.
ALDER grove/wood

ALMSMAN
(elemosinarius) DOR 24.
SFK 14,167
King's BDF 57.
DOR 24.
NTH 17.
King's, French HRT 1,9.
ALMSWOMAN
(prebendaria) of King CAM 32,32.
ALOD (in alod) – See Freehold.
ALTAR
Document of grant
placed on by donor WOR 26,16-17.
Knife put on by way
of grant NFK *14,16.*
Payment to KEN *2,11. 3,15.*
AMBER (ambra) – See Salt.
ANGLO – SAXON
Burgess, having BKM B13.
Holding land TRE
and 1086 (including
kin) BDF 2,5; 7. 3,6; 14. 8,6.
14,1. 17,1-2. 19,3. 21,13. 23,16; 47. 53,23;
28. 55,5. 56,1-8. 57,7-10; 12-19; 21.
BRK 1,10; 40. 3,2. 7,29.
21,20-21. 46,4. 61,1. 65,5; 9; 17; 21-22.
BKM 4,24. 5,21. 11,1.
14,1; 15. 17,15-16; 24. 23,9: 13; 15; 17.
26,1-2. 40,1. 53,1; 9-10. 54,1. 57,1-6; 8-
12.
CAM 1,20-21. 5,*19;* 40.
14,10; 23; 28; 32-33; 49-52; 54. 22,3-4; 9-
10. 23,3-4. 26,19. 30,2. 41,4.
CHS 2,8-12; 22. 5,14.
8,8. 9,13. 20,5.
26,6; 8-11. FD2,6.
CON 4, 17; *18.* 5,13,2; 4-
9; 11. 5,16,1-2. 5,17,1-2. 5,18,1. 5,20,1-2.
5,21,1. 5,22,1. 5,23,1; 3. 5,24,1-3; 5; 9-10;
15.
DBY 17,13; 18; 20. B8.
DEV 3, 91. *13a,2.* 15,6-
7; 58; 61. 16,113; 160. 17,18. 23,25. 25,19.
45,3. 51,15. 52,2-3; 10; 18-19; 27-29; 31;
34-35; 37-38; 40-51.
DOR 8, 6. 11,1. 24,4.
56,1; 7; 9-11; 13; 15-16; 18; 26; 28-30; 34-
35; 37-41; 52-53; 62; 65. 57,22.
ESS 20,44. 23,35. 24,20;
67. 27,9. 30,12-13; 51. 33,3; 6. 37,9. 49,3.
85,1. 87. 88,1. 90,4; 33; 41; 43-45; 49; 59.
GLS 6,6-7. 61,1-2. 78,2-
5; 7; 9-10; 12-17.
HAM 2,5; 7. 3,1; 11.
6,16. 17,2-3. 21,9-10. 23,10. 69,13; 15; 17-
20; 22-26; 33; 36-43; 45; 47; 49-50.
NF9,35-39; 41; 43-44. NF10,4. IoW6,22.
IoW9,1; 3-4; 6-10; 12-14; 16-17; 19-21.
HEF 1,12; 14; 58-59.
10,15; 70-71. 19,6. 24,1-4; 9-10. 29,19.
36,2-3.

HRT 1,6; 10-11; 15; 17.
2,4. 15,8. 17,1. 20,1. 33,5; 16; 19. 34,6; 20.
42,9-11; 13-15.
HUN B10. 29,1-2; 5-6.
KEN M4;6; 8; 13; 16-17;
20. 5,149.
LIN C3; 13. T5. 3,32;
43. 68,16-18; 20; 23-25; 39-41; 45. CK18.
NFK 8,89-90. 9,174;
196. 13,17. 17,49.
27,2. 58,1.
NTH 4,25; 29. 18,91; 95;
97-99. 35,16.
56,30-32; 35.
NTT 1.32. 6,12. 10,55.
30,10; 13; 27; 34;
38-39; 50.
OXF 14,4. 35,25. 58,23-
25; 33.
SHR 3c,8. 4,3,30-31.
4,4,13. 4,5,7. 4,19,9-11. 4,20,2. 4,27,11-
15; 17; 22; 28-29; 32. 5,1; 4; 8.
SOM 1, 21. 8,25; 27; 32.
16,*5;* 8,9; *10.*21,19; 39; 41-42. 35,12. 36,8.
45,16-17. 47,11; 13-19; *21;* 24-25.
STS 8,17. 11,17; 21.
17,1; 3; 7; 17-18.
SFK 3,98-99. 6,178.
7,10; 70; 76. 25,10. 26,10. 27,4-6. 29,4.
32,5. 51,2. 74,8.
SRY 5,6. 8,10-11. 19,41-
42. 36,1-3; 5-6; 9-
10.
SSX 9,8; 111. 10,19; 46.
11,26; 49. 12,12;
24; 38. 13,32.
WAR 16,23; 26. 17,6; 12;
17; 40; 52. 22,11; 27. 27,2. 28,4; 13. 38,1-
2. 43,2. 44,10.
WIL 1,11; 23j. 13,13.
18,1. 19,4. 24,9. 25,4; 15. 26,21; 23. 67,6-
9; 17; 34-35; 39; 41-42; 46; 48; 51; 53-54;
59-63; 66-67; 72; 78; 80-81; 84-87; 89-92;
94; 96. 68,9.
WOR 2,24. 8,26a. 13.
28,1.
YKS 6N48; 55; 65; 67;
70; 83-84; 89; 93; 95-97; 103; 112-113; 129;
135. 9W23; 28; 35; 41; 48; 61-62; 69-73; 75;
85; 108-109. 21W1. 24W11. 25W12; 18.
28W1; 8; 13-14; 27-28; 31-32; 39-41.
29W4-8; 11-13; 15-24; 30-38; 42-44; 47; 49.
29E2-3; 5-6; 8-9; 11-12; 15; 17-20; 23-24;
26-27; 29-30. 29N6; 12.
Living on land 1086 WAR 17,16.
Son of, with 1 plough
only 1086 WOR 16,4.
See also: English; Englishman.

ANIMAL – See Animal; Ass; Bacon pig; Bear;
Beast; Beehive; Bull; Calf; Cattle; Chicken; Cob;

Cow; Deer; Dog; Draught animal; Eel; Fish; Foal;
Game; Goat; Hare; Hawk; Hen; Herring; Horse;
Lamb; Lamprey; Livestock; Mare; Marten; Mule;
Ox; Packhorse; Pig; Porpoise; Ram; Riding horse;
Salmon; Sheep; Sow; Sparrowhawk;Stag; Sumpter
horse; Wether.

ANIMAL	DEV	*2,22. 15,71; 76.*
	16,37; 50; 54; 120. 17,21; 26; 49; 61; 76;	
	83; 86. 19,18. 20,12; 17. 23,22. 25,24.	
	28,12. 32,3; 10. 36,8. 49,1. 51,8. 53,38.	
In a plough	DEV	*17,77.*

See also: Cattle; Draught animal; Third part.

ANNEXATION

House, of	ESS	B3g.
Jurisdiction, of	NFK	1,77.
Land holder, of	ESS	20,79.
Payments, of, in		
King's despite	CAM	1,14.
Woman, by	ESS	90,38.

ANNEXATION of

land (invadere)	ESS	1,6; 27-28. 5,8. 8,8.
	18,43. 20,51-56. 32,28. 89,2-3. 90,1-87.	
	NFK	1,197. 4,26; 51. 9,5;
	92. 10,48; 54; 69; 90; 93. 14,31. 21,1; 8; 35.	
	32,6. 66. 66,35; 51-52; 59; 63; 84.	
	SFK	2,8. 4,32. 5,2. *8,6.*
		73,1. 76,2-3; 13-14;
		17-19.

In despite (super) of:-

Abbess	CAM	21,5.
Abbot	CAM	3,5.
	HRT	10,6.
	SFK	9,2. 76,12.
King	ESS	90. 90,2; 20-21; 30.
	HRT	1,13. 20,2. 42,11.
	SFK	76.
King's hand, from	NFK	66,83.
King's land, of	ESS	90,2-3.
	STS	11,38.
Outlawry, after	NFK	10,77.
Payment for	SFK	73,1.
Persons answerable	STS	11,38.
Wrongfully	WAR	6,9.

See also: Appropriation; Dispossession; free man;
Freeman; Place; Seizure; Taken away.

ANSWER (responsus) – See Return.

ANSWER for (se	Passim BDF; BRK;
defendere)	BKM; HAM;
	HRT; KEN;
	MDX; SRY; SSX.

See also; Hide.

ANTECESSOR – See Predecessor.

APPEAL (revocare) – See Cite.

APPENDAGE – See Manor.

APPROPRIATION (occupare; intercapere)

Dwelling, of	HAM	1,27.
	YKS	C6;9.
Land, of	BDF	57,6.
	DBY	16,1.
	DEV	1,29; 70. *34,5.*
		35.4. 42,4.

	ESS	1,27. 5,12. 20,22;
		73-74; 76; 80.
	HRT	10,9.
	MDX	15,1.
	NFK	21,13.
in despite	CAM	13,2. 22,5. 39,2.
	SFK	4,32.
of Abbot	CAM	5,22. 25,9. 26,7.
	DOR	55,23.
of King	BDF	14,1. 32,15.
	BRK	21,13.
	BKM	18,3.
	CAM	1,16. 19,1. 29,4; 6.
		38,2.
	HAM	44,3.
	HRT	18,3. 31,8. 36,13.
force, by	NTH	55,1.
outlawry, after	ESS	25,5.
wrongfully	BDF	6,1. 24,12. 54,2.
	BRK	1,37. 3,1.
Men and land, of	CAM	13,8.
	HAM	1,27.
Seizure into King's		
hand after	ESS	66,1.

See also: Annexation; Dispossess; free man;
Freeman; Misappropriation; Seize; Taken away;
Usurped.

APPURTENANCE – See Church; Manor.

APULIA, return from	NFK	9,88.

ARABLE (arabilis; seminabilis)

Field	YKS	5N50.
Holding (cultura)	YKS	CW3.
Land	DBY	6,22.
	DOR	34,8.
	LIN	C12. S4. 2,33; 42.
		8,8. 11,3-4. 12,50.
		14,54; 57; 60; 92.
		24,36. 30,14. 38,7.
		CK9.
	NFK	1,70.
	NTH	26,3.
	NTT	5,1.
	STS	10,3.
	SFK	14,167.
	YKS	C22. 2,1. 2W4; 6.

See also: Jurisdiction, full; Ploughland; Town.

ARCHBISHOP
(archiepiscopus)

Acquires land with		
own money	LIN	CK10.
Customary dues of	YKS	C1b
Kitchen of	KEN	3,10.
Spiritual jurisdiction		
(christianitas)	YKS	C37.
Tribute (gablum) of	KEN	*2,18-19.*

See also: Clerk; Court; Crime/offence;
Destruction; Forfeiture; free man; Freeman; Hall;
Hay; Man; Monk; Patronage; Purchase; Reeve;
Revenue; Service.

ARCHDEACON

(archidiaconus)	KEN	M14. 2,14.

	NFK	10,16.
	SOM	*6,14.*
	WOR	2,20; 24; 57.
ARCHENFIELD		
Customs of	HEF	A1-9. 1,49; 53.
ARCHER (arcuarius)	HAM	53.
	OXF	58,2-3.
ARMS (arma)	HEF	1,49.
	LEC	C2.
	SHR	C3.
Custody of	SSX	12,1.
Man-at-arms, for	CAM	B13.
Payments for	OXF	1,12.
ARMY (exercitus)		
Jurisdiction (soca)		
aiding by land/sea	LIN	57,43.
Man-at-arms-1 per 5		
hides	BRK	B10.
Men serving in	HEF	1,53.
Welsh form van-		
guard and rear-guard	HEF	A9.

See also: Campaign; Expedition; Horse; Service.
ARPENT (arpenna) – See Meadow; Vineyard; Woodland.
ARREST (captio)

| Man under King's | SFK | 30,3. 76,14. |

See also: Crime/offence; Evidence; Guarantor.
ARSON – See Crime/offence.
ARTIFICER

(ingeniator)	BKM	42.
	HUN	19,15. 26. D24.
	LIN	47.
	NTH	B17; 21
	OXF	58,1.
ASH wood	NTH	39,4.
(fraxinetum)		
ASS (asinus)	DEV	*23,6.*
	DOR	*55,2.*
	ESS	1,1. 32,16. 33,4.
		34,29. 35,8. 36,1.
		71,2.
	NFK	8,105. 9,233.
	SOM	*5,48. 21,89.*
	SFK	21,5.
ASSART (exsartum)	HEF	1,7; 10a. 10,48-49.

ASSAULT – See Crime/offence.

ASSAYED – See Money.

ASSEMBLY	SFK	27,7.
(placitum)		
Hundred, of	SFK	39,13.
Manor, of in lord's		
hall	CHS	8,16.

See also: Plea; Summons.
ASSENT (concessio) – See Assignment; Consent; Grant; Land.
ASSESSED – See Church; County; Hide; Man; Manor; Value; Vikings.
ASSESSMENT
Evidenced by King's

writ	SRY	6,5.
Land withdrawn from		
(retro)	SSX	9,120.

See also: County; Hide; Hundred; Manor; Value; Will.
ASSIGNMENT (commendatio)
Of land for yearly

| revenue to be agreed | LIN | CK48. |

See also: Commendation; Patronage.
ASSIGNMENT (concessio)

free man, of by King	SFK	37,2.
Land, of	BDF	13,1.
donor's soul, for	SRY	6,4.
	WOR	11,2.
King, by	BDF	17,5.
	GLS	39,8. 59,1. 72,2.
		78,9.
	HRT	9,9.
	NTT	B18.
	SSX	11,42.
Payments, of, by		
King	DEV	1,55.

See also: Gift; Grant.
ASSOCIATE (socius) – See Companion; Joint tenant.
ATTACHMENT – See Appurtenance.
AUTHORITY (potestas: libertas)
Holder's land under

another's	GLS	1,39; 46.
Lack of	HAM	39,4.
Land under holder's		
own free authority	LIN	CW16.

AVOUCH (revocare) – See Cite.

B

BACON pig (baco)   SOM   33,2.
    WIL   24p.
BAKE house
(pistrinum)   NFK   1,66.
See also: Oven.
BAKER (pistor;
panifex)   CAM   44.
    DOR   57,17-18.
    HAM   IoW6,10.
    LIN   S9.
    SFK   14,167.
King's   CAM   *44,1.*
See also: Customary due.
BALE of goods (trusellus) – See Holiday.
BANQUET
(conuvium)   SSX   11,2.
BARBER (tonsor)   HAM   65.
BARLEY (ordeum)
Render of sester   HEF   1,6.
BARON (baro)   DOR   B3.
    KEN   C8.
    SFK   1,102.
    WAR   B2.
Coming into County   SFK   16,34.
King's   DEV   2,2.
    KEN   C8.
    LIN   CK66.
    SOM   *1,31.*
    SFK   14,101. 16,34.
    WAR   B1.
    WOR   10,12.
See also: Domesday survey; Peace; Plea; Pledge;
Prove; Re-purchase.
BARREL (cuva) – See Ale.
BARTON (bertune)
Bishop's   HEF   2,9-10.
Canons'   HEF   2,7.
BATTLE
Hastings, of
   death in   HAM   69,16.
    HUN   D7.
    NFK   66,41.
    SFK   31,50. 76,20.
   reference to   BRK   21,13.
Naval against King
William   ESS   6,9.
Yorkshire, in, by
Harold   ESS   6,15.
See also: Combat; Harold; Ordeal.
BEADLE (bedellus)   BDF   57,3v.
    BKM   57,18.
    CAM   1,20.
    GLS   *1,59-60*
    HEF   1,10a; 39-41; 44.

     2,39. 10,9.
    SFK   74,4.
    SRY   8,12.
    WOR   1,1a.
King's   BDF   57,17.
    CAM   *1,20.*
BEAR (ursus)   NFK   1,61.
Dogs, for   NFK   1,61.
BEAST (bestia/fera silvaticae)
Of the chase   NFK   4,9.
Wild   KEN   5,72.
Woodland   HRT   10,5.
    MDX   10,1.
See also: Enclosure, hedged; Park.
BEEHIVE (rusca; vas   ESS   5,4. 7; 10-11. 8,11.
apium)   9,7; 9. 10,1; 5.
   11,2; 8. 13,1-2. 14,2-3. 20,7-8; 15; 21; 71;
   79. 22,3; 5; 8-9; 11-13; 20. 23,2; 38; 40.
   24,10; 16; 19; 22; 25; 29; 33; 44-46; 49; 53-
   54; 59; 64-65. 25,1-3; 5; 11; 16-18; 22-23;
   25. 26,1. 27,13. 28,11. 30,1; 4-5; 17-18; 27;
   33; 45. 32,1-3; 9; 21; 23-24; 28; 34; 38a;
   42-43; 45. 33,1; 4; 6-7; 11;16; 19-20. 34,7;
   10; 18-22; 27; 29; 33-34. 35,1-4; 11-12.
   36,1; 3; 6; 11-12. 37,1;10. 38,1-4; 6;8. 40,6.
   41,12. 42,3; 6-8. 44,1-3. 47,1-3. 53,1.
   54,1. 56,1. 57,3. 61,2. 67,1. 71,4. 76,1.
     HUN   *4,4.*
     NFK   1,57; 151; 210; 217;
   231. 2,7. 4,2; 30-31; 38. 4,52. 5,4; 6. 7,16.
   8,1; 3; 6; 35; 46; 91-92; 103; 122. 9,2; 9;
   33; 70-71; 73; 75; 77; 80-81; 87-88; 94; 99.
   10,10; 15; 40; 57. 12,17; 27; 30. 13,4; 7.
   14,8; 35. 15,24. 17,17; 53. 19,15. 20,8; 36.
   21,7; 16; 21; 24; 27; 29; 32. 23,2; 5. 25,17.
   31,1; 7-8; 17; 38; 41. 32,1-2; 4; 7. 34,17-
   18. 35,10. 36,5-7. 37,1-2. 46,1. 48,3. 49,2;
   4; 6. 52,1; 4. 61,2.
     SFK   1,23; 46; 49; 51.
   3,9. 4,42. 6,80; 83; 85; 112; 260; 271; 303-
   304; 306; 309; 312. 8,33; 36. 9,3. 12,1.
   14,4-5; 19; 23-24; 32; 48-49; 103; 118-119.
   15,1. 20,1. 21,*1*; 42; 45; 55; 58. 24,1. 25,1-
   3; 5; 61; 79; 85. 26,9-10; 12a; 14. 32,6; 14;
   16; 19. 33,1; 3; 6-8. 34,2-3. 35,1. 37,6.
   39,6. 41,17. 44,1-2. 47,3. 52,5. 53,6. 64,3.
   66,3. 67,28.
Comparative information
   less 1086 than TRE   ESS   23,38; 40. 24,53;
    64. 25,22. 32,42.
    33,19-20. 34,18-19.
    38,2. 41,12. 44,1.
    47,3. 61,2. 76,1.
     NFK   13,4. 21,24. 32,7.
    34,18. 37,2.

	SFK	6,112. 14,32. 34,2-
		3.
more 1086 than	ESS	23,2. 24,10. 25,18;
TRE		23. 30,27; 45.
		35,12. 38,1. 42,7.
		56,1.
	NFK	4,31. 9,87. 13,7.
		21,27. 36,6.
	SFK	35,1. 39,6.
BEEKEEPER		
(mellitarius; custos		
apium)	DEV	23,15.
	HEF	1,47.
	SHR	7,5.
	WIL	1,16.
BEER – See Ale		
BENEFICE	OXF	28,8.
BEQUEST	HAM	69,28.
	HUN	D27.
See also: Death.		
BEREWICK – See Outlier.		
BISHOP (episcopus)		
Evidence by	SOM	1,27.
men of	BKM	5,18.
	HRT	4,1.
Land		
payments for use of	SOM	6,1; 3; 7-8; 9; 14.
taken from in King		
Canute's time	WIL	2,1.
Officer of	CHS	B2.
Patrimony of	NFK	1,61.
Receives fines for		
breach of holy days	CHS	B1-2.
Renders to		
Martinmas, at	WOR	2,80.
penalty for late		
payment	WOR	2,80.
Sons of	NFK	1,69.
Wife of	NFK	10,28.

See also: Barton; Borough; Burgess; Canon;
Chamberlain; Chaplain; City; Clerk; Command;
Corn; Court; Customs; Dispute; Dwelling;
Expedition; Fine; Forfeiture; free man; Gift; Grant;
Holding; Jurisdiction, full; Land; Man; Man-at-
arms; Market; Moneyer; Oswaldslow; Plea;
Protector; Prove; Reeve; Residence; Revenue; Seal;
Separated; Steward; Supplies; Tax.

BISHOP Odo-taking		
and dispossession	LIN	CS13.
BISHOPRIC		
(episcopatus)	HEF	2,1.
	NFK	1,68. 10. 10,78.
		66,39.
	SFK	6,191.
Hidage of	HEF	2,57.
Land		
belonging to	BRK	5,1.
	CHS	G1.
	DOR	3,1.
	NFK	1,61. 10. 10,23; 28;
		30.

	SOM	6,6.
not belonging to	HAM	5a,1.
	HRT	7,1.
	NFK	1,61. 10,21.
	SOM	3,1.
Land of See of		
Chester	CHS	C25. B13. 2,5.
Lincoln	BDF	4,2.
	CAM	3,3.
London	MDX	3,1; 12.
Salisbury	BRK	3,1.
Thetford	NFK	10.
Winchester	BRK	2,2-3.
	HAM	2,1; 5-6; 8-11; 14-
		15; 19-20; 22-23;
		25. 3,23-27. 29,1.
Winchester, not		
part of	HAM	2,24.
Principal seat of	NFK	1,61.
Seat of	SFK	18,1.

See also: Jurisdiction, full; Separated.

BIT of land (parva terra) – See Land.		
BLANCHED (alba; blanca) – See Money.		
BLIND man (caecus)	NFK	17,15.
	NTT	1,25. 30,53.
	WIL	67,53
BLOOD shedding		
Fines for		
had by men/free		
men	CHS	R2,2. R6,2.
land exempt from	CHS	R1,42.
See also: Crime/offence.		
BLOOM (bloma) – See Iron.		
BOARD land (in	NFK	65,17.
mensa)		
BOAT (navis)	CHS	17,1.
	HUN	7,8.
Fishing	CAM	5,8.
	SFK	25,36.
Payment for landing	CAM	5,9.
Small (navicula)	CHS	A3-4.
See also: Ship.		
BOATMAN		
(buzecarlus; batsuein)	WAR	B6.
	WIL	B5.
BODYGUARD (hevewarda; custodia)		
Provided by:-		
Freeman	CAM	5,16. 32,4; 7.
man	CAM	14,39.
Provided for:-		
King	KEN	D22; 24.
sheriff	CAM	5,16. 32,4.
Subject to being given		
victuals	KEN	D22.
BOOKLAND	DEV	3,8.
BOOR (burus)	BRK	1,31.
	BKM	19,2.
	DEV	5,8.
	HAM	1,10; 23.
	HEF	2,12; 25-26; 29-30;
		57.

	OXF	1,6.
	WOR	8,10a.
Defined as freedman		
(colibertus)	HAM	1,10; 23.
	WOR	8,10a.
BOOTY (spolia)		
From land	ESS	89,3.
BORDAR (bordarius) – See Smallholder		
BOROUGH (burgus)	BDF	6,1.
	BRK	B1. 1,42.
	BKM	B2-3.
	CAM	B1.
	CHS	C25. FT2,1; 19.
	DBY	B1; 14. S3.
	DEV	1,1-2; 55. *2,4.*
		16,65. 17,1.
	DOR	B4.
	ESS	1,25. B1.
	GLS	G1; 4. B1.
	HAM	1,28. 17,1. S2.
	HEF	8,1. 9,1.
	HRT	B1. 9,10. 15,1.
	HUN	B1; 14-19. D1.
	KEN	2,2; 41. 3,10.
		5,178. 7,10.
	LEC	C2; 11-12; 16-17.
	LIN	S1.
	NFK	1,61; 63-64; 70.
		9,1.
	NTH	B1-2. 1,5.
	NTT	B1; 3-4; 17. S3.
	SHR	4,1,32.
	SOM	1,30-31. 7,1. *40,1.*
		41,1.
	STS	B1; 10; 12. 10,1.
		11,7.
	SFK	1,116; 122a,c-d.
		3,55. 6,4. 25,52.
		27,8. 31,55. 41,13.
		63,1. 74,9.
	SSX	5,2. 10,1. 12,1.
	WAR	B1-5. 1,6.
	WIL	M1; 3. B1; 5. 3,2.
		13,22.
	WOR	2,49.
Named as such		
Reading	BRK	1,42.
Wallingford	BRK	B1.
Buckingham	BKM	B1-2.
Cambridge	CAM	B1.
Rhuddlan	CHS	FT2,19.
Derby	DBY	B1.
Barnstaple	DEV	1,1. *16,65.*
Exeter	DEV	*2,4.*
Lydford	DEV	1,2.
Totnes	DEV	1,55. 17,1.
Shaftesbury	DOR	B4.
Chelmsford	ESS	B1.
Maldon	ESS	1,25.
Gloucester	GLS	G4.
Winchcombe	GLS	B1.
Southampton	HAM	S.
Twynham	HAM	1,28.
Clifford Castle	HEF	8,1.
Wigmore	HEF	9,1.
Ashwell	HRT	9,10.
Berkhamsted	HRT	15,1.
Hertford	HRT	B1.
Huntingdon	HUN	B1; 14-19.
Fordwich	KEN	7,10.
Hythe	KEN	2,41.
Romney	KEN	5,178.
Sandwich	KEN	2,2.
Seasalter	KEN	3,10.
Stamford	LIN	S1.
Norwich	NFK	1,63.
Thetford	NFK	1,70. 9,1.
Northampton	NTH	B1; 38.
Nottingham	NTT	B1.
Quatford	SHR	4,1,32.
Bath	SOM	1,30-31. 7,1. *40,1.*
		41,1.
Langport	SOM	1,1.
Stafford	STS	B1; 12. 11,7.
Tutbury	STS	10,1.
Ipswich	SFK	1,116; 122a, 25,52.
		74,9.
Lewes	SSX	12,1.
Pevensey	SSX	10,1.
Rye	SSX	5,1.
Steyning	SSX	5,2.
Warwick	WAR	B1. 1,6.
Calne	WIL	3,2.
Malmesbury	WIL	M. B5.
Wilton	WIL	B1, 13,22
Worcester	WOR	2,49.
New	CHS	FT2,19.
	NFK	1,66.
	NTH	B1.
	NTT	B3.
	SSX	5,1.
Small	KEN	7,10.
Town (suburbium)	HRT	B11.
	LIN	T2.
Of town (burbius villae)	HRT	15,1.
Assessment at half hundred	BDF	B.
hidal	HUN	B15.
Bishop's	CHS	C1.
Castle, sited round	STS	10,1.
Custody of	WIL	B1.
Customary dues of	BRK	B1. 1,42.
	DBY	B1.
	HAM	S2.
	HRT	9,10.
	KEN	5,178.
	LIN	S1; 16.
	OXF	B1.
	STS	B12.
Customs of Borough/City	BRK	B1; 7.

	CAM	B10-11.
	CHS	C3-22. B1-2. FT2, 19.
	DEV	C1-2; 4-7. 1,2. 17,1.
	DOR	B1-4.
	ESS	B5-6. 6,89a-b.
	GLS	G1; 4.
	HEF	C2-15.
	HUN	B1; 15-20.
	KEN	D1-6. C1; 3-4; 6-8. 2,2. 5,178.
	LEC	C2-5.
	LIN	S1; 5. T1.
	NTT	B6; 20.
	OXF	B1-11. 1,13.
	SHR	C2-11.
	SSX	11,2. 12,1.
	WAR	B3-6.
	WOR	C1.
Ditch, houses in	NTT	B17.
Evidence by men of	KEN	2,2.
Founding of	NFK	1,66.
Income of (exitus)	NTH	B38. 1,5.
Jurisdiction of King and Earl in	NFK	1,61.
King's	DEV	1,1-2.
	KEN	D1.
	LIN	S1.
Land of		
carucates, taxable attached to	DBY	B1.
	NTT	B1.
divided between certain burgesses	NTT	B1.
free land in	SFK	25,52.
in two Counties	NFK	1,70.
land for ploughs attached to	DBY	B1.
outside borough	DEV	1,2.
	LEC	C17.
	LIN	S7-8; 14.
Lordship, in	DEV	1,1-2. 17,1.
	ESS	B4.
Man of	KEN	2,2.
Measure, standard of	GLS	G1.
Occupied by traders	STS	10,1.
Payments by:-		
to Earl	NFK	1,61.
to lord	WIL	13,22.
nil	SHR	4,1,32.
Payment of:-		
dues (census)	NTT	B3.
land tribute (landgable)	CAM	B10.
	HUN	B16.
mint tax	HUN	B15.
tax for 12 ½ Hundreds	LIN	S1.
tribute (gablum)	OXF	B1.
Payments with		

Hundred	GLS	B1.
Tolls of	CHS	FT2,19.
	HRT	9,10.
	OXF	B1.
exempt from in England	KEN	D5.
Residence outside	LIN	S8-9.
Resources in:-		
fishery	DBY	B9.
mill	DBY	B1-2; 4.
	LIN	S2; 4-5; 7; 10.
villagers	NTT	B1.
Settled by French and English since 1066	HAM	S2.
Strangers dying in with house but no kin	OXF	1,13.

See also: Bridge; Burgess; City; Customs; Danegeld; Ditch; Dwelling; Expedition; Guild; Guildhall; Honey; House; Hundred; Measure; Mint; Quarter; Reeve; Revenue; Service; Sheriff; Ship; Site; Suburb; Tax; Third/two thirds part; Third penny; Wall;Ward.

BOROUGH right (burgherist)	SOM	1,13. 2,2.
BOUNDARY (finis; meta)	HEF	10,2.
	LIN	C26.
	YKS	1N3. 9W64. 24W1. CW1; 3.
Breach, fine for	CHS	R1,41. R5,3.
Measurement – first and most recent	YKS	CW1-2.

See also: Customary due; Reeve; Road.

BOVATE (bovata)	CHS	B11. 1,33. 8,5. 9,15. 17,10. 19,3. 20,6. R1,8; 34-35. R4,1.
	DBY	1,1; 3; 8-9; 11; 17; 19; 22; 26; 30-32; 34-35; 37-38. 2,3. 3,1; 5; 7. 5,2; 4. 6,1-3; 28; 30; 37-38; 41; 43; 48; 52-53; 59-65; 68; 75-76; 82; 84; 88-89; 91; 93-94. 8,1-3; 6. 9,3; 5. 10,3-6; 8; 11-15; 26-27. 12,3-5. 13,1. 14,2; 5; 10. 16,2-8. 17,1-8; 10; 13-14; 17-18; 20-21; 23. B1; 11-12.
	LEC	1,1b; 3-4. 3,10. 4,1. 5,1. 10,7; 13. 13,5-6; 8; 17; 25; 29; 37; 39-42; 53; 58; 63. 14,15; 29; 31-32. 15,7; 12; 16. 16,2; 6; 15; 18; 21. 18,4. 19,13-14; 16; 19. 23,4. 25,2-5. 29,3-4; 18. 35,1. 36,2. 40,1; 11; 25; 36-37. 42,4; 7-8. 43,1; 7. 44,13.
	LIN	1,2-4; 6-7; 13; 15-16; 27-28; 30; 32; 37; 39; 67; 71-73; 75-78; 80; 87; 90; 97; 99-100. 2,2; 4-9; 13; 15; 17-18; 20; 24-25; 27-28; 30; 32. 3,1-4; 6-10; 13-14; 17-21; 25-30; 32-33; 35; 37-40; 42; 45-48; 50; 53; 55. 4,2; 7-9; 11-19; 21-25; 28-35; 38-40; 42-49; 52-54; 56-63; 66-68; 71-73; 75-77; 81. 5,1. 6,1. 7,2; 5-7; 11-12; 14; 17; 19; 22; 25-27; 29; 31-32; 34; 36; 38; 40; 45-48; 50-51; 59. 8,3-4; 10; 13; 19; 21-22; 24; 26-28; 30; 32; 34; 37-38. 9,2. 10,1.

11,7-9. 12,1-3; 5; 8; 10-16; 18-19; 22-23;
29-33; 38; 40; 42-43; 47-49; 52-53; 58; 60-
62; 65; 67-71; 73; 75-76; 79; 81-82; 84; 86-
88; 90; 95; 97. 13,1; 7; 11; 13; 16; 18-19;
21-23; 25-27; 29; 31; 33-34; 36; 40. 14,1; 5-
6; 8-12; 14-17; 19-24; 27-28; 31-33; 36-45;
54-55; 57-58; 60-62; 65; 71; 74; 81-82; 86-
87; 90-92; 94-96; 98; 100-101. 15,2. 16,1;
3; 5-6; 9; 11-22; 24-25; 29-37; 41-46; 49-
50. 17,2. 18,7; 9; 15-19; 21-22; 24; 31.
20,2; 4. 21,2. 22,1-7; 9; 11-12; 14-15; 18-
21; 23; 25; 27; 30-32; 34; 36-37. 23,1. 24,4-
5; 7-8; 11; 14; 19; 21; 23; 28; 31; 33-34; 37;
39; 42; 51-52; 55-56; 58-59; 61; 64; 67-70;
74-77; 81; 87; 95; 97-100; 103; 105. 25,1;
3-6; 8-20; 22; 25. 26,1; 4-5; 7-9; 12-19; 21-
29; 31-33; 36-37; 40-42; 46; 48-51; 54. 27,1-
4; 6; 8-10; 12-14; 17-33; 35-37; 39-42; 44-
46; 51; 53-55; 57; 60-61; 63-64. 28,1-2; 4-
5; 7; 9-10; 12-16; 18-30; 32; 35; 38-41; 43.
29,2-3; 9-22; 24; 26-29; 31-33. 30,1; 6-7;
11-21; 26-27; 32; 34-37. 31,3; 10; 13; 15.
32,2-10; 12-17; 19-26; 29-30. 33,1. 34,1; 3-
12; 16-19; 22-26. 35,1-2; 4-10; 13; 16-17.
36,1. 37,1-3; 6-7. 38,1-4; 6; 13-14. 39,1-3.
40,3-5; 7-13; 16-20; 22-23; 25-26. 41,1-2.
42,2; 6-7; 9-10; 13-16; 18. 43,1; 4; 6. 44,2-
5; 8; 11-13; 15; 17-18. 45,1-4. 46,1-3. 47,1;
3-6; 8-10. 48,1-8; 11-13; 15. 49,1-2; 4-6.
50,1. 51,2-3; 5-6; 8; 11-12. 52,1-2. 53,1-2.
54,1. 55,3-4. 56,8-9; 21-23. 57,1-11; 16; 18;
20; 22; 24; 26-29; 31-35; 39-40; 42-44; 48-
51; 53-55; 57. 58,1-4. 59,1-7; 9; 11-16; 20.
61,1-3; 6; 8-10. 63,1; 5; 8-10; 15; 17-18.
64,1-3; 6; 8; 11; 14-19. 65,1. 66,1-2. 67,2-
15; 17; 20-22; 24. 68,5-6; 9-14; 22; 25-36;
38-46; 48. CS2; 10; 14-18; 22; 25; 29-32;
35. CN3; 5-8; 10; 12; 15; 17; 24; 29. CW2;
5; 7; 10; 13; 17-18; 20. CK1; 5-6; 12-14;
20-21; 26; 28; 30-32; 34-35; 38-39; 41-42;
44; 60; 66; 69.

　　　　　　NFK　　1,69.
　　　　　　NTH　　1,2b; 9; 18. 4,3.
8,6. 18,14; 22; 32; 35. 26,3; 9. 30,15-16.
39,3. 46,5. 48,2. 56,9; 26; 30; 37.

　　　　　　NTT　　B4. 1,2; 4-13; 15-
27; 29; 31-32; 34; 36-38; 40-43; 46; 48-50;
53-54; 56-57; 60-62; 64-66. 2,1-6; 9-10.
3,2-4. 4,1; 3-8. 5,1; 4-19. 6,1-15. 7,1-6.
8,1-2. 9,1-8; 10-35; 37-38; 40-46; 49; 51-
54; 57-59; 62-64; 67-75; 77-94; 96-103; 105-
110; 112-132. 10,1-4; 6-7; 9-18; 21-33; 36-
40; 42; 44-54; 56-63; 65. 11,1-14; 17-25;
28-29; 31-32. 12,2; 4-9; 11; 13-18; 20; 22-
23. 13,1-5; 7-10; 12-14. 14,1-8. 15,1-7; 10.
16,1-6; 8-12. 17,1-4; 7-11; 13-14; 17. 18,1-
7. 19,1. 20,1-3; 5-7. 21,1-3. 22,1-2. 23,1-
2. 24,2-3. 25,1-2. 27,2-3. 28,1-3. 29,1.
30,2-20; 22-29; 31-32; 34-49; 51-56.

　　　　　　RUT　　R17; 19; 21.
　　　　　　YKS　　C33. 1Y10; 15; 19.

1N6; 26; 32; 44; 49; 61; 66-67; 77; 100-101;
104; 114. 1E1-4; 11; 27; 29; 33; 37; 39-42;
50. 1W2; 11; 21; 23; 25; 29; 45; 62. 2,1-2.
2B1; 4-6; 11; 13-14. 2N11; 13-15; 17; 22;
25. 2W4; 6-8; 13. 2E3; 8; 10; 12-13; 18; 20;
23; 30; 33-35. 3Y1; 3-5. 4N1-2. 5N12; 22;
31; 34; 54-55; 61; 65. 5E1-2; 5-6; 8-9; 11;
13; 15-19; 22; 24; 26-28; 33-36; 51; 62; 67.
5W1; 9-12; 17-18; 21-22; 27-28; 30-31; 35-
36. 6N1; 27; 29; 52; 113; 162. 6W2-3; 5.
6E1. 7E1. 8N1-2;·20; 27-28. 8E1. 9W6; 23;
29; 44-46; 70-71; 119-120. 10W7; 17; 19;
27; 30; 33; 36-38; 40. 11E2. 11N1; 7; 19.
11W4. 12W1. 13W6-9; 11; 22; 30. 13E2;
4; 7; 11; 13; 16. 13N2-3. 14E1; 4-8; 11; 14-
16; 24; 29; 42; 46; 48-49; 53. 15E2-3; 10.
16E2. 16N1. 16W1. 18W1. 19W2. 21E5-
7; 12. 21W4; 7; 12; 15. 23W4. 23N1; 33.
23E3; 6; 10; 15; 17; 19. 24W2-3; 7-8; 13.
25W3-4; 7; 17; 29; 32-33. 26E5; 10. 27W1-
2. 28W20; 33. 29W4; 6-7; 28-29; 33. 29E2;
17. 29N1; 9; 11. 29W28-29; 33. 30W4; 9;
18; 21. 31E2-5; 7-8. 31W3-4. 31N5-6; 8;
10. CN2. CE4-8; 12; 14; 17; 24-26; 28.
CW2-3; 8; 11-14; 16; 18; 20; 24; 27; 29; 31;
34; 37-41. SN,Y7. SW,Sk1; 11; 14; 19.
SW,BA2; 5-6; 8-9. SW,Sf1; 5-7; 10; 12-13;
15-18; 20-21; 23-28; 30-33; 36. SW,O1-2;
6-7. SW,St5; 14. SW,Ag9-10. SW,M1; 13.
SW,An1-5; 7; 13-14; 17. SW,Bu8; 20-21;
26; 31; 33; 39-40. SW,H3. SN,L5; 11-12;
15; 19; 23-24; 31-32; 44. SN,D3; 12; 15;
18. SN,Ma2-3; 5-6; 13; 20-21. SN,B5; 9;
13-17; 23; 25; 27. SN,Bi2. SN,A2.
SN,CtA19; 45. SE,He2-3; 5; 7; 9-11.
SE,We12; 5-6. SE,C1-2; 4; 7-9.
SE,How2-5; 8-10. SE,Wei2; 4-5. SE,Sn1;
4-7; 10. SE,Dr4-6. SE,Wa2; 6-7. SE,P4-
5; 7; 9. SE,Hu7. SE,Tu2-3; 7. SE,Bt6.
SE,Sc1-3; 5-7; 9-10. SE,Ac7; 10-11.
SE,Th10-14. SE,So1. SE,Mid1-2.
SE,Ho12-3; 7-10; 13; 15-19; 21-22; 25-26.
See also: Meadow; Woodland.
BOWMAN (arbalistarius; balistarius) – See
Gunner.
BOX wood (buxum)
Rendered for land　　　SHR　　3e,1.
BRAMBLE thicket　　WIL　　13,5.
(runcetum)
BREACH of peace – See Crime/offence;
Customary due; Peace.
BREAD – See Dog; Toll.
BREAKING and entry – See Crime/offence;
Customary due; House breaking.
BRETEUIL – See Customs.
BRETON (brito)　　　BDF　　52.
　　　　　　　　　　BKM　　B8. 43. 44.
　　　　　　　　　　DEV　　*15,12-15*. 16,94.
　　　　　　　　　　　　　　35,4. 39.
　　　　　　　　　　ESS　　38.
　　　　　　　　　　GLS　　W12. 74.

	HEF	10,41; 50.
	HRT	39.
	HUN	28,1.
	LEC	37. 38.
	LIN	42. 46. CK32.
	SOM	*1,19*. 10,2. *19,4; 8;*
		46. 24,5.
	SFK	70.
BREWER		
(cervisarius)	CON	1,2.
	SFK	14,167.
BRIDGE	SFK	21,15.
borough ward on		
other side	LIN	S1.
repair of city's	CHS	C21.
BRIDLE (frenum)	NFK	1,7.
BRINE pit (puteus) – See Salt pit.		
BROTHER (frater)	BDF	16,4. 29. 33. 47,1.
		53,30. 57,7.
	BRK	34. 36,4. 54,2.
	BKM	3a,2. 4,1; 28.
		14,10-11; 16. 17,1;
		30. 18,3. 41,2.
		44,4. 51. 57,15.
	CAM	18,7. 34,1.
	DBY	10,16.
	DEV	*1,41.* 3,40. 15,21.
	DOR	5,2. 26,37. 30,3.
		53,2. 56,13.
	ESS	1,1; 27. 7,1. 30,20.
		34,22. 37. 42,1. 56.
		90,85.
	GLS	1,16; 56. 2,10.
		10,12. 43,1. 52,3.
		53,6; 10.
	HAM	2,10. 6,16. 18,3.
		23,12; 44. 37,1.
		53,2. 69,45; 50. S3.
		IoW1,7. IoW6,2; 4.
	HEF	1,45; 61. 8,7.
	HRT	4,1; 12; 15. 15,10.
		25. 31,3. 36,16.
		37,5. 42,8.
	HUN	1,1; 6-8. 19,8; 15.
		23,1. 24. D21; 27.
	KEN	5,33; 99; 110; 223–
		224.
	LEC	13,63. 42,3.
	LIN	C3. T5. 3,41; 47.
		7,34. 12,4; 31.
		22,26. 26,25; 45.
		28,11. 29,27. 30,3.
		31,17. 51,12. CS6;
		21-22; 38. CN26;
		30. CW16. CK19.
	MDX	18,1. 22.
	NFK	1,192. 9,88. 10,30.
		20,29. 36. 66,103.
	NTH	B26. 43.
	NTT	10,20; 49. 15,5.
	OXF	28,6. 37,1.

	SHR	4,1,15. 4,19,9.
	SOM	2,7. *24,35. 35,19.*
		47,14.
	STS	11,56.
	SFK	1,1; 102; 110. 2,10.
		6,57. 7,24; 37; 67.
		12. 25,79. 30.
		31,60. 39. 41,10.
		66,10. 67,15. 76,3.
	SRY	5,21. 19,37. 25,3.
		36,1.
	SSX	9,31; 130.
	WAR	17,7; 17. 22,18; 25.
		44,11.
	WIL	67,5; 10; 96.
	YKS	1E60. 5E11. 5W24.
		9W45; 103. 29E20.
		CE35; 45. CW2-3.
Being man of his		
brother	HRT	36,16.
Holding land from		
brother	WIL	67,5.
See also: Relations.		
BRUSHWOOD (rispalia) – See Fence.		
BUILDING		
Household		
(aedificium		
dominicum)	NTH	6a,25.
Woodland for	HAM	1,23.
BULL (taurus)	CON	*5,4,13.*
BUNDLE (fascis)	SHR	3e,1.
BURGESS		
(burgensis)	BDF	56.
	BRK	B1.
	BKM	B1; 3-13. 1,3.
		17,17.
	CAM	B1-2; 11. 14,12.
	CHS	C25. FD6,1.
		FT1,1. FT2,1; 19.
		R6,5.
	CON	*4,3.*
	DBY	B1-2.
	DEV	C7. 1,1-2. 3,3; 6.
		5,15. 16,2-3.
		23,27. 24,20.
	DOR	B4. 1,31. 2,1. 30,4.
		55,38.
	ESS	1.25. 20,8. 23,27.
		24,63. B1-2;
		3b,d,p; 5-6.
	GLS	*G1-4. B1.* 1,21; 24–
		25; 43. 3,5. 4,1.
		8,1. 10,14. 12,4.
		20,1. 28,1. 34,3; 8.
		39,2; 6; 12. 41,1.
		46,1. 47,1. 50,3.
		54,1. 58,1. 59,1.
		60,1. 78,10; 14.
	HAM	2,20. 15,1. 23,5.
		32,1.
	HEF	C5; 11; 14. 1,4; 7;

		47. 8,1. 10,7. 13,1.
		19,2. 23,5.
	HRT	B1; 5-6; 10. 9,10.
		10,5. 15,1. 25,2.
		42,7.
	HUN	B1-2; 9; 12; 18. D1.
	KEN	D2-3. C1-3. 2,1; 3;
		16; 24-26; 41; 43.
		3,9. 5,126; 127;
		178. 7,4; 10. 9,9.
	LEC	C2; 16. 3,1; 6.
	LIN	C2; 4; 10-11; 16;
		18. S15. T1-2. 1,9.
		7,56. 27,35. CW3.
	MDX	4,5.
	NFK	1,49; 61; 63; 66-67;
		69-70.
	NTH	B1; 37.
	NTT	B1; 5-6. 6,1.
	OXF	B11. 29,15.
	SHR	C1; 3; 6-8; 14.
		3b,1. 4,5,8. 6,33.
	SOM	1,1-2; 9-10; 19; 28-
		29; 31. 2,1. 5,30;
		66. 7,1. 14,1.
		19,71. 24,17. 36,1.
	STS	B1. 1,9; 30.
	SFK	1,97; 116; 122b-d.
		6,4; 84. 14,120.
		21,47. 25,1; 52.
		27,8. 63,1. 74,8.
	SRY	1,4. 14,1.
	SSX	3,2. 5,1. 7,1. 8,1.
		8a,1. 9,13. 10,1.
		11,2; 104. 12,1; 3;
		6; 44.
	WAR	B3; 6. 18,2. 40,2.
	WIL	M3. 1,1-2; 4; 7; 10;
		18. 3,3-4. 7,6; 11.
		8,3; 10; 13. 9,1.
		10,5. 12,4-6. 23,9.
		24,38. 25,5. 26,7;
		14. 27,9-11; 23.
		40,1. 41,9. 48,11.
		58,1. 67,1; 9. 68,21.
	WOR	4,1. 5,1. 8,1; 13.
		10,10. 12,1. 15,9.
		17,1. 18,6. 19,14.
		22,1. 24,1. 26,1;
		15-16. 28,1.
	YKS	C1a; 2; 40. 1Y10.
		10W3.
Abbey		
given to	SHR	C14.
taken from	HUN	B1.
Agricultural services of		
cultivating/		
working land	DEV	17,1.
	HUN	B18.
	SHR	3h,1.
	YKS	C22.

hay making	HEF	C3.
ploughs, with	BKM	17,17.
	DBY	B1.
	DEV	24,20.
	NTT	B5.
reaping	HEF	C3.
	WOR	19,12.
working like		
villagers	STS	1,30.
	SSX	5,2.
Customary dues		
exempt/not paying	ESS	B3a,b,d.
	HUN	B9.
	KEN	5,178.
	LIN	T1.
held by burgesses	WAR	B3.
paid by burgesses	DEV	3,3.
	ESS	B3a-b,d,h.
	HRT	B6.
	HUN	B1; 9.
	NFK	1,61; 66.
	SFK	1,122c. 25,52.
paid to King	HUN	B12.
	NFK	1,66; 70.
	SFK	1,116; 122c. 6,4.
		27,8. 63,1.
paid to King and		
Earl	NFK	1,61.
Death of	SFK	1,116. 27,8.
King's rights on	HEF	C5.
relief to King on	SHR	C7.
Evidence by	BRK	B1.
	KEN	9,9.
	LIN	C4; 16.
	YKS	C2; 10.
contradicted	LIN	C4.
Devastation of by fire,		
King's tax, officer and		
Earl Ralph's forfeiture	NFK	1,63.
Fine on burning down		
of house	SHR	C6.
Fishing by forbidden	NTT	B6.
Forfeitures (three)		
held by Archbishop	KEN	2,43.
Jurisdiction, full held		
by	WAR	B3.
Land/property of		
chapel	NFK	1,61.
church	NFK	1,61.
	SFK	1,122d. 74,9.
church/land in		
pledge to	HUN	D1.
common property		
for King's service	ESS	B5.
guild	KEN	C3.
guildhall	KEN	D8.
land	DBY	B1.
	DEV	2,1.
	DOR	2,1.
	ESS	1,25. B3a.
	HRT	10,5. 15,1.

	KEN	5,127.
	NFK	1,49; 61; 65-66; 70.
	NTT	B1.
	SFK	1,97; 122c. 21,47.
land, letting	HUN	B18.
meadow	ESS	B3a.
	NFK	1,61.
	SFK	1,97.
mill	ESS	B3a.
	NFK	1,61; 70. 9,1.
property divided in		
common	ESS	B5.
sale-conditions on		
leaving city	HEF	C2.
	LIN	T1.
Living		
outside borough/		
city	CHS	FD5,2.
	DEV	1,1-2. 17,1.
within borough	DEV	1,1-2. 17,1.
at the hall	SFK	1,97.
in the market	SFK	6,191.
London, of	MDX	3,12.
	SRY	14,1.
Lordship, in	NFK	1,66.
	NTH	B1.
	SHR	C7.
	STS	B1.
	SFK	1,97; 122b.
	SSX	10,1. 12,1.
Manor/village,		
belonging/attached to	BKM	1,3.
	CHS	1,1. FD5,2. FD6,1.
	DEV	16,58.
	DOR	2,1.
	ESS	35,5.
	GLS	20,1.
	KEN	2,3; 24-26; 41; 43. 3,9. 7,4.
	LEC	C11. 25,2.
	SHR	6,33.
	SOM	1,19; 28.
	STS	1,30. 8,9.
	SFK	21,47.
	SSX	3,2.
	WAR	1,5.
	WIL	1,2; 10; 18. 3,3-4. 7,11. 8,13. 10,5. 23,9.
Military service		
providing boatman	WAR	B6.
expedition, going		
on	LEC	C2.
	OXF	B2.
	WAR	B6.
horses sent for	ESS	24,63.
	LEC	C2.
horses for carrying		
service	LEC	C2.
payment in lieu of	OXF	B2.
	WAR	B6.

ship, making	ESS	24,63.
Wales, in	HEF	C10.
	SHR	C4.
Payments		
burgess, by in		
another County	BKM	1,3.
dues, free from	GLS	59,1.
excessive burden	SHR	C14.
nothing paid	CAM	B1-2.
	CHS	1,1.
	HEF	1,47.
poll tax	ESS	B3,b,d.
	SFK	1,122c.
smallholders		
contribute to	HUN	B1.
tax (geldum)	LIN	C11.
	SHR	1,1.
toll, from	HRT	15,1.
toll, exempt from	LIN	T1.
tribute gablum)	GLS	G1-4. B1.
	KEN	C1. 2,16. 7,4.
	SHR	C1.
	SSX	10,1.
	YKS	1Y,11.
work, from	NTT	B1.
Payments to King	BKM	B3-7; 9-13.
	HUN	B1; 9; 12.
	NFK	1,61; 66; 70.
nil	BKM	B8; 11.
annually after		
Easter	ESS	B6.
Quitting borough		
for elsewhere	NFK	1,61.
sale of house on	HEF	C2.
	LIN	T1.
Renders by		
corn to King	DBY	B13.
horseshoe (ferrum)	GLS	78,14.
ploughs-loan of	CAM	B11.
ploughshares	GLS	39,12.
	HEF	1,7.
salmon	GLS	10,14.
salt	WOR	26,1.
Render of service		
cartage/carts	CAM	B11.
court, at	GLS	1,24.
	SSX	5,2.
	WOR	19,12.
horse, with, guards		
King whilst		
hunting	SHR	C3.
horse, with, attends		
pleas/Hundred	HEF	C3.
King, to	KEN	2,43. 5,178.
King's hunting	HEF	C3.
	SHR	C3.
pilotage for King	LIN	T1.
providing ship	ESS	24,63.
	KEN	D2.
	LIN	T1.
providing		
steersman	KEN	D3.

Sheriff in relation to:
common pasture
taken by   CAM   B11.
holding burgess for
debt   SFK   63,1.
holding burgess in
pledge   SFK   63,1.
time limit given by
breached   SHR   C8.
Status
could/could not be
another's man   NFK   1,70.
could not with-
draw from lord or
do homage to
another   NFK   1,61.
Abbey/church, of   HUN   B1; 9.
                            SHR   3g,1.
                            SFK   25,52.
Bishop, of   BKM   B3.
                            SHR   1,1.
Count, of   CAM   B1-2. 14,12.
Earl, of   BKM   B4; 11.
                            CHS   FT1,1.
                            SHR   3b,1.
Earl Harold, of   HEF   C11.
                            HRT   B6.
English   NFK   1,61.
                            SHR   C14.
English hold by
previous customs   HEF   C14.
French   NFK   1,66.
                            SHR   C14.
French free from
forfeitures   HEF   C14.
French held by
others   NFK   1,66.
King, of   DEV   3,3.
                            ESS   B3a.
                            HRT   B6.
                            NFK   1,61.
                            NTH   B1.
                            SOM   1,31.
                            STS   B1.
others, of   BKM   B3; 4-11; 13.
                            CAM   B1.
                            CHS   FT2,1.
                            ESS   B3b.
                            HEF   10,7.
                            HRT   B6.
                            HUN   B2.
                            LEC   C11; 16.
                            SHR   3b,1.
                            SOM   1,31.
                            SFK   1,116. 6,4. 25,52.
                                    27,8. 38,3. 63,1.

petty/lesser   WOR   5,1. 22,1. 26,16.
                            DBY   B2.
                            NFK   1,61.
                            YKS   9W64.
poor and cannot
pay tax   SFK   1,122c.
royal   ESS   B6.
slave, being   SFK   25,52.
woman, being   NFK   1,61.
See also: Anglo-saxon; Borough; Cartage; Church;
Claim; Cottager; Grange; Hall; House;
Jurisdiction, full; King's hand; Mercy; Monk;
Pasture; Patronage; Prebendary; Residence; River;
Salmon; Sheriff; Taken away; Tax; Wall;
Withdraw.
BURIAL (sepultura)
Customary due, as   SOM   2,3.
Fees purchased by
mother church   SFK   1,1.
Place of
land holder's   SFK   2,4.
St.Edmund's   SFK   14,167.
Rights   WOR   2,21.
gift, to obtain   HAM   10,1.
BURNING
House, of   HEF   A5.
Town   KEN   D7.
Town/city, in –
liability of
householder from
where fire began   CHS   C13.
See also: Crime/offence; Destruction.
BURSAR
(dispensator)   BRK   41,6.
                            GLS   47.
                            HUN   19,18.
                            KEN   2,10.
                            LEC   C16. 19.
                            LIN   38. CS1; 3; 12; 23-
                                    24; 33-34; 36.
                                    CN22.
                            SOM   5,34.
                            SFK   14,167.
                            WAR   23.
                            WOR   2,13; 19; 49; 67; 73.
                                    9,1d.
BUTLER (pincerna)   BDF   35.
                            CHS   6.
                            DEV   15,16-19; 32-33;
                                    55.
                            DOR   15,1.
                            SHR   4,1,5. 4,6.
                            SOM   19,39; 80; 86.
BUTTER, vessel of (rusca butiri)
Render of   CHS   FT3,7.

C

CALF (vitulus)   ESS   22,3. 30,1. 32,44.
34,1; 4-5; 11-13;
15; 22; 34-35.
41,12. 42,3. 45,1.
48,2. 54,2.
See also: Cow.
CALL/re-call (vocare; revocare) – See Cite.
CAMPAIGN (exercitus)
Horse provided for   ESS   24,63.
See also: Army; Expedition; Service.
CANON (canonicus)   BDF   5,2. 12,1. 13,1-2.
53,32. 57,8.
            BKM   10.
            CAM   16.
            CHS   B12. A1. 1,35.
            CON   1,7. 2,6. 4,2; 23-27.
            DEV   *1,11. 2,2; 5-8; 22.*
10,1-2. 16,89-92.
45,3.
            DOR   22.
            ESS   5,12.
            HEF   2,3; 7; 12-13; 15-16;
55. 6,2. 19,8.
            HRT   13,1-5. 14. 17,14.
34,13.
            KEN   D1. M. P1; 5; 7; 13;
18; 20. 9,9.
            LIN   7,8; 57.
            MDX   3,2; 6; 14-30. 9,4.
15,1.
            NTT   5,3.
            OXF   B10. 14.
            SHR   3d,6. 3g,1-2. 4,1,5.
9,1.
            SOM   6,1; 16-17.
            STS   2,16. 6. 7.
            SRY   2,3. 5,6; 20. 13,1.
17,1; 4.
            SSX   2,1f; 3. 3,10. 9,126.
            WIL   19.
            YKS   C1a; 2; 21; 23-25;
30. 2B4-8. 2W5; 7.
2E1. CE24. CW39.
Bishop, of   SHR   1,2.
Evidence by   SSX   3,10.
            YKS   C25.
Land held as if by   SHR   3d,7.
Manor, of   DEV   1,17.
Payments by   SHR   1,2.
Prebendary of King   STS   6,1.
See also: Barton; Footwear; House; Supplies;
Taken away.
CANUTE – See King.

CAPITAL messuage (caput manerii) – See Head
of manor
CAPITAL punishment – See Crime/offence;
Smith.
CARADOC – See King.
CARGO – See Marten-skins; Ship.
CARPENTER
(carpentarius)   CAM   40.
            DOR   *55,48.* 57,20-21.
            HEF   29,2. 32,1.
            NFK   66,101-102.
            WIL   66,6-7.
            YKS   C20.
CARRIAGE – See Salt.
CARRYING service – See Cartage; Hunting.
CART (currus)   CAM   B11. 14,2. 28,2.
Over-loading, fine for   CHS   S2,2.
Tolls in wich   CHS   S3,2.
See also: Burgess; Ox; Salt.
CARTAGE
service/payments
(avera; averagium)   CAM   B11. 1,2. 14,64.
18,5. 26,7-9. 29,8.
32,35. 35,1-2. 40,1.
41,3.
            HRT   1,6; 9-11; 14-15.
4,1. 5,9-11; 13.
17,4. 31,1. 34,11-
12. 36,8-9; 11; 17.
37,1; 14.
            KEN   1,3. 5,138. 13,1.
            SFK   *66,3.*
three quarters (three
parts) (¾)   HRT   17,4. 36,8.
half (½)   CAM   21,5. 44,1.
            HRT   4,1. 5,10.
one quarter (fourth
part) (¼)   CAM   31,5.
            HRT   36,9; 11. 37,14.
By:-
burgess   CAM   B11.
free man   SFK   *14,92.*
Freeman   CAM   1,2-3; 12; 14. 5,5;
7. 14,2-3; 5; 7; 11; 15; 63; *70;* 71-72; 77;
79; 81. 15,4. 17,2. 18,3; 6; 8. 21,5-6. 26,1;
3; 5; 10-11; 16; 18; 32; 36; 43; 46-47; *51.*
29,4. 31,3; 6-7. 32,4-5; 7; 14; 16; 20-21; 30;
32-33; 38. 44,1.
            HRT   1,9-11; 15. 5,9.
34,12. 36,9; 11.
37,1; 14.
            NFK   9,75.
            SFK   29,1.

Hundred or customary dues, not liable for	HEF	8,1.
Land		
belonging to	NFK	8,51; 58-61.
in exchange for	DEV	2,9-10.
in exchange for site of	DOR	19,10.
	KEN	1,2.
held whilst castle held	YKS	CE20.
Lordship, in	CHS	FT1,1.
Market in	CON	2,6. 4,2.
	SFK	18,1.
Residences outside	LIN	C26.
Sheriff, held by	HEF	8,1.
Site of	HUN	B4; 6.
	WAR	B2.
Small	GLS	1,19.
Taking of	YKS	CN3.
Village land in bounds of	YKS	CW1; 3.
Warden (custos)	SSX	10,2; 22.

CASTLERY

(castellaria; castellatus)	HEF	2,2. 8,1. 10,1-3. 12,2. 13,2. 14,1.
	SSX	9,11.
	WOR	23,14.
	YKS	SN,CtA45.
Church in	HEF	13,2.
Given by King to Count	SSX	9,11.
Land in	YKS	30W3; 30.
Land not belonging	HEF	10,2.
Welsh District belonging to	SHR	4,1,15.

CATCHPOLE

(chacepullus)	MDX	3,9.
CATTLE (animalia)	BKM	20,1.

CON 1,1-5; 8-12; 14-17. 2,4-5; 8. 3,1-4. 4,1-2; 6-7; 9-16; 23-27. 5,1,1-13; 16; 22. 5,2,2; 6; 17-19; 21-22; 24; 27. 5,3,1; 3; 5-9; 11-12; 14; 16-24; 27-28. 5,4,1. 5,5,2-4; 6-7; 9-10; 12; 16-17; 20. 5,6,1-9. 5,7,2-4; 6-10; 12. 5,8,1-4; 6; 9. 5,9,1; 4. 5,10,1. 5,11,1-2; 4; 6. 5,12,3. 5,13,1-2; 9; 11. 5,14,1-2; 3. 5,15,1-5. 5,17,3. 5,20,2. 5,23,1-3; 5. 5,24,1-4; 10; 12; 18; 21-25. 5,25,1-3. 5,26,2-4. 6,1. 7,1.
DEV 1,3-4; 6; 8-9; 11; 13; 15; 17-19; 25-27; 29-31; 33; 36-41; 43-46; 49-72. 2,2; 4; 6-7; 11; 13-15; 17-21; 24. 3,4-8; 12-14; 16-17; 19-23; 25-26; 28; 30-31; 33; 36-38; 40; 44-47; 49; 53; 56; 58-67; 70; 73-78; 80; 85-86; 89-93; 95-96; 97. 4,1. 5,1-6; 8; 11-14. 6,1-5; 7-12. 7,1-3. 8,1. 9,1. 10,1-2. 11,1-3. 12,1. 13a,2-3. 15,2; 5-6; 8-14; 17-18; 23-27; 29-30; 33; 36-37; 39-51; 56; 58; 60-61; 64-67; 70; 75; 77; 79. 16,4-9; 11-12; 14-27; 29-31; 33-36; 39-40; 43-49; 51-53; 55-59; 63; 65; 67-74; 76; 78; 80; 82-91; 94-97; 102; 104; 106-108; 110-114; 116-118; 121-123; 125; 128-133; 136-138; 140-144; 146; 148; 152-154; 158-160; 163-167; 170-172; 175-176. 17,3-8; 10; 12-17; 19-20; 22; 28-36; 41-44; 46; 48; 51; 53-54; 59; 68-69; 73; 78-79; 89; 92; 95; 97; 102-103; 106. 19,2; 4-7; 9-17; 19; 23-27; 29-31; 33; 35; 37-40; 44-46. 20,1; 3; 6; 10-11; 13-15. 21,1; 3-4; 9-10; 12; 14; 16; 19-20. 22,1. 23,1-7; 9-12; 14-20; 21-24; 26. 24,2-3; 5-10; 13-14; 17; 21-23; 25; 27-28; 30; 32. 25,1-2; 4-9; 11-16; 18; 20-23; 25. 28,1-6; 8-10; 13; 15-16. 31,1-2. 32,2; 4; 6-7. 33,1. 34,1-2; 4; 6-7; 10; 14-16; 18-20; 22-27; 29-31; 33; 35; 38-41; 43-44; 46; 48-52; 55. 35,1-5; 7-10; 12-14; 16; 20-22. 36,3; 7; 15-18; 20; 23-26. 37,1. 38,1. 40,2; 4-7. 41,2. 42,1-4; 6-8; 10; 12-14; 16-18; 20-24. 43,2-3; 5. 45,2. 47,1; 5; 7-8; 12-13. 48,3-4; 7-8; 10-11. 49,2; 7. 50,1; 5. 51,1-3; 6-7; 9-16. 52,1; 4-6; 10; 12; 14; 16; 20; 22; 24; 26-29; 31-33; 36-37; 40-41; 43-45; 51; 53.
DOR 1,1-2; 4-5; 7-8; 11-12; 15; 17-19; 21; 28. 11,1. 12,1; 5; 14,16. 13,1; 4; 6; 8. 16,1. 36,1-6; 9-11. 41,1-4. 47,1-3; 6; 8. 48,1. 55,2; 7; 15-16; 19-20; 22; 29; 33; 36; 38; 41.
ESS 1,2-4; 9; 11-13; 19; 21-29. 2,1-5; 7-9. 3,2; 8-10; 12-15. 4,1-2; 5-6; 8-9; 11; 14-15. 5,1-7; 9-12. 6,5; 8; 11; 15. 7,1. 8,1-11. 9,1-2; 7-9; 11-14. 10,1-5. 11,1-3; 6-7. 13,1-2. 14,2-6. 15,1-2. 16,1. 17,1. 18,1-5; 14; 18; 24-25;28; 36-41. 20,3; 8; 15; 19-23; 25-27; 30; 36-37; 39-40; 43-46; 48; 52-53; 55-57; 60; 64; 66-67; 69; 79-80. 22,3; 5-9; 11-15; 20. 23,2; 5; 15; 38-40. 24,1-6; 8-9; 15-26; 28-33; 35; 37; 42-46; 48-49; 53-54; 59-62; 64-66. 25,1-5; 7-8; 10-12; 15-25. 26,1; 3; 5. 27,1-2; 4; 11; 13-14. 28,9; 11; 13; 16-17. 29,1-2; 4-5. 30,1; 4; 16-18; 22; 27; 33; 45-46. 32,1-4; 6-9; 13; 15-17; 19-26; 28; 30; 32-35; 38-39; 43-45. 33,1; 3-4; 6-8; 11-17; 19-20; 22-23. 34,5-6; 10; 18-19; 27; 29; 33-34; 36. 35,1-6; 8-12. 36,3; 6; 8. 37,1-4; 7; 9-11; 13; 16. 38,1-4; 6-8. 40,4. 41,2; 5; 10; 12. 42,1-3; 6-9. 44,1-3. 45,1. 46,1-2. 47,2-3. 49,4-5. 53,1-2. 54,1-2. 55,1. 56,1. 57,2-3; 5-6. 58,1. 60,1-3. 61,1-2. 67,1-2. 68,2; 4; 7. 69,2. 71,2; 4. 81,1. 84,2.
HAM 1,45.
HEF 34,1.
HRT 31,8.
HUN 4,2-4.
KEN 5,57; 84; 124.
LEC 42,10.
NFK 1,2-3; 40; 42; 52; 57; 59; 71-72; 77; 85; 88-89; 94; 105; 123; 128; 135-136; 139; 150-152; 169; 182; 185-186; 193-194; 197-199; 202-203; 205; 209-212; 215-217; 219; 231; 237-239. 2,2. 3,1. 4,1-2; 14; 26; 30-31; 38-39; 41-42; 47; 52.

King's daughter's HAM 67,1.
Queen's BRK 65,16.
CHANCELLOR
(cancelarius) HEF 1,46.
CHAPEL (capella) BRK 44,3.
   HAM 4,1.
   SFK 1,1.
   SRY 8,22. 19,11; 23.
Burgesses, of NFK 1,61.
Built by laymen SFK 1,1.
Church (parish),
under SFK 3,14.
Consecration
(dedicatio) SFK 1,1.
See also: Cemetery; Church, small.
CHAPLAIN
(capellanus) DEV 45.
   GLS 1,42.
   HEF 2,49; 57.
   KEN M9. 13.
   NTH 15.
   SOM 16,4.
Bishop's GLS 2,21.
Earl's NFK 1,66.
   SHR 3c,9. 4,1,5.
King's NTH B14.
Layman's SFK 7,36.
Wife of HEF 34,1.
CHAPTER of Abbey
(capitulum) consent re
land transaction GLS *12,3; 7-8.*
CHARGE (custodia; servare) – See Custody; Land;
Wardship.
CHARTER (carta) – See Title deeds.
CHATTEL (catallum)
Freeman as King's NFK 1,195.
CHEESE (caseus)
Payments
  from OXF 1,7a.
  of BRK 1,32. 5,1. 7,42.
   GLS 60,1.
   KEN 13,1.
   SOM 33,2.
Wey of BRK 1,32. 5,1.
   GLS 60,1.
   KEN 13,1.
CHICKEN (gallina)
Paid to sheriff WIL 24p.
See also: Eggs; Hen.
CHIEF lord
Identity unknown HAM 1,8.
   WAR 3,4.
CHRISTIANS – See Prayers.
CHURCH (ecclesia)
other than Abbey BDF 1,1c; 2b; 3. 4,9.
   BRK 1,2-3; 5; 7-10; 22-
24; 29; 31; 33-35; 39; 44. 2,3. 3,1. 5,1. 7,1;
13-14; 17; 30; 39; 44. 8,1. 12,1. 15,1-2.
17,9. 19,1. 20,2. 21,5; 7-9; 15. 22,11. 23,2.
27,2. 29,1. 36,4. 38,5-6. 40,1. 44,5. 46,1;
3-4. 54,1; 4. 55,3. 63,2. 65,1; 5-6.

   BKM B2. 1,1. 2,1. 3a,1.
   CHS 1,1; 8. 5,10. 13,3.
14,3; 10. 17,7. 27,1; 3. FD1,1. FT1,1; 8.
FT2,1-2; 7; 11; 15. R1,21. R4,1. R5,2.
   CON 2,12-14.
   DBY 1,9; 11; 13-14; 16;
19-20; 27; 29; 37. 2,1; 3. 4,1. 6,6; 24-25;
27; 30; 34; 39-40; 43; 54; 57; 66-67; 69; 95;
97-98. 7,6. 8,1; 3; 5. 9,1; 4. 10,4; 9; 26.
12,2. 17,15. B1; 5-8.
   DEV *1,13; 33.* 2,1; *2.*
15,1.
   DOR 14,1. 18,1-2. 19,10.
24,1-3.
   ESS 1,13. 18,23. 20,13.
27,1. 30,24. 66,1.
B1; 7.
   GLS *G1-4.* W5. 1,1; 13;
21; 37; 60. 9,1.
58,4. 67,1.
   HAM 1,1; 7-8; 16; 19; 30;
40; 44; 47; W4. 2,1; 3; 6; 8-15; 20; 22. 3,1-
9; 11; 13-14; 16; 18; 21. 4,1. 5,1. 5a,1. 6,2-
5; 8-9; 12. 13,1. 14,2. 18,1. 20,1. 21,1; 3;
6. 23,4-5; 18-19; 27-28; 31; 36; 59. 26,1.
28,6-7. 29,1; 3; 5-7. 30,1. 31,1. 35,9. 36,1.
37,1. 38,1. 39,4. 44,3-4. 46,1. 47,1. 49,1.
60,2. 61,1. 67,1. 68,1. 69,1-2; 7. NF9,44.
IoW1,7. IoW2,1. IoW4,1. IoW8,9.
   HEF A1. 1,1; 6-8; 39-40;
48; 62. 2,12. 13,2. 19,6. *26,30.* 29,2; 9.
   HRT B7. 42,11.
   HUN B12-13. 1,1-2; 5; 8;
10. 2,2-5. 4,2. 5,1. 6,1-9; 11-13; 24; 26.
7,1-5; 7. 8,1. 9,1. 10,1. 11,1-2. 13,1. 14,1.
18,1. 19,1; 6; 8-9; 30. 20,1-3; 6; 8. 21,1.
22,1. 23,1. 24,1. 29,1.
   KEN *M3;* 24. C3. P10.
1,1; 3. 2,5-17; 22-23; 25-26; 29; 31-33; 41.
3,1-8; 10-13; 20-21. 4,1-3; 6-13; 16. 5,18;
25; 27; 36; 38; 40-42; 45-46; 51-55; 57-58;
60; 62-63; 66-75; 79-81; 83; 86; 89; 93; 95-
97; 104-105; 118-124; 128-129; 138; 141-
145; 149; 154-155; 158-160; 163; 168; 172;
175; 180; 208; 220; 224. 6,1. 7,5; 7-9; 15;
20-21; 28. 9,3; 6; 10; 12; 22; 24-25; 28; 31;
36-37; 42; 48. 10,2. 11,1. 12,1; 3-4.
   LEC C11-12. 3,1.
   LIN C11; 16; 18. S6; 12-
13. 1,4-7; 9; 17-18; 26; 49; 65; 74; 81; 101-
102. 2,16; 18; 21; 33-34. 3,7; 16. 4,1; 11;
26; 39; 43-44; 50; 56; 69. 7,1; 3; 18; 30; 40;
43; 46; 54; 58. 8,1; 9. 9,1. 10,1. 11,4.
12,14; 21; 43; 47-49; 65; 67-68; 71; 75. 13,1;
5-6; 30-31; 34; 37. 14,9; 18; 23; 47; 63; 66;
71-78; 81; 83; 89; 98. 15,1. 16,8; 47. 17,1-
2. 18,7; 24; 28-29; 31. 19,1. 22,7; 24-25;
28-29. 23,1. 24,1; 5; 10; 12-13; 24; 32; 37-
38; 40; 46-48; 50; 53; 59; 66; 78; 81-82; 90;
92; 102-104. 25,19. 26,7; 23. 27,14; 34.
28,17; 32. 29,8; 11; 22. 30,22; 27. 31,1; 3;

11; 15-17. 32,11; 32; 34. 34,1-2; 12; 15; 17. 35,1; 14. 36,1. 37,2. 38,3; 8. 39,1; 3. 40,17. 42,9; 16. 43,1; 6. 44,5; 7-9. 48,5. 51,11-12. 53,2. 55,1; 3. 56,9; 14; 18. 57,18; 21; 24; 28; 30; 37-38. 58,1-2. 61,1. 63,15. 64,1; 6; 14-15; 17-18. 67,3-4; 7. 68,3-4; 28.

NFK 1,16; 52; 60-61; 68-70; 99; 205-206; 210; 236; 239. 4,38; 40; 42; 52. 6,6. 8,1; 3; 6; 8; 11-12; 14; 22; 27; 37; 71; 82-83; 98-108; 110; 112; 114; 119; 122-124; 126; 128. 9,1-2; 4; 7; 11; 25; 27-32; 36-37; 46; 51; 54; 56; 88; 94-96; 98-100; 134; 208-209; 212; 216; 221; 233. 10,1; 5-8; 15-16; 18; 22; 25; 30; 37; 43; 56-59; 65; 68; 72-73; 76; 83; 86. 12,27; 42. 13,3-7; 10; 13-15; 19; 23-24. 14,8; 15-16; 18; 23-24; 29; 32; 35; 38; 40-42. *15,29.* 17,23; 25-27; 36-39; 43; 50. 19,9; 11; 13; 15; 18; 22; 24-25; 32; 36-37. 20,1; 7-8; 15-16; 24; 26; 29; 33-36. 21,25-26; 29. 22,1; 3-4. 24,5-7. 31,6; 17; 21-22; 25-26; 34; 38; 44. 32,2; 4. 33,2. 36,5. 48,3-4. 49,2; 4-5; 7. 50,12. 61,1-2. 66,9; 16.

NTH 18,80. 21,1.

NTT B4; 15. 1,3; 10; 23; 28; 51; 58; 61. 2,1; 4. 5,4; 10; 13. 6,1; 13. 7,2. 8,1. 9,2; 6; 22; 40; 50; 55; 60; 70; 82; 90; 95; 100; 103; 110; 121-122; 131. 10,1; 5; 16; 29; 56; 65. 11,2; 4; 12; 14; 18; 26. 12,16; 18-19. 13,6; 9. 14,1; 4-5. 17,7. 18,1; 5. 19,1. 22,2. 24,1. 27,1. 30,1; 4; 20.

OXF B6.

RUT R,13; 17; 19-21.

SHR 4,1,10-11; 27. 4,3,3; 26; 31. 4,8,7; 13. 4,21,6. 4,23,3. 5,1. 6,11. 7,4; 6.

SOM 1,10; 19; 21; 29. 5,34. 6,14. 8,37. 12,1. 16,1-4; 6-7; 11. *46,6.*

SFK 1,1-2; 8; 12-13; 16; 20-23; 52; 69; 73; 76; 88; 90; 94-98; 102; 110-111; 113; 115; 118-121; 122d-f. 2,13; 16. 3,1; 3-5; 14; 19; 34; *44;* 48; 52; 56; 93; 95; 105. 4,1; 6; 14; 18-19; 21; 26; 30; 39; 42. 5,1; 3. 6,1-2; 32; 43; 46; 49; 66; 80; 83-85; 90; 96; 112; 120; 130; 133; 138; 143; 159; 161; 170; 172; 181-183; 191-192; 195; 213; 218; 222-223; 238; 249; 260; 271; 281; 287; 301; 303-306; 308; 313. 7,3-4; 28; 37; 60; 67; 70-71; 76; 80; 96-97; 114; 117; 119. 8,5; 22; 31; 35; 48-49; 56; 59. 9,1-2. 11,4. 12,1; 3. 13,2; 6. 14,1-5; 7-10; 12-14; 18-21; 23; 26; 36; 38; 42; 45; 53-55; 58; 60; 62-66; 68-69; 71-82; 85; 87-88; *92;* 93-94; 99; *101;* 102-103; 106; 108-109; 112-113; 120; 131; 137; 139. 15,2; 5. 16,15; 18; 20-22. 17,1. 18,1;4. 19,5; 13-14; 16. 20,1. 21,1; 3; 5-7; 10-11; 15-16; 18; 26; 28; 38-39; 42-43; 45; 54; 83; 85; 95. 22,3. 23,4. 24,1. 25,2-3; 6-7; 10; 27; 32; 34-35; 42; 52-53; 75-76; 78; 85; 93; 97; 100. 26,3; 9; 12a; 13; 16. 27,3; 9-10. 28,1a-b; 3; 7. 29,1; 11-12. 31,9; 21;

41-42; 46; 50; 60. 32,3; 14; 19. 33,1-6; 9-10; 13. 34,2-3; 6; 9; 15. 35,5-6. 37,1. 38,3; 6; 8; 11. 39,5-6; 10; 12. 40,3; 6. 41,1-2; 7; 10; 14. 43,2-3. 44,1-2. 46,1; 3-4; 10. 47,3. 48,1. 52,1; 5. 54,2. 57,1. 60,1. 62,1. 64,1-3. 66,1; 3. 67,3-4; 11. 69,1. 74,9; 13. 76,4.

SRY 1,2-3; 5; 8-9; 12-14. 2.1-5. 3,1. 5,1a; 8-9; 11; 23; 28. 8,1-3; 9; 14; 17; 22; 25; 28; 30. 11,1. 14,1. 15,1. 16,1. 18,3. 19,5-7; 14-16; 21; 26; 32; 36-37; 45; 47. 21,6. 22,1; 5. 24,1. 25,2-3. 27,3. 30,1-2. 33,1. 35,2. 36,5.

SSX 1,1. 2,5-6; 8-9. 3,2-3; 9. 5,1-3. 6,1-2; 4. 7,1. 8a,1. 9,4-5; 7; 11; 14; 31; 60; 82; 104; 107; 109. 10,53. 11,3-4; 7; 10-12; 17-18; 21; 30; 36-37; 41; 48; 55; 57; 59; 63; 67-68; 75-76; 78; 81-84; 88; 93; 96; 105. 12,3-7; 15; 30; 36-37; 39; 42; 48-49. 13,1; 5; 8; 11; 13; 19; 22; 28-30; 34; 38; 49. 14,1.

WIL 1,1; 5-6; 9-13; 15-19; 23a-j. 2,1; 3. 9,1. 17,1. 19,2-3.

WOR 8,1. 10,5. 14,1. 15,9. 26,8; 13.

YKS C2-3; 10-11; 13; 17-18. 1Y1; 5; 7; 9-11; 15-17. 1N65; 105. 1W25; 61. 1L1; 5. 2B1; 3; 6; 11; 18. 2W4; 6-7. 2E12; 23; 26; 38; 41. 3Y4; 10. 4N3. 5N19; 27; 29; 45; 50; 53; 58; 62; 66. 5E29; 55; 66. 5W7-8; 13; 16; 20; 22; 33. 6N1; 13; 18-19; 34; 49-50; 52; 56; 102; 112; 118; 120; 122; 162. 7E1. 8N6. 8W1. 8E1. 9W1-3; 6; 8; 15; 20; 24; 34; 45; 47; 49; 51-52; 54; 56; 64; 70; 94; 115; 118; 139. 10W3; 26; 34. 11E1. 12W1; 4; 12; 26. 13W5; 8; 12; 37. 13E13-15. 13N5; 9; 13; 17. 14E2; 7; 9; 12-13; 24-25; 34; 48; 53. 15E2. 16N1. 16W1; 5. 17W1. 18W1. 20E1. 21E1-2; 5; 9-10. 22W6. 23N19; 23; 27; 32. 23E3; 5; 14-15. 24W12. 25W8; 22; 24. 28W7; 39. 29E13. 29N3; 5; 8. 30W4. CW11; 23.

three quarters (three parts) (¾)	NFK	19,34.
	SFK	6,218. 16,28. 38,11.
	YKS	9W8.
two thirds (two parts) (⅔)	LIN	24,103. 29,28. 40,26.
	NFK	10,90. 14,41.
	SFK	6,18; 206. 14,11; 83; 129.
half (½)	CHS	17,6. 24,5.
	DBY	9,3.
	ESS	9,7. 20,56.
	HUN	7,6. 9,3.
	LIN	1,1. 2,17; 38. 3,4; 33; 37. 14,79; 84. 18,21. 24,93; 97. 26,30; 36-37; 53. 28,11. 32,1. 34,4. 42,1-2. 47,2. 56,20. 57,17. 59,13. 63,1.
	NFK	1,61; 70; 183. 8,2;

33; 84; 106; 108; 132. 9,24. 10,74. 13,6. *15,29.* 17,32-33. 19,40. 20,25. 48,3. 66,14; 21.

NTT 2,7. 9,130. 10,25. 11,28. 13,1; 4; 10. 15,8. 29,2.

SFK 1,73; 118. 3,95. 4,41. 6,30; 114; 225; 311-312. 7,29; 40; 56; 58; 67; 75. 8,33-34; 59; 70-71; 73. 9,3. 14,35; 89; 95; 105; 121. 16,26. 19,15. 21,47. 23,1. 28,6. 30,1; 44-45; 50; 56. 34,10. 36,2. 41,3. 43,3. 51,1. 53,3; 5. 66,2. 76,15.

YKS 1N92. 5N11. 8N1.

one third (one part) (⅓) LIN 3,42. 7,32. 18,15. 27,53. 40,26. 44,10. 48,7; 12. 59,5.

NFK 10,15.

SFK 8,55. 14,17. 25,46. 32,6. 34,12; 18. 46,5.

one quarter (¼) ESS 61,1. B3d.

LIN 12,37. 24,79. 27,57. 39,1.

NFK 8,7. 13,2. 14,16. 20,27. 31,26.

NTT 6,11. 9,3; 125.

SFK 6,18; 28; 38; 75. 7,27; 59; 137. 8,37. 14,72. 16,26; 28; 40; 44. 31,34. 32,5. 34,11. 35,5. 38,5. 43,5. 62,5. 67,5. 71,2.

one fifth (⅕) SFK 5,6. 13,6. 14,46. 16,37; 41.

one sixth (⅙) LIN 3,55-56. 24,97. 48,7. 67,11.

NFK 1,61.

SFK 16,12.

one eighth (⅛) LIN 29,13.

SFK 6,313. 19,2.

one twelfth (¹⁄₁₂) LIN 3,55-56. 67,11.

SFK 2,11.

part of SFK 3,67. 34,9. 58,1.

five parts of SFK 7,15.

City, parish of SHR 3b,1.

Condition/number/type

derelict (vasta)/ruinous/ dismantled CHS FT2,12.

WIL 1,18-19.

free NFK 1,70.

more 1086 than TRE SFK 6,84.

mother HAM 3,16.

SFK 1,1.

new GLS 58,4.

WIL 24,1.

new and beautiful SRY 1,4.

roof damaged WIL 1,18.

small (ecclesiola) BRK 11,1.

DOR 14,1.

HAM 1,19; 29. 2,5; 7. 3,19. 21,7. 42,1.

KEN 1,1. 9,16; 41.

SSX 9,1-2; 122. 11,9. 12,11; 16; 40. 13,25.

wooden (lignea) YKS 11N17.

Custody held by Abbot SFK 25,1.

Customary dues of HRT B7.

free from YKS C37.

received by King LIN C22.

Customs KEN C8.

LIN CK56; 62.

Foundation/building built by lay-man with King's assent NFK 45,1.

founded by Earl NFK 1,66.

land holder could on own land DBY B16.

Held by/belonging to burgess NFK 1,61.

SFK 1,122d. 74,9.

another church NFK 1,69.

SFK 1,12.

free men SFK 1,21.

free woman SFK 1,122f.

King DBY B1.

NTT B4.

King's hand in SFK 76,15.

layman wholly or partly DBY B5-8.

HUN B12.

LIN C4. 2,34. 3,4. 40,26. CK70.

NFK 10,73.

SFK 1,22; 122d-f. 6,18; 206. 7,137. 25,52; 60. 38,3. 74,9.

layman in shares LIN 3,4.

SFK 1,20; 22.

Jurisdiction of RUT R17; 19-20.

(cherchesoch)

Land/resources, of burgesses and houses HUN B12.

free land NFK 21,26.

SFK 1,1-2; 90; 97; 118- 121. 3,3; 5; 14; 72; 93. 4,1. 5,1. 6,1-2; 30; 32; 83; 191; 223; 303. 7,96. 8,33-34. 14,1- 5; 7-9; 12-14; 18-20; 36; 42; 48-54; 58; 60; 62-66; 69; 71; 73-83; 85; 87-88; 93-95; 103. 15,2. 16,12; 26. 17,1. 19,16. 21,10-11; 15- 16; *26; 83;* 85. 25,2; 6; 10; 32; 34-35; 42; 46; 78. 26,9. 27,3; 9-10. 29,1. 31,*9;* 41-42; 44-46. 33,1-2; 13. 34,2-3; 6. 40,3; 6. 41,10. 43,2-3. 44,1. 46,3. 51,1. 54,2. 66,1. 76,4.

land appurtenant to BDF 1,1c; 2b; 3. 4,9.

BRK 1,2; 5; 7-10; 22-24; 29; 31; 33; 35. 7,44. 20,2. 22,11.

BKM B2.

CHS FD1,1.

	SHR	C1; 3; 12. 1,2. 3b,1; 3. 4,1,37. 6,33.
	SSX	11,1.
	WOR	C1-2. 10,17.
	YKS	C1a; 7; 15; 20; 40. 2B2. 22W6. SN,Y1. SW,An16; 18.
Named as such :-		
Chester	CHS	C1.
Exeter	DEV	C1. 2,1. 5,15. 16,1.
Chelmsford	ESS	B2; 6.
Gloucester	GLS	G1; 4.
Winchester	HAM	16,7.
Hereford	HEF	C1.
Canterbury	KEN	C1. 1,4. 2,1. 3,9. 5,125; 144; 147; 160. 7,4; 11.
Rochester	KEN	R1. 5,53; 56; 93; 104.
Leicester	LEC	C1; 3.
Lincoln	LIN	C1; 11; 22; 27.
Oxford	OXF	B1.
Shrewsbury	SHR	C1. 3b,1. 4,1,37.
Chichester	SSX	11,1.
Worcester	WOR	C1. 10,17.
York	YKS	C1a; 40. 22W6. SN,Y1.
Assessment, hidal	CHS	C1.
	SHR	C13. 3g,2.
Breaking into at night	BRK	B11.
Bridge/wall		
County liable for repair at 1 man per hide	CHS	C21.
fine on lord for men not repairing	CHS	C21.
Circuit of	YKS	C29. SN,Y8.
Customs – See Borough.		
Devastated	CHS	C23.
Ditch, houses in	KEN	C1; 6.
	YKS	C7; 15.
Hall in	LIN	C4.
Held		
by King in lordship	HEF	C14.
from Earl	CHS	C24.
Horses provided when King leaves	SHR	C10.
Judges		
fine for not attending Hundred	CHS	C20.
men of King, Earl and Bishop as	CHS	C20.
Jurisdiction, full of King over	KEN	C6.
Land/property		
circuit of, within	YKS	C29. SN,Y8.
near to city	YKS	2B2.
outside pays tax with city	CHS	C1.
	ESS	B2.
	YKS	C22.

not to be sold outside city or kin	LIN	C16.
Lordship, in	HEF	C14.
Payments		
annual lump sum	ESS	B6.
contributions from elsewhere	LIN	T3-4.
King, to	LEC	C3.
King's levy	ESS	B3.
lordship, in	WOR	C2.
tax paid only when other cities pay	DEV	C4.
taxed carucates included in	YKS	C22. SN,Y1.
toll-fine for non-payment	CHS	C18.
Smiths make horse-shoes for King	HEF	C8.

See also: Bridge; Burning; Church; Clothing; Customary due; Ditch; Dwelling; Earl; Escort; Expedition; Field; Honey; Jurisdiction, full; Lodging; Man-at-arms; Marten skins; Meadow; Measure; Narrative; Port; Prebendary; Reeve; Revenue; Sheriff; Ship; Site; Tax; Third/two thirds part; Wall.

CLAIM to land, property or persons

Barred by predecessor's forfeiture	LIN	CS36-37.
Church by layman	ESS	20,56.
	NFK	8,71.
	SFK	1,122f.
jurisdiction divided	LIN	CS11.
Church and priest by Bishop	LIN	1,65.
Customary dues from free men	NFK	13,19.
new, from ship	LIN	CS40.
Denied by jurors	YKS	CN2. CE14.
because land should be King's	LIN	CK59.
	YKS	CE31-32.
Dwelling	LIN	CN,28.
Fishery	GLS	1,64.
	LIN	CS34.
free man	NFK	1,106; 111; 120. 8,19; 129. 9,111; 148; 160. 11,3. 31,12; 15; 17; 29. 34,17. 50,1. 51,2. 53,1. 58,2. 66,86.
	SFK	6,210. 7,64; 68. 16,16. 25,59-60. 64,3. 67,27. 75,3.
half free man	SFK	31,20.
claimed by sheriff to belong to manor elsewhere	NFK	21,22.
chief lord unaware of facts until put in writing	NFK	66,61-62.

Freeman	NFK	1,121. 8,8. 15,10; 13. 19,24.
	SFK	31,44.
half Freeman	NFK	10,19.
House, half	NFK	4,10.
Hundred	CHS	G2.
Jurisdiction	HUN	2,6.
	SFK	14,38.
over free man/persons	DBY	6,62.
	HUN	2,6.
	LEC	14,3. 43,4.
	LIN	3,25. CS17; 25-32. CW15. CK13-14; 16; 26-27; 35; 61; 63.
	NTH	18,1; 31.
	YKS	CE16; 24-25.
Jurisdiction, full	SFK	1,77.
over free men	NFK	14,17.
over land	LIN	CK53.
King		
against	LIN	CS8; 24. CN3. CK34; 59.
by or for	DOR	30,4.
	HUN	2,6; 9.
	LEC	43,5.
	LIN	C21. 12,83. CS6. CK71.
	NTH	30,7. 35,1e.
	STS	8,5. 16,1.
	SFK	25,52.
referred to	BRK	5,1.
	CAM	5,21.
	DOR	36,8.
	LIN	CK50.
Land/property	BDF	3,6. 4,2. 8,2. 16,3. 17,2; 4. 19,1. 21,1; 6. 24,14. 25,7. 28,1. 29,1. 31,1. 32,7. 40,3. 46,1. 54,2. 55,9. 56,2.
	BRK	58,2.
	CAM	28,2. 29,10. 35,1.
	CHS	C25. B13. 1,35. 2,1-2; 5.
	CON	3,2; 7.
	DBY	1,27. 6,27; 99. 16,2. 17,9.
	DEV	3,32.
	DOR	30,4. 36,8.
	ESS	1,2. 4,8. 18,36. 20,56. 23,3. 25,3; 16; 20. 27,14. 28,8. 30,27; 41. 34,19; 30. 43,1. 79,1. 90,76.
	GLS	W18. 1,54; 64. 2,8-10. 28,3. 31,2. 56,2.
	HAM	3,15. 10,1. 21,1.

		23,3. 27,1. 43,6. 44,1. 53,2. 54,2. 67,1. 69,4; 30; 33; 53.
	HEF	14,2. 19,8.
	HRT	B5. 4,21. 24,2. 33,18. 34,13. 37,19.
	HUN	B10; 13. 2,2. 6,3; 7-8. 19,13; 18; 27. 20,3.
	KEN	5,149.
	LEC	14,16. 19,6; 9.
	LIN	C10. 1,9; 65. 3,15; 22; 32. 12,92. 29,7. 30,32. 63,25. 65,5. CS1-40. CN1-30. CW1-20. CK1-71.
	MDX	15,1. 16,1.
	NFK	1,57; 128; 172; 197; *211;* 213. 4,10; 25. 8,29; 37; 137. 9,42; 49. 12,42. 15,2; *22.* 19,24. 21,15. 22,13. 31,6; 11; 20; 23; 26; 29; 44. 35,11. 47,7. 66,35; 37; 40; 81.
	NTH	2,2-3. 4,1. 18,1; 31. 40,2. 41,5. 48,12. 53,1. 56,51; 65.
	NTT	20,4.
	RUT	R7.
	SHR	4,4,23. 4,26,3.
	STS	8,5. 12,1. 16,1.
	SFK	4,13. 6,91. 7,36; 68. 12,6. 14,146. 15,3. 21,45. 25,52-53; 56; 59; 112. 26,14. 31,20. 33,1. 36,6-7. 37,1. 39,3. 70
	SRY	5,3. 19,35. 36,1.
	SSX	11,8.
	WAR	28,19.
	WIL	1,1. 3,1. 7,15. 13,9. 25,2. 30,5. 67,11. 68,25.
	WOR	*9,1a.*
	YKS	C10. CN1-2. CE14; 16-18; 24; 27-28; 31. CW7; 21; 39.
by exchange in Normandy	ESS	22,23.
by lord's men	BDF	25,7. 28,1.
	LIN	CS1-2. CK66; 69.
	NFK	11,3. 66,35; 86.
	SHR	4,26,2.
	SFK	70,1. 76,2.
	SRY	36,1.

	YKS	CE29.	
gift of head manor	LIN	CK27.	
holder unable to			
separate from lord			
TRE	WIL	3,1.	
King's gift and	NFK	8,137. 22,13.	
delivery		31,11.	
King's/Queen's gift			
and/or			
confirmation	BDF	28,1.	
	ESS	38,1; 3. 82,1.	
	HAM	67,1.	
	LIN	57,18.	
	NFK	7,3. 9,1; 102; 233.	
		22,13. 31,11.	
		66,40; 81.	
	SFK	21,45. 25,56. 37,1.	
	WOR	9,4.	
	YKS	CE24. CW39.	
part of			
predecessor's house	LIN	CS25.	
patronage over sub-			
tenants	NFK	4,39.	
patronage over			
woman sub-			
tenant's son	NFK	9,196.	
possession by	BDF	19,1. 24,14. 25,7.	
claimant and/or		28,1. 31,1. 40,3.	
predecessor		46,1.	
	BRK	58,2.	
	CAM	28,2. *35,1.*	
	CHS	B13. 2,1.	
	ESS	27,14.	
	GLS	31,2.	
	HAM	10,1. 23,3. 43,6.	
		53,2.	
	KEN	5,149.	
	LIN	CS11; 18; 23; 25;	
		27-29; 32; 34; 36-	
		37. CN8. CW15.	
		CK35-36; 44; 63;	
		65; 67-69.	
	NFK	1,197; *211.* 4,13.	
		8,29.	
	YKS	CW1.	
possession before			
and after chief			
lord's forfeiture	NFK	1,10.	
possession for two			
years	HRT	24,2.	
possession when			
claimant crossed sea	HRT	37,19.	
possession, prior	NFK	31,44.	
priest's inheritance	LIN	C16.	
purchase price paid			
TRE	LIN	CS5.	
seisin and			
possession and			
receipt of service	YKS	CE34. CW32.	
service and			
payments to manor	NFK	9,49.	

Man			
exchange	NFK	8,19. 31,43.	
	SFK	33,1.	
possession before			
Earl Ralph's			
forfeiture	SFK	6,169.	
CLEAR (adquietare) – See Tax.			
CLEARED of wood – See Assart.			
CLERK/cleric/clergy			
(clericus)	BRK	1,1-3.	
	CON	4,28.	
	DBY	B1.	
	DEV	13a. 17,58.	
	DOR	6,2. 27,2.	
	GLS	62,6.	
	HAM	2,10; 20. 3,16.	
	HEF	2,4-5; 11; 13; 16-17;	
		19; 39-40; 42; 55.	
		14,2.	
	HRT	36,11.	
	KEN	2,1.	
	LEC	13,1.	
	LIN	2,42.	
	NTH	15,1.	
	NTT	5,1; 19.	
	OXF	29,17.	
	RUT	R21.	
	SHR	2,1.	
	SOM	6,3. 19,43. 24,35.	
		36,7.	
	STS	7.	
	SFK	14,13; *14; 87;* 167.	
		25,1.	
	SRY	1,1. 34,1.	
	SSX	2,6. 3,3. 6,1-2.	
		9,11; 72. 10,2; 22;	
		71-73. 11,3; 6; 102.	
	WAR	1,8.	
	YKS	2,1. 2B1; 9. 2E3;	
		40. CE24.	
Archbishop's	LIN	2,42.	
Bishop's	LIN	7,29.	
Count's	ESS	1,28.	
King's	SOM	16.	
Minor (clericolus)	WIL	1,16.	
Village, of	DEV	1,18.	
CLOSE (hega) – See Land.			
CLOTH (pannus)	HRT	31,8.	
CLOTHING (de vestitu)			
Daughter provided			
with from land given			
to Abbey	WIL	13,21.	
King's lordship in			
city, from	GLS	G4.	
Land held by King's			
reeve to supply	BDF	57,20.	
Monks-land held for	DOR	12,14.	
	HAM	3,16.	
	KEN	2,2; *15;* 28; *35.* 3,5-	
		6; *11-14.* 7,21.	
	SRY	2,4-5.	

SSX 2,2; 8.
See also: Footwear; Supplies.
COB (runcinus) CON *1,1-3; 11; 14. 2,9-*
10. 5,1,11. 5,2,17;
22. 5,3,10. 5,4,13;
18.

DEV *1,33; 43-44; 54;*
56; 66; 70-71. 2,2; 4; 6; 11; 18-20; 23. 3,5;
7-8; 21; 24-25; 67; 86; 93; 97. 5,1. 7,1-3.
10,1. 11,1-3. 15,42; 44; 46; 64; 67. 16,3; 7;
14; 17; 19; 52; 58; 63; 76; 83-84; 95-96;
104; 106; 112; 129; 153; 155. 17,21; 29-30;
32-33; 48-49; 51; 69. 19,8; 12; 15; 29-31;
38; 45. 20,10-11; 15; 17. 21,7; 9. 22,1.
23,2; 5; 9; 16-18; 21-23. 24,2-3; 5; 8; 13-
14; 17; 21; 23; 25-26; 28; 30. 25,5; 14-16;
21-22. 32,7. 33,1-2. 34,14; 18; 22-23; 29;
31; 49-50. 40,6. 42,1; 10; 16-17; 22. 49,7.
50,1. 51,1; 3; 6; 8; 12. 52,22; 53.

DOR *1,1-17; 19. 11,1;*
3-6; 12; 15-17. 12,1-5; 7-8; 10; 12. 13,1-4;
6; 8. 36,1-2; 4-5; 7; 9-11. 41,1-4. 48,1. 55,1-
2; 4-6; 9; 15-16; 31; 36-38; 40.

ESS 1,1; 3-4; 9; 11-12;
19; 24-28. 2,1; 3-4; 7-8. 3,15. 4,5-6; 9; 11;
14; 17. 5,2-4; 6-7; 9-12. 6,2; 4-5; 8; 11-12;
14-15. 7,1. 8,1-2; 6; 11. 9,1-2; 7-8; 11; 13-
14. 10,1-2; 4-5. 11,1-2; 6. 13,1; 3-4. 15,1-
2. 16,1. 17,1. 18,1-5; 14; 22; 24; 28; 36-41.
20,7-8; 15; 19-23; 25-28; 36-37; 39-40; 43;
45-46; 52; 55-57; 64; 67; 69; 71; 78-80.
22,5-7; 10-12; 15. 23,2; 5; 38-40. 24,1; 3;
5; 7-10; 15-26; 28-37; 42; 44-46; 49; 53-54;
60-61; 64; 66. 25,1-8; 11-12; 15-16; 18-21;
23-25. 26,1; 5. 27,1-2; 4; 10-11; 13-14; 16.
28,9; 11; 13; 16-17. 29,2; 4. 30,1; 4-5; 17-
19; 22; 27; 45. 31,1. 32,1-4; 6; 8-9; 13-17;
19; 21; 23-26; 28; 32-34; 38-39; 42; 44-45.
33,1; 3; 6-8; 11-13; 15-17; 19-20; 22-23.
34,1; 4-13; 15; 18-22; 27; 29; 33-37. 35,1-
6; 8-12. 36,1; 3; 5-6; 11-12. 37-2; 7; 10-11.
13. 38,1-2; 4; 6-8. 39,1; 4-5; 8. 40,1; 4.
41,5; 9-10; 12. 42,1-3; 6-9. 44,1-3. 45,1.
46,1-2. 47,3. 48,2. 49,4. 52,2. 53,1-2.
54,2. 55,1. 57,1-3; 5-6. 58,1. 60,1-3. 61,1-
2. 65,1. 67,1. 68,2; 4; 7. 69,2. 71,2; 4.
76,1. 81,1. 84,2.

GLS *1,59-60.*
HUN *4,4.*
NFK 1,2-3; 15-19; 32; 40;
52; 55; 57; 59; 71-72; 88; 94; 133; 143-144;
147; 151-152; 185-186; 193; 198; 200-201;
203; 209-212; 215-217; 231; 237-239. 2,2;
4. 3,1. 4,1-2; 9; 17; 26; 30-31; 38-39; 47;
52. 5,4; 6. 6,3; 6. 7,1-3; 16-19. 8,1-3; 6-7;
16; 21-22; 30; 33; 35; 46-47; 55; 62-64; 87;
91-92; 98-100; 102-103; 105; 108-110; 119-
120; 122; 132. 9,2; 6-9; 11-12; 70-71; 74-
77; 80-81; 83; 87-88; 94-96; 98-100; 104.
10,1-3; 5; 8; 11; 15; 20; 22-23; 25; 28; 38;
40; 57-58; 76; 78. 11,1. 12,1; *17;* 27; 30; 32;

42. 13,2-3; 5; 7; 9-10; 12; 14-16; 19; 24.
14,1-2; 6; 8; 11; 13-16; 18; 23; 25-26; 35;
41. 15,1; 4; 7-8; 10; 16-18; 24; 28. 16,1; 4-
5. 17,1-2; 5; 8; 12-13; 16-19; 23; 25; 35; 51;
53-56; 61; 64. 19,4; 11; 13; 15; 18; 21; 32;
36. 20,1; 6-11; 26-27; 29; 34-36. 21,3-7; 14;
16; 21; 27; 29. 22,1; 3-6; 10; 23. 23,1-5; 7-
8; 11-12; 16-18. 24,6-7. 25,12; 17. 28,1-2.
29,5. 31,1-2; 5-6; 8; 10; 17; 20-22; 24-25;
31; 33-35; 37; 41-43. 32,1-2; 4-5. 33,2.
34,1-2; 4-5; 8-9; 17; 20. 35,14-15. 36,1; 5-
7. 37,1-2. 38,2. 39,1-2. 42,1. 43,1. 46,1.
48,3. 49,1; 4. 50,1; 4; 6-7; 9. 51,6; 8; 10.
52,1. 55,1-2. 57,1. 59,1. 66,5.

SOM *1,1; 4-7; 10; 13-14;*
16; 18-29; 32; 34-35. 2,1; 6-8; 10; 12. 4,1.
5,1; 8-9; 14-18; 22-24; 27; 31-35; 37-40; 41;
43-49; 51-52; 54; 56-59; 61-62; 65; 70. 6,1-
13. 7,2-9; 11; 13. 8,1; 3-5; 7; 9-11; 13-14;
16-18; 20-25; 28-34. 9,1; 3-4; 6-7. 10,1; 3;
5. 12,1. 14,1. 15,1. 16,1; 6. 19,4-5; 8-9;
13; 15; 24-27; 29-30; 32; 38-41; 43-44; 47;
49-53; 57-58; 62-63; 66; 69-72; 76; 79-80;
82; 87. 20,1. 21,1; 4; 12; 27; 47; 55-56; 63;
72-73; 89; 93; 96. 22,15; 19. 24,1; 13; 16-
17; 19; 22-23; 25; 27. 25,1; 4-5; 7-12; 16;
29-31; 33-34; 36; 45; 49-51; 54-55. 27,1-2.
28,1-2. 31,3. 32,2-4. 34,1. 35,10; 17; 23.
36,1; 5; 11; 13. 37,5-6; 8. 39,1-2. 40,1-2.
41,1; 3. 44,1; 3. 45,3-4; 7; 11; 13; 15; 18.
46,4; 22. 47,2-3; 6; 8; 14; 17-18; 20-21.

SFK 1,14; 23; 32; 34-35;
44-49; 51-53; 55; 76; 88; 96; 100; 107;
110-111; 115; 118-119; 121; 122b. 2,13. 3,1;
9-10; 34; 46; 56; 61; 69; 74; 94; 98. 4,1; 13;
18-19; 24; 30-31; 38; 42. 5,1. 6,11; 26; 43;
48-49; 57; 62; 80-81; 83; 90; 93; 112; 129;
148; 172; 187; 191-192; 213; 215; 222-223;
264; 271-272; 303; 306-309; 312. 7,1; 3; 5;
13; 18; 47; 56; 58; 60-61; 71; 73; 75-76; 98;
147. 8,1; 7; 11; 31-32; 34; 49; 55. 9,1-3.
11,4. 12,1; 7. 13,2. 14,1-10; 18-20; 23-25;
39; 42; 45; 48-54; 65; 69; 72-76; 105-106;
108-109; 117-120; 129; 139; 163. 15,1-3.
16,2; 21; 26; 40. 17,1. 18,1. 19,16. 21,1; *3;*
5-7; 10-11; 16; 28; 38-40; 42-43; 45; 47; 53-
55; 58; 80; 83. 22,1. 24,1. 25,1-6; 11; 19;
46; 52-53; 55; 61; 63; 76; 79-81; 84-86; 105.
26,6; 8-10; 12a-b; 13; 15-16. 27,9; 13. 28,7.
29,1; 12. 30,1. 31,8; 20; *40;* 56; 60. 32,3-
4; 14; 16; 19; 21. 33,1-4; 6-10. 34,6-9; 12-
13; 15. 35,6. 36,1-2; 4. 37,1; 4-6. 38,4; 11;
16; 22. 39,3; 6-7; 17. 40,3; 6. 41,1-2; 7; 14-
15; 17. 44,1-4. 45,2. 47,2-3. 48,1. 49,1.
52,1; 5. 53,2-3; 5-6. 54,1; 3. 57,1. 60,1.
62,4-5. 64,3. 65,1. 66,1-4; 6. 67,3; 11; 15;
19; 27-28; 30; 33. 68,1. 69,1. 71,1.

At the Hall NFK 4,26.
SFK *21,39.*
COBBLER (sutor) KEN *C1.*
SFK 14,167.

CO-HEIR – See Companion.
COINAGE
Dies – payment for   HEF   C9.
                              SHR   C11.
                              WOR   C1.
Struck for King with
his silver   HEF   C9.
See also: Mark; Money; Moneyer.
COLIBERT (colibertus) – See freedman.
COLLUSION with thief – See Crime/offence.
COMBAT (bellum)
Offered
  by claimant's man
  against Hundred   NFK   66,81.
  by claimant's man
  to prove possession
  of land/free man   LIN   CK66.
                              NFK   9,42; 227.
  by Englishman   NFK   9,227.
  by Hundred against
  claimant's man   NFK   9,227.
  for and against
  claimant   NFK   15,2.
Payment made to
withdraw from   SRY   36,1.
Undertaken after oath   CHS   R1,41. R5,3.
See also: Customary due; Ordeal; Ordeal or
combat; Pledge; Prove; Trial.
COMMAND (jussum; preceptum)
Abbot's   BRK   7,24.
Bishop's   SFK   75,3.
King's   CAM   5,24. 30,2. 32,5.
                              NFK   1,4.
                              SFK   77,4.
                              SRY   5,28. 8,12.
                              WIL   3,1.
  land held without   ESS   6,1.
                              NTH   6a,27.
Lord's   ESS   23,42.
See also: Adjudgment; Pledge.
COMMENDATION (commendatio)
Freeman and land to
King's reeve   BDF   57,20.
Land held from
  Abbot, in   GLS   12,9.
  King, in   LEC   42,9.
                              OXF   55,1-2.
Man/woman to lord   BDF   23,17.
                              BRK   7,24.
Man by King's writ to
protector   BDF   17,5.
Man to reeve for
service   GLS   1,16.
See also: Patronage; Subjection.
COMMISSIONER
(legatus)   BKM   48,1.
                              GLS   49.
Giving possession not
seen by Hundred   NFK   66,64.
Not sent to prove
claim   ESS   18,44.

King's   CHS   C3.
                              GLS   1,63.
                              HEF   1,75.
  who gave
  possession not seen
  by Hundred   HAM   69,16.
  sent to country   ESS   77,1.
  not sent to Hundred
  to prove King's gift   ESS   1,28.
  at transaction, not
  seen by Hundred   CAM   22,6.
See also: Domesday survey; King's officer.
COMMODITIES – See Ale; Barley; Bread; Cloth;
Corn; Fleece; Flour; Fur; Goat skins; Hay; Honey;
Iron; Malt; Oats; Peas; Rye; Salt; Wheat; Wine;
Wood; Wool.
COMMON
Land etc held in   LEC   C11.
                              NFK   1,66.
                              SSX   3,10. 6,1. 10,73.
Land which village
men could sell   BDF   23,43.
Prebend partitioned
after 1066   KEN   M1.
See also: Burgess; House; Pasture; Village.
COMMON people (vili plebe)
Evidence by   HAM   23,3.
COMMUNITY
(communitas)   KEN   P15-16.
COMPANION
(socius)   GLS   53,6.
                              LIN   3,35.
                              NFK   10,33.
                              OXF   6,10.
See also: Joint tenant.
COMPENSATION – See Exchange; Release.
COMPURGATION HEF   A5.
CONCEALED (concelatus) – See Customary due;
Honey; Land; Tax.
CONCERNS (res) – See Sheriff.
CONCUBINE
(concubina)   BDF   24,16.
                              KEN   C4.
CONSECRATION (dedicatio)
Chapel, of   SFK   1,1.
CONSENT (voluntas)
King's not produced   ESS   5,6.
Land held without   BRK   7,31.
                              HAM   IoW1,7.
                              HUN   D8.
                              NTH   6a,27.
See also: Church; Gift; Sale; Tenure.
CONSTABLE
(stalrus;
constabularius)   BDF   1,5. 57,4.
                              BRK   7,7.
                              BKM   2,3. 12,29. 14,29-
                                     30; 45. 17,9. 21,2-
                                     6; 8. 27,1-2. 28,2.
                              CAM   14,29. 15,4. 21,5.
                                     22,2; 6-8. 26,21;

5; 8. 8,1. 9,1; 3. 11,3-4. 12,4. 13,4; 9; 11.
14,*2;* 24; 27; 32; 34; *39;* 43-44; 46; 48; 55-
56; 58-60. 15,4. 16,1. 21,4-5; 8. 22,7-8.
23,3; 5. 24,1. 25,9. 26,20; *23; 25;* 26-27;
30-32; 34-36; 42-43; 47-49. *28,2.* 31,1-2;
6; 7. 32,6; 8; 12; 19-24; 30-33; 35-40. 33,1.
35,1. 38,2-4. 39,1-2. 40,1. 41,13-14; 16.
43,1. 44,2.

DEV *1,4.* 15,21. 17,*29;*
30; 32-33. 47,5.
52,50.

DOR 1,2-3; 6; 12; *15;* 16.
5,2. 8,1; 3. 11,4; *5.* 17,1. 26,49. 31,2. 34,7.
36,6. 55,2. 56,14; 18; 31; 38. 57,21.

HEF 6,3. 7,3. 8,8. 10,9.
14,2.

HRT 1,1-4; 6; 8-11; 13-
15; 18. 4,1-3; 6-16; 19-20; 22; 24. 5,1; 8;
11; 13-14; 20; 23-24. 7,1-2. 8,1. 9,1; 4; 6-
10. 10,2-3; 5-8; 14-15; 17-20. 11,1. 13,3; 5.
14,1-2. 15,5; 8. 16,1-2; 4; 8-9; 11. 17,1; 3-
4; 11; 13; 15. 19,1-2. 20,1; 4-11; 13. 22,1-
2. 23,1-4. 24,1; 3. 25,1-2. 26,1. 28,3-5; 7-
8. 29,1. 31,1; 7-8. 32,1-2. 33,5-6; 9-10; 12-
15; 17. 34,4-5; 10-13; 15; 23. 35,1-3. 36,2-
3; 5; 7; 11; 14-15; 19. 37,5-6; 8-12; 14; 16-
18; 20-21. 38,1-2. 40,1. 41,1. 42,2; 7; 9;
11-13. 42a,1. 44,1.

KEN 2,3; 10. 3,8; 12-14.
5,2; 8; 13; 19-20; 29; 31-32; 34; 93; 95; 124;
138-139; 144. 7,1; 5-6.

MDX 1,2-3. 2,1-3. 3,1-2;
6-7; 12-14; 16; 21; 23-24; 26-28. 4,1-2; 5-
12. 5,1. 6,1. 7,2; 4-6; 8. 8,1; 6. 9,1; 4; 7-9.
10,1. 11,1; 3. 12,1. 13,1. 14,2. 16,1. 17,1.
19,1. 22,1. 24,1. 25,1.

SHR 3c,10. 4,3,2; 68.
4,5,9. 4,10,1.

SOM 1,19; 26; 29-30.
3,2. 5,9; 21; 42; *43;* 47; *49;* 50; 53; 55; 59-
60; *61;* 62; 65; 67; 69-70. 6,15. 8,21-23; 27;
32-34. 19,53; 55; 58-59; 62; *64;* 65. 21,88.
22,4; 18; 27. 24,16; 21; *22;* 23-30; 33-35; 43;
55. 26,5. 28,1-2. 35,5-6; 22. 36,2-3; 12.
37,10; *11.* 45,1; 12-13. 46,21; 24-25. 47,21;
23.

SRY 1,14-15. 2,2. 5,1a-
c,f; 2-3; 6-8. 6,2. 7,1. 8,1-3; 6; 23-24. 10,1.
18,4. 19,15; 26; 31-32. 21,2. 22,1-3. 24,1.
25,2. 27,1-2. 29,1. 34,1. 35,2. 36,7; 10.

SSX 4,1. 5,1; 3. 8a,1.
9,5-11; 13-19; 21-22; 26; 31; 33-34; 51; 60;
64-67; 70; 80; 82-83; 85-86; 89-90; 94; 96;
98; 102-103; 105-107; 109-111; 114-115;
117. 11,48-57; 59; 61-71; 73-85; 90-93; 95-
100; 102-113.

WIL 1,5; 11; 23e. 4,4.
5,7. 7,16. 8,1-2; 4; 6; 8-9; 11-13. 14,1-2.
16,1-3; 7. 18,2. 24,3-4; 9; 19; 28; 31; 33;
36. 25,4. 26,19; 22. 27,23; 27. 28,3; 10; 13.

29,8. 30,5. 36,2. 44,1. 48,6-7. 67,22; 25;
57; 59; 76-77; 89. 68,18.

WOR 8,7; 11; 16-17; 21;
24. 15,8. 19,14.
20,1.

YKS 9W64.

Female   SHR 7,5.
With defined holding MDX 4,5.

CAM *5,47; 50.* 11,3-4.
26,20; *34.*

See also: Sheriff.

COTTAGER (coscet) DEV 2,24. 3,9; 86-87;
91. 5,1; 4. 17,7-8;
10.

DOR 1,8; 28-29. 2,6. 3,8-
10. 11,11-13. 12,12. 13,2. 19,6. 26,15; 31;
56; 58; 60; 68. 31,2. 34,5. 37,4. 46,2. 47,8.
54,9. 55,38. 56,12; 32; 34; 58.

SHR 2,2. 7,4; 6.

SOM 8,30. 19,63. 21,15;
87; 90. 33,1. 34,1.
36,7; 10. 42,2.

WIL M3. 1,1-2; 4-7; 10-
11; 13-15; 20. 2,4-5; 8. 3,5. 5,1. 6,1. 7,2-
4. 8,2-10. 10,1-3. 11,1. 12,1. 13,1-2; 7;
16,1-4. 17,1. 18,1. 19,1; 4. 20,6. 21,1-3.
22,1-3. 23,1-2; 4; 7; 9. 24,1-2; 4-5; 13; 15-
18; 20; 22-23; 25; 30-33; 37-39; 41. 25,5;
11-14; 16-18; 22. 26,2; 4; 7; 16; 18. 27,2;
4; 10-11; 14-17; 21-22. 28,2; 8; 13. 29,1; 5.
32,7-8; 10-12; 16. 36,2. 37,11-15. 41,1-3.
42,1; 6-7. 45,1. 48,4; 6-9. 49,1-2. 50,1; 3.
51,1. 57,1. 58,1. 61,1. 64,1. 65,1-2. 66,1;
3. 67,6-10; 17; 22-23; 25; 35; 43-45; 52; 54;
56; 59-60; 63; 72; 95. 68,3-4; 7-10; 12-13;
21-22; 24; 26; 28-29.

Paying tax with
burgesses   WIL M3.

COUNT (comes) – See Eustace; Jurisdiction;
Jurisdiction, full; Man; Man-at-arms; Patronage;
Servant.

COUNTESS (comitissa) – See Man; Priest;
Steward.

COUNTRY (patria)
Evidence by men of NTT 30,22.
Man leaving   LIN CN,9.
See also: Flight; King William; Leave.

COUNTRYMAN
(rusticus)   DOR *55,24.*
                    HRT 31,1.
                    KEN P8. 8,1.
                    SRY 1,6.
                    WIL 67,66.
                    WOR 10,4.
Land holder serving as WOR 2,57.
Paying tribute   KEN 8,1.

COUNTY (comitatus; scira; scyra)
Customs   BRK B10-11.
                    DBY S1-6.
                    KEN D11-25.
                    LIN C32-33.

	NTH	B36.
	NTT	S1-6.
	OXF	1,12-13.
	WOR	C2-5.
	YKS	C37-40.
Decision by on claim	LIN	CN7.
Evidence		
by (men of)	BRK	1,26-27; 32. 7,38.
		10,1. 14,1. 22,8.
		23,2. 31,3. 44,1.
		46,4. 58,2.
	CHS	C25. B13. 1,35.
		27,3.
	ESS	6,1. 18,32. 32,24.
		52,2.
	GLS	1,11; 13; 60; 63; 65.
		28,3. 32,9. 34,8.
		50,4. 56,2. 59,1.
		72,2.
	HAM	6,1. 27,1. 35,2.
		45,2. 69,4; 33.
	HEF	1,3; 8; 10b. 7,1.
		15,1.
	HRT	1,1; 6; 12-13; 17.
		5,6. 8,3. 17,15.
		26,1. 34,13. 36,13.
		37,21.
	HUN	D5; 14; 19; 23.
	KEN	7.30.
	LIN	65,5. CN3; 27; 30.
		CW10; 16.
	OXF	1,6.
	SHR	4,26,3.
	STS	8,5.
	SRY	1,1c-e. 25,2.
	WIL	1,1.
	WOR	C4. 2,74; 80. 8,1.
		9,4. 19,13. 26,15;
		17. 28,1.
by better/older men		
of	HAM	23,3.
	WOR	23,1.
denial by	HUN	D21.
	LEC	13,23.
does not confirm	CHS	2,5.
	HRT	4,1. 36,9.
does not give		
evidence	ESS	90,28.
evidence of two	DBY	B15.
unaware of facts	BRK	1,26. 7,38. 10,1.
		14,1.
	CHS	27,3.
	ESS	18,36.
	GLS	1,53.
	SHR	4,26,3.
	WAR	3,4.
	WOR	9,5c.
Land		
assessed in another	CAM	1,10; 15; 22.
	HRT	40,1.
	HUN	29,2.

	NFK	1,51.
	SFK	3,1.
assessed and lying		
in another	BRK	33,9.
	SHR	4,28,5.
belonging to church		
in another	SRY	3,1.
	WIL	7,14.
	WOR	9,6a.
belonging to		
Hundred in another	ESS	32,40.
belonging to		
manor/village in		
another	CAM	1,15.
	DBY	1,25.
	DOR	2,6.
	ESS	1,3; 9. 32,40.
	HAM	43,4.
	KEN	5,104.
	LEC	23,2; 5-6.
	NFK	1,51. 8,50.
	SRY	18,1.
	SSX	11,30.
held as long as		
holder had land in		
County	YKS	CE21; 23.
joined to land in		
another	OXF	24,6.
listed in another	SFK	19,2.
lying in another	ESS	40,5.
	HUN	1,2. 29,2.
	SHR	4,1,5.
	SFK	1,38.
	WOR	1,4.
removed and placed		
in another	HAM	69,22.
rendering		
tax/service in		
another	HUN	2,9. D19.
transferred to		
another	HEF	1,72.
Liable to repair city		
bridge/wall	CHS	C21.
Manor assessed in two	BDF	48,1.
Meeting-fine for		
absence from	CHS	R1,40c.
	HEF	A7.
	KEN	D23.
Meeting place	KEN	D23.
Mill in another	SFK	56,6.
Payments of	OXF	1,12.
	WOR	C2.
King, to	LEC	C3.
man-at-arms, to	BRK	B10.
Revenue paid in		
another	WOR	1,5-6. X3.
Witness to land		
ownership	WAR	3,4. 6,9.

See also: Adjudgment; Baron; Borough; City;
Crime/offence; Defence obligation; Earl; Escort;
Exchange; Exile; Honey; Hundred; Jurisdiction;

Jurors; Man; Manor; Meadow; Outlier; Plea; Prove; Revenue; Service; Sheriff; Shire; Tax; Thane; Third penny; Third/two thirds part; Town; Wapentake.

COURT (curia)	ESS	B3b.
Abbot's	BRK	7,6.
Archbishop's	YKS	C21.
Bishop's	NFK	1,61.
Breaking into	OXF	1,13.
Hides,free – belonging to	GLS	11,1.
King's	BRK	1,1; 37.
Land holders – 2 in one court	SRY	19,37.
Poles (virga) for	HUN	7,8.
Repair – obligation	HUN	7,8.
Service at by smallholders	WOR	10,1.
Work/service at by burgesses	GLS	1,24.
	SSX	5,2.
	WOR	19,12.

See also; Adjudgment; Cattle; Horse; House; Judgement; Mill;Plea; Summons.

COW (vacca)	CON	*1,1; 6. 2,1-3; 9-10. 3,5. 4,8. 5,2,15. 5,4,6; 8; 12; 14-16; 18. 5,5,1. 5,7,11. 5,9,2. 5,12,1-2. 5,13,4-5. 5,17,1; 4. 5,24,8-9. 5,25,5.*
	DEV	*2,5. 3,69. 5,4. 7,4. 15,4; 21. 16,92. 21,2; 18. 34,8. 35,23. 48,5. 52,49.*
	DOR	*1,10; 16; 20. 11,2; 15-16. 12,9; 12. 47,5; 7. 55,5; 8-9; 21; 27. 58,2.*
	ESS	6,12; 14. 20,2; 6; 28; 34; 63. 24,7; 10; 37; 45; 59; 62. 27,10; 14. 30,5; 17; 27. 31,1. 32,8; 13; 42. 34,4-5; 8; 11-13; 15; 20; 22; 34-35; 37. 35,8. 36,11-12. 37,15. 38,2; 6. 39,1; 5; 8. 40,1; 3; 6. 41,12. 42,3. 45,1. 48,1-2. 51,2. 54,2. 61,2. 65,1. 67,2.
	GLS	*1,59-60.*
	HAM	IoW 7,15.
	NFK	1,133. 9,9. 13,4; 7; 9. 14,5. 15,1. 19,4. 20,6. 22,10. 29,5. 31,25. 49,2. 50,6.
	SOM	*1,4; 25. 5,4; 12; 28; 34; 59. 8,2; 14. 9,7. 11,1. 14,1. 16,2; 3. 17,8. 19,2; 9; 14; 57; 60; 70-71; 82. 21,5; 12; 14; 22; 71; 78-79; 82; 93; 98. 22,1; 21. 23,1. 25,46; 56. 35,2; 10; 17. 36,3. 39,3. 45,4-5. 46,5; 10; 12; 16.*
	SFK	9,3. 16,30. 25,105. 26,6; 13.
And calf	ESS	34,7-9; 21-22. 36,1; 8. 39,4; 7. 41,9. 47,1; 3. 68,4.
Included in value of village	SOM	16,2.
Pasture for (vaccaria)	YKS	9W87.
monks'	WOR	9,1e.

Render of		
for land	GLS	W2. 1,1-2; 7.
	NFK	31,6.
by Welshmen	SHR	4,3,42.

See also: Crime/offence; Dairy; Dairy farm; Theft.

COWMAN (vacarius)	HEF	1,9; 44.

CRIME/offence
Nature of crime

adultery	BRK	B7.
	HUN	6,3.
	KEN	D19.
	SSX	12,1.
ale-brewing bad	CHS	C18.
arrest – escape/evasion	KEN	D13.
	SRY	1,1b.
arson	HEF	A5.
assault	OXF	1,13.
blood shedding	BRK	B7.
	CHS	C5. R1,40c; 42. R2,2. R6,2.
	HUN	6,3.
	SHR	C9.
	SSX	12,1.
breaking and entry (heinfara)	CHS	FT2,19. R1,41. R5,3.
breaking and entry – pre-meditated	CHS	FT2,19.
collusion with thief (hangewitha)	CHS	C7.
collusion with thief by reeve	CHS	C7.
highway robbery (foristel)	CHS	R1,40b; 41. R5,3.
	HEF	C13.
	KEN	D18. 2,43. 5,178.
	SHR	C2.
	WOR	C4.
homicide	BRK	B11. 31,4.
	CHS	C6. S1,5. FT2,19.
	OXF	1,13.
homicide of King's man	HEF	A3.
homicide of thane's man	HEF	A3.
homicide of Welshman	HEF	A4.
homicide in house by free man	CHS	C4.
homicide in house by householder	OXF	1,13.
housebreaking (heinfara; handsoca)	BRK	31,4.
	CHS	C6. FT2,19. R1,41.
	HEF	C13. A3.
	KEN	D18.
	OXF	1,13.
	SHR	C2.
	SOM	2,2.
	WOR	C4.

measure, false outlaw/exile	CHS	C18.
receiving	KEN	D21.
peace, breach of (gribrige)	BRK	31,4.
	CHS	R1,41.
	HEF	C13.
	KEN	D14-15; 18; 23. 5,178.
	SOM	2,2.
peace, breach of Earl's	YKS	C38.
peace, breach of King's	BRK	B11.
	CHS	C3-4. R1,40b. R5,3.
	DBY	S1.
	LIN	C32.
	NTT	S1.
	OXF	1,13.
	SHR	C2.
	WOR	C4.
	YKS	C38.
peace, King's – killing man in	BRK	B11.
	OXF	1,13.
rape	CHS	R1,40c.
	SSX	12,1.
	WOR	C4.
roads – committed on or near	KEN	D12; 14; 23. C6; 7.
	YKS	C37.
robbery (latrocinium; revelach)	BRK	B7. 31,4.
	CHS	C8.
	ESS	1,3.
	HUN	6,3.
	KEN	2,43.
	LIN	S5.
sexual intercourse, unlawful by girl/ widow	CHS	C9.
theft (latro; latrocinium; furtum)	CHS	C8. S1,5. FT2,19. R1,40b.
	ESS	32,28.
	HEF	A2.
	KEN	D20. 5,178.
	SOM	2,2.
	SFK	6,89b.
theft– animals/ persons	HEF	A2.
	SFK	27,7.
trees – relating to	KEN	D12.
truce (treuva), breach of King's	KEN	D4.
violation/violence to woman	CHS	R1,42. R2,2. R6,2.
violence to woman in house	CHS	C8.

waterways, on	YKS	C37.
Penalty for		
burning of house	HEF	A4.
corporal punishment	BRK	B11.
	LIN	S5.
	OXF	1,13.
	SFK	6,89b.
	WOR	C4.
death	CHS	S1,5.
	ESS	1,3.
	KEN	D17; 20.
dung stool (cathedra stercoris)	CHS	C18.
fine	BRK	B7; 11. 31,4.
	CHS	C3; 5-10; 18. S1; 5. FT1,19. R1,40b-e. 41-42. R2,2. R5,3. R6,2.
	HEF	C13. A2-3; 8.
	HUN	6,3.
	KEN	D4; 12-16; 19; 21.
	OXF	1,13.
	SHR	C2; 9.
	SRY	1,1b. 5,28.
	SSX	12,1.
	WOR	C4.
fine paid through 6 Hundreds	YKS	C38.
fine paid through 12 Hundreds	YKS	C38.
fine paid through 18 Hundreds	DBY	S1.
	LIN	C32.
	NTT	S1.
fine varied by day/season	CHS	C5-6.
forfeiture of land/goods	BRK	B11.
	CHS	C4.
	ESS	32,28.
	KEN	D2O.
	OXF	1,13.
	SFK	6,89b.
outlawry	CHS	C4.
	LIN	C33.
	OXF	1,13.
	SHR	C2.
	WOR	C4.
vengeance by kin	HEF	A4.
Penalty exempt as to King	KEN	D14.
Penalty received by Abbey/Abbot	HUN	6,3.
	WOR	C4.
Archbishop	KEN	D19. C7.
	SSX	12,1.
	WAR	3,4.
Earl	CHS	C3-4.
	DBY	S1.
	LIN	C32.

	CAM	5,38.
	HRT	8,1. 25,2.
	HUN	7,5. 9,2. 19,8.
	WIL	13,10.

Services of

cartage	HRT	31,1.
reaping	WOR	8,7; 11.
reeve, to	SOM	1,17.

See also: Ale; Borough; Burgess; Burial; Castle; Chamber; Church; City; Claim; County; Dog; Dwelling; Force; Forest; Fourth part; free man; Freeman; Hall; House; Hundred; Judge; Man; Manor; Merchant; Monastery; Narrative; Plea; Pledge; Predecessor; Priest; Reeve; Residence; Revenue; Thane; Third penny; Third/two thirds part; Town; Sheriff; Site; Smallholder; Supplies, household; Woodland.

CUSTOMARY rights – See Rights.

CUSTOMS of

Archenfield	HEF	A1-9. 1,49; 53.
Breteuil and Hereford	CHS	FT2,19.
English, land having	HEF	1,61.
Oswaldslow	WOR	2,1; 80. *App V F.*
Pershore Abbey	WOR	9,7.
Welsh	HEF	A1-9.
land having	HEF	1,61.
West Derby (Lancs)	CHS	R1,40-42. R2,2. R4,1. R6,2.

See also: Banquet; Borough; Church; City; County; Dues; Entertainment; Fishing; Law; Salt house; Ship; Wich.

D

DAIRY (vacaria;
wica)   BRK   1,32. 5,1.
                         YKS   9W87.
DAIRY farm
(hardwica; wica)   GLS   W1.
                         HRT   9,6.
DAIRY maid (daia)   HEF   1,45.
DAM (exclusa)
Flooding meadow   HUN   1,2.
Mill   SFK   21,16.
Part of   SFK   6,5.
See also: Weir.
DAMAGE to property – See Destruction.
DANE – man so
described   BKM   19,5. 57,16.
                         ESS   18,37; 39. 23,38;
                                43.
                         GLS   73,1.
                         HAM   32,1.
                         HUN   2,8.
                         NTH   43,7.
                         SOM   6,14. 29,1. 44,1-2.
                         WAR   22,24.
Seizure of land holder
by   YKS   CE34.
DANEGELD –
payments for by
borough   LIN   S1.
DAUGHTER (filia)   BRK   14,1.
                         BKM   19,3. 56,2.
                         HAM   44,4. 52,1. 67,1.
                         HEF   19,6; 10.
                         HRT   44.
                         NFK   46,1.
                         SOM   1,24. 27,3. 37,7.
                         SFK   7,36. 38,9; 11.
                         SRY   1,13. 19,35. 25,2.
                         WIL   13,21. 50,5.
                         WOR   2,33.
Given to Abbey with
land   BRK   14,1.
                         SOM   37,7.
                         WIL   13,21. 50,5.
Land held with   HAM   44,4. 52,1.
See also: Clothing; Gift; Marriage; Relations;
Woman.
DEACON (diaconus)   BRK   1,9.
                         CAM   29,6.
                         DOR   24,5.
                         ESS   1,27. 30,11. 42.
                                61,1. 66. 88.
                         GLS   57.
                         KEN   2,34; 42.
                         LEC   13,72.

                         LIN   68,31; 35. CN9; 11;
                                13; 18; 23. CK14;
                                31.
                         NFK   1,64. 10,19.
                         SFK   7,31; 36. 14,167.
                                21,35. 25,24. 38,22
                                41. 76,20.
                         YKS   C31; 35. 25W14.
                                CE13; 52. CW28.
Being a
    free man   SFK   38,22. 76,20.
    half free man   SFK   7,31.
    man of layman   SFK   7,36.
DEAN (decanus)
Customary dues of   CON   4,26.
DEATH
Division of land on
between sons   SRY   5,27.
    and King   ESS   B1.
    King's service done
    by one with other's
    aid   LIN   22,26. CS38.
    land between 2,
    jurisdiction
    between 3   LIN   CS21.
King's service on   SFK   7,15.
Sudden   NFK   10,33.
Transfer of land on   BRK   7,38.
                         SRY   1,1e.
    on death bed   BDF   13,1.
                         WOR   23,1.
See also: Cattle; Crime/offence; Gift; Narrative;
Tenure.
DEATH duty (relevatio; herietum)
Divided between
Abbot and Earl   LIN   CW9; 11.
Exempt as to King   KEN   D17.
King has land and
goods if heir does not
pay   CHS   R1,40g.
Nature of articles
given to King for   BRK   B10.
                         HEF   C5.
Payable by
    burgess   HEF   C5.
                         NFK   1,70.
                         SHR   C7.
                         YKS   C40.
    free man   HEF   1,49.
    freeholder   KEN   D17.
    Freeman   LIN   S4.
    lawman   CAM   B13-14.
    man under full
    jurisdiction   LIN   S5.

		6. 23,20. 27,1.
		57,14-15; 19.
	LEC	9,1.
	MDX	7,3; 6-7. 8,2-5.
		11,1.
could not	LEC	9,1.

See also: Dispose; Give up; Go away; Go where he would; Grant; Grant and sell; Leave; Put; Remove; Seek; Sell; Separate; Turn; Withdraw.

DOCTOR (medicus)	GLS	1,2.
	HAM	63. NF9,12. S3.
	HEF	7.
	KEN	M21.
	SHR	3d,6. 9.
	SOM	*8,30.* 13,1.
	WIL	1,18. 56.
	WOR	12,1-2.

DOCUMENT – See Altar; Title deeds; Writ.

DOG (canis)	HEF	25,4.
	OXF	1,12.
Bear, for	NFK	1,61.
Customary dues for	BDF	1,1a; 2a; 3.
	WAR	B4.
Kennelling of (nutrire)	BRK	1,38.
Loaves (panes) for	GLS	1,1-2; 7.
Payments for	GLS	1,10.
	NTH	B36.

DOMESDAY Book Called "Book of Winchester"	YKS	31E.
Information given after writing of	YKS	31.
Making, year of	SFK	77,4.
Personal statements in	DBY	12,4.
	DEV	*23,5.*
	DOR	*1,20.*
	ESS	1,3. 36,6. 66,1.
	SOM	*36,7. 40,2.*
	SFK	33,2.
	SRY	22,4.
Structure of:- deletions in	BDF	1,5. 23,36.
	BRK	1,41. 31,1.
	BKM	14,27. 29,1. 35,3.
	CAM	1,22. 14,18. 26,3.
	CHS	22,1.
	CON	5,24,14.
	DBY	1,19. 3,4. 6,93.
	DEV	17,50.
	DOR	33,5. 56,7.
	ESS	2,9. 3,9. 7,1. 8,11.

18,5; 35. 20,6; 28-29; 34; 43; 72. 22,13. 23,34. 25,25. 39,10. 46,1. 52,2. 90,41.

	GLS	19,2.
	HAM	23,42. 28,7. 47,3.
		69,11. NF9,7-8.
		IoW7,8.
	HEF	8,8.
	HUN	B18. 2,2. 15,1.
		17,1.

KEN		5,116.
LIN		1,16. 4,30. 7,7.
		12,48; 50; 96. 13,4.
		16,21. 27,14. 61,6.
		68,21.
MDX		20,1.
NFK		4,20. 8,12-13; 22;

51; 55; 89; 98; 108; 115; 129; 133. 9,30; 59; 87-88. 10,5; 19; 33-34; 61; 74; 76. 14,17; 40. 17,16; 23; 35; 56; 63. 19,2; 36. 20,11; 17; 32. 22,13. 50,9-10. 66,33; 62; 79; 89.

NTT	1,6; 16; 30. 3,1.

5,7. 9,69-70. 10,6; 23; 26. 11,11. 14,6. 15,17. 28,2. 30,1; 31.

SHR	4,11,2. 4,28,1.
SOM	1,12. 8,37. 10,6.
	36,4.
SFK	1,30. 3,34. 6,54; 88;

148; 173; 187; 205; 215; 305; 309. 7,61. 8,55. 14,26; 112. 16,41. 18,4. 21,54-55; 64; 83. 25,37. 26,13; 15. 27,5. 28,1b. 29,12. 31,13; 21; 40; 42. 32,1. 33,6. 34,8-9. 39,10. 66,3. 67,11; 21; 30. 68,2.

SRY	5,1.
SSX	2,5. 9,123. 13,6;
	40.
WAR	14,6.
WIL	25,6.
YKS	1Y18. 1E11; 33.
	5E72. 5W27.
	6N151. 9W66.
	29W7. 29E19.

interlineations as to	BDF	L38. 1,5. 4,2; 5-8.

6,2. 12,1. 16,4-5. 17,4. 20,2. 21,5; 14. 22,2. 23,4; 25; 55. 24,10; 18; 22-23. 25,14. 38. 49,2. 50,1. 53,7; 9. 54,1; 4. 57. 57,1. 19.

persons	BRK	L65. B1; 3-8. 1,1;

3; 5; 8-10; 19; 24; 42. 2,1. 3,2-3. 4,1. 5,1. 7,8; 34. 15,1. 18,2. 20,2. 21,15; 18; 22. 24,1. 49,1. 58,1. 65,20; 22.

	BKM	B4; 9. 1,3-5; 7. 4,5;

8-10; 13; 15; 18-22; 28-29; 31; 34; 37; 40; 42. 7,2. 12,7; 12-13; 24; 31; 37. 14,19; 25; 29; 38; 44-45. 15,2. 16,8. 17,5-7; 31. 19,5. 21,1; 8. 23,2; 5; 10; 14. 26,10-11. 28,3. 30,1. 37,1-2. 39,2. 43,4; 11. 45,1. 51,1-3. 53,2; 8. 57,5; 9; 18.

	CAM	B2. L19. 1,2; 12;

15-16; 18; 20. 3,1; 6. 5,6; 40; 45. 11,2; 6. 13,1-2; 4; 6-7. 14,27; 71; 80. 17,1; 4-6. 18,2-3. 19. 19,1; 4. 21,1; 5. 22,7-8. 25,8. 26,7; 13-16; 18; 20. 22-23; 25; 31-32; 36-38. 27,1. 31,7. 32,1; 4; 8; 11; 21; 23; 35; 38; 43. 35,1-2. 37,2. 38,1; 4-5. 39,1-2. 41,4; 7-8; 13. 42. 44,2.

	CHS	C23. 1,7-8; 13; 22;

24-26; 34. 2,1-6. 3,1. 4,1. 6,1. 7,1. 8,1; 16; 18; 21; 41. 9,1. 10,1. 12,2. 13,1. 14,1. 15,1. 16,2. 17,1-2. 18,1. 19,1. 20,1; 11. 21,1. 23,1. 24,1. 25,1. 26,1. S1,3; 7. S2,1. S3,4.

FD1,1-2. FD6,1. FD8,1. FT1,1; 10. FT2,1;
17; 20. FT3,1; 3. G2.
       CON '1,13. 4,21. 5,1,5.
            5,2,17. 5,4,17.
            5,14,2. 5,24,18.
       DBY 1,20; 27; 30; 37.
3,2. 4,1. 6,25; 29; 40; 59; 65. 7,13. 8,1; 3;
5-6. 11,1. 12. 16,1. 17,13. B9. S5.
       DEV L27. 1,29; 36; 57.
3,6. 5,11-13. 11,1-3. 15,13. 16,1; 7. 18,1.
25,20. 26,1. 28,13. 29,1. 45,1. 51,1. 52,30.
       DOR L54; 57. 1,1-2; 7;
14; 22; 30-31. 2,6. 3,14. 6,2. 7,1. 8,1. 9,1.
13,4. 17,1-2. 19,14. 23,1. 27,2. 28,2.
34,14. 35,1. 37,13. 41,1. 42,1. 43,1. 44,1.
48,1. 49,15. 51,1. 54,6; 8. 55,1. 56,7; 24;
26-27; 30; 36; 66. 57,5; 9; 12; 15; 17; 19-
20.
       ESS   B3a.
       GLS   S1. W8; 15. B1.
L30. 1,5; 14; 54; 60; 62-63; 66. 2,4; 10. 3,7.
5,1. 6,4. 19,2. 23,1. 28,4. 31,6. 34,2. 39,2;
11. 45,3. 50,3. 52,3. 53,4-5. 56,2. 58,4.
59,1. 60,1-2. 61. 61,1. 68,2. 69,7. 72,1.
73,1. 78,11.
       HAM 1,1-2; 8; 13; 16; 19-
20; 25; 27; 29; 32; 40. W10-12; W14-15.
2,8; 10; 16; 18. 3,1; 3; 5; 7; 16; 23. 5,1.
6,12; 16. 9,1. 10,1. 18,2. 20,1-2. 21,2; 6-7;
9-10. 22,1. 23,32; 35; 56; 64. 28,2; 6-7.
29,14. 30,1. 32,1; 4. 41,1. 42,1. 45,1. 47,1;
3. 53,2. 55,2. 56,1; 3. 64,1. 65,1. 66,1.
67,1. 68,11. 69,1; 8; 16; 21; 28; 39-41; 47-
48; 51; 53. NF6,1-2. NF9,12; 20; 23.
NF10,1; 3. S3. IoW1. IoW1,1-3; 5-6; 9.
IoW3,1. IoW6,10. IoW7,1. IoW9,2.
       HEF   C11-12. 1,4; 6-8;
10b; 11; 38; 44; 46-47; 56; 61; 65; 67; 69;
74-75. 2,8; 26; 31-33; 37; 50. 6,8. 7,1; 3-
4. 8,3; 6; 9. 9,3. 10,11; 21; 24-25; 28; 30;
32; 34; 39; 44; 47-51; 54; 56; 58; 63-64; 66;
70; 73. 12,1. 13,1. 14,7. 15,6; 8-9. 17,2.
19,2-5; 7-10. 21,7. 22,1. 23,2; 6. 24,6; 11.
25,3; 5; 9. 29,2; 11; 17-18; 20. 31,1-2. 32,1.
34,1.
       HRT   B3; 6. 1,2-17; 19.
2,1-2; 5. 4,7; 9-10; 12-16; 20; 25. 5,5; 9-
11; 20-24. 6,1. 10,6. 15,2; 10-12. 17,2-3; 6-
9; 12-15. 19,1. 20,4; 9-11. 24,1. 30,1. 31,7.
33,8-9; 17. 34,1; 5-7; 13; 24. 35,1-3. 36,4;
11; 17. 37,1-2; 8; 11-12; 14-15; 19-22. 38,1-
2. 42,14. 42a. 42a,1. 44,1.
       HUN B10; 14. 1,1-2; 5-8.
2,8. 6. 11,2. 13,1. 14. 18,1. 19,14; 25; 27;
30. 20,2-3; 5-6; 9. 21. 24. 25,1. 26,1. 27,1.
28. D7; 17-18; 24.
       KEN D9; 22; 25. M14;
19. C1; 5. P20. 1,1-3. 4,4. 5,4; 25; 29-30;
42; 48; 54; 58-60; 64; 67; 71-73; 79; 84-85;
89; 100; 102; 107-109; 114; 124; 139; 142;

168; 172; 175; 187; 209. 7,10. 9,4; 10; 16-
17; 19; 39. 10,1. 13,1.
       LEC   C17. 1,2. 10,17.
            14,16. 17,33. 19,6.
            40,8. 42,5; 9. 43,5-
            6; 8.
       LIN   C2; 6; 20-21. S4.
1,4-5; 23; 26; 28-29; 31; 34-35; 38; 65; 80-
81; 91. 2,32; 34; 37; 39. 3,4. 7,18; 29; 38.
11,9. 12,7; 43; 47; 49; 60; 76; 83-84; 89; 91.
13,1; 17; 28; 34; 38-39. 14,97. 15,1. 16,50.
18,1; 7; 13; 29. 19,1. 22,27. 24,2; 53. 30,1;
22; 26; 28. 34,12. 35,13. 42,1. 51,11.
56,13-14; 17; 23. 58,8. 59,6. 63,1. 68,25;
31; 35; 38; 42; 46-47. CS20. CN13; 18; 30.
CW14; 16-17. CK23; 31; 34; 38; 40.
       MDX L24. 2,2. 3,3-4; 8-
11. 5,1-2. 7,2; 7-8. 8,3-6. 9,6. 10,1-2. 11,3-
4. 12,1-2. 14,2. 18,1-2. 25,1-3.
       NFK   6,1.
       NTH   B32; 34. 1,4; 21; 26;
31-32. 2,1. 8,1; 4; 8. 15,1. 17,1-3; 5. 18,1;
32. 20,1. 22,9. 23,16. 24,1. 32,1. 41,2.
49,1. 53,1. 56,6; 22. 57,1. 60,1.
       NTT   B1; 3; 13. S5. 1,9;
58-59. 2,5-6. 5,4-5; 9; 11. 6,1; 13; 15. 9,1;
109. 10,3; 5; 16; 27; 35; 39; 56. 11,10. 14,6.
15. 17. 27,1. 30,11; 41; 49.
       OXF   B5; 10. 1,3; 6-7a; 9.
3,1. 5,1. 6,12; 14. 7,4; 10. 9,10. 10,1. 14,6.
15,3-4. 20,5. 29,16-17. 36,1. 40,2. 42,1.
51,1. 56,1. 58,29. 59,14; 23-24; 27.
       RUT   R7-9; 11-13; 16; 18-
            20.
       SHR   C12. 2,2. 3b,2-3.
4,1,2; 5; 14-27; 30-31; 36. 4,2,1. 4,3,1; 16.
4,4,6; 20. 4,5,13. 4,6,1; 5. 4,7,1; 4. 4,8,3.
4,9,1. 4,10,1; 3. 4,11,1; 4; 6; 11. 4,13,1.
4,14,1. 4,15,1. 4,16,1. 4,17,1. 4,18,1; 3.
4,19,1-3; 8. 4,20,1; 8; 18. 4,21,1. 4,22,1; 3.
4,23,1; 16. 4,24,1. 4,25,1. 4,26,1; 7.
4,27,1-2; 17. 4,28,4; 6. 8,1. 9,1.
       SOM L24; 39. 1,12-17;
19; 21; 25; 27-28; 31. 2,1; 10. 3,1. 4,1. 5,34;
51. 6,9; 18. 7,12. 8,7; 26; 37. 9,3. 10,2.
17,1; 7. 19,35; 40; 57; 78. 20,1. 22,23.
24,35. 25,42. 27,3. 35,11. 37,9. 39,1. 45,1;
7-9; 12; 14; 18. 46,12; 16-17; 24. 47,3.
       STS   B9. 1,11-28. 4,2.
5,2. 7,13. 8,1-3; 5; 19; 23; 32. 9,1. 10,3.
11,6; 34; 67-68. 12,1; 5-6; 14; 21. 15,1-2.
       SFK   6,236. 8,63.
            14,108. 26,12c.
            34,5. 35,8.
       SRY   1,1b-c; 4-5; 11; 14.
2,3. 4,2. 5,1; 1b; 11; 17; 19-20; 28. 6,1; 4.
8,18. 14,1. 15,1. 19. 19,25; 32; 39. 20,1-
2. 21,1; 3; 6. 24,1. 25,2-3. 26,1. 29,1-2.
31,1. 32,1. 36,5; 8.
       SSX   1,1-2. 3,10. 8,1-2.
9,4; 6; 11; 14; 21; 26-29; 42-44; 46; 52; 56;

59; 66-68; 72-74; 82; 99; 104; 106-109; 121-122. 10,1-2; 14; 27; 31; 39; 41; 43; 46; 54; 59; 61-63; 83; 86; 93; 115. 11,1; 3; 5; 8-10; 13-14; 16-17; 30; 33; 36-37; 41; 45; 63; 65; 75-76; 93; 95-98; 105. 12,4-5; 9-10; 13; 28; 30; 33; 36; 41-42; 48. 13,6; 9-11; 13; 15; 17-18; 20; 31; 33; 35; 38; 41-42; 46-48; 51; 53; 57.

WAR B2. L38. 1,1; 6-7. 4,3; 5. 8,1. 12,10. 14,2; 6. 15,6. 16,1; 44. 17,10; 15; 48; 60; 63. 21,1. 22,10. 24,1. 26,1. 27,1; 3. 28,1. 29,1; 3. 35,1. 36,2. 37,1; 6. 38,1. 42,1. 43,1.

WIL M5; 12; 16. L40; 66. B4-5. 1,8; 11-19. 2,4. 3,1. 13,2. 17,1. 18,2. 21,2. 23,7. 24p. 24,4. 28,2; 10-11. 30,5; 7. 31,1. 32,2. 40,1. 41,1. 46,1. 47,1-2. 48,1. 49,1a. 50,1. 51,1. 52,1. 55,1. 58,1. 59,1. 60,1. 61,1. 62,1. 64,1. 66,1-3. 67,14-15; 18; 22; 26; 43; 45; 47; 52-53; 61; 75; 77; 100. 68,3; 8-9; 14-15; 23-30; 32.

WOR 1,1a,d; 3b. 2,52; 63; 70-71; 78. 3,3. 8,8; 9b; 25. 14,2. 15,2. 17,1. 18,2; 6. 19,1; 6; 12. 22,1. 23,10. 25,1. 26,4; 13.

YKS C25; 36. 1W53. 2B3-7; 9-14; 18. 2N19. 2W2; 4; 6-7. 3Y10. 4N1-3. 4E1-2. 5N9. 5W8; 14. 6N1. 23N17; 19; 23; 25-27; 29; 33. 25W14. 29W7; 9. 29E7; 12. 30W2. CE11; 13; 18; 27-28. CW24; 42.

interlineations as to other matters of substance	BDF	1,3-4. 5,2. 10,1. 16,2. 19,2. 21,3. 23,36. 24,29. 31,1. 36,1. 44,4. 46,1. 53,26; 32.
	BRK	B1-2; 9. 1,9; 15; 27; 29; 39; 41. 7,2; 6; 18-19. 21,5. 31,1. 36,2. 46,4. 54,2. 55,4.
	BKM	B1. 4,3; 20; 25; 30. 7,1. 12,31. 14,1; 13; 19-20; 27; 30. 26,1. 29,1. 57,6.
	CAM	B11. 1,1; 3; 12; 18. 4,1. 5,6; 27; 29; 37; 49; 57; 60-61; 63. 6,1. 7,11. 9,3. 11,5. 12,3. 13,1-2. 14,3; 7-8; 13; 34; 38; 58; 69. 17,1-2; 8. 21,3; 7. 22,5. 26,3; 23; 26. 28,2. 30,1. 32,27; 32. 41,1. 44,1
	CHS	C3; 6; 8. B13. A1. 1,2; 4; 22; 26. 2,7; 9; 14; 16-18; 20; 28. 3,2. 4,2. 5,9. 8,23; 34. 9,19. 12,1; 3. 14,11. 16,1. 24,7. S2,1. FD5,3. FT3,2. R1,12; 40c; 41. R5,3; 6. R6,1. R7,1.
	CON	1,4. 2,7. 4,22; 25. 5,1,4; 18. 5,2,9-12. 5,3,21; 25. 5,4,12. 5,11,2. 5,13,4.
	DBY	1,11-14; 19; 26-30; 35; 37. 3,1; 4. 4,2. 5,3-4. 6,3; 14-15; 22; 24; 28; 32; 39; 42-43; 48; 63; 66; 77; 79-80;

82; 84; 87-88; 94-96. 7,7-8. 9,1; 3-4. 10,13-15; 17; 25; 27. 17,8. B1; 15-16.

DEV 1,9; 23; 27; 36; 51; 62. 2,8. 3,19; 32; 45; 52; 60. 7,1-2. 15,6; 16; 25; 38; 57; 79. 16,25; 29; 51; 144. 17,13; 15; 22. 19,6; 37. 23,5-6. 24,28-29. 25,8; 20-21. 26,1. 28,8. 29,2. 34,4; 10; 54-55. 35,6; 8-9; 22. 36,22. 39,2; 15. 40,5. 42,10; 16; 21. 44,1. 47,5; 14. 48,2. 49,1. 50,1. 51,5.

DOR B1; 3. 1,1; 3; 22; 31. 2,2. 3,1; 8; 11; 13. 11,4. 13,4; 8. 24,5. 26,1; 8-10; 14-16; 19; 21-22; 33-35; 37; 43; 60; 68. 27,1. 28,5. 30,3. 32,2. 33,2; 5. 34,5; 7. 36,6. 37,4. 39,1. 47,9-10. 50,2. 52,2. 54,3. 55,1; 4-6; 8; 32-34; 42-46. 56,7. 57,1; 3. 58,1.

ESS 1,2; 13; 23-24. 2,4. 3,1; 9. 5,11. 6,1. 7,1. 8,2. 9,7. 10,5. 13,2. 14,5. 18,2; 4-5; 36-38. 20,6; 27; 43; 45; 50-51; 72. 22,6. 23,22; 34-35. 24,25. 25,3; 5; 14. 26,2. 27,14-15. 28,7. 30,36; 44-45. 32,7; 20. 34,1. 35,5; 7. 37,1. 38,5. 39,1; 10. 64,1. 71,4. 83,1. 90,8; 33; 38; 41; 51.

GLS G1. W15. B1. 1,2; 5; 14; 21; 49. 2,13. 3,7. 6,1-2. 11,14. 19,2. 24,1. 26,2. 31,2. 32,5. 35,2. 37,1. 39,17; 20. 41,4. 45,2. 50,4. 53,9-10. 58,3. 59,1. 67,3. 68,8; 12. 71,1. 75,1.

HAM 1,23-24; 27; 32; 35; 39-40. 2,10. 3,1; 5; 9; 14. 4,1. 6,5; 13; 16. 15,1. 16,1. 23,1-2; 5; 40; 42; 68. 28,4; 7. 29,1; 9; 12; 16. 45,4. 53,2. 64,1-2. 67,1. 68,7. 69,6; 13; 29; 48. NF1. NF3,1. NF10,4. IoW1,7; 14-15. IoW2,1. IoW9,3; 11; 15.

HEF C8. 1,3; 7; 40; 69. 2,2; 21. 7,1. 8,8-9. 10,10; 42; 48; 59-60. 15,1; 9-10. 21,6. 24,6-7. 25,1; 7. 29,2-3; 18. 31,7.

HRT B7-8. 1,5; 10; 12; 16; 19. 4,7. 5,25. 10,1. 11,1. 16,2. 17,12. 28,8. 36,1; 8; 15. 37,19.

HUN B17-18. 1,2-3; 6; 10. 2,2-3. 4,1. 6,3; 6; 19. 13,1; 3. 15,1. 17,1. 19,4; 10. 20,7-8. 23,1. 25,1. 28,1. D11; 21; 24; 26.

KEN D2; 4; 8-9; 14; 22. C1-2. P8; 19. 1,3-4. 2,2; 4-5; 16; 32. 3,2; 10. 4,12. 5,6; 13; 29; 43-44; 51; 84; 95; 99; 102; 104-106; 116; 118; 122; 129; 144; 151; 178; 195; 220; 223. 6,1. 7,5.

LEC 1,1a; 2; 4. 2,6. 3,7; 14. 10,1. 13,1. 14,3; 6; 11. 16,9. 18,2. 24,2. 29,1-2. 38,1. 40,28; 39. 43,9. 44,9.

LIN C3; 11; 16-17. S10. T1; 5. 1,3; 5-6; 8; 12-16; 37; 39; 49; 56; 91; 93-94. 2,7; 9-10; 12; 20. 3,1; 7; 16; 22; 32; 34; 37; 44; 47; 52; 54. 4,9; 15; 30; 35; 37; 43; 48; 56-57; 65-66; 71. 7,8; 11; 26; 33; 37; 44; 47; 49; 51; 55. 8,3; 10. 10,2. 12,4; 11; 18; 29; 48; 50; 55; 57-58; 60; 67-68; 72-

73; 75; 92; 95-96. 13,2; 18-19; 29; 33; 39-
40. 14,10; 13; 27; 30; 57; 59; 83; 86; 93;
97; 99. 15,2. 16,2; 11; 17; 23-24; 36; 46.
18,1-2; 9; 17; 32. 22,15; 22; 27; 29. 24,11;
29; 40; 51; 66; 97-98; 105. 25,16; 22. 26,5;
13; 22; 24; 40. 27,1; 5; 26; 30; 37-39; 59.
28,11; 13-14; 29. 29,5; 20. 30,9; 22; 25; 27-
28; 31-32. 31,1-2; 8-9; 11-14; 17. 32,12-
13; 20-21; 24; 31. 34,4; 12; 17. 35,4; 11.
36,1-2. 37,1; 7. 38,5-6. 39,3. 40,7; 26.
41,1-2. 42,7; 15. 44,14. 47,8. 51,1. 56,11;
20. 57,22; 28; 48; 55. 59,12. 61,6; 10. 62,2.
63,15; 19. 64,3; 6; 17-18. 65,2-3; 5. 67,18.
68. 68,6; 45; 47. CS6; 11; 14; 26; 37-38.
CN6; 9; 11; 13; 21; 30. CW10. CK1; 12-
13; 26-27; 33; 42-43; 55; 66-67; 69.

MDX 2,3. 3,12; 18-19.
6,1. 7. 7,3; 6. 18,1.
20,1. 24,1.

NFK L16; 18. 1,2; 62;
192; 220. 4,8-9; 20. 6,6. 7,16. 8,3-4; 6; 8;
11; 16; 22; 26-27; 30; 33; 35; 37-38; 44; 46-
47; 54-56; 63; 67; 82; 84; 91; 93-94; 99-100;
102; 104-108; 112; 116; 122. 9,7; 26; 34;
80; 82; 86; 88; 147; 179; 185. 10,2; 5; 16;
20; 22; 30; 34; 55-56; 59; 66; 68; 72; 77;
79; 83; 93. 11,3. 12,4. 13,2; 4-5; 7; 10; 14-
15; 19; 23-24. 14,8; 11; 16; 35; 38; 40; 42.
17,1; 23; 27; 39; 43. 19,8-9; 18; 27; 32; 37-
38; 40. 20,3; 7; 10-11; 15; 20; 24; 29; 33.
21,3; 6; 15-16; 25; 34; 37. 22,3-4; 6; 12.
23,3-4; 7. 24,7. 25,13. 30. 30,5. 31,4; 6;
44. 32,4. 34,13. 35,12. 43,2. 49,4. 57,1.
61,4. 65,14. 66,5; 9; 33; 35; 57; 62; 67; 79;
87.

NTH 1,10-11; 30. 4,7; 22;
29. 6,11. 6a,6; 27. 12,1. 18,16; 40; 73; 85.
26,7. 30,6; 15. 35,1e; 2; 26. 36,3. 39,13.
43,1-2; 6. 48,2. 54,2. 56,15; 30; 61.

NTT B3-7; 11. 1,2; 4; 6;
8; 12-13; 21; 23-24; 30; 33-34; 41; 45-46;
54. 2,4. 3,2; 4. 4,4. 5,3-5; 7-8. 6,1; 3-4; 8.
9,5; 24-25; 27; 31; 41; 47; 57; 65; 69-70; 75;
79; 88; 91; 94. 10,10; 16; 26; 33; 40; 48;
51. 11,11-12; 25. 12,12; 16. 13,3; 5; 10; 13.
14,5-6. 16,8. 17,15; 17. 19,1. 20,3; 5-6.
22,1. 27,1. 28,2. 30,1; 5; 8; 26; 28; 31; 35;
40; 42; 44; 50-51.

OXF 1,13. 6,4-5; 9. 7,14;
22; 36; 41; 50; 58. 9,4; 6. 17,3. 22,1. 24,1;
4. 28,4; 8; 19. 29,4. 31,1. 34,2. 35,20. 43,1.
58,24.

RUT R1; 7; 10; 17-21.

SHR C2. 3g,10. 4,1,2-3.
4,3,5; 45; 57; 61; 70. 4,4,2; 5; 22. 4,5,12.
4,8,1; 3. 4,10,4. 4,11,2; 13. 4,14,17; 26.
4,20,8. 4,23,8; 15. 4,27,17-18; 22; 29.
4,28,1. 6,3-4; 11; 29; 32. 7,2-3; 6.

SOM 1,3; 10; 12; 17; 20.
2,10. 7,11. 8,5; 11; 18; 21. 10,6. 11,1.
19,76. 21,20. 24,10; 12; 16; 23; 27. 25,13;

33; 46; 55. 27,1. 30,2. 35,19. 36,4. 37,4; 8;
11-12. 39,1.

STS 1,45; 48; 51-53; 58;
61; 63. 2,16-17. 4,3. 7,17. 8,8; 13; 15; 21;
23-25; 32. 11,8-10; 17; 31; 34; 48; 52; 64.
12,2. 15,2. 16,2.

SFK 1,1; 12; 18; 21; 30;
34; 42; 61; 76; 81; 99; 115; 122f. 2,12. 3,4;
94-95; 101. 4,1; 4; 20; 24; 27; 30; 35. 5,1.
6,46; 57; 78-79; 88; 90; 114; 133; 147; 158;
163; 177; 179; 183; 187; 191; 201; 205-206;
215; 271; 274; 287; 305-306; 308; 311-312;
318. 7,4; 17; 36; 38; 56; 71; 75; 112. 8,1;
54-55; 61; 81. 13,7. 14,3; 16; 20; 26; 40-41;
44; 46; 48; 52-53; 55-56; 59; 62-65; 68; 72;
78; 81; 83; 89; 95; 101; 109-110; 112; 116;
119-120; 123; 129-131; 151; 157; 167. 15,5.
16,6; 15; 20-22; 25; 28; 35; 40. 19,14; 16.
21,11; 19; 28; 38-40; 42; 44; 81; 83; 87;
102. 22,3. 25,4; 10; 21; 40; 52-53; 60-61;
63. 26,1; 4-6; 12b; 13; 17. 27,3; 5. 28,1a-
b. 29,1. 31,5; 9; 18; 20; 24; 29; 40-42; 44-
45; 48; 51. 32,1; 6; 8; 14; 19; 30. 33,6; 9.
34,2; 8; 12; 18. 38,11. 39,3; 5. 40,2. 41,7;
10-11. 43,2. 44,1. 46,8. 48,1. 52,5-6; 9-10.
53,3-4; 6. 64,1. 66,3; 9. 67,15; 20-21. 74,4.
76,3.

SRY 1,1d; 10; 12. 3,1.
4,2. 5,1; 3-4; 6; 15; 22; 25; 28. 8,17; 20; 25.
14,1. 18,3. 19,2; 10-11; 15; 31; 35.

SSX 1,1. 2,3. 3,5. 5,1.
6,1. 9,6; 14; 16; 38-39; 47; 76; 83; 86; 92;
106; 109; 122-123. 10,7; 15; 17; 28; 36; 70;
88; 103. 11,8; 10; 18; 21-22; 81; 89-90; 93.
12,1; 38; 41; 43; 45. 13,6; 37; 40.

WAR 6,5. 7,1. 16,46; 52;
54-55. 17,6-7; 10; 12-13. 18,2. 20,1. 31,12.
37,3. 46,9-10.

WIL 1,1; 9; 16. 2,3. 4,3.
5,1; 6-7. 7,2. 8,11. 10,2. 12,3. 13,10. 14,1.
24p. 24,7; 17; 33. 25,24. 26,2; 16; 18; 22.
27,1; 26. 33,1. 41,9. 66,3-4. 67,9; 27; 31;
37; 45; 69; 78; 84; 88; 91. 68,9.

WOR C2; 4. 1,3a; 5; 7.
2,13; 22; 26; 30-32; 48; 55; 78. 6,1. 8,1; 9e;
10a; 11; 22. 9,1a,e. 10,8. 24,1. 26,1; 9; 11;
16.

YKS C3; 26; 31; 33-34.
1Y3-5; 8-11; 13-15; 17-19. 1N13; 19; 67;
77; 92; 110; 125. 1E15; 22; 29; 33; 45. ·1W9;
46; 50; 54; 62; 73. 1L1-3; 6. 2,1-2. 2B1; 4;
18-19. 2N25. 2W2; 9. 2E8; 12; 22; 27; 30.
3Y1; 4; 9. 4N1-3. 5N8; 28; 30; 32; 54; 61;
69; 72. 5E8; 12-13; 15; 18; 42; 44; 46; 53;
65; 72. 5W1; 7-8; 14-15; 18-21; 27; 30; 37-
38. 6N1-2; 7; 11; 18; 26-28; 30-31; 34; 46-
47; 50; 52; 58; 60; 83; 92; 113; 118; 120;
136; 151; 155. 6W2. 6E1. 6N1. 8N1-10;
22-23. 8W1-2. 8E1-6. 9W1; 20-23; 36; 39;
48; 64; 70; 80; 87; 119; 142. 10W1; 19.
11E2. 12W1. 13W7. 13E5. 13N18. 14E1-

2; 4-7; 11; 24. 15E2-3; 6. 16E4. 16N1.
20E3. 21E5. 21W15. 23N1; 8; 10. 23E3.
24W1; 20-21. 25W6; 12. 26E4. 28W36.
29W4-5; 7; 20. 29E13; 15; 17; 19; 29. 29N9.
30W1; 4-7; 9-11; 37; 40. 31E2. 31N10.
CN5. CE1; 24; 30; 33; 49. CW2-3; 11; 18;
20; 24; 26; 32. SN-Passim. SW-Passim.
SE-Passim.

marginal added	BDF	7. 23,24. 24,11.
information		53,22; 24.
	BKM	53,6.
	CAM	26,53. 29,4. 32,5.
	CHS	A18. 1,9; 22. 2,21.
		8,24. 9,27. 11,6; 8.
		17,5.
	DBY	1,17. 10,12.
	DEV	1,33; 50. 3,6.

15,47-52; 79. 17,9; 14; 17. 19,4; 40. 20,1;
7. 23,6. 24,5; 25. 28,16. 34,24; 32; 44-45;
47; 50. 36,1-2. 39,14-15. 48,12.

	DOR	L51. 11,13. 27,10.
		30,4. 32,1. 37,9.
		47,10.
	ESS	8,3.
	GLS	11,14. 12,4. 27,1.
		28,5-6. 36,2. 44,2.
		52,6. 69,7.
	HAM	1,46. 17,1. 23,30.
		28,9. 35,9. 44,1; 3.
		45,9. 47,3. 66,1.
		67,1. 68,5.
	HEF	1,2. 2,5. 23,5. 34,2.
	HRT	5,18. 20,18.
	HUN	7,8.
	KEN	5,117.
	LEC	27,4.
	LIN	1,39. 3,18; 24.

12,38; 41-43; 53; 55; 62; 69; 77; 81; 89-92;
95. 16,21. 29,28. 30,10; 33. 32,26. 56,18.

	MDX	4,7.
	NFK	8,10. 66,17.
	NTH	2,9. 19,2-3. 25,2.
		35,9. 39,2. 57,3.
	NTT	1,53. 2,3; 5; 10.
		5,5-6. 9,6-9; 21; 23;
		47-48. 10,7. 12,12.
		30,10.
	OXF	6,16. 56,1-4.
	SHR	4,14,28. 4,18,3.
		4,19,9.
	SOM	1,27. 19,25; 70.
		46,2.
	STS	1,9.
	SFK	1,101. 6,271. 7,23;
		55; 77; 136. 14,56-
		57; 59; 92-93; 108.
	SRY	6,5. 26,1. 36,10.
	SSX	8a,1. 9,83. 10,84.
	WAR	14,2. 16,20. 22,3;
		10.
	WIL	B5. 1,2. 25,1.

27,10. 51,1. 66,1.
67,37-38.

	WOR	8,16. 15,9. 23,8.
	YKS	1Y7. 1N92. 1E11a.

1W56. 5N1a. 5E39; 43-45; 54-55. 8W2.
9W6-8; 104. 11E6-9. 14E2. 29W8; 25.
SW,BA10-13. SE,Sn8.

marginal signs/		
comments	BRK	1,4. 2,1. 23,2.
	BKM	35,3.
	CAM	32,7.
	CHS	B6.
	DBY	6,27; 48. 12,4.
		16,2. 17,9.
	DEV	1,35; 50. 2,5-8.
		10,1. 11,1. 16,58;
		65. 19,27; 34; 42.
		23,18; 21. 24,23-24.
		34,24; 32; 45; 47;
		50.
	DOR	19,11.
	GLS	1,27-33. 10,8.
	HAM	63,1. IoW7,16.
	HEF	10,37.
	HRT	20,2.
	HUN	2,6; 9. 6,3; 7-8.
		19,9; 16. 20,3.
	LEC	43,2; 7.
	LIN	3,15; 22; 25. 4,7.

7,14-15; 17; 20; 22-24; 29; 48; 54. 8,14; 18-
20; 23; 25; 27-29. 12,92. 14,57. 16,3; 6; 8;
28. 22,19-20. 24,78. 25,10. 27,25; 34; 64.
29,6-7; 33. 30,14. 40,8. 49,1. 61,5. CS11.
CN17. CK21; 28.

	NTH	1,32. 30,4.
	NTT	9,2. 30,3.
	OXF	1,7a. 7,2. 9,10.
	SHR	4,14,12.
	SOM	1,14. 5,43; 50. 9,4-
		5; 8. 16,8. 19,6; 8;
		10; 40. 21,54-55;
		98. 22,20. 25,7-8.
		37,9.
	STS	2,3; 6. 8,29. 11,38.
	SSX	2,5.
	WAR	6,9. 16,5-6. 23,1.
		28,16-18. 30,2.
		31,1-7. 38,1.
	WIL	2,11. 7,15. 12,1.
		13,10-11. 16,5.
		20,6. 25,2. 66,1.
		68,1.
	WOR	2,85.
	YKS	1N29; 136. 1E2; 13;

50. 1W7-8; 11; 21; 23-29; 42; 52-54; 66; 70-
72. 5E15. 25W31. 26E4. 29W2. SW,Sf15.
SW,O3. SE,C5; 8. SE,Sn7.

parchment		
insertions	DOR	1,31. 36,4-11. 42,1.
	HAM	4,1. 6,13-17.
	SRY	8,23-27.

signs – "gallows"   BDF   4,9.
BRK   B2-6; 9-11. 3,1.
7,2-5; 7-11.
BKM   B4-11; 13.
CHS   C4-13; 15; 17-26.
S2,2. FT2,19.
FT3,2-5. R1,39;
40b-g; 41-42; 44.
DBY   B5-16.
DOR   1,30-31.
ESS   1,1-7; 9-15; 18-31.
2,1-9. 3,1-16. 4,1-18. 5,1-12. 6,1-15. 7,1.
8,1-11. 9,1-2; 4; 6-9; 11-14. 10,1-5. 11,1-
8. 12,1. 13,1-2. 14,1-7. 15,1-2. 16,1. 17,1.
18,1-30; 32-33; 35-38; 40-43; 45. 19,1.
20,1-8; 10-14; 16; 18-20; 22-27; 29-41; 43-
80. 21,1-4; 8-10. 22,1-12; 14-20; 22-23.
23,1; 3-8; 11-16; 28; 30-34; 36-43. 24,1-67.
25,1-6; 8-26. 26,1-5. 27,1-6; 8-18. 28,1-
18. 29,1-5. 30,1-51. 31,1. 32,2-45. 33,1-
23. 34,2-37. 35,2-14. 36,2; 4-12. 37,2-16;
18-20. 38,2-6; 8. 39,1-5; 7-12. 40,1-4; 6-9.
41,2-3; 5-9; 11-12. 42,2-9. 43,2-6. 44,2-4.
45,1. 46,2-3. 47,2-3. 48,2. 49,1-4. 51,2.
52,2-3. 53,1-2. 54,2. 55,1. 57,1-5. 59,1.
60,1-3. 61,2. 62,4. 63,1-2. 64,1. 65,1. 66,1-
2. 67,1-2. 68,1-8. 69,1-2. 70,1-2. 71,2-4.
72,1-3. 73,1. 74,1. 76,1. 77,1. 78,1. 79,1.
80,1. 81,1. 82,1. 83,1-2. 84,1-2. 85,1.
86,1-2. 87,1. 88,1. 90,1; 4; 10; 15; 19-20;
22; 29-31; 34-36; 38-39; 41-44; 46; 48-49;
59; 79-87. B1-3a,c-g,k-t; 5-6.
GLS   G3-4. S2. W2-19.
1,2; 8. 19,2.
HEF   C7; 13. A2-8; 10.
1,1-2; 5; 8; 40.
HRT   B3-10.
HUN   B2-8; 10; 13-14.
D2-29.
KEN   D4-5; 9-10; 24. C3-
4; 8. P2-4; 19-20. 1,1. 5,128; 167. 6,1. 7,19.
9,35.
LEC   C17.
LIN   C5-11; 13-17; 19-
25; 33. S8-16. 22,27. CS22-39. CN3-30.
CW2-3; 5-20. CK2-71.
MDX   L25. 1,4.
NFK   1,2-16; 18; 20-29;
31-42; 45-51; 53-54; 56-57; 59-60; 62-65;
68; 70; 72-76; 78-87; 90-96; 98-125; 127-
140; 142-146; 148-149; 151-167; 169-172;
174-180; 182; 184-188; 191-193; 197; 200;
202-203; 205; 208; 210-211; 213-214; 216;
218; 220-230; 233-234; 236-240. 2,2-11.
4,2-8; 10-21; 23-25; 27-37; 39; 41; 44-45;
48-50; 53-54; 56-57. 5,2; 4. 6,3; 5. 7,2; 5;
8-9; 11-14; 16; 18; 21. 8,1-7; 9-20; 22-33;
35-46; 48-53; 55-58; 60-84; 86-87; 90-97;
99-106; 108-116; 118-136. 9,2; 5-9; 12-17;
19-23; 25-50; 52-57; 60-64; 71; 74; 76; 78-
81; 86-87; 89; 94-96; 98; 100; 105-108; 110;

112-113; 120-121; 123-125; 129; 137-139;
144; 146-149; 151-156; 158; 160-166; 169-
173; 180; 182-183; 186; 200. 10,2-19; 21;
23-24; 29-33; 35; 37-42; 44-45; 47; 49; 51;
57-59; 61-66; 68-81; 83-91; 93. 11,2; 5.
12,2-6; 8-18; 20-26; 28; 31-45. 13,1-11; 13-
22. 14,2-4; 6-33; 35-37; 39-43. 15,2-29.
16,2-6. 17,2-13; 15-16; 18-28; 32-33; 35-
40; 43; 45-65. 18,1. 19,1-2; 5; 7-9; 12; 14-
15; 19-21; 24-26; 28-30; 37. 20,2; 8-9; 11;
13; 17-18; 21; 24-25; 27; 31. 21,6; 11; 14-
15; 17-18; 25; 28-30. 22,3-5. 23,10-13; 15-
18. 24,2-6. 25,2-8; 10; 13; 15-22; 25-28.
26,3-5. 28,2. 29,2-11. 30,3-5. 31,2; 4; 6-
11; 13-18; 21-22; 25-33; 39-42; 44-45.
32,3-6. 33,3-4; 6. 34,2-3; 6; 8-11; 16-19.
35,3; 5; 7; 9-11; 14-18. 36,3-4; 7. 37,3.
38,4. 43,2-3. 47,4-5; 7. 48,5-7. 49,2; 5; 8.
50,3; 5; 7-8; 10; 13. 51,2-3; 6-7. 56,2; 6.
64,2-4; 6-9. 65,2-3; 7; 9-10; 16. 66,2-6; 8;
13; 15; 24-26; 35; 39; 41; 43-44; 51-53; 55-
58; 63-65; 67; 69; 71-72; 76; 78; 80; 83-91;
95; 99-101; 103-108.
NTH   B37-38. 4,4-36.
5,3-4.
NTT   B8-14; 16-20. 4,4.
5,1; 4. 9,7; 25.
12,3; 5.
OXF   B6-9. 1,13.
SHR   C5-10.
STS   2,22.
SFK   L74-76. 1,1-2; 7-8;
12-13; 16; 23; 32; 44; 48-52; 61-64; 66; 68;
74-76; 88; 90; 95; 100; 105; 109; 111; 116-
121. 2,1-2; 7; 12; 14; 17-19. 3,2-3; 5; 8-10;
15-16; 36-39; 46; 49; 56-58; 61; 63-64; 67-
68; 71-72; 74; 86-87; 93; 95-99; 103. 4,2;
13-15; 20; 24; 30; 37-38; 42. 5,1-3; 8. 6,1;
4-5; 11; 17; 24; 26; 28; 32; 42; 45; 49; 57;
70; 76; 78; 80; 83-89; 92-94; 100-108; 113-
114; 116-119; 121-124; 129; 133; 135-136;
143; 155-157; 159; 170; 176; 179; 192; 214;
223-224; 245; 248; 251; 262; 264; 271; 304-
307; 309. 7,3; 5-8; 10; 14-16; 18-34; 36-39;
42; 47; 56; 58; 62; 64-65; 67; 70-71; 73; 77;
79-80; 82-96; 98-113; 115; 117-122; 138-
140; 143-146; 148. 8,4; 6; 9; 13-14; 21; 33;
35-36; 47; 55; 67; 80-81. 9,1; 3-4. 12,4; 6.
13,4-5. 14,1-33; 35-42; 48-55; 57-106; 108-
132; 134-136; 138-140; 146; 148-164; 166-
167. 15,1-5. 16,1-2; 6-15; 17-38; 40-48.
17,1. 18,1-6. 19,1-21. 20,1. 21,1-13; 15-
50; 52; 54-72; 74-88; 90-105. 22,1-2. 23,1-
2; 4. 24,1. 25,1-13; 15-64; 67-68; 71-87;
89-112. 26,1-20. 27,1-13. 28,1-7. 29,1-14.
30,1. 31,1-9; 11-23; 25-29; 31-34; 36-38;
40-58; 60. 32,1-27; 29-31. 33,1-13. 34,1-
10; 12-18. 35,1-8. 36,1-14; 16-17. 37,1-7.
38,1-9; 11-23; 25-27. 39,1-13; 16-17. 40,1-
6. 41,1-19. 42,1-2. 43,1-9. 44,1-4. 45,1-3.
46,1-5; 8-9; 11-12. 50,2. 52,2-4; 8; 10.

53,3-4; 7. 56,2-6. 61,2. 62,2-3. 64,2. 66,2-
5; 7-11; 13; 16-17. 67,2-6; 8; 11-18; 20-26;
28-32. 69,2; 4. 74,2; 4-8; 10-16. 75,1-2; 4-
5. 76,3-6; 9-10; 13-15; 19-22. 77,4.
   SRY 1,1c-f; 6; 14. 5,1c-
        e; 28.
   SSX 1,1. 2,1b-g; 10.
        3,3. 9,6; 14. 11,2.
        12,1.
   WAR 6,9. 12,4-11. 17,23-
70. 18,9-16. 19,5. 22,12-28. 27,2-6. 28,2-
14. 29,3-5. 30,2. 31,7-12. 37,2-9. 39,2-4.
44,6-8.
   WIL M2-16. B5. 1,1;
        23a-j.
   WOR 1,4. 8,9c-g; 10,b-e;
        11; 26b-c. 9,1c-e;
        5b; 7.
   YKS C1b; 2-20; 22-35;
39-40. 1Y1-2; 15. 2B1-2. 3Y1; 12. 5W7.
CN2-5. CE1-4; 6-33. CW1-26; 30-36; 38-
40.
signs –
transposition (first
of pair only)
   BDF 22,4. 53,24. 57,19.
   BRK 20,2. 28,2. 34,3.
        49,2.
   CAM 5,33. 32,1.
   CHS C12. 5,13. 8,22-23.
        9,10. S3.
   CON 4. 5,4,18. 5,6,6.
   DBY 6,28. 10,11.
   DEV 1,45. 3,19; 56; 76.
        16,94. 49,6.
   DOR L51. 1,30. 12,16.
        19,7; 10. 36,3.
        41,5. 50,4. 57,19.
   GLS W2. 11,14. 24,1.
        26,1. 27,1. 28,5.
        32,7; 12. 72,2.
   HAM 3,26. 6,1. 21,7.
        23,25; 31; 61. 47,2.
        NF9,40. IoW7,16.
   HEF C9. 1,2. 6,6. 10,5;
        40.
   KEN M17. 2,39.
   LEC 6,3.
   LIN 3,16; 28. 4,5; 11;
21; 46; 56. 8,9. 12,44. 13,31. 14,35. 16,17.
18,4. 22,5; 26; 36. 24,21; 59. 26,7; 11; 24.
30,9. 32,4. 35,11.
   NTH 19,1. 23,1.
   NTT 1,53. 4,5. 9,6; 20;
        80; 90.
   OXF 29,21. 55,1. 58,12.
   SHR 3b,3. 4,14,27.
        4,26,6. 6,27; 31.
        7,4.
   SOM 45,2.
   STS 1,25.
   SRY 22,4. 27,3.

   WAR 3,5. 16,61. 44,3.
   WIL 1,3. 13,10. 16,5.
        26,12. 50,5. 67,37.
   WOR 8,22. 12,1. 18,5.
        19,14.
   YKS 1N2; 21. 12W20.
        25W28. 29E26.

DOMESDAY survey
Barons sent to inquire
into lands   DEV 5,5.
        WOR App V.F.
Commissioners of   GLS 1,63.
        HEF 1,75.
        WOR App V.F.
  order seizure of
  land   ESS 66,1.
Reference to   CHS FT2,19.
        GLS 1,63.
        HUN B21.
        KEN 2,2.
        SHR C12.
        WOR X2-3.
See also: Baron; Recorded; Return.
DOWER/dowry (dos)
Excluded from
husband's forfeiture   OXF 1,13.
Land
  claimed not to be
  included in   BDF 55,9.
  given in before
  witnesses   ESS 30,16.
  held in   BDF 57,7.
        GLS 39,18.
        HAM 6,16.
  part of   BDF 55,11.
See also: Marriage portion.
DRAG net (tracta)   MDX 12,2.
See also: Fishing net.
DRAPER (draparius)   KEN C1.
DRAUGHT animal
(afrus)   GLS 3,7.
DRENG   CHS R2,1-2. R3,1.
        YKS C3.
DUEL (bellum) – See Combat.
DUES (census)
King's   ESS 77,1.
        HRT 31,8.
Land
  held at   ESS 1,11-12. 33,22.
        STS 4,8.
  purchase price not
  covered by   ESS 23,2.
  sold for purchaser
  to receive   ESS 23,2.
Payment   DBY B1.
        DEV 3,8.
        ESS 1,4; 27.
        NTT B1.
        WOR 10,1.
  elsewhere   NTT B3.
        WOR 8,9.

land which did not		
pay	GLS	1,56.
	OXF	28,28.
not paid	OXF	24,6.
not paid to revenue	GLS	1,15.
Remitted by King	CHS	R1,39.
Sheriff's	DBY	B15.
Villagers		
fishery in dues of	SHR	4,18,2.
paying	HEF	2,24; 53.

See also: Borough; Burgess; Enclosure; House; Mill; Revenue; Rider; Salt house.

DUNG stool

(cathedra stercoris)	CHS	C18.

DWELLING

(mansura; masura)	BRK	B1-4. 15,2.
	CAM	B1-9.
	HAM	1,28. 16,7. 17,1-2. 23,16. 29,5. 39,3. 69,25.
	HEF	C3-4; 6. 2,1; 32. 13,2.
	KEN	D8-9. C3-5. 2,1-2; 16. 4,15. 5,124; 144-145; 147; 151; 198; 220. 7,10.
	LIN	CN28.
	NFK	1,61; 70.
	NTT	20,4.
	OXF	B5-10.
	SHR	C14. 1,1.
	SOM	*19,70.*
	STS	B1-10.
	SFK	32,7.
	SRY	1,5. 2,3. 15,1-2. 19,1-2; 15; 17; 21. 29,1.
	SSX	5,2. 11,1. 12,6.
	WAR	B2-3. 18,3.
	WIL	M1-17. B5.
	WOR	10,17. 23,12.
	YKS	C1a-b; 3-21.
half (½)	WIL	M2-3; 6-7; 11-12; 14.
quarter (¼)	WIL	M13.
free	OXF	B9-10.
house-contrasted		
with	NFK	1,70.
	WIL	M1.
Appertaining to		
another borough	BRK	B2.
manor in another		
County	BRK	B3.
	OXF	B5.
manor/village		
elsewhere	BRK	B2-3.
	CHS	FD1,1.
	HAM	23,16.
	HEF	2,32.
	KEN	2,16. 4,15. 5,124; 144-145; 198.

	OXF	B6-9.
	STS	B4; 6; 8.
	SFK	31,55.
	SRY	1,5. 15,2. 19,15. 29,1.
	WAR	B2.
Assessed in land		
where it belongs	WAR	B2.
Condition		
derelict/waste/		
unoccupied (vasta)	CAM	B1-5; 8-9.
	CHS	FD1,1.
	ESS	1,25.
	NFK	1,66.
	OXF	B5; 7-10.
	SHR	C14. 1,1.
	STS	B1-2; 4; 6-7; 9. 8,19.
	SFK	1,122c. 38,3.
	WIL	M2; 11-12; 17. B5.
	WOR	10,17.
destroyed	KEN	2,16.
empty (vacua)	DOR	B4.
	NFK	1,61; 69-70; 210.
	SOM	*40,1.*
	SFK	25,52. 39,12. 41,13.
	YKS	C1b.
inhabited		
(hospitata)	KEN	2,2.
	STS	B1; 8.
	SFK	39,12.
	SSX	12,1-2.
	WIL	M1.
	YKS	C1a-b; 21.
uninhabited		
(inhospitata)	SSX	12,1-2.
	YKS	C1b.
waste through		
castle site	SHR	C14.
	WAR	B2.
	YKS	C10.
Custody given by		
sheriff	YKS	C20.
Customary dues		
burgesses		
having/with full		
jurisdiction	KEN	C3.
	WAR	B3.
burgesses, canons,		
judges having	YKS	C1a.
exempt	HAM	16,7.
	OXF	B9.
	YKS	C2.
lost by King	KEN	D8.
paid by dwelling	CAM	B2-5.
	SFK	31,55. 41,13.
	YKS	C1b.
paid by		
derelict/empty		
dwelling	CAM	B9.

	SFK	41,13.
Dimensions of	YKS	C10.
Forfeiture of	KEN	D9.
	YKS	C10.
Jurisdiction, full, of	LIN	CN28.
King's revenue, of	WIL	M16.
Lordship, in	STS	B1.
	SFK	31,55.
Manor, removed		
from	SRY	29,1.
Owned/occupied by		
Abbot	SFK	38,3.
	WAR	B2.
Bishop	SHR	1,1.
clergy in guild	KEN	2,1.
free man	SFK	76,10.
Frenchman	BRK	B1.
	YKS	C1b.
lord (dominica)	SRY	5,8.
moneyer	YKS	C4.
monks	WAR	B2.
nun	WAR	B2.
priest	YKS	C3; 6; 16.
reeve	YKS	C10.
smallholder	HAM	1,27. IoW1,7.
villager	HAM	1,27.
woman	NFK	1,61.
Payments		
levy (scotum)	SFK	1,122c.
none	CAM	B2; 6-7.

	HAM	39,3.
	OXF	B9-10.
	YKS	C1b.
none from empty	YKS	C1b.
uninhabited, by	YKS	C1b.
Services of		
reaping/hay		
making	HEF	C3.
rendering none	OXF	B9-10.
	WIL	M2; 16.
Situation		
borough wall,		
within	STS	B4.
castle, in	HEF	13,2.
city wall,		
within/outside	HEF	C1; 3; 6.
ditch, within	YKS	C7; 15.
Tax		
paying	STS	B11.
not paying	SHR	C14.
Tribute, paying	HAM	1,28.
	WIL	M1.
Wall dwelling	OXF	B5; 9-10.

See also: Appropriation; Castle; Claim;
Destruction; Herring; Jurisdiction, full; Plot; Tax.

DYKE (fossa)

Making of near road	KEN	D12.
	NTT	B20.
Protection of	NTT	B20.

DYKE builder (fossarius) – See Ditcher.

E

EARL (comes)
Abbey, building	SHR	C14. 3b,1.
Banishing man from area may recall him	YKS	C39.
Fines/penalties in city had by Earl	CHS	C4; 15-21.
	YKS	C38.
Giving land to establish borough	NFK	1,66.
Hand of, person in	SFK	1,110.
Holding whole County	SHR	4,1,37.
Household of – supply of salt to	CHS	S1,1.
Officers of	CHS	C3; 18. S2,2.
	HUN	B18.
Payments to	KEN	D7.
	NFK	1,61.
	WOR	C1.

See also: Burgess; Castle; Chaplain; Church; City; Cook; Crime/offence; Customary due; Death duty; Division; Exile; Falconer; Fine; Fold; Forest; Forfeiture; Fourth penny; free man; Freeman; Goldsmith; Harold; Holding; House; Jurisdiction; Jurisdiction, full; Man; Manor; Monk; Patronage; Peace; Plea; Reeve; Salt house; Servant; Thane; Third/two thirds part; Wapentake.

EARL Ralph – See Claim; Forfeiture; Rebellion.

EARLDOM (consulatus)	ESS	52,2.
Land in	NFK	1,70.
ECCLESIASTICAL land	NFK	10,32.

ECCLESIASTICAL matters – See Abbess; Abbey; Abbot; Alms; Altar; Archbishop; Archdeacon; Benefice; Bishop; Bishopric; Burial; Canon; Cemetery; Chapel; Chaplain; Chapter; Church; Clerk/cleric/clergy; Consecration; Deacon; Dean; Ecclesiastical land; Excommunication; Festival; Holy days; Man; Mass; Monastery; Monk; Nun; Palm Sunday; Parish; Parishioner; Peter's pence; Prayers; Prebend; Prebendary; Priest; Psalms; Registrar; Sacristan; Saint; Territory; Tithe.

EDWARD, King – See King.

EELS (anguillae)	CAM	14,73.
	OXF	6,7. 13,1.
	WOR	2,72.
Renders of	DBY	6,30.
	HEF	1,5; 10b.
by fisherman	CAM	5,56. 6,2. 7,12. 9,4. 18,9.
by fishery	BRK	1,15; 18. 7,32.
	BKM	1,5. 3,1. 3a,4. 4,15; 18. 19,1. 23,2-3; 7.
		26,4. 29,2. 51,1. 52,1-2. 53,7.
	CAM	1,1. 5,45-50; 52; 55; 57; 59. 7,11. 14,55; 68. 41,1.
	GLS	59,1.
	HAM	23,36.
	HEF	1,21; 28. 29,2.
	HRT	32,2.
	HUN	8,2. 19,29.
	KEN	2,11; 26. 3,5; 11. 5,26; 57; 97. 11,1.
	LIN	13,37. 14,99. 18,29. 37,6. 42,1.
	NTT	9,116; 122.
	OXF	6,1b. 7,32; 37. 28,12.
	SHR	4,19,2.
	SOM	9,1.
	STS	1,11.
	SRY	8,14; 28. 22,4.
	SSX	11,21.
	WOR	2,66; 68. 10,10. 19,6. 20,5.
	YKS	2E1. 5E25; 35. 13E4; 13-14. 23E2.
by fishpond	CAM	14,73. 22,6.
	MDX	5,1. 13,1.
	YKS	12W25.
by garden	SOM	19,26.
by land	KEN	6,1.
	SHR	4,6,5.
by marsh	CAM	1,9. 9,2. 14,59. 17,1. 23,5. 24,1. 32,37-38; 40. 39,2.
by meadow	CAM	4,1.
by mill	BDF	4,6. 8,5. 21,1; 9; 17. 23,3; 5; 7; 10-12; 29; 36. 25,9. 26,2. 32,4. 53,9; 13.
	BRK	1,16; 18. 7,32.
	BKM	5,13; 15. 12,35. 14,13. 16,9. 23,32.
	CAM	1,3; 12. 4,1. 5,14. 14,63; 74. 17,2; 4.
	DOR	6,3.
	HAM	1,38. 23,52. 27,2. 45,1. 51,1.
	HEF	1,4-5; 10a. 7,3-4. 8,2. 10,9; 29. 12,2. 19,2.
	HRT	15,10. 26,1.
	KEN	5,12; 57. 12,1.

54

	LIN	34,2.
	MDX	5,1. 11,1.
	NTH	4,1-2; 4. 6,10a; 11-
		12. 6a,29.
	OXF	6,6. 7,2; 10; 22; 32;
		37. 29,16.
	SHR	4,3,52. 4,11,2.
		4,19,2. 6,11.
	STS	1,24.
	SSX	2,1a. 10,56; 60;
		111. 11,9; 14; 18-
		19.
	WAR	3,2-3. 4,2. 6,18.
		11,1; 3. 22,9.
		28,14. 29,4. 37,1;
		4.
	WOR	2,15. 9,1a. 10,3.
by weir	CAM	32,6. 38,2; 3.
	HEF	1,39.
	HRT	5,25. 16,10-11.
		17,14. 33,13.
		34,13.
	MDX	11,1.
Large, rendered by		
fishery	SHR	4,1,21.
Stick of (stica)	HEF	1,4; 10a; 39. 7,3-4.
		8,2. 10,9; 29. 12,2.
		19,2.
	KEN	D24.
	OXF	6,1a-c.
	SHR	4,19,2. 6,11.
	WAR	3,3. 4,2. 11,1; 3.
		22,9. 28,14. 29,4.
		37,1; 4.
	WOR	2,15; 66; 68; 72.
		9,1a. 20,5.

See also: Customary due.

EGGS (ova)
Rendered to sheriff   WIL   24p.
See also: Chicken; Hen.

EMISSARY (nuncius)
King's not seen   SRY   23,1.

ENCLOSURE/   CHS   B8. 1,8; 25-27. 2,7;
hedged enclosure   13; 30-31. 5,8; 12;
(haia)   14. 8,11; 13-14; 19;
24-26; 29-32; 36; 39-42. 9,17-18; 20; 24.
13,4. 14,4-6; 9; 13. 16,2. 17,7. 18,1; 3; 6.
20,12. 24,9. 26,8-10. 27,4. R5,1.

	GLS	1,34. 10,11. 16,1.
	HEF	2,23; 25; 27; 30-31.
		9,2. 29,16. 31,1.
	SHR	3c,2; 5; 7-8. 4,1,27;

36. 4,3,1; 46. 4,4,4; 10. 4,8,13. 4,11,4.
4,13,1. 4,14,4; 7; 20. 4,15,1. 4,20,2-3; 5-
6; 21-23. 4,23,2; 6; 9; 11. 4,24,1. 4,26,3.
4,27,11; 33. 5,1; 5-6. 6,16.

	WAR	16,17.
	WOR	2,7.
half (½)	CHS	13,5.
	SHR	4,4,21. 4,5,12.
Dimensions of	WAR	16,17.

Fourth penny of dues
shared King/Earl   SFK   1,12.
King's – woodland in   BRK   1,1.

	HEF	1,43. 2,9; 24.
	OXF	1,4-5.
	WAR	27,3.

Obligation to build
  men's   CHS   R6,2.
  thane's   CHS   R1,40a.
Purpose of
  catching wild
  animals   HEF   29,16.

	WOR	18,4.
keeping what is		
caught	HEF	29,16.
taking roe deer	SHR	4,8,10. 6,14.
Solid (firma)	SHR	4,3,15.
Wood/woodland, in	BRK	1,1.
	GLS	1,34.
	HEF	14,7. 24,6.
	SHR	3c,5. 4,1,27; 36.
		4,4,20. 4,18,3.

ENCLOSURE
(sepes; defensus;
defensio)   BDF   16,3.
Land in King's   HEF   2,2; 56.
Woodland put in   WOR   18,3.
See also: Deer.

ENCROACHMENT
(superfactum)   SSX   3,2.

ENGINEER (artifex;
machinator)   HAM   S3.

	NFK	55.

ENGLISH
Abbot   WIL   8,12.
Evidence by   DEV   *5,5.*

	ESS	18,6. 30,16.
unaware of facts	ESS	18,6-7.
Free	DOR	19,1.
Lands of	CAM	B2.
repurchase by	SFK	14,39.
Man-at-arms	BRK	40,1.
	HRT	23,3.
	WAR	17,68.
	WIL	3,1.
Woman	ESS	24,35.
	WIL	8,6.

See also: Anglo-saxon; Burgess; Customs; free
man; French and English; Hide; Hundred (long);
Return; Thane; Value.

ENGLISHMAN
(anglicus)   BDF   3,7; 13. 15,3.

	BRK	7,11; 26. 41,5.
	BKM	4,24. 5,11. 14,15.
		17,1. 23,15. 54,1.
	CAM	14,46. 26,32; 41.
	DEV	*5,5.* 20,9; 13-14.
	ESS	6,3. 23,2. 30,16;
		47. 35,14. 76,1.
	GLS	*G1-4.*
	HAM	2,1. 69,19. S2.

HEF	10,40.
HRT	2,4. 10,19. 17,11. 23,3. 26,1.
LIN	37,2. 68,37.
MDX	7,8. 9,6. 12,1.
NFK	1,61; 66. 9,75; 78; 81; 227. 14,9.
NTH	6a,22.
NTT	5,1.
SOM	5,28. 6,10. 7,11. 36,7. 45,12. 47,13; 15; 17.
STS	8,7; 17. 9,1. 11,37; 48.
SRY	8,7; 11. 22,5.
SSX	10,117. 11,98.
WIL	1,10-12. 2,10. 3,1. 13,3; 13. 14,1. 15,1-2. 24,17; 19. 27,5. 32,14.
YKS	9W138.

ENMITY (inimicitia) – See Feud.
ENTERTAINMENT (pasticius)
Payment for   SSX   11,2.
ENTRY into land
Forfeiture for non-
payment on   CHS   C11.
See also: Death duty; Possession; Reeve.

ESCORT (inwardus)	CAM	14,23; 40; 49. 26,2; 7-9; 18. 29,8. 32,35. 35,2. 38,1.
	HEF	C4.
	HRT	1,6; 9-11.
	KEN	D24. 1,3.

Provided by
Freeman   CAM   1,12; 14. 5,5; 7; 16. 13,8. 14,2-3; 5; 7; 10; 15; 21-22; 27; 63; 69; 71-72. 17,2; 4. 18,3. 21,4-5. 23,2. 26,1; 5; 10; 12; 16; 18; 21; 32; 34; 36; 42; 44-47; 49; 51. 31,2-4; 7. 32,4-5; 8; 10; 14; 16; 19-21; 25-27; 30; 32-33; 38. 41,4.
    HRT   1,9-11.
priest   CAM   14,21.
Provided for
court when King in
city   HEF   C4.
King when in
County/sheriffdom   CAM   1,14. 5,5. 26,51.
sheriff   CAM   5,7; 16. 13,8. 14,2-4; 20-21; 27; 39; 63; 71-72. 17,2. 21,5. 23,2. 26,5; 16; 18; 21; 47; 49. 31,3-4; 7. 32,4; 9; 19; 23; 25-27; 30; 38-39.
See also: Payment.
ESTABLISH a claim (deratiocinare) – See
Adjudge; Prove.
ESTATE (terra) –
land delivered as   SFK   76,20.
EUSTACE, Count
100 manors of   ESS   3,2. 20,4-5.
EVASION of arrest – See Crime/offence.
EVIDENCE (dicere; testare; testificare)

Given by
limited number of
people   ESS   33,17.
named persons   BRK   21,17. 41,5.
    ESS   23,3. 36,9.
    NFK   1,201. 4,39. 6,1.
    SFK   6,92.
    WOR   11,2.
un-named persons
(ut dicunt)   BDF   1,4.
    BRK   7,15. 21,18.
    GLS   1,64. 41,1.
    HAM   1,8; 13.
    HUN   D18.
    SRY   2,3.
    SSX   9.121. 12,41; 48.
    YKS   C2. 1Y15. 1W26.
Hearsay   BDF   1,4.
    HUN   D26.
    LIN   CK27.
    SFK   31,53.
    YKS   9W26. 10W42.
King's needed to
prove possession   HAM   69,16.
Man under King's
arrest cannot give   SFK   30,3.
No one able to give   SFK   76,22.
Proved a lie   SFK   74,11.
See also: Bishop; Borough; Canon; Claim;
Common people; Country; County; Deliverer;
English; free man; French; Holding; Hundred;
Landholder; Lathe; Law; Man; Monk; Nun; Oath;
Peers; Priest; Reeve; Riding; Sheriff; Sheriffdom;
Tenure; Thane; Town; Villager; Wapentake;
Welshmen.

EXACTION (tailla)   LIN   2,5; 11; 29; 33-34; 36-37. 3,2; 16. 4,1-3; 5; 11; 31; 40; 42-43; 57; 67; 72; 74. 6,1. 7,8; 14; 17-21; 23-24; 27-28; 30; 36; 38-39; 56. 8,1; 4-5; 8; 15; 20; 22-23; 28; 31. 11,3. 12,1; 4; 7; 14; 17; 19-21; 42-43; 47-49; 60. 13,1; 10; 17; 33-34. 14,1; 9; 13; 16-18; 25-26; 29-31; 39; 41; 46; 58-59; 64-66; 84; 89; 97. 16,1; 22; 33; 43. 17,2. 18,1; 3; 7; 11; 13; 20; 24-25. 20,1. 21,1. 22,1; 3; 7; 22; 25-26; 28-31. 24,1; 10; 12; 14; 17; 20; 22; 24-25; 33; 72-73; 78; 82. 25,1; 3; 5; 8-9; 13; 15. 26,1; 4; 10-11; 17; 22-23; 25; 30; 40; 44; 46-47. 27,1; 5; 7; 10; 14; 34; 38; 41-43; 47; 57. 28,1; 11; 13-17; 20. 29,1. 30,1; 9; 18; 20; 28; 31. 31,1; 3; 7. 32,1; 7; 13; 15; 17; 19-21; 29; 32. 33,1. 34,1-6; 12; 24. 35,3-4; 6; 9; 14; 16. 36,2-3. 38,1; 14. 39,1; 3. 40,5; 23. 41,1. 42,1-2. 43,1. 44,1-2; 7-10. 47,1; 8. 48,1-2; 4-5; 11. 49,1. 51,1-4; 12. 55,1. 56,1; 9. 57,1; 5; 7; 28; 30; 38; 45. 58,1; 6. 59,4; 9; 15. 61,1; 6; 9. 62,1. 63,1-2; 5-7; 12; 15. 64,1; 18. 68,2.
    NTT   9,74.
    YKS   12W28.
Payable in another
manor   LIN   31,16.

EXCHANGE (escambium; commutatio)
Church for castle site DOR 19,10.
Dispossessed land holder
  not given land in
    exchange   LIN C4.
  to be given land in
    exchange   SHR 3d,7.
Fishery for land   LIN 14,27.
House
  for church/
    waterway   SRY 5,28.
  for land   HAM 6,9.
New land, of   NFK 8,64.
Land, of   BDF 3,8; 10-11. 23,7; 16;
                      41-43; 55. 25,1; 4.
            BKM 5,10; 18. 19,1.
            CAM 32,10; 25.
            DEV 1,23-24. 2,10.
                      34,54. 35,4. 44,2.
                      48,2; 12. 51,2-3; 5-
                      10.
            DOR 3,14-18. 56,36.
            ESS 6,11. 8,9. 9,10.
22,14-15; 19; 21. 23,29. 26,3-4. 30,4; 17.
32,29; 31; 34-35; 38a; 41-45. 33,3; 5; 18; 23.
34,32. 36,11-12. 37,17; 19-20. 39,12. 52,1.
90,7-9.
            HAM 69,20; 40.
            HEF 1,46. 2,8. 25,9.
                      30,1.
            HRT 37,19.
            KEN P20.
            LEC C12.
            LIN 4,42. 14,27; 35.
                      CK13; 19.
            NFK 8,18; 23; 28; 32; 37-
38; 40; 48; 52-53; 88; 96. 9,25; 32; 86.
12,17. 14,35. 23,9. 31,11-12; 17-18; 23; 26;
29; 32; 39; 44-45. 51,5.
            NTH 23,3.
            OXF 28,16.
            SOM 8,31; 41. 19,86.
            SFK 7,4. 15,3. 31,50-51;
53-54; 56. 33,1-2; 4-6; 8; 12-13. 36,6-7.
66,11. 76,18.
            SRY 6,1. 19,27.
            WIL 1,3. 3,5.
            WOR 9,4. 11,1.
Land, of by
  King   ESS 30,47.
            LEC 29,1; 15; 19-20.
            YKS 31N10.
  King's order   BKM 17,2.
            SHR 3d,7.
Land in England for
land in Normandy ESS 22,23-24.
            SFK 56,1.
Land for land in   NFK 1,201. 8,2-4; 10;
another County   12-13; 26; 56; 68-
                      70; 80; 84; 90; 112;
                      133. 38,3.

            SFK 26,1-3; 5.
Manor
  for castle   DEV 2,9-10.
  for King's house
    unjustly   HAM 6,1.
Mill for land   HAM 1,21. NF10,2.
Park for land   KEN 5,67. 7,6.
Persons held by
  free man   NFK 31,8; 33. 52,1.
            SFK 29,1. 31,51.
  Freeman   SFK 29,1.
  man   NFK 14,32. 31,43.
Unfair   KEN P20.
See also: Castle; Claim; Forest; free man; Freeman;
Release.
EXCOMMUNICATION
Threat of   WOR 23,1.
EXEMPT (quietus)
Land   BRK 7,16.
            CHS 24,5. R2,1.
            DOR 2,6.
            GLS 1,6; 31-33.
            HAM 69,30. S2.
            HEF 1,44.
            WOR 8,1.
            YKS CW22; 36.
                      SE,Sn10.
  apart from tax CHS R1,29; 39.
Land holder, for 3
years   CHS R4,2.
See also: Death duty; Hide; House; Hundred;
King's hand; Levy; Service; Sulung; Tax; Tribute.
EXILE (exul)   DBY S2.
            KEN D9.
            NTT S2.
            SHR 3d,7.
            WOR *1,2.*
Imposed by King/Earl
and County for crime LIN C33.
Restored to peace by
King alone   DBY S2.
            LIN C33.
            NTT S2.
See also: Crime/offence; Harold; Outlaw.
EXPEDITION (military) (expeditio)
Payments
  from house for
    King's mercenaries ESS B6.
  to King by
    burgesses/borough,
    for   LIN S1.
            OXF B2.
            WIL B5.
Penalty
  fine for non-
    attendance   HEF C10.
            OXF 1,13.
            SHR C4.
            WAR B6.
            WOR C5.

fine for non-
attendance of
substitute BRK B10.
    WOR C5.
forfeiture of land
for non-service BRK B10.
    WOR C5.
Persons exempt SOM 2,3.
Persons rendering
service on
  burgesses LEC C2.
    OXF B2.
    WAR B6.
  burgesses providing
  horses LEC C2.
  free men WOR 2,21.
  men HEF 1,49.
    LIN CS38.
  men of manor with
  men of Hundred HUN D14.
  men with men of
  Bishop SOM 2,2.
Places rendering service on
  borough to like

extent as others DEV 1,2. 17,1.
manor supplying
horses LIN CK53.
town BDF B.
Rate of service
  city as for 5 hides DEV C5.
  County – 1 man per
  5 hides BRK B10.
    WIL B5.
Wales, into HEF C10. A8.
See also: Army; Battle; Burgess; Death; Tenure.
EXPEDITION
(military) by sea BDF B.
    DEV C5. 1,2. 17,1.
    ESS B6.
    LEC C2.
    WAR B6.
    WIL B5.
    WOR 2,21.
Burgesses provide
boatmen WAR B6.
See also: Ship.
EXPLOITED – See Stocked.
EYRIE (area) – See Hawk.

F

FACE value (ad numerum) – See Money.
FAIR (feria; forum)   CON   2,2.
  third (⅓)   SFK   34,18.
Annual held
wrongfully   CON   *2,2.*
FALCONER
(accipitrarius)   BRK   60.
    CAM   *32,28.*
    HAM   68,11. 69,49.
    HUN   D8.
    KEN   12,2.
    NFK   63.
    SOM   *47,10.*
    SSX   11,38.
Earl's   NFK   1,131.
FAMILY (parentes)
unable to sell land
outside   LIN   C16.
See also: Relations.
FARM (firma) – See Revenue.
FARTHING (minuta;
ferdingus; quadrans)   CHS   S3,2.
    HRT   5,9.
    KEN   3,17.
    NFK   1,57; 136; 144; 194;
206; 233; 238. 4,41; 52. 5,6. 6,6. 7,16-17.
8,7; 132. 9,73; 94; 97; 103. 10,23. 12,33-
34. 14,8; 40. 17,10; 64. 19,15. 20,6; 10-11;
13; 26. 24,7. 25,9. 31,41. 32,3. 33,2. 34,9.
35,12. 40,1. 48,1. 51,8. 61,1. 64,1.
    SHR   4,8,9.
    SFK   1,88; 115. 3,3. 6,42;
47. 7,1; 6; 19. 12,1. 14,32; 70; 73; 76; 78-
79; 82-83; 87; 93; 95; 109. 21,40; 54. 27,10.
36,4. 37,6. 48,1. 66,1.
  half farthing   NFK   8,128.
See also: Halfpenny; Money; Penny.
FATHER (pater)   BDF   4,2. 14,1. 56,5-6.
       57,7; 16-17.
    BRK   3,2. 7,29. 65,5.
    CHS   26,9-10. R1,40g.
    DBY   B8.
    DOR   56,13; 18; 28-30;
       53. 57,22.
    ESS   20,44. 24,20; 59-
       60. 40,9.
    GLS   16,1. 56,2. 61,1-2.
       78,5; 16.
    HAM   6,16. 69,17-20; 25;
       38-39; 47; 50; 52.
       NF9,36-39; 41; 44.
       IoW1,6. IoW9,7.
    HEF   10,3; 15; 37; 66; 70-
       71.

    HRT   7,1.
    HUN   D8.
    KEN   M8; 16; 20. 5,149.
    LIN   C3. T5. 22,26.
       CS21; 38. CK18;
       29.
    NFK   1,197. 4,39. 8,29.
       9,196. 66,60.
    OXF   34,3. 35,25.
    SHR   3c,8. 4,1,12. 5,1.
    SOM   8,41. 16,9. 47,14;
       21; 25.
    SFK   3,98-99; 101. 7,15-
       17; 79; 144. 16,15.
       25,60. 27,4-7. 38,6.
       51,2. 73,1. 75,4.
    SRY   36,9.
    WAR   17,6; 15; 32; 62.
       38,1.
    WIL   1,11; 23j. 13,13.
       19,4. 67,6-9; 42;
       46; 54; 59; 66-67;
       72; 78; 84-85; 91-
       92; 94.
    WOR   19,1-2; 7; 10.
    YKS   7E2. CE29.
Daughter holding
land from   HEF   19,6.
Son holding land
from   HAM   69,52.
    YKS   7E1-2.
See also: Relations.
FEAST – See Festivals.
FEE (feudum) – See Holding.
FENCE (sepes)
Materials for repair of   WIL   13,10; 18.
Nuisance, being   KEN   D12.
Village, of   CAM   *5,28.*
Wood/woodland
  brushwood
  (rispalia) for   HRT   35,2.
  carts for, from
  King's woodland   CAM   28,2.
  for making (ad   BRK   1,16; 27; 34; 36.
  clausuram)   7,33. 17,5. 21,6.
       22,8; 10. 26,2.
       38,1. 41,3. 58,2.
    BKM   B2. 14,2. 16,7.
    CAM   3,6. 5,36; *37.* 7,2-3;
       5. 13,11. 14,23; 26;
       43; 45-46; 48-51;
       53. 25,7; 10. 26,34;
       36; 41-42. 27,1.
       31,7. 32,20-25; 32-

pasture in	HAM	1,38. 22,1.
Woodland		
in	HAM	1,28; 38. 22,1.
		23,51; 65. 45,1.
		NF3,8-9. NF5,1.
		NF9,35; 43.
		NF10,1; 4.
	STS	12,10-11.
	WIL	2,52-54; 56-57; 60-
		61; 78-79; 81.
		23,14. 26,3.
in King's	HEF	10,19. 21,6.
	STS	7,6. 12,10-11.
in, assessed in pigs	HAM	NF9,43. NF10,1.
put in by Earl	CHS	26,6. FD9,1.
		FT3,6.
put in by King	WOR	1,1c; 2. 26,5.
taken in, to		
deterioration of		
manors	CHS	FD9,1.

See also: Claim; Gift; Honey; Mare; Woodland.

FORESTER

(forestarius)	GLS	*1,59-60.*
	HAM	1,2; 23; 31.
		NF9,24. IoW7,20.
	HEF	1,42; 44.
	OXF	1,6.
	SOM	46,3.
	STS	13.
	SRY	1,2. 27,1.
	WAR	1,9. 44,1-6.
King's	WIL	67,99.
King's woodland, of	ESS	1,24.
Revenue of	HAM	1,23.

See also: Pigman.

FORFEITURE (forisfactura)

Holder's		
predecessor's, bars		
third party claim	LIN	CS36-37.
Husband cannot		
forfeit wife's land	YKS	CE15.
King retains land		
despite acquittance	NFK	66,82.
King's right to	KEN	6,1.
	LIN	S4.
Land, of		
by free men	SFK	67,30.
to third party		
paying tribute	BDF	46,1.
sub-tenants paying		
on holder's		
forfeiture	NFK	9,196.
Land forfeited	SFK	21,13.
taken on payments		
to reeves	NFK	17,22.
which should not		
be redeemed	SFK	67,30.
Persons of		
Hardwin	SFK	21,16.
Humphrey of St		
Omer	NFK	8,8.

Odo, Bishop	LIN	CS13.
Ralph (Earl)	HRT	16,2. 35,3.
	NFK	1,7; 10; 57; 63; 77;
		81; 106; 111; 120-121; 131; 136; 161; 172;
		181-182; 194-195; 197; 209; 216; 226. 4,*15-*
		16; 42; 44; 51; 56. 8,1; 71. 9,30; 49; 111;
		160; 196; 198; 200. 10,19; 69. 12,32; 34;
		45. 15,18; 17,30. 19,2; 20. 25,15. 26,5.
		27,2. 34,17. 38,2. 47,7. 58,3. 65,17. 66,42;
		64; 80-81; 83-85; 98; 102.
	SFK	1,62. 3,40-41; 57;
		59. 4,32. 6,169. 7,19; 44. 16,3; 33. 25,104.
		74,8. 76,13; 17. 77,4.
Ralph Wader	NFK	1,215.
Walter of Dol	SFK	4,15. 6,212; 215.
		14,146. 16,34.
		31,34.
Withgar	SFK	76,5.
Reason for		
holder accused		
before King	LIN	CW12.
King's tax not paid		
although land		
exempt	HRT	36,9.
non-repair of city		
wall	OXF	B10.
refusal of tribute	BDF	46,1.
unspecified	BDF	6,1.
	BKM	57,18.
	LIN	CS12; 36.
	NFK	8,8. 17,22. 66,82.
	SFK	8,53. 67,30.
	YKS	C10.
widow's re-		
marriage within		
year	NFK	10,67.
Thane, of – land and		
money shared		
King/Earl and		
wife/heirs	DBY	S4.
	NTT	S4.

See also: Burgess; Claim; Crime/offence;
Dwelling; Entry; Expedition; Fine; Hundred;
Jurisdiction; Residence; Ship; Thane; Thief;
Third/two thirds part.

FORFEITURES

Held by		
Abbot	WOR	9,7.
King throughout		
England	SHR	C2.
King's, granted to		
Abbey	WOR	C4.
Three		
defined	HEF	C13.
	KEN	2,*41;* 43.
	SHR	C2.
held by Abbey over		
Freeman	NFK	26,5.
held by Archbishop		
over burgesses	KEN	2,43.
held in lordship	HEF	C13.

	SHR	C2.
Four		
held by Archbishop		
except King's four	WAR	3,4.
held by King		
throughout		
kingdom	WAR	3,4.
Six		
Freeman not having	NFK	31,35.
held by Abbey	SFK	8,35. 16,1. 21,40-
		41. 25,17; 19; 27;
		78; 102; 111. 33,1-
		3. 53,7.
held by King and		
Earl	NFK	9,87.
	SFK	33,6-7.
jurisdiction of	NFK	19,14.
Six over Freeman		
held by Bishop	NFK	10,28.
held by King	NFK	9,75.
held by King and		
Earl	NFK	7,16-17.
FORGE (forgia;		
ferraria)	HAM	23,38.
	HEF	C8.
	SSX	10,102.
	WAR	16,24.

See also: Smithy.

FOURTH part.		
Of customary dues		
held by King	SFK	1,40.
Of market held by		
King	SFK	1,40.
FOURTH penny		
Of dues of enclosure		
shared by King/Earl	SFK	1,12.
FOWLER		
(aucuparius)	GLS	*1,59-60.*
FREE (liber)		
Holder being free		
with land	DOR	40,7.
	SHR	4,3,3-4; 6-8; 13; 48;
		64; 66. 4,4,1; 13.
		4,21,6. 4,24,4.
	WAR	14,2; 5-6.

See also: Dwelling; Exempt; Go where he would; House; Land; Man-at-arms; Manor; Sale; Slave.

FREE jurisdiction (frigesoca) – See Jurisdiction, free.

FREE LAND (libera		
terra)	DEV	24,18.
	DOR	40,7.
	ESS	13,1. 90,14.
	GLS	37,4.
	HEF	1,46.
	KEN	3,2. 5,65; 85; 124.
	NFK	1,99. 6,6. 9,32; 196;
		221. 10,33; 73.
		15,2; *29;.* 17,49.
		21,26.
	SFK	1,1-2; 90; 97; 118-

121. 3,3; 5; 14; 72; 93. 4,1. 5,1. 6,1-2; 30; 32; 83; 107; 124; 130; 191; 223; 303. 7,96. 8,33-34; 36. 14,1-5; 7-9; 12-14; 18-20; 36; 42; 48-54; 58; 60; 62-66; 69; 71; 73-83; 85; 87-88; 93-95; 103. 15,2. 16,12; 26. 17,1. 19,16. 21,10-11; 15-16; *26; 83;* 85. 25,2; 6; 10; 32; 34-35; 42; 46; 52; 78. 26,9. 27,3; 9-10. 29,1. 31,*9;* 23; 41-42; 44-46. 33,1-2; 13. 34,2-3; 6. 35,7. 40,3; 6. 41,10. 43,2-3. 44,1. 46,3. 51,1. 54,2. 62,6. 66,1. 76,4. 77,4.

See also: Borough; Land.

FREE man (free man)	BRK	1,7; 10-12. 10,1.
(liber homo)		17,4; 6; 8; 10; 13.

20,1. 21,4; 8; 10; 12-13. 22,10. 23,2-3. 27,2-3. 28,2. 31,5. 33,3-4. 34,1. 35,5. 36,2-3. 40,2. 41,4-5. 43,1. 44,3-5. 45,2-3. 46,2. 47,1. 48,1. 49,2. 55,2-4. 62,1. 65,4; 8; 13.

	CHS	C4. B1. 1,2-3; 14;

18-21; 23; 27-28; 31-33; 36. 2,7-10; 14-15; 17-19; 21-31. 3,1-8; 11. 4,1. 5,1-2; 4-10. 6,1-2. 7,1; 4. 8,1; 3-4; 6-7; 9-15; 17-20; 22-40; 42; 44. 9,4-6; 9-12; 14-17; 19-20; 28-29. 10,4. 11,1; 3-6; 8. 13,1-3; 5-6. 14,3-5; 7-8; 10-13. 15,1. 16,1. 17,1; 3-4; 6-9; 12. 18,1; 3; 5-6. 19,1-3. 20,1-2; 4; 10. 21,1. 22,1. 23,1-3. 24,1-9. 25,1. 26,1-2; 7. 27,1-2; 4. FD2,1-4. FD3,1-2. FD5,1-3. FD7,1. FD8,1-2. R2,2. R6,1-2.

	DEV	24,28-29. 25,25.
		34,5.
	DOR	24,5. 49,5. 57,16-
		18.
	ESS	1,1; 4; 6-7; 14-16;

17-17a. 3,6; 8-10; 13. 4,6; 9-10; 14-15; 17-18. 5,7-8; 12. 6,12. 8,8. 9,5. 11,2-3; 6. 13,1-2. 14,1-2; 6-7. 18,1-10; 12; 16-18; 20-23; 25; 27-30; 32-33; 35-37; 42-45. 20,1-3; 7; 13-15; 18-29; 31; 33-36; 38; 40; 43; 45; 49; 56-57; 60-62; 69; 72-76; 80. 21,1; 4; 6-7. 22,2-3; 6; 10-12; 14-15; 21-23. 23,1; 3; 28. 24,3; 5-6; 8-9; 11; 13; 18-19; 22; 24; 26-30; 32; 34; 37; 44-48; 50-51; 55; 57; 59. 25,2-5; 9; 13-17; 25. 26,1-2. 27,1; 4; 6-7; 10; 12; 14; 17. 28,3; 7; 9-10; 12-13; 17. 29,3. 30,1; 10; 20-22; 34; 37; 39-41; 44; 46-47; 51. 32,1; 3; 5-19; 21-23; 25; 27-28; 38a; 45. 33,2-3; 6; 8; 10; 12-13; 18; 20; 22-23. 34,1; 4; 6; 8; 10; 14; 16-17; 21; 24-25; 27; 29; 35-37. 35,2-3. 36,1-4; 6-8; 11-12. 37,2-4; 6-7; 9; 11; 13-16. 38,1-2; 5; 7-8. 39,1-4; 10. 40,2-5; 9. 41,5-6; 10-11. 42,1; 5. 43,1-6. 44,1-2. 45,1. 46,1-2. 47,1; 3. 48,1. 49,3. 50,1. 52,2. 53,1. 54,1. 57,3-6. 58,1. 59,1. 60,2. 61,1. 62,2. 63,1-2. 64,1. 66,1-2. 67,1. 68,4-5. 69,1-3. 70,1. 71,1-2; 4. 72,1; 3. 73,1. 75,2. 78,1. 83,1. 84,1-2. 87. 89. 90,2; 4-5; 7-8; 12-13; 18; 22-23; 25-27; 30; 33; 35-37; 39-46; 48; 50-56; 58-60; 67; 74; 76-79; 83-84; 106-112; 116-120; 127-131. B1.

	GLS	1,2; 7-8; 15; 51.

4,1. 12,1; 3-4. 19,2. 20.1. 39,9; 12. 61,2. 63,1.

HAM 1,33; W1; W6; W8; W17; W20-21. 2,21. 6,16. 7,1. 15,1. 21,1. 23,1-3; 37; 49; 53-54. 27,1. 28,3. 35,4; 7-8. 43,1. 45,3. 50,2. 56,3. 68,7-8; 9-10. 69,16; 34. IoW7,2-3; 14. IoW8,4-5; 13.

HEF 1,49; 51. 2,10. 7,8. 8,3. 10,5; 25; 30; 32; 54. 15,9. 21,2.

HRT 12.1.

KEN *C1. 3,1.* 5,61; 136; 218; 223.

LEC 16,9. 19,2. 28,1. 40,7; 17.

NFK 1,2; 4-6; 9; 13; 16; 19; 21; 41; 43-48; 50; 54; 56-60; 71-73; 75-81; 83; 86-87; 93; 96-113; 116; 119-120; 122; 125; 127-131; 133-134; 136-137; 141-149; 155; 163; 166-173; 179; 182-193; 195; 197-200; 202-206; 208; 210; 217; 221-222; 225; 232; 237; 239-241. 2,1; 8; 11. 4,1-3; 6-7; 18; 26-27; 29-34; 36; 38-47; 51-57. 5,1-5. 6,1; 4-7. 7,1; 5-10; 12-18; 20-21. 8,1-8; 11-14; 16-19; 21-28; 31-33; 38; 42-44; 47; 49-63; 66-70; 72-73; 75-90; 93-96; 99; 102; 104; 109; 112; 114; 117; 119-122; 129-130; 137. 9,3; 5; 8-9; 14-15; 18-20; 22-24; 30; 32; 48; 62; 66; 74; 76-77; 80; 86-93; 99-102; 104; 106; 109; 110-111; 114-116; 119-123; 126-129; 132-133; 137-139; 142; 146; 155-165; 171-172; 174-175; 179-180; 182-223; 226-227; 229-233. 10,20; 27; 34-35; 37; 42-43; 46-48; 50; 52-53; 55; 60; 62-63; 65-66; 68; 70; 72-76; 78-83; 85-93. 11,1-5. 12,1-4; 6-7; 9; 15; *17;* 18-20; 22; 27-38; 42; 45. 13,3; 9-10; 12; 14-16; 19. 14,3; 9; 16-17; 23; 31; 33; 40-43. 15,7-8; 10-13; *28.* 16,2. 17,8-10; 14-15; 22; 53; 55-56; 58; 60; 61; 63-64. 19,1; 3; 8-9; 13; 15-16; 23; 25; 27; 32-33; 35. 20,1-7; 10-11; 14; 16-19; 24-26; 28-29; 32; 35; 45-46. 21,1-5; 8-15; 18; 22; 24; 26-29. 22,9; 14; 17. 23,4; 7-8; 13-15; 17-18. 24,1-4; 6-7. 25,1-9; 12-13; 15-19; 24-26. 26,1; 3; 5-6. 27,1. 28,1. 29,1-4; 7-8; 11. 30,2-4; 6. 31,1-2; 4-6; 9; 11-17; 19-20; 23; 26-30; 32-33; 38; 41-42; 44. 32,1-6. 33,1; 4-5. 34,4-8; 10-12; 14; 17; 19-20. 35,2-5; 8-10; 12; 14-16. 36,2-3. 37,1-2. 38,2-3. 39,1. 41,1. 43,1; 4. 47,1-7. 48,1-8. 49,1; 3; 5-6; 9. 50,1-5; 8; 13. 51,1-2; 4-5; 8-10. 52,1-4. 53,1. 54,1. 55,1-2. 56,6-7. 57,3. 58,1-2. 59,1. 60,1. 61,4. 64,3-9. 65,4-5; 7; 9-12; 14; 17. 66,1-16; 18-36; 38-49; 52-55; 57; 64-66; 70; 72-78; 80-82; 84; 87-88; 92; 94-95; 98; 100; 102-104; 106-107.

NTH 1,30. 22,1. 40,2.

OXF 1,7b. 8,1. 11,1. 12,1. 15,2. 28,2. 35,3. 47,1. 50,1.

SHR 3c,12. 3f,3. 4,1,8.

4,3,1-2; 9; 11-12; 17; 19-20; 26; 57; 59-61; 63; 65; 67-68; 70-71. 4,4,2-5; 7; 11; 14-15; 17-19; 21; 24. 4,5,1; 4; 6-11; 15. 4,6,5. 4,7,3; 5. 4,8,1-2; 4-6; 13; 15. 4,9,2-3. 4,10,1-2; 4. 4,11,1; 5; 7-8; 10; 12. 4,12,1. 4,14,1; 4-11; 13; 16; 26-28. 4,15,1-3. 4,16,1. 4,17,1. 4,18,1. 4,19,7; 9-13. 4,20,1-3; 6-7; 9; 12-15. 4,21,1-5; 7-16; 18. 4,22,2. 4,23,3; 6-15; 17-18. 4,24,1-3. 4,25,1-2; 7. 4,26,5-6. 4,27,1; 5; 10-13; 17; 19-28; 30; 35. 4,28,2-3. 5,2; 8. 6,1; 3; 6-8; 31. 7,1; 3-6.

SOM 1,4; 25. 3,1. 19,27.

STS 1,8. 3,1. 4,7. 7,2-5; 10; 15. 8,4; 6; 8-10; 14-15; 18-20; 22; 24-27; 31-32. 10,4; 8. 11,1-2; 5; 8; 10-11; 14-20; 22-33; 35-36; 38-41; 44-47; 50-53; 56; 58-60; 62-66. 12,2; 5; 7; 9; 11-13; 15-17; 20. 13,1-3; 5-9. 14,2. 15,1-2. 17,3; 6; 10-11; 13-14; 17-18.

SFK 1,7; 9; 11; 13; 15-16; 18-19; 23-31; 43; 45-64; 68-75; 77-83; 86-87; 89-90; 93; 95; 105; 107; 110-114; 119; 121. 2,6-7; 10-13; 15-16; 18-20. 3,1; 4-13; 16-17; 19; 21-24; 26-29; 31-43; 45-47; 50-54; 56-57; 59-66; 80; 82-83; 86-87; 89-104. 4,2-9; 13-25; 27-29; 31-42. 5,1-2; 4; 6-7. 6,6-17; 19-21; 23-25; 29-30; 32-40; 42; 44-54; 56-62; 64-65; 67-69; 71; 73-79; 81-83; 85-87; 90; 92-94; 96-101; 103; 106-107; 109-114; 116; 118-120; 123; 126-127; 129-130; 132-141; 143; 145; 149-151; 153-154; 156-159; 161-162; 164-168; 170; 172; 174-175; 177-180; 183-184; 186; 188-203; 205-206; 208-219; 222-228; 230-234; 236-268; 270-277; 280-284; 286-293; 297; 309; 311-313. 7,1-5; 9-10; 13; 15; 17-19; 22-30; 32-33; 36-37; 40-45; 48-52; 54-68; 75-76; 79-87; 89-91; 95; 98-102; 106; 108; 110-112; 114-115; 117-134; 136-138; 140-151. 8,*1;* 4-9; 12; 14; 19; 22-32; 35-36; 38-47; 49; 53; 55-72; 74-78; 80. 9,2-4. 10,1. 11,1. 12,1-2; 7. 13,2-7. 14,1; 3; 9; 13; 17; 20-21; 25; *26-27;* 29; 31; 34; 38-46; 48-68; 70-72; 75; 77-95; *100-101;* 104; 106; 116-118; 122-132; 134; *135;* 139-140; 143; 146-149; 151-152; 154-161; 164; 166. 15,2; 4. 16,1-47. 19,2-20. 21,16-17; 19; 22-23; 25-29; *30-31;* 32-37; 39-41; 45-49; 58-59; 62-66; 69; 71-76; 78-84; 86-88; 90-95; 99-100; 104. 22,2; 3. 23,1-2; 4; 6. 24,1. 25,19-21; 25; 27; 34; 43-50; 56-57; 59-60; 67-70; 72-75; 78-80; 82-103; 105-112. 26,6-8; 10; 12a-b; 13-18; 20. 27,3; 7; 11; 13. 28,3-5; *6.* 29,1; 3-11; 13. 30,1-2. 31,1-2; 4-5; 7; 9-13; 14-36; 40; 49-50; 56-58. 32,2; 5; 8-23; 25-26; 28-30. 33,1-6; 8; 10; 12. 34,2-3; 9; *12.* 35,3; 5-8. 36,3-7; 9-10; 12-15; 17. 37, 1-7. 38,4-8; 10-12; 14; 16; 18; 20-22; 27. 39,1-3; 5-10; 12. 40,1; 3-4. 41,3-7; 9-12; 14; 16-18. 43,3; 5; 7-9. 44,2-3. 45,1-3. 46,1; 8-11. 48,1. 50,1.

51,1-2. 52,1; 3-7; 9-11. 53,1-7. 54,3. 56,1-6. 57,1. 58,1. 59,1-2. 60,1. 61,1. 62,1-5. 64,1; 3. 66,1-4; 6; 8-9; 11; 13-14; 16. 67,2-4; 6-23; 25-32. 68,3-5. 69,3-4. 70,1. 71,1. 74,1-5; 7; 10-13; 15. 75,1-5. 76,1; 12; 16; 18-19; 21-23. 77,2-4.

	SRY	5,1a; 24. 19,44; 48. 23,1. 25,2.
	SSX	9,9; 19,20; 48; 51;

61-62; 64; 69; 76-77; 79; 83; 85-87; 97-98; 103; 110; 112-117. 10,4; 7; 15; 78. 11,24-25; 40; 43; 47; 50-53; 66; 71; 73-74; 78-92; 94; 99-103; 105-109; 112-115.

	WAR	2,1. 4,1-6. 14,2-6.

16,2-3; 6; 8-19; 22-27. 17,7; 15; 17; 27; 61; 69. 23,4. 36,1.

	WOR	C5. 2,21; 83. 8,9b; 15-17; 22-23. 9,4; 7. 15,5; 9. 26,1.
	YKS	9W47.
whole (integer)	NFK	1,172. 9,27; 29; 37; 43-44. 12,11-12; 14; 19.
	SFK	4,42. 6,169; 188; 267; 274. 7,60. 21,75. 26,16. 52,5.
half (½)	NFK	1,99; 106; 108; 110-111; 120; 122; 131; 180; 202-203; 239. 2,12;

27. 4,44; 53. 6,5. 7,13; 18. 8,18; 24; 55-56; 131. 9,13; 17; 27; 29; 39; 42-45; 48; 56-58; 60; 99; 161-162; 182; 184; 187; 191-194; 196; 202; 208-209; 212-214; 216. 11,2. 12,9; 11-12; 14; 19-20; 22; 36-37; 43. 14,31; 33; 40. 17,53. 19,30; 37; 40. 20,14; 22. 24,7. 25,9. 26,5. 29,8. 31,20; 23. 34,17. 36,5. 48,4-6. 52,3. 53,1. 64,2. 66,14; 34-35; 40; 80-81; 83; 85; 97.

	SFK	1,9; 62; 78-80; 110-111; 113. 2,10. 3,23; 35; 37-41; 43; 48; 100.

4,5; 15; 25; 42. 6,11; 16; 33; 42; 48; 59; 63; 85; 90; 98; 106; 110; 155; 161; 165-169; 177; 180; 188; 210; 214-215; 244; 264; 267-268; 274; 284; 292. 7,31; 37; 60; 75; 98; 100; 125; 136; 143; 145; 148. 8,1; 8-9; 12; 19; 22; 25-26; 30-31; 38; 49. 14,20; 21; 41; 65; 72; 78; 82; 84; 96; 101; 118; 139; 151; 164. 16,6; 16; 19; 26; 38. 19,17. 21,31; 56; 71-75; 91; 94; 101-102. 25,60. 26,15-16. 31,19; 20; 25; 52. 32,14. 34,15. 35,7. 39,10. 43,5. 45,3. 52,1; 5. 66,2; 4; 6. 67,10; 24; 27; 29; 32. 76,11.

quarter (¼)	NFK	31,6.
	SFK	6,169. 21,75.
sixth (⅙)	SFK	16,30.
Acquisition of		
by land holder	ESS	20,43.
	NFK	29,4.
by sub-patronage	SFK	6,34.
for land	NFK	29,11.
Annexation of	ESS	6,8. 18,44. 20,49. 41,8-9; 12. 45,1.

		90,10; 15-17; 38; 81-82; 85.
	NFK	4,51. 9,13. 10,48. 21,5; 7-8; 14. 66,12; 16; 44; 51; 83; 105.
	SFK	4,32. 14,152. 20,1. 76,4; 6-7.
from King	ESS	30,21. 90,15.
in King's despite	ESS	6,8. 90,15.
by woman	ESS	90,38.
Appropriation of	ESS	18,22. 20,34.
	NFK	30,2. 66,49.
Assessment/valuation of	NFK	1,103. 31,30.
	SFK	1,42. 8,46.
elsewhere than his holding	NFK	1,103; 149; 168; 191. 4,27. 9,13; 41; 180. 31,27. 47,6.
	SFK	1,77; 93. 3,16; 33; 45; 48; 50; 62-63; 136-137; 149; 154. 8,25. 31,14.
with Freeman	NFK	9,146.
unable to pay	SFK	7,133.
Assignment of, by King	SFK	37,2.
Charge of – under another's	NFK	64. 66,81.
Customary dues		
Payment of	ESS	1,2; 4.
	NFK	8,129. 13,7. 21,2; 4. 66,3.
	SFK	1,42; 62; 105. 7,3. 14,26; 49-52; 71; 115. 21,83.
1086 but not TRE	SFK	1,17.
elsewhere	SFK	14,136.
to secure pasture	NFK	66,15.
not paid	ESS	1,2. 90,19.
Evidence by	SFK	75,1.
Exchange, held by	NFK	31,8; 33. 52,1.
	SFK	29,1. 31,51.
Gift of to Abbey	SFK	8,8.
Had for land	NFK	35,15.
Holding (feudum), belonging to	ESS	90,17.
	NFK	9,14-15; 28; 111. 25,15. 66,68; 76.
	SFK	6,209. 7,64. 25,59-60. 75,1.
not belonging to	NFK	66,62.
	SFK	25,60.
Hundred		
free man in	SFK	25,70.
free man in different from his holding	SFK	6,118.
Land of		
area of holding	SFK	6,73. 68,3.
held as a free man	CHS	1,4-7; 11-12; 16-17;

35. 2,11-12. 5,14. 8,8. 9,13; 18; 22-27.
12,3-4. 14,2; 6. 17,5. 22,2. 26,6; 8-9; 11-
12. 27,3. FD2,6. FD7,2.

                      SHR   4,20,8.

held elsewhere
from dwelling   SFK   1,122b.
less land 1086 than
TRE   NFK   27,2.
free man not on
land 1086   ESS   1,16.
Lordship, in   ESS   39,11-12.
                      NFK   8,8. 19,6. 66,69.
                      SFK   3,16; 62; 94. 6,252.
7,3. 8,59. 25,60. 31,1-2; 21; 43; 45; 48; 51.
36,15. 38,17. 52,7; 9. 53,4. 67,10; 12.
Made man of another   ESS   34,2.
voluntarily   ESS   30,47.
Man of or held by/
under
  Abbey/Abbot   NFK   1,226. 8,128. 9,13;
16; 167; 180. 10,84. 12,44. 14,23; 32.
15,10-11; 13. 16,6. 17,15. 20,32. 43,2. 48,8.
65,15.

                      SFK   2,1-2. *3,33*. 8,1-2;
4; 6; 8; 10; 17; 20; 42; *56*. 14,26-27; 33; 35-
37; 49-51; 71; 97; 106; 110-115; 137; 141-
142. 21,1-2; 8-9; 16; 51-52; 55; 93-94; 96.
25,27. 26,1-3. 31,40. 32,1. 47,2. 64,3.
67,30. 76,10-11.
  Abbot's Holding
but not so   SFK   75,1.
  Archbishop   NFK   1,105.
  Earl   SFK   12,4. 25,58.
  free man   NFK   1,116; 206. 8,102.
9,13-14; 17; 54; 212-214; 216. 10,43; 53;
74; 82; 87-88. 12,42. 21,13. 66,87.
                      SFK   1,107. 6,170; 178;
247; 268; 301; 313. 13,6. 14,129. 16,4.
19,14; 16. 21,58; 84; 91. 25,85. 26,12b.
66,3-4; 13.
  Freeman   NFK   17,9.
  King   ESS   89.
                      NFK   9,149. 14,40.
20,11. 65. 66,69;
89.
                      SFK   1,21. 8,49. 16,18.
30,1. 74,13.
  King Edward   NFK   6,7. 9,228. 22,13.
29,6. 30,4. 31,12.
66,60.
                      SFK   1,16; 18. 2,9. 7,33.
8,51. 16,18-19; 26.
66,5. 76,7.
  priest   SFK   7,122.
  Queen   SFK   7,14. 37,2.
  woman   SFK   3,81. 6,209. 31,54.
33,13. 38,9.
  another   ESS   18,21a. 24,57. 33,2.
39,11-12. 41,8.
69,2. 90,85.
                      NFK   1,1; 4; 6; 19; 59; 95-

96; 98-99; 111; 119; 131; 148-149; 155; 169;
172; 177-178; 195; 202-203; 224; 226-227;
230; 241. 2,5; 8; 12. 4,19; 22-23; 34; 38;
40-41; 49; 51; 53; 55. 6,5-6. 7,9-10. 8,8;
11-14; 18; 33; 40-41; 46; 55; 58; 70; 123-
128; 132-134; 137-138. 9,3; 13; 15-16; 26;
32-47; 49-50; 52-54; 56-57; 59-60; 63-65;
67; 69; 103; 105; 107-108; 115-118; 124;
130-131; 134-136; 140-141; 143-154; 157;
161-162; 166-167; 169-170; 173-174; 176-
178; 180-182; 184; 186; 196; 198-199; 201;
211; 218; 224-225; 228-229; 231; 234.
10,13; 26; 33; 43-45; 49; 51-53; 55; 57-58;
62; 64; 66-67; 69; 71; 84; 90. 11,4-5. 12,8-
17; 23-25. 14,16-17; 23; 40. 15,10-11; 13;
25. 17,18. 19,6; 9-10; 20; 28; 30-32; 36-38;
40. 20,1; 7-8; 10-13; 22; 24; 26; 31-32; 34-
36. 21,22; 26; 33. 24,7. 25,23; 25. 26,3.
27,1-2. 29,1; 6; 8-9. 30,2. 31,3; 5; 16-18;
45. 32,3. 33,2; 6. 34,13. 35,1; 6; 8-9; 13;
16. 36,1; 5-7. 43,3. 47,4. 48,3; 6. 49,6; 8.
50,9. 51,6. 53,1. 57,1. 61,2-3. 64,1-2; 9.
65,2-3; 7-8; 13-16. 66,2; 17; 42; 44; 48; 56;
58; 61-62; 71; 79; 85-87; 89-91; 93; 96-97;
99; 101; 108.
                      SFK   1,44-51; 53; 61-62;
108. 2,3-6; 17. 3,16; 18; 25; 31; 59; 62; 70;
93. 4,15; 40; 42. 6,3; 5; 17; 30; 37; 58; 61;
78-79; 93; 97; 106; 110; 117; 124-125; 127;
138; 143; 155; 159; 165; 169-170; 175; 177;
179; 183; 190; 209; 212; 215; 219; 226; 236;
245; 250-252; 257; 261-262; 271; 280; 284;
289; 291-292; 295-296; 299; 301-302; 312;
314; 316-319. 7,4; 13; 16; 23; 36-37; 49;
51; 63; 75; 77; 88; 92-94; 96-99; 101-102;
104-105; 107; 109; 113; 117; 119; 124-125;
133; 136; 140; 143-144; 146-148. 8,*1*; 3-4;
6; 9; 11; 15; 17; 42; 47; 50-51; 59; 70. 14,11;
14; 16; 22; 24; 27; 36; 54; 63; 68; 72; 81-
83; 86-87; 90; 92-93; 95-99; 101; 111; 115;
119; *151*; 152. 16,4; 6-7; 11-13; 35. 19,1;
17. 21,16; 49; 64; 71; 83; *94*; 100. 25,30-
32; 42; 56; 65; 67. 26,4-5. 29,1. 30,3. 31,20;
36-37; 43; 45-48; 51-53. 32,1. 33,11. 38,17.
40,6. 41,7. 42,1. 43,4-6. 46,7. 51,1. 52,7;
11. 55,1. 64,1; 3. 66,10. 67,7; 9-11; 20; 23.
75,2. 76,2; 4-5; 16; 20-23. 77,1.
half man of another   SFK   7,77; 79; 90.
of another under
  third person   NFK   9,43-44.
Manor/village – free man:
  added/joined to   ESS   18,2; 5. 20,1; 25;
27; 43. 24,9. 40,9.
                      NFK   1,29; 57; 149; 197;
202; 229; 239. 6,5-6. 8,2; 56. 9,99. 12,42.
19,36. 20,10-11. 26,3; 5. 36,5. 48,2. 52,1.
66,50.
                      SFK   1,66-67. 2,10; 13.
3,56; 97. 6,28; 42-44; 92; 94; 110. 7,5-7;
18; 64; 71; 147. 8,35; 49; 81. 9,1. 20,1.
21,16; 28. 25,53; 57; 59. 26,12c; 13. 28,6.

196. 12,6.

SFK 4,15. 6,62; 212.
7,38. 14,138.
31,38.

Manor/village,
belonging to
NFK 1,209.
SFK 8,21.
elsewhere NFK 12,21.
See also: Grant and sell; Jurisdiction, full;
Patronage.
FREEDMAN
(freedman)
(colibertus) BRK 7,6.
CON 1,1.
DEV 1,50; 56.
DOR 1,2; 4-5. 8,1.
GLS 1,15; 21; 24; 31; 47;
53. 3,1. 7,2. 8,1.
14,2.
HAM 1,10; 15; 17; 21; 23;
28; 38; 41-43; 47.
3,7. 16,1. 69,53.
HEF 1,4-6.
SHR 4,1,30. 5,1.
SOM 1,2; 4; 6; 8-9; 19-
20; 23; 27-30. 2,1.
8,5-6; 15. 12,1.
27,1. 33,2.
WAR 14,1.
WIL 1,1-4; 6-7; 10; 12;
16-18. 3,1. 7,1.
8,11. 12,4. 13,5; 9-
10; 18-19. 15,1.
24,22. 27,26.
WOR 8,7; 10a.
Defined as "boor" HAM 1,10; 23.
WOR 8,10a.
FREEHOLD (in alod) BRK 1,17-18; 21; 24; 28.
7,34; 38. 14,1.
17,6. 21,5. 22,8-11. 23,2. 26,1-2. 27,1.
28,1; 3. 30,1. 34,4. 35,3-4. 38,1-2; 4. 39,1.
40,1. 41,1. 44,2. 45,1. 46,1. 48,1. 50,1.
51,1. 52,1. 53,1. 54,1-3. 55,1. 57,1. 58,1.
59,1. 60,1. 63,1. 65,4; 9-12.
HAM 1,6; 18; 32-35; 39;
W1-2; W6-10; W13-14; W16-21. 8,1. 9,1-
2. 10,1. 21,1; 3-4; 8. 22,1. 23,1; 3; 25-29;
31-34; 36-42; 44-53; 55-60; 65. 27,1-2.
28,1; 3-6. 29,12-14. 32,2-4. 34,1. 35,2-3;
6; 8-9. 36,1. 37,2. 38,1. 39,5. 43,1-5. 44,2-
3. 45,1-4; 6-7. 46,1-2. 47,2-3. 50,2. 51,1.
53,1. 56,3. 57,1. 60,1. 61,1. 62,1-2. 63,1.
68,1; 5-6; 9-11. 69,3; 5; 8-13; 15-36.
NF7,1. IoW2,1 IoW6,11-19. IoW7,1-5; 7-
8; 10-11; 13; 15. IoW8,1; 3-5. IoW9,8-13;
15.
KEN C3. 5,187; 190.
7,24. 9,9.
SSX 10,51-54; 56-58; 60;
62; 64; 67-70; 75; 78-80; 91-92; 95; 110-

111; 115. 11,9; 17-18; 20-25; 27; 29; 31; 34;
38; 43-44; 46. 14,1.
Land not so held HAM 1,W10. 23,2; 54.
FREEHOLDER (alodiarius)
BRK 7,4. 13,1. 21,20.
64,2.
HAM 23,61-62, NF3,1.
NF7,1. NF8,2.
NF9,5-6; 19; 29.
NF10,2. IoW2,1.
IoW9,23.
KEN D16-17.
SRY 5,19.
SSX 12,9; 14; 46. 13,35;
47.
FREELY – See Freeman; Land; Thane.
FREEMAN
(freeman) (francus
homo) ESS 1,16a. 25,5.
HAM 2,21. 40,1.
LEC 42,3.
LIN 26,53.
NTT 10,59.
SHR 4,3,24; 29.
SFK 6,84. 33,10.
WAR 17, 27.
WOR 8,28. 9,7.
YKS 2E34.
Belonging to manor SFK 33,10.
FREEMAN BDF 2,3; 5; 7; 9. 3,2-4;
(socmanus) 6; 14. 6,2-3. 16,1-
2; 6-9. 17,1-2. 19,2. 21,1; 4; 7; 11; 16-17.
23,1; 7-12; 14; 16; 21; 23; 27; 30-31; 34; 37-
41; 44-45; 49-50; 53-55; 57. 24,8; 10-11; 13;
17; 19; 21-22; 24; 26-30. 25,4; 7; 9-11; 13;
15. 32,4; 6; 11; 13; 16. 33,1-2. 34,1. 39,2.
42,1. 43,1. 44,1. 47,4. 48,1-2. 51,2-3.
53,1; 3; 20-22; 24; 26; 29. 54,2. 55,1; 7; 11.
57,3iii, vi; 20.
BKM 1,1-3. 5,12; 17.
17,10; 27. 18,1.
CAM 1,2; 6; 14; 16; 21-
23. 2,3. 3,4. 4,1. 5,9-11; 16-17; 24; 27; 29;
33; 45; 51-52; 54-55; 60-63. 7,5. 13,8-10.
14,2; 7; 10-11; 15; 21-22; 26; 31; 42; 48; 54-
57; 59; 63; 69-71; 75; 77; 79; 81. 17,4. 18,6;
8. 19,3. 21,4-5. 22,6. 23,2-4; 6. 25,3; 9-10.
26,1; 3; 5; 7; 10-12; 18-19; 21; 40; 48; 52-
54. 28,2. 29,12. 31,1; 3; 5; 7. 32,5; 7; 18;
21; 22; 23; 30; 37. 35,2. 41,4.
DBY 1,2; 4; 7; 16; 21-22;
26. 2,2. 5,5. 6,21; 38; 68. 7,6. 8,3. 10,2; 4-
5; 19; 26. 13,1-2. 17,5-6; 22. B3.
ESS 1,2-5; 9; 19; 21a;
24-25; 27. 6,8. 7,1. 9,11. 13,1. 14,5. 15,1-
2. 17,2. 18,10-11; 13. 20,1; 8; 28; 36-37;
39; 80. 21,5; 7. 23,2; 4-5; 7-26. 24,1; 24;
44. 25,1; 5; 12; 18-19. 30,1; 4; 27; 34. 32,9;
24. 33,5; 11. 34,5. 35,5; 7-8; 13-14. 41,4.
44,1; 3. 48,1-2. 49,2. 66,1.

114-118; 120; 123-124; 126; 131-132. 10,3-
5; 7-11; 13-14; 17; 19; 22; 25; 34-35; 39;
46-47; 50; 57; 59-61; 64. 11,2-3; 5; 7; 10-
12; 14; 19; 22-23; 25; 27-32. 12,2; 4; 8-10;
12; 17-18; 20; 23. 13,1; 4; 6; 8-9. 14,1; 3-
5; 8. 15,1; 5; 8. 16,1; 5-8. 17,1; 3; 5; 7-11;
15; 17-18. 18,1-2; 4-5. 19,1. 20,1; 3-8.
21,2. 22,1-2. 23,1-2. 24,1. 26,1. 27,1-2.
28,1-2. 30,1; 4-5; 8; 13; 21; 28; 37; 43; 46-
49.

| | RUT | R6; 20. |
| | SFK | 1,1; 3-6; 12; 66; 70; |

88; 91; 109; 115; 118-120. 2,7-8. 3,17; 34;
58. 5,5. 6,1; 42; 71-72; 121-122; 131; 191;
207; 236; 269; 283; 285; 287; 308; 313. 7,72.
8,53; 81. 14,1-5; 7-9; 18; 23; 26; 30; *42;
43-44; 45; 48-53; 63;* 69-70; 72-76; 77; *81;*
93; 103; 106; 120; *139; 164;* 165. 15,2.
16,6; 33. 18,2-3. 21,10-11; 13; 26; *29;* 43-
44; 54; 80; *83.* 24,1. 25,4-18; 22; 26; 39;
42; 59. 27,1-2. *31,18-19.* 32,30. 33,5. 34,8.
35,1; 4-5. 37,5. 67,12.

| | SRY | 17,4. 21,3. |
| | YKS | 1Y2-3; 11-13; 15. |

2,1. 2B1; 18. 2W4; 6-7; 9. 3Y1; 4; 6; 9.
4N1; 3. 4E2. 5N54. 5E8-9; 15; 55; 65. 5W8;
11; 16; 18-19; 21-22; 30. 6N1; 35. 6E1.
7E1. 8E1. 9W6; 16; 22; 25; 44; 82-83.
10W1; 8; 22-23. 12W3-7; 9-11; 13-28.
13N5. 14E2; 4-7; 11; 15. 15E4. 16W1.
18W1. 19W3. 21E5-6. 21W3. 23E14.
24W19-20. 25W18. 27W2. 29W4; 9; 25.
29N9.

whole (integer)	NFK	9,31.
half (½)	LIN	27,20-21. 38,2.
		59,16.
	NFK	1,27; 57; 185; 193;

203; 216. 2,7. 4,9; 11; 27; 29. 7,4; 19. 8,10;
115. 9,31; 81; 134; 165; 208. 10,19. 12,17.
17,33; 53-54. 20,19; 30. 31,1; 7; 43-44.
35,9.

	SFK	*14,53; 59; 139; 164.*
		37,1.
quarter (¼)	NFK	1,57.
Annexation of	ESS	1,27. 20,69; 77.
		90,31.
in King's despite	ESS	90,31.
	NFK	1,195.
Appropriation of	ESS	20,26; 71. 90,34.
Assessment/valuation		
of	NFK	1,121.
elsewhere than his	NFK	1,149. 4,27-28.
holding		14,34. 15,28.
		20,19.
with free man	NFK	9,146.
Customary dues of	ESS	1,4; 25; 27-28.
		41,4.
	HRT	5,23. 34,17. 36,9;
		13. 42,14.
	NFK	1,1; 3; 182; 216.

8,37; 39-40; 62; 98; 108. 9,75-76; 79. 14,15;

35. 15,1; 7-9. 20,7. 25,25. 31,39. 48,2.
49,3. 66,94.

| | NTT | 1,32. |
| | SFK | 1,1; 12. 6,71. 9,2. |

14,2; 4-5; 8-9; 18; 23; 69-70; 72; 75; 120.
25,1; 17-18; *59;* 104. 31,44; 49. 67,12.

except the 6		
forfeitures	NFK	31,35.
not paying except		
service	ESS	1,13a.
Exchange, held by	ESS	1,27. 32,24. 33,17;
		20. 39,4.
	SFK	29,1.
Gift of	NFK	1,59; 216.
Held by/of/under		
Abbey/Abbot	CAM	32.2; 36; 43.
	NFK	1,209. 8,39-40. 9,8;

79. 14,8; 28; 30. 15,19; 21. 17,33; 44-45;
49-50; 59. 20,31-33. 21,32. *23,16.* 25,27-
28. 31,4. 35,18.

| | SFK | *8,8.* 9,2. 14,2; 12; |

69-70; 72-73; 75; 82; 106; 146. 16,6. 21,12;
21; 29. 22,2. 40,5.

Earl	CAM	26,4.
	ESS	82,1.
	NFK	17,50.
free man	NFK	1,100; 155.
	SFK	14,82.
Freeman	NFK	1,159; 162. 22,2.
King	ESS	17,2. 90,31.
	HRT	1,17. 42,14.
	HUN	1,3.
	LEC	18,1.
	NFK	7,3.
King Edward	BDF	55,3. 57,1; 3ii.
	CAM	1,3. *14,39.* 21,6.

26,45-47. 29,4; 12. 31,3; 6. 32,14; 16; 19;
25-26; 38. *38,2.* 41,10.

| | HRT | 4,6; 16. 5,23. |

15,13. 28,1. 34,8; 18-19; 25. 36,9. 37,14;
17. 38,2.

	MDX	9,2. 11,2.
	SFK	31,50.
King William	BDF	57,13.
	ESS	1,8.
	HRT	36,9.
thane	LIN	1,9.
woman	SFK	6,311. 25,104.
another	ESS	1,4; 28. 20,69; 71.

23,2; 34. 24,36; 54. 30,42; 48-49. 33,6; 17.
34,10. 39,4.

| | NFK | 1,1; 3; 7; 11; 52; 55; |

57; 59; 81; 117; 121; 153; 194; 211; 215-
216; 223. 2,6. 4,8; 10; 15; 20; 37; 42; 51.
5,1. 7,4; 9. 8,1; 8-10; 37; 48; 64-65; *81-84;*
106; 108; 113; 116. 9,8; 99; 105; 145-146;
160; 165. 10,12-13; 16; 18-19; 26; 28-29;
33; 40. 12,5; 7. 14,28; 30. 15,1; 7; 28.
17,21; 33. 20,10; 19; 31. 21,4; 14; 34. 22,11-
12; 21. 23,9; 11; *16. 24,4.* 25,10-11; 25.
26,4. 31,39; 43. 35,7; 17. 37,3. 40,1.

	SFK	1,1; 102.
more on manor		
1086 than TRE	ESS	15,1. 30,45.
	NFK	1,81; 182. 8,64.
		9,11. 20,14.
	SFK	15,2.
Payments of	HRT	37,10.
	NFK	10,29. 15,17.
		21,25.
to office holder		
during tenure	NFK	1,7.
tribute, not paying	NFK	1,7.
Plough		
with plough in		
another manor	LIN	35,10.
without plough	YKS	9W25.
who does not		
plough	YKS	14E1.
Render of corn to		
church	BKM	3a,1.
Revenue, belonging		
to	ESS	30,4.
Sale of		
as King's chattel	NFK	1,195.
for a bridle	NFK	1,7.
Seeking lord where he		
would	LIN	S4.
Service of, to		
Abbey	SFK	14,15.
manor elsewhere	SFK	14,12.
sheriff	BKM	1,3.
sheriff, King's	BKM	1,1.
Status of		
Archbishop's reeve	HRT	43,1.
canon	MDX	9,4.
free	BDF	23,9.
	NFK	8,39.
free man	ESS	20,26.
	NFK	15,10; 13. 31,43.
free with land	NFK	8,37.
Guard (huscarl)	HRT	15,2.
King's reeve	HRT	36,13.
with nothing	LIN	34,18.
	NTT	12,14.
Taken	ESS	17,2.
Value of	NFK	1,135. 31,39.
less 1086 than TRE	NFK	31,39.

See also: Bodyguard; Cartage service; Church; Claim; Crime/offence; Death duty; Delivery; Do what he would; Escort; Exchange; Fold; Forfeiture; free man; Go where he would; Grant; Jurisdiction; Jurisdiction, full; King's hand; Patronage; Plea; Possession; Prove; Residence; Sale; Sell; Sheriff; Taken away; Third/two thirds part; Tribute; Withdraw.

FREEMAN'S land

(terra sochemanorum)	DBY	1,8.
	HUN	6,3. D4.
	KEN	6,1.

FREEWOMAN

(sochemanna femina)	SFK	6,264.

FRENCH and English

Evidence by	DEV	34,5.
Man-at-arms	MDX	12,1.

See also: Borough; Hundred.

FRENCHMAN

(francigenus)	BDF	3,7. 25,11.
	BRK	B1.
	BKM	5,12.
	CAM	B6. 7,4. 25,9.
		32,32.
	CHS	B3. 1,1; 15; 22. 2,3.

3,3; 8; 11. 4,1. 8,1; 7; 16. 9,4-5. 13,3. 14,7; 10. 16,2. 18,5. 20,12. 23,1. 25,2. 27,3. FT1,2. FT2,11-12.

	DEV	42,6.
	DOR	26,9. 54.
	ESS	23,40. 24,3; 17; 19.
		33,13.
	GLS	G1-4. 8,1. 10,5; 7.

31,7. 34,2; 8. 52,4. 59,1. 60,4. 68,1.

	HAM	S2.
	HEF	1,1; 7; 11; 26; 55;

61. 2,12; 34; 36. 6,6-7. 7,3. 10,14; 56; 59. 11,1. 14,5. 19,4. 29,5; 9.

	HRT	1,9. 5,9; 21; 24.

10,1-2; 4-7; 9; 15-16. 11,1. 15,3; 10-11. 20,13. 21,2. 23,4. 24,3. 25,2. 26,1. 28,4. 34,15; 19. 37,10. 42a,1. 44,1.

	KEN	M3. 2,12. 5,78;
		102.
	LEC	2,6. 13,1; 17; 37;

51; 53. 15,10-11; 13; 15. 16,1; 8. 17,9. 18,2. 19,13. 40,15; 26.

	LIN	30,29.
	MDX	2,1-2. 3,12. 4,8.
		5,1. 7,6. 10,1.
		11,1-2. 12,1. 24,1.
	NFK	31,16-17.
	NTH	30,18. 35,1e. 40,2.
	OXF	6,13. 7,46. 9,6.
		41,1.
	SHR	3b,3. 3g,8. 4,1,23.

4,3,4; 7; 13; 22-23; 32; 45; 51; 53; 58; 61; 68; 71. 4,8,7. 4,11,1. 4,21,4; 6; 14. 4,25,7. 5,3. 6,9. 9,1.

	STS	2,20-21.
	SFK	6,84.
	SSX	11,10; 17-19; 21-22;
		83. 13,33.
	WAR	12,5. 16,18; 40.
		18,2; 11. 40,2.
	WIL	24,3. 26,3. 27,3; 7.
	WOR	2,17; 21; 70. 8,1; 6;

10e; 11; 20-21; 23. 9,5b. 10,3; 5; 8; 11; 16. 15,8. 20,2-4. 26,12. 27,1.

	YKS	C1b.
Customary dues of	SFK	6,84.
Evidence by	DEV	2,2.
Man dwelling under	MDX	7,6.
Serving with plough	SHR	3g,3.

See also: Burgess; Dwelling; Man; Reeve; Servant; Value.
FRIEND (amicus) WOR 23,1.
FUEL (focus)
Wood (nemus) for CAM 44,2.
See also: Fire wood.
FUGITIVE (fugitivus)
Fine for SSX 12,1.
FULL jurisdiction (soca et saca) – See Jurisdiction, full.
FUR – See Marten.
FURLONG CON 5,1,14-21. 5,2,2-4;
(ferdingus; ferlingus) 7-10; 19-21; 23; 26;
29-33. 5,3,2; 4; 16-17; 25. 5,4,2-12; 17; 19-20. 5,5,1; 5-6; 14; 18; 22. 5,6,10. 5,7,1-2; 4-5; 7-8; 10-13. 5,8,3-5. 5,9,4. 5,11,3; 5-7. 5,12,1-3. 5,13,6; 10. 5,14,3-6. 5,15,1-2; 4-5. 5,16,1. 5,17,1-2; 4. 5,18,1. 5,19,1. 5,20,1-2. 5,21,1. 5,23,3-4. 5,24,1-2; 6-11; 13; 15; 17-18; 20; 22-25. 5,25,4. 5,26,1-4. 6,1.
DEV 1,4; 26; 31-33; 41;
57. 3,5; 13; 43; 46; 55; 59; 62; 73; 76; 82; 95; 98-99. 5,1; 4. 6,6. 7,4. 15,6-7; 15-16; 31; 53-54; 57. 16,7; 24-25; 35-36; 47; 77; 85; 92; 122; 126; 134-135; 144; 147; 151. 17,5; 15; 17-19; 74; 88; 98-99; 104. 18,1. 19,27. 20,7-8; 15. 21,10-12. 23,5; 11. 24,5-6; 12. 25,8; 10; 19. 29,1; 7. 30,2. 34,3-4; 9; 14; 21; 37; 42-43; 47. 35,8; 12; 19; 24; 30. 36,6. 39,3. 40,4. 42,2; 4; 12; 21. 44,1. 45,1. 47,6-7. 50,1; 3-4. 52,2-3; 20; 28; 37.
HAM NF10,4. IoW1,8.
SHR 7,4.
SOM 1,12; 32. 5,5; 19.
16,4. 21,5-6; 22; 42; 50; 52; 57; 59; 68. 22,5; 12; 18. 25,19-20; 35. 35,7. 37,10. 44,1. 45,1. 46,7; 11; 15. 47,13.
SSX 9,107. 10,117.
11,22.
defined HAM NF10,4.
See also: Quarter.
FURLONG CHS 8,15; 27; 38-39.
(quarentina) 14,13. 27,1. R2,1.
R5,3. R6,1.
CON 1,3-5; 10-11. 2,11.
5,2,27-28. 5,12,2.
DBY 1,16; 18; 21; 35-37.
2,1. 3,3; 5. 5,1; 3-5. 6,2-7; 9; 13-15; 17-20; 27; 29; 38; 56; 63-64; 68-71; 74; 79; 86; 96; 99. 7,3-6. 8,2. 9,5. 10,1; 8; 14-16; 19; 21-22. 11,4. 12,1; 3-4. 13,1-2. 14,2-3; 7. 16,2. 17,1-2; 5; 9; 12; 18; 20. B2.
DEV 1,4; 6; 8; 14; 16; 18; 21; 26; 34-35; 45; 48; 53-54; 57-58; 70; 72. 2,5; 7; 12; 16. 3,9-10; 12-14; 21; 88. 4,1. 5,1. 6,1-2; 4; 7; 9; 12. 7,2-3. 13,1. 14,2. 15,23; 37; 44; 46; 51; 56; 64; 67; 70; 72; 78. 16,3; 8; 11; 13; 18-19; 26; 29-30; 33; 36; 39; 59; 77; 107-108; 110-111; 121-122; 153; 160; 172. 17,4-8; 10; 13; 16-17; 19; 21; 38;

69; 79-81; 84-85; 89-90; 93; 97-101; 104-105. 19, 15,17; 19; 27; 34; 42; 44. 20,12; 15. 21,16; 19-21. 23,1; 7; 10; 11-12; 15. 24,5-7; 20; 23-25; 32. 25,2;15; 26; 28. 28,8-9; 16. 29,9. 32,6. 34,7; 23-26; 32; 44; 55. 35,1-7; 9; 13; 25; 29. 36,6; 18. 37,1. 39,18-21. 40,1; 5. 42, 18; 24. 45,2. 47,6. 48,10. 51,15-16. 52,10-11; 28; 31; 36; 40; 53.
DOR 1,1; 7-11; 13-24;
26-31. 2,1-4. 3,1; 3; 5-11; 13-16; 18. 4,1. 5,1-2. 6,1-4. 7,1. 8,1-6. 10,2-3; 5-6. 11,1-6; 10-17. 12,1; 3-4; 8-10; 12; 14-15. 13,1-8. 15,1. 16,1-2. 17,1. 19,2-7; 9; 12-13. 20,2. 21,1. 22,1. 23,1. 24,4-5. 25,1. 26,3-10; 14-23; 26-27; 30-37; 39-40; 45-52; 54-55; 57-68; 71. 27,1-3; 5-11. 28,3-6. 30,2-4. 32,1-5. 33,4. 34,1-2; 5; 7-15. 35,1. 36,1-11. 37,1-2; 4-8; 13-14. 38,2. 39,1. 40,1; 4-9. 41,1-5. 42,1. 43,1. 45,1. 46,1. 47,1-10. 48,1-2. 49,1; 3-4; 8-11; 14-17. 50,1; 2-4. 51,1. 52,1-2. 53,1-2. 54,1; 3; 6-12. 55,1-8; 11; 13-14; 16-17; 19; 21-22; 25-27; 29-30; 33-38; 40-41; 46. 55a,1. 56,1; 7-8; 12; 14; 16-17; 19-21; 23-24; 28-29; 31-33; 37-38; 45; 48; 50; 54; 57-58; 60; 64. 57,1; 3-4; 8-15. 58,1-2.
GLS 1,27. 2,1; 10. 6,1.
10,1-2; 10. 11,3. 14,1. 19,2. 20,1. 32,10. 38,1. 42,1. 46,3. 52,3. 53,10. 54,1. 68,9. 69,7. 72,3. 78,9-10.
HEF 2,8-9; 13; 27; 51.
9,2; 5. 10,48-49.
27,1.
HUN 1,7-8. 4,2-3. 6,1; 3;
6; 12; 20; 25. 12,1. 13,3. 14,1. 19,3; 11; 30. 20,2-3; 8-9. 29,1.
LEC C17. 1,3; 7; 9-11.
2,1. 3,11-12. 5,2. 6,1; 3. 9,3. 10,1; 3-4; 6; 9; 11; 16. 12,2. 13,4; 20-22; 26; 39-42; 44-46; 56; 65; 67-68; 70; 72. 14,3; 18-19; 26. 15,1-3. 17,24; 28; 30. 18,1. 19,2; 4; 12; 20. 21,1. 22,1. 25,2-4. 28,1-2. 29,3. 39,2. 40,9-10; 19; 21-22; 24; 26; 29; 32; 41. 42,1; 5. 43,1-2; 6.
LIN 1,12; 14; 26; 31; 35;
38; 79; 81. 2,42. 4,17; 20;79. 7,10; 56. 8,1-2; 8. 9,2. 11,3. 13,1; 44. 17,2. 18,1; 6. 22,10. 24,36; 80. 30,23. 31,11; 16. 34,12. 35,13-14. 42,1-2. 55,3. 56,2; 6-7; 9-10; 13-14; 16-18. 63,7; 13. 64,13. 65,2-4. 67,25.
NFK 1,16; 18; 23; 26; 28-29; 35; 57; 71-72; 77-78; 81-82; 86; 88; 95-96; 105; 124; 132; 144; 153; 160-161; 179; 183; 186; 191; 193-195; 200; 202-203; 206; 216; 218; 221; 225-226; 228; 233-234; 236; 238. 2,1; 5; 9; 12. 3,1. 4,2-3; 7; 9; 16-17; 26; 31; 34; 41; 56. 5,2; 6. 6,2; 6. 7,2; 9; 11; 19. 8,3; 21; 30; 40; 45-46; 50; 52; 58; 62; 68; 72; 84; 87; 89; 91; 98; 102-104; 108; 110; 112; 114; 128; 130; 132. 9,2; 6; 11; 23; 28; 31-32; 46; 59; 63; 68-70; 82; 87; 94; 97-

36; 53-54; 56; 59-61; 67; 70; 72; 77-78; 85.
8,1; 7-8; 9e; 11; 14; 16; 20. 10,13. 15,7; 11.
16,1-3. 18,1-4. 19,3; 10. 20,5. 23,2; 9; 14.
26,1; 3; 12; 15.

        YKS   C32. 1Y10; 15-17.
1N54; 76, 1W25. 2B1; 3; 11. 2N4. 2W1-
4; 6. 2E17. 3Y1-2. 4N2. 5N1; 8; 11; 14; 18;
32; 53-54; 59-60; 66. 5W1, 3-6; 11-14; 16-
.21; 23; 25; 30. 6N3; 17; 28; 32-33; 47; 55;
65; 92; 103; 108; 116; 124; 129; 138; 141;
143; 146; 162. 6W2. 8N4-6; 22-23. 8E2.
9W2-4; 9; 11; 17; 35; 39; 45; 58; 60; 63; 68;
74; 76; 79; 91; 95; 97-98; 106; 111; 115;

117; 121; 125; 128; 135; 137; 139; 141-143.
10W1-4; 8; 10-12; 14; 17-18; 20; 23-24; 26-
32; 37-39; 43. 11W1. 12W2-6; 8-17; 19-23;
26. 13W1-7; 17; 27; 30; 33. 13E5. 13N9;
11-12; 16-17. 14E1; 11; 17; 21; 29-30; 36-
37; 46-47; 50; 52; 54. 15E4; 8. 16E3. 16N2.
16W1; 3; 6. 17W1. 19W1. 21E5-7; 9.
21W1-2; 12-14. 22W3. 23N1; 4; 8-11; 13;
15-16; 18; 26-30. 25E2; 4. 24W7. 24E1.
25W6; 10; 12; 14-15; 17-18; 20; 28; 30.
28W11; 33. 29W3-4; 9; 13.

FURNACE (furnus) – See Salt.

FYRD – See Army; Expedition.

G

GAME/Game beating – See Beast; Deer; Hunting.

GARDEN (hortus; ortus)	CAM	*5,14; 41. 14,27; 73. 21,4. 26,26-27. 32,5; 9; 32; 35; 41. 38,2.*
	DEV	3,45. 10,1.
	DOR	B4. 34,5. *36,4. 55,16.*
	HRT	B5.
	KEN	P11.
	LIN	7,36. CN20. CK20-21; 34.
	MDX	3,12. 4,1.
	NTT	1,44.
	OXF	28,28.
	SOM	19,26.
	WAR	1,6.
	WIL	66,6.
Belonging to manor/village elsewhere	NTT	9,9. 12,3.
Destroyed for King's pool	YKS	C22.
Leased	HRT	B5.
Little (hortulus)	NTH	41,5.
	WAR	1,6.
Taken over for a mill	LIN	CN20.

See also: Dwelling; Eels; Taken away.

GATE (porta)	ESS	7,1.

GELD (geldum) – See Tax.

GIFT (donum)
Nature of gift

Bishop's new gift	KEN	5,12; 16; 18; 40; 44; 49-50; 104; 209.
church given by King	ESS	6,1.
	NFK	1,61; 66.
	YKS	C2.
church given by layman	HEF	1,39.
	NFK	1,66.
free man given by King	ESS	49,3.
	NFK	5,2. 9,14; 16; 23; 160. 12,1. 20,7. 50,1. 51,2. 58,2.
	SFK	8,46.
free man given by King with his land	SFK	14,26.
gate in London given by King	ESS	7,1.
jurisdiction	LIN	CS22.
	NFK	20,31.
jurisdiction given		

by King	HUN	D4.
	SFK	14,38.
	YKS	CE33.
jurisdiction by King with patronage/ customary dues	SFK	14,26; 28.
jurisdiction with donor's wife	NFK	8,8.
jurisdiction not witnessed	LIN	CK16.
jurisdiction, full by nun	LIN	1,9.
jurisdiction, full with patronage over men	SFK	14,37.
land or property	BDF	40,3. 46,1. 57,8.
	BRK	1,45. 12,1. 14,1.
	BKM	7,1.
	CHS	R1,43. R4,2. R5,6.
	DOR	10,1. 23,1. 47,7.
	ESS	5,5-6. 6,1; 15. 12,1. 20,56. 24,5. 30,16.
	GLS	1,56; 59-60. 2,10. 11,14. *12,1-4; 7-8.* 35,2. 56,2.
	HAM	1,8.
	HEF	1,4-5; 39; 61; 65. 5,2. 8,8. 9,2. 10,66. 29,1; 18. 31,1; 7.
	HRT	1,13. 31,8.
	HUN	2,7-8. 8,4. 20,6. D2.
	KEN	5,12; 16; 18; 40; 44; 49-50; 104; 209.
	LEC	5,2.
	LIN	CK27.
	NFK	1,75. 6,1. 10,30. 17,49
	NTH	46,6.
	OXF	1,6.
	SHR	3d,7.
	SOM	13,1.
	STS	5,2. 11,8.
	SFK	2,10. 15,3. 35,7. 77,1.
	SRY	19,10.
	SSX	12,13; 30.
	WAR	8,1.
	WIL	8,12.
	WOR	6,1. 11,2. 15,9.
land by dying man before witnesses	WOR	23,1.
land/property by		

78

King/Queen
BDF 5,1. 12,1.
BRK B1. 1,38. 31,4.
    65,7.
BKM 56,1-2.
CHS B7.
DEV 10,2. *12,1*. *16,1*.
    27,1.
DOR 17,1. 56,19.
ESS 1,11. 3,10-11. 5,7.
6,1. 8,9. 11,7. 15,1. 24,1; 59-60. 30,18; 40.
32,8; 25. 34,2; 8. 38,1; 3. 42,7. 60,3. 81,1.
90,20.
GLS 1,8; 37; 42; 44; 50-
    51; 64. 12,1. 24,1.
    69,7.
HAM 2,17. 6,17. 45,1.
    69,33; 41.
    IoW9,15.
HEF 1,12. 10,50; 66.
    19,1. 22,8.
HRT B10. 36,19.
HUN D4; 18.
LEC 13,21.
LIN C12; 22-23; 25.
    57,18. 68,37.
    CS30-31. CK71.
NFK 1,61; 64; 71. 4,1.
    7,3; 14. 8,14; 91;
    137. 9,1; 50; 88; 92;
    102; 104-105; 167;
    183; 233. 47,7.
    66,40; 81.
NTH 1,10.
OXF B9. 1,3. 13,1.
    28,24.
SHR 3d,7.
SOM 24,6. 32,5. 40,2.
STS B12.
SFK 1,115. 7,19; 44.
    8,46. 14,28; 68.
    21,45. 23,1. 25,56.
    32,1. 37,1; 3.
    39,16. 61,1. 67,1.
SRY 10,1.
WAR 42,3.
WIL 17,1.
WOR 8,1. 9,1c; 4.
YKS C1a; 2. CE24.
    CW39.
land with King's
consent
GLS 10,13. 16,1.
HAM 7,1.
HEF 2,58. 10,5; 37.
NFK 8,10. 45,1.
NTH 56,61.
WOR 15,9.
land by Abbot/
without chapter's
consent GLS *12,7-8*.
land freely ESS 24,59.
land with full
jurisdiction HUN D14.

land with
jurisdiction and
holder HUN D29.
land, gift intended
but not effected HUN D3.
land, gift confirmed
by King's grant NFK 17,24.
lordship, of NFK 17,51.
manor with son's
consent SFK 25,1.
market by King SFK 7,3. 18,1.
money to lady of
manor HEF 1,6.
SHR 4,1,21.
service by King ESS 77,1.
Persons, of, with land
donor's daughter to
Abbey BRK 14,1.
SOM *37,7*.
WIL 13,21.
donor's daughter in
marriage DEV *16,44*.
SOM 27,3.
SRY 25,2.
TRE holder's
daughter BKM 56,2.
WOR 2,33.
donor's niece in
marriage HRT 25,2.
villager/
small-holder HEF 10,5.
widow of former
holder GLS 34,8.
Purpose of gift
to maintain widow WOR 2,33.
to provide donor
with necessities BRK 7,38.
for King's well
being DBY 3,6.
to wife for
maintenance GLS 1,63.
Reason for gift (consideration)
donor's affection
for King HUN D8.
keeping Forest BRK 31,4.
kennelling dogs BRK 1,38.
service rendered. HUN D4.
Soul (anima), gift for soul of:-
donor BRK 30,1.
DOR 55,47.
HAM 6,10.
LIN 11.9.
SFK 64,2.
SRY 8,30.
WAR 14,2.
donor with sons'
consent WAR 6,9.
donor's brother HEF 1,61.
donor's father GLS 16,1.
donor's husband GLS 10,13.
donor's predecessor SHR 4,3,8.

WOR 3,1. 11,2. 15,4-11.
16,2-4. 17,1. 18,1; 3-4. 19,11; 14. 20,1-5.
21,1; 3. 26,9; 11.

could without
permission   KEN 5,7.
could not   BRK 7,2-3; 15. 18,1.
                      HAM 1,8. 2,1; 2; 5; 7-8;
10. 3,3; 5-6; 8-9; 12. 6,6. 11,1. 18,2. 23,7;
35. 41,1. 57,2.
                      SSX 9,123.
could not without
permission   BRK 7,24. 33,9.
                      HAM 21,10.
                      SRY 8,18.
could with land   BRK 41,6. 64,1.
                      DEV 23,23. 24,29.
                      DOR 1,31. 58,3.
                      GLS 11,14.
                      HAM 18,1.
                      HEF 1,40.
                      KEN 5,10; 12; 18; 43; 80;
158; 174. 9,5.
                      LEC 15,7.
                      STS 11,48.
                      SRY 5,1d,f; 2-3; 26-27.
17,4. 19,18; 28; 46;
48. 21,5.
                      SSX 9,2-6; 9; 15; 24;
111. 12,24; 46.
                      WOR C5.
could not with land BRK 21,15.
                      HAM 23,3.
                      WAR 2,2.
could with land to DEV 1,32; 49. 3,8; 11;
another lord   19; 22; 40. 13a,2.
15,14-23; 31; 47-48. 16,5; 7; 10. 17,11-13.
24,23; 28-29. 34,34. 36,1-2; 25. 40,1; 3.
42,12; 21.
                      DOR 1,18-20. 55,8; 25;
32.
                      SOM 5,43. 24,16.
                      WIL 41,4.
could not with land
to another lord   DOR 9,1.
could to another
lord   DEV 1,15; 46. 2,10.
3,26; 40; 98. 13a,2. 15,11-12; 20; 28-30;
38; 48-52; 54. 16,5; 10. 24,14. 25,28. 28,3.
34,5; 44; 49. 35,22. 40,7. 47,7.
                      DOR 1,29. 15,1. 36,4;
10-11. 47,1; 10-12.
48,2. 55,8; 34; 48.
56,66.
                      HEF 1,3.
                      SOM 2,9. 25,3. 27,1.
                      WIL 28,4.
could not to
another lord   HAM 28,2.
so free he could
with full
jurisdiction   ESS 23,30.

See also: Dispose; Do; Give up; Go away; Grant;
Grant and sell; Leave; Put; Remove; Seek; Sell;
Separate; Turn; Withdraw.

GOAT (caper)   CON 1,1; 5; 14; 17. 3,1;
3; 5. 4,10-12; 15; 28. 5,1,1; 4; 9. 5,2,2-3;
5; 7; 11; 17-18; 24-25. 5,3,3; 7; 10-11; 13-
14; 17-19; 22. 5,4,11-12; 14-16. 5,5,2; 7-9;
11; 17-18. 5,6,2. 5,7,9. 5,8,1-2. 5,10,1.
5,11,1-6. 5,12,1. 5,13,2-5. 5,14,1. 5,15,6.
5,17,3. 5,19,1. 5,20,1-2. 5,22,1. 5,23,3.
5,24,3; 12; 15; 21; 23-24. 5,25,3.
                      DEV 1,14; 23-30; 37-39;
46-47; 51; 57; 59; 65; 69. 2,2; 4; 15; 23.
3,4; 8-9; 12-13; 23; 26; 28; 30-31; 33; 36-
38; 40; 43-45; 47-49; 53; 56; 58-60; 62-64;
66; 73; 75; 77; 80; 86; 92; 99. 4,1. 5,1-5;
7-8; 11-12; 14. 6,5; 7-8; 12. 7,2. 10,2. 11,1-
2. 13a,3. 15,3; 5-6; 8; 10-12; 18; 25; 36-
37; 39-40; 44-46; 49; 56; 58; 65; 67; 70-71;
74; 79. 16,6-7; 12; 14-15; 20-21; 23; 25;
27; 32; 34; 36; 39-40; 44; 47; 57; 63; 65-
67; 72-73; 76; 78; 83; 87; 94; 104-105; 107-
108; 111; 116; 118; 121-123; 128; 130; 137;
140-141; 148; 152-154; 158; 160; 164; 166;
170; 175-176. 17,5; 7; 13; 20-21; 31-32; 36;
41; 43-44; 49; 57; 59; 63; 73; 76; 97; 102.
19,5; 10-18; 23; 33; 37; 40-41; 44-46. 20,1;
3; 10; 13-14. 21,1; 3; 7; 9; 19. 22,1. 23,2-
3; 5-6; 9-12; 18-23; 26. 24,2; 10; 13-14; 17;
22. 25,2; 7; 9; 13-14; 23-25. 27,1. 28,1-2;
3-5; 7-10; 13; 15-16. 31,2. 32,2; 6. 34,6;
10; 14; 16; 20; 22; 25-26; 28; 31; 33; 38-
39; 44; 50-52. 35,3; 5; 8; 14; 21; 23. 36,3-
4; 17-18. 37,1. 40,2; 5; 7. 41,2. 42,2-4; 8;
13; 19; 23. 43,2-3. 46,2. 47,5-6. 48,3; 7-8;
10-11. 51,7; 9. 52,20; 24-26; 32-33; 37; 42;
45; 53.
                      DOR 1,3-6; 8; 10; 12; 15-
17; 21. 11,11-14; 16-17. 12,2; 10; 14. 13,3;
6. 36,4; 6; 11. 41,5. 47,6; 8. 55,16; 21.
                      ESS 1,9; 11; 28. 2,4; 8.
3,13. 4,8-9; 12; 15. 5,3-4; 7. 7,1. 8,1; 3; 6-
7. 9,7; 11. 10,4. 11,1; 3; 7. 14,3-4. 15,1-
2. 18,5; 39. 20,3; 6-8; 23; 36-37; 39; 64; 71;
79-80. 22,6; 9. 23,15; 38. 24,10; 17; 19; 22;
31; 33; 43-44; 46; 48; 53-54; 64. 25,3; 15;
17-18; 21; 23. 27,10-11; 14. 16. 28,13; 16-
17. 29,4. 30,5; 17-18; 27; 45-46. 32,4; 6;
16; 21-26; 38a-39; 44-45. 33,6; 8; 14; 23.
34,4; 6; 9; 11; 22; 27; 29; 33; 36. 35,3-5; 8;
12. 37,10-11. 38,1; 3. 39,4. 40,4. 41,2; 5.
42,2-3; 6-7; 9. 44,1; 3. 45,1. 46,1-2. 47,2-
3. 53,1. 54,1. 55,1. 56,1. 57,1. 58,1. 61,2.
67,1. 68,4; 7.
                      HRT 31,8.
                      NFK 1,3; 52; 57; 71; 77;
85-87; 128; 136; 169; 192-194; 212; 216;
219; 228; 231; 237. 3,1. 4,9; 31; 39; 41. 5,6.
6,2; 4; 6. 7,2; 17-18. 8,1-2; 35; 62; 87; 91;
103; 119; 122; 130; 132. 9,12; 24; 73; 80-
81; 87-88; 168. 10,5-6; 15; 28; 40; 76. 11,1.

13,19. 14,13; 16; 18; 23; 39. 15,17; 24.
17,5; 25; 51. 19,18; 21-22; 32. 20,9-10; 23;
26. 21,27; 29-30. 22,1. 23,1; 8; 18. 26,2.
29,8; 10. 30,5. 31,1-2; 5; 34; 38. 32,7. 33,1-
2. 34,17; 20. 35,15. 36,6-7. 43,1. 50,9.
51,5-6; 8. 54,1. 57,1. 58,2. 59,1. 61,1.

SOM *1,9; 11; 13; 16; 20-
21; 23; 26; 28-30. 2,10. 3,2. 4,1. 5,4; 6; 8-
9; 13; 22; 25; 27-28; 32; 34; 37; 43; 52-55;
60; 67. 6,1; 4; 6; 9; 13; 17. 8,1-2; 11; 14;
18; 20; 22; 24; 27; 30; 32. 9,1. 13,1. 17,6.
19,1; 4; 7-8; 16; 18; 20; 24; 26-29; 37; 52-
53; 63-64; 68. 20,1. 21,12; 14; 19; 29; 33;
44; 47; 50; 54; 56; 59-60; 62; 64; 70. 22,8;
12-14; 21; 24. 24,15; 22; 30. 25,7-9; 12-
14; 22; 24-25; 38-40; 42-43; 49; 51. 27,2.
29,1. 30,1. 32,2. 34,1. 35,5; 19-20; 23.
37,1; 3; 10. 39,2. 40,1. 42,1. 44,3. 45,11.
46,8-9. 47,7; 13; 21.*

SFK 1,8; 16; 23; 47; 49;
53; 75-76; 88; 90; 100; 110; 120-121; 122b.
2,6. 3,1; 3; 10; 46; 69; 74; 98. 4,1; 13; 18;
20; 30; 42. 5,5. 6,11; 28; 43-44; 48; 57; 62;
80-81; 85; 90; 192; 213; 215; 222; 260; 262;
303-306; 309. 7,4; 6; 15; 19; 37; 42; 56; 64;
73. 8,31; 34-36; 55. 9,3. 11,4. 14,1; 5; 20;
32; 38; 42; 47; 52; 72-73; 75-76; 102-103;
105-106; 119. 16,16; 21; 29. 17,1. 18,1.
19,16. 21,1; 3; 15-16; 39; 42; 47; 58; 95.
25,4; 6-7; 49; 63; 79; 81; 84. 26,3; 10; 12a-
c. 27,3; 6; 10-11. 28,7. 30,1. 31,8; 42; 50;
56; 60. 32,14; 19. 33,4; 6-8; 10; 13. 34,3;
6; 12. 35,1; 5. 39,6. 40,2; 6. 41,7; 10; 17;
43,3. 44,1-2. 46,4. 47,3. 49,1. 52,1; 5.
53,3; 6. 54,1. 55,1. 57,1. 58,1. 62,4. 66,3.
67,15; 27; 30; 33.

Skins – render of   NFK   1,70.
GOATHERD
(caprarius)   HAM   33,1.
GODSON (filiolus)   OXF   1,3.
See also: Relations.
GOLD – See Mark; Ounce; Queen.
GOLD embroidery/fringe (aurifrisium)
Land assigned to
teacher of donor's
daughter   BKM   19,3.
Maker of, for King
and Queen   WIL   67,86.
GOLDSMITH
(aurifaber)   BRK   7,8. 63. 65,5.
                           CAM   1,18.
                           ESS   1,11-12. 81. B3j.
                           NFK   65,8.
                           OXF   58,17-19.
                           SFK   1,97.
                           SRY   36,6.
                           WIL   67,43-44.
Earl's   NFK   66,98.
GOODS (pecunia) – See Chattel; Crime/offence;
Forfeiture; Livestock; Stock.
GOSHAWK (asturco) – See Hawk.

GRAIN (frumentum) – See Corn.
GRANARY keeper   WIL   68,29.
(granetarius)
GRANGE (grangia)   SFK   3,55.
  burgesses, of   SFK   1,122b.
  lordship, in   SFK   1,122b.
  Queen, of   SFK   1,122b.
GRANT of property (concessio)
Bishop, by   NFK   10,78.
King, by   ESS   36,11.
                         HAM   67,1. S3.
                         HEF   19,1.
                         KEN   2,5.
                         NFK   14,15-16. 17,24.
                         NTH   1,21.
                         SOM   2,9. *13,1.*
                         SFK   33,2.
  acknowledged by   SOM   2,9.
  at grantee's request   NFK   9,49.
  of full jurisdiction
  over free man   NFK   14,17.
  to layman for soul
  of King's son   HRT   36,19.
  to family of TRE
  sheriff   HUN   B10.
  not seen by
  Hundred   NFK   10,28.
  to be written in
  records   SOM   2,9.
Layman, by   NFK   10,27. 14,35.
                                 17,21.
                         SRY   1,1c; 13.
Queen, by
  of free man   SFK   37,2.
Holding, of   NFK   17,51.
Land, of
  for donors' souls   SFK   64,2.
  in exchange for life
  tenancy of other
  land   SFK   15,3.
  from fear of grantee   WOR   *2,12; 69.*
  to King to establish
  a borough   NFK   1,66.
  as in Normandy   GLS   W16.
  witnessed by
  Hundred   BDF   56,5.
See also: Altar; Assignment; Gift; Recovery; Writ.
GRANT of land
Cleric could not away
from church   SFK   25,1.
Freeman
  could   BDF   21,10.
                         CAM   26,49. 32,27.
  could not   CAM   32,30.
  could not without
  permission   BDF   21,5.
                         MDX   9,4.
  could not and
  cannot without
  permission   CAM   5,62.
  could except for

jurisdiction
could not because
part of chief lord's
lordship   CAM   32,40.
could to whom he
would   BDF   6,2. 16,9. 18,6.
                           21,4. 23,14; 22-23;
     30; 34; 41. 24,21-22. 25,13. 32,2; 4; 6; 11;
     13; 16. 39,2. 43,1. 53,1; 20. 55,7; 10. 57,3ii;
     13.
                 CAM   1,2. 14,59. 22,6.
Land holder
could   BDF   47,3. 57,18.
                 CAM   5,40. 14,32; 38.
                          25,1. 26,39. 32,18;
                          22. 41,14.
                 SFK   14,100.
could not   CAM   36,1.
                 HRT   15,4.
could without
permission   CAM   22,1.
could not without
permission   CAM   *14,80.*
could to whom he   BDF   1,4. 3,6; 13. 4,8.
would   6,1. 10,1. 15,5.
     16,3-4. 17,5-7. 18,5-7. 21,8; 14. 22,2. 23,4;
     18; 22; 25; 28. 24,6; 20; 23. 25,5-6. 32,7.
     34,3. 41,1. 44,2; 4. 49,1; 4. 53,14. 54,1.
     55,8; 12. 56,1-4. 57,2; 4; 6; 8-9; 17.
                 BKM   35,3.
                 CAM   3,1. 12,1-3. 13,1; *6;*
     12. 14,39; *40;* 65; 67; *68.* 15,3. 19,4. *25,8.*
     26,15; 21. 28,1. 30,1. *32,3.*
                 HRT   42,13.
could where he
would   BDF   4,7.
                 CAM   32,38.
GRANT and sell (land) (dare vel vendere)
free man
could 1086   SFK   7,3.
could   NFK   17,8.
                 SFK   14,1; 9; 11; 13-14;
     16-17; 20-22; 24-27; 29; 31; 49-50; 52-68;
     72; 75; 77-96; 98-99; 101; 104; 110; 112-
     114. 25,78; 102.
could not   NFK   10,13; 26.
                 SFK   *8,81.* 14,129.
                          31,23.
could not without   NFK   1,226. 9,167. 35,4.
permission   43,2.
                 SFK   14,11; 14; 52; 97;
                          104.
could not 1086
without permission NFK   9,60.
could not away
from his lord   SFK   53,6.
swears he could not
away from his lord ŞFK   25,105.
could not away
from Abbey   NFK   29,7.
                 SFK   8,8.

in monastery to
such extent he
could not   NFK   10,87.
free woman
could not   SFK   14,138.
could not away
from Abbey   SFK   11,4.
Freeman
could   BDF   2,3; 5; 7. 3,11.
     16,8. 21,1; 11; 16. 23,31; 37; 40; 44. 24,11;
     26; 28. 44,1. 51,2. 53,3-4; 22; 29. 54,2.
                 BKM   4,3.
                 CAM   1,21. 2,4. 4,1. 13,8.
     14,42; 46; *56;* 58. 18,8. 21,5. 23,3. 25,9.
     26,3; 19; 21; 35; 41-42. 28,2. 31,1; 3; 7.
     32,7-8; 10; 16; 23; 30; 40. 37,2. 38,3.
                 HRT   5,14. 33,17.
                 MDX   7,1. 11,2.
                 SFK   14,26; 30.
could not   BDF   21,1. 23,9.
                 CAM   31,1.
                 NFK   10,28. 14,24.
                 SFK   6,148; 176; 236.
                          21,80. 22,2. 35,1. ⌐
could without
permission   BDF   3,2; 14. 17,1.
                 CAM   7,5. 23,6.
                 MDX   9,9.
                 SFK   14,18.
could not without
permission   BDF   3,3. 17,1.
                 CAM   5,7; *61-62. 31,1.*
                          32,1.
                 MDX   3,13. 11,3.
                 SFK   14,1-5; 7-9; 12; 15-
     16; 23; 69-70; 72-
     73; 75; 93. *21,12.*
could to whom he   BDF   2,9. 3,4. 6,3. 16,6-
would   7. 17,2. 19,2. 23,1;
     7; 16; 21; 38. 24,8; 10; 13; 17; 19; 27; 29.
     25,4; 11; 15. 33,2. 42,1. 47,4. 55,3; 6; 11;
     13. 57,3vi.
                 BKM   1,1. 19,1.
                 CAM   1,3. *14,11.* 26,24-
     25; 27. 29,12. 31,1.
could to whom he
would without
permission   BDF   25,10.
                 CAM   *26,37.*
could where he
would   BDF   3,7.
could not outside
Abbey   CAM   44,2.
                 NFK   1,220.
could not outside
Abbey without
permission   CAM   26,48. *44,2.*
could not outside
manor   BKM   12,5.
                 MDX   5,1.
could and withdraw BDF   53,29.

	CAM	28,2.
Land holder		
could	BDF	2,1-2. 19,3. 21,3. 23,13; 24. 24,4. 32,10. 53,4; 6; 18. 57,7; 11; 16.
	BKM	5,20. 14,29. 26,9. 41,3.
	CAM	1,16. 5,40. *12,2.* 14,62; 64. 17,5. 21,9. *22,1;* 4; 8-9. 24,1. 25,1; 5. 26,18; 21; 31. 31,2. 32,11-12; 23. 35,1. 37,1. *41,14.*
	HRT	1,10.
	MDX	23,1.
	SHR	4,3,18.
	SFK	9,2. 14,167.
could not	BDF	21,1.
	BKM	23,19.
	CAM	1,20. 14,66. 32,29.
	SFK	8,37.
could without permission	BDF	24,15.
	CAM	22,2-3. 27,1.
could not without permission	BDF	3,5; 9. 4,4. 51,4.
	BKM	3a,2. 14,30. 21,3. 22,2.
	CAM	17,1. *36,1.*
	MDX	3,2; 4. 5,2.
	NFK	*20,18.*
	SFK	14,1; 3; 106.
could to whom he would	BDF	3,15. 15,1. 24,1; 9. 52,1. 54,2. 55,4. 57,3i; 5.
	BKM	4,1. 12,30. 19,3.
	CAM	14,*17;* 29; 49. *15,2.* 22,7. 26,14; 22. *41,9.*
	DBY	13,2.
	GLS	1,3.
	HUN	D18.
could not to whom he would	SFK	67,15.
could to whom he would without permission	MDX	3,2.
could not away from Abbey	CAM	18,7.
	HRT	17,1.
	SFK	31,13a. 47,3.
could not away from lord	SFK	53,6.
could not except to lord	HAM	23,44.
could not away from manor	BKM	4,17; 43.
	CAM	*26,23.*
	HRT	15,5.
could not away from manor without permission	MDX	8,1.

could not without permission of holder of another manor	BDF	53,32-33.
in monastery to such extent he could not	NFK	10,90.
Church and house-holder could	HRT	B7.
Land of King's jurisdiction holder could without permission	BDF	3,3.
Or separate land from Abbey-holder could not	CAM	26,7.

See also: Dispose; Do; Give up; Go away; Go where he would; Grant; Leave; Put; Remove; Seek; Sell; Separate; Turn; Withdraw

GRAZING

(herbagium)	BRK	20,3.
	CAM	39,2.
	HAM	1,8; 15-17; 27; 44; 47; W3. 2,1; 4; 15. 3,1. 6,9. 29,3; 7. 49,1. 69,2; 42.
	KEN	2,17; 31. 5,138.
	MDX	3,20. 6,1. 8,6. 12,1. 25,1.
	SSX	2,1a. 10,1; 3. 11,3; 6; 112-113. 12,49.
Pigs, for	SRY	1,7; 9-10; 13. 2,5. 5,11; 20; 22. 6,5. 8,17; 19; 21. 16,1. 19,1-2; 4; 11; 23; 44; 47. 20,2. 21,4; 6-7. 36,4; 7.
	SSX	2,1a-c,e; 5. 3,1; 3-4; 8. 6,2. 8,1. 9,1-2. 10,94; 96-97; 100; 102; 105; 111-112; 115. 11,44.
ratio of render to pigs grazed	SRY	19,11; 23.
	SSX	2,5. 3,1; 3-4; 8. 6,2. 4.
Village, for	CAM	1,11. 29,7.

See also: Meadow; Pasture.

GROOM (equarius)

King's	BDF	57,2.

GROVE (grava) – See Copse.

GRUFFYDD – See King.

GUARANTOR (advocatus; ad warantum)

Cannot answer whilst in King's custody	SFK	76,14.
King called upon as	DEV	*23,6.*
	NTH	46,5.
	SFK	1,103.
Land held without	SFK	74,10.
For reeve adding free men to revenue	SFK	1,7. 74,4; 7.
Sheriff as	SFK	1,7; 122f.

See also: Cite; Patron; Surety; Warrant.

GUARD (huscarle)	BRK	B1.
	DOR	B1.
	GLS	34,3.
	SOM	47,24.
	SFK	67,10; 13.
	SRY	21,6-7.
King's	DOR	B2-4.
King Edward's	BDF	46,1. 53,12.
	BKM	12,36. 13,2. 14,35.
		18,1. 43,11. 46,1.
		49,1. 53,4.
	GLS	1,59.
	HRT	15,2. 22,2. 27,1.
		34,15.
	MDX	7,2; 8. 11,1. 17,1.
	NFK	49,7.
Earl's	BDF	23,20.
	CAM	41,11.
	HRT	34,7.
Earl Harold's	ESS	30,16.
	GLS	1,66.
	MDX	8,3.
Payment by		
borough/town for/to	DOR	B1-4.

See also: Bodyguard; Escort.

GUARD duty

Mail-clad men		
(loricati) found for	BKM	40,1.
Men of manor, by	CAM	1,18.

See also: Payment.

| GUARD penny | | |
| (warpenna) | CAM | 1,18. |

GUARDIANSHIP (custodia) – See Custody; Sea; Wardship.

GUILD (gilda)

Burgesses, of	KEN	C3
Clergy, of	KEN	2,1.
Town, of	KEN	C3. 5,205.

| GUILDHALL | | |
| (gihalla) | KEN | D8. |

GUNNER		
(arbalistarius;		
balistarius)	DEV	47. 48. 49,7.
	ESS	79.
	GLS	W3; 9. 58.
	LIN	1,36. 48. 61. CK41.
	NFK	1,3; 61; 66. 15,18;
		21. 17,43. 26,5. 51.
		52. 53. 54.
	SOM	32,1.
	SFK	6,191; 238. 21,11.
		68. 69. 76,16.
	SRY	35,1-2.
	SSX	9,14.
	WAR	B2. 40.
	WIL	68,30.
	YKS	C17. 26E. CE32.
		SE,P8. SE,Bt2; 7.
		SE,Ac3; 6-8; 11-12.

H

Manor of	BRK	1,46.
	GLS	1,24; 52. 19,1.
	HAM	3,9.
	HEF	1,61.
	KEN	5,192.
	LIN	57,14. CK27.
	NFK	20,10.
	NTH	18,8.
	NTT	20,7.
	SHR	4,3,15.
	SSX	9,4. 12,6.
	WOR	2,41; 55.
value of	NFK	20,10.
	SFK	3,34.

HEARTH tax
(herdigelt; fumagium) HEF   1,49.
                       SSX   13,1.

HEATHLAND
(bruaria)   DOR   10,2.
HEDGED enclosure – See Enclosure.
HEIR (heres)   HAM   29,3.
                      LIN   CW12.
See also: Claim; Death; Death duty; Forfeiture;
Inheritance; Service, King's; Sheriff.
HEN (gallina)
Rendered by
woodland/pasture   GLS   39,6.
See also: Chicken; Eggs.

HERIOT (herietum)	CAM	B13-14.
	LIN	S4-5. CW9; 11.
	NFK	1,70.
	SFK	73,1.

See also: Death duty; Relief.

HERRING (allectus)	KEN	2,2. 5,160.
	NFK	1,216.
	SFK	1,12. 6,84. 31,7; 21-34.
	SRY	15,2. 19,21.
	SSX	7,1. 12,3-4; 13.
dwelling, from	SRY	19,21.
fishery, from	KEN	5,160.
gift, as	SFK	6,84.
tribute, as	SSX	12,13.

More rendered 1086
than TRE   SFK   14,120; 163.
HIDATED (hidata)
Land which is   CHS   26,5. FT2,18.
not/never was   FT3,1; 6.
                      HAM   1,9; 11; 17; 36; 42;
                            47; W5.
                      SHR   4,20,4. 5,8.
                      SOM   *1,6.*
                      SSX   11,42.

HIDE (corium) – See Skin.
HIDE (hida) (land
measure)   KEN   3,15. 5,104.
                      LEC   1,6; 9-10. 3,2. 6,1.
9,1. 10,1. 13,1. 18,3. 25,1-2. 29,3. 38,1.
39,2. 43,3. 44,3-4; 6.
Passim; BDF. BRK. BKM. CAM. CHS.
CON. DEV. DOR. ESS. GLS. HAM.

HEF. HRT. HUN. MDX. OXF. NTH.
SHR. SOM. STS. SRY. SSX. WAR.
WIL. WOR.

Acreage of	CAM	25,10.
64 acres when		
ploughed	GLS	6,3.

Assessment
land not paying tax,
not assessed	WIL	1,2-5; 7.
exempt	BRK	7,3.
	GLS	*9,1.* 12,1. *19,2.* 41,1.
	SRY	19,25; 28.
	SSX	8,3. 13,55.
	WOR	*10,10.* 19,12-13.
exempt and free	GLS	11,8.
free	GLS	11,1; 12. 12,7.
	HEF	5,1.
	SRY	5,25.
	WOR	*9,4.* 10,1-3; 5-6;10. *28,1.*
Better	DOR	14,1.
Carucates in	CHS	R1,44.
	LEC	29,3. 38,1. 44,6.

Land not divided into DOR   2,6. 3,1; 9.
Number of hides
land unnumbered in
hides	SSX	13,52.
no evidence given		
about	HAM	1,2; 17; 21; 41.
not known	HAM	1,27; 43-44.
	SOM	1,1-10; 20.
	WIL	1,1.
not known as land		
paid no tax	DEV	1,7; 11; 14. *23,5.*
	DOR	1,2-6.
	WIL	1,1.

Reduced
by King	BRK	7,15. 21,16; 18.
	CAM	22,6.
	GLS	1,65.
	HAM	3,12.
because sheriff		
oppressed by a		
higher assessment	CAM	22,6.
Welsh/English	HEF	2,15; 56.

HIDE/sulung – Comparative information
Assessment (se defendere)
less 1086 than TRE   BDF   1,1a. 32,1.
                      BRK   1,6-8; 10-13; 15-16;
21; 24; 28. 2,1-3. 3,1. 5,1. 6,1. 7,1; 6-7;
10; 12-13; 15; 17; 21; 23; 27; 30-33; 35-37;
39; 42; 44-45. 8,1. 9,1. 10,1. 12,1. 14,1.
15,1. 16,1-3. 17,3; 5-11; 13. 18,1. 19,1.
20,2-3. 21,1; 3; 5; 8-9; 13; 16; 18-19. 22,2;
5; 10; 12. 23,2. 24,1. 25,1. 26,1; 3. 27,1.
28,1-3. 30,1. 32,1. 33,3-6. 34,1; 3-4. 35,1-
4. 36,6. 37,1. 38,3; 6. 39,1. 40,1. 41,2; 4-
5. 42,1. 43,2. 44,3-4. 45,1-3. 46,1-3; 5-6.
48,1. 49,1; 3. 50,1. 51,1. 52,1. 53,1. 54,1-

4. 55,1-3. 57,1. 58,1. 60,1. 61,1. 62,1.
63,1-3; 5. 65,1; 4; 6-7; 10-13; 15; 19.
CAM 1,11. *5,39; 41.
13,4. 14,61; 67; 74. 18,8. 26,42. 29,1-3.
32,31. 41,1.

HAM 1,1; 4-6; 8; 12-15;
18-20; 24-26; 29-33; 35; 39-40; 46; W1-2;
W8-21. 2,1; 3-4; 11; 14; 18; 25. 3,3; 5; 7;
9-12; 14; 16; 19-22; 25-27. 6,3; 9; 11-16.
7,1. 8,1. 9,2. 10,1. 13,1. 14,1-4; 6. 15,1-
3; 5. 16,1-5. 17,3. 18,1; 3. 19,1. 21,1; 3; 6;
8. 22,1. 23,4-7; 18-20; 26-28; 37; 41-42;
44-45; 49; 51-52. 24,1. 26,1. 28,7; 9. 29,2;
4; 11; 13-14; 16. 30,1. 32,1-2. 35,1-2; 4; 7-
9. 38,1. 39,1-2; 5. 40,1. 41,1. 42,1. 43,5.
44,1; 3-4. 45,1. 48,1. 50,1-2. 51,1. 53,2.
54,1-2. 55,2. 56,1-3. 57,1-2. 58,1. 59,1.
60,2. 61,1. 62,2. 65,1. 67,1. 68,1-3; 5; 7;
10. 69,1-2; 5-6; 14; 16; 23; 31-33; 36; 40;
42; 45-47; 52. NF1,1. NF2,1. NF3,2-4; 8-
16. NF4,1. NF5,1. NF6,1-2. NF7,1.
NF8,1-2. NF9,1-2; 11; 13; 35-36; 38; 40;
44. NF10,1; 3-4. IoW1,1-5; 7-10; 12-15.
IoW2,1. IoW3,1. IoW5,1. IoW6,1; 4-6;
12; 15; 17. IoW7,1-3; 5-6; 17-18; 21.
IoW8,3-4; 6; 8-9. IoW9,2.

HRT 7,1. 10,9; 11. 17,1.
19,1. 21,1. 22,1. 32,1.

KEN 2,6; 9; 21-23; 32;
41. 3,1-2; 4; 7; 15-16; 20-21. 4,1-2; 5-14;
16. 5,19; 93; 102; 128; 159; 225. 9,22; 36-
37; 42. 12,1.

SHR 3d,6-7.

SRY 1,4; 7-13. 2,1-6.
3,1. 4,1. 5,1b-c,e; 2-3; 5; 8; 11; 15; 17; 19-
22; 24; 26-27; 29. 6,1-3; 5. 7,1. 8,1-6; 9;
13-14; 17; 19-21; 25; 27-30. 9,1. 11,1. 12,1-
2. 14,1. 15,1-2. 16,1. 17,1; 4. 18,1-4. 19,1-
12; 14-15; 17; 19; 21-24; 26; 29; 31-32; 35-
36; 38-39; 44-45; 47. 20,1-2. 21,1; 4; 6-7.
22,1-5. 24,1. 25,1-3. 26,1. 27,1-3. 28,1.
29,1-2. 30,1-2. 31,1. 32,1-2. 34,1. 35,1-2.
36,3-10.

SSX 2,1a; 2; 5-9. 3,2; 4.
4,1. 5,1-3. 6,2. 7,1. 8,1. 8a,1. 9,2; 4; 15;
18; 23-25; 32; 107; 120; 122. 10,3; 18-20;
22; 27-28; 31; 44; 89; 93. 11,3-4; 6-7; 25;
40-41; 48; 72-73; 85; 89; 110-113. 12,3-9;
23; 26; 36; 40; 42-44; 48-49; 54-55. 13,4-9;
12-15; 17-20; 22-25; 27-28; 30; 33-35; 39-
42; 46-47; 49-51; 53; 56.

WIL 1,11.
same 1086 as TRE BRK 1,9; 14; 19; 41. 4,1.
7,8; 16; 18; 20; 22; 24-26; 28-29; 34; 38; 40-
41; 43; 46-47. 10,2. 11,1. 17,1; 4. 20,1.
21,2; 4; 7; 11-12; 14-15; 20-22. 22,1; 3-4;
6-9; 11. 23,1-2. 26,2. 27,2-3. 29,1. 31,1-
2; 5-6. 33,2; 7-8. 34,2. 35,5. 36,1-5. 38,1-
2; 4-5. 40,2. 41,1; 3. 44,2; 5. 46,4; 7. 47,1.
49,2. 55,4. 56,1. 58,2. 59,1. 61,2. 63,4.
64,1-2. 65,2-3; 5; 8-9; 13; 20.

BKM B1. 1,1-3; 6. 5,1.
CAM *5,44.* 22,6. 28,2.
HAM 1,3; 28; W6-7;
W22. 2,2; 5-10; 12; 15-16; 19-24. 3,1-2; 4;
6; 8; 13; 15; 17-18; 24. 6,2; 4-8. 9,1. 14,5.
17,1-2. 18,2. 20,1. 21,2; 4-5; 7; 9-10. 23,1;
3; 8-17; 21; 23-24; 29-36; 38-40; 43; 46-48;
50; 53; 55; 57-68. 25,1. 27,1-2. 28,1-6; 8.
29,1; 3; 5-8; 10; 12; 15. 32,4. 34,1. 35,3;
5-6. 36,1-2. 37,1-2. 39,3-4. 43,1-4; 6. 44,2.
45,3-8. 46,1-2. 47,1-3. 49,1. 51,2. 52,1.
53,1. 60,1. 62,1. 63,1. 64,1-2. 66,1. 68,6;
9; 11. 69,3; 7-11; 13; 15; 17-22; 24; 26-27;
29-30; 34-35; 37-39; 41; 43-44; 48-50; 53-
54. NF9,34; 39; 41-43. NF10,2. IoW1,6.
IoW6,2-3; 7-9; 13-14; 16; 18-20; 22.
IoW7,4; 7-8; 10-15; 19-20. IoW8,1; 5; 7;
10-12. IoW9,1; 4-12; 14-24.

KEN 2,3. 6,1. 8,1. 9,45.
10,1-2. 11,1-2.
12,3-4. 13,1.

MDX 2,2. 3,17; 20; 30.
NTH 56,20a.
SRY 1,5-6; 15. 4,2. 5,4;
7; 9-10; 13-14; 23. 8,12; 18; 22. 19,13; 16;
37; 46; 48. 21,2-3. 33,1. 36,1.

SSX 1,1-2. 2,3. 3,1; 3;
5-9. 6,3-4. 7,2. 8,2. 9,1; 3; 5-13; 16-17; 19;
21-22; 26; 28; 30-31; 34; 82-84; 103-105;
109-111; 121; 123-124; 129-131. 10,2; 4-7;
9; 11-12; 14-15; 17; 23-26; 29; 33-34; 38-
43; 46-50; 52-53; 59; 86-88; 94-95; 105; 111;
113; 118. 11,5; 8-24; 27; 29-39; 43-47; 49-
50; 52-55; 61-63; 67-69; 74-76; 78-84; 86-
88; 90; 92-93; 95-105; 107-108; 114-115;
12,10; 12-13; 15-16; 18; 22; 27; 29-35; 37-
39; 50-51; 56. 13,26; 31-32; 37; 45; 54.
14,1-2.

WIL 26,2.
assessed TRE but BRK 1,4; 10; 12-13; 15;
nil 1086 18; 37-40; 43-45;
47. 3,3. 13,1-2. 17,2; 12. 18,1. 21,17. 41,6.
43,1. 65,14; 16-17; 21.

HAM 1,12-15; 24; 30.
2,18. 6,9. 13,1. 14,6. 19,1. 29,4. 39,5. 48,1.
68,1-2. NF1,1. NF6,1-2. NF7,1. NF8,1.
NF9,1. NF10,3. IoW1,7. IoW3,1. IoW6,5.
IoW7,1.

SRY 1,5; 8; 10-11; 13.
5,1b-c,e; 2-3; 29. 8,4; 25. 9,1. 11,1. 17,1;
3-4. 18,1. 19,22; 46. 21,3. 22,4. 26,1. 31,1.

SSX 9,25; 32. 10,22; 27-
28. 12,36; 55. 13,6; 13; 17-18; 20; 23-25;
27; 41; 47; 50-51; 56.
less 1086 than there BKM 12,31.
CAM 5,61. 7,5. 8,1.
14,55. 23,6. 32,23.
HAM 2,15.
HRT 33,17.
MDX 3,12; 14. 4,1. 7,5.
18,1. 20,1. 24,1.

25,1.
more 1086 than
there   CAM   32,23.
             MDX   2,1. 3,1. 4,12. 5,1.
                        6,1. 7,6. 8,4-6. 9,1;
                        8-9. 10,1. 11,1.
                        12,1-2. 13,1.
same 1086 as there   MDX   4,9-10. 9,7.
Land held for
less 1086 than TRE   CAM   32,33.
             ESS   1,24. 4,9. 8,9. 10,2-
                     3. 15,1. 37,20.
more 1086 than
TRE   ESS   48,1.
             NFK   1,138.
same 1086 as TRE   ESS   1,13; 19; 29. 5,7-
12. 15,2. 18,38; 45. 20,43-44; 52; 64; 74.
22,14-15. 23,30. 30,6-7; 10-12; 14; 16. 40,9.
46,1-2. 60,3. 68,7. 69,1. 70,2. 74,1. 81,1.
Land taxed at
less TRE than there   CON   1,2-4; 6-10; 14-17.
1086   2,2-4; 5; 6-10. 3,3;
5. 5,1,1-12; 14-20; 22. 5,2,1; 2-6; 9-15; 17-
21; 23-24; 27-33. 5,3,2-10; 12; 14-15; 18-
22; 24-28. 5,4,1; 3-18; 20. 5,5,2-9; 14-20.
5,6,1; 3-5; 7-10. 5,7,3-11. 5,8,1-9. 5,9,1-
4. 5,10,1. 5,11,1-7. 5,12,1-3. 5,13,1-4; 7-
12. 5,14,1; 3-5. 5,15,1-6. 5,16,1-2. 5,17,3-
4. 5,18,1. 5,19,1. 5,20,1-2. 5,22,1. 5,23,1;
3-5. 5,24,1-5; 7-8; 12; 15-22; 24-25.
5,25,1-4. 5,26,1-3.
             DEV   3,48; 96. 5,4. 7,3-4.
15,,35; 49; 58; 77. 16,35; 118. 17,69. 19,6.
20,4. 21,12. 24,5. 28,8. 34,25. 36,19; 23-
25. 52,10.
             DOR   11,16. 12,16. 36,2.
                     55,35.
             SOM   1,21-22; 24; 27; 29-
30. 2,1-8. 5,6; 26; 40; 64. 7,7. 8,20-21.
17,7. 19,5; 13; 20; 29. 21,10; 90. 22,13;
25. 24,9. 25,9; 47. 27,2. 35,12. 47,16.
more TRE than   CON   4,6; 10. 5,2,7-8; 16.
there 1086   5,4,1-2; 19. 5,7,2.
5,21,1. 5,23,2. 5,24,9-11; 15; 23. 5,26,4.
             DEV   1,4; 16; 25; 28-29;
37-38; 43-44; 52; 56-57. 2,11; 13; 15. 3,54;
62; 65-69; 73; 92-93. 5,1; 3; 10. 7,1. 12,1.
15,10; 12-13; 25; 55; 68. 16,6; 12; 28; 32;
34; 36; 45; 72-75; 80; 92; 96; 132-133; 136-
139; 148; 155. 19,27; 31. 20,14. 21,4; 14.
23,10-12; 26. 24,2; 6-7; 32. 28,1. 31,1-2;
4. 32,4-5. 34,2; 10; 18; 28. 35,6; 22. 36,1;
6. 42,4; 6; 10-13. 43,3. 47,5-6. 48,1; 3-5;
7. 49,7. 50,1; 15. 52,4; 11-14; 26; 36; 40;
43.
             DOR   1,16; 19-20. 11,1;
6; 12-13. 36,4-5. 47,4-5. 55,11; 16; 40.
             SOM   1,14; 49. 5,19; 21;
37; 45; 68. 6,10; 13-14. 7,3; 9. 8,2; 5; 11;
17-18; 25. 9,6. 12,1. 13,1. 14,1. 15,1.
19,10; 43; 50; 86. 21,47; 67. 25,5; 33; 41.

33,1-2. 35,11. 37,4; 8-10. 39,3. 45,7. 46,4;
16; 22. 47,12; 21.
same TRE as there   CON   1,5; 11. 2,1; 11.
1086   3,1-2; 4. 4,5; 7-8;
18. 5,1,13. 5,2,22. 5,3,1; 11; 13; 16-17; 23.
5,5,1; 10; 12-13. 5,6,2. 5,7,12. 5,13,5.
5,17,1-2. 5,24,13.
             DEV   1,10; 12-13; 15; 17-
21; 23-24; 26-27; 30-36; 39-42; 45-51; 53-
55; 58-72. 2,2; 4-8; 12; 14; 16-24. 3,4-9;
11; 13-14; 16-26; 28; 30-31; 33; 36-47; 49-
53; 55-61; 63-64; 70; 74-77; 79-81; 83; 85-
91; 94-95; 97. 4,1. 5,2; 5-9; 11-14. 6,1-5;
7-12. 7,2. 8,1. 9,1. 10,1-2. 11,1-3. 13,1.
13a,2-3. 14,1. 15,2-5; 8-9; 11; 14; 17-20;
22-24; 26-27; 29-34; 36-48; 50-52; 54; 56-
57; 60-67; 70-76; 78-79. 16,3; 5; 14-27; 29-
31; 33; 37; 39-44; 46-71; 76-78; 82-90; 93-
95; 97; 100-117; 119-131; 140-147; 149-
154; 157-166; 169-173; 175-176. 17,3-10;
12-17; 20-24; 26-68; 71-83; 85-107. 18,1.
19,5-6; 8-21; 23-26; 28-30; 37,40; 44; 46.
20,1; 3; 5-6; 10-13; 15-17. 21,1-3; 6-10; 13;
15-21. 22,1. 23,1-3; 6-7; 9; 14-23. 24,1; 3;
8-10; 13-15; 17; 19; 21; 23; 25; 27-30. 25,1-
9; 11-17; 20-25. 27,1. 28,2-4; 6-7; 9-13;
15-16. 32,1-3; 6-7; 9-10. 33,1-2. 34,1; 6-8;
12; 14-16; 19-24; 26-27; 29-31; 33; 35; 38-
41; 43-44; 48-52. 35,1-5; 7-10; 12-18; 20-
21. 36,1; 3-4; 7; 10; 12-18; 20; 26. 37,1.
38,1-2. 40,1-7. 41,1-2. 42,1-3; 5; 8-9; 14-
18; 20-24. 43,1-2; 5. 46,1-2. 47,1; 7-8; 11-
14. 49,1-2; 5-6. 50,5. 51,1-3; 5-13; 16. 52,1;
5-6; 16-23; 25; 27-29; 31; 34-35; 38; 41-
42; 44; 52-53.
             DOR   1,7; 9-15; 17; 24;
26-27. 11,2; 4-5; 10-11; 14-15; 17. 12,1-5;
7-12; 14. 13,1-4; 6. 16,1-2. 36,3; 7-11.
41,2-5. 47,2-3; 6-9. 48,1-2. 55,1-2; 4-6; 9-
10; 17; 19-20; 22; 26-27; 30-34; 36; 38; 41;
43; 47. 58,1-2.
             NTH   56,23; 45.
             SOM   1,11-13; 15-19; 23-
26; 32-35. 2,10-12. 3,1-2. 4,1. 5,2-5; 7-18;
22-25; 27; 31-37; 39; 41-44; 47-54; 57-67;
69-70. 6,1-9; 11-12; 15-17. 7,2; 4-6; 8; 10-
11; 13. 8,1; 3-4; 6-10; 12-16; 22-35. 9,2-4;
7-8. 10,1-5. 11,1. 16,2; 6; 8. 17,1-6; 8.
18,1-4. 19,1-4; 7-9; 11-12; 14-16; 18-28;
30-32; 34-42; 44-49; 51-60; 62-68; 70; 72-
73; 75-81; 87. 20,1-3. 21,1-2; 4-8; 12-15;
19; 21-28; 31-33; 37-41; 43-45; 47; 49-51;
54-60; 60-65; 68; 70-77; 79-82; 86-89; 92-
93; 95-96. 22,1-5; 8-12; 14-15; 17; 19-24;
26-28. 23,1. 24,1; 3-5; 7-11; 13-25; 27,34;
37. 25,1; 3-4; 6-8; 10-18; 21-22; 25-31; 34-
35; 37-39; 43-45; 48-56. 26,2-6; 8. 27,1; 3.
28,1-2. 29,1. 30,1-2. 31,1-4. 32,1-5; 8.
34,1. 35,1-2; 4-7; 10; 13; 16-18; 20; 22-23.
36,1-2; 4-5; 9-11; 13-14. 37,1-2; 5; 7; 11-
12. 38,1. 39,1-2. 40,1-2. 41,1-3. 42,2. 43,1.

Defined CHS C5.
free man working on CHS B1.
Loading within city
territory on CHS B2.
Merchant opening
bale on CHS B2.
Slave breaking CHS B1.
HOLY days
Defined CHS C5-6.
Penalties for offences
on CHS C5-6.
See also: Abbey; Bishop; Peace; Truce.
HOMAGE (hominatio; homagium)
Burgess could not
render without
permission NFK 1,61.
Claim to NFK 8,134.
NTH 35,1j.
HOMICIDE (homicidium) – See Crime/offence.
HONEY (mel)
Concealment of HEF A6.
Payments for CAM 1,1-5; 7; 9.
NFK 1,52.
Render of CAM 1,7.
sester of CAM 3,5.
DBY 1,11; 15; 29.
DEV 23,15.
DOR 12,12. 37,9.
ESS B6.
GLS G1. W2-3; 19. 1,7.
19,2. 28,1.
HAM 1,27.
HEF A6. 1,1; 8; 10a; 38;
48; 51; 53; 55; 58-61. 10,1-2; 16. 13,2. 14,1.
17,1. 19,1. 29,20.
KEN 7,4.
LEC C1.
NFK 1,11; 32; 52; 61; 70;
139; 143; 216. 8,54.
NTT 1,1; 45.
OXF B1. 1,12.
SFK 1,122g.
SSX 13,1; 14.
WAR B4-5.
WIL 12,4. 24p.
WOR 2,8; 76; 83. 8,10a;
28.
Render of, from
bee keeper DEV 23,15.
borough ESS B6.
NFK 1,61; 70.
SFK 1,122g.
WAR B4-5.
city GLS G1.
LEC C1.
OXF B1.
County OXF 1,12.
forest HAM 1,23.
HEF 1,8; 52.
mill WOR 2,76.
royal manors WAR B4.

sheriffdom WAR B4-5.
Welshmen HEF 1,8; 48; 55; 58; 61.
10,1; 16. 19,1.
woodland HAM 1,27.
NTH 1,6.
WOR 2,15.
Render of
one day's SFK 1,12.
half (½) day's NFK 1,5.
SFK 1,8.
one night's NFK 1,19.
Revenue of BDF 1,1a; 2a; 3.
HAM 1,23.
part of 3 days' CAM 1,1-2.
Sester
borough measure GLS G1.
King's measure GLS 19,2.
larger measure WAR B5.
value of ESS B6.
WAR B4-5.
See also: Customary due.
HONOUR (honor) BDF 24,14.
CON 5,6,6. 5,24,14.
DEV *15,11; 15-22; 29-
31; 47-52. 19,35.
23,23-24.*
HRT 24,2.
SHR 4,1,5.
SOM *36,2. 45,2.*
STS B1; 6.
SFK 25,52; 75.
Church, in SHR 4,1,5.
Manor not part of SFK 32,19.
HORSE (equus) ESS 20,6. 37,3.
GLS *1,59-60.*
HEF 1,49.
LEC C2.
NFK 1,42; 70. 8,107. 9,2;
24; 32-33; 46; 168. 10,33. 12,17; 20. 21,24-
25. *31,20.* 32,7. 35,3; 7.
SOM *8,5.*
SFK 2,6. 6,3. 8,35; 46;
48. 12,3. 14,102-103. 15,5. 18,4. 20,1.
21,7. 25,7; 34; 47. 27,3-4. 31,40-41. 33,13.
34,1; 5. 38,1; 6. 41,10. 43,3. 46,1. 54,2-3.
55,1. 76,4.
Army/campaign for,
burgesses supply ESS 24,63.
Burgess with
guards King whilst
hunting SHR C3.
attends Hundred
with sheriff HEF C3.
Court, of BKM 19,2.
Expedition, supplied
by manor for LIN CK53.
Hall, at NFK 1,169; 182; 219;
230. 2,7. 9,59; 63. 20,23. 29,8. 33,6. 34,15.
35,9. 41,1. 52,4.
SFK 1,97-98. 6,1. 12,5-
6. 16,10. 21,3; 6; 10-11. 27,5-7. 28,1a-b; 3.

31,42. 32,1. 34,2-3. 35,1-2. 42,1. 43,1.

Hire of – city dwelling paying for	HEF	C3.
King provided with		
by way of service	BRK	B1.
	CAM	22,6.
when leaving city	SHR	C10.
when in sheriffdom	CAM	1,14.
Lord, held by	HRT	16,9.
Overloading – fine for	CHS	S2,2.
Payments for		
packhorse	BDF	1,1a; 2a; 3.
	LEC	C4.
	NTH	B36.
	OXF	1,12.
	WAR	B4.
	WIL	B2.
	WOR	C2.
passage of	KEN	D3.
supplies to	LIN	12,43; 47-49.
Saddle, with and without	BRK	B10.
Stolen, found in man's home	SFK	27,7.
Taken away	BDF	17,1.
Type		
hunting	NTH	B36.
packhorse (summarius; caballus)	CHS	S2,2.
packhorse, King's	NTH	1,5.
riding (palefridus)	CAM	B13.

See also: Bridle; Cartage service; Cob; Crime/offence; Draught animal; Foal; Mare; Meadow; Pasture; Purchase and sale; Service, King's.

HORSE – cloth (feltrum) – payment for	NTH	1,5.
HORSE shoe (ferrum) Making of by city smiths for King	HEF	C8.
Render of by burgesses	GLS	78,14.
HORSEMAN (eques)	NTT	B9-10.

See also: House.

HOUSE (domus)	BRK	B7; 9. 58,2.
	CHS	C2; 4; 8; 13; 23. B12. A1. 13,2. 17,8. S1,3.
	CON	4,3.
	DEV	C1; 3. 1,1-2; 40. 2,1; 4. 3,1-2. 5,15. 15,1. 16,1; 65. 17,2. 19,1. 23,27. 30,4. 32,6. 34,58. 35,31. 36,27. 39,22. 43,6. 47,15.
	DOR	B1-4. 1,31. 2,5. 14,1. 26,54. 27,4. 31,1.
	ESS	3,16. 9,7. 34,6. B3a-t; 6-7.
	GLS	G2. 3,1. 24,1.

	HAM	1,46. 23,19. S2. IoW1,7.
	HEF	C2-3. 1,39; 41.
	HRT	B2-5; 7-10.
	HUN	B5; 9; 12-14. D2.
	KEN	D8-9. C2-3. 5,44; 53; 56; 58; 78; 81; 93; 125.
	LEC	C6-15; 17.
	LIN	C20-22. S10. CS25.
	NFK	1,61; 70. 51,9. 66,107.
	NTH	B2-35.
	NTT	B8-14; 16-17.
	OXF	B10. 1,13.
	SHR	C1.
	SOM	5,20. 21,81. 40,1. 41,1.
	SFK	14,167. 16,35; 47. 27,7. 41,13.
	SRY	1,1d-g. 5,8; 28.
	SSX	10,1. 11,1.
	WAR	B1-2. 3,1; 3. 17,69. 18,14. 22,4; 8. 26,1. 28,17-18.
	WIL	M1. 3,2. 7,2. 24,20. 28,1. 32,1. 41,1. 45,1. 49,1. 51,1. 68,24.
	WOR	C1. 1,2; 3a. 2,49-51; 68; 82. 14,1. 15,13. 26,2.
	YKS	C1a; 2. SN,Y1.
half (½)	ESS	B3a.
	HUN	B9.
	NFK	4,10.
	WIL	26,19.
compared to waste land	WIL	M1.
contrasted with dwelling	NFK	1,70.
	WIL	M1.
free	NFK	1,70.
	OXF	B10.
Appertaining to court	CAM	7,4.
manor/village	DEV	16,1.
	DOR	31,1.
	ESS	6,8. 7,1. 9,8. 17,1. 20,36; 39. 31,1. B3j-m,q-r.
	KEN	5,53; 58; 78; 81; 93; 125.
	LEC	C7-8; 11; 13-15.
	NTH	9,6.
	SRY	1,1d-e. 5,8.
	WIL	3,2.
	WOR	1,2; 49-50; 68.
Building materials for	HUN	7,8.

woodland for	HAM	1.23.
Burning down –		
penalty	SHR	C6.
Condition		
derelict/unoccupied		
(vasta)	CHS	9,17. 20,3.
	DOR	B3.
	LEC	C12.
	NFK	1,64.
	NTH	B4; 6-7; 9; 11-12; 15; 19-20; 27.
	OXF	B4; 10.
	SOM	1,31.
fortified	HEF	10,46. 25,9.
(defensabilis)		
inhabited	OXF	28,8.
neglected	DOR	B2.
new	SHR	4,1,32.
not to be left empty	HEF	C2.
removed	NFK	66,106.
very good	WIL	24,1.
Customary dues		
paying	DEV	C1. 3,1-2. 5,15. 9,2. 17,2. 19,1. 39,22. 47,15.
	ESS	3,16. B3b,e-g,j-t.
	HAM	S3.
	HRT	B2-4; 7; 9-10.
	SFK	41,13.
paid to King	DEV	35,31. 36,27.
	ESS	B1.
not paying/		
exempt/kept back	CHS	B12. A1.
	DEV	3,2. 5,15. 9,2. 17,2. 19,1. 23,17; 27. 39,22.
	ESS	B3e-g,j-s.
	HRT	B3.
	YKS	C2.
not paying except		
King's tax	HRT	B8; 10.
King's kept	DEV	23,27. 30,4. 34,58. 35,31. 43,6.
back/not had		
	NFK	1,61.
Destroyed		
castle, for	CAM	B1.
cause unstated	DEV	C3. 1,1-2. 3,1; 3. 16,2. 28,17.
	DOR	B1; 3-4.
	GLS	G4.
	OXF	B4.
fire, by	DEV	2,1.
mills, to make	CAM	B12.
monks, by	KEN	C2.
Held		
in common with		
King	LEC	C11.
in pledge	LIN	C21.
in pledge from		
burgess	DEV	5,15. 23,27.
Land pertaining to	ESS	B1.

Owned/occupied by		
Abbess	ESS	B3s.
	HAM	16,7.
Abbot	DEV	5,15.
	ESS	B3a.
Baron of King	WAR	B1.
burgess	ESS	1,25.
	HRT	B5; 10.
	NFK	1,61.
	YKS	C2.
canon	CHS	B12. A1.
	SHR	3g,1.
	YKS	C21.
church registrar	CHS	B12.
church warden	CHS	A1.
horseman	NTT	B9-10.
King	DEV	C1.
	ESS	1,25.
	HAM	6,1; 9. NF9,41.
land holder	SRY	5,8. 19,37.
man	MDX	4,1.
man-at-arms	MDX	4,1.
merchant	NTT	B9.
reeve	SFK	14,167.
villager	MDX	3,3.
woman	ESS	B3a.
	SRY	1,1d.
Lease of	HRT	B5.
Lordship, in	DEV	3,1.
	SFK	14,167.
	WAR	B1.
	WOR	2,49.
Payments		
dues (census)	WOR	C1.
exempt	DEV	3,2. 9,2.
	HAM	S2.
levy (scotum)	ESS	3,16.
lump sum divided		
between each	ESS	B6.
mercenaries of		
King, for	ESS	B6.
nil	HEF	1,41.
	NTH	B17; 21.
	OXF	B10.
	SRY	1,1g.
nil through poverty	OXF	28,8.
Renders		
ploughshare	HEF	1,41.
salt	WOR	2,50; 82.
Repair		
forbidden	KEN	C2.
materials for	WIL	13,10; 18.
	WOR	2,31.
obligation to	HUN	7,8.
wood for	CAM	7,2-4. 14,49-51; 53. 26,42. 32,23-25.
	HRT	10,4. 36,3.
Revenue, in	ESS	31,1.
Sale-conditions of	HEF	C2.
	LIN	T1.
Seized on re-marriage		

of widowed holder   SRY   1,1d.
Service
  answering for every
  service of King   DOR   B1-2.
  King, to   HEF   C2.
  not performed from
  poverty   HEF   C2.
  repairing city wall OXF   B10.
  work at the court   WOR   2,49.
Situation
  castle, occupied by GLS   G4.
  Earl's land on in
  new borough   NTT   B3.
  inside/outside city KEN   C2.
  market place, in   WOR   2,51.
  wall, below   ESS   B3a.
  wall within/
  without   ESS   B3q.
                      OXF   B4. 28,8.
  waterway on   KEN   D9.
Taken away   KEN   C2.
  from borough   SOM   1,31.
  with garden from
  burgess   HRT   B5.
Tax
  paying   CHS   C2.
                      OXF   B4. 28,8.
                      YKS   C22.
  paying King's   LEC   C10.
                      WAR   B1.
  not paying   LIN   C20-21.
                      OXF   28,8.
                      WIL   M1.
  unable to pay   DOR   B2.
                      OXF   B4.
Toll, with its own   YKS   C2.
Tribute (gablum)
  paying   BRK   B7.
                      KEN   C2.
                      OXF   28,8.
                      WIL   M1.
  not paying   OXF   28,8.
See also: Annexation; Burning; Crime/offence;
Croft; Destruction; Ditch; Dwelling; Exchange;
Forfeiture; Jurisdiction; Jurisdiction, full; Keeper;
Manor; Marriage; Mercy; Mill; Pledge; Purchase;
Reeve; Residence; Road; Timber; Waste land;
Widow.
HOUSE breaking (heinfara) – See Crime/offence.
HOUSECARL (huscarle) – See Guard.
HOUSEHOLD (famulus)
Member of King's   NFK   1,10.
HOUSEHOLD land (terra dominica)
Of King   BRK   1,37.
See also: Manor; Revenue.
HOUSEHOLD revenue (firma dominica) – See
Lordship revenue.
HOUSEHOLD supplies – See Supplies.
HUNDRED (hundredum)
Attendance/service at   HEF   C3. 1,72.
  fine for non-

attendance   CHS   C20. R1,40d.
                      HEF   A7.
                      SFK   6,89a.
Borough, of   GLS   B1.
Circuit, within   BKM   3a,1.
Customary dues
  of manor/village   DEV   1,23.
  not paid in   SFK   2,6-7.
Dimensions of half
Hundred   SFK   1,40.
Evidence by (men of)   BDF   3,6. 4,2. 5,1. 6,1.
8,2. 10,1. 14,1. 16,3. 17,1-2. 19,1-2. 22,1.
23,12. 24,12. 25,7. 29,1. 31,1. 32,15. 40,3.
54,2. 56,3.
                      BRK   1,11; 37; 39; 43.
                             20,2. 21,13; 16.
                             41,6.
                      BKM   4,17. 12,5. 17,20.
                             18,3. 38,1.
                      CAM   1,16. 3,5. 5,3; 22;
26; 32-33. 13,2. 18,3. 21,5. 22,5-6. 25,9.
26,18; 30; 33; 57. 28,2. 29,4; 6; 10; 12. 35,2.
37,2. 38,2. 39,2. 40,1.
                      DEV   15,67. 16,74.
                      ESS   1,28. 3,8; 10. 5,8.
9,14. 10,3; 5. 18,34. 20,51; 56. 22,8. 23,33;
42. 25,3; 16; 20. 27,14; 17. 30,3; 15-16; 23;
27; 39; 41. 32,28. 34,19; 28. 37,9. 47,3.
66,1. 90,9; 17; 64-65.
                      GLS   11,14.
                      HAM   1,2. 4,1. 6,16. 18,2.
20,1. 21,7. 23,16; 44. 27,1. 28,1. 29,9.
32,3. 43,4-6. 44,1. 45,2. 53,2. 54,2. 56,3.
68,4. 69,6; 16; 30; 33; 40.
                      HRT   1,6; 9. 2,1. 10,6;
12. 16,1. 17,1. 19,1. 24,2. 32,1. 35,3. 36,9;
11. 37,9; 19. 38,2. 42,11.
                      HUN   19,15.
                      KEN   1,1. 5,149. 9,9.
                             13,1.
                      LIN   35,12. 68,22.
                      MDX   15,1. 25,2.
                      NFK   1,52; 96; 106; 120;
128; 136; 172; 197; 211; 216; 218; 229. 4,10;
20. 8,5; 8; 17; 29; 71; 137-138. 9,42; 49;
111; 160; 167. 10,21; 59; 93. 13,19; 21.
14,15. 15,2; 18. 16,1. 17,18. 19,24. 20,10.
21,15; 22. 23,16. 24,1; 4. 25,15. 27,2. 28,1.
31,11; 20; 28. 34,17. 35,11. 43,2. 47,7.
65,16. 66,64; 67; 80-82.
                      SFK   1,77; 97. 2,6; 8.
4,13. 7,5; 13; 55. 8,63. 14,104. 16,3; 34.
18,4. 25,40; 52-53; 105. 26,12d; 14. 27,7.
31,13a; 34; 48-49; 53. 35,3. 38,3. 39,3; 10.
41,11. 52,1. 53,6. 67,30. 76,2. 77,4.
                      SRY   1,5; 9. 4,2. 5,3;
25-26. 6,5. 8,4; 18; 29. 11,1. 19,25; 27; 35.
23,1. 25,1-2. 28,1. 36,4.
                      SSX   10,99. 11,8.
by better and old
men of   HAM   23,3.

J

		29,1.
of manor	NFK	9,68.
King's land, of		
annexation from	CAM	29,12.
	ESS	49,6.
in another County	NTH	46,5.
not had	YKS	5E28.
Land		
held without (sine)	STS	12,14.
of the jurisdiction		
(de soca)	DBY	1,35. 6,48. 16,1.
	LEC	42,4.
	LIN	12,47-50; 60. 37,2. CW17.
	NTH	6a,14. 8,1-3; 7-9; 11. 35,1e-g,i; 19b. 48,6. 56,10; 12; 19; 20c,e-f; 32; 45; 56; 63.
	NTT	13,5.
of King's		
jurisdiction (soca		
regis)	BDF	3,3. 57,15.
	BKM	17,7-8.
	CAM	1,2. 32,9; 15; 21.
	ESS	22,24.
	HRT	4,1; 9. 34,17. 42,9.
	HUN	19,4. D15-17; 25; 29.
	LEC	1,5.
	NTH	46,5.
	NTT	11,17.
	OXF	58,14.
over land of		
Abbey's work		
(werche)	LIN	8,38.
withdrawn	OXF	1,2.
Lordship, over	SFK	40,3.
Lost by previous		
holder	NFK	1,135.
Manor/village/land, of		
in manor etc		
elsewhere	BDF	23,24. 53,3.
	DBY	1,2-8; 19; 26. 3,1.

6,28; 53. 8,3. 9,3. 10,13-14; 26. 14,5-6.
16,8.

	ESS	18,32; 34. 37,20. 90,9.
	HRT	1,8; 10-11; 13-14. 34,11.
	HUN	3,1. 5,1. 6,18. 13,5. 19,7; 15; 17-20. 20,5.
	LEC	1,11. 13,5; 24. 19,9. 27,2. 29,11-12; 21. 43,3. 44,11.
	LIN	1,3; 10; 13-23; 25;

27; 32; 36-37; 39-63; 67-80; 82-90; 92-106.
2,2; 4; 7; 10; 17; 20; 22-24; 31; 35; 38. 3,10-
12; 14-15; 18-19; 23; 26; 28; 30; 34; 38; 44-
45; 49; 54. 4,7; 12; 18; 22; 24; 27; 31; 35;
37; 44; 52; 58; 60; 62-64; 66; 68; 71. 7,4-5;
7; 9; 12; 25; 31; 40-41; 45-46. 8,2; 10; 16;
18; 20; 25-26; 30; 36-37. 9,2. 10,2-3. 11,9.
12,2; 5-6; 15-16; 22; 32; 38-39; 45-46; 54;
63-68; 71; 73-79; 81; 84-85; 87; 95; 97. 13,9;
18-19; 23; 32; 37; 43. 14,2; 4; 10; 19; 37;
47; 67-83; 86; 88-91; 96; 101. 15,2. 16,11;
13; 16-17; 21; 29; 31; 38; 50. 18,8; 19. 22,5;
11; 17; 19-20; 23; 27; 36-38. 24,6; 14-15;
18; 29; 35; 38; 42-45; 60; 77; 79; 84. 25,3;
12; 18; 20. 26,12-13; 19; 24; 29; 32; 34; 51;
54. 27,4; 10; 13; 21; 23; 28-29; 31-32; 39;
46-47; 63-64. 28,6; 9-10; 13; 21; 26; 36; 39;
43. 29,5-7; 14; 21; 26; 33. 30,2; 4; 11; 13;
25; 28; 30; 37. 31,4; 12; 18. 32,5; 34. 34,10;
13. 35,7; 17. 36,4. 37,2; 7. 38,6; 9. 39,2.
40,3; 8; 11; 16. 42,6; 14-15; 18-19. 43,3-4;
6. 44,3; 12-13; 15; 18. 46,2. 47,9. 48,9; 16.
49,6. 51,5. 54,2. 55,2. 56,15-16; 20-21.
57,2; 8; 11; 16; 21; 25; 31; 34; 39-40; 49;
51. 58,3; 7. 59,1; 6; 10; 15; 21. 60,1. 61,2.
62,2. 63,9; 11; 16; 18-19; 21-23; 25. 64,3;
14; 16; 19. 67,2; 16; 18. 68,14; 22; 36. CS8;
12; 15-16; 30-32; 35-37. CN10. CK17; 21;
25; 27; 42; 49.

	MDX	8,2. 17,1. 18,1.
	NFK	1,79; 135; 146; 204.

4,46-47. 5,4. 6,1. 8,8; 58; 60. 9,63; 129-
133. 10,5; 17; 53. 11,2. 13,17. 15,12. 19,8.
20,5; 7-9; 11; 30. 21,17. 24,3. 25,1. 29,6.
31,40-41. 37,3. 49,6. 66,74-75; 77; 90; 95.

	NTH	1,9; 22; 28. 2,5-6;

10-11. 4,19; 23. 6a,11; 15; 17; 30. 12,4.
18,4; 24; 30; 37; 41; 44; 54; 57-58; 61-62;
75; 83-84; 86; 95. 22,6-7. 26,5. 30,8; 13.
35,2; 3b; 14-15; 20; 25. 41,7. 43,11. 60,3.

	NTT	1,2-8; 10-16; 18-21;

30; 46-50; 65. 4,4. 5,8; 14-16. 6,2. 9,7-8;
13; 24-25; 29-30; 38; 42; 47-48; 56; 71; 75;
81; 83; 99; 109; 117-118; 123. 10,10; 19; 26;
45-46; 50. 11,3; 15-17; 19; 27. 12,1; 13; 20.
13,4-5; 13. 17,5; 10; 13-14; 16. 24,3. 25,1.
27,2. 28,2. 30,26; 44; 49; 55.

	SFK	1,92; 114; 119.

3,68; 70; 80-82. 5,6-8. 6,69-70; 311-313.
8,36-37; 42; 46. 14,161. 16,35-37; 41; 46-
47. 21,45-46. 25,64-67; 69-70; 72-73; 75;
77. 28,5. 32,5; 8. 35,3. 38,21. 40,3. 44,2.
58,1. 61,1. 64,3. 71,1-2. 75,3; 5.

	YKS	1Y1-4; 6-11; 14-16;

18-19. 1N18; 86; 97; 108. 1E43. 1W25-26;
30-31. 2,4. 2B11; 18. 2N25. 2W8-9. 3Y1-
2; 4; 6; 8-9; 12. 4N1-3. 4E1. 5N8; 11; 17;
22; 28-29; 32; 51; 54; 61; 68. 5E6; 8; 12;
15-16; 22; 24-26; 28; 31-33; 37; 60-64; 67.
5W7-8; 18; 30-31; 38. 6N1-2; 8-9; 26-27;
29-31; 34; 50; 111; 123-124; 127; 138; 162.
6W5. 6E1. 7E1. 8E1. 9W1; 62; 64; 78-80;
82; 96; 125. 10W1; 9; 12; 17; 19; 27; 29; 40;
43. 11E6-9. 11N12. 12W1. 13W7; 14; 16;
18; 28-29; 36-37. 13E3; 6; 16. 13N3; 6; 13.

14E1-2; 4-9; 11; 24. 15E3; 6. 16N1. 16W6.
19W2. 20E3. 21E5; 7; 12. 21W3. 23N3.
24W1; 8; 10; 19-20. 25W3; 5; 11; 27. 26E3.
28W36. 29W10; 25. 29E4. 29N2; 4. CE4-
5; 7; 11; 24; 30; 33. CW2-3; 11-14; 16; 25;
33-34. SW,M14.

in manor else- where except for house	SFK	16,35.
in King's manor	NFK	1,144; 186. 4,28.

elsewhere
8,55-57; 59; 69-70;
72; 79. 9,5; 126-127. 14,9. 15,11; 12. 17,20.
19,8; 32. 20,10; 12. 24,1-2. 25,1-2; 4; 6; 8.
32,1. 34,5-6; 20. 39,2. 49,5. 58,1. 66,24-
25; 38; 76.

Manor/village/land in, under or with	DBY	1,21-22. 2,2. 5,2. 6,41; 68; 93. 9,5. 10,2-3. 13,1.
	ESS	1,11.
	HUN	1,9. 6,18. 13,2-5. 19,4-5; 7; 15; 17- 20.
	LIN	1,8-9; 11-12; 37;

64. 2,15. 3,1. 4,45; 48. 7,47-51. 8,7. 12,23-
28; 30; 33-36; 41; 72; 82. 13,1-8; 10; 12-17;
28; 31; 33-34. 14,1; 15; 17-18; 23; 25; 29;
31-32; 36; 38; 46; 59; 66; 84-85; 93-94; 99-
100. 16,19; 23-24; 26. 17,3. 18,1-3; 9-10;
14; 21-24. 20,3. 22,2; 4; 12-15; 18; 31.
24,3-4; 7; 20; 28; 30-34; 39-41; 46-51; 63-
64; 67; 69-70; 78; 85-93; 95-105. 25,6; 16-
17; 21-24. 26,33; 38-39. 27,9; 17-18; 20; 22;
36; 43; 49-50; 62. 28,22-24; 27-28; 30-31;
40-41. 29,3; 13; 24-25. 30,15. 31,13-14.
32,2; 14; 22-23; 25. 34,14-22. 35,8; 10; 12.
37,4. 38,2. 40,13; 18-19; 22; ;24-25. 42,4-
5. 44,1. 51,8. 56,2-3; 10. 57,3-4; 26; 31;
43; 52-53. 58,4-5. 59,13. 61,3; 7-8; 10.
63,4; 13-15. 64,4-9; 11-12; 17. 65,1-3; 5.
67,3-4; 7. 68,3; 9; 12. CN6. CK12; 34; 47.

	NFK	64,2.
	NTT	1,29; 54-57. 3,2.

5,4. 6,2-4; 14. 9,4; 14; 27; 44; 49; 58; 63;
67-68; 78; 86-87; 91; 124; 132. 10,8-9; 11;
13-14; 37-38; 42; 60. 11,5; 7; 10; 21; 23;
28-32. 12,14; 17. 14,3-4; 8. 16,10. 17,11;
17. 18,2. 20,2. 30,21; 51.

	YKS	1N66. 1W12; 73.

2B18. 2E35. 5W19; 37. 11W4. 13E10.
29W4. 29N9. 31E1. CE25. CW40.

except parish church	YKS	1Y16. 1W25.
except hall and village	SFK	7,122.
Manor/village/town with/free with	NFK	1,174.
	SFK	1,97; 99.
	SRY	22,4.
Persons-free man in/under/at	NFK	13,7. 15,7-8. 21,2- 3. 31,26.

	SFK	1,105. 4,3. 8,49.

14,127; 146-147. 15,2. 19,6-8. 21,1; 19; 31-
35. 26,2. 43,4.

Jurisdiction over, held by:-		
Earl	SFK	4,4. 16,9.
ecclesiastical body/person	NFK	8,19; 44; 46. 9,180. 13,7. 24,4. 26,5. 66,4; 8; 16; 46.
	SFK	1,75. 2,1; 3-5. 3,93.

4,4. 5,1. 6,28; 32. 7,2. 8,45; 66; 68; 80-81.
12,2. 14,24; 40; 42-43; 46; 122; 125-127;
130-132; 134; 136-137; 140; 143; 148.
16,27; 30-33. 19,14-15. 20,1. 21,9; 17; 22;
26-28; 36; 71; 75; 78-79; 84. 25,34. 26,3-4.
28,4. 32,28-29. 33,12-13. 34,2. 43,3. 53,7.
66,11. 67,4; 6. 76,4; 21.

King	ESS	90,85.
	NFK	1,97-99; 182. 10,13; 26; 48. 23,14.
	STS	12,17.
	SFK	2,6. 7,18. 8,66; 68. 12,7. 38,6. 74,1-2.
King and Earl	NFK	8,51. 9,198. 14,42. 17,54. 20,35. 50,1. 55,2.
	SFK	4,43. 6,213. 7,10. 14,39. 29,1. 31,45- 48. 32,1. 38,7; 17.
King and Earl except for patronage	SFK	6,211.
layman	ESS	43,6.
	NFK	1,5; 96-97; 99; 239.

8,51; 70. 9,169; 200. 10,80. 14,20-21. 19,6.
31,32. 34,4. 66,71; 87.

	SFK	1,75; 77. 3,100. 4,4;

15. 6,2; 191; 193; 216. 7,10. 8,46. 15,4.
19,14; 17. 27,3. 34,2-3. 35,7. 76,23.

woman	SFK	1,67; 73.
Persons-free man Jurisdiction over lying in:-		
Hundred	NFK	12,16.
	SFK	7,55. 31,51. 41,12.
Hundred to third penny	NFK	1,101.
King's manor	NFK	8,55-56. 9,80. 20,11. 24,4.
manor/village	ESS	11,6.
manor/village	NFK	9,77; 80. 20,11.
manor/village elsewhere		39,1. 52,1. 58,2. 59,1.
Persons-free man Jurisdiction over, detained	NFK	10,48.
Persons-Freeman at	NFK	31,25.
Jurisdiction over held by:- ecclesiastical body/person	CAM	14,30. 31,2.

	NFK	1,220. 8,37; 39.
		26,5.
	SFK	14,75.
King	CAM	5,9.
	HRT	4,16. 5,9. 33,19.
	NFK	1,153. 21,14.
King and Earl	NFK	7,16-17. 10,19.
layman	HRT	33,11.
	NFK	1,77; 216; 220.
		23,10. 34,1.
	NTH	1,21.
	SFK	6,308.
woman	CAM	1,12.
Persons-Freeman		
Jurisdiction over		
lying in:-		
Hundred	NFK	1,154; 157; 159.
		17,9.
	SFK	31,42.
King's manor		
elsewhere	NFK	1,185. 15,15.
manor/village		
elsewhere	BDF	53,4.
	CAM	23,4. 26,18. 32,10.
	NFK	1,195; 220; 223.
	SFK	6,308.
Persons-man		
in/at	NFK	14,42. 31,21.
Jurisdiction over		
held by:-		
Abbot over men		
seeking fold	NFK	17,3.
ecclesiastical		
body/person	CAM	5,56. *6,2. 7,12. 9,4.*
	NFK	8,*16;* 18.
King	HRT	5,11. 33,19. 34,6.
		36,8. 42,9.
layman	LIN	26,45.
	NFK	9,6. 26,2.
	SFK	1,102.
Persons-man		
Jurisdiction over		
lying in:-		
Hundred	NFK	17,3.
manor/village		
elsewhere	CAM	21.7.
	SFK	33,10.
Persons-priest		
Jurisdiction over		
held by:-		
Abbot	SFK	16,30; 34.
King	HRT	42,9.
	SFK	26,5.
layman	LIN	57,17.
Persons-villagers		
jurisdiction in		
manor elsewhere	SFK	40,3.
Persons-woman		
Jurisdiction over:-		
free man's wife held		
by Abbot	SFK	66,13.

free woman held by	SFK	25,33. *32,26.*
Abbey/Abbot		66,13.
woman held by		
Abbot	SFK	16,48.
Ploughs on	NFK	1,186.
Remaining despite		
sale of		
land/withdrawal		
in/with		
King	CAM	14,64. 21,4. 26,18.
lord	BDF	4,2. 17,4.
	CAM	3,2; 4. 5,24; 27; 29;
		40. 7,5. 14,17; 27;
		30; 57. 22,3-4; 8.
		26,17-19; 27; 29;
		48. 28,2. 31,1.
		32,5; 8; 12; 22; 30-
		32; 35-36; 39; 43.
		41,14. 43,1.
	ESS	35,13-14.
	NFK	*15,7-8.*
	SFK	14,24-25; 27; 29-31;
		52-57; 59; 68; 72;
		75; 77; 112-114.
manor/village	CAM	26,19. 32,8.
	ESS	24,22. 25,18-19.
Render/payment of or		
for (suit)	ESS	30,40. 32,7.
	LEC	3,7-8.
	LIN	16,24. 24,81.
	NTH	1,32.
	SFK	33,10.
	WOR	2,1; 30.
elsewhere than		
where owed	YKS	CE7.
free man by,		
according to law	SFK	1,105.
free man by taken		
without lord's		
knowledge	SFK	14,37.
Freeman by, in		
King's manor	ESS	1,9; 13; 24.
nothing except		
army service	LIN	57,43.
Resources, over		
fishery	LIN	CS34.
hall	LIN	CN25.
King's house	NTH	B9; 14.
mill	LIN	1,23. 16,9. 27,11.
		49,3. CS9.
mill in		
manor/village	LIN	67,15. CS35.
elsewhere		CK64.
plot (tofta)	LIN	CS34. CN21.
		CW18.
watermeadow	LEC	44,2.
wood in manor		
elsewhere	LIN	18,26.
Shared	CAM	26,18. 33,21.
	LIN	8,9. 29,6-7.
	NFK	1,51. 4,38-39. 13,7.

		20,31. 66,8.
	SFK	4,3; 6; 8. 6,19-22;
		227; 311. 8,66.
		21,30. 25,40. 43,7.
		62,5. 67,3-4.
		74,10.
over free man	NFK	9,88.
	SFK	4,4.
over Freeman	NFK	10,19.
	SFK	6,308.
over woman	SFK	66,13.
Value of	NFK	1,215. 15,16.
	SFK	3,44. 21,52.

Value of manor
without   NFK   1,135.

See also: Annexation; Borough; Church; Claim; Death; Force; Freeman; Gift; Go where he would; Grant; Jointly; Land; Patronage; Pledge; Sell; Third penny; Third/two thirds part; Withdraw.

JURISDICTION,	LIN	2,37. 8,39. 26,51.
free (frigesoca)		51,4. 59,4-5; 9; 12.

JURISDICTION, full (saca et soca)

Bishopric over, held by layman	SFK	6,191.
Church over, held by Bishop	LIN	C11.
City over, held by King	KEN	C6.
Forfeiture of thane having	DBY	S4.
	NTT	S4.
Hall with	LIN	3,7.

Held by
burgess by King's gift	KEN	D2.
Earl/Count	DBY	S6.
	LIN	T5.
	NTT	S6.
	SFK	3,13.
ecclesiastical body/person	CAM	14,59.
	DBY	B4; 11-12. S6.
	HUN	B3.
	KEN	7,30.
	LIN	C11. T5. 1,9. 5,3.
		8,12. 11,5. CN30.
		CK43.
	NFK	1,226. *8,89. 49,6.*
	NTT	B4. S6.
	SFK	2,9. *3,57.* 6,114;

116-117; 299. 7,1. 12,1; 4. 14,100; 111; 119; 121; 129; 154; 157-158; 163. 15,3; 5. 18,4. 19,19. 21,4; *8-9;* 14; 41; 47. 25,103. 27,3; 7. 28,1b. 31,*12;* 40. 34,1. 38,2. 41,10. 46,1. 53,1; 6. 54,3. 59,2. 66,9. 75,2.

	WAR	3,4.
	YKS	2N20.
free man	NFK	1,98.
	SFK	*2,2.* 26,1.
	WOR	C5.
Freeman	NFK	17,11.

King	HUN	19,12. D18.
	NFK	21,13. 22,6.
	NTH	39,15.
	NTT	B4.
	SFK	1,116. 26,12d.
King and Earl	NFK	10,79. 12,20. 55,1.
	SFK	1,77. 8,50. 16,11.
		25,53. 26,14.
		41,11.
lawman	LIN	C2-3. S5.
layman	CAM	14,18.
	DBY	S6.
	ESS	20,80.
	HUN	11,1-2. 19,11; 16.
		29,2. D11.
	KEN	D25.
	LEC	1,10. 2,4; 6. 3,12;

15-16. 13,3; 6. 17,21. 19,12-14; 17. 24,2. 28,5. 29,3; 14. 36,2. 40,26; 41. 43,11.

	LIN	T5. 1,9. 3,6. 14,9.

24,9; 59. 30,33. CS13; 18. CN28; 30. CW1; 9; 14. CK69.

	NFK	1,226. 8,93. 9,87;

167. 17,18. 19,19. 24,6. 31,6-7. 43,2.

	NTH	1,27. 2,1-2. 3,1.

4,1; 8-9; 11. 5,2-3. 16,2. 18,1. 22,9. 23,9. 35,9. 39,15. 44,2. 46,6. 48,4; 10-11. 56,15; 25; 36; 40; 47. 58,1.

	NTT	S6. 9,128. 20,6.
		30,39.
	STS	11,43-44. 12,8; 15;
		18-19; 23; 26-29.
	SFK	1,116; 118-119.

4,14. 6,112-114; 307-308. 7,3. 8,51. 15,1. 19,9. 25,32; 102. 33,1; 4. 34,2-3. 35,1-2. 39,16. 43,2-3.

	YKS	C36. 5E46. 6N3-4;
		7-8; 11; 29; 53.
		CE17.
layman from King	SFK	6,148.
moneyer	HEF	C9.
nun	LIN	1,9.
Queen	LIN	T5.
thane	CAM	29,8.
	HUN	19,32.
woman	LIN	1,9. 36,5.
	NTH	35,1j; 7.
	STS	12,27.

Hundred over, held by
Abbey	SFK	*21,52.* 59,2. 66,1.
King	NFK	1,149.
King and Earl	NFK	1,42.
King's manor	NFK	1,42.
layman	NFK	1,226.

Hundred, lying in	SFK	1,65. 29,1.
of manor/village	NFK	9,55. 24,6.

for holders of 30
acres   NFK   1,181.

Hundreds, 22, of	KEN	6,1.

Land holder
with, but no hall	NTT	9,113. 30,39.

with, has fines for
crime SRY 5,28.
with, except King's
tax HUN B3.
LIN C11.
without LEC 24,2.
STS 8,7.
Manor/village/land of
in manor etc
elsewhere LEC 15,16.
NFK 9,167. 43,2.
SFK 6,82. 26,12a.
YKS 2B18.
in manor elsewhere
for use of King/Earl SFK 6,82.
Manor, lying in
for holders of under
30 acres NFK 1,181.
Persons-burgess
over HUN B1-2; 12.
NFK 1,61.
SFK 1,116.
Full jurisdiction
over held by:-
King KEN C1.
SFK 1,116.
King and Earl NFK 1,61.
layman HUN B2.
SFK 25,52. 27,8.
Persons-free man
under SFK 3,4. 21,2. 25,50.
Full jurisdiction
over held by:-
Count SFK 26,12a.
ecclesiastical
body/person NFK *8,16; 46; 54.*
SFK *2,16. 5,2.* 6,301.
8,47; *81.* 10,1. 14,49; 52; 71; 97; 115. *16,20;*
27. 19,15. 21,*17; 22; 76;* 83. 31,40. *67,9;*
11-12; 15. 76,5.
King NFK 14,17.
King and Earl NFK 1,163.
SFK 26,13. 31,7.
King over all in
Hundred NFK 9,156.
layman NFK 1,226. 10,66. 28,1.
SFK 7,3. 8,47. 19,16-17.
25,42-49; 78; 111.
33,2; 4. 76,6.
woman SFK 16,10.
Full jurisdiction
over, lying in
Hundred SFK 8,53.
manor elsewhere NFK 1,225.
Persons-Freeman
under NFK 1,216.
SFK 29,1.
Full jurisdiction
over, held by:-
ecclesiastical
body/person NFK *24,4.*

SFK 14,2; 4-5; 7-9; 12;
15-16; 18; 23; 69-
70; 72; 93.
King BDF 17,2.
HRT 36,11.
NFK 22,7-8.
King and Earl NFK 1,154; 163.
layman SFK 28,2. 67,12.
Full jurisdiction
over, lying in
manor elsewhere NFK 1,223.
Persons-man
under LIN CW9; 15.
under, except for
tax etc LIN S5.
Full jurisdiction
over, held by:-
Abbey SFK 14,1; 3; 48; 106.
Earl for men
seeking his fold NFK 1,163.
King STS 11,12.
layman HUN D9.
SFK *66,4.*
Persons-small-holders
Full jurisdiction
over held by:-
Bishop,and over
those seeking the
fold NFK 10,25.
layman, and over
hall SFK 8,49.
Persons-woman
Full jurisdiction
held by Abbot
over:-
free man's wife SFK 14,68.
free woman SFK 11,4.
Remaining with lord
despite sale of land ESS 35,13-14.
SFK 9,2. 14,1; 3; 9; 11;
13-14; 16-17; 20-
22; 49-50; 78-96;
98-99; 101; 110.
Render of
by men WOR 2,21.
in manor WOR 2,67.
Residence without LIN C10.
Resources,over
arable land LIN 38,7.
dwelling, house,
residence, plot DBY B9-10; 14.
HUN B3-5; 14.
KEN C3-4.
LEC C7; 12-13.
LIN C6-9; 11. S5. 36,5.
NTT B14.
WAR B3.
fishery DBY B9.
lordship of hall SFK 31,42.
plot LIN CW18.
site (haga) except

K

KEEPER (custos) of
Hundred	ESS	32,25.
King's house	HAM	NF9,41.

KING

Aethelred
gift by	GLS	12,1.
time of	SHR	4,1,12.

Canute
land taken by	ESS	3,9.
time of	CHS	B13. 2,1.
	SHR	3c,2.
	WIL	2,1.

Caradoc destroys
villages	GLS	W2.

Edward
charter and seal of	KEN	5,149.
date of death	SHR	3d,7.
death of	ESS	24,23; 25; 29; 35.
illness of	WIL	1,3.
"illustrious" (gloriosus)	SFK	33,13. 34,5. 40,2.
judicial process at Christmas court of	SHR	3d,7.
kinsman (cognatus) of	HEF	1,41.
land held before reign of	DEV	2,2.
	SHR	4,26,3.
predecessors of	HRT	17,15.
sister of	SRY	14,1.
wronged by King Gruffydd	CHS	B7.

Gruffydd
customary dues	GLS	W4.
gift to and land recovered from	CHS	B7.
lays land waste	HEF	1,49.
payments to	CHS	FT3,7.

William
acquires England	DEV	1,23; 41.
barons sent by to inquire into lands	DEV	5,5.
battle, naval, against	ESS	6,9.
coming/arrival of	ESS	20,41; 52. 24,43; 48; 55; 59. 42,7. 52,2. 66,1. 79,1. 83,1.
	NFK	1,2; 4; 144. 15,1. 52,3.
	SFK	8,51. 18,1. 25,1. 76,4; 6.
coming/arrival of in England	BDF	32,1; 15. 46,1. 56,2-3.

	BKM	3a,1. 56,1.
	DEV	C3. 1,1-2. 19,35.
	ESS	1,25. 5,6; 12.
	GLS	2,4.
	KEN	D7.
	NFK	1,121; 230. 9,79. 10,77. 17,18.
	STS	11,37.
	WIL	25,23. 32,17.
coming to country/ district/"this land"	ESS	1,25; 27. 5,7. 6,9. 8,8. 20,56. 24,65-66. 30,16. 90,64-65.
	NFK	9,5. 10,67. 21,13-14.
	SFK	1,110.
conquers England	NFK	1,120.
crosses sea	ESS	3,11. 6,11.
	HAM	53,2.
	OXF	1,6.
daughter of, service to	HAM	67,1.
holds England	DEV	19,35.
London, in	ESS	30,18.
Normandy, goes to	GLS	78,9.
rebellion against	CAM	19,4.
siege of Sainte-Susanne, at	OXF	28,24.
son of, grant for soul of	HRT	36,19.
son of takes land away from Abbey	DOR	3,6.
throne, obtains	DEV	1,23.
visits St Edmund's Abbey	NFK	14,16.
Windsor, at	BRK	41,6.

KING

Obligations to,
exemption from	HRT	36,9.

Offence against
	ESS	83,1-2.

Officer of (legatus; minister)
	CHS	C18. S2,2.
	ESS	77,1.
	GLS	G4.
	HUN	B18.
	KEN	D13.
	LIN	12,83. CS6. CK25; 71.
	OXF	24,6. 58.

See also: Acquire; Administration; Alms; Almsman; Annexation; Arrest; Assessment; Assignment; Baker; Baron; Beadle; Bodyguard; Borough; Burgess; Canon; Cartage; Chamber; Chamberlain; Chaplain; Chattel; Church; Cite;

Performed as reeve
orders NTH 1,3.
See also: Citizen.
KINSMAN (cognatus; consanguineus)
Inheritance from LIN C16.

King Edward's HEF 1,41.
See also: Relations.
KITCHEN (coquina)
Archbishop's KEN 3,10.
KNIGHT (miles) – See Man-at-arms.

L

LABOUR service – See Service.
LADY of manor
Gift to by reeve HEF 1,6.
LAKE (lacus; mara) – See Mere.
LAMB (agnus)
Render of to sheriff WIL 24p.
See also: Customary due; Sheep.
LAMPREY (lampridula)
Render of by fishery SRY 8,14.
LAND
Abandoned GLS 44,2.
Bit of (parva) HAM S3,
SSX 10,1.
Claimed by none DEV *52,51.*
Close (hega) NFK 66,83.
Concealed BKM 18,3.
DEV *15,14.* 19,6.
ESS 90,41-42.
NFK 65,16.
Cultivated HUN B18.
LIN 3,1; 19. 22,33.
56,4. 57,57. 60,1.
CK2.
SHR 3h,1.
YKS C22. 1W53.
21W12-13. 22W6.
24W8; 11. 29W17.
uncultivated NTT 9,101.
YKS 28W13.
with manor
elsewhere LIN 56,4.
Custody/charge of DBY 1,29.
NFK 1,71.
NTT 10,23-24; 32; 48.
SFK 1,1; 96; 100; 120.
76,14.
WAR 14,6. 18,1.
WOR 8,12.
for King DBY 1,32; 35-36.
NFK 1,71; 127; 209.
66,84.
SFK 1,1; 61; 96-97; 100;
106; 120; 122.
74,15. 76,14.
Dispersed in other
land/divided OXF 9,7.
Free with the
jurisdiction ESS 30,6.
Handed over to chief
lord DEV 15,31.
Held against lord's
will (ab invito) SOM 10,2.
Held with assent/
command/permission ESS 83,2.

Bishop of SFK 29,9.
King, of BDF 57,1; 3.
CAM 5,24. 30,2. 32,5.
ESS 30,30.
NFK 17,24.
NTH 6a,27.
SOM 8,20. 27,3. 45,14.
SFK 21,29-30.
King's not obtained NFK 17,22.
Held in absolute
freedom HEF 1,47.
Held freely DBY B1.
DEV 2,10. 3,19; 22; 40.
15,*23;* 26-27; 38; 49-50; 79. 16,144. 17,17.
19,40. 20,1. 24,8. 25,*20;* 27. 28,16. 34,49;
55. 35,8. 38,1.
DOR 26,71. 55,34.
56,56.
ESS 1,20. 5,1. 18,36.
20,41. 21,9. 22,4. 24,65. 26,4. 30,40.
33,20. 34,28. 36,12. 37,2; 19. 44,3. 70,3.
75,1. 90,69-71.
GLS 1,4.
LEC 5,1. 13,19; 67; 72-
73. 14,28; 30-33. 15,16. 17,3-5; 8. 19,3; 12-
14; 19. 21,1-2. 29,2; 10; 14; 18; 20. 32,1-2.
38,1. 40,9; 14. 41,3. 44,5-6; 8; 10; 12.
NFK 10,56. 12,1. 64,1.
NTH 2,4; 7; 12. 4,2; 4-5;
7; 24-25; 30-31; 33-36. 5,1; 4. 13,1. 14,3.
18,2; 4-6; 9-14; 16; 22-25; 27-31; 33-35;
39; 42-49; 52; 54-58; 60-61; 63-67; 69; 72;
76-77; 79-81; 86; 88-89; 92; 96; 98. 19,1-
3. 21,1. 22,1; 8. 23,2; 5; 8; 10; 13; 15; 17-
18. 24,1. 25,2. 26,1; 6-7; 10-11. 27,1. 28,1.
29,1. 30,16; 18. 31,1. 33,1. 34,1. 35,3g; 10;
13; 15-16; 21-23; 26. 36,2; 4. 38,1. 39,17.
40,1; 4-6. 41,2-7; 9. 42,3. 43,2-4; 6-8; 10.
45,3. 46,7. 47,1c. 48,2-3; 12; 16-17. 51,1.
54,1-3. 55,3. 56,7-8; 23; 28-32; 38; 49; 51;
60; 66. 57,1-2. 58,2. 60,2.
OXF 6,16. 7,1; 3. 16,1.
18,1. 20,1. 23,1-2. 24,2; 5. 26,1. 27,2-3.
28,6. 33,1-2. 34,1. 35,3; 6-7; 9; 13; 19; 21-
22; 25. 40,1. 43,1-2. 44,1. 45,3. 47,1. 48,1.
49,1. 50,1. 52,1. 53,1-2. 54,1. 55,1-2.
56,1; 3-4. 58,17-19; 21; 23-25; 32; 37-38.
59,2.
SHR 3e,2. 4,3,69.
SOM *1,28.* 8,2; 20. 17,6.
35,4. 36,7; 13.
37,12. 45,3. 46,2.
STS 16,2-3.
SFK 12,5. 14,38. 25,55.

3,1; 3; 34; 46; 56; 85; 95; 100. 4,1; 6; 13-14;
31; 35; 38. 6,26; 43; 82-83; 85; 90; 112; 114;
129-130; 148-149; 156-157; 166; 171; 179;
191; 209; 247; 260; 262; 271; 275; 303-306;
308; 311. 7,3-4; 13; 15; 19; 37; 40; 42; 47;
56; 58; 60; 69; 76-77; 79-80; 86; 92. 8,7;
34-35; 46; 48; 55-56; 58. 12,6-7. 13,2.
14,6-7; 18-21; 23-24; 38; 42-43; 45; 48-49;
51-52; 62; 70; 72-77; 81-82; 87-88; 98; 101;
103-106; 120; 167. 15,1-2; 5. 16,10-11; 15;
41. 17,1. 18,1. 19,13-14. 20,1. 21,*1*; 5-6;
10-11; 16; 26; 28; 38-40; 42-43; 45; 80.
25,1-3; 5a; 35; 42; 55; 61; 76; 81; 84; 93.
26,9; 12d. 27,6; 13. 28,1a-b; 3. 29,1. 31,8-
9; 20; 41-42; 44-45. 32,19. 33,3-4; 6-7; 13.
34,2-3; 5; 13. 35,1; 5. 37,1. 38,6; 8; 11.
39,6. 41,1; 7; 14. 42,1-2. 43,2-4. 44,1-2.
45,2. 46,1; 3-4. 47,3. 48,1. 49,1. 53,2; 5.
54,1; 3. 57,1. 64,1. 66,1-2. 67,3; 19; 27;
29-32. 68,4-5.

        WAR 1,1-5; 7-9. 2,2. 3,1;
6. 4,1. 6,1; 5; 8; 10; 18. 10,1. 11,2. 12,8-
9. 14,1; 3. 15,1-2; 4; 6. 16,4; 16-18; 22-24;
42-44; 50-51. 17,1; 4; 6-9; 14-16; 49; 70.
18,3; 6-7; 13. 19,1. 22,6-9; 19; 25-26. 23,2;
4. 24,1. 26,1. 27,1; 3-6. 28,2; 9; 16; 19.
31,5-8. 37,6. 38,1. 39,4. 42,1-2. 44,7; 14.

        WIL 1,1-7; 9-13; 16-22.
2,1-2; 7; 9-10. 3,1-2. 7,1; 3-4; 6-7; 9; 11;
14; 16. 8,2; 6-7; 10-13. 10,2-3; 5. 11,1. 12,2-
6. 13,1-2; 5-7; 9. 14,1-2. 15,1-2. 16,1; 3; 6.
17,1. 18,1-2. 20,1; 6. 21,2. 23,9-10. 24,10;
15; 19; 22; 27; 33. 25,1; 22. 26,7; 9; 12-14;
20. 27,1; 15; 17; 23. 28,1; 11. 30,1. 31,1.
32,12. 33,1. 34,1. 36,2. 37,1-2; 7. 38,1.
41,5. 42,2; 8-10. 44,1. 47,1. 48,3-4; 8.
56,1-2; 4. 59,1. 60,1. 64,1. 66,7. 67,6; 9;
14; 32; 39; 86; 92; 94. 68,3.

        WOR 1,1a,c; 2; 6. 2,2;
5-7; 9; 15; 22; 25-26; 30-31; 34; 38; 48; 52;
62; 66; 68; 70-71; 77-79; 81-82; 84-85. 3,1;
3. 8,1; 8-9a,g; 11; 14; 19-20; 23; 26a. 9,1a;
2; 5a. 10,4; 10. 14,2. 15,4; 7; 9; 11-13.
16,2. 17,1. 18,2-4. 19,1-2; 10; 12-14. 23,1-
3; 5; 9-11. 24,1. 26,2; 4-6; 12-13. 28,1.

        YKS C23-24; 27-28; 30-
33; 35. 1Y1-7; 9-11; 14-15; 18-19. 1N1; 3;
5; 11; 38; 54; 56; 68; 105. 1W30. 2,1-2. 2B1-
3; 6-7; 9-11; 13; 17. 2N3-4; 14; 21; 24-25.
2W1; 3-4; 7-9; 12. 2E1-2; 14; 17. 3Y1-2;
4; 8-11; 15; 17-18. 4N1-3. 4E1-2. 5N1-9;
11; 14; 17-18; 26; 28-30; 32; 45-46; 49-50;
52-54; 58; 60; 63; 65; 67; 76. 5E7; 11; 17;
29; 34-36; 59; 65-66. 5W1-3; 5-8; 11; 14;
16-25; 32-34; 38. 6N1-13; 15-16; 18-21; 23-
39; 44-52; 55-88; 90-102; 104-107; 109;
112-113; 115-126; 130; 132; 134-141; 147;
151-152; 162. 6W1; 5. 6E1. 7E1. 8N2; 4-
5; 7-8; 10; 22-23. 8W1. 8E2; 5. 9W1-5; 12;
14-16; 24-26; 34-40; 45; 48-50; 54; 58-60;
64-67; 69-70; 75; 77-82; 85-87; 89-90; 92-

97; 101-103; 105; 107; 109-110; 112-114;
116; 118-124; 126-127; 129-130; 133-134;
137-138; 140; 142. 10W1-2; 4; 6; 8; 16; 18;
23; 26; 30-31; 35-36; 38; 41. 11E1. 11W1.
12W1; 27. 13W3-6; 9-12; 14; 16-18; 27-28;
30; 33-35; 37-38. 13E4-5; 13-16. 13N9; 13;
15; 17-18. 14E8; 11-13; 15-25; 28-30; 32-
34; 36; 38-39; 42-48; 50-54. 15E4; 8; 12-15;
17. 16E1; 4. 16N1-2. 16W1; 3; 5-6. 17W1.
18W2-3. 19W3. 20E1; 4. 21E2; 5-7; 9-11.
21W1-2; 5; 12-14. 22W2-3. 23N1-2; 4; 6-
9; 11; 13; 15-16; 18; 20; 25-27; 29-31; 34.
23E2-5; 8; 10; 12; 14; 18. 24W1; 6; 10; 12;
15-16; 18-19. 25W1-3; 6; 8-12; 14-16; 19-
20; 24; 29. 26E8; 10. 28W1; 5-6; 10-11; 13;
30-32; 35; 37. 29W1-3; 5-7; 9-10; 24; 26.
29E11; 28. 29N3; 5; 8.

LEASE (prestare; accommodare; adcensare) of

free man (adcensare)	NFK	1,131; 197; 226.
	SFK	25,53.
Land/property	CAM	*5,58.* 28,2.
	DBY	3,2.
	DOR	1,30. 34,8. 55,23.
	GLS	1,2. 34,8.
	HEF	1,4. 29,1.
	HRT	B5.
	KEN	1,1.
	LIN	60,1. 62,2. CW16. CK36.
	NFK	1,*211;* 217. 9,88. 17,18.
	SHR	4,14,12. 6,11.
	SOM	35,1.
	SFK	1,88. 4,15. 14,49.
	SRY	1,9. 4,2.
	WIL	7,5. 8,12. 32,11. 45,2.
	WOR	2,1; *8;* 20; 24; *56-60; 67; 82.* 10,13. 26,16.
	YKS	2E26. 29E20.
in exchange for writing services	WOR	*2,60.*
Manor to free man and wife	SFK	68,5.
through sheriff outside King's revenue	SRY	4,2.
LEAVE-holder could not with land	LEC	14,28.
	STS	11,10.
LEAVE land Holder could not because jurisdiction	NTH	4,29. 45,2.
elsewhere	NTH	43,11.
Holder could on payment to King	CHS	R1,40f.
Man so doing	LIN	CN9; 11; 13; 23.
	NFK	1,226. 10,83.

See also: Country; Flight; Transferability.

LEAVE his lord-
holder could not   HEF   34,1.
LEET (leta)   NFK   1,71. 15,1.
LEGAL and social matters – See Adjudge;
Adjudgment; Agreement; Assembly; Bequest;
Blood shedding; Borough; Burgess; Burning;
Cartage service; Cite; City; Claim; Combat;
Commendation; Commissioner; Compurgation;
County; Court; Crime/offence; Customary due;
Customs; Death; Death duty; Debt; Deliverer;
Delivery; Dispossession; Dispute; Division;
Dower; Evidence; Exile; Feud; Fine; Fold; Force;
Forfeiture; Freehold; Fugitive; Gift; Grant;
Guarantor; Heriot; Holding; Homage; Honour;
Hundred; Installer; Intestacy; Jointly; Judge;
Judgment; Judicial enquiry; Jurisdiction;
Jurisdiction, full; Jurors; Land; Law; Lawman;
Lease; Legal proceedings; Loan; Lordship; Manor;
Manor/village/land; Marriage; Measure; Mercy;
Narrative; Oath; Offender; Officer; Ordeal;
Outlaw; Patronage; Peace; Plea; Pledge; Port;
Possession; Postponement; Predecessor;
Protection; Protector; Prove; Punishment;
Purchase; Reeve; Relief; Re-purchase; Return;
Revenue; Riding; Right; Sale; Seal; Service;
Sheriff; Sheriffdom; Shire; Summons; Tenure;
Theft; Third/two thirds part; Third part; Third
penny; Title deeds; Trial; Truce; Wapentake;
Wardship; Warranty; Wich; Widow; Wife; Will;
Woman; Writ.
LEGAL proceedings
taken by lord's men   SHR   4,26,2.
See also: Adjudge; Claim; Judicial enquiry;
Narrative; Plea; Prove; Trial.
LET – See Lease; Reeve.
LEVY/King's levy
(scotum)   BRK   33,9.
                          KEN   3,2. 5,133. 7,28.
  city, of   ESS   B3.
  exemption from   KEN   7,28.
  not paid   KEN   P16. 3,3. 5,133.
See also: City; Dwelling; House.
LIFE tenure – See Tenure.
LIVERY – See Delivery.
LIVESTOCK (pecunia)
Acquired with land   HRT   31,8.
None   DOR   55,32.
                          WIL   68,12.
                          WOR   8,25.
See also: Destruction; Goods; Pasture; Stock;
Value.
LOAD (carricare) – See Holiday.
LOAD (summa) – See Corn; Manload; Packhorse;
Packload.
LOAF (panis)
Render of   GLS   W5. 1,1-2; 7.
See also: Dog.
LOAN (accommodare)
Of land   SRY   1,9.
See also: Lease.
LODGING

(hospitatio;
hospitium)   BRK   1,42.
                          KEN   2,16.
In city from King's
lordship   GLS   G4.
Small   YKS   C11.
LODGING house
(mansio ad hospitia)   YKS   C15-17.
LOOK after (servare) – See Custody.
LORD (dominus)
Man not able to have
any save King   KEN   5,1.
See also: Assembly; Borough; Burgess; Cite;
Claim; Command; Commendation;
Crime/offence; Customary due; Delivery;
Dispossession; Freeman; Go away; Go where he
would; Grant; Grant and sell; Hall; Jurisdiction;
Jurisdiction, full; Land; Landholder; Leave; Legal
proceedings; Man; Meadow; Mill; Ordeal;
Outlaw; Pasturage; Patronage; Plea; Protector;
Reaping; Restoration; Riding man; Sale; Seek; Sell;
Separated; Tax; Tenure; Theft; Turn; Villager;
Withdraw; Woodland.
LORDSHIP (dominium)
Animals in   ESS   1,1-2; 9; 11; 21; 26-
                          27; 29. 2.1. 3,1; 3. 6,4-5; 8. 10,5. 18,4; 22.
                          20,26; 34; 39; 48. 24,59. 25,22. 26,1. 32,8;
                          12. 42,1. 46,2. 71,4.
                          HAM   1,45.
                          NFK   8,34. 9,32; 168.
                          10,3. 14,41. 17,18.
                          26,2.
                          SFK   1,97. 3,9; 94.
                          16,29. 21,16.
Borough in   DEV   1,1-2. 17,1.
Burgess in   NFK   1,66.
                          NTH   B1.
                          SHR   C7.
                          STS   B1.
                          SFK   1,97; 122b.
                          SSX   10,1. 12,1.
Castle in   CHS   FT1,1.
Church in   DBY   B1.
                          NTT   B4.
City in   HEF   C14.
City payments in   WOR   C2.
Dwelling in   STS   B1.
                          SFK   31,55.
Fishery in   GLS   1,56; 64.
                          NFK   1,210.
Forest in   OXF   1,10.
Forfeitures, three in   HEF   C13.
                          SHR   C2.
Free man in   ESS   39,11-12.
                          NFK   8,8. 19,6. 66,69.
                          SFK   3,16; 62; 94. 6,252.
                          7,3. 8,59. 25,60. 31,1-2; 43; 45; 48; 51.
                          36,15. 38,17. 52,7; 9. 53,4. 67,10; 12.
Freeman in   LIN   S4.
                          SFK   3,58. 6,171; 191.
                          31,42; 44; 49.

67,12.

Grange in SFK 1,122b.
Hall of SFK 1,97. 31,42.
House in DEV 3,1.
SFK 14,167.
WAR B1.
WOR 2,49.
Hundred in WOR 2,1.
King's
  land of ESS 30,39.
  GLS G2.
  WIL 25,23.
  manor of WOR C2.
  village of CAM 1,2-6; 9.
Land
  given out of KEN 7,17.
  held without KEN 5,181.
  in more than one NTH 48,11; 16.
  part of lord-ship SFK 6,31-32; 41; 55;
  manor/village/hall 204; 235; 294. 7,74.
  elsewhere 8,52. 16,33; 48.
    21,14; 37. 36,16.
    41,8. 52,9. 66,13;
    15.
  taken away from SFK 3,57.
    WIL 8,12.
Land/manor/village BDF 2,1. 3,1-2; 7; 11.
in 5,1. 6,2-3. 8,1-3;
  7-9. 9,1. 10,1. 11,1. 12,1. 18,1. 19,1. 20,1.
  21,1-2; 4; 6. 23,3-5; 10-12; 15. 24,14-15;
  27. 25,9-10; 13; 15. 27,1. 30,1. 32,4; 13.
  33,1. 34,1. 35,1. 36,1. 39,1. 40,3. 41,1-2.
  47,1-2; 4. 48,1-2. 49,1-4. 51,2. 52,1. 53,5;
  20; 29. 54,3. 55,2; 6.
    BRK 1,1-12; 14-29; 31-
  41; 44. 2,2. 3,1. 5,1. 7,6; 18; 28; 39; 44.
  10,2. 28,2.
    BKM 1,3-5; 7. 2,1-3.
  3,1-2. 3a,1. 4,13; 18; 20; 39. 5,2; 6; 12-14;
  20. 7,1-2. 8,1-3. 9,1. 10,1. 12,3; 6-7; 29;
  35. 14,5; 7; 9; 13; 21; 23; 38. 15,1. 16,5-6;
  9. 17,17; 27. 19,1-2. 20,1. 21,1; 3-4; 6.
  22,1. 23,7; 12; 14. 24,1. 25,1. 26,3-4; 8.
  27,1-2. 28,2-3. 29,1-3. 31,1. 35,2. 37,1-2.
  38,1. 43,1-2; 9; 11. 44,2-3. 45,1. 46,1. 48,1.
  51,1. 52,1-2. 55,1. 56,1-2. 57,3-4; 17.
    CAM 1,2; 4-5; 18. 2,1-2;
  4. 3,3. 5,1-4; 6; 9; 12; 14-15; 18; 20-21; 23;
  25; 27-29; 31; 34; 36; 38-39; 41-42; 44-48;
  50-53; 55; 57; 59-63. 6,1; 3. 7,2-11. 8,1.
  9,1-3. 10,1. 11,1-4; 6. 13,1-2; 4; 8-9; 11.
  14,1-2; 7; 11; 13-14; 27; 37; 44; 48; 53; 55;
  59; 67; 71; 74; 78. 15,1. 16,1. 17,1. 18,3.
  21,3; 5. 22,6. 25,9-10. 26,7; 17-18; 26-27;
  30; 33; 42; 56. 28,2. 29,3; 5; 7; 9. 31,1-2.
  32,4-5; 7-8; 23; 33; 40-42. 35,1-2. 38,1-3.
  39,2. 40,1. 41,1; 4; 7.
    CHS 1,1; 22; 34. FD1,1.
    R1,45. R2,1. R3,1.
    R7,1.
    CON 1,1-12; 14-17. 4,1;

3; 16. 5,25,4.
    DEV 1,1-2; 19; 21; 34-
35; 48. 2,2. 3,11-12; 30; 41-42; 50; 54; 64;
68; 98-99. 5,9. 7,1. 14,1. 15,22-23; 34; 46;
62; 78. 16,30; 62; 77; 87; 149; 151; 169.
17,62; 71; 77; 81; 85; 87; 90; 94; 96; 98-
101; 104-105. 19,36. 20,16. 21,13. 24,8; 15;
29. 25,4; 20; 22. 32,9. 34,48. 35,6; 17-18.
36,2; 6. 38,1. 41,1. 42,5. 43,1. 47,14. 48,1;
5; 9. 51,7. 52,46.
    DOR 1,7; 9-21; 24; 26-27;
30-31. 2,2-3; 6. 3,1-8; 10-11; 13; 18. 4,1.
5,1. 6,1; 3-4. 8,1; 3-5. 9,1. 10,2-3; 6. 11,1;
3-6; 10-17. 12,1-5; 7-12; 14; 16. 13,1-4; 6.
14,1. 15,1. 16,1-2. 17,1-2. 19,1-10; 12-14.
20,1-2. 21,1. 22,1. 23,1. 24,4. 25,1. 26,20.
28,1-2. 30,1. 31,1-2. 32,1. 34,8-9; 11.
36,3. 38,2. 40,8. 49,12. 55,1; 23; 34; 44.
56,19.
    ESS 1,1; 9; 13. 3,9-10;
12-14. 7,1. 10,1-2. 18,2-3; 15-17. 20,1; 7-
10; 16; 19; 23; 25; 37-38; 43; 45-46; 59; 63-
64; 71; 77-78; 80. 21,7. 22,1; 5-6; 17; 22.
23,1-2; 12; 16; 27; 30; 39-40; 43. 24,10; 13;
15-18; 20-24; 49; 53; 57; 59; 61. 25,4-5; 13;
15; 18-19; 22; 25-26. 27,3-4; 8-10; 14.
28,11; 13. 29,1-4. 30,1; 5; 18; 25; 27; 34;
39; 42; 45. 31,1. 32,1; 8-10; 16-17; 19-21;
27; 30; 38. 33,3; 6-7; 12; 19-20. 34,4; 8; 11-
12; 16; 18-20; 23-25; 31-32; 35. 35,1-2; 5-
6; 8-10. 36,1; 5-6; 9-11. 37,3; 9; 11-12; 16.
38,2; 4-8. 39,1-2; 4-5; 7-9. 40,9. 41,3.
42,2-4; 7. 43,3. 44,3. 45,1. 48,2. 49,1; 3.
52,1-2. 53,1. 54,1-2. 56,1. 68,7. 71,2; 4.
90,11. B4.
    GLS G2. W11. 1,2; 24;
50; 53; 55-56; 61-62. 2,10. 3,1. 11,10. 26,4.
39,6; 17. 66,5.
    HAM 1,1-2; 8-9; 21; 25;
27-28; 30; 36; 39; 41-44; 47; W1-8. 2,1; 3;
5-6; 8-12; 14-15; 20; 25. 3,19. 6,13; 16-17.
21,6. 23,63. NF2,2-3. NF3,11. IoW1,1-8.
IoW2,1. IoW6,1; 21. IoW7,3.
    HEF 1,3; 10a; 55. 8,2.
    10,41.
    HRT 1,1-6; 9; 18. 2,3.
3,1. 4,2-3; 22. 5,8; 10. 7,1-2. 8,1-3. 9,1; 4-
5; 7; 10. 10,1-11; 15-16; 18-20. 11,1. 12,1.
13,1-5. 14,1-2. 15,1; 3; 10. 16,2; 9-10. 17,1;
3; 12-13; 15. 22,1. 23,2-4. 24,3. 25,2. 26,1.
28,4. 29,1. 30,1-2. 31,3; 7. 32,1-2. 33,2-3;
17-18. 34,7; 12-13; 15-16. 35,1-2. 36,7; 11;
14-15. 37,8; 14; 21-22. 41,1. 42,1-2. 42a,1.
43,1. 44,1.
    HUN 2,9. 4,1-3. 6,1-2; 4-
9; 11; 13; 21. 8,2. 19,27. 20,1-4; 6. D8.
    KEN 1,3. 2,3-4; 8-11; 14;
16-23; 25-26. 5,120-122; 124; 128-129.
9,10. 13,1.
    LEC 1,3-4; 11. 13,1.
    14,1-2; 6.

LIN   C12. S+. T2. 8,7.
12,47-50. 13,1. 26,33. 27,50. 60,1. 67,7;
21. CS21. CN6. CW10. CK13.

MDX   2,1-2. 3,1; 3; 5;
7-9; 12; 14; 16; 18-25; 29-30. 4,1; 3-10; 12.
5,1. 6,1. 7,5-6. 8,4-6. 9,1; 7-9. 10,1. 11,1.
12,1-2. 13,1. 16,1. 17,1. 18,1-2. 20,1. 22,1.
24,1. 25,1.

NFK   1,66. 4,27; 51. 8,56;
108. 9,1; 13; 67-68; 97; 149; 233. 10,1-3; 5-
6; 8; 10; 14-15; 30. 14,21; 26; 43. 15,10.
16,4. 17,18; 51. 19,1; 3-5; 28. 21,2; 36.
26,4. 33,3. 34,2; 5. 35,11. 50,10. 53,1.
57,2. 64,7. 66,59; 62.

NTH   1,5; 9; 32. 18,1; 5;
7; 9-11. 19,2. 23,17. 25,3. 26,2. 35,1; 6-7.
39,18. 41,1-2. 42,1; 4-5. 45,1. 46,4. 48,11.
49,1. 51,1. 56,7; 20a.

NTT   5,4.

OXF   1,6. 6,1a,c; 5-6; 16.
7,2-3. 9,1-3; 9a-b. 10,1. 17,1. 28,3-4; 6.
29,3-4; 13; 18. 35,7. 51,1. 58,1; 25. 59,17-
18; 23-24.

RUT   R2.

SHR   4,1,2-3; 5; 35; 37.
4,4,20. 4,11,4. 4,19,1. 5,4.

SOM   1,11-19; 21-24; 27-
29; 32-33; 35. 2,1; 10-12. 4,1. 5,4; 6; 9; *37;
43; 64.* 6,1-17. 7,2-3; 5-7; 9; 13. 8,1-4; *5;*
6;7; 11; 13; *14;* 16-18; 21-33; 35. 9,2-7; *8.*
10,1-2. 11,1. 12,1. 13,1. 14,1. *16,2.* 17,1;
4-5; 7-8. 18,4. 19,1-2; 5; 7; 9-10; *14; 19;
22; 26;* 50; *83;* 86. 20,1; *2-3.* 21,1-2; *4; 10;
17; 28; 31; 33; 39-40; 54; 62; 67-68; 75-77;
87-88. 22,9; 21; 23.* 24,9; 11; 17; *24; 32.
25,1; 6; 9; 18; 22; 28; 30; 32; 35; 52.* 26,2.
27,3. 35,2; 7. 41,2. 45,17. 47,7; *16.*

STS   2,11.

SFK   1,12; 78; 85; 88; 94;
97; 101; 122b. 2,11-14. 3,1; 3; 10; 16; 34;
44; 46; 57-59; 63; 82; 86; 89; 91-93; 95; 97;
103. 5,2. 6,5-7; 11; 31-32; 41-42; 54-56; 71;
101-102; 123; 125; 132; 137; 142; 177; 191;
204; 216; 235; 264; 266-267; 294; 300. 7,3;
72; 74; 143-144; 149-150. 8,7; 27; 41; 52;
55; 80; 82. 13,2. 14,26; 42; 49; 63-64; 66;
144; 153. 16,33; 48. 21,4; 14; 18; 20; 23-
24; 28; 37; 40; 44; 83; 97; 105. 25,38; 53;
74. 26,12d. 27,11-12. 29,2-6; 11. 30,1-2.
31,1-2; 7-8; 13a-14; 18; 21; 26; 34; 37; 39;
41; 43-45; 48-49; 51; 53; 58-59. 32,4.
33,10. 34,8; 12-13; 15; 17-18. 36,8; 15-16.
38,7; 10; 13; 17; 19. 39,5. 40,3. 41,1-2; 7-
8; 10; 14; 18-19. 43,9. 44,1; 3. 52,9; 11.
53,4. 62,3. 66,13; 15. 67,3; 7; 10-15. 68,5.
76,20.

SRY   1,2-3; 6-14. 2,1; 3.
3,1. 5,1a,f; 2-3. 8,14; 21. 19,1; 16; 39; 47.
33,1.

SSX   1,1-2. 2,5-7. 3,1-4;
6-8. 5,1. 8,3; 11; 16. 9,1; 4; 11; 13-15; 38.

10,2-3; 22; 27-28; 43; 50; 59; 90; 93. 11,3;
6-7; 30; 37-38; 55; 59. 12,3-6; 49. 13,7; 9;
30; 52.

WAR   27,1-2.

WIL   1,5; 10-22. 2,1-12.
3,1-5. 4,1-3. 5,1-7. 6,1-2. 7,1-4; 6-12; 14-
16. 8,3-13. 10,1-5. 11,1. 12,1-6. 13,1-2; 5;
7-12; 14; 16-20. 14,1-2. 15,1-2. 16,1-3; 6-
7. 17,1. 18,1-2. 19,1. 20,1-2; 5-6. 21,1-3.
22,3-6. 23,1-2; 4-5; 7-10. 24,1; 3; 7; 10; 13;
18-19; 21-25; 27-28; 31; 33; 36; 38-39; 41.
25,1; 5; 8; 11; 22-23; 27. 26,1; 3-5; 7; 9-14;
18; 22. 27,1-5; 7-20; 23-26. 28,1-3; 7-9;
11-13. 29,2; 6-9. 30,1-2; 4-7. 31,1. 32,1; 4-
5; 7-10; 12-13; 15; 17. 33,1. 34,1. 36,1-2.
37,1-2; 7-8; 11-12; 15. 38,1. 39,2. 40,1.
41,1-3; 5; 7; 10. 42,1-2; 8; 10. 43,2. 44,1.
45,1; 3. 47,1. 48,1; 6-11. 49,1-3. 50,2; 4.
52,1. 53,1. 54,1. 55,1. 56,1-2; 4. 58,1-2.
59,1-2. 60,1. 61,1. 63,1. 67,1.

WOR   1,1a; 2. 2,1; 4-6; 11;
15; 18; 22; 31; 38; 48; 68; 72. 8,1; 7-9a; 11;
13; 21. 9,1b,d; 4-5a.

YKS   C37. 1Y15; 19.
2B1. CE13; 20-23; 26; 30. CW8.

Man in   ESS   1,20.

    HAM   S1.

Mill in   BKM   14,46.

    DEV   23,22.

    NFK   20,22.

    STS   1,31.

Plough in   BDF   1,1a,c; 2a-b; 3; 5.
2,3; 9. 3,4-5; 10; 12. 4,1. 5,2. 8,5. 15,2; 5-
7. 16,1-4; 7-9. 18,2; 4; 6. 21,5; 9; 12-13;
17. 22,1. 23,17-23; 26-27; 29-30; 36-42; 45;
49. 24,1; 3; 5; 8-10; 16-19; 22; 24; 29. 25,1-
2; 4; 7; 11. 26,1-3. 29,1. 31,1. 32,1-3; 5-6;
8-9; 16. 33,2. 34,2. 37,1. 39,2. 42,1. 45,1.
46,2. 53,1; 3-4; 8; 11; 13; 15; 17; 26. 54,2;
4. 55,3; 7; 13. 57,5.

BRK   1,1; 4-12; 15-41; 44;
47. 2,1-3. 3,1-3. 4,1. 6,1. 7,1-4; 6-8; 10;
12-13; 15; 17; 20-21; 23-25; 27-28; 30; 33-
40; 42-45; 47. 8,1. 10,1-2. 11,1. 12,1. 14,1.
15,1-2. 16,1-3. 17,3; 5-6; 8. 18,1-2. 19,1.
20,2-3. 21,1-11; 14-20. 22,1-3; 5-12. 23,1-
3. 24,1. 25,1. 26,1; 3. 27,1-3. 28,1; 3. 29,1.
30,1. 31,1-3; 5-6. 32,1. 33,2-4; 6-8. 34,4.
35,1-3; 5. 36,1-2; 4-6. 37,1. 38,1-6. 39,1.
40,1-2. 41,1-6. 42,1. 43,1-2. 44,1-5. 45,2.
46,1-4; 6-7. 47,1. 48,1. 49,1-3. 50,1. 51,1.
52,1. 53,1. 54,1-4. 55,1-4. 56,1. 57,1. 58,1.
59,1. 60,1. 61,1-2. 62,1. 63,1-5. 64,1.
65,1; 3-5; 7; 9-12; 15; 18-20.

BKM   B2. 1,1-2; 6. 3a,2;
4. 4,1-2; 5-6; 10; 12; 14-16; 19; 21-23; 27;
29-38; 40; 42. 5,1; 3; 5; 7-10; 15. 6,1-2.
12,2; 8; 12; 30-31; 36-37. 13,1-2; 4. 14,2-
4; 6; 8; 10-12; 14; 16-17; 20; 22; 24-27; 29;
31-32; 34-37; 39-43; 45-46; 48-49. 15,2.
16,1-3; 7-8; 10. 17,2; 4-7; 9-10; 16; 18-19;

22-26. 18,1-3. 19,3-4; 6-7. 21,5; 7-8. 23,2-
5; 8; 16; 18; 22; 26; 29; 31-32. 24,3. 25,3.
26,9. 29,4. 32,1. 34,1. 35,1. 36,1. 39,1-2.
40,1. 41,1-2; 4; 6. 43,3-8; 10. 44,4. 47,1.
49,1. 50,1. 53,1; 3; 8. 57,1; 13.
　　　　　CAM　1,1-9; 11-12; 17.
2,3. 3,4; 6. 4,1. 5,5; 8; 10-11; 13; 49. 7,2.
12,1; 4. 13,6. 14,8-9; 15; 17; 19; 23; 26;
28-29; 31; 36; 49-50; 58; 60-63; 65; 67-70;
73; 80-81. 15,2-4. 17,2; 4. 18,1-2; 6-8.
20,1. 21,1; 8. 22,3-4; 7-8. 23,6. 24,1. 25,3;
7. 26,16; 36; 43; 46-47; 49; 51; 53. 28,1-2.
29,1-2; 8; 10. 30,1. 31,3; 7. 32,1-2; 6; 12;
14; 16; 20-22; 24; 30-32; 34; 37-40; 43.
37,2. 38,5. 41,9; 16. 44,1-2
　　　　　CHS　B3-5; 9. A2-6; 9-
11; 15-18. 1,1; 3-4; 8; 13-15; 22-23; 25; 34-
35. 2,1-8; 14-15; 17-19; 22-25; 29. 3,1-3; 6-
7. 4,1. 5,1-2; 5-7; 9-10; 12. 6,1. 7,2-4. 8,1-
2; 6-10; 16-17; 19; 21; 24-26; 28-31; 35-37;
40; 42. 9,1; 4-7; 9; 17-20; 24-26. 10,3-4.
13,1-2. 14,1; 3; 6; 11. 15,1. 16,2. 17,1; 3;
8. 18,2-3. 19,1. 20,1; 11. 21,1. 23,1. 24,1-
3; 9. 25,2-3. 26,6-7; 9; 12. 27,3. FD1,1.
FD5,2. FD6,1. FT1,1. FT2,1-4; 6-7; 12;
14-15. FT3,1; 7. R1,43; 45. R3,1. R5,5.
R6,5. R7,1.
　　　　　CON　2,1-11. 3,1-3. 4,5;
7; 10. 5,1,1-13; 22. 5,2,1-2; 11-13. 5,3,1;
3; 8. 5,15,6.
　　　　　DBY　1,9; 16; 20; 27-28;
36-38. 3,1-7. 4,1. 5,4. 6,4-7; 12; 14; 17-18;
24-28; 31-32; 34-35; 37-40; 43; 45-47; 51;
54-55; 57; 62-67; 69; 76; 78; 80; 83; 85-86;
88; 90-92; 94-99. 7,1; 3-4; 6-9. 8,1-3; 5.
9,1; 3-4. 10,1; 4-5; 7; 10-11; 19; 21-23; 25.
11,1-2; 4. 12,2; 4. 13,1. 14,1-4; 6-7. 16,8.
17,6; 10; 15.
　　　　　DEV　1,3-8; 10-18; 20;
23-34; 36-47; 49-71. 2,4-7; 11-19; 21-24.
3,4-9; 13-14; 16; 18-26; 28; 30-31; 33; 36-
40; 43-47; 49; 52-53; 56-63; 65-67; 69-70;
73-74; 76-77; 80-81; 83-88; 90-93; 96-97.
4,1. 5,1-2; 4-8; 10-14. 6,1-5; 7-12. 7,2-4.
8,1. 9,1. 10,1-2. 11,1-3. 12,1. 13,1. 13a,2-
3. 15,4-5; *6;* 8-14; 17-20; 26-27; 32; 35-45;
47-50; *51;* 56-58; 61; 64; 66-67; 70; *71;* 72-
76; 77. 16,3-9; 11-15; 17-24; 26-27; 29; 31-
37; 39-40; 42-45; 47-48; *50;* 51; 55-57; 63;
65; 69-71; 73; 75-76; 78; 80; 83-86; 89; *90;*
93-96; *100-101; 103;* 106-114; 118-119; 121-
122; 128-131; 133; 136; 138-143; *145-147;*
148; 150; 152-153; 155; 159; *160;* 162-166;
170-173; *175;* 176. 17,3-10; 13-17; *19;* 21-
22; *25;* 26; 29-30; 32-33; 36-38; 41-42; 45-
46; 48-51; *52;* 56; *58;* 59-60; 64; 67; 69; 73;
79; 92; *93; 105; 107.* 18,1. 19,4-8; *9;* 10-
12; 15-17; 20-21; 25-26; 28-31; 35; 37-40;
44; 46. 20,1; 3-4; *6;* 10-11; *12;* 13-15. 21,1-
4; 6-7; 9; *10;* 12; 14-17; *18;* 19-21. 22,1.
23,2-3; 5-7; 9-12; 14-22. 24,1; 3-6; 8; 14;

17; 19; 21; 23; 30. 25,1; *2; 3;* 5-6; 9; 13-16;
17; 23-24. 27,1. 28,1-11; 13; 15-16. 29,2-
6. 30,1; 3. 31,1-2. 32,1-7; 10. 33,1-2. 34,1-
2; 6; 8; 10; 12; 14; 16; 18-19; 21-23; 25; 27-
31; 39-41; 43-44; 49-52; 55. 35,1-2; 4-5; *8;*
9-10; *20; 22;* 26; 29. 36,1; 10; *17;* 19-20.
37,1. 38,1-2. 39,1; 4-5; 12; 14-15; 17-21.
40,4-5; 7. 42,1; 6; 10; 16-17; 20; 23. 43,2-
3; 5. *46,2.* 47,1; 5; 11. 48,7-8; *11.* 49,1-2.
50,1; *5.* 51,2-3; 5; 8; 10-13; 16. 52,10; 13;
18; 34; 52-53.
　　　　　DOR　1,1-6; 8. 2,1-2; 4; 6.
3,1; 9; 15. 5,2. 8,2-3. 11,2. *13,5.* 24,5. 26,1;
3-4; 6; 8-9; 14-15; 18; 26; 28; 32-33; 44-
46; 49-52; 59; 61-64; 66-67. 27,1; 3-7; 9;
11. 28,4. 29,1. 30,3-4. 32,2; 5. 33,1-2; 4.
34,1-2; 5-8; 10; 12-13; 15. 35,1. 36,1-2; 4-
11. 37,1; 5; 13. 38,1. 39,1-2. 40,1-3; 9.
41,1-4. 42,1. 43,1. 44,1. 45,1. 46,1-2. 47,1;
3-9. 48,1-2. 49,1-6; 9-11; 14-16. 50,4.
51,1. 52,1-2. 53,1-2. 54,1; 3-6; 8-9; 11-12.
55,2-6; 8-11; 16-17; 19-20; 22; 24-31; 33;
35-36; 38; 40-41; 45. 56,1-2; 7-9; 14; 17;
28-29; 31; 35-36; 38; 44-45; 48; 57-59; 62.
57,9-11; 13; 15. 58,1-2.
　　　　　ESS　1,1-4; 8-9; 11-13;
19; 21-24; 26-30. 2,2-5; 7-9. 3,1-3; 5-16.
4,1-2; 4-6; 8-12; 14-15; 17. 5,1-5; 7; 9-12.
6,1; 5; 8-12; 14-15. 7,1. 8,1-11. 9,1-2; 7-9;
11; 13-14. 10,1-5. 11,1-4; 6-8. 12,1. 13,1-
2. 14,2-5; 7. 15.1-2. 16,1. 17,1. 18,1-5; 11;
14-15; 17-18; 22; 24; 27; 29-30; 34; 36-38;
40-41; 43. 19,1. 20,1-4; 6-10; 12-13; 15-16;
19-28; 30; 32-33; 36-41; 43-46; 48-52; 54-
59; 62-72; 74-75; 77-80. 21,1-4; 8. 22,3-11;
15; 18-20; 22. 23,1-4; 6-8; 10; 28; 30-32;
38-42. 24,1-6; 8; 10-11; 13; 16-26; 28-31;
33; 35-36; 42; 44-46; 49; 53-54; 57; 60-61;
64. 25,1-6; 11-21; 23; 25-26. 26,1-5. 27,1-
5; 8; 10-14; 16. 28,2; 5-9; 11-13; 15-17.
29,1-5. 30,1-7; 9-11; 14; 16-20; 22-24; 27-
40; 44-46; 48; 50-51. 31,1. 32,1-9; 13-19;
21; 23-26; 28; 30; 32-36; 38-42; 44-45. 33,1;
3-8; 11-20; 22-23. 34,4-12; 14-16; 18-23;
26-27; 29-30; 33-37. 35,1-5; 8-13. 36,1-3;
5-9; 12. 37,1-4; 7; 9-12; 14-17; 20. 38,1-8.
39,1-5; 7-9. 40,1-4; 6; 8-9. 41,3; 9-12. 42,2-
4; 6-9. 43,1; 3-6. 44,1-3. 45,1. 46,1-2.
47,1-3. 48,1-2. 49,1; 3. 50,1. 51,2. 52,1-3.
53,1-2. 54,1-2. 55,1. 56,1. 57,1; 3; 5-6.
58,1. 59,1. 60,1-2. 61,1-2. 64,1. 65,1. 66,1.
68,4. 69,2. 71,2; 4. 72,2-3. 74,1. 76,1.
77,1. 78,1. 79,1. 81,1. 82,1. 83,1. 84,1-2.
86,1. 90,4; 7; 22-23; 26; 29-30; 35; 50; 53;
57-58; 65. B1.
　　　　　GLS　W13; 15-16; 18-19.
1,1; 3; 7; 9-17; 20-27; 34-35; 37; 43; 45; 47-
49; 53-55; 57-62; 65-67. 2,1-8; 10-13. 3,1-
5; 7. 4,1. 5,1-2. 6,1-9. 7,1-2. 8,1. 9,1. 10,1-
11; 13. 11,1-12; 14. 12,1-9. 13,1. 14,1-2.
15,1. 16,1. 17,1. 18,1. 19,2. 20,1. 21,1.

22,1. 23,1-2. 24,1. 26,1-4. 27,1. 28,1; 4.
29,1. 30,1-3. 31,1; 7-11. 32,1-7; 11; 13.
33,1. 34,1-11. 35,1. 36,1; 3. 37,1-3; 5.
38,1-4. 39,1-9; 12-21. 40,1. 41,1-5. 42,1-
3. 43,1-2. 44,1. 45,1-3; 5-6. 46,1-3. 47,1.
48,1-3. 49,1. 50,1-3. 52,1-7. 53,1-11. 54,1-
2. 55,1. 56,1-2. 57,1. 58,1-2; 4. 59,1. 60,1-
7. 61,1-2. 62,3-6. 63,1-4. 64,1-3. 65,1.
66,1; 3-6. 67,1-7. 68,1-10; 12. 69,1-7.
70,1-2. 72,1-3. 73,1-3. 74,1. 75,1. 76,1.
78,1; 5-13; 15-17.

HAM   1,1-3; 8-47; W1;
W3-4; W8-15; W19; W21. 2,1-11; 13-15;
19-25. 3,1-11; 13-16; 18; 20-22; 24. 4,1.
5,1. 6,1-9; 11-17. 7,1. 9,2. 10,1. 11,1. 13,1.
14,2-6. 15,1-4. 16,1-6. 17,1; 3. 18,1. 19,1.
20,1. 21,1-7; 9-10. 22,1. 23,1; 4-36; 38-42;
44-53; 55-60; 64-65; 68. 24,1. 25,1. 26,1.
27,1-2. 28,2; 5-7; 9. 29,1; 3; 8-9; 11-13; 15-
16. 30,1. 31,1. 32,1-2; 4. 33,1. 34,1. 35,1-
9. 36,1-2. 37,1-2. 38,1. 39,2-4. 40,1. 41,1.
42,1. 43,1; 3-4. 44,1; 3-4. 45,1; 3; 6-7.
46,2. 47,3. 48,1. 49,1. 50,1-2. 51,1-2. 52,1.
53,1-2. 54,1. 55,1-2. 56,1-3. 57,1-2. 58,1.
60,1-2. 61,1. 62,2. 63,1. 64,1. 65,1. 66,1.
67,1. 68,1-3; 5-7; 10. 69,1-8; 14-20; 22-24;
26-29; 32-33; 36; 41-42; 45; 47-48; 52.
NF3,8; 11-13. NF9,13; 34; 37-38; 40; 44.
NF10,1; 4. IoW1,1-5; 7-8; 10; 12-13.
IoW2,1. IoW3,1. IoW6,3-6; 8-9; 12-16;
18; 20-21. IoW7,3-8; 11; 13-14; 17; 22-23.
IoW8,1; 3-9; 11. IoW9,1-7; 9-13; 18-21;
23-24.

HEF   1,1-2; 4-10a,c; 11;
13; 15-18; 20-24; 26-34; 39-48; 53-54; 56;
60-62. 2,4-21; 23-40; 42; 44-46; 48-51; 56-
58. 5,1-2. 6,3-6; 9. 7,1-4; 6-9. 8,1; 3; 5-8;
10. 9,1-7; 9-11; 15-19. 10,1; 4-6; 8-9; 11;
14; 16-17; 19-21; 24-37; 40; 42; 44; 46-51;
54; 56-61; 63-64; 66-70; 73-74. 11,1. 12,2.
13,1. 14,1-6; 8; 10; 12. 15,1-2; 5-10. 16,1-
4. 17,1-2. 18,1. 19,1-3; 5-10. 20,1. 21,1-
7. 22,1; 4-5; 7-8. 23,1; 4-5. 24,1-2; 7-12.
25,1-3; 8. 26,1-2. 27,1. 28,1. 29,1-3; 8; 11-
13. 31,4-5. 32,1. 35,1. 36,1.

HRT   1,12. 2,1-3. 4,6; 8-
17; 19-20; 24. 5,1; 4; 13-14; 16-17; 20; 23-
24; 26. 9,6; 8-9. 10,12. 15,5-6; 8; 11-12.
16,1; 11. 17,2; 8; 11. 19,1. 20,1-2; 7-8; 11;
13. 21,1-2. 22,2. 24,1. 25,1. 27,1. 28,3; 5;
8. 31,1; 6; 8. 33,5; 8-9; 11; 15; 20. 34,4; 10;
17; 22; 24. 35,3. 36,2-3; 16; 19. 37,11.
38,1-2. 42,11.

HUN   1,1-2; 5; 7; 10. 2,1-
8. 4,1-4. 5,1. 6,1-9; 11-16; 18-20; 22-26.
7,1-6. 8,1-2. 9,1-3. 10,1. 11,1-2. 12,1. 13,1.
14,1. 15,1. 16,1. 17,1. 18,1. 19,1-3; 6; 8;
14-15; 17-20; 23-24; 29-30. 20,6-9. 21,1.
22,1-2. 23,1. 24,1. 25,1-2. 26,1. 28,1. 29,5.

KEN   M6-8; 11-12; 14;
19-20; 22; 24. 1,1-4. 2,3-38; 40-43. 3,1-21.

4,1-14; 16. 5,1-3; 5-9; 12-13; 16; 18-34; 36-
46; 48-49; 51-60; 62-64; 66-78; 80-93; 95-
111; 115-120; 122-124; 126-129; 131; 134;
136; 138-147; 149; 152-153; 155; 158-160;
162-168; 170-172; 174-176; 179-180; 183;
185-187; 191-195; 197; 199-202; 206; 208;
210; 215; 217-220; 224-225. 6,1. 7,1-9; 11-
13; 16-21; 23; 29. 8,1. 9,1; 3-4; 6; 9-10; 12;
16; 18; 22; 24-25; 28; 30-31; 36-37; 42; 45;
47-50. 10,1-2. 11,1-2. 12,1; 3-4.

LEC   1,1a-b; 2; 4; 6-7; 10;
12. 2,1-6. 3,1; 6; 8-9; 11-15. 4,1. 5,1-2.
6,1; 3; 5-6. 7,2. 9,1; 3; 5. 10,1; 3-4; 6-9; 12;
15-17. 11,1-2. 12,1-2. 13,1-2; 4-7; 12; 15-
23; 26-30; 32; 34-35; 37-41; 43-44; 47-48;
50-51; 53-58; 60-67; 69-70; 74. 14,5; 9-11;
13-14; 16; 20; 23-24; 26-27; 29; 31-33.
15,1-5; 8-16. 16,1-9. 17,4; 6-9; 12-14; 18-
24; 26; 28; 30; 32-33. 18,3-5. 19,1; 5; 11-
13; 15; 17-19. 20,1-2; 4. 21,1-2. 22,1. 23,1;
4. 24,1; 3. 25,1; 3-5. 27,1; 3. 28,1-2; 4-5.
29,1-3; 5-6; 10; 13; 15-19. 31,1. 32,1-2.
33,1. 34,1. 35,1. 36,1-2. 37,1; 3. 38,1.
39,1. 40,10; 12-13; 15-19; 21-24; 26-29; 32-
34; 36; 39-41. 41,2-3. 42,1-3; 7. 43,1-6; 9;
11. 44,1-4; 6-7; 9-13.

LIN   1,38; 55; 65-67; 70;
81; 91. 2,1; 3; 5-6; 11-12; 16; 33; 42. 3,3.
4,17; 26; 44; 65; 69. 7,1; 4; 8; 10; 43; 48;
50; 56. 8,1; 4-5; 7; 11. 10,1. 11,1; 3-5; 9.
12,3; 8; 42; 47-49; 55; 57-58; 61; 67; 70;
96. 13,5; 10; 17; 20; 28; 34. 14,1; 23; 46;
54; 90; 97-98. 15,1-2. 16,46. 17,2. 18,2; 7;
25; 27; 29; 31. 20,1. 22,1; 7; 22; 24; 26.
24,1; 12-13; 26; 36; 40-41; 43; 46; 73; 78;
81-82; 86; 100; 103. 25,1. 26,1; 10. 27,7;
34. 28,1; 13; 15. 29,1; 8. 30,22; 29. 31,1;
11; 17. 32,1; 17; 32. 34,14-15; 17. 35,6.
36,1-2; 4. 37,1-2. 38,1; 3; 5; 8. 39,1; 3.
42,1; 9. 43,1-3. 44,16. 48,1. 55,1. 56,11;
13. 57,12; 14; 22-24; 27-29. 58,1; 8. 63,3-
4; 15. 64,3; 18-19. 65,3. 67,15; 19. 68,1.

MDX   3,2-6; 8; 13; 16; 18-
19. 4,2; 11. 7,2; 4; 7. 10,2. 11,2-3. 19,1.
21,1.

NFK   1,1-3; 11; 15-17; 19;
21; 29-30; 32-33; 40; 42; 52-53; 55; 57; 59;
71-73; 77-78; 82; 85-87; 89; 92; 94; 105-106;
114; 123; 127-128; 131-133; 135-147; 150-
152; 169; 175-176; 182-183; 185-186; 188;
192-194; 197-203; 205-206; 208; 210-212;
215-219; 228; 230-231; 236-239. 2,2-5; 7;
12. 3,1. 4,1-2; 9; 14; 16-17; 23; 26; 29-33;
35; 37-39; 41-42; 45; 47; 49-50; 52. 5,1-4;
6. 6,1-4; 6. 7,1-3; 7; 9-11; 16-19. 8,1-3; 6-
7; 13; 16; 18; 21-22; 24-28; 30; 34-35; 37;
40; 46-47; 50; 54-55; 58-64; 67-68; 87; 91;
94-95; 99-100; 102-103; 105; 108-110; 115;
119-122; 130; 132. 9,1-3; 6-12; 24-25; 31-
33; 46-48; 56; 63-64; 70-78; 80-81; 83-84;
87-88; 94-96; 98-100; 102; 104; 117; 129;

136; 145-146; 149; 153; 155; 157; 167-169; 174; 177; 182; 218; 221. 10,1-11; 15-16; 19; 21-25; 28; 30; 33; 36; 38; 40; 56-57; 67; 76; 78; 90. 10a,1. 11,1-2; 4. 12,1; 17; 27; 30; 32; 42. 13,2-7; 9-10; 12-16; 19; 23-24. 14,1-2; 4-8; 11-12; 14-16; 18; 21; 23-26; 29-30; 35; 37; 39-41. 15,1-2; 4; 7-11; 14; 16-18; 23-26. 16,1; 3-5. 17,1-3; 5-14; 16-19; 23; 25-27; 35-41; 43; 51; 53-56; 61-65. 18,1. 19,1; 4-5; 7-9; 11-13; 15; 17-19; 21-22; 24; 32; 36. 20,1-2; 4; 7-10; 12; 14; 23-24; 26-27; 29; 34-36. 21,2-7; 9-10; 16; 19; 21; 23-25; 27-30; 32-34. 22,1; 3-6; 10; 16; 23. 23,1-5; 7-8; 10-13; 15-18. 24,5-7. 25,1; 7; 12; 17; 21. 26,2-3; 6. 27,1. 28,1. 29,1-6; 8; 10. 30,1-2; 4-5. 31,1-2; 5-8; 10; 17; 22; 24-25; 31; 33-35; 37-39; 41-44. 32,1-2; 4-5; 7. 33,1-2; 6. 34,1-4; 7-10; 15; 17-18; 20. 35,2-3; 5-10; 12-15. 36,1-2; 5-7. 37,1-3. 38,1-2; 4. 39,1-2. 40,1. 41,1. 43,1. 44,1. 46,1. 47,4. 48,2. 49,1; 3-4; 6. 50,1; 4-9; 11-12. 51,3-6; 8; 10. 52,2-4. 55,1-2. 57,3. 58,1-3. 59,1. 60,1. 61,1-2. 65,8. 66,22; 64; 87; 95.

NTH　1,1; 4; 6-8; 11-20; 23-26; 30-31. 2,1-2; 4; 7; 11-12. 3,1. 4,1-17; 20-27; 30-34; 36. 5,2-4. 6,1-8; 10a,c; 11-13; 15-17. 6a,1-2; 4-7; 10-11; 13-16; 20; 22-25; 27-30; 32-33. 7,1-2. 8,13. 9,1; 4-6. 10,1-2. 11,1-2; 4-6. 12,1; 3. 13,1. 14,1-2; 5-6. 16,1. 18,1; 3-5; 13-15; 17-21; 23; 27-28; 30-31; 34; 36-37; 44-45; 47-48; 52; 55; 57-59; 65; 69; 75-76; 80; 82; 85-86; 88-90; 92-93; 96. 19,1-2. 20,1. 21,1-3; 6. 22,1-6; 8-9. 23,2-5; 7-14; 16-19. 24,1. 25,1-2. 26,1; 3-6; 8-10. 27,1. 28,1-2. 29,1. 30,6; 9-10; 14; 17. 31,1. 32,1. 33,1. 34,1. 35,3a; 4-6; 8-10; 12-13; 16; 19a; 21-24; 26. 36,1-4. 38,1. 39,2; 6-9; 11-18. 40,1-4; 6. 41,4-9. 42,3. 43,1-2; 4; 6-11. 44,1a. 45,2; 4-5; 8-9. 46,1-4; 6-7. 47,1a; 2. 48,2-6; 8-9; 11-12; 14-16. 50,1. 52,1. 53,1. 54,1-3. 55,1-4; 6. 56,1; 8; 15-18; 21-23; 25-27; 29-30; 35-40; 45-46; 49-51; 59; 61; 64-66. 57,1-2. 58,1-2. 59,1-4. 60,1-2.

NTT　1,1; 23; 61. 2,6. 4,2-3. 5,1; 3; 5; 7; 11; 13; 18. 6,1. 8,1-2. 9,16; 39-40; 43; 51; 55; 60; 65-66; 74; 82; 84; 90; 95; 97; 100; 103-104; 107; 115. 10,1; 3; 5; 9-10; 15-16; 18; 34; 36; 43; 46; 56; 59; 61. 11,2; 4; 6; 9-10; 12; 14; 17-18; 20; 26; 33. 12,11-12; 16. 13,6; 9. 14,5. 15,8. 16,1; 5; 7. 17,4; 9; 15. 18,1; 5-6. 20,1; 7-8. 22,2. 23,1. 24,1. 25,1. 30,12; 36.

OXF　1,1-7a; 8-9. 2,1. 3,1-2. 4,1. 5,1. 6,1b; 2-5; 7-16. 7,1; 4-11; 13-15; 17-18; 20-22; 24-27; 29-33; 35-37; 39-41; 43-53; 56-62; 64-65. 8,2-4. 9,6-8; 10. 11,1. 13,1. 14,3-4; 6. 15,1-5. 16,1-2. 17,2-8. 18,1-2. 19,1. 20,1; 3-9. 21,1. 22,1-2. 23,1-2. 24,1-5. 26,1. 27,1-4; 6-8; 10.

28,2; 7; 9-10; 12-23; 25-27; 29. 29,1-2; 5-23. 30,1. 31,1. 32,1-2. 33,1-2. 34,1-3. 35,1-6; 8-11; 16-22; 24-29; 31-32; 34. 36,1. 37,1. 38,1-2. 39,1-3. 40,1; 3. 41,1-2. 42,1. 43,1-2. 44,1. 45,1-3. 47,1. 48,1. 49,1. 50,1. 52,1. 53,1-2. 54,1. 55,1-2. 56,1; 3-4. 57,1. 58,2-5; 7-10; 12; 15-18; 20-24; 27-33; 35-38. 59,1-2; 5-6; 8-9; 11-12; 14-17; 19-22; 24-29.

RUT　R5-6; 19-21.

SHR　1,4-8. 2,1-2. 3b,2-3; 5. 3c,2-11. 3d,6. 3f,2-3. 3g,3-8; 10-11. 4,1,1; 4-12; 14; 16-32; 36. 4,2,1. 4,3,1-4; 6; 8-9; 11-31; 38-39; 44-45; 48-50; 52-58; 60-61; 63-71. 4,4,1; 3-5; 10-24. 4,5,1; 4; 6-10; 12. 4,6,1; 3; 5. 4,7,1-2. 4,8,1; 4-7; 9-16. 4,9,1-3. 4,10,1-4. 4,11,1-8; 10-12; 15-19. 4,13,1. 4,14,3-4; 8-9; 11-12; 14; 16; 18; 22-25; 28. 4,16,2. 4,17,1; 3. 4,18,2-3. 4,19,2; 5-8; 10; 12-13. 4,20,1-3; 5-8; 13-17; 24; 26. 4,21,2-4; 6-12; 14-16; 18-19. 4,22,2-3. 4,23,1-6; 8-10; 12-14; 16-18. 4,24,1-2; 4. 4,25,1-3; 6. 4,26,3-4. 4,27,1-2; 9; 19; 21-23; 26-27; 29; 35. 5,2; 4; 8. 6,1-2; 5; 7-12; 14; 16; 19-21; 23-25; 33. 7,1; 3-6. 9,2.

SOM　1,1-10; 20-21; 25-26; 28; 30. 2,6-8. 3,2. 5,1-3; 5; 8; 10-11; 13-18; 20; 22-28; 31-37; 39-63; 65-67; 69-70. 6,1; 9-10; 13-14. 7,4; 8; 10-11; 14. 8,5; 9-11; 15-18; 20; 23-24; 28; 30; *31;* 33-34. 9,1. 10,2; 4-5. 15,1. 16,1; 3; 6; *13.* 17,2-3; 6. 18,1-2. 19,3-4; 8; 11-13; 15-16; 18; 20-21; 24-25; 27-35; 37-41; 43-49; 51-60; 62-68; 71-72; *74;* 75-82; 85; 87. 21,5-8; 12-15; 19; 22-27; 29; 32; 34; 37-38; 41-43; 45-47; 49-51; 55-56; 61; 63; 70-74; 78-79; 81-82; 85-86; 89-90; 92-96; 98. 22,1-6; 8; 10-15; 17-22; 24-28. 23,1. 24,1; 3-5; 7-8; 10; 12-16; 18-23; 25-31; 33-34. 25,1; 3-5; 7-17; 21; 24-27; 29-31; 33-34; 37-41; 43-45; 47-51; 53-56. 26,3-6; 8. 27,1-3. 28,1-2. 29,1. 30,1-2. 31,1-4. 32,1-6; 8. 33,1-2. 34,1. 35,1; 4-6; 10-13; 15-20; 22-23. 36,1-2; 4-5; 9-14. 37,1-3; 5-12. 38,1. 39,1-3. 40,1-2. 41,1; 3. 42,1-2. 43,1. 44,1-3. 45,1-4; 7; 18. 46,4; 6; 9; 16; 21-23; 25. 47,1-6; 8; *9;* 12; *14;* 17.

STS　1,1-2; 6-8; 11-17; 19-20; 23-24; 26-27; 29; 32. 2,1-3; 5; 10; 15-18; 20; 22. 3,1. 4,1-5; 7. 5,1. 7,2; 13-15; 17-18. 8,1-13; 15; 17; 22-25; 27-28; 30; 32. 9,1. 10,2-6; 9-10; 8-11; 13-16; 18; 20; 24-25; 27-31; 33; 36-50; 52; 54; 56-58; 60-63; 65-68. 12,1; 4-13; 15; 17-18; 20-22; 24; 26-31. 13,2-3; 6; 9. 14,1-2. 15,1-2. 16,1; 3. 17,6; 13; 18-19.

SFK　1,1-2; 8-9; 12; 14; 16; 18; 23; 32-36; 45-51; 53; 56; 60; 75-76; 88; 90; 96-98; 100-102; 110-111; 115; 118-121; 122b. 2,6-7; 9-10; 13. 3,1; 9-10; 34; 46; 56; 61; 67-70; 72-74; 79; 88; 93-94; 98-

99. 4,1; 10; 13; 15; 18-22; 24; 26; 30; 35; 38; 40; 42. 5,1; 3-7. 6,1-3; 11; 26-27; 32; 42-44; 49; 62; 80-81; 83-85; 88; 90; 92-93; 110; 112; 129; 135; 148; 156; 172; 191-192; 213; 220; 222-223; 260; 264; 271-272; 303-309; 312-313. 7,1; 3-7; 10; 13-15; 18-19; 26; 29; 36-38; 47; 51; 56; 61; 67; 70-71; 73; 75-76; 98; 122; 147. 8,1; 7; 11; 13-14; 20-21; 31-37; 46-49; 55-57; 9,1-3. 10,1. 11,4. 12,1; 3-7. 13,2-3; 6-7. 14,1-10; 18-21; 23-25; 32; 38-39; 42-43; 45; 47-53; 55; 64-65; 68-70; 72-77; 96; 98; 102-103; 105-106; 108-109; 114; 117-120; 128-129; 139; 163-164. 15,1-2; 5. 16,2; 10-12; 22; 25-26; 30; 37; 40; 44-45. 17,1. 18,1; 4. 19,1-2; 16; 21. 20,1. 21,1; 3; 5-7; 10-11; 15-16; 26; 28; 38-40; 42-43; 45; 47; 53-55; 80; 95. 22,1. 23,2-3. 24,1. 25,1-3; 5-10; 19; 33-34; 36; 52-53; 55-57; 59; 63; 66; 75-76; 79; 81-82; 84-85. 26,3; 5-6; 8-10; 12a-c; 13-15. 27,3-7; 9-10; 13. 28,1a-b; 3; 6-7. 29,1; 11-12. 31,3; 7-8; 20; 28; 40-42; 50; 53; 56; 60. 32,1; 3-4; 6; 14; 16; 19; 21. 33,1-4; 6-10; 12-13. 34,1-3; 4-8; 12-13; 15. 35,1-2; 5-6. 36,1-2; 4; 8. 37,1; 4-6. 38,1; 6; 8; 11; 16. 39,6; 12; 17. 40,2-4; 6. 41,1-2; 7; 10; 14; 17. 42,1-2. 43,1-7. 44,1-4. 45,2-3. 46,1-4; 7. 47,2-3. 48,1. 49,1. 50,1. 51,1. 52,1; 5. 53,1; 3; 5-6. 54,1-3. 55,1. 57,1. 58,1. 59,1-2. 60,1. 64,1; 3. 65,1. 66,1-4; 6; 10. 67,2-3; 10-11; 15; 27. 68,1; 5. 69,1. 71,1-2. 76,4; 23.

SRY   1,2-14. 2,1-6. 3,1. 4,1-2. 5,1a-b; 4-9; 11; 15; 17-23. 6,1-3; 5. 7,1. 8,1-3; 6; 9; 14; 17-19; 21-23; 25; 28; 30. 10,1. 11,1. 13,1. 14,1. 15,1-2. 16,1. 17,1. 18,1-4. 19,1-12; 14-17; 19-21; 23; 26; 29; 31-32; 35-39; 41; 44-47. 20,1-2. 21,1; 3-7. 22,1-5. 24,1. 25,1-3. 26,1. 27,1-3. 28,1. 29,1-2. 30,1-2. 31,1. 32,1-2. 33,1. 34,1. 35,2. 36,1; 3-10.

SSX   1,1-2. 2,1a-f; 2-3; 5-10. 3,1-10. 4,1. 5,1-3. 6,1-4. 7,1-2. 8,1; 3. 8a,1. 9,1-11; 13-15; 17-19; 22-24; 26; 31-32; 34-35; 54; 58-60; 64; 66; 70; 72; 74; 77; 80; 82-84; 87; 90; 96; 103-107; 109-111; 120-125; 129-130. 10,2-7; 11-12; 14-19; 22; 24-27; 29-31; 34-38; 41-43; 45; 47; 49; 53; 58-60; 65-67; 69; 72; 74; 77; 86-89; 91-95; 109; 111; 113; 115-118. 11,3-28; 30-41; 43-46; 48-57; 59; 61-68; 70-74; 76-88; 91-93; 95-96; 100; 102-106; 108-111; 113. 12,3-11; 13-16; 18-19; 21-23; 26-28; 30-44; 46-48; 51; 53-56. 13,1; 3; 5-15; 17; 19-23; 25; 28-32; 34-35; 38; 41; 43-49; 53; 56. 14,1-2.

WAR   1,1-4; 6-7. 2,1-3. 3,1-6. 4,1-2; 6. 5,1. 6,2-5; 7-8; 10-12; 14-20. 7,1. 8,1. 9,1. 10,1. 11,1-4. 12,1-6; 8-10. 13,1. 14,1-3. 15,4-6. 16,1-2; 5-16; 18; 20-23; 25-26; 29-36; 38-42; 44-47; 49-50; 52-54; 56-64; 66. 17,1-2; 5; 7-8; 10-12; 14-15; 19; 21-22; 25-26; 28-35; 37-41; 51-52;

56-62; 64-66; 70. 18,2-6; 8; 11-12; 14. 19,2-4; 6. 20,1. 21,1. 22,1-5; 8; 11-17; 19-26. 23,1. 24,1. 25,1. 26,1. 27,2-6. 28,1; 3; 6-8; 10-11; 13-14; 16-19. 29,1; 3-5. 30,1-2. 31,1-7; 10-11. 33,1. 34,1. 35,1-2. 36,1-2. 37,2-9. 38,1-2. 39,1-4. 40,1-2. 41,1. 42,1; 3. 43,1-2. 44,3; 5-11; 14; 16. 45,1.

WIL   1,1-9. 3,3-4. 7,2. 8,1-2. 18,2. 19,2. 20,3. 22,1-2. 24,2; 4-5; 11; 15; 26; 30; 34-35. 25,2-3; 7; 15; 19; 26. 26,2; 16; 19. 27,5-6. 29,1; 5. 30,3. 32,2-3; 11. 39,1. 41,6; 8. 42,5. 43,1. 48,3-5. 50,5. 51,1. 53,2. 64,1. 65,1. 66,1; 3-4; 8. 67,2; 5-9; 11; 14; 16-17; 28; 32-33; 39; 43-44; 48; 54; 59-63; 72-73; 77; 80; 89; 94-95. 68,3; 6-10; 15-16; 18; 20-22; 24-27; 29-30.

WOR   1,1a,c; 2; 5-6. 2,2; 5; 7-11; 14; 17-21; 23; 25; 45-46; 62; 64-66; 76; 78-79; 81-85. 3,1-3. 8,1-4; 7; 9c,e; 10a,c; 11; 14-20; 23-24; 26a. 9,1a; 2-4; 5c; 6b. 10,1; 3; 5-11; 13-14; 16. 11,1-2. 12,2. 14,1-2. 15,1-2; 4; 6; 8-13. 16,1-3. 17,1. 18,1; 3-4. 19,1-8; 10-12; 14. 20,1-6. 21,3. 23,1-3; 5-12. 24,1. 26,1-4; 6-13; 15-17. 27,1. 28,1.

YKS   C28. 1N54; 65; 92. 2,1-3. 2B1-2; 4; 6-7. 2N2; 23. 2W1; 4; 6-7. 2E1-2; 7-8; 12; 23; 28; 38; 41. 3Y1; 4; 9-10; 13. 4N1; 3. 4E1-2. 5N11; 17-19; 27-28; 45; 47; 53-54; 58-59; 63; 66-67. 5E1; 5; 10-11; 15; 17-18; 31-32; 34-36; 38; 65-66. 5W6; 8; 10; 12-14; 30; 32. 6N1-3; 8; 12-13; 15; 19-20; 27-28; 31-32; 36; 52-58; 92; 101; 103; 112-113; 129; 134; 136; 138. 7E1. 8N1; 54-5. 8E1; 3. 9W1-2; 8; 19; 23-28; 35; 37; 39; 54. 10W1-4. 11E1. 12W1-3; 12; 18. 29W25. 29N13.

Resources		
nil	BRK	5,1. 7,19. 17,1; 4. 33,1. 34,1. 46,5. 58,2. 65,17.
	GLS	1,50. 31,2; 5. 38,5. 51,1. 78,14.
	HAM	IoW7,21.
	HEF	10,45; 53.
	KEN	5,35; 47; 79; 112; 121; 207. 7,22.
	LIN	4,50.
	MDX	3,17.
	NTT	B19.
	STS	12,25.
	SRY	21,7.
	SSX	13,42; 54.
	WOR	8,9g. 23,13.
2 beasts only	HAM	1,45.
Salt house in	NFK	1,203.
	SSX	10,77.
	WOR	1,3b.
Thane in	OXF	1,76.
Warland in	OXF	58,25.
Wood/woodland in	HEF	2,11. 8,7.

SHR   4,3,28.
STS   11,62.
WIL   1,2.

See also: Borough; City; Gift; Household;
Jurisdiction; Mill; Plough; Revenue; Sheriff;
Taken away; Tax; Villager; Woodland.
LORDSHIP revenue (dominica firma) –

See Revenue.
LORIMER
(lorimarius)   ESS   1,2. 9,7. 64.
                          NFK   1,61.
LOSS of land – See Land.
LOWY (leuga) – See Territory.
LUMP (massa) of iron – See Iron.

M

MAIL-clad man
(loricatus) BKM 40,1.
Found by land-holder
for guard duty BKM 40,1.
MALT (brasium)
Measure of GLS 1,7.
Mill rendering BKM 12,3.
SHR 4,4,11.
Packload (load) of BKM 12,3.
SHR 4,4,11.
Payments for CAM 1,1-5; 7; 9.
Peck of WIL 24p.
Render of CAM 1,7.
Revenue, part of 3
days' CAM 1,1-2.
Sester of WIL 24p.
See also: Customary due.
MAN (homo) BDF B1. 3,6. 4,2. 5,1.
6,1. 10,1. 14,1. 16,3. 17,1-2; 4. 19,2. 21,6.
23,12; 43. 24,12. 29,1. 31,1. 32,1; 15.
53,19. 54,2. 56,3.
BRK B7; 10-11. 1,39.
7,12; 27; 31; 36; 38; 42. 8,1. 10,1-2. 21,22.
34,2. 41,6. 58,2.
BKM 4,5; 26. 5,21. 16,7.
17,17; 20. 18,3. 22,2. 23,6; 13. 57,11.
CAM 1,6; 11; 16; 18. 3,2;
5-6. 5,22; 32; 40; 56. 13,8. 18,3. 21,5. 22,5-
6. 26,8; 9; 30; 33; 42; 57. 29,4; 6; 12. 31,2;
7. 32,32. 35,1-2. 40,1.
CHS C4; 6; 15-16; 21.
B2; 6. A15. 1,24. 2,1; 10. S1-2; 4. S2,2; 4.
S3,2-3. FT3,7. R1,41; 43. R2,1-2. R3,1.
R4,2. R6,2. R7,1.
DBY 1,14. 13,2.
DEV 3,84. 16,74.
DOR 2,2. 3,10-11. 8,3.
36,6. 57,17.
ESS 1,1-4; 6; 9; 11-13;
19-20; 22-31. 2,2-4; 7-8. 3,1-3; 5-16. 4,1;
4; 8-9; 11; 14-15; 17. 5,1-5; 7-12. 6,1-2; 5;
8-12; 14-15. 7,1. 8,2-4; 6-11. 9,2; 5; 7-9;
11; 13-14. 10,1-5. 11,1-3; 6-8. 12,1. 13,1-
2. 14,2-5; 7. 15,1-2. 16,1. 17,1. 18,1-5; 11;
14; 17; 22; 27; 29-30; 36-38; 40-41; 43-44.
19,1. 20,1; 3; 6-9; 12; 15; 17; 19-20; 25-27;
32; 34; 36-41; 43-46; 48; 50-52; 54-59; 62-
72; 74-75; 77-80. 21,1-4; 8-9. 22,3-8; 10-
11; 13; 19-20. 23,1-4; 6-7; 10; 28-31; 38;
40. 24,1-5; 8; 10; 15-17; 20-26; 28-31; 33;
42; 44-46; 53-54; 57; 60-61; 64. 25,1-5; 11-
12; 14-20; 23; 25-26. 26,1; 3-5. 27,1-5; 10-
14; 17. 28,5; 8-9; 11-13; 15-17. 29,1-5.
30,1-7; 9-11; 14; 16-20; 22-23; 27-32; 34-

35; 38; 40; 44-46; 50-51. 31,1. 32,1-4; 6-9;
13-14; 16-19; 21; 23-26; 28; 30; 32-35; 38-
39; 41; 44-45. 33,1; 3-7; 11-20; .22-23.
34,4-13; 15-16; 18-23; 26; 29; 33-37. 35,1-
6; 8; 10-13. 36,1-3; 5-6; 8-9; 12. 37,1-3; 7;
9-12; 16; 20. 38,3-6; 8. 39,1-5; 7-9. 40,1-
2; 4; 6; 9. 41,3; 9-10; 12. 42,2; 4; 6-9. 43,1;
3-4. 44,1; 3. 45,1. 46,1-2. 47,1-3. 48,1-2.
49,1; 3. 50,1. 52,1-3. 53,1-2. 54,1-2. 55,1.
56,1. 57,1; 3; 5-6. 58,1. 59,1. 61,1-2. 64,1.
65,1. 66,1. 69,2. 71,2. 74,1. 76,1. 77,1.
79,1. 81,1. 83,1. 86,1. 90,7; 22-23; 26; 35;
49; 53; 57-58; 63; 65. B3m.
GLS W4; 13; 16; 18. 1,2;
11; 13; 15-16; 48; 53; 60. 3,1. 6,5. 8,1.
11,14. 19,2. 27,1. 28,1; 7. 50,4. 68,4.
HAM 1,42. 2,9. 3,1. 6,3;
5; 16. 15,1. 18,2. 21,7. 22,3. 23,44; 49.
53,2. 54,2. 69,16; 28. NF3,1. NF5,1.
NF10,2. S1. IoW1,7. IoW2,1. IoW8,5.
HEF C1-4; 10; 13. A2-3;
5. 1,7; 11; 44; 49; 53-54; 57. 2,1; 26-28; 49;
56. 3,1. 6,8. 8,1; 4. 9,4. 10,2; 42-44. 19,1-
2; 5. 21,1; 3. 24,13. 29,9; 20.
HRT 4,1. 10,6. 17,1.
19,1. 24,2. 26,1. 34,13. 36,9. 37,9; 19.
HUN 6,17. 19,32. 20,1.
D14.
KEN D2; 11; 14; 19; 24.
P13; 15. 2,2; 11. 3,10. 4,16. 5,1; 7; 43; 74;
149. 9,5; 52.
LEC 13,1; 14; 49. 27,2.
LIN C33. T1; 4. 3,17;
56. 12,59; 90. 22,5. 29,21. 30,28. 31,3.
32,35-36. 35,12. 40,15; 18; 24. 65,5. 68,22.
CS. CS1; 6; 9-16; 19-22; 24; 29; 38; 40.
CN3; 8. CK15; 40; 52; 55; 67-68; 70.
MDX 2,2. 3,29. 4,1. 7,6.
NFK 1,2-3; 11; 15-17;
19-21; 29-33; 40; 42; 50; 52-53; 55; 57; 59;
61; 66; 70-73; 77-78; 81-82; 85-89; 92; 94;
98; 105; 111; 115; 120-123; 128; 131-132;
135-137; 139-144; 146-147; 150-152; 155;
169; 175; 182-183; 185-186; 188; 192-194;
197-203; 206; 209-212; 215-219; 228; 230-
231; 236-237; 239-240. 2,1-4; 7; 12. 3,1.
4,1-2; 9; 14; 16-17; 20; 23; 26; 29-33; 35;
37-39; 42; 45; 47; 49-50; 52. 5,1-4. 6,1-4;
6. 7,1-2; 6-7; 9; 11; 13; 15-18. 8,1-3; 5-7;
13; 16-19; 21-22; 26; 28; 30; 33-35; 37; 40;
44; 46-47; 50; 54-55; 58-64; 67-68; 71; 87;
98-100; 103; 105; 107-110; 115; 119-122;
130; 132; 138. 9,1-3; 6-9; 11-12; 14-15; 24;
27; 31-33; 45-49; 56; 63; 70-78; 80-81; 83-

84; 87–88; 94–95; 98–100; 102; 104; 109;
117; 129; 136; 145–146; 148–150; 153; 155;
157; 168–169; 174; 177; 179; 182; *204;* 208;
221; *232;* 233. 10,1–5; 7–11; 15–16; 19–25;
28; 30; 32–33; 35–36; 38; 40; 48; 56–57; 61;
67; 76; 78; 81; 87; 93. 10a,1. 11,1–3. 12,1;
17–18; 27; 30; 32; 41–42. 13,3–6; 9–10; 12–
14; 16; 19; 24. 14,1–2; 4; 6–8; 11–16; 18; 23–
26; 29–30; 32; 35; 37; 39–42. 15,1–2; 4; *5;*
7–12; 14; 16–18; 23–26; 27. 16,1; 3–4; 6.
17,1–13; 16–19; 23; 25–27; 35–41; 43; 51; 53–
56; 62–65. 18,1. 19,4–5; 7; 9; 11; 13; 15; 17–
19; 21–22; 24–26; 32; 36. 20,1–2; 4; 6–14;
19; 23–24; 26–27; 29; 34–36. 21,2; 4–5; 7; 9–
10; 14; 16; 19; 23–30; 32–34. 22,1; 3; 5–6;
10; 16; 23. 23,1–5; 7–8; 10–18. 24,5–7. 25,1;
3; 7; 12; *15;*17; 21. 26,1–3; 5–6. 27,1. 28,1.
29,1–6; 8; 10. 30,1–2; 4–5. 31,1–2; 5–8; 10;
12; 14–15; 17; 21–22; 24–25; 31; 33–35; 37–
39; 41; 43–45. 32,1–2; 4–5; 7. 33,1–2; 6.
34,1–2; 4–5; 7–10; 15; 17–18; 20. 35,1–4; 6–
7; 9; 12–16. 36,1–2; 5–7. 37,1–3. 38,1–2; 4.
39,1–2. 40,1. 41,1. 42,1. 43,1–2. 44,1.
46,1. 48,2–3. 49,1–3; 6. 50,1; 4–9; 11–12.
51,3; 5–6; 8; 10. 52,2–4. 53,1. 55,1–2. 56,1–
4. 57,1; 3. 58,1–3. 59,1. 60,1. 61,1–2. 65,8.
66,22; 48; 57; 64; 80; 84–87; 91; 95.

NTH	1,3; 8. 43,5; 8; 11. 55,5.
NTT	B3. 30,22.
OXF	1,6; 13. 6,1a; 4. 7,41. 28,28. 34,3.
SHR	C3. 1,8. 3c,12–13.

3e,1. 4,1,5. 4,2,1. 4,3,32; 34; 47. 4,23,10.
4,26,7. 6,11. 7,4; 6.

SOM	1,27; 31. 6,9. 10,2. 26,6.
STS	2,20. 4,6. 10,1. 17,4.
SFK	1,1–2; 8–9; 12; 14;

16; 18; 23; 32–34; 36; 44–50; 53; 56; 60–61;
75–77; 88; 90; 96; 98; 100–103; 110–111; 115;
118–121; 122b. 2,6; 9–10; 13. 3,1; 3–4; 9–
10; 34; 46; 55–56; 61–62; 67–68; 70; 72–74;
79; 93–94; 98–99. 4,1; 13–15; 18–22; 24; 26;
30–31; 35–36; 38; 40; 42. 5,1; 3; 7. 6,1–3;
5; 11; 26; 32; 42–44; 48–49; 62; 80–85; 90;
92; 110; 112; 129; 148; 156; 172; 191–192;
211; 222–223; 260; 262; 264; 271–272; 300;
303–309; 312. 7,1; 3–4; 6–8; 13–15; 18–20;
26; 29; 36–37; 42; 47; 51; 56; 61; 67; 70–71;
73; 75–76; 78; 121–122; 137. 8,1–2; 7; 11;
14; 20–21; 31; 33; 35–37; 42; 46–47; 55–56.
9,1–3. 11,4. 12,1; 3–7. 13,2; 6–7; 14,1–10;
18–20; 23–26; 32; 38; 42–43; 45; 47–55; 67–
70; 73–76; 96; 98; 100; 102–103; 105–106;
108–109; 117–120; 128–129; 132; 139; 163–
164; 167. 15,1–2; 5. 16,2; 10–11; 22; 25; 37;
40; 44. 17,1. 18,1; 4. 19,1; 16; 21. 20,1.
21,1; 3; 5–6; 10–11; 15–16; 26; 28; 38–40;
42–43; 45; 47; 53–55; 80; 95. 22,1. 23,2–3.

24,1. 25,1–3; 5–8; 10; 34; 53; 56–57; 59–61;
66; 76; 79; 81–82; 84–85. 26,3; 5; 8–10; 12a–
c; 13–16. 27,3–7; 9–10; 13. 28,1a–b; 3; 6–7.
29,11–12. 30,1. 31,3; 7–8; 15; 20; 28; 34;
40–42; 50; 53; 56; 60. 32,1; 3–4; 6; 14; 16;
19; 21. 33,1; 3–4; 6–10; 13. 34,1–3; 5–6; 8;
12–13; *15.* 35,1–2; 6. 36,1–2; 4; 6. 37,1; 4–
6. 38,1; 3; 6; 8; 16. 39,3; 6; 12; 17. 40,3–4;
6. 41,1–2; 7; 10; 14–15; 17. 42,2. 43,1–3; 5–
7. 44,1–4. 45,2–3. 46,1–2; 4–5; 7. 47,2–3.
48,1. 49,1. 50,1. 51,1. 52,1; 5; 9. 53,1; 3;
5. 54,1–3. 57,1. 58,1. 59,1. 60,1. 64,1; 3.
66,2; 6; 13. 67,1–3; 10–11; 28. 68,1. 69,1.
70,1. 71,1–2. 75,1. 76,4; 7.

SRY	1,1a–c,e–f; 5; 9. 4,1–

2. 5,3; 6; 28. 6,5. 8,4; 8; 12; 22; 29. 11,1.
19,22; 25; 27; 35; 39. 21,3. 22,4. 23,1.
25,1–2. 28,1. 36,1; 4.

SSX	3,6; 8. 5,1. 9,111;

130. 10,5; 22; 27; 66; 75. 11,55. 12,1; 3; 6;
35 13,38.

WAR	16,55. 17,18; 20; 60.
WIL	B5. 2,12. 3,4. 7,1–2; 11. 8,7–9. 10,2. 12,3. 15,1–2. 41,4.
WOR	C5. 2,1. 8,12; 17;

26c. 9,7. 10,1. 15,12. 23,1. 26,16,

YKS	C3; 10; 12; 26; 33.

5N65. 5E18; 25; 33; 43; 61. 6N1; 125; 151.
23N36. 29E29–30. CN2. CE13–15; 20; 32;
34. CW1; 7; 17; 23–24; 31–32; 38–39.

whole (integer)	NFK	1,122.
	SFK	32,24.
half (½)	NFK	1,122. 19,26. 20,13. 31,3; 14. 66,85.
	SFK	4,15. 7,36; 79; 90. 32,24. 39,9. 67,17.

Abbey, not belonging to TRE	SOM	9,8.
Assessed in manor elsewhere	NFK	31,1.

Being man of

Abbess	BKM	17,9.
Abbot	BDF	16,5. 34,3. 53,25.
	BKM	12,12; 17–18; 22.
	CAM	3,5. 5,*2;* 5; 7.

13,11. 17,1–3. 26,2; 27; 41; 48–51. 27,1.
30,3. 31,2. 32,1; 21–23; 27–28; 31–33; 35;
39–40. 40,1.

HAM	6,5.
HRT	1,17. 4,15. 10,3. 17,1. 34,2. 37,13.
HUN	6,7.
KEN	9,9.
LIN	8,4; 7–9; 15; 19–20; 22–23; 27; 31; 34; 36.
MDX	8,2.
NFK	1,61; 66. 65,13.

	SOM	8,2.
	SFK	14,54. 18,4. 40,5. 67,30.
	SSX	8,1.
	WOR	9,1d.
Archbishop	BDF	16,5.
	BKM	4,3; 15; 17. 12,5; 21; 23. 17,3-4. 29,1. 33,1.
	CAM	2,4. 26,23; 26; 41. 28,2. 31,7. 32,8; 10; 13-14; 21. 44,1.
	ESS	6,8.
	HRT	1,10. 2,1; 3; 5. 4,4; 6; 11; 17. 5,8; 10; 13-17; 21; 23; 26. 7,2-3. 10,11. 16,8. 17,5. 23,1-2. 34,14. 37,5-6; 10; 16. 41,1-2. 42a,1. 43,1.
	KEN	2,16; 21; 26; 34. 3,2; 8.
	LIN	2,3; 5-6; 8-9; 11; 17-18; 21; 27; 29; 34; 36-38; 40. CK16.
	MDX	18,1.
	OXF	29,16.
	SRY	2,1.
	YKS	2,3.
Bishop	BDF	3,10-11. 4,2; 4-5. 24,23. 28,2. 34,2.
	BKM	5,18. 14,43; 48-49. 26,1. 43,6. 53,7-8.
	CAM	B1. 14,58.
	CHS	C20. B2; 6.
	DEV	25,3.
	ESS	1,27. 7,1. 18,34. 48,2.
	GLS	W13.
	HEF	2,57. 28,1.
	HRT	4,1; 25. 42,11.
	LIN	3,5-8; 20; 27; 31; 33; 35-37; 39-41; 48; 50-51; 53. 4,2-4; 7-8; 10-11; 13-16; 23; 28; 31; 38-43; 46; 50-51; 54; 56-57; 59; 61; 67; 72; 74; 76; 78-79. 7,4; 14; 16; 18-19; 21-23; 27-28; 30; 32; 34; 38-40; 51-54. CS1-2; 28.
	MDX	3,13.
	NFK	1,61. 10,11; 48; 53; 78.
	NTT	6,13; 15. 7,1-3; 5-6.
	SHR	1,8.
	SOM	2,2.
	SFK	6,93. 18,4. 64,3.
	SRY	3,1. 36,1.
	SSX	3,7.
Count	BKM	12,19.
	CAM	14,18; *82*.
	CON	4,22.
	DEV	1,23.
	ESS	90,87.
	HRT	10,6. 24,2.
	LEC	44.
	LIN	12,4; 7; 14; 18; 20; 31; 37; 40; 51-53; 55-58; 64-65; 80; 82; 85; 88-93; 96. CK66; 69.
	NFK	1,197. 4,25; 51.

		9,49. 10,19. 66,86.
	NTT	2,4; 9. 4,5; 7.
	SFK	21,1.
	SSX	10,2-3.
	YKS	6N36; 53; 56-58; 147; 151. SN,CtA45. SE,Sn1.
Countess	BDF	21,1. 22,2.
	BKM	53,5.
	HUN	D18.
	LEC	C17.
	LIN	56,6; 12-13; 18.
Earl	BDF	23,4; 47. 24,14. 35,2. 40,3. 44,1. 49,2-3. 50,1. 53,2; 7; 9; 31-33. 54,1. 57,2.
	BKM	B11. 3a,3; 5. 4,3; 5; 7-9; 13; 15; 19-20; 22; 34-35; 40-42. 5,10. 6,1-2. 12,2; 6-7; 11-13; 24; 37. 14,19; 25. 15,2. 17,5-7. 23,2; 5; 10. 26,10-11. 28,3. 30,1. 37,1-2. 39,1. 43,3-4; 11. 45,1. 51,1-3. 53,2.
	CAM	1,6. 3,6. 13,3; 8; 11-12. 14,27; 47; 71. 17,5-6. 21,5; 7-9. 25,8. 26,6; 13; 16; *22*; 23-24; 26; 31-32; 42. 31,7. 32,4; 8; 10; 14; 21; 23; 40. 35,1. 37,1-2. 38,3-5. 39,1-3. 41,3-5; 12-16. 43,1.
	CHS	C20; 25. 1,22; 34.
	GLS	1,8. 5,1. 28,7. 68,2.
	HEF	1,46.
	HRT	B6. 1,10; 13-16. 4,9-10. 5,5; 9; 20-21; 23; 25. 6,1. 15,2; 10-11. 17,2; 4; 8-9. 19,2. 24,1. 26,1. 30,1. 31,7. 33,7; 17. 34,1; 5; 13. 36,11. 37,2; 8; 11-12. 14-15; 18; 20. 42,14. 44,1.
	HUN	D10.
	LIN	13,17; 20-22; 24; 26; 30-31; 33; 38-39; 41-42; 45.
	MDX	2,3. 5,2. 8,4. 9,6. 11,3. 14,2. 18,1-2. 25,2-3.
	NFK	1,7; 19; 64; 131. 9,13.
	NTH	22,9. 53,1.
	NTT	3,3.
	RUT	R16.
	SHR	4,26,2.
	STS	12,14.
	SRY	18,2.
	SSX	6,1. 9,59.
	WAR	29,3.
ecclesiastical body	CAM	26,49. 32,40.
	HEF	1,44.
	HRT	10,17. 31,2. 33,1. 37,8.
	MDX	4,11.
	NFK	4,39. 9,180.
	NTH	6a. 16,2.
	SFK	18,4. 21,2. 76,19.
	WIL	13,9.
free man	GLS	4,1.
Frenchman	GLS	31,7.
King	BDF	4,6. 23,51. 53,23; 28. 57,10; 12.

CAM   26,34; 36. 32,35.
44,1.
CHS   C20. B6.
DEV   15,67.
HEF   A3. 1,49.
KEN   D10.
LIN   CS38. CN2.
NFK   4,25. 8,71; 138.
20,11. 66,89.
SFK   37,2.
SSX   12,1.
King Edward   BDF   2,6. 3,8; 10-11. 4,6-
7. 14,1. 15,1; 7. 21,3. 23,4; 35-36; 56. 25,8.
41,1. 53,4; 8; 10; 14; 17-19; 34-36. 57,3iv;
8.
BKM   5,15; 20. 12,15.
14,31. 17,13. 24,1. 36,2. 39,2. 41,7. 43,1.
44,3. 47,1. 57,15.
CAM   3,2. 13,8. 14,39-40;
64; 72. 15,4. 17,2. 26,16; 24; 32; 34; 36;
42-44; 49. 29,6. 31,2; 4; 7. 32,1; 3-5; 8; 10;
16; 20; 22-23; 27; 30; 32-33; 35; 37; 39; 43-
44. 38,2. 44,1.
HRT   5,23. 17,4; 15.
20,2. 25,1. 28,7. 31,3. 34,3. 37,10. 44,1.
MDX   8,4. 9,3. 11,2. 14,1.
16,1. 20,1. 22,1. 23,1. 25,1.
NFK   1,70.
SFK   7,33. 8,6.
SSX   12,1.
King Gruffydd   CHS   FT3,7.
lawman   LIN   S5.
layman/laywoman   BDF   1,4-5. 2,4; 8, 3,3;
6-7; 9; 13-15; 17. 16,3. 17,1; 4-6. 18,2-7.
19,3. 21,5; 9-10; 13-15. 23,13; 16; 22; 24;
42; 55. 24,2; 6-7; 20; 25. 25,1-3; 5-7. 28,1.
32,2; 6; 9. 33,2. 44,2; 4. 47,1. 53,27. 54,4.
55,4; 8; 10; 12-13.
BRK   31,3. 58,2.
BKM   B4-9. 4,1; 3; 5-7;
21; 24-25; 28; 31; 43. 5,4; 12-14; 16-17; 19-
20. 7,2. 12,1-2; 4; 9-10; 12; 25-29; 31-35;
38. 14,1; 20; 28-30; 33; 44-47. 16,7. 17,6;
8-9; 11-12; 14; 18; 20-22; 25; 28-31. 18,3.
19,1. 21,2-4; 6-8. 23,6; 11; 13; 15; 17-18;
21-23; 25-28; 30-31; 33. 25,2. 26,3; 5; 7.
28,2. 29,4. 36,1; 3. 41,3; 5. 43,2; 4. 44,1-
2; 5. 47,1. 53,3; 6. 57,17.
CAM   1,12. 13,2; 11.
14,1; 3-7; 11; 27; 29-31; 34; 45; 46; 49; 57-
58; 62; 64-66; 68; 71; 76. 15,4. 18,3. 21,5.
22,6; 8. 23,2. 25,5. 26,16; 21; 28; 34-36;
38-39; 49. 29,10. 30,1. 31,7. 32,3; 8; 10-
12; 16; 20; 23-24; 30-32; 44. 35,1-2. 40,1.
44,1.
CHS   B6. 17,7. 18,2.
20,4.
DBY   6,2. 16,1.
DEV   15,40.
DOR   55,3.
ESS   6,12. 9,14. 10,5.

18,23. 23,29-30. 30,2-3; 40; 47. 33,17.
34,2; 22. 88,2. 89,3. 90,17; 76-77.
GLS   W18. 2,9. 6,1.
69,6-7. 72,3.
HAM   23,31; 34. 68,5.
HEF   1,35; 52. 8,4. 15,9.
21,7. 24,13.
HRT   2,2. 4,6-7; 12-16;
18-20; 23; 25. 4,6-7; 12-16; 18-20; 23; 25.
5,7; 10-11; 13. 15,5; 7. 16,3-6; 11-12. 17,1;
4; 6-7; 10-11; 14-15. 19,1. 20,2-5; 7-12.
22,2. 24,2. 25,2. 26,1. 28,3; 5; 7. 29,1.
31,1; 3; 7. 33,1; 3; 5-6; 8-10; 12-20. 34,6-
7; 9-12; 23. 35,3. 36,1-2; 4-5; 8; 11; 16-17.
37,1; 4; 10; 12; 19. 38,1-2. 42,6; 12.
HUN   19,5; 7; 13.
KEN   1,3. 5,93.
LEC   10,17. 17,8; 11.
25,2. 29,20.
LIN   14,3; 5; 9; 11-17;
20; 25; 28; 30-34; 38-41; 43-45; 58-59; 63-
65; 84; 87; 92-93; 95. 15,1. 16,1-4; 7; 9-10;
12; 14; 27-28; 32-33; 35; 39; 43-45; 47. 17,1.
18,12; 15; 17; 20; 24; 31-32. 21,1. 22,3; 8;
10-14; 25; 28-29; 31-36. 23,1. 24,1; 7; 10;
12; 22; 24; 27; 36; 41; 54; 61; 66; 68; 72-
74; 76; 80-81; 83-84; 86; 92. 25,2; 5-6; 11;
13. 26,11; 17; 20; 22; 27; 30; 33; 35-38; 40;
43; 46-48; 53. 27,1-3; 5; 12; 14; 20; 22-25;
37; 40; 44; 47-48; 50-51; 53; 56-61. 28,2-
3; 5; 7; 15-16; 19-20; 25; 29; 32-33; 35; 37-
38; 42-43. 29,18; 27. 30,3; 5-7; 9; 12; 17-
20; 22; 25; 30; 33; 36. 31,2-3; 5; 8-9; 18.
32,3-4; 6-9; 11-12; 15; 27-28; 31. 34,3-6;
8-9; 24. 35,11; 13. 36,1-3. 37,2. 40,2; 4; 6-
7. 41,1. 44,2; 5; 8. 46,1. 47,3-7. 48,2; 6;
9; 11; 13. 51,2-4; 6; 10. 57,1; 5-7; 10-11;
13; 15; 18-19; 22; 24; 33; 39; 48; 55. 59,2;
4-5; 7; 9; 11-12; 14-20. 61,4; 7. 63,1-2; 7.
64,2-3; 6; 15. 67,1; 20. 68,2. CN1; 14; 19.
CW9. CK57; 66.
MDX   7,1; 3; 7-8. 9,4-6.
11,2-4. 15,2. 18,1. 25,2.
NFK   1,19; 61; 106; 111;
148; 195; 203; 208. 4,20; 26; 39-41; 56. 5,1.
8,31; 33; 37; 137-138. 9,42; 179-180; 196;
227. 11,3. 13,19. 14,31. 15,2. 19,2. 20,11;
19-20. 21,14; 22. 24,5. 30,2. 31,39. 34,18.
66,35; 51; 59; 63-64; 67; 81; 89; 91.
NTH   4,7. 35,1j. 56,65.
NTT   9,2-3; 6; 10; 18-20;
22; 26; 31; 33; 36-37; 44-46; 50; 52; 55; 57;
59; 62; 64; 66; 69-70; 89-90; 107-108; 110-
111; 116; 118-120; 122; 126-127; 129; 131.
10,2; 22; 25; 39; 51. 11,22; 25. 12,1. 14,7.
15,3-5; 7; 9. 17,3; 7; 16. 19,1. 21,1.
OXF   7,16.
RUT   R15.
SOM   21,58.
SFK   2,17. 4,15; 32. 6,5;
92-93; 106. 7,13; 36-37; 102; 111; 114; 119.

		8,6. 9,2. 14,146. 21,1. 26,12d; 15. 31,34. 37,2. 39,9. 64,3. 67,11-12; 17. 70,1. 75,2. 76,2-3.
	SRY	1,1b. 5,19. 19,2; 27-28. 21,7.
	SSX	10,89. 12,6.
	WAR	17,6.
	WIL	60,1.
	YKS	C26. 1W53. 9W2. 14E6-7; 30; 32-33; 36-40; 42-48; 50-53. 16W3. 21E4; 7; 9; 11. 23N9-11; 13; 15-16; 24; 28; 30-31. 23E6; 9; 14. 24W4; 12; 18. 24E2. 25W2-3; 6; 9; 11; 13; 16; 19-20; 24; 28-30. CW32. SW,Bu49.
lord	KEN	D14.
man-at-arms	CHS	2,3. R7,1.
	GLS	52,3.
	HEF	2,28.
monk	HEF	1,44.
	HRT	10,12.
priest	SFK	2,17.
	WOR	8,8.
Queen Edith	BDF	1,4. 2,1. 23,28-29; 32. 49,4. 57,6.
	BKM	4,11. 14,6; 27; 40. 16,2. 19,1. 23,14; 20. 25,1. 26,3; 8. 41,1. 43,11. 56,2.
	HRT	7,1. 15,5. 33,2; 4. 42,7. 46,7.
	SFK	37,2.
rider	HEF	2,28.
riding man	GLS	1,15.
sheriff	BDF	17,7. 23,25.
sheriffdom	BDF	17,4.
thane	BDF	18,2. 23,22. 32,6. 55,6; 13.
	CAM	23,6. 32,23.
	HEF	A3.
	HRT	29,1. 31,1; 7.
two others'	SFK	7,36. 67,17.
County, of	BRK	7,38. 10,1. 21,22.
	GLS	1,11; 13; 53; 60. 28,7.
	HAM	22,3.
	HRT	4,1. 34,13. 36,9.
	HUN	D14.
	LIN	C33. 65,5. CN3; 17; 19.
	SRY	1,1d. 25,2.
	WOR	23,1.
	YKS	CE15.
Customary dues- paying	NFK	31,21.
Evidence by	SFK	1,60.
men of country	LIN	31,3.
	NTT	30,22.
King's men	DEV	15,67.
lord's men	GLS	72,3.
sworn men	DBY	13,2.
village, men of	SFK	1,77.
God, of (homo dei)	BKM	5,17; 19. 25,2.

Holding nothing	HEF	1,11.
Hundred, of	BDF	3,6. 4,2. 5,1. 6,1. 10,1. 16,3. 17,1-2. 19,2. 21,6. 23,12. 24,12. 31,1. 32,15. 54,2. 56,3.
	BRK	1,39. 41,6.
	BKM	17,20. 18,3.
	CAM	1,11; 16. 5,22; 32. 18,3. 21,5. 22,5-6. 26,30; 33; 57. 29,4; 6; 12. 35,1-2. 37,1. 40,1.
	DEV	16,74.
	ESS	7,1.
	GLS	11,4.
	HAM	6,16. 18,2. 21,7. 22,3. 53,2. 54,2. 69,16.
	HRT	10,6. 17,1. 19,1. 24,2. 37,9.
	HUN	6,17. 20,1.
	KEN	1,1.
	LIN	35,12. 68,22.
	NFK	8,71. 9,49. 66,64.
	SFK	7,78; 121. 38,3.
	SRY	1,5; 9. 4,2. 5,3; 28. 6,5. 8,29. 11,1. 19,25; 27; 35. 21,3. 23,1. 25,2. 36,4.
Half Hundred, of	BDF	29,1.
Of whom King might do as he please	ESS	9,5.
Living freely	ESS	9,5.
Lordship, in	ESS	1,20.
	HAM	S1.
Manor/village belonging/attached to	NFK	19,36. 31,21.
	SFK	4,14.
belonging to manor elsewhere	NFK	10,10. 31,1.
More on land 1086 than TRE	NFK	1,71.
None on land	SHR	4,3,47.
Paying nothing	HEF	21,1; 3.
Not ploughing	LIN	40,15.
Poor	SFK	6,84.
Riding, of	LIN	CS9-16; 19-20; 24-25; 29; 40. CN8. CK67-68; 70.
	YKS	CW39.
Value of	ESS	7,1.
	SFK	14,54.
Wapentake, of	LIN	12,59; 90. 22,5. 31,3. CS1; 6; 21-22; 24-25; 38. CK40; 55.
	YKS	CW1; 7; 17; 23-24; 31; 38.
Young (juvenis)	GLS	34,8.
	WOR	25,1.

See also: Assessment; Borough; Claim; Country; County; Crime/offence; Deacon; Delivery; Evidence; Exchange; Fold; free man; Freeman; House; Hundred; Jurisdiction; Jurisdiction, full; Lordship; Meadow; Monk; Patronage; Possession;

Priest; Purchase and sale; Reeve; Riding; Theft; Value; Village; Wapentake.

MAN-at-arms (miles)
BDF 3,4. 18,1; 4. 26,2-3. 46,1.
BRK B10. 1,22. 7,15. 22,5. 29,1. 31,6. 33,1. 46,3-4. 64,1.
BKM 5,3. 14,10. 17,18. 43,10.
CAM B13. 7,1. 14,17; 20; 64; 75; 77. 15,4. 26,5; 21; 24; 32; 35; 38; 40-41. 31,4. 32,*14;* 22-23; 33; 35.
CHS 2,1-4. 9,17. 17,5. R5,6. R7,1.
DBY 1,27. 6,27; 69.
DEV *2,2.* 5,1; 4; *13.* 17,33. *19,33.* 20,13-14. 21,2. *23,16.* 28,8-9. *48,10.*
DOR 3,13; 17. 8,2. 9,1. 11,13. 47,7. 55,32; *33; 35; 43.*
ESS 3,15. 9,7. 18,6. 20,56. 21,5. 23,3; 11; 13. 28,11. 30,21; 27. 32,22. 34,4. 41,12. 42,1; 5-6; 8-9. 90,7; 25.
GLS W15. *3,1.* 11,5-6. 12,2; 9. 21,1. 52,3. 53,2. 67,1. 68,9.
HAM 3,12. 21,1.
HEF 1,40; 48. 2,4; 10-11; 13; 16; 21; 26-28; 30; 33; 37; 39-40; 44; 47-48; 57. 8,8. 19,1-2. 21,4. 29,2.
HRT 4,2; 16; 21-22; 25. 10,9. 17,7. 27,1. 28,4; 7-8. 31,1. 33,18; 20. 34,3; 7; 16-17.
HUN 2,8. 6,18; 22; 26. 10,1. 13,1. 15,1. 17,1. 19,8.
KEN 2,5; 10-11; 21. 3,18. 5,2; 7; 128; 136; 138; 146; 165; 192. 7,8-9.
LEC 1,10. 2,4. 3,12. 5,3. 13,1; 33; 51; 53; 57; 66; 69. 15,10. 16,9. 22,1. 28,4-5. 44,4; 7.
LIN 7,1; 56.
MDX 2,1-2. 4,1. 5,1. 7,8. 8,3. 11,1-2.
NFK 1,66. *15,14.*
NTH 4,5. 6a,1; 6; 10; 12; 14-15; 19; 24; 30-31. 18,23; 57. 22,1-2. 23,3; 9. 35,2; 10. 43,1.
NTT 5,1; 4.
OXF 6,1a; 2-3; 5-6. 9,9b. 29,4. 44,1. 59,23.
SHR 2,2. 4,1,5. 4,3,40-41; 59. 4,4,20. 4,11,4; 18. 4,19,1; 4. 4,20,8; 18. 4,23,16. 4,26,5. 5,4. 6,11; 16; 18.
SOM 5,40. 6,3; 6; 8. 12,1. 19,86. 25,9; 13; *30.* 35,5. 37,2.
STS 7,13. 8,5; 7. 10,10. 11,6; 57.
SFK 66,3.
SRY 5,27. 6,1. 18,3. 19,23; 36-37.
SSX 3,2-3. 9,1; 6; 8.

11,3. 12,5; 41; 43. 13,6; 9; 20; 22; 28; 30; 38; 42-43; 46; 49.
WAR 16,30; 34; 51-52; 55; 60. 17,23; 61. 18,3. 19,4. 23,3. 30,1. 33,1. 37,4. 38,2.
WIL 2,1; 7; 10. 3,1. 7,16. 8,4; 6; 8. 12,2. 13,2. 14,1. 22,3. 26,1. 30,4-5. 37,13. 54,1. 68,14.
WOR 1,1c. 2,33; *42-44;* 72. 9,3. 15,10. 18,4. *26,15-17.*
YKS 2,1. 2B1; 3; 9; 18. 2E1; 26; 28; 36; 39. 6N134; 136-138. 13W36. 14E31. 21E10.

Death duty of   BRK   B10.
Free as a thane   HEF   1,40.
King's command, by   WIL   3,1.
Land for use of   DEV   *5,1; 4. 42,16.*
                     SOM   6,3; *8;* 9.
Proven (probatus)   MDX   12,1.
Rate of pay   BRK   B10.
Service of   BRK   B10.
                     KEN   2,5. 5,165.
                     SRY   5,27.

Smallholders dwelling
under   MDX   11,1. 12,1.
Status
  English   BRK   40,1.
                     HRT   23,3.
                     MDX   12,1.
                     SFK   14,167.
  French   CAM   31,3.
                     DOR   *11,13.*
                     KEN   7,9.
                     MDX   12,1.
                     SFK   14,167.
  Abbey/Abbot, of   GLS   12,9.
                     HUN   6,1.
                     NTH   6a,3; 7-8.
                     SFK   14,69.
                     WIL   8,8.
  Archbishop, of   KEN   2,5; 28.
                     YKS   2B1.
  Bishop, of   DOR   3,1.
                     ESS   18,22-23.
                     HEF   2,18; 49.
                     HRT   4,21.
                     OXF   6,1a; 2-3; 5.
                     WOR   2,33.
  Earl/Count, of   ESS   20,56.
                     LEC   43,1.
                     SHR   4,1,6.
  King Edward, of   DOR   49,12.
                     KEN   5,136.
  King's household,
  of   BRK   B10.
  layman, of   BDF   46,1.
                     DBY   9,1. 11,3.
                     ESS   27,17. 39,7.
                     GLS   52,3. 53,2.
                     HEF   1,48. 8,8. 19,1. 29,2.

	HRT	1,13.
	LIN	20,1; 4. 28,17. 31,16-17. 35,3. 64,5; 14.
	NFK	*8,37.*
	OXF	29,4.
	SHR	4,1,8.
	STS	10,10.
	WIL	30,5. 68,14.
	WOR	16,1. *26,15-17.*
	YKS	10W1; 3. 14E11; 34; 48.
sheriff, of	GLS	53,2.
	HRT	1,13.
	HUN	19,2.
wife, of	ESS	39,7.
Tax paid by city for use of	DEV	C4.

See also: Arms; Army; Expedition; House; Man; Mercenary; Soldier.

MANLOAD (onus hominis)	CHS	S2,4.

MANOR (manerium)

Amalgamation TRE	LEC	13,63.
Appendage of (appendentium)	YKS	10W1. 14E1; 11.
Appurtenances of (adjacentia)	LIN	14,66; 83.
	YKS	14E8 23N21; 24; 32.
Assessment in 2 Counties	BDF	48,1.
none because holders exempt for 3 years	CHS	R4,2.
Custody of	ESS	1,1-2.
	HUN	1,1-2; 5-8.
Customary dues of	CON	*1,1.*
	DEV	1,23.
	DOR	1,2; 6.
	ESS	1,24; 27.
	SOM	1,4; 12. 30,2.
	SFK	6,84.
remaining in manor despite sale of land	NFK	9,100.
Dependencies of (appendicia)	BRK	3,1.
	DBY	2,3.
	DEV	*1,21. 16,3.* 23,5.
	DOR	1,2-6; 8.
	LEC	43,1.
	NTH	1,13e; 15; 32. 35,1j; 19h. 56,1; 20k.
	SOM	1,1-2; *9.*
	STS	1,6; 30. 2,16. 11,6.
	WIL	1,3; 5; 9; 11-12; 18. 12,4.
Described as such	BDF	1,1-3; 5. 2,1; 9. 3,1-5; 7; 10-11. 5,2. 7,1. 8,1-3; 5; 7-8. 9,1. 10,1. 11,1. 12,1. 15,2; 4; 6. 16,1-2; 4; 6; 8-

9. 17,2. 18,4; 6. 19,1. 20,1. 21,1; 6; 17. 22,1. 23,1; 3-5; 10-12; 14-23; 27; 29; 37-38; 40; 42; 45; 49. 24,1; 3; 5; 8-10; 13-18; 22; 24; 27. 25,1-2; 4; 9-11; 13; 15. 26,1. 31,1. 32,1; 4-6; 8; 13. 33,1-2. 39,1. 40,3. 41,1-2. 44,4. 45,1. 47,1. 48,1-2. 49,1-3. 51,1-3. 52,1. 53,1; 3-5; 20; 29-30. 54,2-4. 55,2; 6. 57,3iv.

BRK B1-2. 1,1-3; 5; 7-10; 14; 24; 26-27; 31-34; 37; 39. 2,1; 3. 3,1. 7,2-3; 7; 11; 14; 18; 22-23; 38; 42. 8,1. 10,1. 13,2. 17,4. 22,10. 23,2. 26,2. 30,1. 33,4. 34,1; 4. 35,4. 37,1. 38,6. 40,2. 41,1. 43,1. 44,2. 46,2. 48,1. 54,2-3. 55,3. 58,1-2. 59,1. 65,1; 11; 18.

BKM 1,1-7. 2,1-3. 3a,1-2; 4-5. 4,1-2; 5-6; 10; 13-16; 18-20; 22-23; 27; 29-38; 40; 42-43. 5,1-3; 5-10; 12-15; 18; 20. 6,1-2. 7,1-2. 8,1-3. 9,1. 10,1. 12,2-3; 6-8; 16-17; 19; 24-25; 29-31; 35-37. 13,1-4. 14,2-14; 16-17; 19-39; 41-42; 44-46; 48-49. 15,1-2. 16,1-3; 5-10. 17,2; 4-7; 9-10; 16-18; 22-28; 30. 18,1-3. 19,1-2; 4; 6-7. 20,1. 21,1; 3-8. 22,1. 23,1-3; 5; 7; 12; 14; 16; 20; 22; 26; 29; 31-32. 24,1; 3. 25,1; 3. 26,4; 8-9; 11. 27,1-2. 28,3. 29,1-4. 30,1. 31,1. 34,1. 35,1-2. 37,1-2. 38,1. 39,1-2. 40,1. 41,1-7. 42,1. 43,1-5; 7-11. 44,1-4. 45,1. 46,1. 47,1. 48,1. 49,1. 50,1-3. 52,1-2. 53,3-5; 7-8; 10. 55,1. 56,1-2. 57,1-4; 13.

CAM 1,1-7; 11-12; 18. 2,1; 3. 3,3. 5,1-2; 4; 6; 14; 23; 25; 28; 38-39; 41; 44-45; 47; 50-52; 55; 57; 59-63. 7,2-5; 8-10. 8,1. 9,1-2. 13,11. 14,1-2; 11; 13-14; 27; 53; 55; 59; 61; 67; 74; 78. 15,1. 16,1. 17,1-2. 18,1; 3; 8. 21,3. 22,6. 25,9. 26,42. 28,1-2. 29,1-3; 5; 7; 9-10. 32,1; 4-5; 23; 32-33; 37. 39,2. 41,1; 7.

CHS B4; 13. 1,1; 4-5; 8; 15; 21-22; 25; 31; 33-34. 2,1-3; 5-7; 9; 14; 20-21; 26. 3,2. 5,4; 6-7; 9. 7,4. 8,5; 14; 16; 22-25; 27-29; 31-32; 34-36; 38; 42. 9,3-4; 9; 15; 17; 20. 11,3. 12,2. 13,5. 14,11. 16,2. 17,5; 7. 23,2. 24,9. 26,1; 9. 27,1-4. S1,1. FD2,2; 4. FD5,2-3. FD6,1. FD7,1. FD9,1. FT1,1-2. FT2,1; 18-19. FT3,1; 6-7. R1,1-2; 10; 12; 15; 17; 19; 21; 23; 35; 39; 43; 45. R2,1-2. R3,1. R4,1-2. R5,2-3; 5-6. R6,1-4. R7,1.

CON 1,1; 4; 6; 15; 18. 2,2; 6. 3,7. 4,2; *3; 21;* 26. 5,2,1. *5,8,10.* DBY 1,1; 9-16; 18-20; 27-37. 2,1; 3. 3,1-7. 4,1-2. 5,3-5. 6,2-14; 16-40; 42-47; 49-67; 69; 71-73; 75-80; 82-99; 101. 7,1-13. 8,1-6. 9,1-4; 6-10; 1; 4-11; 16-25. 11,1-5. 12,1-5. 13,1-2. 14,1-4; 7-11. 15,1. 16,1-8. 17,1-22. B3.

DEV 1,4-6; 11; 15; 17; 19-21; 23-25; 29; 32-34; 37; 40-41; 45-46; 49; 55; 60; 63; 66-67; 70. 2,2; 9-10. 3,8; 19; 26; 30; 76; 80. 5,1-2; 4; 8. 7,4. 10,1-2.

15,12; 38; 40; 57; 67. 16,3; 5; 7; 33; 58; 71-72; 80; 83; 92; 94; 144. 17,13; 17; 33; 92; 105. 19,6; 16-17; 37; 40. 20,10. 22,1. 23,5-6; 20; 23. 24,5; 8. 25,3. 28,2; 16. 33,1-2. 34,10; 14; 34; 43; 46; 49; 52-55. 35,10. 36,18; 21-23; 25-26. 38,1; 10; 14. 40,4-5. 42,16; 21. 43,3. 44,1. 51,2-3; 5-10.

DOR 1,1-17; 24; 30-31. 2,1; 6. 3,1-9; 18. 8,1; 3. 9,1. *11,4-5. 12,15.* 13,1; 4. 17,1. 19,10; 14. 26,20; 60. 27,6; 9. 30,4. 31,1-2. 35,1. 36,2; *4-6.* 38,2. 39,1. 47,7. 53,2. 55,8; 17; 39. 56,61. 57,1. 58,1-3.

ESS 1,1-4; 9; 11; 13; 19-20; 22; 24; 26-30. 2,2-9. 3,1-3; 5-15. 4,1-4; 6-15; 17-18. 5,1-5; 7-8; 10-12. 6,4; 6; 9; 11-12; 15. 7,1. 8,1-10. 9,1; 7-8; 13-14. 10,1-5. 11,2-3; 7-8. 12,1. 13,1-2. 14,2; 4-5. 15,1-2. 17,1. 18,2; 5; 18; 30; 32-33; 35-36; 38-43. 20,1-3; 5-10; 12-13; 15-17; 19-20; 22-27; 30; 32; 36; 38-40; 43-51; 53-57; 60; 62-75; 77-78. 21,1-2; 8. 22,3; 5; 7-8; 10; 15-20. 23,1-4; 6; 28; 31-32; 38-41. 24,1-3; 5; 7-11; 13-37; 42-43; 45-46; 49; 53-62; 64-66. 25,1-8; 10-23; 25-26. 26,1-3; 5. 27,1-8; 10-18. 28,1-6; 8-9; 11-18. 29,1-5. 30,1-12; 14; 16-20; 22-40; 44-46; 50-51. 31,1. 32,1-9; 12-36; 38-45. 33,1; 3-9; 11-20; 22-23. 34,2-24; 26-27; 29-37. 35,1-6; 8-13. 36,1-8; 10-12. 37,1; 3-5; 7; 9-14; 16; 18; 20. 38,1-8. 39,1-5; 7-10. 40,1-4; 6-9. 41,1-3; 5-7; 9-12. 42,2-9. 43,3. 44,1-4. 45,1. 46,1-2. 47,1-3. 48,1-2. 49,1; 3. 50,1. 51,2. 52,1-2. 53,1-2. 54,1-2. 55,1. 56,1. 57,1; 3-6. 58,1. 59,1. 60,1-3. 61,1-2. 62,1; 3-4. 63,1. 64,1. 65,1. 66,1-2. 67,1-2. 68,1; 3-4; 7-8. 69,2. 71,1-2; 4. 72,1-3. 74,1. 76,1. 77,1. 78,1. 79,1. 80,1. 84,2. 90,5; 7; 10; 22-23; 35.

GLS 1,1-3; 7; 9-13; 15-17; 21-22; 24; 34-41; 47-48; 50; 52-53; 55-63; 65; 67. 2,1-3; 5-10; 12-13. 3,1; 4; 6-7. 4,1. 6,1; 3. 7,1. 10,1; 7-8; 13. 11,14. 13,1. 16,1. 19,1-2. 20,1. 22,1. 28,7. 31,1; 7. 33,1-2. 35,2. 38,2. 39,1; 5; 12; 18; 20. 41,2-3; 5. 43,2. 45,3. 46,3. 52,3. 53,1; 3; 6-7; 10; 12. 54,1. 56,1-2. 59,1. 60,3. 61,1-2. 62,1. 65,1. 66,2. 67,2-3. 68,2-3; 6-9; 11-12. 69,1-5; 7-8. 70,2. 71,1. 75,1-3. 76,1. 78,1; 6; 8.

HAM 1,1-2; 7-8; 10-11; 16; 19; 21-23; 25-27; 29; 36-37; 42; 44; 47; W4; W8; W17; W19-21. 2,1; 4-5; 8-10; 12; 14-15; 19-21. 3,1; 3; 5-6; 8-9; 11-12; 16. 6,1; 3; 12-13; 16. 13,1. 18,2-3. 19,1. 21,1; 3-4; 6; 8. 22,1. 23,1; 3; 12; 16; 33; 37; 40-41; 46; 49; 51-52; 56. 27,2. 29,3-4; 11-12; 16. 32,2. 35,3-4; 6-7. 43,1-6. 44,1. 45,1; 3-4; 7. 47,2. 51,1. 53,1-2. 54,2. 56,3. 60,1. 61,1. 68,5; 7-8; 10. 69,4; 6; 11; 16; 18; 21-23; 26-28; 30; 32; 36; 47. NF2,3. NF3,2;

7. NF4,1. NF9,19; 36. NF10,1. IoW1,6-10; 13. IoW2,1. IoW6,7. IoW7,1; 6-8; 22. IoW8,3-4. IoW9,13.

HEF 1,1-10a,c; 39-47; 51; 61-63; 67; 69-71; 73-74. 2,1; 8; 10-12; 17; 21; 23-26; 30-33; 39-40; 49-51. 7,1; 3. 8,2; 5-9. 9,2; 4; 13-14. 10,5; 10-11; 15-16; 32; 34; 40; 59; 61; 72. 11,1-2. 14,2. 15,1; 3. 16,3-4. 19,2-3; 6; 8; 10. 20,2. 21,1. 22,7. 23,3; 5. 24,3; 5; 7. 25,8. 27,1. 28,1-2. 29,1-4. 30,1. 31,5; 7. 35,1.

HRT 1,1-6; 9; 18. 3,1. 4,2-3; 6; 8; 11; 13-14; 16-17; 19; 22; 24. 5,1; 8; 14; 17; 20; 24; 26. 7,1-2. 8,1-3. 9,1; 4-5; 7; 9-10. 10,1-4; 6-11; 15-16; 18-19. 11,1. 12,1. 13,1-5. 14,1-2. 15,1; 3; 5; 10-12. 16,2; 7; 10. 17,1-3; 8; 11; 13; 15. 19,1. 20,7; 11; 13. 21,1. 22,1-2. 23,2-4. 24,1; 3. 25,1-2. 26,1. 27,1. 28,4; 8. 29,1. 30,1. 31,1; 6-7. 32,1-2. 33,2-3; 8-9; 12; 15; 17-18. 34,5; 7; 10; 12-16; 24. 35,1-3; 7; 11; 14; 16; 19. 37,8; 11; 14; 21-22. 38,2. 41,1. 42,2; 6-7. 42a,1. 43,1. 44,1.

HUN 1,1-2; 5-8; 10. 2,1-8. 3,1. 4,1-5. 5,1. 6,1-9; 11-16; 19-26. 7,1-6. 8,1-2; 4. 9,1-3. 10,1. 11,1-2. 12,1. 13,1. 14,1. 15,1. 16,1. 17,1. 18,1. 19,1-3; 6; 8; 11-14; 23-25; 27-30. 20,1-4; 6-9. 21,1. 22,1-2. 23,1. 24,1. 25,1-2. 26,1. 28,1. 29,1; 3; 5. D10.

KEN M2. 1,1-4. 2,3-4; 9-16; 21; 25-26; 29; 31-32; 41-43. 3,2; 5; 6; 8; 15; 18. 4,1-2; 15-16. 5,1-4; 6; 9-10; 12; 16-18; 26; 28-29; 33; 35; 40; 44; 53-54; 56; 58-59; 67-68; 70; 74; 76; 78; 81; 93; 96-97; 99; 102-105; 122; 124; 128-129; 138; 144-147; 149; 152; 155-156; 159; 175; 182; 185; 187-188; 198; 204; 207; 218; 224. 6,1. 7,1-2; 4-6; 8-9; 15; 19-20; 23. 8,1. 9,1; 39; 51. 12,1. 13,1.

LEC 1,1a; 2. 13,23; 26; 63. 14,31. 15,2; 7. 29,3. 43,1; 6.

LIN T2. 1,1; 4-7; 9; 14; 26; 29; 31; 35; 38; 65; 81; 91. 2,1; 3; 5-6; 8-9; 16-18; 20-21; 27-29; 32-34; 36; 38; 40; 42. 3,1-9; 13; 16; 20-22; 25; 27; 31; 33; 35-36; 39-43; 48; 50-52. 4,1-5; 8-11; 13-17; 23; 26; 28; 31; 34; 36; 38-43; 46; 50; 53-57; 59; 61; 65; 67; 69; 72-79. 6,1. 7,8; 10; 14-24; 26-28; 30; 32; 34; 36; 38-39; 43-44; 52-54; 56-57. 8,1; 4-5; 8-9; 11; 13-15; 17; 19; 22-23; 27; 31; 34; 39. 9,1. 10,1. 11,1; 3-5; 9. 12,1; 3-4; 7-9; 13-14; 17-21; 29; 31; 37; 40; 42-43; 47; 49; 51-53; 55-58; 60; 62; 80; 85-86; 88-93; 96. 13,1; 17; 22; 24; 26; 28; 30-31; 33-34; 38-39; 41-42; 44-45. 14,1; 3; 5-6; 8-9; 11-18; 20; 22-27; 29-34; 38-46; 58-60; 62-66; 84; 87; 92-93; 95; 97. 15,1. 16,1-4; 7-10; 12; 14; 18; 20; 22; 27-28; 30; 33; 35-36; 39; 41; 43-47; 49. 17,1-2. 18,1; 3-4; 6-7; 11-13; 15; 17-20; 24-25; 27-29;

31-32. 19,1. 20,1. 21,1. 22,1; 3; 7-8; 10; 16; 21-22; 24-26; 28-35. 23,1. 24,1; 5; 10; 12-13; 17; 20; 22; 24; 36-37; 54; 61; 68; 72-74; 76; 78; 80-82. 25,1-3; 5-9; 11; 13; 15; 19; 25. 26,1-4; 7-8; 10; 14; 16-17; 20; 22-23; 25-27; 30-31; 33; 35-37; 40; 43-50; 53. 27,1-3; 5; 7; 10; 12; 14-15; 19; 22; 24-27; 30; 33-35; 37-38; 40-45; 47-48; 50-51; 53-61. 28,1-3; 5; 7-8; 11-12; 14-17; 19-20; 25; 29; 32-33; 35; 37-38; 42. 29,1; 4; 8-11; 18; 22; 27-30. 30,1; 3; 5-9; 12; 17-20; 22; 25-29; 31-33; 36. 31,1-3; 5; 7; 9-11; 15-17. 32,1; 3-4; 6-9; 11-13; 15; 17; 19-21; 24; 26-29; 31-33. 33,1-2. 34,1-9; 12; 24; 27. 35,1-4; 6; 9; 11; 13-16. 36,1-4. 37,1-2; 6. 38,1; 3; 8; 10; 12-14. 39,1; 3. 40,1-2; 4-7; 9-10; 12; 15; 17; 20; 23. 41,1. 42,1-2; 9; 13; 16. 43,1; 5. 44,1-2; 4-5; 7-11; 16. 45,1-3. 46,1; 3-4. 47,1-7; 10. 48,1-2; 4-5; 8; 10-15. 49,1-2; 4-5. 50,1. 51,1-2; 4; 7; 12. 52,1-2. 53,1-2. 54,1. 55,1; 3. 56,1; 5-9; 11-14; 17-19. 57,1; 5-7; 10; 12-15; 18-19; 22-24; 27-30; 33; 36-38; 41; 44-48; 50; 54-56. 58,1-2; 6. 59,1-5; 9; 11-12; 14; 16-20. 61,1; 4-6; 9. 62,1. 63,1-2; 5-8; 12; 15; 20; 24. 64,1; 15; 18. 66,1-2. 67,1; 5; 7-10; 12-13; 20; 22-24. 68,1-2; 4-5; 8; 13; 15-24; 26-27; 30-35; 37-48. CK19; 25; 38; 40; 71.

MDX 2,1-2. 3,1-2; 12; 14; 16-18; 20-21; 25-26; 30. 4,1; 3-10; 12. 5,1. 6,1. 7,2; 4-8. 8,4-6. 9,1; 7-9. 10,1-2. 11,1-3. 12,1-2. 13,1. 14,1. 15,1. 16,1. 17,1. 18,1-2. 19,1. 20,1. 21,1. 24,1. 25,1.

NFK 1,1-4; 15; 19; 32; 50; 57; 71; 81; 93; 124; 132; 135-136; 139; 143; 145; 147; 150; 152; 169; 182-183; 192; 197; 201-202; 209-210; 212; 215; 231; 238-239. 2,4. 4,1; 9; 14; 39; 49. 6,4; 6. 7,1-2. 8,2; 6-7; 16; 24; 63; 91; 98-101; 103; 105; 107; 109-110; 115; 119-121; 128; 132. 9,1-2; 6-7; 24; 46; 70; 73; 76; 78; 80-81; 87-88; 96; 99; 168; 174; 232. 10,1-3; 5-8; 10-11; 15-16; 20; 22; 28; 30. 12,20; 30; 32. 13,2-4; 16; 22; 24. 14,1; 14-15; 16; 17-18; 23-24; 29-30; 40. 15,1; 6; 11; 17; 28. 16,1; 3; 5. 17,10; 13; 55; 64. 18,1. 19,1; 4-5; 13; 15; 24; 36. 20,7; 10-11; 14; 19; 23. 21,2; 5-7; 9; 19; 26-27; 32. 23,5; 12; 16-18. 24,6. 26,2; 5. 29,4; 8. 30,1. 31,1; 6; 8-9; 17; 21-22; 25; 28; 34; 39; 43-44. 33,1. 34,1-2; 5; 9; 13. 35,9. 36,5; 7. 37,3. 39,2. 40,1. 48,2-3. 51,5-6. 52,1. 53,1. 54,1. 55,2. 59,1. 65,17. 66,62-63; 83.

NTH 1,1; 8-9; 11-13a; 15l; 16-19; 30. 6,10a; 25; 28. 35,1a,j; 19a,h; 25. 43,5. 44,1. 47,1. 54,3. 56,20; 36; 45.

NTT 1,1; 9; 17; 23; 45; 51; 58-59; 61. 2,1-4; 6-9. 3,1; 2-4. 4,1-3; 5-7. 5,1; 3-7; 9; 11; 13. 6,1; 5-13; 15. 7,1-6. 8,1-2. 9,1-3; 5-6; 10-12; 15-20; 22; 26; 28; 31-37; 39-41; 43-46; 50-55; 57; 59-60;

62; 64-66; 69-70; 72-74; 76-77; 79-80; 82; 84; 88-90; 92; 94-98; 100-108; 110-112; 114-116; 118-122; 125-127; 129; 131. 10,1-5; 15-18; 20; 22-25; 27-35; 39-40; 43-44; 47-51; 53-59; 61-62; 64-66. 11,1-2; 4; 6; 8-12; 14; 18; 20; 22; 24-26; 33. 12,11-12; 15-16; 18-19. 13,1-2; 6-11. 14,1-3; 5; 7. 15,1; 3-9. 16,1-9; 11-12. 17,1-4; 7-9; 12; 15-16. 18,1; 3-7. 19,1. 20,1; 3; 5-8. 21,1-2. 22,1-2. 24,1. 25,1. 26,1. 27,1. 28,1; 3. 29,1-2. 30,1-12; 14; 16-20; 22-24; 27-28; 30-38; 40-41; 43; 45-47; 50-52; 55.

OXF 1,1-7b; 9. 6,1a-b; 10; 12-13. 28,3; 6; 8.

RUT R5-20.

SHR 1,3; 8. 2,1. 3a,1. 3d,3; 6. 4,1,1-6; 8-12; 17; 19; 21-22; 30; 37. 4,3,1; 5; 10; 27; 29; 34-36; 43-44; 62; 65; 70. 4,4,2; 17; 20; 23. 4,5,1; 3; 14-15. 4,7,5. 4,8,3. 4,9,2; 4. 4,11,1; 3-4; 13; 19. 4,12,1. 4,14,1; 4-5; 7; 11; 18; 23. 4,15,1-3. 4,16,1-2. 4,17,3. 4,18,1-2. 4,19,1; 10; 12. 4,20,1; 3-5; 8. 4,21,4; 6; 8; 10; 14; 18. 4,23,3; 7-8; 14; 18. 4,24,4. 4,25,2; 6. 4,26,3-4; 6. 4,27,2; 4-5; 16; 18-19; 26; 29. 4,28,4-5. 5,8. 6,1-3; 14; 20; 32-33. 7,4; 6.

SOM 1,1-13; 17; 19-21; 25; 27-29; *34.* 2,1. 3,1. 4,1. 5,1-2; 5-7; *9;* 10-12; 15; 18; 34; 37; 40-41; 43; 48; *52;* 53-54; 57; 62; 64. 6,1; 3; 6-10; 13-14; 18-19. 8,1-2; 17-21; 24-27; 31; 36; 39-41. 10,1-2; 6. 13,1. 16,10. *17,8.* 19,2; *15;* 17-18; *20;* 23-27; *32;* 57; *63-64.* 20,1-2. 21,2; 6; 35; 37; 47; 54; *65;* 85; 92; *98.* 22,*5;* 14; 20-21. 24,*8;* 10-11; 16; *17;* 30. 25,1; *7-8;* 9; *13;* 18; 30; 33; 46; 55. 26,3; 6; 8. 27,1; 3. 28,1. 30,2. 32,4-5. 35,1-2; 4. 36,2; 5; 7; 13. 37,4; 8; 12. 44,2. 46,*3;* 5; 21. 47,5; *12.*

STS B8. 1,1; 6-7; 30; 32. 2,2; 9-10; 16; 20-22. 8,5; 9; 28; 31. 10,9. 11,6; 37; 56. 12,1.

SFK 1,1-2; 8-10; 12-14; 16-19; 23; 32; 36; 42-44; 46-53; 55-56; 60; 71; 73; 75-77; 82; 88; 90; 98; 100; 102-103; 110-112; 115; 118-121. 2,6; 10-14. 3,1; 3; 9-10; 13; 31; 34; 39; 44; 46; 56-57; 61; 65; 67-83; 88; 93-95; 98-100; 103. 4,1-2; 10-11; 13-16; 19-22; 30; 35-36; 38; 40; 42. 5,1; 3; 6-7. 6,1-2; 10-12; 26-28; 32; 42-46; 48-49; 57; 69; 78; 81-85; 90; 92-96; 98; 100; 102; 109-110; 112; 125; 129-130; 143; 148; 155; 165; 172; 184; 191-192; 201-202; 213; 216-217; 221-223; 225; 227-228; 238-239; 247; 251; 260-262; 264; 271-272; 276; 303-308; 311-312. 7,1; 3; 5-8; 10-11; 13-19; 26; 29; 37; 40; 42; 47; 51; 54; 56; 58-61; 64; 67; 70-71; 73; 75-76; 96-98; 119; 122; 138; 140-141; 145-147. 8,1-4; 7-9; 11; 13-14; 20-21; 31-37; 46-47; 49; 55-57; 66; 81. 9,1-3. 10,1. 11,1-2. 12,1; 5-7. 13,2; 4-6. 14,1-10; 18-21; 23-25; 32; 38-39; 42-43; 45; 48-52; 54;

65; 69-70; 72-76; 102-103; 105-106; 108-
109; 118; 120; 139; 163. 15,1-3; 5. 16,2-3;
10; 14-15; 17; 20; 22; 25-26; 28-30; 35-37;
40-42; 44-46. 17,1. 18,1; 4; 6. 19,13-17.
20,1. 21,5-6; 10-11; 15-16; 26; 28; 38-40;
47; 49; 53-55; 58; 62; 71; 80; 90; 95. 22,1-
2. 23,2-3. 25,1-4; 34; 52-53; 55-57; 59; 61;
63-69; 71; 74-76. 26,6; 8-10; 12a-b; 13-16.
27,3-7; 9-10; 13. 28,1a; 3; 6-7. 29,1-3; 10-
12. 30,1; 3. 31,3; 8; 13a; 27-28; 40-42; 49-
50; 53; 56; 60. 32,1; 3-4; 6; 14; 16; 19; 21.
33,1; 3; 6-10; 13. 34,1-9; 12-13. 35,1-3; 5-
6. 36,1-2; 4-14. 37,1; 4-6. 38,6; 8; 11; 16;
21-22. 39,3; 6-7; 12; 16. 40,2-4; 6. 41,1-2;
10; 14-15. 42,1-2. 43,1-3; 5-7. 44,1-4.
45,2-3. 46,1-5; 7. 47,2-3. 48,1. 49,1. 50,1.
52,1; 5. 53,1-3; 5-6. 54,1. 57,1. 58,1. 59,1.
60,1. 62,1-2; 4-5. 64,1. 66,1-4; 10. 67,2-6;
10; 15; 20-21; 27-31; 33. 68,1; 5. 69,1-2.
71,1-2. 76,14; 17; 23.

           SRY   1,1d-e; 2; 4-6; 9; 11;
13-14. 2,1; 3. 3,1. 4,1-2. 5,1a; 3; 6; 8; 19;
24; 29-30. 6,1. 8,7; 29. 11,1. 13,1. 14,1.
15,2. 18,1-2. 19,5; 15; 17; 27; 29-30; 33-35;
37; 39; 46. 21,3-4; 7. 25,1. 29,1. 36,4; 9.
           SSX   1,1. 2,1; 3-7; 10.
3,1-9. 5,1-2. 6,1-2. 8,1-2; 9. 9,1; 4; 6; 8;
11; 13-16; 19; 24; 38-40; 42-45; 47; 60; 120.
10,2-3; 8; 15; 17; 20; 22; 26-27; 31-32; 34-
38; 47-49; 61; 79; 99; 112; 115. 11,3; 5-8;
10; 17; 20-22; 27-31; 37-38; 40; 44; 47; 50-
51; 55; 62; 76; 83. 12,2; 4; 6; 11; 14; 20;
23; 53. 13,6; 9; 28; 38-40; 44.
           WAR   1,2; 5; 7; 9. 12,3-4.
16,21; 55; 60; 64-65. 31,1.
           WIL   1,1-13; 15-18. 2,1;
5; 12. 3,1-4. 5,1. 7,1; 3-4; 8; 11; 16. 8,13.
12,4. 13,2; 10. 17,1. 20,6. 21,1-2. 22,1-5.
23,8-10. 24,19. 25,9; 28. 32,16. 42,10. 50,3
56,1-4. 67,11; 98. 68,23.
           WOR   1,1a-c; 2; 4-6. 2,2;
6; 15; 18; 22; 31; 38; 45; 68; 72; 77; 84-85.
8,1; 28. 9,1a; 6a. 10,5. 11,2. 14,1. 15,1-6;
10; 12. 18,2; 4; 6. 20,4-5. 23,1; 5; 8; 10; 14.
26,3; 7; 9; 12.
           YKS   C26-28; 30. 1Y1-
12; 14-19. 1N1-5; 8-13; 15-85; 87-96; 98-
107; 109-110; 112-137. 1E2-3; 5-20; 22-25;
27-34; 36-37; 39-41; 44-60. 1W1-11; 13-26;
29-30; 32-33; 35-38; 40-48; 50-66; 68-70;
72-73. 1L2-8. 2,1-3. 2B1; 3-13; 16-19.
2N2-5; 7-14. 2W1-4; 6-7; 12. 2E1-2; 6; 12;
14-17. 3Y1-2; 4-5; 7; 9-11; 13-18. 4N1-3.
4E1-2. 5N1-36; 38-43; 45-50; 52-53; 55-
60; 62-67; 69-73; 75. 5E1; 4-5; 7; 10-11;
17-21; 23; 25; 27; 29-30; 32; 34-36; 38-45;
47-55; 57-59; 65-66; 68-73. 5W1-26; 28-30;
32-36; 38. 6N1-5; 9-10; 12-13; 15-21; 23-
27; 29-32; 34-37; 45; 48-52; 54-59; 61-67;
70-77; 79-84; 86-88; 90-110; 112-113; 115-
122; 125-126; 129-136; 138-141; 143-148;

150-152; 155; 157-159; 161-162. 6W1-3; 5-
6. 6E1. 7E1-2. 8N2-17; 19; 22; 24; 26.
8W1. 8E1-2; 4-6. 9W1-9; 11-13; 15-18; 20-
30; 33-78; 82-83; 85-92; 94-103; 105-124;
126-143. 10W1-8; 10-36; 38-39; 41-42.
11E1-5. 11N1-7; 9-11; 13-23. 11W1-3.
13W1-13; 15-17; 19-45. 13E1-2; 4-5; 7-9;
11-16. 13N1-2; 4-5; 8-19. 14E1-5; 7-13; 15-
45; 48-53. 15E1-4; 7-10; 13-17. 16E1; 3-5.
16N2. 16W1-5. 17W1. 18W1-3. 19W1; 3.
20E1-2. 21E1-12. 21W1-2; 6; 8-16. 22W4.
23N1-2; 4-7; 9-11; 13; 15-17; 19; 22-23; 25-
31; 33-36. 23E1-12; 14-19. 24W1-7; 9; 11-
13; 15-16; 18; 21. 24E1-2. 25W1-3; 6; 8-
13; 15-26; 28-33. 26E1-2; 4-5; 7-12. 27W1-
2. 28W1; 5-6; 8-23; 25-35; 37-40. 29W1-7;
9; 12-50. 29E1-20; 22-30. 29N1; 3; 6; 8;
12. 30W1; 3-32; 34-40. CN5. CE1; 11; 35-
39; 41-52. CW2-3; 18; 20; 24; 32. SW,Sk1.
SN,CtA45.

half (½)	HAM	23,41.
small (maneriolum)	LIN	C11.
Destroyed/ dismembered (confusum)	GLS	1,38.
Earl's – King has nothing from	YKS	C37.
Formed from separate lands	GLS	1,55; 60.
free man for making up	NFK	9,45-46; 48. 21,26. 29,4; 7. 34,17.
	SFK	55,1.
Held		
freely	DEV	*15,23-25. 25,25.*
	ESS	23,32. 24,9; 42-43;
61-62. 26,3. 30,4. 32,2. 34,32. 40,9. 41,1. 68,1.		
by holder's free authority (propria libertate)	LIN	CW16.
Hundred-manor comprising	CHS	R4,1. R5,3.
making payments with	CHS	R5,5.
	GLS	1,10; 12.
	SHR	4,1,2; 4; 6.
placed in/belonging to	GLS	1,12.
	SHR	4,1,4-6; 9-11.
wrongfully in	GLS	11,14.
with land in 6	NTH	1,32.
King's	BDF	1,5. 57,4.
	CAM	1,1.
	DBY	14,6.
	DEV	3,32. *13a,1; 3.*
16,56; 74; 80. 24,22. 43,1. 45,1. 51,2.		
	ESS	17,2. 23,28. 41,4.
	HAM	43,4-5.
	HEF	15,3-4. 16,3-4.
	HUN	1,2. 5,2. 19,15; 17; 19.

26,16; 22. 42,10.
WOR 11,2. 15,1; 6; 10;
12. 18,2; 4. 20,4-5. 23,5; 14. 26,3; 7; 9; 12.
YKS 1Y16. 1N5; 19; 26;
28; 38; 40-42; 59; 65; 67-68; 77; 80; 87; 91;
99; 102; 104; 110; 113-115; 123. 1E5; 11;
15-18; 29; 32; 40; 45; 50; 52-54; 56; 59-60.
1W9; 13-14; 17-19; 25; 30; 33; 37; 42; 47;
50-51; 59; 64. 1L4-5; 7. 2B8. 2N2-4. 2E15.
5N6; 19; 30; 47-48; 53; 57; 59; 63; 66-67.
5E1; 11; 17-18; 23; 29-30; 34; 36; 39; 42-
45; 51. 5W17; 20-21; 25-26; 30. 6N26-27;
56; 58; 67; 88; 90; 98; 100; 107; 113; 116;
134-136; 138; 141; 151; 155. 8E4. 9W3; 6-
8; 11-12; 16; 18; 24; 34-35; 39-40; 45; 47-
48; 50-52; 63; 68; 77-78; 86-87; 94; 96; 98;
100; 103; 106; 110; 115; 119-122; 124; 129;
135-136; 138-140. 10W3; 6; 8; 12-14; 16;
27; 39; 42. 11E2-3; 5. 11N4. 13W1-3; 12;
17; 25; 35. 13E2; 4-5; 7; 12. 13N8; 10; 12;
18-19. 14E13; 17-19; 26; 28-29; 31-32; 34;
36; 48-49; 52-53. 21E1. 21W10. 23N4; 11;
28-29. 23E2; 6; 8-9; 17. 24W5; 9; 15; 21.
25W1-3; 6; 8-10; 15; 19-20; 23-24; 29-31.
26E4-5; 8; 12. 27W1. 28W11; 30. 29W2; 7;
14; 17; 20; 35-36; 47. 29E12; 16-17; 20; 27.
30W15; 17; 22; 26-27; 29-30; 38-39. CE35;
45; 49.

comprising more
manors 1086 than
TRE   BRK 33,4.
               DEV *39,6; 14-15.*
               ESS 27,6.
               KEN 5,18.
               NFK 9,11. 48,3.
               SOM 3,1.
added to manor NFK 26,5.
added/in manor to
which it did not
belong TRE   BDF 1,1b. 57,4.
               BKM 57,10.
               ESS 52,2.
               HRT 16,3. 22,2. 33,4.
               MDX 7,1; 3; 7-8. 8,2.
comprising a manor
before 1086   YKS 2N5.
lying in manor in
another Hundred CHS 1,1.
               GLS 4,1.
               NFK 14,1.
               NTH 43,5.
               SFK 6,11. 14,69. 38,24.
not in any manor KEN 9,39.
               SRY 1,13. 19,35; 48.
not held as a manor SRY 19,35.
placed in manor
with King's assent BDF 1,4.
removed and put in
another County   HAM 69,22.
land/resources/men
put out-side manor HEF 1,4; 39-42; 44-46.

wrongfully in
another manor   DEV 1,40.
wrongfully and by
force put in another
manor   HRT 1,17.
Lordship – Earl has
nothing from   YKS C37.
Making of   NFK 1,201. 6,6.
Making up-land for
unknown manor NFK 34,18.
Man not belonging to KEN 5,1.
Meadow/mill/houses
held as   OXF 28,8.
Member of outside GLS 1,13.
Money
  owed/paid from
  another manor DEV 1,11; 37.
  paid to visiting wife
  of lord   SHR 4,1,21.
Royal (regale; de
regno)   HAM 1,42; 47.
               NFK 1,71.
               WAR B4.
Tax
  paid in Hundred HUN D14.
  paid with land of
  another landholder WIL 25,2.
  not paid with
  manor   KEN *2,30.*
Transfer of hall/stock
to another   BRK 58,2.
Unjustly received HAM 6,1.
Unoccupied   SHR 1,3.
Value
  deteriorated by loss
  of wood-land for
  Forest   CHS FD9,1.
  if well managed NTH 6a,27.
Villager/small holder
added to   NFK 9,87.
Villagers holding MDX 3,17.
Villages held as more
than 1 by same holder OXF 28,3; 6. 29,3; 5.
               HEF 1,63.
Waste   YKS SN,CtA45.
Work of   SRY 1,13.
See also: Manor/village/land and cross references
thereunder.

MANOR/village/land
Abbey, land lying in
TRE but not 1086 CAM 21,5.
               HEF 15,1.
Accounted in another
(computare)   HAM 20,2.
               LEC 43,7.
               LIN 5,3.
               SFK 6,308.
               SRY 13,1.
Assessed in another
(appreciare)   BDF 51,4.
               CAM 1,14; 19. 5,24; 29;

43; 45. 12,4. 14,3;
82. 32,5; 44.
ESS　　1,22. 34,31. 44,4.
HRT　　9,6. 42,3.
HUN　　20,5.
LEC　　14,4.
LIN　　1,7-8; 25. 3,37.
7,34. 12,85. 27,48. 30,5. 32,33.
MDX　　9,8.
NFK　　1,12-13; 16-17; 40;
48; 51; 53-55; 57; 59-60; 79; 83-84; 91; 104;
132; 137-138; 149; 165; 183; 190; 194-195;
207; 214; 227-230; 232-236. 2,5; 9-10. 4,3;
7; 11; 15; 17; 21; 34; 54; 56. 7,21. 8,12; 73-
74; 79; 81; 88; 104; 117-118. 9,85; 108; 146;
170; 179; 181-182. 10,7-8; 14. 12,3; 14,3;
38; 42. 15,15; 28. 17,1; 24; 33; 45; 48.
19,10; 23; 30; 33, 20,19-22; 32; 35. 21,36.
22,10-13; 15; 20-23. 26,4-5. 31,40. 33,6.
36,7.
NTH　　4,6. 18,8. 54,3.
56,53.
SHR　　4,8,3. 4,28,5. 6,3-
4. 7,2.
SFK　　1,64; 78-80; 82; 87;
92-93. 3,1-2; 4; 7; 13; 16-17; 20; 31; 33; 45;
49-50; 52-53; 62; 80; 83; 105. 4,12. 6,11; 22;
69; 71; 104; 106; 136-137; 149; 154; 255-
257; 264; 266-270; 288-289; 308; 310. 7,12;
26; 34; 43; 52; 63; 132. 8,25; 43; 55. 21,20-
21; 24. 22,2. 23,1; 6. 25,36; 40; 54; 62.
29,6. 31,14; 35. 34,10; 18. 38,23; 25. 39,13.
47,1. 52,9. 56,5. 62,6. 68,2.
SRY　　5,30.
SSX　　10,8; 23.
WAR　　42,2.
WOR　　2,41.
YKS　　10W43.
lying/joined to
manor/village in
another County
DBY　　1,25.
ESS　　1,3; 9. 32,40. 40,5.
LEC　　23,2; 5-6.
NFK　　1,51. 8,50.
OXF　　24,6.
SHR　　4,1,5. 4,28,5.
SFK　　19,2. 51,2.
in another because
ploughed by
ploughs of that
village
KEN　　9,8.
in revenue of
another
SHR　　4,8,8. 4,28,4.
Attached/belonging/
lying/held or placed
to/in another
manor/village
BDF　　17,3. 23,7; 52.
32,10. 51,4. 53,29-
30.
BRK　　58,3. 65,18.
BKM　　3a,1. 11,1. 17,30.
CAM　　1,14; 19-20. 5,2.
13,2; 5. 14,37. 17,6. 23,1. 25,9. 26,20.

32,13.
CHS　　8,21; 36; 41. 27,3.
FT1,1-9. FT2,1-16. FT3,2-6.
DBY　　1,1; 9; 11-16; 18-20;
26-29; 32; 35; 38. 3,1. 4,2. 6,48; 53; 57; 59;
89; 91. 8,3. 9,3. 10,4; 12; 15; 17. 17,14; 23.
DEV　　1,5-6; 11; 15; 29;
40-41; 46; 49; *50;* 66-67. 2,10. 3,8; 11; *12;*
19; 26; 30; *40;* 72; 76; 80. 5,2; 8. 15,12;
16; 29-31; 38; 40; *47; 49-50;* 53; 57; 79.
16,33; 56; 74; 83; 92; 94; 144. 17,*11-12;* 13;
14; 17; 92; 105. 19,*3-4;* 6; *16;* 18; 36-37;
40; 43. 20,7; 10. 21,11. 23,*3;* 5; 20; 23-24.
24,5; 8; 18; *24.* 25,20; 25. 28,16. 34,10; 14;
34; 43; *44;* 45-46; 49; 55; 57. *35,5-9; 22.*
36,*2;* 18; *23;* 25-26. 38,1. 39,10; 14; *15;* 16.
40,4; 7. 42,5; 14; 16; 21. 43,3. 44,1. *49,7.*
50,1. 52,33.
DOR　　1,2; 8. 3,18. 27,6.
34,14. 35,1.
ESS　　1,4; 6; 19. 2,2.
18,11. 20,25; 36; 51; 63. 23,28. 28,6. 30,3;
23. 32,16; 40. 37,3. 46,2. 52,1. 87,1.
GLS　　1,17; 24-25; 34-37;
41; 48; 54. 2,8-9. 3,1; 3; 5; 7. 4,1. 34,2.
HAM　　1,22; 31. 2,1; 10.
3,5; 8-9. 6,13. 21,10. 23,18; 44. 27,1. 29,4.
32,3. 69,6.
HEF　　1,3; 7-8; 10c; 11-36;
44. 2,31.
HRT　　1,1-9; 12. 7,4. 15,5.
16,11. 25,2. 28,1-3; 6. 34,13. 36,4; 6. 39,1.
44,1.
HUN　　7,7. 9,4. D19.
KEN　　2,21; 24-25; 30; 33.
5,171.
LEC　　1,1b-c; 3-4; 7. 2,1.
6,4. 8,5. 9,4. 10,7. 13,2; 26. 14,3-4. 15,2;
7; 10. 25,4. 29,3; 18. 35,1. 43,1; 6. 44,1-2.
LIN　　1,2; 7-8; 64; 66.
11,8. 14,72; 95. 16,8; 48. 22,15. 24,9.
51,11. 57,55. 65,5. CK20; 41.
MDX　　8,3. 9,8. 15,1.
NFK　　1,2; 29-31; 33-35;
40-42; 51; 53; 55; 57; 71; 76; 87; 90-91; 93;
104; 114; 126; 132; 135; 143; 147-148; 150;
164; 176; 183; 192; 206; 209-210; 212; 218;
228; 230; 232; 236-237; 239-240. 2,1; 3-4.
4,9; 14; 17; 48. 6,6. 7,2. 8,8; 10; 37; 62;
108-109; 118; 130. 9,2; 85; 87-88; 167.
10,5; 8-9; 12; 15; 20; 30; 39; 41; 65; 77.
12,3. 13,16. 14,3; 22-23; *38.* 15,4; 10; 15;
28. 17,21; 48. 19,28. 20,22. 21,19; 31; 36.
22,10-11; 13; 16; 23. 23,5; 13. 24,6. 25,21-
22. 26,5. 31,9; 40. 34,3; 9; 14; 16. 36,7.
49,4. 66,41; 67.
NTH　　1,1-2; 8; 13; 15-19.
4,3; 10. 5,2. 6,10b-c. 6a,9; 12; 16; 18-19.
12,2. 18,7; 80. 23,3. 39,11. 44,1b-c. 47,1b-
c. 54,3. 56,1; 16-18; 20b-j; 45; 53.
NTT　　1,8; 26; 66. 5,4; 11;

18. 9,21; 85-87; 91; 118. 10,21; 41. 12,22.
13,3; 14. 21,3. 23,1-2. 24,1. 27,3. 28,2.
30,15.

	OXF	1,7a. 7,58. 24,6.
	SHR	4,11,13. 4,26,2.

4,28,4-5. 5,9. 6,3. 7,2.

SOM 1,4; 6; 11-12; 17;
27-28. 2,8-9. 4,1. 5,2; 15; 18; 37; 40-41; 43;
47; 48; 52; 53; 59; 62; 69. 6,7; 14; 19. 8,1;
5; 11; 14; 20; 23-24; 30. 19,*13-14;* 20; *26;
29;* 35; 57; *59; 63-64; 68; 72-73; 78; 81.*
21,6; 35; 37; 47; 54-55; *85;* 90; 92; 97.
22,*13;* 14; *19;* 20; *28.* 24,11; *14;* 30. 25,1;
3; 6; 13; 15; 18; *27; 30;* 33; *40; 43; 45;* 46;
55. 26,3; *8.* 27,1; 3. 35,1-2; 4; 12; 14; 24.
36,2; 5; 7; 13. 37,4; 6; 12. 44,2. 45,1-3; *5;*
12. 46,*4;* 5; 11; *14;* 21. 47,5; 25.

STS 1,1-3; 6-7. 2,2; 4; 6-
8; 11; 13-14; 16; 20-22. 7,2. 8,16; 21. 10,4.
11,5-6; 56; 67. 12,22.

SFK 1,11; 41; 64; 78; 85;
100-101; 108; 115. 2,8. 3,95. 4,12. 6,11-13;
43; 82; 104; 256. 7,6; 20; 26; 34-36; 46; 53;
63; 72; 75-76. 8,*6;* 37; 43. 9,2. 11,5. 14,135.
16,5; 33. 21,*22;* 80. 25,39; 41. 28,1b. 34,6;
16. 38,23; 25. 43,1-2. 46,6. 47,1. 52,9.
62,6. 65,1. 67,8; 15. 76,17; 20.

SRY 1,11; 15. 5,13.
19,39. 29,2.

SSX 9,120. 10,66; 81-82;
84; 101; 103-104; 106-110; 116. 11,37.
12,10; 20-21; 23; 28-29; 33; 53. 13,7; 10;
15-16; 37-38; 46-47; 51-53.

WAR 1,8-9. 16,49. 27,6.
WIL 8,6. 12,4. 29,5.
WOR 1,1b-c. 2,3-5; 7; 13-
14; 16-17; 19-21; 23-25; 29-30; 32-37; 39;
41; 47; 52; 55; 58; 69-71; 73-75. 8,28. 10,5.
18,6.

YKS C33. 1Y2; 17.
1E26; 35; 38. 1L1-3; 6. 2W1; 8. 3Y3. 5E9.
5W24. 6N35. 8N5. 9W1; 26; 28; 70; 81;
93; 131. 10W43. 11E5. 11N8. 13E10.
13N13. 14E10. 15E5; 11. 21E5. 23N8; 12;
14; 18; 20-21; 24; 32. 23E4; 13. 24W17.
26E6. 29N7. 30W1; 37. CW9-10; 40.
SW,H9. SW,Cr5. SE,How6.

Belonging rightly in
another
	DEV	*42,16.*
	WOR	26,15.

Dependency of
(appendicium)
	DOR	18,2. 19,10.
	LEC	14,2.
	NTH	6,7-8. 16,1. 23,9.

35,1i-j.
	SOM	2,1.
	STS	1,13; 15-18; 20-21;

23-25; 27; 29; 33; 42. 4,3; 5; 8. 8,12; 22.
11,19; 23.
	WIL	27,3.

Dimensions of
	CHS	1,12. 2,2-6; 10.

26,9. G3.
	DBY	1,30. 9,5. 10,16.
	LIN	1,26; 31; 34-35; 38;

81. 4,17; 20. 7,8; 10; 56. 8,1; 17; 20. 12,21.
13,1. 14,46; 83.

NFK 1,1; 6; 9; 11; 16-23;
25-26; 28-29; 32-33; 35; 42; 51-52; 57; 59;
70-73; 77; 81-82; 85-88; 93-96; 105; 124;
128; 132-133; 136; 139; 142-144; 146; 150-
154; 157; 159-161; 174; 179; 182-183; 185-
186; 191-203; 206; 209-212; 215-216; 218-
219; 221; 225-226; 228; 230; 232-234; 236-
239. 2,1-2; 4-5; 9; 12. 3,1. 4,1-3; 7; 9; 16-
17; 26; 29-31; 34; 39; 41; 45; 47; 50; 52;
56. 5,1-3; 6. 6,1-3; 5-6. 7,2; 9; 11; 15-19.
8,1-3; 6-8; 16; 18; 21-22; 30; 34; 40; 44-47;
50-52; 56; 58; 61-62; 64; 68; 72; 84; 87; 89;
91; 98-99; 102-105; 108; 110; 112; 114; 121;
128; 130; 132. 9,2; 6; 9; 11-12; 23-24; 26-
29; 31-33; 46; 59; 63; 68-71; 73; 75; 78; 80;
82; 87; 94-95; 97-99; 103-104; 109; 146;
149; 154; 162; 166; 174-175; 178-179; 185;
212; 216. 10,1-10; 15; 18; 20-25; 28; 30; 33;
35; 38; 40; 45; 57-58; 65; 72-74; 81; 90-91.
11,5. 12,1; 5; *17;* 20; 26-27; 33-34; 36; 42.
13,2; 4-6; 8-10; 14-15; 18-19; 23-24. 14,1-
2; 8; 12-15; 17-19; 21; 23-24; 29-30; 35; 38-
41. 15,1-3; 7-10; 16-18; 24-26. 16,1; 4-5.
17,3; 5; 8-13; 15-19; 23; 25-27; 32; 35-38;
40; 43; 49; 51; 53-54; 56; 62; 64. 18,1. 19,3;
9; 11; 15; 18; 21; 24; 32; 36. 20,1-2; 6-11;
13; 15-16; 23; 25-26; 29; 31-36. 21,2-6; 10;
17; 19; 21; 23-27; 29; 33-34. 22,1; 6; 13; 20;
23. 23,1-3; 12; 15-18. 24,4-7. 25,1-2; 6; 9-
12; 15-17. 26,1-3; 5. 27,1-2. 28,1. 29,5-6;
8; 11. 30,5. 31,1-6; 8; 10-11; 17; 22-23; 28-
29; 33-34; 36; 38-39; 41-43. 32,1; 3-4; 7.
33,2. 34,1; 3-5; 7-9; 16-17; 20. 35,10; 12;
16. 36,5-6. 37,1. 39,1. 40,1. 41,1. 46,1.
48,1-2; 4; 6. 49,2; 5. 50,1; 7. 51,3; 6; 8.
52,3. 53,*t.* 54,1. 55,1-2. 58,1-2. 60,1. 61,1-
2. 64,1. 65,14. 66,16.

	RUT	R18-20.
	SFK	1,1-2; 8; 23; 40; 75-

77; 88; 90; 94; 96-97; 99; 104; 106; 111; 115;
118-121; 122b. 2,6; 10; 13; 16. 3,1; 3-4; 13;
34; 46; 55-56; 61; 67; 69; 72; 74; 85; 94-95;
98; 100. 4,1; 6; 13-14; 31; 35; 38; 42. 5,1.
6,1-2; 26; 30; 42-43; 47; 82-83; 85; 90; 112-
114; 129; 135; 148-149; 156-157; 166; 171;
179; 191-192; 209; 213; 222; 225; 238; 247;
260; 262; 271; 275; 287; 292; 303-308; 310-
311. 7,1; 3-4; 6; 13; 15; 19; 37; 40; 42; 47;
56; 58; 60; 69; 75-77; 79-97; 99-100; 104;
110; 118-120. 8,7-8; 11; 13-14; 34-35; 46;
48; 55-56; 58-59. 9,1-3. 12,1; 3; 6-7. 13,2.
14,1-21; 23-28; 32; 38; 42-43; 45; 48-55; 57-
60; 62-83; 85-88; 93; 95; 98-99; 101-106;
108-114; 117; 120; 139; 162; 167. 15,1-2; 5.
16,2; 6; 10-11; 15; 18; 40-41; 45. 17,1.
18,1. 19,13-14. 20,1. 21,1; 3; 5-7; 10-11;

15-16; 26; 28; 38-40; 42-43; 45; 53-55; 64; 80; 95. 23,5. 24,1. 25,1-3; 5a; 35; 42; 49; 53; 55; 57; 59; 61-62; 67; 76; 78; 81; 84; 93. 26,9; 12d; 13. 27,3-7; 9-10; 13. 28,1a-b; 3; 6-7. 29,1; 12. 31,8-9; 11; 20; 40-42; 44-47; 49; 56; 60. 32,3; 6; 19; 21; 28. 33,1-4; 6-7; 9-10; 13. 34,2-3; 5-6; 13. 35,1-3; 5-6. 36,1-2; 4. 37,1; 6. 38,6; 8; 11. 39,6-12. 40,3-4; 6. 41,1-2; 7-8; 10; 14; 17-18. 42,1-2. 43,1-4. 44,1-4. 45,2. 46,1-5. 47,3. 48,1. 49,1. 53,2; 5. 54,1-3. 57,1. 58,1. 62,5. 64,1. 66,1-3; 6. 67,3; 5; 12; 14-15; 18-19; 27,32. 68,4-5. 71,1. 76,4.

        YKS   C23-24; 27-28; 30-33; 35. 1Y1; 3-7; 9-11; 14-15; 17-18. 1N3; 5; 11; 38; 48; 54-56; 66; 68; 105. 1W30. 2,2. 2B2-3; 6-7; 9-11; 13; 17. 2,N3-4; 24. 2W1; 3; 7; 9; 12. 2E1-2; 14. 3Y1-2; 4; 8-11; 15; 17-18. 4N2-3. 4E1-2. 5N1-9; 11; 14; 17-18; 26; 28-30; 32; 45; 53; 58-60; 63; 65-66. 5E7; 17; 29; 59; 65-66. 5W1-8; 11-14; 16-25; 32-34; 38. 6N2-13; 15-21; 23-37; 39; 45-52; 55-88; 90-92; 95-109; 112-113; 115-126; 129-130; 132; 134-135; 137-138; 141; 143; 146-147; 151-152; 162. 6W1; 5. 8N2; 5; 7-8; 10; 22-23. 8W1. 8E2; 5. 9W1-5; 24-25; 34-38; 48-50; 64; 70; 119. 10W1; 4; 41. 11E1. 11W1. 13W1-7; 9-12; 14; 16-18; 27-28; 33; 35; 37. 13E5; 13-15. 13N9; 13; 17-18. 14E8; 11-25; 28-30; 32-34; 36; 38-39; 42-48; 50-54. 15E4; 12-15; 17. 16N1-2. 16W1; 3. 17W1. 18W2-3. 19W3. 20E4. 21E2; 5-6; 9-11. 21W1-2; 12-14. 22W2-3. 23N1-2; 4; 8-11; 13; 15-16; 18; 20; 25-31; 34. 23E2-5; 8; 12; 14; 18. 24W1; 6; 10; 12; 15-16; 18. 25W1-3; 6; 8; 10-12; 15-16; 19-20; 24; 29-30. 26E8; 10. 28W1; 5-6; 10-11; 13; 30-32; 35; 37. 29W1-7; 9-10; 24; 26. 29E11. 29N3; 5; 8.

Held/shared by more/others than those enumerated   NFK   1,221. 9,26; 59. 10,30; 74. 14,13; 15; 17. 15,8; 25. 17,12; 16-19; 40. 32,7. 60,1. 64,1.

        SFK   1,20; 22; 115. 2,10; 16. 3,4; 69; 72; 100. 4,6. 5,1. 6,1-2; 113; 166; 271; 308. 7,56; 92; 96-97; 99; 119. 8,34; 48. 9,2. 14,1-2; 11; 14-21; 24-28; 54-55; 60; 65-66; 69; 73-75; 77-83; 85-86; 93; 98-99; 102; 104-106; 108; 110-112; 114. 16,6; 11; 15; 41. 19,14. 21,39-40; 42; 45; 53-54. 22,3. 25,2; 42; 61-62. 26,16. 31,20-21; 56. 32,21; 28. 33,1-3; 7. 34,13. 38,6; 8. 42,2. 53,2. 54,1. 58,1. 64,1. 66,2-3. 68,4. 71,1.

Land

 added/attached/   ESS   1,3; 9; 13. 11,2.
 belonging to   14,5. 15,1. 17,1. 20,7; 19; 23; 25; 43; 45. 22,3; 8. 23,2. 24,9; 22; 48; 59. 25,2; 5. 28,7. 30,21; 27; 34; 39. 32,9. 33,1; 6. 34,10. 35,2. 36,3; 6. 37,3; 9.

42,1. 44,1. 48,2. 49,1. 52,2. 83,1. 84,1. 90,79.

        NFK   1,4; 10; 28. 9,1; 78. 13,2. 14,1. 17,10; 18. 19,15. 29,3. 31,28.
        SFK   4,25. 25,55. 26,15. 40,3. 47,3.

added/lying where   DEV   *19,3-4. 35,5-9.*
it did not belong   *36,2. 39,6. 40,1; 3. 44,1. 48,2; 8-11.*
        NFK   22,13.
        SOM   *45,5.*

could not be put outside its own   CAM   26,23.
making up, for   NFK   8,117; 120-121. 9,8. 13,10. 25,24. 34,13; 18-19.

making up in another Hundred   SFK   7,55.
resources/men
added to   ESS   1,3. 3,8.
        GLS   1,1-2; 10; 14.

taken from or not
belonging   BRK   1,14.
        BKM   12,19. 38,1.
        CAM   5,2.
        CON   1,4; 6. 2,13-14. 4,1; 26. *67.* 3,11; *12;* 32; 92. 7,4. *15,57.* 16,7; *9;* 80; 92. 22,1. 23,5; 20. *24,24.* 34,2. 39,10.
        DEV   1,5; 22; 25; 34; *50;*
        DOR   1,13. 35,1.
        ESS   20,6. 30,23. 33,17.
        GLS   1,11; 19.
        HAM   1,2.
        HRT   1,1. 15,4-6; 9. 16,1. 34,13. 39,1. 44,1.
        HUN   D10.
        KEN   1,1.
        OXF   1,3.
        SOM   1,1-2; 4-5; 7; 9; *11;* 20-21; 27. 5,5. 10,1. 19,2; *15. 21,65.* 24,8. 25,7; 55. 46,5. 47,25.
        SRY   1,2; 9. 29,1.
        WOR   1,1b.

Member of
(membrum)   BDF   49,3.
        GLS   1,2; 9; 12-13; 15; 21. 3,1. 10,1.
        HEF   1,5; 10a. 29,2.
        LEC   1,3. 29,3.
        NTH   1,2a; 6; 13a; 15a. 35,1a. 56,20a.
        SHR   2,1. 7,4; 6.
        SOM   1,2.
        STS   1,6-7. 2,11; 16; 20; 22. 11,6.
        WOR   2,31; 45; 48. 9,2.

Reduced/lacking in
resources   HEF   1,1.
        NTH   1,11-12; 14.

Wrongfully in/ joined

to/removed from
another CON 3,7.
DEV 1,*40*; 41. *15,14-15.*
25,25. 40,6-7.
SRY 1,11. 8,29.
See also: Assembly; Burgess; Canon; Church;
Claim; County; Crime/offence; Customary due;
Deliverer; Delivery; Eustace; Exaction; Exchange;
Expedition; Fine; free man; Freeman; Gift; Grant;
Guard; Hall; Head; Herring; Holding; Honour;
House; Hundred; Jurisdiction; Jurisdiction, full;
Lady of manor; Land; Lease; Lordship; Man;
Market; Meadow; Mercy; Mill; Obligations;
Outlier; Priest; Reeve; Remove; Resident;
Resources; Revenue; Salt house; Separated;
Sheriff; Site; Smallholder; Tax; Third part; Third
penny; Third/two thirds part; Throne; Tithe;
Tribute; Value; Village; Villager; Welshman;
Withdraw; Woodland; Work.
MARCH – See Welsh March.
MARE (equa) CON *4,10.*
DEV *16,36; 50.*
DOR *47,8.*
ESS 34,27. 35,8.
HRT 31,8.
NFK 8,21. 9,12. 21,4.
31,33. 34,4.
SOM *5,4. 8,17. 24,27-28.*
SRY 22,4.
Foal, with DOR *55,16.*
NFK 13,15.
Forest, person having
charge of King's SRY 22,4.
Unbroken (equa CON *1,1-3; 16. 4,7.*
indomita) *5,1,1-2; 4-5; 7-8;*
11-13. 5,3,1; 20; 22; 27-28. 5,4,18. 5,5,9.
5,6,2-5; 7-8. 5,13,2; 5. 5,14,4. 5,23,1.
5,25,1.
DEV *15,36. 16,164.*
34,6; 14.
DOR *47,3.*
SOM *1,20. 5,24; 33; 40-*
41; 43. 6,9; 15. 8,9; 13; 30. 19,24; 26; 51;
53; 68. 21,23. 24,12-13. 25,9; 14. 36,1.
42,1.
Wild (equa silvatica) CON *1,1; 14. 2,1. 5,1,10.*
5,3,3.
DEV *1,46; 57. 10,1.*
16,5; 31. 19,16. 23,18; 21. 24,13-14. 25,1.
52,40.
NFK 1,200. 4,38; 41.
8,98; 107; 119. 9,71; 88; 94. 13,7. 14,2.
21,14. 34,17.
SOM *24,34. 25,9; 26; 55.*
SFK 1,115. 7,1. 14,23.
27,4. 37,1.
See also: Foal; Horse.
MARGINAL entries/notes/signs – See Domesday
Book.
MARK
Gold, of CAM 22,6.
CHS C24.

DOR 1,24.
GLS 1,21.
HAM 21,6. 69,12.
HEF 1,44.
HRT 42,6.
KEN P19.
LIN 13,1. CW4. CK18;
39.
NFK 17,18; 22.
SOM 1,31.
SFK 1,103. 14,39.
SRY 5,6. 6,4. 36,1.
SSX 11,3; 7.
WOR 11,2.
Silver, of BKM 17,30.
CHS C2. 1,6.
CON 5,1,5; 7-8; 13.
DBY 6,33. S3.
DEV C4. 1,14. 2,1.
DOR B1-4.
ESS 5,11. B6.
GLS 1,10; 21.
HEF 1,44.
KEN 5,162.
LIN C21. 8,13.
NTT S3. 9,73; 114.
12,18. 17,16.
SOM 19,9.
SFK 32,19.
SRY 12,2.
YKS 10W41. CN4.

MARKET
(mercatum; portus) BDF 1,2a. 18,6.
BRK B7.
CON 2,6. 4,2-3. 5,1,2.
5,2,11.
DEV *11,1.* 16,3.
GLS 1,7; 15; 24; 47.
HAM 1,2; 42; 45.
HEF 2,8.
KEN 1,4. 2,27. 8,1.
LEC 29,3.
LIN 7,56. 14,97. 24,13;
45.
NFK 1,19.
NTH 6,10a. 35,1a.
OXF 1,6.
SOM 1,8; 10; 20; 26. 2,1.
9,3.
STS 10,1.
SFK 1,1; 12; 40; 97.
6,191. 7,3. 14,120.
18,1. 25,1.
WIL 12,4.
half (½) LIN 1,64.
NFK 1,212.
third (⅓) SFK 42,2.
quarter (¼) NFK 13,16.
Bishop's SFK 18,1.
Burgesses dwelling in SFK 6,191.
Castle, in CON *2,6. 4,2.*

	SFK	18,1.
Day of	BRK	B7.
	CON	2,6.
	DEV	*11,1.*
	SFK	18,1.
changed	SFK	18,1.
Dependency of	SOM	1,10.
King, given by	SFK	7,3. 18,1.
Meat (macellum)	YKS	C3.
Men living in	GLS	1,15.
New	BRK	1,3.
	GLS	1,7.
	LIN	14,66.
Place (forum)	LIN	24,91.
	NTH	1,8.
	WOR	2,51.
houses in	WOR	2,51.
Queen, set up by	GLS	1,24.
Rights (thol et theim)	DBY	S5.
	HUN	B14.
	LIN	C2; 11. T5.
	NTT	S5.
	WAR	3,4.
	YKS	C36.
Shared between King		
and Abbot	SFK	14,120.
Smallholders, in	SFK	42,2.
Stall (bancus)	YKS	C3.
Taken away from		
manor	CON	4,2.
Tolls	BDF	1,1a.
Value	SFK	42,2.
reduced because of		
nearby market	CON	2,6.
	SFK	18,1.

See also: Fourth part; Merchant; Port; Third
penny; Trading.

MARRIAGE	NFK	21,14.
	SFK	7,36. 14,38.
	SRY	1,1d.
Forfeiture		
of house on		
widow's re-		
marriage	SRY	1,1d.
of land on widow's		
remarriage within		
one year	NFK	10,67.
Land given on	DEV	*16,44.*
	GLS	68,13.
	HRT	25,2.
	SOM	27,3.
	SFK	7,36.
	SRY	25,2.
	WOR	2,33. *11,1.*
by King/Queen	BKM	56,2.
	DEV	27,1.
	GLS	34,8.
	OXF	58,34.
Mill given on	OXF	58,34.
Payment by wife to		
King by reason of	SHR	C5.

Portion (maritagium)		
land given as	HRT	25,2.
land of, held by		
husband	BDF	24,18.
	CAM	21,9.
land, part of	BDF	55,12.
land of, held by		
wife	BDF	55,5-8.
Wife – right to her		
own property before		
and after separation	YKS	CE15.

See also: Dower; Gift; Widow; Wife.

MARSH (mariscus;	CAM	1,9. 5,9; 39. 7,8.
maresc)		9,2. 14,2; 59. 17,1.
		23,5. 24,1. 32,37-
		38; 40. 39,2.
	ESS	21,3. 29,1. 36,3.
		66,1. B1.
	HUN	4,1. 6,6; 11.
	KEN	7,29. 9,7; 13-15;
		20-21.
	LIN	1,3. 7,43; 50. 11,3-
4. 12,81. 24,14; 54; 57-58. 26,52. 63,26.		
64,10; 13. 67,4.		
	NFK	1,208. 15,1. 65,17.
Dimensions unknown	NFK	15,1.
Man going into	NFK	1,197. 35,16.
Rendering plough-		
shares	CAM	*5,9. 14,2.* 17,1.
Sheep, for	NFK	12,42.

See also: Eels.

MARSHAL		
(marescal)	CON	5,1,3.
	ESS	30,16. 62.
	HAM	56,3. 62.
	SFK	65.
	WIL	M12. 59.
	YKS	CW17.
MARSHLAND		
(broca; brocus)	DBY	1,26.
	YKS	2W6.

See also: Water meadow.

MARTEN skins		
King's right of pre-		
emption	CHS	C17.
Timber of	CHS	C22.
MASON		
(cementarius)	HAM	3,1.
	HEF	2,27.
MASS sung		
by priest	NFK	1,195.
for King/Queen	BDF	57,19.
	HEF	A1.
	NFK	1,196. 45,1.

See also: Prayers; Psalms.

MAST (paisso) – See Fodder; Woodland.

MEAD keeper		
(medarius)	CAM	*3,5.*
MEADOW (pratum)	BDF	8,2. 25,7. 29,1.
	BRK	1,1-3; 5-11; 15-23;
25-28; 30-42; 44-45; 47. 2,1-2. 3,1. 4,1.		

67,1; 3-6. 68,7; 9-10. 69,6-7. 70,2. 74,1.
75,1. 78,5; 12-13; 15-16.
      HAM 1,1-3; 8; 11-22; 25-
30; 34-39; 41-47; W3-4; W8; W13-15; W19.
2,1-11; 13-15; 18; 20; 23; 25. 3,1-11; 13; 16-
20; 24-26. 4,1. 5,1. 5a,1. 6,1; 3; 5-9; 12-
17. 7,1. 8,1-2. 9,2. 10,1. 12,1. 14,1-6.
15,1-5. 16,1-5. 17,1-3. 18,1-3. 19,1. 20,1.
21,2-4; 5-9; 22,1. 23,1-8; 10; 12-20; 22-23;
25-26; 33-34; 36-38; 40; 42; 49; 51-59; 62;
64-68. 27,1-2. 28,6-8. 29,1-3; 5-6; 10-16.
30,1. 31,1. 32,1; 4. 35,1-3; 6-7; 9. 38,1.
39,1; 3. 42,1. 43,1-2; 4; 6. 44,1; 3-4. 45,1-
2; 5-6; 8-9. 46,1. 47,3. 49,1. 50,1-2. 51,1-
2. 52,1. 53,2. 55,1-2. 56,1-2. 58,1. 60,2.
61,1. 62,1-2. 63,1. 66,1. 68,1; 6-7; 9; 11.
69,1-5; 7; 9; 11-12; 17; 22; 27-29; 32; 35-
39; 41-43; 45-47; 50-52. NF2,3. NF8,2.
NF9,2; 11-13; 36-40; 43; 45. NF10,3.
IoW1,1-7; 10; 13-15. IoW2,1. IoW5,1.
IoW6,1-8; 14-16; 19. IoW7,5; 7-8; 17-18;
21. IoW8,3; 6; 8-9; 11-12. IoW9,1-2; 5; 8;
11-12; 17-20; 23-24.
      HEF 1,4. 2,4; 6; 8; 11-
17; 19-21; 23; 25-36; 39-40 42-46; 49-51.
7,1; 3-4. 8,2; 5. 15,6-9. 19,9-10.
      HRT 5,26. 15,3. 43,1.
      HUN B18. 1,1-2; 5-10.
2,1-8. 3,1. 4,1-4. 5,1-2. 6,1-9; 11-16; 18-
26. 7,1-7. 8,1-4. 9,1-4. 10,1. 11,1. 12,1.
13,1-5. 14,1. 15,1. 16,1. 17,1. 18,1. 19,1;
3-6; 8-9; 11; 13-15; 17-19; 23-25; 28-32.
20,1-9. 21,1. 22,1-2. 23,1. 24,1. 25,2. 26,1.
28,1. 29,1; 3; 5-6.
      KEN C1. P3; 19. 1,1-4.
2,3-17; 19-20; 22; 25-26; 28-30; 32-33; 35-
36; 41. 3,1-6; 8-9; 11-21. 4,1-3; 5-6; 8-14;
16. 5,1-2; 5-6; 9-20; 23-24; 27; 29-33; 38-
51; 53; 56-60; 63; 65-68; 70-72; 74; 77-80;
82-91; 93-106; 108; 110-111; 113-114; 123-
124; 128-129; 138; 142; 144-146; 158; 162-
168; 170; 172; 175; 185; 191; 208. 6,1. 7,2-
7; 9; 11-14; 17; 19; 27. 8,1. 9,1-5; 16-18;
22; 24-25; 28; 30-33; 36; 42; 49; 53. 10,1-
2. 11,1-2. 12,1; 3-4. 13,1.
      LEC C17. 1,1a-c; 2-10;
12. 2,1-2; 4-5. 3,1-2; 6-9; 12-16. 5,1-3. 6,1-
3; 5-6. 7,2. 8,1; 4-5. 9,1; 3. 10,1; 3-4; 6-7;
9-11; 15-17. 11,1. 13,1-2; 4; 7-8; 13; 15-17;
20-24; 26; 28; 30; 32; 34; 38-41; 50; 53-58;
60-64; 66; 69-70; 72-73. 14,1-2; 4-7; 12-14;
16; 20; 22-24; 29; 31-33. 15,1-3; 7-13; 16.
16,3-4; 6-9. 17,1; 4-5; 14; 16; 18-19; 21;
23-26; 29-30; 32-33. 18,1-5. 19,1-3; 6; 9;
11-15; 17-20. 20,1-4. 22,1. 23,1; 4-6. 24,1;
3. 25,1-5. 27,2. 28,4-5. 29,2-5; 10-11; 13-
20. 30,1. 31,1. 32,1-2. 33,1. 34,2. 35,1-2.
36,1-2. 37,1. 38,1. 39,2. 40,1-4; 6; 11-13;
15-19; 21-24; 26; 28-29; 31-36; 40-41. 41,2-
3. 42,1-3; 5-9. 43,1-6; 9-11. 44,1; 3-6; 8-
9; 12-13.

      LIN C12; 14. S9. T2.
1,2-13; 17-32; 34; 36; 38; 40-42; 44; 48; 50;
52-53; 55-58; 60-61; 63; 65-70; 75; 77; 79-
82; 84; 86; 88-97; 99-103; 105-106. 2,1-7;
11-14; 16-17; 19-23; 26-29; 32-38; 40-42.
3,2-9; 12-18; 20-22; 25-27; 31-36; 38; 41-
42; 44; 46-49; 51-54. 4,2-3; 5; 7-17; 20; 23-
24; 26; 30-32; 34-36; 38-40; 42-47; 50-59;
63-69; 71-81. 5,1. 6,1. 7,3-8; 10-11; 14;
16-17; 19; 23-25; 27-28; 30-34; 36; 38; 40;
43; 45-48; 50-54; 56-59. 8,1; 3-9; 11; 14-
15; 17-20; 22-23; 27-28; 31; 33-34. 9,1-2.
10,1-4. 11,1; 3-6. 12,1; 4-7; 11-12; 18-25;
28-29; 34-40; 42-44; 47; 49-50; 52-53; 55-
62; 64-68; 70-77; 79-80; 82; 84-93; 95-97.
13,1-10; 13-16; 18-19; 21-24; 26-35; 38-42;
44-45. 14,1; 3-6; 9-20; 23-26; 31; 33; 36;
39; 41-60; 62-90; 92-96. 15,1-2. 16,1; 6-12;
14; 16-20; 22-23; 28; 30; 33; 36; 39; 41; 43-
44; 46-47; 49. 17,1-3. 18,1-4; 7-17; 19-20;
22-23; 26; 28-32. 19,1. 20,2. 21,1. 22,1; 3-
5; 7; 10-14; 16-19; 22-36; 38. 23,1. 24,1-2;
4-7; 10; 14; 17-19; 22; 24-27; 31-32; 36-40;
42-48; 50-51; 54; 56; 62-68; 70-74; 76-77;
80-89; 92-93; 95-100; 102-105. 25,6-9; 11-
13; 15-18; 20; 22; 24-25. 26,3-4; 8-11; 13-
14; 16; 20; 22-28; 31-36; 38-41; 43-52.
27,1-3; 5; 7; 9-10; 14; 19-20; 22-25; 27; 30;
32; 34; 38-44; 47; 50-51; 53-62; 64. 28,1-
3; 7; 11; 13-15; 17; 20-21; 23; 25-31; 41.
29,1; 3-12; 14-15; 18-21; 23-24; 28-30; 32.
30,2-4; 6; 9-14; 17-20; 22; 26-27; 29; 31-33;
36-37. 31,1-2; 5; 7-12; 14-18. 32,1-3; 5-9;
11-12; 14-18; 21-22; 24; 26-27; 29; 31-32;
34. 33,1-2. 34,1-3; 6-10; 12-17; 20-25; 27.
35,1-4; 6-7; 9; 11-15; 17. 36,1; 4. 37,1-2;
5-7. 38,1-5; 8-13. 39,1-4. 40,2-10; 12; 16-
17; 20-21; 23; 25-26. 42,1-5; 7; 9-10; 13-
17; 19. 43,1-5. 44,4-5; 7-8; 10-11; 16-18.
45,1; 3-4. 46,1-4. 47,1-5; 7-8; 10. 48,1; 4-
6; 8-15. 49,1-2; 4. 50,1. 51,1-4; 6-8; 11-
12. 52,1-2. 53,1-2. 54,1-2. 55,2-3. 56,1-3;
5; 8-11; 13-14; 17-20. 57,1; 3-7; 10; 12; 14-
16; 18-19; 21-33; 35; 37-38; 41-42; 44-50;
55-56. 58,1-8. 59,1-5; 7-8; 10-11; 16-20.
60,1. 61,1; 3-4; 6; 8-10. 62,1-2. 63,1-3; 5-
7; 15. 64,1; 3-7; 12-19. 65,2-5. 66,1-2.
67,1-2; 4-10; 13-14; 16; 18; 20-26. 68,1-5;
9-25; 27; 29-30; 32-35; 37; 40; 42-43; 45;
48. CN4; 21. CK2; 61.
      NFK 1,1-5; 9; 11-13; 15-
19; 21; 23; 26; 28; 30; 32-33; 40; 42-47; 50-
57; 59-62; 64-65; 69-71; 73-74; 76-77; 79;
81-82; 85-89; 91-96; 98-101; 105; 108-112;
114-120; 122-124; 128-133; 135-146; 150-
164; 169-171; 173-174; 178-179; 182-183;
185-187; 189; 191-206; 208-212; 214-219;
221-228; 230-231; 234-241. 2,1-2; 4; 7-8;
11-12. 3,1-2. 4,2-3; 6-9; 14-18; 20-21; 23-
24; 26-35; 37-42; 44-53; 55-56. 5,1; 3-6.
6,1-7. 7,1-4; 6-13; 15-20. 8,1-4; 6-18; 21-

114-115; 117-121. 2,1; 6-7; 9-11; 13; 16-
17. 3,1; 3-5; 8-11; 13-14; 17; 24; 26; 34; 36-
39; 41; 46-48; 55-57; 59; 61; 67; 69-70; 72-
74; 76; 79; 81-84; 88; 94; 96; 98-100; 104.
4,1-4; 6; 10; 12-24; 26; 30-31; 35-39; 42.
5,1-2; 4-7. 6,1-3; 5; 11; 14; 26-29; 32; 42-
44; 46; 48-50; 57-58; 60-62; 64-65; 69; 71-
72; 76; 78; 80-83; 85-86; 90-96; 98; 100;
106; 109-110; 112; 116; 119-121; 125; 128-
131; 135; 138; 141; 143; 147-149; 156-157;
159; 161-163; 165; 170-172; 176; 178-180;
183-184; 186-195; 201-202; 209-210; 212-
217; 219-225; 228; 235-236; 238-239; 242;
247; 251; 253-255; 260-262; 264-265; 267-
268; 271-273; 276-277; 283-284; 287; 291;
293; 299-301; 303-309; 311-319. 7,1; 3-8;
10-11; 13-15; 17-19; 24; 26-30; 37; 40-42;
45; 47-49; 54-56; 60-61; 64; 67; 70-71; 73;
75-77; 79-86; 88-92; 97-104; 106-108; 110;
114-115; 117-123; 126; 128; 133; 138-141;
143; 145-147. 8,1-14; 19-22; 27; 31-37; 40;
42; 44-49; 55-59; 66; 70; 80-81. 9,1-3. 10,1.
11,1; 4. 12,1-7. 13,2-7. 14,1-19; 21-27; 29-
32; 35-39; 41-49; 51-59; 61-85; 87-88; 90-
96; 98-103; 105-112; 114-115; 117-132;
134; 137-139; 146; 156-157; 163-164; 166.
15,1-3; 5. 16,2-4; 6-7; 9-12; 14-15; 17-22;
25-30; 32-33; 35; 37-38; 40-41; 45-46. 17,1.
18,1; 3-4; 6. 19,1-2; 7; 9; 12-19; 21. 20,1.
21,1; 3-8; 10-12; 15-17; 19; 26; 28-30; 38-
40; 42-47; 49; 53-55; 58; 62; 64-66; 69; 71;
78; 80-81; 83-86; 90-91; 95; 99. 22,1-3.
23,1-3. 24,1. 25,1-7; 9-12; 14; 16-17; 19-
20; 27; 31-33; 36-37; 41-44; 46-49; 52-53;
55; 57; 59-61; 63; 65; 67; 71-72; 74-76; 78-
87; 90; 92-93; 97; 99-100; 103; 105-107.
26,1-2; 5-6; 9-12b; 13-16. 27,1-7; 9-13.
28,1a-b; 2-3; 6-7. 29,1-5; 9-11; 13-14. 30,1.
31,3; 5; 7-9; 12; 14-15; 18; 20-21; 25; 27-
28; 32; 35; 38; 40-51; 53; 56; 60. 32,1; 3-6;
9; 14; 16; 19; 21-30. 33,1-3; 5-10; 12-13.
34,2-3; 5-9; 12; 15. 35,1-3; 5-7. 36,1-2; 4;
7-13. 37,1; 3-6. 38,1; 4-8; 11; 16-17; 22;
24; 27. 39,1; 5-6; 8-10; 12; 16-17. 40,1-4;
6. 41,1-4; 7; 10-11; 14-15; 17-18. 42,1-2.
43,1-5. 44,1-4. 45,2-3. 46,1-5; 7-10. 47,2-
3. 48,1. 49,1. 50,1. 51,1. 52,1; 4-5; 9; 11.
53,1-3; 5-7. 54,1-3. 55,1. 56,1-2. 57,1.
58,1. 59,1-2. 60,1. 62,4-5; 7. 64,1; 3. 66,1-
4; 6-7; 10; 13; 16. 67,1-3; 5-7; 9-12; 14-21;
26-31; 33. 68,1; 3; 5. 69,1. 70,1. 71,1-2.
72,1. 74,13-14. 76,1-7; 23. 77,4.

SRY   1,2-14. 2,1-5. 3,1.
4,1. 5,1a; 2-3; 6-7; 10-11; 13; 15; 20; 22-
23; 26-27. 6,1; 5. 8,3; 6; 9-12; 14; 17-26; 28;
30. 11,1. 12,2. 13,1. 14,1. 15,1-2. 16,1.
17,1; 3. 18,2-4. 19,1-2; 4; 10-11; 15-16; 19-
20; 23; 27; 29; 31; 36-39; 41; 44-45; 47.
20,2. 21,1; 2-4. 22,2-4. 24,1. 25,1-3. 26,1.
27,1-2. 28,1. 29,1. 30,2. 31,1. 32,2. 33,1.
35,1. 36,3-4; 6-7; 9-10.

SSX   2,1a-b,e; 2; 5; 7; 10.
3,1-6; 9. 4,1. 5,1-3. 6,1; 3-4. 7,1-2. 8,1; 3;
8; 10. 8a,1. 9,1-3; 5-6; 8; 11; 13-16; 18-19;
21-22; 24; 26; 64; 74; 82-84; 86-87; 89; 92;
96; 103-106; 109-112; 120-123; 125; 129-
130. 10,2-4; 7-8; 11; 20; 22; 27; 30-31; 35-
38; 43; 60; 65; 69; 75; 83; 86; 105; 111; 113;
115. 11,3-4; 6-10; 12; 14; 16; 18-23; 25; 27-
28; 32; 37; 39; 42; 44-45; 53-55; 59-62; 64;
66; 68; 72-82; 84-87; 89; 92-93; 95; 103-
104; 108; 110. 12,3-9; 14; 19; 27-28; 30-31;
33-34; 36-37; 39-42; 44; 47; 49; 55. 13,1; 5;
7; 9-14; 20; 22-24; 29-31; 33-42; 45; 48-49;
53-54; 56. 14,1-2.

WAR   1,1-4; 6-7. 2,1-3.
3,1-3; 6-7. 4,1-6. 5,1. 6,2-5; 7-8; 11-18; 20.
7,1. 9,1. 11,1; 3-4. 12,1-6; 8. 14,1-3; 6.
15,2-4. 16,1-2; 5-6; 8; 10-16; 20-23; 26; 28-
41; 44-47; 50; 52-54; 56-60; 63. 17,1-2; 4-
14; 17-21; 23-25; 28; 30-35; 37-41; 43-59;
61-64; 66-70. 18,3-6; 8-9; 11. 19,1; 4-5.
20,1. 21,1. 22,1; 3-4; 17; 19; 24-27. 23,1-
3. 24,1-2. 25,1. 26,1. 27,3. 28,1; 3; 5-8;
10-19. 29,1; 3-5. 30,1. 31,1; 3; 6-7; 9-12.
32,1. 33,1. 34,1. 35,1. 36,1-2. 37,1-5; 7;
9. 38,1-2. 39,1-4. 41,1. 42,1; 3. 43,1. 44,1;
3; 5-9; 12; 14.

WIL   1,1-22; 23a,e. 2,1;
3-12. 3,1-5. 4,2-4. 5,2-4; 6. 6,1-2. 7,1-12;
14-16. 8,1-13. 10,1-5. 11,1. 12,1-6. 13,1-
14; 16-19. 14,1-2. 15,1-2. 16,1-4; 6-7. 17,1.
18,1-2. 19,1-2; 4. 20,1-6. 21,1-3. 22,1-3;
5-6. 23,1-2; 4-5; 7-10. 24,1-7; 9-10; 16; 18-
23; 25; 27-33; 36-38; 40-42. 25,1-5; 7-8;
11-14; 18-20; 22-23; 25-28. 26,1-5; 7; 9-19;
21-22. 27,1-3; 5-6; 8-11; 13-27. 28,1-3; 5;
7-13. 29,1-3; 5-8. 30,1-2; 4-5; 7. 31,1. 32,1-
3; 5; 7; 9-13; 16-17. 34,1. 35,1. 36,1. 37,1-
2; 4-13; 15. 38,1. 39,1-2. 40,1. 41,1-5; 7-
10. 42,1; 5-8; 10. 43,1-2. 44,1. 45,1. 47,1-
2. 48,1-2; 4-6; 8-12. 49,1-3. 50,1-5. 51,1.
52,1. 53,1-2. 56,1-4; 6. 57,1. 58,1-2. 59,1.
62,1. 64,1. 65,1. 66,1-4; 6. 67,1-2; 6-9; 14-
15; 17; 20; 22-23; 25-27; 31-32; 37; 39-40;
43-46; 54; 59-63; 68; 72; 76-77; 81; 83; 86-
90; 94; 98. 68,1; 3; 13; 15-16; 18-22; 24-
30; 32.

WOR   2,2-3; 5-7; 10-11;
13-15; 17-19; 21-23; 27-36; 38-42; 45-48;
52-53; 56; 58-68; 70; 72; 75-79; 85. 8,1; 3-
9a,d-g; 10a; 11; 14-17; 19-20; 22-24; 26a.
9,1a; 2-3; 5a. 10,1; 3; 5-11; 13. 15,11-12.
19,1; 13. 23,14. 27,1.

YKS   C22; 30-32. 1Y2; 4-
7; 11-13; 16; 18. 1N5; 9; 12-13; 15; 19; 38;
54; 66. 1W25. 2,1-2. 2B1-3; 7; 11; 19. 2N2-
4; 14; 21. 2W1-4; 6-8; 10; 12. 2E23; 29; 32-
33; 38; 40. 3Y1; 9; 15. 4N1-2. 5N1; 5-9;
17-18; 21-22; 26-27; 47-48; 53; 58-60; 63;
65; 67. 5E17; 29; 59; 65. 5W1; 4-5; 8; 13;
15-16; 18. 6N1-2; 11-13; 15-17; 21; 27; 32-

33; 36; 46; 49; 51; 56; 59; 92; 102; 104-105; 113; 120; 122; 125; 136-138. 6W1-2; 5-6. 6E1. 7E2. 8N1; 5-8; 10; 22. 8W1. 8E3. 9W1-6; 8; 16-19; 23-24; 26-28; 31-32; 34; 37-40; 42-43; 45-46; 49-50; 56-57; 59-61; 64; 66-68; 74; 76; 79-80; 96; 98-99; 104; 108; 116; 119; 121; 125; 139; 142. 10W3; 8; 15; 24-25; 28; 31; 38-39; 41. 11N4. 12W5. 13W1-2; 6-7; 9-12; 14-18; 26; 28; 31; 33; 35. 13E5; 13-14; 16. 13N2; 4-5; 12; 14; 18. 14E1-2; 4-5; 7-9; 11-25; 27-30; 32-34; 36-40; 42-48; 50-53. 15E14. 16E3-4. 16N1. 16W6. 19W1; 3. 20E1. 21E10. 21W6. 22W3. 23N4-5; 13; 16; 20-21; 24-25; 28-29; 31-33. 23E10; 12; 14; 18-19. 24W4. 25W1-2; 6; 9-10; 12; 15-16; 18-20; 22; 28-30. 26E1; 11. 28W33; 39-40. 29W6-7; 14; 25; 36. 29E5. 29N1; 8; 12. SN,Y5. SW,An18.

Belonging to		
burgesses	ESS	B3a.
	NFK	1,61.
	SFK	1,97.
manor in another		
County	LIN	2,26.
men	NFK	49,2.
Comparative information		
less 1086 than TRE	ESS	68,2.
	NFK	31,7.
	SFK	1,1.
more 1086 than		
TRE	NFK	1,139.
Enough for 1 hide	WIL	68,1.
Flooded by dam	HUN	1,2.
Grazing for King's		
horses	KEN	C1.
Hay from, for oxen	GLS	59,1.
Horses, for	BKM	3a,4. 19,2. 23,2.
	HRT	16,9.
Lease of	DOR	1,30.
Lord		
held by	LIN	24,56.
for use of	HRT	33,12.
Manor, to maintain	GLS	7,1.
Measures of		
arpent	WOR	50,1. 68,4; 7; 10.
bovate	LIN	67,6.
carucate	LIN	64,13.
corner (angulum)	HAM	23,16.
hide	HRT	15,3.
virgate	CHS	8,27. FD2,1. FD8,1.
	LIN	18,28.
	NTT	1,34. 16,3. 30,9.
	WIL	28,10.
None	HRT	37,6.
	YKS	C24.
Ox, for	BDF	1,4. 3,17. 13,2.

21,7-8; 11. 23,34; 45; 50-55. 24,7. 32,15. 53,6. 56,8. 57,8; 10.
BKM 5,17. 17,29. 26,10.

53,2. 57,5.
CAM 5,3; 10. 6,1. 7,7. 11,2. 12,3. 14,15; 33-34; 36; 39-40; 42; 45; 47; 51; 57; 72; 75; 78; 80. 18,1. 21,6. 22,7; 10. 23,1-2. 26,2; 23; 24-25; 33-34; 37; 38; 44; 53. 30,3. 31,4; 7. 32,17-19; 27; 29. 36,1. 41,3; 14-15. 44,1-2.

CHS	1,25.
HEF	7,3-4. 8,5. 10,9; 27. 14,2-3.
HRT	1,1; 3. 2,1. 4,6; 8;

10-11. 5,10-11; 24. 13,3. 16,1; 7; 12. 17,9-10. 20,8; 12. 23,1. 33,16. 34,5; 17. 36,2; 5; 12. 37,16-19; 23. 42,9.
MDX 3,13. 4,12. 7,6-7. 8,3. 11,2-3. 25,2.
WOR 2,16.

Plough (team), for BDF 1,1a,c; 2a; 3; 5. 2,1-4; 6-9. 3,1-2; 4-5; 7-8; 10-11; 13. 4,1-7. 5,2. 6,1-3. 7,1. 8,1-3; 5-8. 9,1. 10,1. 11,1. 13,1. 14,1. 15,1-2; 4-7. 16,1-4; 7-9. 17,2; 4-5; 7. 18,1-2; 4; 6. 19,1. 20,1. 21,1-6; 9; 12-17. 22,1. 23,1; 4-5; 7-21; 26-29; 35-37; 39-43; 49; 56-57. 24,1; 3-6; 8-10; 13-30. 25,2; 4; 7-15. 26,2-3. 29,1. 30,1. 31,1. 32,1-6; 10-11; 13; 16. 33,1-2. 34,3. 39,2. 40,1; 3. 41,1-2. 42,1. 43,1. 44,1-2; 4. 45,1. 46,1-2. 47,1-4. 48,1-2. 49,1-4. 51,1-3. 52,1-2. 53,1; 3-5; 7-9; 11-15; 17-18; 20-26; 28-33; 35-36. 54,1-4. 55,1-13. 56,2-3. 57,3i-iii; 5-6; 18.
BKM B1-2. 1,1-7. 2,1-3. 3,1-2. 3a,1-2; 4; 6. 4,1-2; 5-6; 10-11; 13-16; 18-19; 21-23; 25-29; 31-42. 5,1-3; 5-9; 11-16; 18-21. 6,2. 7,1-2. 8,1-3. 9,1. 10,1. 11,1. 12,1-4; 6-12; 14-15; 24-25; 28; 30-31; 33-38. 13,1-4. 14,2-49. 15,1. 16,1-3; 5-10. 17,2; 5; 7; 9-10; 12; 15-18; 20; 22-27. 18,2-3. 19,1-2; 4-5; 7. 20,1. 21,1-6; 8. 22,1. 23,1; 3-6; 8-18; 20-25; 28-29; 31-33. 24,1-3. 25,1; 3. 26,1; 3-4; 7-9; 11. 27,1-2. 28,2-3. 29,1-4. 30,1. 31,1. 34,1. 35,1-3. 36,1-2. 37,1-2. 38,1. 39,2. 40,1. 41,1-7. 42,1. 43,1-7; 9-11. 44,1-3; 5. 46,1. 47,1. 49,1. 50,1. 51,1-3. 52,1-2. 53,3-10. 55,1. 56,1-3. 57,1-4; 7-9; 12-13; 16-18.
CAM 1,1-7; 9; 12; 14; 17-18. 2,1-4. 3,1; 3-5. 4,1. 5,4; 8; 11-12; 14; 18; 20; 23; 25; 28-31; 34; 36; 39; 41-42; 44-55; 57; 59-63. 6,1. 7,1-2; 4-6; 7; 8-11. 8,1. 9,1-3. 10,1. 11,1; 3-4; 6. 12,1-2; 4. 13,1-2; 4; 6-9; 11. 14,1-2; 4; 7-9; 11; 13-14; 16; 19-20; 22-23; 26-27; 29; 31-32; 41; 42; 43-44; 46; 48-50; 53-56; 58-60; 63-71; 73-74. 15,1-4. 16,1. 17,1-4. 18,6-8. 20,1. 21,1; 3-5; 7-9. 22,1-2; 4; 6; 8-9. 23,3-4; 6. 24,1. 25,3-7; 9. 26,6; 14; 16-19; 21; 26-27; 30-32; 34; 35-36; 40-43; 45-49. 27,1. 28,1-2. 29,2; 5; 7; 9-10. 30,1-2. 31,1-3; 6-7. 32,1-2; 4-8; 10; 12; 14; 16; 20-23; 28; 30-34; 36-40; 43.

23,5; 7; 14; 32. 24,1. 25,1. 26,2-3; 8. 29,1-2. 31,1. 35,1. 41,2; 4; 6. 43,2; 7-9; 11. 44,1-2. 46,1. 52,1-2. 56,1. 57,3; 13.
CAM B12. 1,1-3; 5; 12. 2,1; 4. 3,1. 5,6; 14; 18; 23; 25; 31; 34. 7,9. 11,3-4. 12,1. 13,4; 6. 14,1-2; 8-9; 11; 13-14; 16; 26-27; 29; 32; 34-35; 40; 55; 63; 65-69; 74. 15,1-2; 4. 17,1-2. 18,7-8. 20,1. 21,3; 5-6. 22,2; 5; *6;* 9. 25,3. 26,17; 19; 30; 32; 34. 28,2. 29,4-5; 9-10. 31,1. 32,1; 4-5; 7-8; 16; 32. 38,3. 41,7.
CHS 1,15; 22. 2,5-6. 9,5. 13,3. 14,1. 16,2. 18,2; 5. 21,1. FT1,1. FT2,1-2; 7.
CON 1,14. 4,10. 5,1,2; 22. 5,3,24.
DBY 1,9; 16; 19-20; 27-29; 37. 2,1; 3. 3,3. 4,1. 5,1. 6,7; 14; 16; 24-25; 27; 30; 34; 39-40; 43; 46-47; 50; 54-57; 66-67; 69; 76; 80; 86; 92; 95. 7,6. 8,1. 9,1; 4. 10,1; 4-5; 9. 12,2. 14,4. 17,11; 15; 22. B1-2; 4.
DEV 1,7; 11; 13; 26; 33; 35; 46; 53-54; 56; 70. 2,2; 12-14; 21. 3,3; 8; 70-71. 5,4. 10,1. 11,1; 3. 15,23; 26; 57; 61. 16,3; *45;* 58; 69; 76; 95; 102; 105-106; 109; 111; 122; 129; 135; 159; 163-164; 166. 17,48. 19,31; 37. 21,6. 22,1. 23,5-6; 9; 18; 22. 25,15; 17; 28. 32,2. 34,22-29; 50-52; 57. 35,1-2. 36,18; 26. 40,5. 41,2. 42,16; 24. 48,5. 49,2. 51,8. 52,34.
DOR 1,2-8; 12-13; 15-16; 18; 20; 26; 31. 2,1-4; 6. 3,1; 3-6; 8-11; 13; 16. 5,1-2. 6,1; 3. 8,1-2. 9,1. 10,2; 6. 11,1; 5; 12; 14. 12,1-2; 4-5; 7; 14; 16. 13,1-4. 14,1. 16,1. 17,1. 19,2-7; 9; 12; 14. 20,1-2. 22,1. 24,5. 26,3; 7-8; 10; 14-15; 21-22; 24; 26; 28; 32; 40-41; 43-44; 46; 52-53; 56; 59; 63-64. 27,1-2; 6-7; 9. 28,1-2. 30,1; 3-4. 31,1-2. 33,4. 34,2; 8-10. 35,1. 36,1-2; 4-7; 11. 37,9. 38,1-2. 39,2. 40,1; 3; 6; 8-9. 41,5. 42,1. 43,1. 46,1-2. 47,2; 6-7; 9. 48,1. 49,12; 16. 50,1; 4. 53,2. 54,5-7. 55,1-6; 15; *16;* 19-20; 22; 27; 29; 35; 38; 44; 48; 53. 57,1; 11; 13-14; 21. 58,1.
ESS 1,2; 4; 9-13; 19; 24-26; 28; 30. 2,1-4. 3,3; 5; 7-8; 12-13; 15-16. 4,9; 14. 5,5; 10-11. 6,5; 7-9; 14. 9,1; 7; 13-14. 10,5. 11,1-2; 8. 12,1. 14,4. 15,1-2. 18,1; 14; 40-41; 43. 20,6-7; 19; 21; 25; 31; 36-37; 43; 56; 79. 21,6. 22,4; 6; 11; 13. 23,2-4; 7; 12; 26; 34; 36; 38-40. 24,19-20; 26; 31-33; 48; 53; 57; 59; 64. 25,4; 21. 26,1. 27,2; 11. 28,2; 13. 29,4. 30,4-6; 9; 16-18; 22; 30-31; 45. 32,3-4; 7-8; 14; 16; 18-19; 24-26; 36; 38; 42. 33,1; 3-6; 11-13; 16; 22. 34,4-8; 12; 18; 20-21; 29; 33. 35,1; 5; 8. 36,1; 3; 5; 10-11. 37,3; 9; 12. 38,5; 7. 39,1; 4-5. 40,1; 3; 6. 41,3; 7. 42,3; 6; 9. 43,1; 6. 44,1; 3-4. 46,1-2. 47,2-3. 49,1; 3. 53,1.

54,2. 55,1. 60,2. 64,1. 65,1. 74,1. 84,1. 87,1. 90,15; 22; 30; 65; 67-68. B1; 3a; 7.
GLS W15-18. *B1.* 1,1-2; 7; 9-10; 12-13; 15; 17; 21-22; 24; 34; 36-37; 41; 47-50; 55-58; 66-67. 2,2-3; 8-9; 11-12. 3,1-5; 7. 6,5. 7,2. 8,1. 10,1; 3-4; 10; 12-14. 11,1-2; 8; 14. 12,1; 5. 13,1. 14,1-2. 16,1. 19,2. 20,1. 23,1-2. 24,1. 26,1-2. 28,1; 4. 31,1; 5; 7; 11. 32,7; 11. 34,4; 8-9; 11. 35,1. 36,3. 38,2-3. 39,5-6; 8-9; 12; 15-18; 20-21. 41,2. 45,5-6. 46,1-3. 47,1. 48,1. 50,3. 52,3-5; 7. 54,1-2. 55,1. 56,1-2. 58,3-4. 59,1. 60,1-2. 61,1-2. 62,5. 63,1-2; 4. 64,2-3. 66,1; 4. 67,4-6. 68,1; 5; 7; 9; 12. 69,2; 5-6. 72,3. 73,1-2. 74,1. 78,1; 8; 10; 14-17.
HAM 1,1-2; 8; 13-17; 19-23; 25-30; 38-39; 41-43; 45; 47; W3-4; W14. 2,1; 3-6; 9-13; 15; 20; 23; 25. 3,1-3; 5-11; 13-15; 20; 26-27. 5a,1. 6,4; 6; 8-9; 11-12; 14-17. 8,1. 14,1-2; 4-5. 15,1-2; 4. 16,1-2; 4-7. 17,1. 18,1-2. 19,1. 20,1. 21,1; 9. 22,1. 23,4-6; 8; 12-13; 18-19; 22; 26; 33-34; 36; 40; 42; 44; 50; 52; 62; 66; 68. 24,1. 25,1. 27,1-2. 28,7. 29,3; 5-6; 8-9; 11; 15. 32,1. 35,3-4; 6. 36,2. 38,1. 41,1. 43,4; 6. 44,1; 3-4. 45,1; 6. 49,1. 50,1. 51,1. 53,2. 55,2. 58,1. 62,1-2. 63,1. 66,1. 68,1; 9. 69,1-2; 5; 9; 17; 22-29; 32; 35; 42. NF5,1. NF8,2. NF9,40-41. NF10,2. IoW1,1; 7; 10; 15. IoW2,1. IoW6,4; 6-7; 15; 22. IoW7,5; 18; 21. IoW8,6; 8-9. IoW9,17.
HEF 1,1-2; 4-10a,c; 23; 28-29; 39-40; 42; 46-48. 2,5; 8; 14; 17; 21; 24; 26; 28-31; 33-35; 39; 42; 49; 51. 5,1. 6,3. 7,3-4; 9. 8,1-2; 7; 10. 9,7. 10,9; 24; 27-30; 32-33; 47; 60; 63; 67; 70. 12,2. 15,6. 17,1. 18,1. 19,2; 6; 8. 21,3-4; 7. 23,4. 24,12. 25,8. 29,1-2; 8; 11.
HRT B11. 1,1; 3; 8-9; 18. 2,2. 4,2-3; 22. 5,1; 10-11; 17; 24-26. 7,2. 8,1. 9,1; 4; 8-10. 10,1; 3-7; 9-11; 15-16; 19. 14,2. 15,1; 5-6; 10. 16,2; 9. 17,1; 8; 10; 15. 19,1. 20,13. 22,2. 23,3-4. 24,3. 25,2. 26,1. 27,1. 28,4. 31,1; 8. 32,1. 33,2; 5; 15; 17-18. 34,4; 11; 20-21; 24. 36,11; 14; 16; 19. 42,1; 10. 42a,1. 43,1. 44,1.
HUN B17. 1,1; 8; 10. 2,4; 8. 4,4. 6,3-4; 8-9; 13; 16. 7,5. 8,2. 11,1. 13,1. 18,1. 19,12. 20,6; 8. 22,2. 28,1.
KEN D10. M3. C1. P13; 19. 1,1-4. 2,1; 3-13; 16-17; 19; 21-26; 29; 31-32; 36; 41. 3,1; 3; 5; 7-9; 11-17; 21. 4,2-3; 5; 7; 9-10; 13-14. 5,1; 4; 12; 15-18; 20; 22-23; 25; 28-29; 34; 36; 39-40; 42-43; 46-47; 51-52; 56-58; 63-64; 67-71; 74; 78; 83; 85-86; 88-89; 93; 95-99; 102-105; 107; 116; 118-119; 122; 124; 128-129; 138; 141; 143-145; 158-159; 162; 164; 168; 183; 185-186; 188; 192. 7,2-3; *4;* 7-8; 17; 20. 8,1. 9,3; 6; 9; 16-17; 24-25; 30; 32; 36-37; 40; 42. 10,1-2. 11,1-2. 12,1; 3.

11; 15; 21; 23-27. 24,9; 16-19; 21; 23; 30-31. 25,1-2; 7-10; 13; 17; 31; 33; 36; 38-39; 43; 45; 50; 53; 55. 26,2-3; 5-6. 27,1-2. 28,1. 31,2-3. 32,3-4. 33,1. 35,10-11; 17-18; 20; 22-23. 36,1; 5; 9-10; 13. 37,1; 5; 8; 11. 39,2. 40,1-2. 41,1; 3. 42,2-3. 44,3. 45,6; 10-11; 17. 46,5; 9; 21-22. 47,6; 10; 16-21.

STS 1,1; 6-7; 17-18; 20; 22; 24; 26-27; 29-32. 2,1; 3; 5; 10; 16; 22. 4,8. 5,2. 6,1. 7,14; 18. 8,1-2; 5; 7; 19; 32. 9,1. 10,3. 11,6; 12; 15; 29; 33; 35; 39; 42; 44; 49-51; 57-58. 12,6; 8; 15; 26-27; 29-31. 14,2.

SFK 1,1-2; 71; 97-98; 100; 110; 115; 118-120. 2,6. 3,5; 56; 69; 72. 4,1; 10; 13-14; 19; 35. 6,26; 42; 65; 79; 83; 110; 112; 129; 135; 143; 160; 172; 176; 189; 191; 223; 225; 239; 260; 272; 312; 314-315. 7,1; 6; 61; 76; 106; 118; 121; 139. 8,37; 55. 9,1; 3. 12,1; 3-4. 13,2. 14,4; 7-10; 12; 18; 23; 49; 53; 69; 77; 80; 83; 88-89; 98-99; 101; 106; 108-109; 118; 129; 167. 15,2-3; 5. 16,2-3; 35; 41; 45. 18,1; 4. 19,1-2. 20,1. 21,10; 15-16; 26; 43; 54; 80; 90; 95. 22,1-2. 23,3. 24,1. 25,1-3; 35; 42; 45; 52; 76; 78; 81; 85-86. 27,3-7; 9; 13. 28,1a; 3; 6-7. 29,1. 31,8; 20; 41; 48; 50; 53. 32,5; 14; 19. 33,1; 3; 7-8; 12. 34,1-3. 35,1; 3; 6. 36,1-2; 4. 37,1. 39,6-7; 12; 17. 40,3; 6. 41,10. 42,1. 43,2. 44,2-3. 46,4-5. 47,3. 51,1. 53,1. 55,1. 56,6. 58,1. 59,1-2. 60,1. 66,1; 10. 67,5; 12; 28; 31. 76,7.

SRY 1,2-3; 5-14. 2,1; 3; 5. 3,1. 4,1. 5,1a-b,f; 8; 19. 6,1-2; 5. 8,6; 9; 17; 28. 11,1. 15,1-2. 16,1. 18,2-3. 19,1; 4; 12; 14-16; 21; 23; 26; 32-33; 36-37; 39; 47. 21,1; 4; 6-7. 22,2-3. 25,2. 27,1-3. 28,1. 29,1. 32,2. 33,1. 36,3-5; 9.

SSX 1,1. 2,1a,c-d; 2; 7. 3,8-9. 5,2. 6,1-2. 8,16. 9,1-2; 86; 89. 10,1-3; 22; 26-31; 56; 60; 65-67; 95; 105; 109; 111; 117-118. 11,1-3; 5-11; 14; 18-23; 26-27; 30; 35; 39; 41-44; 48-49; 52-53; 55; 59; 64; 74; 78; 82; 92; 105-106; 110-111. 12,3; 6; 30; 34; 36; 39; 42; 48. 13,6; 10; 12; 20; 23; 30; 38; 43; 49; 51-52; 56. 14,1-2.

WAR 1,1; 3-6. 2,2-3. 3,1-3; 6. 4,1-2. 6,2; 8; 10; 15; 18. 9,1. 10,1. 11,1; 3-4. 12,1; 4-5; 8. 14,1-2. 15,4; 6. 16,1-2; 9-10; 12; 14; 18; 21; 50; 63. 17,6-7; 13; 15; 25; 47; 49; 51-52; 54; 56; 60; 62; 69. 18,2-5; 9. 19,1-2; 4. 22,1-3; 7; 9; 11; 16; 25. 23,1-4. 26,1. 27,1; 3. 28,10; 16. 29,4. 30,1. 31,4-6; 10. 32,1. 34,1. 35,2. 37,1; 4-6. 39,1; 4. 40,2. 42,3. 43,1. 44,15-16.

WIL B5. 1,1-14; 16-18; 21; 23h. 2,1-2; 4; 6-7; 9-10; 12. 3,1-4. 4,3-4. 5,2-3; 6-7. 6,1-2. 7,1-4; 6-7; 9; 15-16. 8,2-3; 5-10; 12-13. 10,1; 3; 5. 11,1. 12,1-6. 13,1-3; 5; 8-14; 16; 19-20. 14,1-2. 15,1-2. 16,1. 17,1. 18,1-2. 20,6. 21,1. 22,1; 4; 6. 23,1; 7; 9. 24,2; 5; 7; 19-21; 25; 27-28; 33; 36; 38; 40-41. 25,1-2; 5; 7; 14; 22. 26,2-5; 10-12; 17-18; 20-21. 27,1; 3; 6-7; 11; 15-17; 19; 23-25. 28,1-2; 11; 13. 29,1; 5. 30,1-2; 7. 31,1. 32,1-2; 5; 9; 12; 17. 34,1. 36,2. 37,1-2; 7; 15. 40,1. 41,5; 8-9. 42,1; 5-8. 44,1. 45,1; 3. 47,1. 48,8; 12. 49,1. 50,2; 4. 51,1. 53,1. 56,1-2. 58,1. 59,1. 60,1. 64,1. 67,2; 6-9; 14; 17; 32-34; 37; 43; 48; 54; 56; 59-61; 77; 80; 86; 92; 94-95. 68,12; 20-22; 25-26; 28; 32.

WOR 1,1a; 2. 2,4; 6; 13-15; 18; 21-22; 25; 31; 38; 43; 45; 48; 57; 59; 63-66; 68; 72; 76; 78; 81-83; 85. 8,1; 7; 9c,g; 10c; 23. 9,1a-b; 3; 5a-c; 6b. 10,1; 3; 5-6; 10-11. 14,2. 15,6; 9; 12-13. 18,1. 19,1; 4; 8-9; 12. 20,1. 21,3. 23,11. 26,3; 7-9; 15; 17. 28,1.

YKS C22. 1Y1; 7; 9-10. 2,3. 2B1; 6; 9. 2N2; 21. 2W7. 2E1; 10. 3Y1. 4N1. 4E2. 5N19; 53. 5E5; 31-32; 65-66. 5W6; 8; 12-14. 6N13; 21; 32; 51; 122; 137-138. 8N1; 5-6. 8E1-2. 9W1; 6; 8; 26; 35; 41; 47-48; 51-52; 61; 64; 77; 96; 119. 10W3-4; 13-14; 26. 12W1; 5. 13W1-2; 26; 32-33; 35. 13E2; 15-16. 13N12; 17. 14E13; 34; 37. 16N1. 17W1, 19W3. 23N9; 19; 33. 23E2-3; 14-15; 18. 25W24. 26E10. 29N8. CW3.

three-quarters (¾)
(3 parts)

DOR	57,4.	
LIN	14,12.	
NFK	1,61. 2,12. 9,160; 178. 25,18. 31,22.	
SFK	4,19. 6,312.	

two-thirds (⅔) (2 parts)

ESS	21,10.	
LIN	4,57; 72. 27,7. 42,2.	
NFK	1,74. 9,136. 25,12. 50,6.	
SOM	5,15.	
SFK	9,1. 14,82. 25,27.	
WIL	26,22. 38,1. 67,43.	

half (½)

BDF	23,27. 25,12. 53,8.	
BRK	21,5; 10. 23,1. 44,2. 46,4. 47,1. 64,1.	
BKM	5,15. 53,7.	
CAM	1,3. 4,1. 5,11. 11,1. 17,4. 21,5. 31,2. 32,1-2.	
DEV	34,23.	
DOR	1,29. 11,9. 26,4. 37,10. 52,2.	
ESS	1,1. 6,1. 14,3. 20,8. 24,46. 25,1. 29,2. 30,24. 34,20. 47,1. 69,2. 90,70. B1.	
GLS	6,1. 11,14. 41,5. 69,6. 78,1.	
HAM	1,2. 2,18. 6,1; 15. 14,6. 15,2. 17,3. 69,27-28.	

MINSTER (monasterium) – See Monastery.

MINT (moneta)	CHS	FT1,1. FT2,1.
	ESS	B6.
	GLS	G1.
	LIN	C27.
	NFK	1,70.
	NTT	B7.
	OXF	1,12.
	SOM	1,31. 2,1.
	SFK	1,122g.
	SSX	10,1.
	WIL	B5.
New	SSX	12,1.
Tax on	LIN	C23.
borough (geldum		
monete)	HUN	B15.

See also: Money; Moneyer.

MISAPPROPRIA-
TION (preoccupare)

of land	ESS	1,24. 6,12. 18,36.
	WAR	17,16.
in King's despite	HAM	54,2.
	WAR	17,16.

See also: Appropriation.

MONASTERY
(monasterium)	BDF	10,1.
	BRK	46,4.
	BKM	7,2. 17,30.
	CAM	5,26; 32. 26,18; 30.
	CHS	B11.
	GLS	1,27.
	HAM	3,2-3; 5-6; 12-14;
17-21. 6,8; 13-14; 17. 10,1. 29,9. 41,1.
NF2,2-3. IoW5,2,1. IoW5,1.
	HRT	1,3.
	KEN	M3.
	MDX	4,1.
	NFK	1,70. 10,87; 90.
		17,9.
	SHR	3b,1.
	SOM	7,12.
	SRY	5,28.
	SSX	11,30.
Abbey, given to	SHR	3b,1.
Customary due paid		
to	BKM	7,2.
Layman, held by	NFK	1,70.

See also: Grant and sell; Monk; Sell; Supplies; Tax;
Tenure.

MONEY

Method of calculation
assayed and
weighed (arsuras et		
pensatas)	BKM	1,1-2; 5-6.
	CAM	1,1-5; 7; 9; 14; 17.
	CON	1,1-4.
	DEV	C2. 1,7; 11; 13; 23;
		34-35; 41; 45; 53-
		54. 17,1.
	GLS	1,16.
	HAM	1,W3.

	HRT	B11. 1,9; 19.
	KEN	C1.
	LIN	1,1; 4.
	SRY	1,14.
	SSX	1,1.
blanched (alba;		
blanca; candida)	DOR	1,1.
	ESS	20,36-37; 43; 45.
	GLS	1,56; 58.
	NFK	1,11; 52; 61; 67; 70;
81; 87; 94; 128; 136; 139-141; 143; 150-152;
163; 174; 179; 182-183; 185-187; 192-194;
197-200; 203; 208; 212; 216; 219; 237-238.
	RUT	R4.
	SFK	1,1; 75-76; 88.
blanched pence	HEF	C15. 1,3-4; 6; 8.
face value (ad		
numerum)	BRK	B8. 1,37.
	BKM	1,1-6. 52,2.
	CAM	1,1-2; 4-9; 17.
	CON	1,14.
	DEV	C2. 1,1; 10; 50; 57-
		59; 64-65; 68. 17,1.
	GLS	G1. B1. 1,10; 47;
		50; 62.
	HAM	1,1; 28-30. 20.1.
	HEF	C15.
	HRT	B11. 1,9; 18-19.
	HUN	1,10.
	KEN	D7. C1. 1,1; 3. 6,1.
	LEC	C1; 4.
	LIN	C27.
	NFK	1,19; 28; 52; 57; 59;
61; 67; 70; 77; 139; 143; 147; 152; 163; 182;
185-186; 198-199; 226.
	NTH	1,20; 24-25; 30; 32.
	NTT	1,51.
	OXF	B3. 1,2-6; 12.
	SOM	1,26-29; 31.
	SFK	1,1; 12; 75-76; 90;
		96-97; 99; 103; 115.
	SRY	1,2; 14.
	WIL	1,5; 7; 10-13; 16.
	WOR	C2.
fired and weighed	KEN	1,3.
(ad ignem et ad		
pensam)		
pure silver	DBY	1,15.
reckoning (ad	NFK	1,150-151.
compotum)		
weighed (pensum;		
ad pondus)	BDF	1,1a; 2a; 3.
	BRK	1,4.
	CON	1,5-12.
	DEV	1,1-3; 5-6; 8-10; 12;
14-21; 29-31; 33; 36-41; 43-44; 46-49; 51-
52; 55-56. 23,5.
	ESS	1,24-25.
	GLS	1,14.
	HAM	1,1; 16; W3.
	KEN	1,1.

	LEC	C3.
	LIN	1,5-6; 9.
	NFK	1,5; 11; 32; 52; 70. 22,8.
	NTH	B36. 1,32.
	OXF	1,12.
	SFK	1,2; 8; 12; 96; 103; 118-120.
	SRY	1,2-3.
	WAR	B4. 15,4; 6.
	WIL	B3-4; 6; 8-13.
	WOR	C2. 1,1b; 2.
	YKS	C20.
weighed by King's weight	NFK	1,61.
weighed to land holder's standard	HRT	17,1.
white (alba; blanca; candida)	ESS	20,43; 45.
	GLS	1,58; 61.
	HAM	1,W6.
white pence/coin	CAM	1,1; 4; 7; 9.
	HEF	1,1-2; 9.
	HRT	17,1.
white pounds	HAM	1,W4.
	NFK	1,82.
	NTH	B36.
white silver	BDF	1,1a; 2a; 3.
	BKM	B1. 1,3-4; 6.
	CAM	1,2-3; 5.
	SOM	1,10-15; 17-25.
Minting of	BRK	B1.
Rouen pence	DEV	10,2.

See also: Farthing; Gift; Halfpenny; Mark; Mint; Moneyer; Ora; Ounce; Penny; Premium.

MONEY changer (cambitor)	SFK	6,89c.
MONEYER (monetarius)	CHS	C19.
	ESS	B6.
	HEF	C9. 2,1.
	HUN	B19.
	LEC	C5.
	NFK	1,64.
	NTT	B1.
	OXF	B10.
	SFK	1,97.
	WOR	C1.
	YKS	C4.
Bishop, of	HEF	C9. 2,1.
	NFK	1,64.
Exempt from dues whilst he makes coin	BRK	B1.
Free house of	OXF	B10.
Full jurisdiction, having own	HEF	C9.
King, of	SHR	C11.
Mints coin for King from King's silver	HEF	C9.
Payments by	ESS	B6.

	LEC	C5.
	NTT	B1.
	SFK	1,122g.
change/renewal of money, on	CHS	C19.
	DOR	B1-4.
	HEF	C9.
	SHR	C11.
	SSX	12,1.
	WOR	C1.
date due	SHR	C11.
not fully met	SFK	1,122g.

See also: Coinage; Death duty; Dwelling; Mint; Third penny.

MONK (monachus)	BDF	19,1. 38,2. 55,8.
	BRK	2,1. 7,25; 38. 10,2. 33,5.
	BKM	3,1. 12,6; 8; 29. 14,37.
	CAM	5,29. 14,60. 17,1-2. 42,1.
	DBY	3,6. 6,24-25.
	DEV	1,4. 16,93. *34,53.*
	DOR	2,5. 3,1-9. 12,14. 13,1; 4. 57,8.
	ESS	1,2. 90,79.
	GLS	1,55-56. 10,14.
	HAM	3,1; 5; 10; 15-16; 23. 29,9. 69,28. IoW1,7.
	HEF	1,44.
	HRT	10,12.
	HUN	8,3. 18,1. 28,1.
	KEN	C2. 2,2; 11; 15; *16;* 27; 28; 35. 3. 5,149. 7,*2; 12;* 20; *21;* 24.
	LIN	C3. 3,4. 7,55. 13,44. 42,13. CW16.
	NFK	*1,211.* 8,17. 14,17. 17. 17,6; 22; 43.
	NTH	6a,25; 27.
	OXF	6,6. 16,2. 35,33.
	SHR	3b,1-2. 3c,2. 4,1,5-6. .
	SOM	2,11. 7,12. 8,20; 26; 35. 9,8. 32,5.
	SFK	3,14. 14,163; 167. 15.
	SRY	2,2; 4-6. 8,22; 30. 9,1.
	SSX	2,2; 8. 9,13; 102. 10,1. 11,3. 12,3.
	WAR	B2. 31,1.
	WIL	2,3-4. 8,6.
	WOR	2,23; 29; 41; 44; 46; 63;85. 8,6. 9,1b,e. 11,2.
Abbey French, held		

N

NAIL, iron – See Iron; Ship.
NARRATIVE entries

Affairs concerning Woodchester	GLS	1,63.
Building of chapel and rights of mother church	SFK	1,1.
City dwelling-ownership	YKS	C10.
City house-exempt from customary dues	YKS	C2.
Courtship and marriage of Wihenoc's man	NFK	21,14.
Death-bed transaction	WOR	23,1.
Dispute re stolen property	SFK	27,7.
Founding of St John's, Clare	SFK	25,1.
Gift of land TRE to Evesham Abbey	WOR	26,16.
History of Bromfield	SHR	3d,7.
Outlaw devolution of land following outlawry	NFK	9,49.
pardoning and reconciliation of Edric of Laxfield	SFK	6,79.
Plea frustrated by King Edward's death	SHR	3d,7.
Tenure of Alveston	WAR	3,4.
Waterways/tolls/moorage at Southwark	SRY	5,28.

NAVAL battle – See Battle.
NAVIGATION – See Mill; River; Ship.

NEPHEW (nepos)	BDF	2,9.
	BRK	65,19.
	DOR	55,45.
	ESS	18,25. 65. B3h.
	GLS	2,3. 27,1.
	HAM	IoW7,7-8. IoW9,10.
	HEF	22,5-6.
	KEN	D10. 1,1. 5,38; 63; 79; 145; 184.
	LIN	C4; 22-23. 64,1-2; 7-8; 10; 15.
	NFK	1,192. 8,51. 15,12. 17,18. 49.
	NTH	B25.
	NTT	7,6
	OXF	43.
	SFK	6,216; 233. 8,50. 15,3. 26,13.
	SRY	19,12.
	WIL	3,1.
Holding land from uncle	HAM	IoW7,7.

See also: Relations.
NET – See Drag net; Fishing net.

NIECE (neptis)	DEV	3,89.
	GLS	68,13.
	HRT	25,2.
	NFK	10,81.

See also: Relations.
NIGHT's provisions (noctis de firma) – See Honey; Revenue.
NORMANDY – See Exchange; Grant.
NORSE – war against WOR 26,16.
NOTHING – See Freeman; Land; Lordship; Man; Recorded; Settler; Smallholder; Village.

NUN (monialis)	BDF	53,1; 3-4.
	CAM	11,2.
	GLS	23.
	HAM	14,6. 44,1.
	HEF	1,10b. 2,17.
	LIN	1,9.
	SFK	14,167.
	WIL	16,5.
Evidence by	WOR	2,67.
Holding land/property	GLS	78,8.
	HRT	15,4.
	KEN	7,11.
	LIN	67,27.
	MDX	17,1.
	NFK	47,7.
	SOM	16,12-13.
	WAR	B2. 43,1.
	WOR	2,54; 67.
Poor	NFK	47,7.

See also: Dwelling; Jurisdiction, full; Supplies.

O

OAK (quercus)	WAR	12,11.
	WOR	2,13.
Third oak in Earl's		
revenue	DOR	1,2.
OATH		
Evidence given on	KEN	C8.
	LIN	C4.
	SFK	25,105.
	YKS	CN2. CE13-14; 21; 30-32; 34.
Place for making	SOM	2,4.
See also: Combat; Evidence.		
OATS (avena)		
Packload of	BDF	24,5.
Peck of	WIL	24p.
Sester of	WIL	24p.
Sowing of	HEF	1,7.

OBLIGATION (wara) – See Defence obligation.
OCCUPATIONS – See Almsman; Almswoman; Archer; Artificer; Baker; Barber; Beadle; Beehive keeper; Beekeeper; Boatman; Bowman; Brewer; Bursar; Butler; Carpenter; Castle warden; Catchpoll; Chamberlain; Chancellor; Church Registrar; Churchwarden; Cobbler; Commissioner; Concubine; Constable; Cook; Corn dealer; Cowman; Crossbowman; Dairy maid; Deliverer; Ditcher; Emissary; Engineer; Falconer; Fisherman; Forester; Fowler; Goatherd; Gold fringe maker; Goldsmith; Granary keeper; Groom; Guard; Gunner; Harper; Harvester; Horseman; Hunter; Huntsman; Installer; Interpreter; Jester; Keeper of King's house; Larderer; Lawman; Lorimer; Man-at-arms; Marshal; Mason; Mead keeper; Mercenary; Merchant; Messenger; Mill keeper; Miller; Minister; Money changer; Moneyer; Officer; Orphrey worker; Pigman; Ploughman; Prebendary; Purveyor; Reeve; Registrar; Rider; Riding man; Robe maker; Sailor; Salt boiler; Salt worker; Scribe; Scullion; Servant; Shepherd; Sheriff; Smith; Soldier; Steersman; Steward; Summoner; Tailor; Treasurer; Usher; Valet; Vavassor; Vine dresser; Washer; Watchman; Woodland keeper.
OCCUPIED (hospitata) – See Dwelling; Inhabited.
OFFENCE – See City; Crime/offence; Fugitive; Hunting; King; Outlaw; Road; Shore; Waterfront.
OFFENDER – land of

Held by reeve who pays offender's fine	ESS	83,2.
Taken by reeve through sheriff	ESS	83,1.
OFFICE		

(ministerium)	NFK	1,122; 124.
Belonging to Hundred	NFK	1,142.
OFFICER (minister)		
Gift to by reeve	HEF	1,6.
Payments to	NFK	1,7.
Possession of land not given by	LIN	CS19.

See also: Abbot; Bishop; Earl; King; Sheriff.

OPEN land (planum)	BDF	4,2. 54,2.
	CHS	2,7.
	DBY	1,8.
	GLS	1,57. 10,11.
	HEF	1,4.
	HRT	10,9.
	SFK	3,59.
	WOR	8,6. 9,2. 10,10.
	YKS	1Y2. 2B1. 2N14. 4N1. 5N52; 67; 76. 6N93-94; 136; 139-140.

OPPRESSION (vastare) – See Sheriff.

ORA	BDF	57,6.
	BKM	7,2. 12,30.·14,3. 41,6. 43,2.
	CAM	B10. 1,5. *5,6.* 25,1. 26,19. *41,6.*
	CHS	C13. 2,3. R1,40a.
	DEV	1,28.
	GLS	G1. B1. 1,56; 58; 61.
	HAM	1,20; 28-30; W4; W15; W20.
	HEF	1,6; 38-39; 41-42.
	KEN	D7. 1,1. 5,1. 6,1.
	LEC	C1; 5.
	NFK	1,24; 29; 148. 9,159. 25,28. 31,44. 34,19. 66,79.
	NTH	B36. 1,8-9; 32.
	OXF	B3. 1,12.
	SHR	4,1,16; 21; 32.
	SOM	1,1-9; 31.
	SFK	1,94. 6,89a. 14,29.
	SRY	16,1.
	WIL	B2.
	WOR	C2. 1,2; 4-5. 2,81. 23,8. 26,6-7; 10; 13; 17.
Silver, of	BKM	24,1.
	LIN	S5.
Value of	CAM	*41,6.*

155

ORCHARD
(pomerium;
virgultum) DEV 15,1.
DOR 55,47.
NTT B18.
ORDEAL (judicium [dei])
Offered by
Abbot's steward NFK 66,41.
claimant's man NFK 8,37. 10,19.
defendant's
villagers against
Hundred and
County HAM 23,3.
Englishman NFK 9,227.
free man SFK 6,92. 7,13.
Hundred and
claimant's man
against each other NFK 13,19.
King's man in
support of claimant NFK 8,71.
King's man that
free man belonged
to King's manor NFK 8,138.
member of King's
household NFK 1,10.
pardoned outlaw
that he returned to
his lord SFK 6,79.
priest LIN C4.
woman NFK 1,213. 66,80.
Pledge given with
regard to NFK 9,227. 13,19. *15,2.*
See also: Combat; Ordeal or combat; Prove; Trial.
ORDEAL or combat offered
By claimant's man NFK 9,42.
against Hundred NFK 66,81.
By Hundred against
claimant's man NFK 9,227.
By King's man
against Hundred NFK 4,25.
For and against
claimant NFK 15,2.
ORDER – See Command.
ORPHREY (aurifrisium) – See Gold embroidery.
OSWALDSLOW –
customs WOR 2,1; 80. *App V F.*
OUNCE (uncia)
Gold, of BDF 1,1a; 2a; 3.
BRK 36,2.
CAM 18,3. 22,6.
ESS 25,22. 38,2. 48,2.
55,1.
HEF 1,2.
HRT 21,1.
KEN 4,1-2.
LEC 13,21; 61.
MDX 24,1.
NFK 1,66.
SFK 9,1. 31,20.
OUTLAW (utlagus;
ex lex) ESS 24,65.
GLS 1,6.

KEN D9.
NFK 9,49.
OXF 1,13.
SFK 6,92.
WOR C4. 9,1b.
Abbot outlawed BRK 46,4.
Death of in York ESS 30,16.
Denmark, living in NFK 10,77.
free man
could return to
patronage after
pardon SFK 6,79.
outlawed ESS 18,23. 25,5.
NFK 66,5; 78.
Land and person
seized by King SFK 6,79.
Person imposing
outlawry NFK 66,78.
Priest on outlawry
becoming another's
man SFK 7,114.
Receiving KEN D21.
Restored to peace
only through King CHS C4.
YKS C39.
Return of, to his lord
not seen by Hundred SFK 6,79.
Slayer of, receives
outlaw's goods OXF 1,13.
See also: Annexation; Crime/offence; Earl; Exile;
Reeve; Sheriff.
OUTLIER (berewica) BDF 23,2. 54,3. 55,9.
CAM 1,17. 5,45; 48-49;
53. 7,1. 14,48.
CHS 8,21; 41. 11,7.
FT1,2-9. FT2,1-18. FT3,2-5. R1,1; 31.
R2,1. R3,1. R5,3.
DBY 1,1; 9; 11-16; 18-20;
24-25; 27-29; 37-38. 2,1. 3,1. 4,2. 6,12; 27;
74; 86; 89. 7,5. 10,4-5; 15; 17.
ESS 1,3; 19; 27. 10,5.
12,1. 20,25; 36; 63. 32,16. 37,3. 46,2.
GLS 1,15. 2,4. 19,2.
HAM 1,17; 27; 45. 64,2.
HEF 1,8. 7,1.
HRT 15,12. 16,10. 17,1.
30,2. 36,15.
HUN 1,6. 4,5. 8,3. 10,1.
20,8. D22-23.
KEN 5,138.
LIN 1,2; 8; 10-11; 30;
64-65. 3,11; 47; 52; 55. 7,29. 8,6-7; 29; 32;
35. 9,2. 11,2; 6-7. 12,5; 10-12; 44; 50; 61;
67; 70; 83; 94. 13,11; 25; 35-36. 14,28; 86;
98. 15,2. 18,30. 20,2. 21,2. 24,2; 8; 11; 19;
23; 26-27; 40; 43; 52; 55-59; 62; 65; 71; 75;
83. 25,10; 14. 26,9; 15; 18; 28; 41-42; 52.
27,4; 6; 8; 52. 28,13; 18. 29,2; 12; 15-17;
19-20; 23; 31-32. 30,10; 14; 23-24. 31,6; 8.
32,10; 16; 18; 30. 34,23; 25-26. 35,5. 37,5.
38,4-5; 11. 40,21. 41,2. 42,3; 7; 10; 17.

43,2. 44,17. 45,4. 48,3; 6-7. 56,15; 22.
57,35; 42. 59,8. 61,7. 62,2. 63,3-4; 10; 17;
22. 64,2; 6; 10; 19. 65,4-5. 67,6; 11; 14-15;
17. 68,6; 10-11. CK10.

MDX 4,5. 9,8. 11,2.

NFK 1,2; 16-20; 29; 33-36; 40; 42; 52; 55; 57; 71; 84; 87-88; 90-91; 93; 104; 114; 132; 137-138; 143; 147; 150; 164; 176; 179; 192-193; 210; 212; 218; 228-230; 236-239. 2,3-4; 10. 4,9; 17; 30. 6,6. 7,2. 8,62; 108-109; 130. 9,2; 78; 85; 87-88; 94; 98. 10,5; 8; 15; 20; 24; 30; 65. 13,19. 14,1; 23. 19,23; 32. 22,3-6; 10; 16; 23. 23,5; 13. 24,6-7. 26,2. 29,7. 34,3; 9. 40,1. 49,4.

NTH 18,64.

NTT 1,1; 17; 23; 27-28; 47; 52; 60. 5,1; 3-4; 7; 10. 6,1. 9,85. 10,36; 63. 13,3. 17,6. 24,1. 27,3. 30,15.

RUT R7; 17-20.

SHR 4,1,1-2; 5-6; 11-12; 16-17; 21-23; 26-27; 29-30; 37. 4,3,32-33; 39-40. 4,4,20. 4,8,3. 4,14,9. 4,18,3. 4,19,1. 4,20,21. 4,22,1. 5,9. 6,10.

STS 2,20; 22. 11,6.

SFK 1,33-35; 37; 76; 85; 100-101; 115. 4,12. 6,11; 43; 135; 156-157; 187; 264; 308. 7,21; 76. 14,53; 55. 21,80. 25,35. 26,12c. 28,1a. 43,1-2. 65,1.

SSX 11,70. 15,3; 7; 46.

WAR 1,2.

WOR 1,1a; 2. 2,3; 78; 81-82; 84. 8,22-23. 9,1a. 10,5. 23,1. 28,1.

YKS 1Y2-4; 6-8; 10-11; 14-15; 18-19. 1E22; 26; 35; 38. 1W9; 31; 67; 71; 73. 2,1-2. 2B1; 9; 11; 18. 2W4; 6-7; 12. 2E1; 14; 16; 18-36; 38-41. 3Y1; 4; 14. 4N1; 3. 5N8. 5E24; 65. 5W27; 38. 6N1; 32; 50; 52; 56; 85; 92; 111; 118; 120. 6W2. 9W1; 4; 8-9; 13; 15; 20; 81-84; 86; 93; 130. 10W41; 43. 11N8. 13W9; 14; 28; 39-41; 44. 13E10-11. 13N17. 14E1; 11; 14; 54. 15E2; 5; 11. 16E2. 16N2. 16W1. 20E3-4. 21E5. 23N6; 8; 12; 18; 20-22; 24; 27; 29; 32-34. 23E3; 13-15. 24W17; 21. 25W32-33. 26E6. 29W5-7; 42. 29E12. 29N7. 30W1. CE40. SW,Sk2. SW,BA1-2. SW,Sf1. SW,Ag1. SW,M5-6.

Counted (enumerata) SFK 21,80.

Equivalent to a member GLS 1,15.
STS 2,20; 22.

Lying in different County from its manor ESS 1,3; 26; 28.
SHR 4,1,5.
SFK 1,96.

Lying in different Hundred from its hall/manor ESS 12,1.
SFK 7,71. 14,53; 55.

Manor, being HUN 4,5.

NFK 7,2.
NTT 1,17.
See also: Member; Revenue.

OUTSIDER (extraneus) – See Merchant; Stranger.

OVEN (furnus)
Earl's HAM IoW6,10.

OVERSEAS – See Service, King's.

OX (bos) BDF 13,2. 17,6. 21,7-8; 11. 22,2. 23,6; 44; 52; 55. 32,12; 15. 52,2. 53,19; 24-25. 56,5; 7-8. 57,10; 12; 19.

BRK 13,2. 30,1.

BKM 5,4. 12,34. 14,26. 17,3; 29.

CAM 5,46. 13,2. 14,24; 39; 47; 51. 17,5. 21,4; 6. 22,10. 23,1-2. 26,2; 16; 22; 32; 34; 37; 44. 30,3. 31,5. 32,11; 18-19; 27. 41,14-15. 43,1.

CHS 3,8. 8,20. 9,10. 12,1. 20,4-5; 8. FD2,3. FT3,3. R7,1.

CON 3,6. 4,28. 5,2,7; 19. 5,3,14; 16-17; 26. 5,4,2; 6; 11-12. 5,5,1; 8; 10; 13. 5,6,6. 5,7,7. 5,8,1-2; 9. 5,12,1-2. 5,13,1; 9-10; 12. 5,14,3-5. 5,15,2; 4. 5,17,3. 5,18,1. 5,20,1-2. 5,21,1. 5,23,1; 5. 5,24,3; 8; 15. 5,25,2.

DBY 6,82.

DEV 3,74; 76; 87-88. 15,14; 22; 33; 37. 16,8; 49; 82. 17,9; 12; 17; 42; 61; 66. 33,2. 35,7; 23. 36,17. 42,2.

DOR 11,5. 55,40.

ESS 18,17. 36,6. 57,1. 90,73.

GLS 1,21. 59,1. 60,1.

HAM 2,9. 12,1. 23,43. 29,2.

HEF A7. 1,49-50. 24,7.

HUN 2,1. 3,1. 13,1; 4. 19,25.

KEN M21. 5,10; 15; 45; 54; 66; 137.

LIN 1,29-31; 34; 56; 60; 62-63; 74; 76. 2,7-9; 17-18; 21; 31. 3,5; 18-19; 28; 36; 47; 53. 4,25; 42. 7,27; 47. 8,7; 10. 12,9; 14; 42; 79. 14,6; 42. 22,34. 24,11; 44; 75. 26,32-33; 35; 54. 27,2; 4. 28,18; 29. 29,13; 27. 30,3. 37,3. 40,24. 41,1. 58,1; 3-4. 59,3. 64,2; 9; 15. 67,5; 8; 24. 68,22; 46.

NFK 1,2; 16; 57; 73; 81; 90; 106; 109; 119; 140; 142; 144. 2,7. 4,22; 54. 7,2-3; 13. 8,11; 54. 9,4; 8; 22; 28; 51; 58; 61; 77; 92-93; 98; 118; 128-129; 135; 163; 199. 10,11; 70. 13,1; 6; 10. 14,1; 7; 32; 42. 15,12. 16,1. 17,13; 19. 18,1. 19,3; 9-10; 20,5-6. 21,1. 22,16. 24,6. 31,12; 33. 35,10; 18. 38,1. 48,6. 49,8. 50,4. 61,2. 66,62; 64; 73; 75; 82; 90; 99.

NTH 1,22. 6,16. 18,2. 30,18. 41,10.

NTT 1,52. 5,3. 7,6. 9,7; 128. 10,6; 60.

11,18.
SHR 4,4,16. 4,14,17.
    4,17,2.
SOM 21,30; 40; 54; 85.
    25,6; 56. 36,9.
    47,15; 24.
STS 8,5; 14.
SFK 1,12; 18; 51; 119.
2,3-4. 3,6-7; 62. 4,3. 6,5; 23; 49; 123; 202;
214; 227; 248; 313; 315. 7,18; 57; 59; 66-
67. 8,35; 42-43; 49; 51; 63. 14,7; 21; 34; 70.
16,24; 41. 19,17. 21,27; 43; 52. 25,10; 17;
38; 51; 67; 82. 26,5; 8. 29,6; 8; 11. 32,11;
27. 34,8. 36,7; 12-13. 37,4-5. 38,2; 8; 16;
20. 41,11. 64,3. 66,6. 67,21; 23. 74,3. 75,1;
4.

SRY 1,10. 8,12. 19,8; 30;
    33; 39.
SSX 9,98-99; 118. 10,12;
    15; 47-48; 68; 72.
    11,33. 13,37; 49.
WOR 2,71.
YKS 2E27. 5E21-22; 25.
    5W9. 6N124.
    14E8. 15E3. 23E1.

half (½) BDF 57,9.
    LIN 14,41. 27,20-21.
Death duty, as HEF 1,49.
Drawing stone to
church WOR 10,5.
Fine, as HEF A7.
King's HAM 69,4.
Land for BDF 3,16-17. 13,2. 17,6.
21,7-8; 11. 22,2. 23,31; 34; 44; 55. 25,3.
32,12; 15. 44,3. 53,19; 25. 56,1; 4; 7-8.
57,9-10; 17; 19.

BRK 3,2.
BKM 12,18; 23. 17,13;
    21; 29. 25,2. 26,10.
    57,5.
CAM 1,21. 5,2; 19; 37;
40. 7,7. 11,5. 12,3. 13,2-3; 10; 12. 14,6; 10;
17; 20; 24; 31; 39; 47; 51-52; 57; 72. 17,5-
6. 19,1-2; 4. 21,4; 6. 22,10. 23,1-2. 25,8.
26,1-2; 7-8; 12; 13; 15-16; 18; 22; 28; 32-
33; 37-39; 44; 50; 55. 29,11. 30,3. 32,13;
15; 18-19; 26; 29. 36,1. 41,5; 6; 14-15.
CHS 8,41. 9,22; 27.
    13,6-7.
DBY 1,5; 9; 23; 26; 31-
32; 34. 5,2. 6,2-3; 19; 21; 26; 29; 42; 47;
56; 61-62. 9,3. 10,3; 8; 14; 27. 12,3. 13,1.
14,5. 17,1; 8-9; 14; 18; 21.
DOR 40,13. 55,12; 18.
56,25; 41; 49-51; 63; 66. 57,2; 7; 18.
ESS 89,2.
HRT 1,7. 2,5. 5,2; 22.
7,3. 15,9. 17,5; 7. 31,2; 5. 33,16; 19. 34,2;
6; 8-9. 36,1; 9-10. 39,1. 42,5; 12; 14-15.
HUN 2,6-7. 3,1. 6,3; 10.
8,3-4. 13,2. 19,4-5; 13. 20,9. 29,2; 4; 6.

KEN 5,11.
LIN 1,27. 2,18; 22; 25;
32; 38. 3,1-2; 9-10; 13; 16-17; 20-21; 25-
26; 28; 30; 33; 42; 46; 48; 50; 52. 4,4-5; 9;
14; 22; 28-31; 35; 46; 49; 52-53; 56; 59; 62-
64; 67-68; 71; 73; 75-76; 78; 80-81. 5,2-3.
7,5; 11; 27; 36; 45; 48-49; 51; 59. 8,3-4; 6;
10; 14; 26-28; 30-32; 38. 10,1; 4. 11,1; 7;
9. 12,3; 6; 10; 13; 15; 22; 38; 42; 45; 52-54;
57-58; 61-62; 75-79; 81-84; 86-88; 95-96.
13,11; 16; 19; 21-23; 25; 35-36; 43. 14,6;
10-12; 14; 16; 22; 24; 33; 36; 43-45; 55; 62;
71; 74; 82; 87; 90; 94-96; 100. 16,3; 5-6; 9;
12-13; 18-20; 24; 30; 38; 41; 45-46; 49.
17,2. 18,15-18; 21. 20,2; 4. 21,2. 22,3-4; 6;
11-13; 15; 18; 23; 27; 30-34. 24,4-5; 11; 21;
29-31; 35; 42-43; 55-56; 58-61; 65; 67; 69-
70; 74; 77; 88-89; 98. 25,10; 12; 15-16; 18-
19; 22. 26,3; 12; 14-16; 18; 20-22; 27-29;
31-32; 34; 37-38; 43; 45-46; 51; 54. 27,2-
4; 6; 8; 12; 19; 23-27; 29-32; 36-37; 40-41;
44-46; 51-57; 59-64. 28,2-4; 7-8; 14-15; 20;
23-24; 26; 28; 30; 32-33; 36-37; 39; 41.
29,2-4; 10; 12-22; 24; 26-28; 30; 33. 30,7;
10-11; 13-17; 25; 32-33; 36. 31,3-4; 10; 18.
32,2-6; 8-9; 11-20; 23; 25; 29-30. 33,1-2.
34,3-5; 7; 9-12; 16; 19; 22-27. 35,5; 8; 10;
13; 17. 37,1; 3; 5-7. 38,2; 4; 6; 10; 13. 39,3.
40,2; 4-6; 9-10; 16; 18-19; 21. 41,2. 42,2;
5-7; 14; 18-19. 43,4-6. 44,1; 8; 12; 15-16;
18. 45,1-4. 46,2-4. 47,3-6; 10. 48,5-8; 11-
13; 15. 49,1; 4-6. 50,1. 51,2-3; 5-6; 8; 10.
52,1-2. 53,1. 55,4. 56,15; 21; 23. 57,3-5;
11; 19; 23; 25-27; 29; 31; 33-34; 42; 44; 46-
50; 56. 59,1-13; 16; 20. 61,1-3; 8-10. 63,3;
8; 10; 17-18. 64,6; 8-11; 16-17. 65,1. 66,1-
2. 67,1-5; 8-12; 14-15; 17; 20-22; 24-25; 27.
68,5-6; 8-14; 17; 22; 25-26; 29-36; 38-39;
43-44; 46-47.

MDX 9,5. 25,2.
NFK 12,2. 66,64.
NTH 18,22; 40. 21,3-4.
30,18. 41,10. 43,10. 45,3. 56,28; 53. 57,3.
NTT 1,6; 18; 29; 46; 60;
62. 2,7-8. 3,4. 4,2; 8. 5,10; 16. 6,4-6; 10;
14-15. 7,1; 3. 9,5; 7; 13; 27; 35; 38; 42; 52;
54; 69; 71; 73; 89; 92; 94; 105; 123; 126;
128. 10,2; 11; 17; 22; 27; 35-36; 39-40; 51;
53-54; 63. 11,11; 23. 12,2; 4; 7; 15. 13,11-
12. 14,4. 15,5-6. 16,4-5; 10; 12. 18,2; 4.
24,2-3. 25,2. 28,2-3. 29,1-2. 30,2-3; 27; 30-
32; 35; 37-40; 43; 45; 49-50; 52; 56.
OXF 58,22.
SOM 21,9; 16. 25,19.
STS 2,21.
SRY 8,12.
WIL 24,37. 26,8. 28,10.
29,3-4. 56,6. 67,21; 49; 53; 74; 79; 88.
68,17.
YKS 1N7. 1E3; 6; 14; 21;
42. 1W41; 49. 2E19-20; 22; 30. 8N20.

29W12; 27; 29; 34. 29E9.

Land, free, for   KEN   5,85.
Land for, ox not there HRT   36,1.
                     MDX   25,2.
Ploughing oxen/oxen
in a plough/ploughing
with oxen   BDF   15,3.
                     CHS   2,16. FT1,9.
                     CON   *5,5,11; 14. 5,8,3.*
                     DBY   1,4. 6,20; 65. 9,2.
                                  17,14.
                     DEV   *3,37; 44. 15,29.*
16,4. 17,98. 19,34. 21,1; *18. 28,10. 34,32;*
35. 48,9; 11. *52,46.*
                     HAM   3,6. 21,9. 69,6.
                     HUN   1,3. 3,1. 19,4-5; 7;
                                  22-23. 29,2.
                     KEN   7,24. 12,1.
                     LEC   25,3.
                     LIN   2,15; 23; 25; 27; 35.
3,25; 30; 33; 40; 43; 46; 48. 4,19; 21-22; 28;
32; 35; 41; 45; 51; 64; 79; 81. 5,2. 7,14; 45;
57. 8,19; 21; 29-30; 32. 12,5-6; 10; 12; 18;
47; 53; 57; 83; 92; 96. 13,27. 14,3; 10; 14;
19; 24; 34; 38; 44-45; 60. 16,8; 10; 13-14;
18-19; 22; 27-28; 30; 33; 40; 47; 50. 18,16-
17. 22,3-4; 12; 20. 24,4; 19; 29; 39; 43; 55;
57-58; 65. 25,2-3; 8; 14; 22. 26,5; 11; 16.
27,6; 8; 13; 20-21; 30; 37; 45; 49; 55; 61.
28,7-8; 14; 19; 23; 30-32; 38-41. 29,12; 14;
17; 19-21; 23-24; 26; 32. 30,6; 11; 14-16;
18; 37. 31,5. 32,3-4; 8-10; 12; 14; 16; 18;
22; 24; 32-33. 33,1. 34,5; 7-10; 14; 19; 21;
23; 25. 35,4-5; 11. 36,3. 38,2; 5-6. 40,2-5;
7; 10-12; 17-18. 42,5. 43,2-5. 44,1; 16; 18-
19. 45,1; 3. 46,1. 47,2-4; 6; 10. 48,7-8; 12-
13. 49,4. 51,4-6. 56,21. 57,14; 18-19; 29;
31; 34-35; 43; 47; 51. 59,2; 11; 15-16; 18;
20. 63,3. 64,2. 66,1-2. 67,9; 12. 68,2; 12;
19; 30-31; 33-34; 38; 42; 44-45.
                     NFK   2,7. 7,11. 9,21; 35;
38; 40; 47; 56; 65; 146; 156; 166. 10,29; 31;
80-81; 92. 12,25. 14,30. 19,28. 20,20. 52,3.
64,9. 65,9. 66,61; 93.
                     NTH   56,56.
                     NTT   1,25; 31; 41. 6,12.
9,1; 10; 86; 114. 11,23-24; 27-29; 31. 13,4.
15,3. 20,3; 6-7. 21,1. 30,2-3; 23; 25; 37-38;
46; 48.
                     RUT   R18.
                     SHR   4,3,29. 4,4,9.
                     SOM   *8,14. 46,9.*
                     SRY   19,22.
                     SSX   9,12. 10,78. 11,90.
                     WAR   18,16.
                     WIL   13,3. 28,10.
                     WOR   10,5.
                     YKS   5N17. 5W1. 7E2.
                                  10W5.
Render of   CON   1,15.
See also: Crime/offence; Customary due; Hay;
Meadow; Pasture; Purchase and sale; Salt; Theft.
OX cart   CHS   S2,2. S3,2.
OX hide-render of   NFK   1,70.

P

PACKHORSE (caballus; summarius) – See Horse; Salt.
PACKLOAD/load (summa) – See Church; Corn; Fish; Flour; Freeman; Malt; Peas; Oats; Salt; Wheat.
PALFREY (palefridus) – See Horse.
PALM Sunday
Render of box wood
on   SHR   3e,1.
PANNAGE (pasnagium) – See Pasturage; Pig.
PARAGE (in paragio) – See Jointly.
PARCEL (particula) – See Land; Measure; Piece.
PARISH (parochia)
Of mother church   SFK   1,1.
PARISHIONER (parochianus)
Transferred to
another church   SFK   2,8.
PARK (parcus)   CHS   26,6.
                    ESS   24,17.
                    GLS   1,48.
                    HAM 55,2. 56,1.
                    HEF   10,48.
                    KEN 5,67; 124. 7,5-6.
                    MDX 9,9.
                    SHR   C3.
                    SOM 19,24.
                    SFK   6,83; 191; 303. 66,1.
                    SSX   1,2. 9,19. 11,81; 85; 112-113.
                    WOR 5,1. 9,1d. 14,2.
   half (½)   SFK   1,101.
Beasts of the chase,
for   NFK   4,9.
King's   BKM 19,3.
                    HAM IoW5,1.
                    SRY   1,3.
Meadow in   HAM IoW5,1.
Wild/woodland
beasts/animals, for BDF   23,4.
                    BKM 14,5.
                    CAM 14,78. 41,1.
                    DEV   1,64.
                    HAM 2,9.
                    HEF   1,41.
                    HRT   10,5. 26,1. 36,7.
                    KEN 5,72.
                    MDX 10,1.
See also: Deer.
PASTURAGE (pasnagium)
Dues for, lord exempt SRY   4,1.
free men receiving
from their men   CHS R2,2.
King's woodland,

from only through
sheriff   HAM 69,4.
Pigs, from   GLS   W8.
                    HAM 1,3; 29.
                    KEN 5,138. 7,7; 9. 12,4.
                    OXF   1,7a.
                    SRY   1,10. 5,22. 6,5. 20,2. 21,6.
                    SSX   2,10. 3,1. 7,2.
See also: Pasture (and cross references thereunder); Pasture land.
PASTURE (pastura)   BDF   24,29. 32,13. 53,5.
                    BRK   1,41. 7,6; 23. 21,18.
                    BKM 4,37.
                    CAM B11-12. 5,6. 26,16. 29,10.
                    CHS 20,10.
                    CON 1,1-12; 14; 16-17.
2,1-6; 9-11. 3,1-6. 4,1-8; 10-20; 23-24; 26-27. 5,1,2-22. 5,2,2-3; 5-6; 8; 10-14; 17-19; 21-31; 33. 5,3,1-28. 5,4,1-4; 6-11; 13-19. 5,5,1-22. 5,6,1-10. 5,7,1; 3-13. 5,8,1-10. 5,9,1-4. 5,10,1. 5,11,1-6. 5,12,1-3. 5,13,1-5; 7-12. 5,14,1-6. 5,15,1-6. 5,16,1-2. 5,17,1-4. 5,18,1. 5,19,1. 5,20,1-2. 5,21,1. 5,22,1. 5,23,1-5. 5,24,1-13; 15-23; 25. 5,25,1-3; 5. 5,26,1-4. 6,1.
                    DBY 6,74.
                    DEV   1,3-9; 11; 13-15;
17-20; 24-34; 37; 39-42; 44-61; 64-67; 70; 72. 2,2; 4-5; 7; 11-21; 23-24. 3,4-14; 16; 18-25; 27-30; 33; 35; 37-58; 60; 62-67; 69-70; 73-77; 80-81; 85-93; 96-97; 99. 4,1. 5,2-6; 8-14. 6,1-2; 4-5; 7-12. 7,1-4. 8,1. 10,1. 11,1-3. 12,1. 13,1. 13a,3. 14,1-2. 15,4-5; 8-10; 12-18; 21-25; 32-34; 36-37; 39-40; 43-48; 50; 52-54; 56-61; 63; 67-68; 70-71; 74; 78-79. 16,3-12; 14-17; 19-27; 29-31; 33-36; 40; 43-48; 50-54; 56-59; 63; 65-72; 74-78; 80-90; 92-95; 97-98; 101; 104-105; 107-113; 116-124; 128-133; 135; 138-151; 153-154; 156; 158-160; 162-172; 175-176. 17,3-7; 10-17; 19-23; 26-27; 29-36; 38; 40-41; 44; 48-50; 53; 56-57; 59-60; 64; 66; 69-70; 73; 79-81; 85; 88-92; 95-98; 100-106. 18,1. 19,2; 4-6; 8-21; 24-27; 30-31; 33; 35; 37-42; 44; 46. 20,1; 3-6; 10-15. 21,1-4; 6-7; 9; 13; 15-16; 19-21. 22,1. 23,1-7; 9; 10-15; 17-21. 24,1-3; 5-16; 19-20; 23-24; 26; 28-32. 25,1; 3-6; 9-10; 12-13; 15-16; 20-22; 24; 26; 28. 27,1. 28,1-7; 9-13; 15-16. 29,1-2; 8-9. 31,1-2. 32,2-4; 5; 6-7; 10. 33,1-2. 34,1-2; 4-7; 10; 14-22; 24; 26-29; 31-33; 35-36; 38-

160

39; 43-44; 46; 48-51; 53; 55. 35,1-21; 23;
25-26; 28-29. 36,1-7; 10; *12;* 13-16; 18; 20;
24-26. 37,1. 38,1-2. 39,1; 4-14; 16-17; 19-
21. 40,1; 4-7. 41,1-2. 42,1-8; 12; 15-16; 18;
20; 23-24. 43,1-5. 44,1-2. 45,2. 47,1-2; 4-
8; 11-14. 48,1; 3-5; 7-12. 49,2-3; 5-7. 50,1;
3; 5. 51,2-3; 5-9; 11-16. 52,2-6; 8-10; 12-
14; 16; 19-20; 22-29; 31-36; 39-41; 43-45;
47; 51-52.

DOR 1,1-8; 10-12; 14-20;
22-24; 26-31. 2,1-4; 6. 3,6; 8-11; 13-18.
4,1. 5,1-2. 6,1-4. 8,2-6. 9,1. 10,1; 3; 5-6.
11,1-6; 10-17. 12,1-4; 7-9; 11-12; 15-16.
13,1-6. 14,1. 16,1-2. 17,1-2. 19,2-8; 10;
12-14. 20,1-2. 21,1. 22,1. 23,1. 24,5. 25,1.
26,3-10; 12; 14-22; 24-28; 30-34; 36-39;
41-42; 44-52; 54-68. 27,2-5; 7-11. 28,2-6.
29,1. 30,1; 3-4. 31,1-5. 33,4. 34,2; 5-13;
15. 36,2-3; 5-11. 37,1-2; 4-9; 11; 13-14.
38,1-2. 39,1. 40,2; 4-5; 7-9. 41,1-5. 42,1.
43,1. 44,1. 45,1. 46,2. 47,2-10. 48,1-2.
49,1; 3-12; 14-17. 50,1; 3-4. 51,1. 52,1-2.
53,1-2. 54,1; 3-4; 6-13. 55,1-9; 11; 13; 15-
17; 19; 21-22; 24-27; 29-38; 46. 55a,1.
56,8-9; 13-14; 16; 19-20; 23-24; 28; 31-38;
44-46; 48; 50-51; 53-55; 58-60; 62; 64.
57,1; 3; 8-10; 12-15. 58,2.

ESS 1,2. 7,1. 20,7-9.
24,14; 44. 26,1. 34,7. 37,3; 9. 40,1. 55,1.
B4.

GLS 39,6. 41,2. 73,1-2.
HAM 1,19; 23; 45; 47.
2,5. 3,9. 4,1. 6,8; 17. 21,6. 22,1. 29,1.
HEF 1,5.
HRT 5,20. 8,1. 23,3-4.
24,3. 28,4. 33,9. 44,1.
HUN 1,5; 10.
KEN P11-12. 1,1; 3. 5,8;
15; 27; 29; 38; 42-43; 45; 57; 85; 88; 91;
105; 110; 119; 122; 124; 126; 138; 144; 166.
LIN 1,105. 57,55.
CK15.
MDX 9,1.
NFK 1,10; 62; 69-70.
16,1. 18,1. 21,37.
NTH 1,10. 4,30-31; 34.
23,16-19.
OXF 1,1-3; 7a; 9. 2,1.
6,4-7; 14. 7,2-4; 9-10; 18; 20; 26-27; 32;
35-37; 40; 51; 53; 58-59; 64. 8,2; 4. 9,6; 9a.
11,1. 13,1. 14,6. 15,2-4. 16,2. 17,3-5. 18,1.
20,4-6. 24,3-4. 27,2-3; 10. 28,1; 4-7; 9-10;
12; 14-15; 19-20; 25. 29,1; 5-6; 8; 16; 18;
21; 23. 30,1. 32,1-2. 35,6; 24-25; 28. 39,1;
3. 40,1; 3. 45,1-3. 50,1. 54,1. 55,1-2. 58,4;
8; 20-22; 31; 35. 59,6; 10-13; 18; 20; 25-
27; 29.

SOM 1,1-3; 6; 8-12; 14-
18; 20-23; 25-29; 35. 2,1; 8-11. 3,1-2. 4,1.
5,1; 4-11; 13-15; 18; 21-22; 24-27; 30; 32-
37; 39-43; 49-50; 53-56; 59-60; 62-63; 65-

66; 70. 6,1-10; 13-15; 17. 7,2-4; 9; 11-12.
8,1-3; 5; 8-9; 11; 16-17; 20-21; 23-28; 30-
32; 35. 9,1-2; 4-7. 10,1-2. 11,1. 12,1. 13,1.
14,1. 16,2-3; 6; 12. 17,1-2; 4; 6-8. 18,1; 3-
4. 19,4; 7; 9; 12-14; 16; 20-22; 25-26; 28;
32; 35; 37; 39; 43-44; 46; 49; 51; 53; 62; 66;
75-76; 87. 20,1-3. 21,1-2; 4-7; 12-15; 17-
20; 22-25; 28-29; 34; 39-41; 43-47; 49-50;
53-54; 56-65; 67-68; 71-73; 81-83; 90; 92-
95. 22,1-4; 8-16; 20-24; 26; 28. 23,1. 24,1;
11-13; 16; 18-19; 21; 23; 25; 27-31; 33.
25,2-3; 6-19; 23-25; 27-34; 37-41; 43-44;
47; 49-54; 56. 26,3-4; 6; 8. 27,1-3. 28,1-2.
29,1. 30,1-2. 31,1-4. 32,1-6; 8. 33,1-2.
35,4; 6-7; 10-11; 13; 15; 17; 20; 22. 36,4-
5; 10-13. 37,1-2; 10. 38,1. 39,1-2. 40,2.
41,1; 3. 42,2. 43,1. 44,1. 45,3; 5; 11. 46,4;
9; 11-12; 18-19; 21-25. 47,6-8; *9;* 10; 12;
14; 16-17; 19; 21; 23.

STS 12,30.
SFK 1,73.
SSX 10,1-2; 35; 43; 67;
85. 11,60; 64; 92. 12,3. 13,29; 52.
WAR 1,6. 16,31; 33.
18,8. 24,1. 33,1. 42,3.
WIL 1,1-20; 22. 2,1-5; 7;
9-12. 3,1-5. 4,1-4. 5,1-5; 7. 7,1-3; 6-8; 10-
12; 14-16. 8,1; 5-6; 8-10. 10,1-5. 11,1. 12,1-
6. 13,1-3; 5-13; 16-20. 14,1-2. 15,1-2. 16,1-
4; 6-7. 17,1. 18,1-2. 19,1. 20,1-2; 4-6.
21,1-3. 22,1-4; 6. 23,1; 4-5; 7-10. 24,1-7;
9-13; 15-16; 18-25; 27-30; 34-37; 39; 41-
42. 25,1; 3-5; 7-8; 11; 13-17; 22; 24; 26-27.
26,1; 3-5; 7; 9-13; 16-17; 20-21. 27,1-3; 6-
10; 14-16; 18-20; 22; 25. 28,1-3; 5; 7-9; 11-
12. 29,1-3; 5-8. 30,1-2; 6-7. 31,1. 32,1-3;
5-11; 17. 33,1. 34,1. 36,1-2. 37,1-2; 5; 7-
8. 38,1. 39,1-2. 40,1. 41,1-2; 5-6. 42,1-10.
43,1-2. 44,1. 45,1. 47,1. 48,1-8; 10-12.
50,2; 4-5. 51,1. 52,1. 53,1. 54,1. 55,1.
56,1-4; 6. 57,1. 58,1-2. 59,1-2. 60,1. 61,1.
63,1. 64,1. 66,2-4; 6-7. 67,2; 5-9; 12; 14-
17; 20; 22-23; 25; 27; 31-32; 35-37; 39-40;
43-44; 46; 52; 59-63; 68; 72; 76-77; 80; 83;
85-86; 89; 92; 94. 68,1-2; 9-10; 13-16; 18;
21-22; 24-26; 28-29.

WOR 2,48.
Animals, for
  cattle KEN 5,124.
  cows YKS 9W87.
  horses BRK 1,26.
  livestock (pecunia) BKM 2,1.
CAM 10,1. 11,6. 14,49;
63. 22,3; 7. 26,18; 31; 43; 48. 29,1. 31,1.
32,5; 28-29; 31; 37-38. 38,2. 39,2.
HRT 1,3; 18. 2,2. 3,1.
4,1-2; 6; 11-12; 14-20. 5,1; 4; 8; 14; 17; 20;
23. 7,1. 8,1-3. 9,1; 4-8; 10. 10,1-4; 6-12;
15-16; 18-19. 11,1. 13,1-5. 14,1. 15,2; 10-
13. 16,1; 4; 9-11. 17,2-4; 10; 12-14. 20,1-
2; 7-9; 11; 13. 21,1. 22,2. 28,3-4; 7. 33,2-

104; 146. 10,18. 15,1. 17,23; 38; 43; 49; 53.
25,11. 29,11. 31,8; 41. 55,2. 61,1.

NTH 3,1. 25,1. 26,10.
35,8; 22. 39,17. 43,9. 46,4. 48,2; 17. 56,38;
45. 59,1.

NTT B20. 1,20; 42.
9,126. 16,9.

OXF 9,3. 17,5. 27,1.
29,21.

RUT R13.

SOM 19,15. 22,27.

STS 13,4. 17,17.

SFK 1,77; 90; 99. 8,56.
33,4; 6. 41,8.
67,25.

WAR 6,6. 11,4. 22,19.
29,1; 3. 33,1.

YKS 5E66. 12W16.

PERMISSION (licencia) – See Burgess; Consent;
Go away; Grant; Land; Monk; Sale; Withdraw.

PERSONS – Classes of – See Anglo-saxon; Baron;
Boor; Breton; Burgess; cottage-man; cottager;
Cottager; Countryman; Dane; Earl; Englishman;
Fleming; free man; free woman; freedman;
Freeholder; freeman; Freeman; Freewoman;
Frenchman; Guard; Man; Man-at-arms;
Mercenary; Relations; Rider; Riding man; Slave;
Smallholder; Thane; Vavassor; Villager;
Welshman.

PETER'S pence SOM 2,2.

PETITION (requisitio)
To King to retain land DOR 54,8.

PIECE of land
(mansio terrae) ESS B1.
See also: Land; Measure of land; Parcel.

PIG (porcus) CAM 1,2.

CON *1,1; 5; 16. 2,5.
3,4-5. 4,10; 25. 5,1,1; 4; 6; 11. 5,2,2; 6-7;
12; 17; 19; 21-22; 25; 27. 5,3,1; 7-10; 12-
13; 16-20; 23-24; 27-28. 5,4,5; 8; 12; 14.
5,5,2-3; 7; 10; 12; 16-17. 5,6,1-3; 5-8; 10.
5,7,4. 5,8,1-2; 6. 5,10,1. 5,11,1-2; 4; 6.
5,12,1-3. 5,13,1; 4; 9; 11. 5,14,1-2. 5,15,3-
5. 5,20,1. 5,23,5. 5,24,15; 23-24. 5,25,1; 3;
5. 6,1.*

DEV *1,18; 25; 30; 33;
37-40; 50; 56-59; 64-67; 70; 72. 2,2; 4-5;
13; 15; 18; 23-24. 3,4-5; 13; 16; 19; 21; 23;
33; 36-40; 43-50; 52-53; 56; 58-62; 66; 69;
73-78; 80; 84; 86; 90-93; 97. 4,1. 5,1-6; 8.
6,3-5; 8-9; 13. 10,1. 11,1. 13a,3. 15,4-5; 8;
10; 14; 18; 21; 23; 26-27; 34-46; 48-50; 56;
58; 61; 66-67; 70; 74. 16,4; 7-8; 11-12; 18;
21-23; 26-27; 32-33; 35-37; 39-40; 43-44;
53; 56-57; 59; 65; 67-72; 76; 80; 82-85; 87;
90; 94-96; 99; 102-103; 105; 110-111; 114;
122; 129-130; 135; 138; 141-143; 148-150;
152-154; 158; 164; 166-167; 170; 175-176.
17,5; 8; 13; 15; 17; 20; 28-34; 42-43; 48-
49; 54-55; 57; 63; 68; 73; 78-79; 89; 91;
93; 95; 97; 102. 18,1. 19,4; 6; 10-12; 14-*

*19; 21; 27; 31; 33; 35; 37; 40; 44. 20,1;
11; 13-15. 21,1-2; 4; 10; 18-20. 23,2-3; 5-
7; 10-11; 16-18; 20-24. 24,5; 7-10; 13-14;
17; 19; 22-23; 28; 32. 25,1-5; 11; 13; 15;
24-25. 27,1. 28,1-10; 13; 15-16. 31,1. 32,5;
10. 33,1-2. 34,1-2; 6-8; 10; 14-16; 18; 20;
22-24; 26; 28; 31; 33; 38-40; 44; 48-52; 55.
35,1-5; 8; 10; 12; 14. 36,4; 15-17; 20; 23-
24; 26. 37,1. 40,2; 4; 6. 41,2. 42,4; 6; 8;
10; 13-14; 16; 18; 21; 23-24. 43,2-3. 46,1.
47,5. 48,7. 50,1; 5. 51,3; 5; 7-9; 11-12.
52,10; 16; 21; 24; 29; 38; 41; 45; 53.*

DOR *1,1-11; 13; 16-17;
19-21; 24; 26-27. 11,1; 3-7; 10-12; 15-16.
12,2; 4; 7; 9-10; 14; 16. 13,1-4. 16,1-2. 36,1-
8; 10-11. 41,1; 4-5. 47,1-9. 55,1-2; 4-5; 8-
9; 11; 15-16; 19-22; 26; 29; 31; 35-36; 38;
42. 58,2.*

ESS 1,1-4; 9; 11-13; 19;
22; 24-28. 2,1-5; 7-9. 3,1-2; 8-10; 12-15.
4,2; 5-6; 8-9; 12; 14-15. 5,1-5; 9-12. 6,1; 5;
8; 11-12; 14. 7,1. 8,1-3; 5-11. 9,1-2; 7-9;
11; 13-14. 10,2-5. 11,1-3; 6-8. 13,1-2.
14,2-6. 15,1-2. 16,1. 17,1. 18,1-5; 14; 22;
25; 28; 36-39. 20,1-3; 6-9; 15; 19-20; 22-
23; 25-26; 28; 34; 36-37; 39-40; 43; 45-46;
52-53; 57; 64; 66-69; 71-72; 74; 77-80.
22,3; 5-15; 19-20. 23,2; 5; 15; 38-40. 24,1-
3; 6-9; 15-26; 28; 30-37; 42-46; 48-49; 53-
54; 59-62; 64-66. 25,1-5; 7; 10-12; 15-25.
26,1; 3; 5. 27,1-4; 10; 13-14; 16. 28,5; 9;
11; 13; 16-17. 29,2; 4-5. 30,1; 4-5; 16-19;
22; 27; 33; 45-46; 50. 31,1. 32,1-9; 13-26;
28; 30; 32-35; 38-39; 41-45. 33,1; 3-4; 6-8;
11-17; 19-20; 22-23. 34,1; 4-13; 18-22; 27;
29; 33-34; 36-37. 35,1-6; 8-12. 36,1; 3; 5-
6; 8; 11-12. 37,1-4; 7; 9-11; 13; 15. 38,1-
4; 6-8. 39,1; 4-5; 7. 40,3-4; 6; 8. 41,2; 9-
10. 42,1-3; 6-9. 44,1-3. 45,1. 46,1-2. 47,1-
3. 48,1-2. 49,4-5. 51,2. 52,2. 53,1-2. 54,1-
2. 55,1. 56,1. 57,1-6. 58,1. 60,1-3. 61,1-
2. 65,1. 67,1-2. 68,2; 4; 7. 69,2. 71,2; 4.
76,1. 81,1. 84,2.

GLS W2-3; 19. 1,1-2; 7;
59-60.

HEF 10,2.

HRT 8,1-3. 31,8.

HUN 4,1-4.

NFK 1,1-3; 15-16; 18-20;
30; 32; 40; 42; 52; 57; 59; 71-72; 77-78; 81-
82; 85-89; 92; 94; 105; 123; 128; 132-133;
135-136; 138-139; 144-145; 147; 150-152;
169; 182; 185-186; 192-194; 197-203; 205;
208-212; 215-216; 219; 228; 230-231; 237-
239. 2,4; 7. 3,1. 4,1-2; 9; 14; 17; 26; 30-
31; 38-39; 41-42; 47; 52. 5,1-4; 6. 6,1-4; 6.
7,1-3; 15-19. 8,1-3; 6-7; 16; 21-22; 30; 34-
35; 46-47; 55; 62-64; 87; 91-92; 98-100;
102-103; 105; 107-110; 115; 119-122; 132.
9,2; 6-7; 9; 11-12; 24; 32-33; 46; 59; 70-71;
73-77; 80-81; 83; 87-88; 94-95; 98-100;

2,2; 4; 11; 18; 21. 3,5-6; *14;* 20; 22. 5,8.
11,3. 13,1. 15,46. 16,*43-46;* 58; 78; *80;*
140; 141. *17,21.* 19,5; 15; *17.* 20,14-15.
23,5; 9; 15; *18.* 28,13. 39,20. 42,6; 16; *23.*
44,1. 52,10.

| | HEF | 1,42-43. |
| | SOM | *1,9; 23. 6,12-13.* |

22,3. *24,17.* 25,9. 36,5. 47,21.

PIGSTY (sudis) – See Road.

PLACE (mansio)	ESS	71,4.
Annexation of	ESS	90,1.
Taking away	ESS	60,1.

See also: Dwelling; Residence.

PLAGUE – See Cattle.

PLEA (placitum; querela)
Absence from

fine for	CHS	R1,40d.
illness, through	SFK	76,19.
Adjournment of	SFK	75,5.

Between Bishop and

| woman | SFK | 75,5. 77,4. |

Concerning
ownership of

Freeman	NFK	1,195.
possession of priest	SFK	16,34.
stolen horse	SFK	27,7.

County, of –

payments for	HEF	C15.
	SHR	4,1,37.
	WAR	B4. 1,6.
	WOR	C2.
Customary dues of	DEV	15,67.
Entering into	DEV	*2,2.*
	KEN	*2,5; 30.*
	SRY	1,5. 5,28.
	WOR	*App V H.*

freemen, of
(francorum hominum) WOR   8,28.
Held by

| barons | KEN | C8. |

bishop, thrice

yearly	SOM	2,2.
chief lord over men	HEF	10,2.
Earl	CAM	13,8.

Earl in

| County/Hundred | CHS | C24. |

Hundred

attendance at	HEF	3,1.
	SFK	39,3.
held in	WOR	X3.
payments for	CHS	S1,7.
	ESS	1,2. 24,41a; 52.
	HEF	C15.
	WOR	C2.
revenue, in	WIL	B5.

right given/

received at	HEF	3,1.
service rendered at	HEF	C3.
	WOR	2,21.

King Edward's death

| not terminating | SHR | 3d,7. |

Land, of

| income from | BRK | 2,3. |

land dealt with

| without plea | BRK | 1,43. |

Lord fails to give

| support in | WAR | 44,12. |

Men lent for holding

| of | CAM | 13,8. |

Sheriff's jurisdiction

| excluded | WOR | 2,1. |
| Withdrawal of | SRY | 5,28. |

See also: Adjudgment; Claim; Combat; Dispute;
Judicial enquiry; Legal proceedings; Ordeal;
Prove; Reeve; Revenue; Summons; Third penny;
Trial.

PLEASURE, land held at – See Will.

PLEDGE	ESS	90,1-2; 29; 41-42;
(vadimonium)		74; 76. B3a.
	KEN	1,1.
	LIN	CW4.
	NFK	1,192; 197. 4,51.

9,227. 13,19. *15,2.* 65,13; 17. 66,5; 84; 86;
106.

	SFK	21,95. 32,16. 74,4.
		75,1-2. 76,13; 15;
		17.

Bequeathed to monks	HAM	69,28.
Burgess in, to sheriff	SFK	63,1.
Englishman, given by	NFK	9,227.
House held in	DEV	5,15. 23,27.

Instead of service/

| payments | ESS | 1,8. |

Jurisdiction over land

placed in	LIN	CS29.
Land given in	NFK	66,36.
	SFK	14,39.
Land held in	BDF	32,15. 56,3.
	BRK	7,7.
	BKM	5,6.
	DOR	1,24. 34,6; 14.
		35,1.
	GLS	78,15.
	HAM	67,1. 69,13.
	HRT	2,4. 4,1.
	LEC	13,33.
	LIN	C21. 57,12. CW3.
		CK33; 49; 55.
	MDX	4,11.
	NFK	1,213; 240. 66,107.
	OXF	58,31; 33.
	SOM	1,35.
	SFK	6,318. 14,39.
		31,53. 74,10.
	SRY	5,6. 6,4.
	WAR	17,13; 15; 68. 28,1.
	WIL	67,15.

by King's grant/

| order | ESS | 36,9; 11. |

subject to King's

| customary dues | ESS | 36,9. |

Land held because

predecessor had it in
pledge   NFK   66,107.
Land pledged to
Abbey for money to
redeem holder from
capture   NFK   17,18.
Land pledged by
Abbot to King's
barons   SFK   14,101.
Land placed in   CAM   22,6.
                          HRT   36,11.
                          HUN   D1.
    for 9 years   LIN   68,21.
Mill held in   ESS   40,3.
Money given in for
land   LIN   CK18.
Purpose for which pledge given:-
    to do justice   NFK   1,195.
    as to payments to
    revenue   SFK   74,11.
    to pursue claim by
    judgment/combat   LIN   CK66.
    to prove possession   LIN   CK69.
                          NFK   9,227.
Redeemed/discharged
(adquietare)   BDF   32,15.
                          DOR   34,6.
                          LIN   57,12. CK49.
                          NFK   1,213.
    not redeemed   DOR   1,24.
PLEDGE (a person)
(mancipius;
fideiussor)   CAM   1,12.
                          SFK   74,4.
PLOT (masura; tofta)   DBY   B4; 14.
                          HRT   28,1. 36,4.
                          HUN   B3.
                          LIN   C16; 22-23; 25. 1,9;
64. 3,7. 14,9; 31. 25,5; 7. 27,25. 28,32.
30,17; 33. 32,12. 34,4-5; 24. 36,1. 40,1.
47,3; 5. 48,4. CS34. CN21. CW18.
                          SHR   3b,3.
                          SOM   26,6.
                          YKS   22W6.
Tax due on, not paid   LIN   C20.
See also: Dwelling; Jurisdiction; Jurisdiction, full.
PLOUGH (caruca)   Passim.
Half (½)   BDF   1,3-4. 2,4; 6-8. 3,8;
17. 4,1; 3; 5; 8. 6,1. 7,1. 8,6; 9. 14,1. 15,3.
18,3; 7. 21,15. 23,9; 25; 43; 45; 47-48; 56-
57. 24,5-7; 19-21; 23; 28-29. 25,2; 5; 8; 14.
26,3. 32,5; 7; 10-11; 16. 34,1. 38,2. 40,2.
42,1. 43,1. 44,2; 4. 46,1. 47,3-4. 52,1. 53,3;
7; 12; 18; 21; 23; 28-29; 36. 54,1-2. 55,1;
4; 8; 13. 56,5-6. 57,2; 3ii-iii,v; 4; 8; 11-13;
15; 18; 20.
                          BRK   1,7. 2,1. 3,3. 7,3;
9-10; 18; 22-23; 25; 28-29; 34; 42. 17,2; 6;
10. 18,1. 21,2; 4. 23,2. 26,1; 3. 27,3. 28,2.
31,2. 33,2-5. 34,1; 4. 35,1; 3. 36,2; 6. 38,4.

39,1. 40,1. 41,1; 4; 6. 45,3. 46,1; 7. 48,1.
49,1. 51,1. 55,1. 59,1. 64,1. 65,2-4; 16-17.
                          BKM   B1. 1,4. 3a,3; 5-6.
4,7-9; 18; 26; 31; 36; 39. 5,4-5; 16-17. 12,1;
5; 9; 17; 20; 22; 26; 30; 32; 35-37. 14,2; 15;
26-28; 39; 44. 16,4; 6; 9. 17,1; 12; 15; 17-
19. 18,2. 21,5; 7-8. 22,2. 23,6; 19-21; 26;
28-30; 32. 28,1-2. 33,1. 35,2. 40,1-2. 41,7.
43,3; 10. 47,1. 51,2. 53,2; 5. 56,3. 57,3;
10; 12-13.
                          CAM   1,20. 3,6. 5,13-15;
29; 31; 34; 41; 44. 6,1. 7,6; 8. 11,2; 4. 12,4.
13,7-9. 14,9; 21; 28; 30-31; 33; 36-37; 40-
45; 49-50; 76. 15,3. 18,5-6. 21,3; 7. 23,3;
6. 25,1. 26,5; 10-11; 20; 23; 27; 29; 31; 41;
43; 45; 48. 30,2. 31,6. 32,6; 8; 10; 20; 22;
24-25; 27-28; 34-35; 38; 43. 35,2. 38,1.
39,2. 40,1. 41,8-9; 13. 43,1.
                          CHS   B3-4. A6-7; 10; 17;
22. 1,3; 9. 2,4; 24; 31. 3,4; 7; 9; 11. 5,6; 8;
10. 7,3. 8,4-6; 11-12; 16; 18; 20; 23; 35-
36; 39; 43-44. 9,2-4; 11; 19; 21; 25. 10,1-
2. 11,4; 6. 12,4. 13,4. 14,3-4; 7; 10-13.
16,2. 17,7. 19,3. 20,2-3; 6-7; 9; 12. 24,1;
4; 6-7; 9. 25,3. 27,2-4. FD1,1. FD2,1-2.
FD4,1. FD5,1. FD6,1. FD7,2. FT3,3.
                          CON   2,8. 4,20; 24-25;
27. 5,2,23; 27. 5,3,4; 14-16. 5,4,3; 12; 17;
20. 5,5,9; 11; 13-14; 17. 5,6,1; 3-4; 8. 5,7,1;
3; 5; 7; 11. 5,8,1-3; 7; 9-10. 5,9,1. 5,11,4.
5,12,1; 3. 5,13,3; 8-9; 11. 5,14,1. 5,15,3.
5,16,1. 5,17,1; 3. 5,20,1-2. 5,23,2; 5.
5,24,3; 5; 12; 15; 22; 24. 5,25,3. 6,1.
                          DBY   1,13-14; 18; 21; 36.
3,1; 3. 6,38; 41; 45; 52; 60; 84. 7,6; 9. 8,1-
3. 10,7; 15; 23; 26. 12,1. 14,5; 9-10. 16,3-
4. 17,6; 9-10; 18; 22.
                          DEV   1,4; 11; 14; 20-21.
3,17-18; 33; 35-36; 38-40; 49; 59-60; 65-66;
72; 80-81; 93; 96; 98. 5,1; 8-9. 6,12. 13a,2.
15,11-13; 26-27; 30; 34; 36-38; 42; 44; 50;
53; 55; 62; 67; 72-73. 16,6; 25-26; 30; 37-
38; 40; 48-49; 51; 56-57; 64-65; 77; 79; 87;
92; 94; 99; 110; 115; 123; 125; 135; 138;
141; 144; 149; 158; 161; 167; 170-171; 173.
17,5; 7; 12-13; 17; 23; 33; 40-41; 43-45; 62;
68; 71; 73-74; 81-82; 85; 93; 99-104; 107.
19,6; 20; 23; 25-27; 43; 45. 20,15; 17.
21,11. 23,4; 24. 24,1; 5; 18; 19; 24; 27.
25,3-4; 10; 12-13; 18-20; 24-25. 28,8; 10;
16. 29,1. 32,2. 33,2. 34,21; 23; 32; 42; 46;
49; 51-52. 35,8; 10; 12; 23; 27-28; 30. 36,3-
4; 13; 15; 20-22; 24-25. 37,1. 39,2-3; 11;
14. 40,3-6. 41,1-2. 42,7-8; 15; 19; 21. 47,6;
9-10. 48,9-10; 12. 49,1. 50,3-4. 51,2; 9.
52,21; 31; 39; 46; 51.
                          DOR   1,8-9; 14; 24. 3,1.
7,1. 11,2; 4. 12,11. 17,1. 19,1. 24,2. 26,1;
7; 17; 19; 21; 25; 31; 33; 37; 39-40; 49; 51;
60; 62; 65. 27,2; 5; 7; 10-11. 30,3. 32,2; 5.
33,2; 4. 34,3. 35,1. 37,3; 5; 10; 12. 39,1.

40,2. 41,1; 4. 47,1; 6; 11-12. 49,2; 9; 16-17. 50,1; 4. 54,1-2; 9. 55,7; 9; 15-17; 19-21; *26;* 27-28; 30; 32; *34;* 36-40; 43; 47-48. 56,3-5; 12; 19-21; 27; 31; 33; 35; 40; 44-45; 47; 55; 64. 57,3; 6; 10-11; 14; 20.

ESS   1,3; 6-7; 15; 19-20; 23-25; 27. 2,4. 3,3; 5-7; 10; 13. 4,9; 11; 16. 5,8-10. 6,7-8; 12-13. 7,1. 8,1-2; 8; 10. 9,3; 6; 8; 10-11. 11,5; 8. 16,1. 18,11; 15; 19-20; 33; 35; 41; 43-45. 20,1; 3; 14; 18-21; 23; 32; 37; 39; 43; 45; 54-55; 58; 62-63; 65-66. 21,1-2; 7; 9-11. 22,3-4; 9; 14; 17; 19-20; 23-24. 23,2-5; 7; 10; 25; 28-30; 35-36. 24,1; 4-5; 8-9; 18-19; 27; 30-31; 37-38; 40-42; 44; 48; 50; 56; 61; 67. 25,9; 12-14; 17; 19; 21. 26,1. 27,1; 3; 5; 7; 9-14; 17. 28,3; 6-7; 13; 15-16. 29,2-3. 30,1; 3; 5-6; 11-13; 15; 17; 19; 21; 23; 26-28; 30; 34; 40; 42; 44-45; 47; 50-51. 32,2; 6; 8-11; 13; 20; 25; 28; 30; 34-36; 39. 33,1-2; 5-6; 14; 17; 22. 34,5; 10-11; 13; 15-16; 22; 25-28; 35. 35,6-7; 12. 36,2-3; 9; 12. 37,2; 4-7; 9; 18; 20. 39,2; 4; 6. 40,2; 5; 9. 41,8-9. 42,2. 43,1-2; 4. 44,1; 3. 45,1. 46,1. 47,3. 49,1-3. 52,2. 57,2; 5-6. 61,2. 62,1; 3-4. 63,2. 64,1. 66,1-2. 67,1-2. 68,5-6. 69,1-2. 70,3. 71,1. 75,1-2. 80,1. 82,1. 83,1. 84,1. 85,1. 86,1. 87,1. 90,10; 15-17; 22-23; 26; 37; 44-45; 52; 55; 65; 73; 75; 84-85.

GLS   W18. 1,15; 42. 6,1. 12,3. 19,2. 21,1. 27,1. 31,7. 32,2. 37,2-3. 39,7; 19. 48,3. 53,11. 64,2. 66,5. 68,9. 69,4-6. 73,3. 76,1.

HAM   1,1; 3-4; 12-15; 21-22; 28-30; W8; W10; W18. 2,2; 5; 7; 12-13; 15-16; 18; 20; 24. 3,5; 25. 6,3; 16. 9,1. 11,1. 14,1; 6. 16,2; 4. 17,2. 18,1-2. 21,2; 5; 9. 23,3; 7-8; 14; 16; 22-23; 30; 33-35; 38; 40; 60; 64; 67-68. 28,4. 29,10. 31,1. 35,1; 4-8. 39,1; 5. 40,1. 43,3. 45,1-2; 5; 8-9. 46,1. 52,1. 54,2. 55,2. 56,3. 58,1. 62,1-2. 64,2. 65,1. 66,1. 68,7-8; 10. 69,6; 8; 15; 18-19; 23-24; 26-27; 31-33; 35; 37-38; 40; 43-45; 50; 52. NF3,2. NF9,36; 42; 44. NF10,4. IoW1,1; 4; 12. IoW2,1. IoW6,3; 9; 11-14. IoW7,1; 6-8; 13-14; 21. IoW8,4; 6; 8-11. IoW9,1; 3-4; 6-10; 12-14; 19-23.

HEF   1,11; 22; 24; 40; 42; 45; 56-57; 61; 70. 2,5; 10-12; 16-18; 25; 42; 44-46; 49-50; 57. 6,3; 5. 8,4;9. 9,2; 17-18. 10,15; 19; 25; 32; 40; 45; 48; 55; 59; 61; 64. 14,1; 3; 10. 15,1. 16,1. 19,3-4; 9. 20,2. 21,7. 24,2; 10. 29,8-9. 33,1.

HRT   1,6; 10; 13; 15-17. 2,2-3. 4,1-2; 4; 7; 9; 13; 15-16; 18; 23-25. 5,6; 17; 19; 21; 23; 25. 6,1. 7,4. 9,2-3; 7. 10,2; 10; 20. 11,1. 12,1. 13,4. 15,4; 6-8. 16,8; 12. 17,2-4; 8; 11-12. 18,1. 20,5-7; 10-12. 23,1-2. 26,1. 28,1-2; 6. 31,1. 32,1. 33,1; 5-7; 9-12; 14; 18. 34,7; 11; 13; 16; 19; 21;

23; 25. 36,5; 8; 13; 15; 17-19. 37,5-6; 8-9; 11; 14; 16; 20; 22. 41,1-2. 42,1; 7.

HUN   2,2; 8-9. 5,2. 6,7; 14. 7,7. 9,4. 13,4. 19,3; 6; 11; 13-14; 17-18; 20; 26-28; 30-31. 23,1. 28,1.

KEN   M3-5; 8; 10-12; 14-16; 18; 20. P3-5; 7; 15; 18. 2,10-11; 14; 16-17; 19-20; 26; 30; 33; 39; 41-42. 3,2; 6; 8-9; 12; 14; 16-18; 21. 5,16-17; 20; 22; 39; 41; 43; 49; 64-65; 68; 74; 76; 78; 80; 83; 85; 93-94; 99; 105; 107-108; 110; 112-113; 121; 123; 126; 128; 130; 136; 139-140; 146-149; 152; 155; 158; 162-163; 165; 168; 171-172; 174; 176; 179; 182-183; 191; 193; 200-201; 207-209; 213; 215; 217; 219; 224. 7,4; 14; 18; 21-23. 9,1; 4-5; 27-30; 44; 47. 11,1.

LEC   1,1a,c; 4; 7. 2,4. 3,3. 4,1. 7,1. 8,1; 3. 9,2. 10,2-3; 13. 13,2-3; 9-10; 14; 23-25; 32-37; 42-43; 45; 49-50; 52-53; 55; 59; 62; 68-69; 73. 14,5; 16; 27; 29; 33. 15,6; 9; 13-14. 16,6. 17,3-7; 10-11; 22; 24; 33. 18,4. 19,1; 3-4; 7; 15; 18. 20,2. 21,2. 23,3; 5. 25,5. 27,3. 28,2. 29,2-3; 17-19. 32,1-2. 35,1. 37,3. 40,13; 23; 25; 28; 31; 35; 39. 41,1-2. 42,1-3; 6; 8. 43,1-2; 8; 10. 44,5; 13.

LIN   1,3-4; 14; 16; 27; 34; 42; 50; 53-54; 59; 71-72; 77; 79-81; 89-90; 92; 95-97; 99. 2,1-3; 5-6; 8; 10; 13; 15-17; 19-20; 22; 32; 35; 37. 3,3; 6-8; 13; 16; 21; 27; 32; 34; 39-41; 49-50; 52; 55. 4,1-2; 6-7; 12; 19; 23; 32-33; 37-38; 44-49; 51; 54; 56; 59-61; 67; 69; 77. 6,1. 7,1; 6-7; 16; 18; 21; 26; 29; 33-34; 46; 48; 50; 54; 59. 8,4-7; 13; 16; 19; 22; 29; 34; 37-39. 9,2. 10,4. 11,1-2. 12,5; 8; 13; 17; 19-22; 24-25; 29; 37; 41; 48; 51; 54-55; 57; 62; 66; 68; 78; 80-81; 87; 89; 93; 95. 13,4; 7; 12; 15; 17-18; 26; 29; 36-37; 39; 42. 14,5; 8; 15; 17; 20; 23; 25; 30; 36; 39-40; 43; 45; 65; 79; 86-87; 89; 93-94. 16,2-4; 7; 9-10; 12; 23-24; 32-33; 35-36; 38-40; 43; 46. 18,3-4; 6; 12-15; 20; 24; 30. 20,3. 22,3; 5; 13; 21-22; 26; 28; 30. 23,1. 24,2; 7; 14-15; 27; 32-34; 48; 63; 67; 72; 76; 87; 90; 96-97; 100. 25,3; 6; 11; 13; 18-19; 24-25. 26,1; 3; 7-9; 11; 17; 20-24; 30-32; 34; 36-37; 40; 42; 45; 48-49. 27,1; 5; 14-15; 22-23; 25; 32-33; 39-40; 44; 46; 48; 52-54; 59-60. 28,2-3; 15-16; 19-21; 25; 29; 32-33; 35-36; 43. 29,10; 16; 22. 30,1; 19; 25; 30. 31,2-3; 5; 8; 13; 17. 32,5-9; 17; 20; 24; 27-28; 31. 34,3; 6; 12; 22; 28. 35,3; 7; 9-10; 13-14; 17. 36,1-2; 4. 37,2. 38,3-4; 9; 14. 39,1-2. 40,1-2; 5-6; 8; 16; 23; 25-26. 42,1; 3-4; 9-10; 19. 44,3; 10; 12. 47,1; 8. 48,1; 4-5; 15. 50,1. 51,1; 3-4; 7; 10. 53,2. 54,1. 55,3-4. 56,6; 8. 57,1-2; 5-6; 15; 25-26; 28; 30; 32-33; 39; 41; 44; 48; 53; 55-56. 59,1-2; 5; 7-9; 14; 19-20. 60,1. 61,5-7; 10. 63,1; 3; 7; 10; 19-20. 64,5; 17. 65,1; 5.

67,10-11; 14-18; 22. 68,2-5; 8; 14; 17; 25; 32; 34; 36; 42; 48.

MDX 3,3; 7-8; 15-16; 18-20; 22-24. 4,4; 10. 5,2. 7,2-3. 8,1; 3; 6. 9,3-4. 10,2. 11,4. 14,2. 18,1. 23,1. 25,3.

NFK 1,1-2; 4; 7-10; 13; 17-18; 20-21; 28-29; 43-45; 47-48; 51-52; 54-55; 57; 59-60; 72; 74; 76-78; 80; 84; 86-91; 93; 95; 97; 113-120; 123-124; 127-128; 132-133; 136-137; 141-145; 148; 150; 152-155; 159; 171-172; 174-177; 182-183; 185-186; 188; 194-195; 202; 208-209; 212; 214; 216-218; 227; 230; 237-239; 241. 2,2-8; 10-12. 3,1. 4,5; 9; 11; 13; 15; 17; 19-21; 23; 26-27; 29; 31; 33-35; 38-40; 42-43; 45; 51-53; 55-56. 5,2-3; 5. 6,1; 4-7. 7,1; 3-5; 7; 9-10; 12-16; 18; 20-21. 8,2-4; 7-10; 12-13; 16-19; 21; 25-28; 30; 33-34; 36; 40; 46-47; 50; 53; 55; 59-61; 65; 68-69; 82; 94; 99; 108-109; 119; 121; 130-132; 135-136. 9,3; 7-10; 14-17; 19-20; 23; 26-28; 30-31; 34; 36-37; 39; 42; 46; 48; 53-54; 60; 63-64; 67; 72-75; 77-78; 81; 87-88; 90; 94-95; 98; 100; 102; 105-106; 109-110; 116; 120-122; 125; 127; 130-133; 135-137; 139-140; 142; 145-146; 149-150; 152-155; 157-159; 161; 163-165; 169-173; 175-178; 189; 194-202; 204; 207-208; 213; 217-218; 220-221; 225; 228-229. 10,1; 3; 6-7; 14-17; 20; 24-25; 28; 30-31; 33-34; 36-39; 41-42; 45; 47; 50; 55-58; 62-64; 67; 70-74; 76; 78-80; 83-85; 87-91; 93. 11,1; 4-5. 12,5-13; 15; 17-20; 22-23; 27; 29; 32-33; 35-36; 38-40. 13,3; 5; 9; 13; 16-17; 21-22; 24. 14,7-10; 12-14; 24-25; 28; 30; 33; 35-36; 40-42. 15,2; 5-6; 10-12; 14-15; 17-19; 25; 29. 16,2-3; 6. 17,1; 6-7; 9-12; 14-19; 22-23; 25-27; 31-32; 37-41; 45; 49; 53-57; 59; 61-65. 19,3-5; 7; 9-11; 13; 15-16; 19; 21-25; 29; 32-33; 36-40. 20,1-3; 5-11; 13; 17; 19; 22-26; 28-29; 31-36. 21,2-5; 7-14; 16-19; 23-24; 26-27; 29; 31-32; 34. 22,3; 6; 9; 14; 16-17; 22-23. 23,1; 4-5; 7-8; 10-11; 13-16; 18. 24,4-7. 25,4; 7; 9; 14; 17; 20; 23; 28. 26,2-5. 27,1. 29,4-8. 30,4. 31,1-6; 10; 12; 15-18; 22; 24-25; 28; 34; 37; 39; 43-44. 32,1-3; 5. 33,1-2; 6. 34,2; 8-11; 15; 18. 35,3-4; 6-10; 12; 14; 16-17. 36,3; 5; 7. 37,2-3. 38,1-2. 39,1. 40,1. 41,1. 43,1-2; 4. 44,1. 47,4-5. 48,2-4; 8. 49,4; 9. 50,3-5; 8; 11; 13. 51,2; 7; 10. 52,1-3. 53,1. 55,1-2. 56,4-7. 58,3. 61,1-2. 63,1. 64,2; 5-8. 65,1-6; 8; 10-11; 15. 66,2; 4; 11; 16; 20-21; 23; 25; 27-28; 38; 40; 43; 53; 60; 66-67; 70; 73; 77; 79-82; 85; 89-90; 92-93; 95; 97; 99; 104.

NTH 1,2a; 8; 15a; 29-30. 2,7-8. 4,1-2; 4-5; 7-10; 19; 23; 29; 35. 6,4; 10b-c. 6a,1; 7; 9-10; 13; 16; 19; 21; 24; 27-28. 8,3; 7-11. 9,1-3. 10,2. 12,1. 14,1; 4; 6. 17,1; 5. 18,4; 7; 11; 24-26; 29-31; 38; 46; 49-50; 54-55; 59; 63; 65; 68-72; 77-78; 81;

84-85; 88; 95-96; 98. 21,1. 22,2-3; 7-8. 23,2-3; 6; 9; 11; 15. 25,2. 26,3-5; 7-9. 28,2. 30,2-4; 8; 12-13; 15-17. 31,1. 35,1a; 12; 14; 16; 19a,d-e,g; 20; 23; 25. 39,2; 11. 40,1; 3; 6. 41,2. 43,1. 45,2-3. 46,2. 48,6-7; 12. 51,1. 54,1. 55,2-3; 6. 56,3-5; 10; 14; 19; 20c,f; 23; 25; 29; 34-36; 40; 44; 50-52; 55-56; 58; 60-61; 65. 57,4. 58,1-2. 60,3.

NTT 1,7; 10; 12-13; 15; 23; 52; 55-56; 61-62. 2,2-3. 3,1; 3-4. 4,6-7. 5,1; 4-5; 16; 18. 6,1; 3-4; 6-7; 10; 13. 7,1-2; 4-5. 8,2. 9,1-2; 4; 11; 22; 26; 29-30; 32-33; 37; 39-40; 57; 59-60; 64; 66-67; 70; 73; 76; 79; 85; 87; 89; 95-97; 114-118; 121; 123-124; 126-127; 130-131. 10,9; 17-18; 22; 24-25; 31; 33; 35; 40; 47; 49; 57-58; 61-62. 11,5-6; 8-11; 19; 22. 12,9; 11; 17; 23. 13,1; 4; 7-8; 10; 13. 14,2. 15,4; 8-9. 16,1; 5; 11. 17,1-2; 8; 17-18. 18,3-4; 7. 19,1. 20,3; 6. 21,2. 23,1. 24,2. 29,1. 30,4; 6; 9; 15; 34; 37; 39; 41; 43; 46; 51-52.

OXF 1,10. 6,4; 15. 7,11; 13; 21; 28; 30; 33; 41; 49; 52; 57-58. 9,3; 10. 12,1. 15,1. 17,8. 20,4; 9. 21,1. 22,2. 27,3; 5; 7. 28,9-11; 16; 21; 28. 29,9; 12; 14; 20-21. 33,2. 34,3. 35,33. 45,1. 56,4. 58,4-5; 21; 26-27; 35; 38. 59,13; 15-16; 27.

RUT R9.

SHR 1,4; 6. 3c,2; 8. 3d,1. 3e,1-2. 3f,2; 6. 3g,2; 6; 11. 4,1,8; 19; 36. 4,3,1; 4; 12-13; 23; 26-29; 31-32; 48; 50-51. 4,4,3; 5-6; 14; 20-21; 23-25. 4,5,1; 3-4; 13. 4,6,1-2; 4. 4,8,2; 6; 8; 12; 14. 4,9,2. 4,10,2. 4,11,1; 3; 11. 4,14,3; 8; 10; 16; 18; 28-29. 4,16,2. 4,19,1; 13. 4,20,1-2. 4,21,4-6; 8-9; 12; 14; 17. 4,23,4; 6; 13; 15; 18. 4,24,1-2. 4,25,3. 4,27,1-2; 9; 14; 17; 19; 21; 34. 5,2. 6,1; 6; 10; 12; 21; 23; 26; 33. 7,4. 9,2.

SOM 1,6; 12; 21; 28-29; 34. 2,7-8. 3,1. 4,1. 5,1; 4; 43; 46; 50; 53-54; 60; 64-65; 69. 6,9. 7,15. 8,4-5; 8; 10; 12; 15; 20; 24; 27-28; 30. 9,5; 8. 16,3; 6. 17,3; 6. 19,4-5; 12; 19; 21; 34-35; 43; 55; 59; 74; 81. 20,2. 21,1-2; 4; 11; 13; 17-19; 24-25; 32-37; 39-42; 44; 46-49; 52; 54; 57-59; 61-65; 67-68; 71; 80-81; 84. 22,1; 7; 9-11; 14-15; 20; 27. 24,4-5; 12-13; 18; 24; 29-30. 25,1; 3; 12-13; 15; 17; 20; 22; 26; 36; 40-42; 44; 47; 55-56. 26,5. 28,1. 31,4. 35,4; 6-7; 12; 14. 35,20-21. 36,5-6; 9; 12. 37,12. 38,1. 45,4; 14; 17. 46,1; 5; 10; 14; 23. 47,9; 11; 14; 15; 22; 24.

STS 1,3; 8; 14; 30; 44. 2,5; 11; 18-19. 4,2. 5,2. 7,3-5; 15. 8,4; 6; 17; 26; 30. 10,7-8. 11,11; 13; 33; 39; 41-42; 45; 48; 50. 12,5; 10; 26. 13,5-6. 14,2. 16,2. 17,12; 18-20.

SFK 1,1-2; 5; 7-9; 12; 14-16; 18; 26; 34-35; 38; 44; 46; 48; 50; 53-58; 60; 64; 68; 75-76; 78-80; 90; 92-93; 95;

107; 110; 112; 115; 117; 119; 121. 2,1; 3; 5; 9-10; 13; 16-20. 3,1-3; 13-14; 16; 26-28; 31; 33; 40-41; 43; 49; 51; 56; 65; 70; 72; 74-75; 77-78; 81-83; 86; 88; 93-99; 101. 4,2-3; 15; 18; 20-21; 27; 29; 36-37; 40-41. 5,8. 6,1; 3; 5; 11; 14-15; 20; 23; 32-34; 42-46; 48; 50; 52; 54; 57-58; 61-62; 65; 68; 71; 73-74; 78-79; 83; 86; 88; 90; 92; 94; 97-98; 110; 116; 118-119; 122-123; 127; 132; 137;155; 157; 165-166; 168-169; 172; 174-175; 177-178; 180; 186; 189-191; 193-194; 198; 202; 205; 209; 211-213; 215-220; 223-227; 229-230; 236; 238-239; 245-246; 248; 251-254; 260; 262-263; 267-268; 271-272; 276-277; 280-284; 290; 292-293; 296; 300; 303-305; 308-309; 312; 315; 317-318. 7,1; 6; 10; 13; 15; 17-18; 22; 25-26; 28-30; 36-38; 44-45; 47-48; 51; 54; 56; 58-60; 64; 71; 73; 75-76; 88; 90-92; 99-100; 111-112; 119; 122; 126; 136; 138-139; 141-146. 8,2; 4-6; 8-10; 25; 31-33; 35; 37-40; 42; 46-47; 49-51; 55-57; 61; 69; 71; 80. 9,1-2; 4. 10,1. 11,3. 12,4. 13,6-7. 14,9; 15; 18; 20-22; 26; 32; 36; 38; 42-43; 45; 59-60; 66; 70; 75-76; 90-91; 96; 98; 105; 118-119; 122; 127-132; 134; 138. 15,4. 16,1-4; 7; 9; 11-13; 15-16; 18; 20; 22; 26; 29; 35; 37-38; 41. 18,1; 5. 19,2; 4-6; 9; 11-12; 14-19. 20,1. 21,4; 8-9; 11; 19; 26; 30; 36; 39-40; 44; 50; 58-59; 62; 65-66; 69; 71-72; 74-75; 79-81; 86; 90-91; 94; 98; 100. 23,4; 6. 25,1; 3; 5-6; 8; 10; 15; 17-18; 21-22; 28; 30-34; 36; 40; 51; 57; 59; 63-64; 66-74; 79; 81; 84-85; 87; 90; 95-97; 104; 111. 26,4; 8; 10; 12a-b; 13; 15-17. 27,1-3; 7; 9. 28,3; 6. 29,1; 5; 7; 9; 12-14. 30,1. 31,1-6; 15; 17; 22; 24; 26; 28-30; 33-35; 50-51; 53-54; 56-57; 60. 32,1; 4-5; 8; 15-16; 20; 25. 33,1-4; 12. 34,8; 18. 35,5; 7. 36,1; 5; 7-8; 10-14. 37,4. 38,5-7; 11; 14; 20-22. 39,1; 4-6. 40,3; 5. 41,3; 6; 11; 14. 42,2. 43,1-3; 6. 44,2. 45,3. 46,8. 47,2. 48,1. 51,1-2. 52,1; 4-5. 53,2-3; 5-6. 56,2-3. 57,1. 58,1. 59,1. 60,1. 61,1. 62,1; 4-5. 64,1; 3. 66,1-3; 6-7; 11-13; 16. 67,2; 4-6; 8-10; 12; 15; 18-21; 27-30; 32. 68,1-3; 5. 69,2-4. 73,1. 74,3; 7. 75,1; 4. 76,6; 16; 19. 77,3.

SRY   1,10. 2,6. 4,1. 5,6; 16; 21; 27. 6,4. 8,11; 13; 20; 26. 12,2. 17,4. 18,2. 19,1; 8-9; 13-14; 17; 21; 29; 31; 36-37; 39. 21,3. 22,2. 26,1. 27,3. 34,1. 36,4; 6-7.

SSX   2,9-10. 3,2; 4; 7-9. 5,2. 6,1; 3. 7,2. 8,1; 5. 9,1; 14; 17; 97; 108-109; 120; 130. 10,2-3; 5; 7; 15-17; 19; 27-29; 31; 33; 35; 37; 43; 48; 50; 58; 60; 63-66; 69-70; 74; 87-88; 91-94; 101; 105-106; 108; 110; 116-117. 11,3; 11; 17-18; 21-22; 32-33; 37; 41; 50; 52; 58; 80; 83; 88; 91; 98. 12,6; 13-14; 19; 25; 27-28; 33; 35-36; 50-52; 55. 13,2-3; 6-7; 9; 23; 26; 33; 39; 43-48; 55.

WAR   4,4. 6,7; 20. 12,2; 6-7. 15,1. 16,13-14; 24; 26-27; 30-32; 51; 56; 58; 62; 64. 17,2; 4; 8; 11; 29; 31; 33; 35-39; 42; 44-47; 53; 55; 58; 68. 18,4; 6; 9-10; 15-16. 19,4-5. 22,7; 11. 27,4. 28,1; 8; 10. 29,3. 30,2. 33,1. 35,1. 37,8. 38,1. 39,3. 41,2. 44,2; 5; 7. 45,1.

WIL   1,9. 3,5. 5,1; 4. 7,1; 12; 15. 8,9. 10,1. 11,2. 15,1. 20,3-5. 21,1-2. 24,6; 13; 17; 30; 39; 42. 25,2; 12; 17-18. 26,19. 27,4; 12; 15; 22. 28,3-5. 29,5; 9. 30,1. 32,6; 14; 17. 33,1. 35,1. 36,1. 37,8-10; 12-13; 15-16. 41,2. 42,2. 46,1. 48,6-7; 10-11. 50,2; 4. 53,1. 55,2. 56,2-3. 62,1. 66,2. 67,9; 13; 15; 18; 22-27; 31; 36; 45; 50-52; 56-57; 65; 67-70; 75; 78; 82-84; 86-87; 89; 91; 96. 68,9; 14; 18; 26; 31.

WOR   1,1c-d; 2; 6. 2,18; 20; 63; 70; 75; 83. 8,8; 10d; 11; 14; 19; 24. 14,1. 15,9. 16,1; 3. 19,10; 14. 21,3. 23,1; 4; 6; 12. 26,6.

YKS   C23; 25; 32. 1Y1; 3; 11. 1N10; 12-15; 25; 31; 33-34; 39; 42; 51; 55; 57; 63; 65-66; 73; 79; 84; 89; 95; 104; 106; 128; 132; 134; 137. 1E1; 20; 34; 55. 1W1; 6; 12; 15; 20-22; 24; 32; 34; 38; 43; 45-46; 48. 2,1-2. 2B1; 6; 14. 2N2; 26. 2W2; 6. 2E12; 20; 23; 34. 3Y1; 9. 5N14; 16; 47; 58; 66; 74. 5E3; 9-10; 34-35; 38; 65. 5W7; 10; 13; 16; 19; 21; 23; 38. 6N1; 32; 49; 52; 56; 59; 116; 119; 147. 6W3. 8N9; 12; 15; 17; 19; 21. 9W7; 21-23; 30; 37; 45-46; 50; 52-53; 56; 58; 60; 72-73; 82; 87; 95; 113. 10W3; 7; 15; 26; 29; 37-38; 41. 11E2. 11N9. 11W2. 12W5; 7. 13W8-9; 36. 13E4; 7; 10-12. 13N1-2; 7; 11; 14. 14E2; 7-8; 13; 18; 36; 40. 15E3; 6; 16. 16E3. 18W1-2. 19W2. 20E2. 21E5; 7-12. 21W3; 6. 22W1. 23N7; 14; 16; 24; 28; 30-32; 35. 23E1; 7; 11-13; 16; 18. 24W11; 14. 24E1. 25W11. 28W8; 23-25; 27; 34. 29W2; 4; 9; 11-13; 15-16; 21; 23-24; 27-28; 33. 29E3; 5; 10; 15; 18-19; 21-25. 29N2; 13. SN,CtA45.

Added to manor/village by reeve   GLS   1,54; 61.

Anonymous holder of   BDF   24,18.

Burgesses with   BKM   17,17.

   DBY   B1.

   NTT   B5.

Could be had on land/manor/village   NFK   1,35-37; 39; 136-137; 192; 210-211. 7,3. 8,40. 12,42. 15,18. 19,32. 20,8. 21,18. 22,23. 23,3. 24,4. 31,33. 32,1. 34,5. 41,1. 50,7-8; 12.

   SFK   6,129.

Could be restored   ESS   7,1. 8,4. 20,15. 23,2; 6. 24,13; 53. 26,1. 30,34-35; 39. 32,7. 41,3.

   NFK   1,2; 19; 57; 69; 77-78; 86-87; 143; 145; 188; 212; 215; 236. 4,9. 8,99; 105. 9,12; 48; 71; 74-75; 77-78; 83-

84; 99; 106. 10,5; 9; 11; 57. 13,17. 15,11-
12; 1; 4. 16,5. 17,64. 19,13; 15. 20,8-9; 24;
26. 21,10; 19. 25,7. 29,2; 5. 31,15; 39. 46,1.
47,4. 58,2.

	SFK	1,101-102. 3,34.

4,19; 24. 6,191; 260; 308. 18,4. 20,1. 21,38.
27,9. 46,5.

Diminished through cattle plague	ESS	1,2-3.
Idle (ociosa)	HEF	2,46.
Land cultivated by land holder's own ploughs	HRT	36,6.
ploughed with lordship land	LIN	67,21.
worked with plough from another manor/ village	HRT	31,3.
	LIN	CK2.
Lord's	DBY	5,1.
	WIL	13,3.
More than ploughable land	HEF	2,5.
None on the land/"not there"	BDF	15,4. 32,7. 38,2.

47,3. 50,1. 53,27.
55,8. 56,6. 57,7.

	BKM	4,5; 9; 43. 14,47.

28,1. 53,4; 6.

	CAM	3,5. 14,3. 31,4.

32,11; 17. 33,1. 37,1. *38,1.* 41,10-11.

	ESS	1,7; 14; 20; 28.

4,14; 17. 6,4. 8,8. 14,1. 18,6; 16; 19; 31;
44. 20,52. 22,3. 23,28; 33. 24,4; 9; 58.
25,2. 26,3-4. 28,5; 14. 30,12-13; 15; 26; 44;
46; 49-50. 32,6; 28; 45. 33,13; 17. 34,2.
35,11. 37,20. 39,9-10. 40,9. 41,4; 10. 46,3.
62,1. 68,6; 8. 70,1-3. 71,3. 90,5; 16; 27-
28; 37; 75. B1.

	HRT	4,25. 5,3; 10-11;

25. 10,17. 15,13. 18,1. 20,3-4; 6. 24,2.
28,1-2. 33,4; 6. 36,5. 37,2; 9; 12. 42,3; 13.

	KEN	9,17.
	MDX	3,9. 25,3.
	NFK	1,80; 113; 147.

4,29. 7,5; 13. 9,48; 106. 10,52; 80. 12,10.
15,12. 16,6. 19,31. 20,7. 23,18. 25,14.
29,7. 31,5; 14; 35; 39. 32,3. 34,5. 35,1.
47,5. 66,6.

	OXF	35,33.
	SFK	1,58; 60. 3,55. 4,2;

31. 6,57; 87; 96; 109; 113-114; 117; 120-
121; 171; 216; 226-227; 246. 7,55-56; 60;
67. 8,2-4; 6-7; 10; 14; 40; 46; 50; 77. 11,4.
16,14. 21,12; 62; 94; *100.* 23,6. 26,2; 4.
29,1. 31,17; 32-33; 42; 50. 32,1; 28-30.
33,11. 34,5; 17. 35,3; 6. 38,6; 12; 14; 16;
18. 39,4-5. 40,4-5. 62,7. 67,1; 5-6; 10; 12;
15; 20. 69,4. 76,2; 16.

	SSX	10,20. 13,27.

		WOR	8,25.
None in lordship		BDF	2,9.
		CAM	5,12.
		ESS	4,4. 5,1. 18,30.

20,24; 44; 67. 23,32. 32,40. 41,3. 90,26.

	HRT	15,11.
	KEN	5,112; 121; 145.
	LEC	28,4.
	NFK	1,78. 9,98. 14,21.

21,29. 26,3. 30,4.

	SFK	1,1; 60. 6,32; 85;

88; 129. 8,14; 57. 16,25. 32,19. 40,4. 68,1.

	WAR	27,1.
None recorded	CAM	5,12. 25,10.
	DOR	12,13.
None there except lordship ploughs	HRT	34,17.
Number possible/ which can plough land/for ploughing	YKS	C22-26; 28-35. 1Y1-11; 14-18. 2B1-19. 2N2-6;

14; 19-25. 2W1-12. 2E1-2; 4-9; 11-12; 14-
17. 3Y1-5; 8-15. 4N1-3. 4E1-2. 5N1; 2-30;
32; 45-46; 49-50; 52-54; 58-62; 65-67; 73;
75. 5E1; 3-5; 7-8; 10-11; 13-15; 18-21; 23;
27; 29-32; 34-36; 38-40; 42-44; 55-56; 65-
66; 68; 71-72. 5W1-26; 32-36; 38. 6N1-13;
15-111; 113-141; 143-152; 161-162. 6W1-
6. 6E1. 7E1-2. 9W1-5; 9-19; 24-31; 33-38;
40-87; 89-103; 105-143. 10W1-43. 11E1-5.
11N1; 3-7; 14-17; 24. 11W1. 13W1-38.
13E1-16. 13N1-5; 7-19. 14E1-28;30-45;
47-50.

Reduced through Ralph Wader	NFK	1,215.

See also: Animal; Borough; Burgess; Cattle;
Freeman; Frenchman; Hall; Jurisdiction; Lordship;
Man; Meadow; Ox; Ploughland; Smallholder;
Tax; Villager.

PLOUGH – comparative information

Less ploughs 1086 than TRE	ESS	1,1-4; 7; 9; 11; 13-15; 19-20; 23-28;

30. 2,2; 6. 3,2; 8-13; 15. 4,4; 9; 14; 17. 5,1;
8; 10-11. 6,2; 4-5; 7-8; 11-12; 15. 7,1. 8,3-
4; 7-9. 9,7-11; 14. 10,2; 5. 11,1; 6; 8. 12,1.
14,1; 4-5. 16,1. 18,2-3; 6-7; 10; 16; 19; 28;
30-31; 33; 35-36; 41; 43-45. 20,3; 6-9; 13;
19; 23-25; 27; 32; 36-39; 43-44; 52; 55-57;
62-69; 74-75; 77-78. 22,3-6; 8; 13-14; 17-
18; 21. 23,1-2; 6; 28; 32-33; 38-41. 24,4;
9-10; 13; 18; 20; 24; 31; 33; 38; 45; 49; 58.
25,2-3; 6; 11-12; 17; 19; 21; 23; 25-26. 26,1;
3-5. 27,2-4; 6; 11; 13-14; 16-17. 28,5-6; 9;
11; 13-17. 30,1; 5-6; 10-13; 15; 17-20; 24;
26-28; 34-35; 38; 40; 44-47; 49-51. 32,3; 6-
7; 9; 13-14; 16; 19-20; 24-25; 27-28; 35;
38-42; 45. 33,1; 3-4; 6-7; 13-14; 16-17; 22.
34,2; 4; 11-13; 22; 26-27; 29; 32-34. 37.
35,1-2; 9; 11. 36,2-3; 11-12. 37,2; 9; 15-18;
20. 38,4. 39,1-2; 4-5; 7-10. 40,1-3; 6-7; 9.
41,3-4; 9-10; 12. 42,2-3; 7-8. 43,4. 44,1-3.
45,1. 46,1-3. 47,2-3. 49,3. 51,2. 52,1-3.

53,1. 54,1-2. 57,2-3. 61,1-2. 62,1; 3. 63,1-
2. 64,1. 65,1. 67,1-2. 68,5-6; 8. 69,2-3.
70,1-3. 71,2-3. 74,1. 77,1. 80,1. 85,1. 87,1.
90,4-5; 7; 15-17; 23; 25-28; 36-37; 40; 65;
75. B1; 3b.

LEC   9,1. 11,3. 12,1-2.
14,3; 5; 16; 19; 23; 26; 31-32. 15,2; 4-8.
16,1-3; 6; 8. 17,5; 11-13; 19-21; 23-24; 26;
28-30; 33. 18,3; 5. 19,13-14. 27,2-3. 28,2;
4-5. 29,2-3; 5-6; 11; 19. 30,1. 32,1-2. 33,1.
34,1. 35,1. 36,1-2. 37,1-3. 38,1. 40,2-4; 6-
7; 10; 13; 18; 21; 23; 26-29; 31; 40-41. 42,1.
43,6. 44,3; 5; 7-9.

NFK   1,1-5; 17; 21; 32-33;
40; 45; 51; 53; 57; 59; 69; 71-74; 77-78; 80;
86-92; 94; 96; 105-106; 113-114; 120; 123;
127-128; 131-133; 135; 137; 139; 142-143;
145; 147; 150; 155; 171; 175; 177; 179; 182-
183; 185; 188-195; 197-198; 203; 205; 208-
212; 214-216; 218-219; 222; 226; 231; 233-
234; 236-239. 2,2-5. 4,2; 9; 21; 28-32; 34-
35; 38-39; 42-43; 47; 52; 56. 5,1; 3; 6. 6,3-
6. 7,3; 5; 10; 13; 16-18. 8,6; 10; 21-22; 25;
38; 40; 46; 61-63; 65; 78; 80; 82; 84; 91;
95; 99; 105; 107-109; 132. 9,11-12; 26; 28;
46; 60; 70-71; 74; 78; 83-84; 87; 94; 98-
100; 102; 116; 129; 131; 135-136; 139; 172;
196-199; 205; 209; 211-215; 217-218; 225.
10,6; 9-11; 14; 19; 21; 24-25; 28; 33; 35; 49;
60; 74; 79-80. 11,5. 12,10; 27; 30; 34; 42.
13,3; 6; 13; 16-17; 21-22; 24. 14,1; 14; 16;
21; 25; 31; 40. 15,1-2; 6-9; 11-12; 14; 24;
25; 26. 16,6. 17,7; 14; 16; 18-19; 22-23; 54;
56; 64-65. 19,1; 4-5; 9-11; 13; 18-19; 24; 31-
32; 39-40. 20,1-2; 7-9; 14; 18; 23-25; 29-
31; 36. 21,2-5; 7; 10-11; 14; 18-19; 21; 23-
24; 26-27; 29-30; 32. 22,3; 6; 14; 16; 23.
23,1-5; 9; 11; 17-18. 24,1-2; 4; 6. 25,4; 7;
9-10; 14-16; 20; 22-23. 26,1-5. 27,1. 28,1.
29,3; 6-10. 30,1; 4. 31,1-2; 5-6; 8; 11-12;
14-15; 22; 25; 28-29; 33; 35; 38-39; 44.
32,1-4. 33,2; 6. 34,1; 4-5; 8; 10; 15; 18.
35,1; 4; 6-7; 9; 15; 18. 36,5. 37,1. 38,2-3.
39,1. 40,1. 41,1. 42,1. 43,1-2. 46,1. 47,3;
5. 48,2. 49,1; 6-7. 50,1; 4-5; 8. 51,5; 7-8.
52,1; 4. 58,1-2. 66,6; 9; 14; 16; 21; 26-29;
40; 87; 89-90; 97; 99; 104.

NTH   6,7-8. 6a,4; 6. 41,1.
SHR   2,2.
STS   10,2. 14,1.
SFK   1,1-2; 12; 15-16; 18;
23; 26; 29-30; 32-36; 42; 44-47; 50-51; 54;
58-60; 76; 96; 100-102; 107; 110; 115; 117-
119; 121; 122b. 2,3-6; 10; 16-17; 19. 3,1-2;
4; 24; 31; 34; 36-37; 39-41; 46; 55-57; 65;
69-70; 77; 93; 95; 98; 101. 4,1-2; 4; 6; 13-
14; 19-21; 23-24; 27; 31; 35; 37-38; 42. 5,1;
3-4. 6,1; 5; 11; 14; 26-27; 30; 32; 42-47; 49;
57; 73; 78; 82-83; 85; 87-88; 94; 96; 98;
109-110; 112-114; 116-117; 120-121; 129-
130; 133-134; 137-139; 143; 148-149; 155-

157; 159; 163; 166; 169; 171-172; 174; 176-
177; 179; 183-184; 186; 188-191; 193-194;
198; 202; 211; 213-218; 220; 224-227; 238-
239; 246-247; 251; 254; 260; 262; 267-268;
272; 274; 276-277; 282; 292; 303-306; 308;
312-315; 318. 7,6-7; 13; 15; 18; 29; 41; 55-
56; 58; 60; 64; 67; 71; 73; 75; 85; 126; 145.
8,2; 4-7; 9-11; 14; 20; 22; 25; 27; 29; 31-
32; 35-40; 44; 46-47; 49-51; 55-57; 66; 70;
77; 80. 9,1-2. 11,1-4. 12,2; 5; 7. 14,20-21;
23-24; 26; 36; 44; 48; 65; 70; 74-77; 79; 81;
92; 110; 115; 118. 15,2; 5. 16,3-4; 6; 9-10;
12; 14-16; 20-22; 25-27; 29; 35; 38; 40; 43;
45. 18,1; 4. 19,1-2; 13-16; 18; 21. 21,1; 3;
5-6; 12; 16-17; 26; 28; 38; 42-45; 54; 58; 62;
64; 66; 72; 75; 79-80; 83-84; 86; 90-91; 94-
95; 99; *100*. 22,3. 23,2-4; 6. 25,1-2; 4; 6-7;
20; 31-32; 34; 43; 46; 53; 59; 63; 71-72; 76;
84-86; 106. 26,2-4; 6; 12a; 15-16. 27,3-6;
9-10. 28,1a-b; 3; 7. 29,1; 11-13. 30,1. 31,8-
12; 15; 17-18; 21; 24; 26; 32-35; 40-44; 46-
47; 49-50; 53; 56; 60. 32,1; 3-5; 11; 19; 21;
27-30. 33,1; 3-8; 11-13. 34,2-3; 6; 8; 12-13;
15; 17. 35,1; 3; 5-6. 36,1-2; 4; 6; 8-10.
37,6. 38,5-7; 11-12; 14; 16-18. 39,4-8; 10;
12; 17. 40,2-6. 41,7; 10-11; 14-15; 18. 42,2.
43,2. 44,2. 46,1-5; 7-9. 47,2. 50,1. 51,1.
52,1; 3; 5. 53,2-3; 5. 54,1-3. 56,1-2. 57,1.
58,1. 59,1. 60,1. 62,1; 4-5; 7. 66,1-3; 6; 10-
11; 13. 67,1-6; 10-12; 15; 17-21; 28-31; 33.
68,1; 5. 69,1-2; 4. 70,1. 76,2; 4; 7; 16; 21.
77,3.

More ploughs 1086   ESS   1,28-29. 3,5. 5,2; 5.
than TRE   6,13. 7,1. 8,2. 9,1-
2. 10,4-5. 15,1-2. 17,1. 18,14; 36. 20,15;
21-22; 40; 54. 22,3; 15; 19; 23. 24,17; 21-
22; 26-28; 41; 46; 48; 53; 57; 61. 25,5. 27,1.
29,2. 30,4; 16; 45. 31,1. 32,8-9; 18; 24; 30.
34,5; 8; 10; 23. 35,3; 8. 36,5. 37,4. 44,1.
48,1-2. 55,1. 57,5. 66,2. 83,1. 90,10; 22;
52-53; 55; 58.

LEC   14,1-2; 6; 9-10; 13-
14; 20; 31; 33. 15,3. 16,7. 17,4; 22; 32.
18,4. 19,15. 29,10; 13-14; 18. 40,8; 16; 19;
24; 33. 42,3. 44,4.

NFK   1,1; 11; 52; 62; 100;
139; 144; 151-152; 156; 199; 212; 230. 4,1;
7; 9; 38; 56. 5,1. 6,4. 8,7; 16; 36; 53; 57;
59-61; 63; 98; 119-121. 9,24; 32; 48; 50; 63;
75-76; 78; 88; 94; 146; 150; 154; 162; 169;
171; 174; 180; 196; 228. 10,1; 4; 15; 55; 57;
73. 11,2. 12,33. 13,19. 14,2; 9; 11-13; 19;
41. 15,17; 25. 17,1; 63. 19,7; 21; 36. 20,1;
7; 11. 21,3; 24; 37. 22,11. 23,16. 29,5.
30,5. 31,10; 44. 34,7; 15. 35,7. 36,5. 37,1.
48,4. 49,4. 50,6; 11. 52,2-3. 55,1. 57,1.
58,3. 61,1-2. 66,101.

STS   7,1.
SFK   1,14; 120. 3,9; 61;
74-75; 81; 88; 96. 4,3; 18; 30. 6,3; 157; 177;
187; 191-192; 307. 7,36; 45; 47; 76. 9,1.

14,1; 35; 49-50; 52; 69; 72; 105-106; 120.
16,26. 17,1. 19,17; 19. 21,11; 40. 25,5; 36;
52; 79-80; 97; 111. 26,9-10; 14; 16. 32,19.
33,9-10. 37,5. 38,11. 39,16. 43,1-3. 48,1.
52,1. 66,2.
Same ploughs 1086 as ESS   1,6; 10; 12-13;
TRE   19-20. 2,1; 3-4;
8-9. 3,1; 3; 6; 16. 4,1; 3; 5-8; 10-12; 15-16;
18. 5,3-4; 7-8. 6,6; 14. 8,1; 5-6; 10-11. 9,3;
5; 12-13. 10,1; 3; 5. 11,2-3; 5. 13,1-2. 14,2-
3. 18,1; 4-5; 8-9; 15; 20-21a; 23; 26; 29;
37. 19,1. 20,1-2; 4-5; 10; 12; 14; 16; 18-20;
26; 28-31; 33-34; 37; 39; 43; 53; 61; 76; 80.
21,1-4; 6-7; 10. 22,7; 9-12; 16; 20; 22; 24.
23,3-5; 7-18; 20-26; 29-31; 34; 36. 24,1-3;
5-9; 11; 14-17; 19; 23; 25; 29-30; 35; 37; 39;
42-44; 50; 54; 60; 64; 67. 25,1; 4; 9; 13; 16-
18. 27,5; 7; 9; 15. 28,1-4; 7-8; 13; 17. 29,1;
3-5. 30,1-3; 9; 14; 21-23; 25; 27; 29-33; 36-
37; 39; 42; 48. 32,1-2; 4-5; 10-12; 15-17;
21-23; 25-26; 34; 36; 45. 33,1; 3; 5-6; 8;
10-12; 19-21; 23. 34,3-4; 6-7; 9; 14-19; 21-
22; 27; 36. 35,2; 4-7; 12-13. 36,1; 4; 6-10;
12. 37,1; 3; 5-7; 11-13; 19. 38,1-3; 5-8.
39,3-4. 40,4. 41,1-2; 6; 8; 12. 42,1; 9. 43,1-
3; 5-6. 44,3. 46,1. 47,1; 3. 49,1. 50,1. 51,1.
57,1; 4-6. 60,1-2. 62,4. 66,1. 68,1-4; 7.
69,1-2. 71,1; 4. 72,1-2. 73,1. 75,1-2. 81,1.
82,1. 84,1-2. 89,3. 90,8; 20; 29-30; 33; 35;
39; 44-47; 49-51; 54; 56-57; 68-70; 79; 83-
85. B1; 7.
              LEC   14,11-12. 15,1.
16,4. 17,18. 18,1-2. 28,1; 3. 29,1; 4; 8; 15.
40,1; 15; 17; 22; 32; 34-36. 44,6; 10-13.
              NFK   1,2; 4; 7; 11; 15-16;
19; 28-30; 32; 40-42; 46-48; 50; 52; 55; 71;
77; 80-81; 85; 87; 90; 93-95; 97-99; 101; 104;
108; 110-112; 115-119; 124; 128-133; 136;
138-141; 143; 145-146; 149; 151-155; 157-
162; 169-170; 172-174; 177-178; 183; 185-
187; 191-196; 198-200; 202-206; 212; 215-
218; 220-221; 223-225; 227-230; 237-240.
2,1-2; 4-8; 10; 12. 4,8-10; 14-17; 19-20; 26-
27; 29; 33-34; 37-39; 44-46; 49-50; 52-53.
5,2-5. 6,1-2; 6. 7,1; 4; 6-15; 17; 19. 8,1-4;
8; 11-12; 16; 18-19; 23-28; 30; 33-34; 39-
44; 46-47; 50-52; 54-56; 58; 60; 62; 66-70;
74; 78; 81; 83; 85-90; 92; 94; 96-103; 108-
110; 112; 116; 119-124; 126; 130; 133-135.
9,1-2; 6; 8; 10-11; 13-21; 23-25; 27; 29-40;
42; 45; 47; 52-54; 56-57; 60; 64; 67; 72-73;
77; 81-82; 85-91; 95; 98-100; 102-103; 116-
117; 119; 123; 126; 130; 132; 137-138; 140;
142; 145-147; 149; 151-153; 157-161; 164-
170; 173; 177; 179; 182-183; 188-191; 194;
196; 198; 201-202; 206; 208; 216; 219; 221;
228-229; 233-234. 10,2-3; 5-6; 8; 15-17;
19-20; 22-23; 25; 28; 30; 32; 36-40; 43-45;
50; 55; 58; 62; 64-65; 67-69; 71; 73-74; 76;
78; 81-88; 90-93. 10a,1. 11,1-4. 12,1; 6-9;
11-14; 17-20; 22-25; 27-28; 30-32; 35-40;

42; 44. 13,3; 7; 9-10; 12-16; 24. 14,1; 4; 6;
8; 16-18; 23-24; 26; 28-30; 33; 35; 37-38;
40; 42. 15,2; 4; *9;* 11; 17; *18;* 19; 21-22;
*27;*28. 17,1; 5-6; 8-11; 15-17; 19; 21; 23;
25; 27; 31; 33; 35-38; 45; 49; 51-53; 56-57;
62; 64. 18,1. 19,6; 9-11; 15; 17; 22-23; 25;
27; 29-30; 32; 34; 36. 20,4-8; 10; 15; 17; 19;
22-23; 26-27; 32-36. 21,4; 9-10; 12-14; 16-
17; 22; 24-25; 27-29; 31-32; 34. 22,2; 5; 10;
12-13; 16; 23. 23,5-8; 10; 12-14; 16-18.
24,3; 5; 7. 25,1-3; 6-8; 11-13; 25-28. 26,1-
2; 6. 29,2-4; 7. 30,2; 4. 31,1; 5; 7; 10; 12-
13; 16-18; 20; 22-24; 31; 34; 37; 41-45. 32,3.
33,1-2; 5-6. 34,1-2; 9; 11-13; 17; 20. 35,3;
5; 8; 10; 16. 36,3-4; 6. 38,1; 4. 39,1-2. 41,1.
43,3-4. 46,1. 47,1; 4. 48,2-3. 49,2-3. 50,2-
3; 6-7; 9; 12. 51,1; 3-4; 6; 8; 10. 52,1; 3-4.
53,1. 55,2. 56,1-7; 9. 57,3. 58,1-2. 59,1.
60,1. 61,1-2; 4. 64,1-9. 65,9-11. 66,1-2; 10-
13; 20; 24; 30; 32; 49; 70; 77-78; 80-81; 87;
91-93; 95; 100.
              SFK   1,1; 3-4; 9; 12-13;
16; 18; 24-25; 44; 46; 48-49; 51-53; 55; 61-
62; 64; 66-67; 69-70; 73; 75; 77-78; 88-90;
93; 95; 98; 108; 110-112; 114-115; 120;
122b. 2,1-2; 7; 9; 11; 13; 18; 20. 3,3; 10-
11; 16; 19; 21-22; 26-27; 33-35; 38-39; 47;
52; 57-59; 61; 63; 68; 72; 82-83; 86; 93-94;
97; 99-100; 103. 4,12; 18-19; 28; 35-36; 39;
42. 5,2; 4-7. 6,2-3; 15; 19-20; 28-29; 32-
34; 48-49; 57-58; 60-61; 64-65; 75; 77-78;
80; 82-84; 90; 92-94; 97; 100; 106; 110; 125;
128; 130; 143; 161-162; 165; 170; 175; 180;
184; 201; 209-210; 217-218; 222-223; 228-
229; 236; 239; 245; 247; 261; 264; 271; 273;
280; 283-284; 291; 296; 299; 301; 316-317.
7,3; 5; 7; 10; 17; 20; 23; 25-26; 28; 30; 32-
33; 37; 39-40; 42-43; 45; 49; 54; 58; 64; 75;
77; 79-80; 82; 98; 102; 109-111; 117-119;
122; 133; 136; 142-144; 148. 8,1; 6; 8; 12-
13; 17; 45; 48-49; 53; 59; 66; 81. 9,2-3.
11,4. 12,1; 4; 6. 13,3-4; 7. 14,1-19; 21-23;
25; 27-28; 32; 36-37; 41-46; 48-55; 57-62;
65-78; 80; 82-91; 93-104; 106; 108-109;
111-114; 117-121; 125-126; 129-132; 134;
138-139; 146; 155; 166. 15,1-2; 4. 16,2; 7-
8; 11; 13; 15-16; 18-19; 22; 26; 30; 32-33;
35; 37; 41. 19,4-5; 9; 14-17. 20,1. 21,7-11;
15; 26; 29; 36; 39; 46-47; 53; 55; 71; 81; 90.
22,1. 23,1. 25,1-2; 9; 11-12; 14; 16; 27-30;
33; 37; 39-42; 44-45; 48; 51; 57-61; 67-70;
73-74; 78; 92; 96; 100; 103-105. 26,1; 4-5;
7; 10-12c. 27,7; 12-13. 28,2; 4. 29,1-5; 9.
30,3. 31,20; 25; 27; 29; 32; 40; 48; 51; 54.
32,6; 9; 14; 16; 20; 22. 33,1; 6; 10; 12-13.
34,1; 3; 5; 7; 12. 35,1-3; 5; 7. 36,5-6; 15.
37,1; 3; 5-6. 38,4; 8; 11; 21-22. 40,3. 41,3-
4; 14; 17. 42,1. 43,1; 4-5. 44,3-4. 45,2.
46,1. 49,1. 51,1. 52,1; 9. 53,1; 3; 6. 55,1.
56,3. 57,1. 61,1. 66,1-4; 7-9; 12. 67,12; 14;

19; 27. 68,4. 69,3. 71,1-2. 74,1-2; 13. 75,5.
76,1; 5-6. 77,4.

Less ploughs than　　BDF　1,1c; 4. 2,1-3; 6; 9.
plough land　　　　　　4,7. 5,1-2. 7,1. 8,2-
3. 11,1. 12,1. 14,1. 15,1-2; 5. 16,1-2. 19,1.
20,1. 21,1; 6; 15. 22,1. 23,11; 17; 21-22.
24,1; 5; 10; 13; 15-19; 28. 25,5; 13-14. 26,2-
3. 28,1. 29,1. 30,1. 31,1. 32,1-2; 6; 11; 13;
16. 33,1-2. 40,3. 41,1-2. 48,1-2. 49,2. 51,1.
52,1. 53,5; 7; 11; 13; 17; 20-21; 30. 54,2-
3. 55,1; 11. 57,3v.

　　　　　　　BRK　1,10-11; 15; 21; 24;
27-30; 35-36; 38-39; 44. 2,1. 7,1; 6; 8-9;
14-16; 22-23; 27-35; 37-38; 42-45. 8,1. 9,1.
10,1. 15,2. 16,2. 17,1; 6; 8. 18,1-2. 19,1.
20,2-3; 5; 9; 11; 13; 15-16; 18; 20. 22,2-3;
6; 11-12. 26,1; 3. 28,1-3. 29,1. 33,5-6; 8,
34,1-4. 35,1; 3; 5. 36,2; 4; 6. 38,2-4. 39,1.
41,1; 4-6. 44,3-5. 46,3; 6. 47,1. 48,1. 50,1.
51,1. 52,1. 55,1-2. 59,1. 63,2-3; 5. 65,3-4;
7; 12; 17; 19.

　　　　　　　BKM　B1. 1,1-2; 4; 6-7.
2,1. 3,1-2. 3a,5. 4,1; 4-5; 14; 27; 30-31; 33-
34; 36-40; 42. 5,2-5; 17; 20. 6,1. 7,1. 8,2-
3. 12,1; 6-7; 17; 24; 30-31; 36-37. 13,2-3.
14,2; 16; 20; 25-29; 33; 39-40. 16,5; 7-9.
17,3; 6-7; 10; 12; 18. 18,2. 20,1. 21,1; 7-8.
23,18; 20; 26; 29; 31-32. 25,1. 26,3; 11.
27,2. 28,2-3. 29,1. 31,1. 35,1-2. 36,2. 37,1.
38,1. 39,1. 40,1. 41,3-4; 6-7. 43,6; 8-11.
46,1. 47,1. 48,1. 49,1. 51,1-2. 56,2-3. 57,2-
3; 7; 10.

　　　　　　　CAM　1,2; 4-7; 9; 11-12;
17. 2,2; 4. 3,1; 3-6. 5,1; 3-4; 6; 12; 29; 31;
34; 38; 41-42; 57; 60-63. 7,4-5; 8; 10. 9,2-
3. 12,4. 13,9; 11. 14,1; 27; 44; 49; 55; 73-
74. 15,1-2. 18,2-3. 20,1. 21,5. 26,21; 23;
27; 31; 49. 28,2. 29,10. 30,2. 31,2; 7. 32,4-
5; 7-8; 10; 22-25; 27; 31; 33-35; 37-38; 40.
35,1. 38,1. 39,2. 41,1; 3; 9; 12-13. 43,1.
44,2.

　　　　　　　CHS　B4-5; 8-9. A2-4;
6-7; 9-10; 12; 16-17. 1,1; 3-4; 7-8; 14-15;
21-23; 25-26; 34-35. 2,2-7; 14-15; 17-21;
23-24; 26-29; 31. 3,1-11. 4,2. 5,1-3; 5-8;
10; 12-14. 7,1; 3-4. 8,1; 3-4; 6-8; 11-12;
16; 19; 21-28; 31-32; 34; 36; 38-39; 42-44.
9,4-5; 9; 17; 20; 25-26. 10,4. 11,3. 12,4.
13,1-5. 14,1; 3-7; 9-12. 17,1-4; 7-8. 18,1-
3; 5-6. 19,1. 20,1; 11-12. 22,1. 23,2-3.
24,1-3; 5-6; 9. 25,2-3. 26,1; 6-7; 9; 11. 27,3.
FD1,1. FD7,2. FT3,3.

　　　　　　　CON　1,1-3; 5-12; 14-18.
2,1-11. 3,1; 3-6. 4,1-7; 10-20; 23-25; 27.
5,1,1-13; 22. 5,2,1-2; 5-6; 10-14; 16-19; 21;
23-25; 28. 5,3,1; 3-8; 10-24; 26-28. 5,4,1;
2; 3; 5-10; 11; 12-18; 20. 5,5,1-7; 8; 9-20.
5,6,1-5; 7-10. 5,7,1; 3-12. 5,8,1-2; 4; 6-7;
9-10. 5,9,1-4. 5,10,1. 5,11,1-2; 4; 6.
5,12,1-3. 5,13,1-5; 8-9; 10; 11-12. 5,14,1-
4. 5,15,1-6. 5,16,1. 5,17,1-4. 5,20,1.

5,22,1. 5,23,1-2; 5. 5,24,1-5; 8; 12; 15; 17,
20-23; 25. 5,25,2-3; 5. 5,26,2-4. 6,1.
　　　　　　　DBY　1,1; 12-14; 22; 25;
28-29; 36-37. 3,1-2. 4,1. 5,1; 5. 6,12; 96.
7,5; 9. 9,3-4; 6. 10,5; 21-22. 11,3. 15,1.
16,6. 17,11. B3.
　　　　　　　DEV　1,4-11; 13-18; 20-
21; 25-31; 33-36; 38-42; 45-46; 48-56; 60-
63; 65; 67-68; 70-71. 2,5; 7; 9; 11-12; 14-
15; 17-19; 21; 23-24. 3,4-5; 8-11; 13-14; 16-
21; 23; 25; 28; 30-31; 33; 35-40; 42-50; 52-
61; 63-67; 69-70; 72-77; 79-81; 83-84; 86-
90; 92; 96; 98. 5,1; 4-8; 11; 13. 6,1; 3-4; 7-
12. 7,2-4. 10,1. 11,2. 12,1. 13,1. 13a,2.
14,1-2. 15,2; 5; 8-14; 17; 20-23; 26-30; 34;
36-39; 41-47; 49-52; 54-59; 62-65; 67-68;
70-77; 79. 16,3-6; 8; 10-15; 18-22; 24-27;
29; 31-37; 39-40; 42-45; 47-48; 50-54; 56-
57; 60; 64-71; 74-79; 81-83; 85-86; 88-90;
93-96; 103-104; 107-115; 117-123; 125-131;
133; 135-136; 138-143; 148-153; 155; 158-
159; 161-164; *167;* 170-171; 173; 175. 17,4-
5; 7; 9-10; 12-17; 19-23; 26; 28; 32; 35; 38-
42; 44; 46; 48-49; 58; 61-62; 64; 67-68; 73;
75-77; 79-83; 85; 87-89; 91-93; 96-101;
103-105; 107. 18,1. 19,4-8; 10; 20; 23; 25-
28; 30; 33; 35; 37-40; 42; 44-46. 20,1; 3-6;
10-17. 21,1-4; 6; 9-10; 13-21. 22,1. 23,2-5;
7; 9-12; 14-15; 17-24. 24,1; 3; 5; 16; 19-20;
23-25; 27; 31. 25,9-10; 13; 15; 17-18; 23;
26. 27,1. 28,1-6; 8; 10-12; 15-16. 29,3; 5-
6; 8. 30,1; 3. 31,1-2; 4. 32,2-3; 6-7. 33,1.
34,1-2; 5-6; 16; 18; 21-22; 24-25; 27-28;
32; 40-41; 46; 48-50; 52; 55. 35,4-5; 7-9;
11-13; 15; 20-23; 25-30. 36,1; 3-4; *6;* 7-8;
10-15; 17-19; 21-26. 37,1. 38,1-2. 39,1-5;
7-11; 14-21. 40,3; 5; 7. 42,1-2; 4-10; 15-
16; 18; 20-21; 23-24. 43,1-2; 4. 44,1. 46,2.
47,1; 4-8; 11-12; 14. 48,1; 3-4; *5;* 6. 8-11.
49,2; 6. 50,1. 51,2; 9-10; 12-14. 52,6; 10-
15; 18-21; 23; 26; 28; 34-36; 41-43; 46; 51.
　　　　　　　DOR　1,2-3; 5-9; 12-15;
18; 24; 26-27; 30-31. 2,2; 4. 3,6-7; 10; 15;
17. 4,1. 5,1-2. 6,3-4. 8,1-5. 9,1. 10,1; 6.
11,2-3; 6; 11-12; 16-17. 12,1-3; 7-8; 10-12;
16. 13,2. 14,1. 15,1. 16,2. 17,1-2. 19,1; 3.
20,1-2. 21,1. 22,1. 24,4-5. 25,1. 26,1; 6-7;
10; 14-15; 18; 20-22; 26; 28; 31-33; 40; 44;
46; 50-51; 61; 66-67; 69. 27,3; 5-7. 28,1-2;
4-5. 29,1. 30,1; 3. 32,1-2. 33,2; 4. 34,2; 5-
8; 11-12; 15. 35,1. 36,6; 8. 37,1; 4-5; 13.
38,1. 39,1. 40,1; 3; 9. 41,1-4. 42,1. 45,1.
46,1-2. 47,1-2; 4-8. 48,2. 49,3; 9-10; 12;
15-16. 50,4. 51,1. 53,2. 54,3; 6. 55,1-3; 5-
6; 8-9; 11; 16; 19-20; 26-27; 29; *34;* 36; 38;
40. 56,1-2; 14; 19; 28-29; 31; 33; 35; 38; 44;
46; 57-58; 64. 57,14-15. 58,2.
　　　　　　　HAM　1,3-4; 14-15; 17-18;
27; 42; 45; W3; W16. 2,1-2; 7; 16; 19; 22.
3,5; 10; 15; 22; 24. 5,1. 6,1-2; 5; 13; 15-16.
7,1. 9,1. 11,1. 13,1. 14,1; 4. 16,4; 6. 18,2-

3. 19,1. 20,1. 21,1-2; 5; 9. 23,1; 4; 7-8; 22;
31; 34; 39-40; 43; 53; 57-60; 64; 68. 27,2.
28,7-8. 29,1-2; 5-7; 13-14; 16. 30,1. 31,1.
32,1; 4. 35,2-4; 6-7; 9. 36,1. 37,1-2. 39,1.
41,1. 42,1. 43,1; 5. 44,8. 45,8-9. 47,2.
52,1. 54,1. 55,2. 56,3. 58,1. 60,2. 64,1-2.
68,1; 5; 10. 69,1; 7; 11; 13-16; 23; 27; 30-
31; 34; 44; 46; 48; 53-54. NF1,1. NF2,1-3.
NF3,2; 6-7; 9; 14-15. NF4,1. NF5,1.
NF6,1-2. NF7,1. NF8,1-2. NF9,1; 3-7; 9-
11; 18-22; 24-33; 36. NF10,3; 5. IoW1,1-
2; 4-5; 12; 14-15. IoW5,1. IoW6,3; 22.
IoW7,1; 5; 8; 11-12; 15; 17-18; 20-21.
IoW8,3-6; 10. IoW9,5; 8; 11-12; 20-22.
      HRT   1,1-6; 9-12; 18. 2,2-
3. 4,2; 4-5; 7-8; 10-13; 15; 17-18; 22. 5,1;
4; 14; 16-18; 20; 23-24; 26. 7,1. 8,1-3. 9,1;
4-5; 9-10. 10,1-6; 8-9; 15-16; 18-19. 11,1.
12,1. 13,1-5. 14,1-2. 15,1-2; 4-5; 10. 16,4-
6; 9. 17,1; 3. 20,2; 8-9; 11. 21,2. 22,1-2.
23,2-4. 24,1; 3. 25,1-2. 26,1. 27,1. 28,3-5;
8. 30,1-2. 31,1. 32,1-2. 33,2-3; 8; 12; 15;
17-18; 20. 34,1; 4-5; 7; 11-13; 15-16; 18-
19; 21-22. 35,1-3. 36,11; 13; 16; 19. 37,4;
21-23. 38,2. 41,1-2. 42,1-2; 9; 11. 42a,1.
44,1.
      HUN   1,1-3; 6; 10. 2,1-2;
4; 6; 8. 4,1-3; 5. 6,1-6; 9; 11-16; 18-19; 24;
26. 7,2-6. 9,1-3. 10,1. 11,2. 13,4. 14,1.
16,1. 19,1-8; 14; 18-20; 23; 25; 27; 29; 31.
20,2-3; 5; 7-9. 21,1. 22,1. 23,1. 24,1. 25,1-
2. 28,1.
      KEN   2,9; 17; 19; 23. 3,4;
16. 5,13; 15; 18-19; 33; 47; 51-52; 54-55;
67; 71-73; 76; 79; 83; 86; 89; 98; 105; 115-
116; 120; 123; 126; 128-129; 139; 141-142;
144-146; 155; 159; 166-168; 171-172; 208;
220. 6,1. 7,5; 15; 17; 19. 9,5; 16; 19; 29;
31; 42; 47-49. 11,1. 12,4.
      LEC   1,12. 3,7-9. 4,1.
5,1-2. 7,1. 10,9; 12-13; 16. 11,1. 13,2-3; 8-
9; 11-13; 21-22; 28-29; 41; 48-49; 51; 58; 62;
65; 69; 74. 15,9; 12-16. 17,10; 15. 19,3.
21,1. 22,1. 23,2; 6. 25,3. 42,8.
      LIN   1,3; 6-8; 10; 12; 26;
31; 34-36; 65; 80; 90; 106. 2,2; 6-8; 10-12;
19-20; 23; 28; 38-39. 3,6-7; 11-12; 14-15;
20; 22-23; 34-36; 41; 49; 53. 4,2-3; 7; 12;
16; 27; 34; 55; 57; 60-61; 65; 67-68; 77.
5,1-2. 6,1. 7,7; 17; 19; 21-22; 25; 48; 51;
57. 8,3; 15-17; 20; 23; 25; 28; 31; 39. 10,3.
11,4. 12,1; 4; 7; 14; 23-30; 32-33; 35-36;
40; 51; 60; 63; 68; 71-76; 80; 84; 89; 96.
13,5; 7-8; 12-13; 15-19; 28; 34-35; 37; 39.
14,2; 30; 32; 35; 44; 49; 84; 86; 89; 93; 99.
15,2. 16,1-2; 4; 11; 18; 23; 30; 33; 35; 39;
44; 46. 17,2. 18,2; 7-9; 12; 20; 29-30; 32.
21,1. 22,5; 8; 12; 25; 28; 30. 24,4; 7; 12-13;
36; 44; 48; 50-51; 58; 65; 76; 78; 80-81; 85;
96-97; 102. 25,7-8; 21-22; 25. 26,23-24; 33;
35; 39-40; 42; 49-50; 53. 27,10; 14-15; 26;

33; 38; 43; 45-46; 62; 64. 28,5; 15-16; 19;
21; 25; 35; 39. 29,5; 7; 13-14; 17; 19; 21.
30,1-2; 5; 11-12; 14-20; 27-28; 30. 31,1; 14.
32,7-8; 16-18; 20-22; 27-28; 31. 33,1. 34,7;
13-14; 16-21; 23; 25. 35,7; 9; 16. 36,1-2; 4.
37,1; 4-5. 38,6; 9; 11-14. 39,2. 40,1; 5; 10;
15; 18; 23; 26. 41,1. 42,3; 10; 13. 43,3.
44,5; 9. 45,1; 3. 46,1. 47,4; 10. 48,2; 4; 9;
14. 49,1-2. 51,1; 7; 10; 12. 54,1. 55,2-3.
56,1-2; 6-7; 10; 17; 19; 21. 57,6; 12; 15-16;
24; 28-32; 37; 41; 53. 58,1; 7. 59,3; 11-12;
14. 60,1. 61,5. 62,1. 63,1-3; 5; 16. 64,1; 3;
5-7; 15-16; 18-19. 65,1-2. 66,1-2. 67,9; 12;
16; 23. 68,2; 12; 24; 30; 38; 44; 46; 48.
      MDX   2,1-2. 3,3; 7-8; 12-
14; 16-22. 4,1; 3; 6; 8; 12. 5,1. 7,2-4; 6; 8.
8,3-6. 9,1; 4; 7; 9. 10,1. 11,4. 12,1-2. 14,2.
15,2. 18,1-2. 20,1. 21,1.
      NTH   1,1; 2a,g; 3-4; 7;
11-13a; 13d; 14-15a; 15l; 16-19; 24; 26; 29-
30; 32. 2,4; 7-8; 11-12. 4,4-5; 10; 12-13;
30-31; 36. 5,1-2. 6,2; 4; 7; 10c; 11; 15; 17.
6a,4; 11; 13; 16; 22-23; 25-27; 29; 32. 7,2.
8,9. 10,3. 12,1-2. 13,1. 14,3; 6. 18,1; 7; 9-
11; 14; 17; 19-20; 26; 28-31; 33-34; 36-39;
46; 48; 50-52; 54-57; 59; 64-65; 74; 79-80;
86; 88-89; 91; 95. 19,2. 21,1; 6. 22,1; 3; 6-
9. 23,3-6; 8-12; 16; 18-19. 26,1-8; 10. 28,1.
30,2; 4-5; 15; 17. 31,1. 33,1. 34,1. 35,5; 9;
19a-b,d-e; 20; 24-25. 36,4. 38,1. 39,8-12;
15; 18. 40,1. 41,3; 6. 42,2. 43,5-8; 11.
44,1a. 45,2; 5. 46,1-2. 47,1a. 50,1. 52,1.
53,1. 54,3. 55,2; 6. 56,1; 8; 20j; 21-22; 34-
36; 38; 57; 64-65. 58,2. 59,3. 60,2.
      NTT   1,9-10; 12; 28; 55.
5,5; 9; 18. 6,8. 7,4-5. 8,2. 9,4; 11; 16; 33;
117; 124. 10,66. 11,4; 6; 10-11. 12,11.
13,10. 14,8. 16,1. 30,6; 19-20; 40.
      OXF   1,1; 8-9. 5,1. 6,2-3;
12-13; 16-17. 7,4-8; 11; 16-18; 21-22; 26-
27; 30; 33; 36; 39; 41; 43-44; 50; 52; 56;
58; 61; 65. 8,2-3. 9,3; 5; 7; 9a; 10. 10,1.
11,1. 12,1. 14,6. 15,4-5. 16,1. 17,4-5.
18,1. 20,1-4; 7-10. 21,1. 24,1; 3. 27,3; 5.
28,4; 12-14; 16-17; 23. 29,1; 3-4; 8; 16-17;
22-23. 30,1. 31,1. 34,1-3. 35,3; 7; 11; 18-
20; 22; 30; 32. 36,1. 37,1. 38,2. 39,3. 41,1.
42,1. 43,1-2. 45,1-3. 49,1. 50,1. 53,1-2.
56,1; 3-4. 58,4-5; 7-8; 10; 12; 15; 24-25;
33; 37. 59,1-2; 11; 13; 15-17; 19; 23; 26-28.
      RUT   R12; 15.
      SHR   3e,2. 3f,4-5. 4,1,5;
8; 12. 4,3,32-37; 40; 53; 59; 71. 4,4,9; 20.
4,5,3. 4,6,6. 4,11,4; 9-10; 14; 17-19. 4,14,1-
17; 22-25. 4,15,1-3. 4,16,2. 4,17,3. 4,18,1-
3. 4,19,2; 4-8; 10; 13. 4,20,1; 3; 6-8; 13-
18; 24; 26. 4,21,1-6; 8-10; 12; 14; 18-19.
4,22,1-3. 4,23,1; 3-6; 9-14; 16-18. 4,24,1-
2; 4. 4,25,1; 3; 7. 4,26,3; 6. 4,27,1-3; 9; 11;
15; 17; 19-21; 25-27; 29; 32-34. 5,1-4; 8-

9. 6,1; 7-8; 10; 12-14; 18-21; 23-26. 7,3-5. 9,1-2.

SOM 1,1; 3; 6-9; 11-17; 19-21; 25-30; 32-34. 2,1; 10-11. 4,1. 5,1-2; 5-7; 10-11; 15-16; 18; 20; 25; 34; 37; 39; 41; 43-45; 47; 53; 57; 60; 63-65. 6,1-8; 10-13; 15; 17. 7,2; 5-6; 9; 13. 8,1-2; 4; 6; 8; 10-11; 14-18; 20; 22-24; 28-32; 35. 9,4; 7. 10,1-2; 4. 11,1. 14,1. 16,2-3; 8; 13. 17,2; 4-7. 18,1-3. 19,2-5; 8; 10-11; 13; 15; 18; 20-22; 24; 28-29; 31-32; 34-35; 37; 40; 43; 45; 48; 50; 54-60; 63-65; 68; 72; 78; 85; 87. 20,1. 21,7; 13; 19; 37; 39-40; 46; 49-50; 54; 56-62; 64-65; 67-68; 70-73; 76-79; 81; 85-87; 91; 93-95. 22,1-3; 5; 8; 10-15; 19-20; 24; 27. 24,1; 3; 9; 11; 14-16; 23; 29-31. 25,1; 6-7; 9; 14-15; 17-18; 23; 26; *28*; 39-41; 44; 47; 49-54; 56. 26,4-5. 27,2-3. 28,2. 30,1. 31,2-4. 32,1-2; 4-6. 33,1-2. 34,1. 35,1-2; 5; 7; 11-12; 18; 22-23. 36,4-5; 7; 9-11; 14. 37,1-2; 5-6; 9. 38,1. 39,3. 40,1-2. 41,1. 43,1. 44,3. 45,4; 6; 10. 46,21; 23. 47,1-6; 8; *9*; 12; 16-17; 19; 21.

STS 1,4; 6; 10; 13; 16; 18; 20-23; 25; 27-28; 31-32. 2,1-2; 5; 8; 14; 16; 18. 4,2-3. 6,1. 7,2. 8,1-3; 5-9; 12; 14; 17; 19-25; 28; 30. 10,4; 9. 11,1-2; 6; 8-13; 17-24; 27-29; 31-34; 37-40; 42-43; 45-47; 49-50; 54-55; 57-58; 64-67. 12,5-6; 8; 10-11; 17; 19-20; 22-23; 25; 27-28; 30. 13,1-2; 5-6; 8-9. 14,1-2. 16,1-2. 17,1-2; 8; 12-13; 18-20.

SFK 1,12.

SRY 1,4-5; 8; 14. 2,3. 5,2; 5; 11; 22-23; 27. 6,4-5. 7,1. 8,1-2; 13; 20-21; 25. 13,1. 14,1. 15,2. 17,1. 19,2; 8; 21; 24; 26; 32; 38; 44-45; 47-48. 20,1-2. 21,6-7. 22,1. 24,1. 25,1. 26,1. 27,3. 34,1. 36,8.

SSX 2,8-9. 3,2-3. 4,1. 7,1. 9,1; 4; 18; 21. 10,4-5; 7; 11-12; 15; 17-20; 25-26; 28-32; 34-38; 42; 47-50; 52; 61; 63; 65; 68-69; 78; 87-90; 92-95; 99-100; 102; 106; 109; 111-112. 11,7; 10; 12; 14; 16; 23; 25; 27; 30; 32-36; 39-41; 43; 49-50; 54; 57; 75; 98; 102; 104; 107; 113. 12,3; 9; 11; 15-16; 23; 27; 31-32; 35-36; 39-41; 43; 48-50. 13,6-7; 10; 13-14; 17; 23; 27; 33; 48-49.

WAR 1,1; 6-7. 2,1; 3. 3,5; 7. 4,1-2; 4. 6,2-5; 7; 12; 14-16; 18-19. 8,1. 9,1. 11,1; 4. 12,1; 6; 9-10. 14,1-3; 6. 15,1-3. 16,1-3; 5; 7; 13-15; 18; 20-21; 23-24; 26; 29-31; 33; 35-38; 41; 44; 48; 50; 52-53; 56; 58; 62-63; 66. 17,2-4; 6; 9; 13; 16; 19; 22; 28; 30; 38; 41; 45; 47; 50; 54; 56; 67; 69. 18,6; 8-10; 14. 19,1; 3; 5. 20,1. 22,1; 6-9; 11; 13; 15-16; 19; 24-25. 26,1. 27,1-3; 5-6. 28,1; 3; 6; 8; 11; 14. 29,1; 3; 5. 30,1-2. 31,2-7; 10-11. 33,1. 34,1. 35,1. 37,3-6; 9. 38,1. 39,1. 41,1-2. 42,1. 44,1-2; 5; 7; 12; 16.

WIL 1,3; 5-7; 10-12; 15; 17; 19; 22. 2,1-2; 5-6; 8-10. 5,3; 6. 6,1. 7,1-4; 6-9; 11-12; 14-15. 8,5; 7; 9-10; 12-13. 10,1-3. 12,4-5. 13,2; 7; 14; 16. 14,1. 15,1-2. 16,1. 19,1. 20,3; 5-6. 21,1. 22,1; 4; 6. 23,1; 4-5; 8-10. 24,1-2; 22; 25; 30; 33; 35; 41. 25,5; 7-8; 13; 19; 26-27. 26,1; 3; 7; 13-14; 16; 19; 21-22. 27,4; 6; 8; 10; 17; 19-20. 28,1-3; 7-9; 11. 29,9. 30,1; 7. 31,1. 32,2; 5; 7; 15; 17. 33,1. 36,1. 37,1; 8. 39,1. 41,1-2; 6. 42,2-3; 8. 43,2. 48,7-8. 49,1-3. 50,1; 4. 51,1. 54,1. 55,1. 56,2-3. 59,1. 60,1. 65,1. 66,4. 67,1; 9; 17; 28; 31; 36-38; 43-44; 54; 59-60; 62-63; 77; 89. 68,14; 16; 18; 25-26; 30; 32.

YKS C26; 28; 30; 33. 1Y1; 3-4; 6-7; 10-13; 15; 18. 1N38; 66; 93. 1W25. 2,1-2. 2B2; 6; 8-9; 11. 2N2; 14; 19; 21-22. 2W2-4; 7-9; 11-12. 2E1; 8-9; 14; 28; 36. 3Y1; 4; 9. 4N1; 3. 4E1-2. 5N17-19; 28; 45; 50; 54; 59-61; 66. 5E1; 3; 5; 8; 11; 18; 23; 27 29; 32; 34; 39; 42; 65. 5W1; 10-11; 14-15; 18; 21; 30. 6N1-3; 12-13; 15; 21; 24-25; 29; 31-32; 34-36; 46; 50-51; 56-58; 63-65; 92; 104; 109; 117-118; 120; 123; 125; 131; 139-140; 147; 150; 152. 6W5-6. 6E1. 7E1. 8N4; 7; 10. 8W1. 8E3-4. 9W3; 7; 9; 12; 16; 20; 32; 47; 58; 60; 63-64; 68-69; 75-77; 80; 82-83; 93; 99; 115; 120. 10W8; 16-17; 21; 28; 31; 41. 11E2. 13W11; 17; 20; 35; 37. 13E2; 7; 13-16. 13N5; 18. 14E1-2; 4-9; 11-13; 15-16; 19-20; 24-25; 27; 31-34; 36-40; 43; 45; 50; 52-53. 15E2-3; 12. 16W3. 18W1. 20E1; 3. 21E1; 9-10. 22W2-3; 5. 23N2; 5; 8; 17; 20-21; 30; 33. 23E6; 8-9. 24W12; 20. 25W1-3; 9-15; 17-20; 24; 28; 30. 26E1; 8. 28W1; 6; 10-11; 14; 29; 31; 37. 29W6-7; 13; 15-16; 20; 24-25. 29E13-15; 28-29. 29N3; 9.

More ploughs than   BDF 21,2. 23,45. 24,8.
plough land   27,1.

BRK 1,6-9; 18; 20; 33; 41. 7,12-13; 17-18; 24; 39-40. 10,2. 11,1. 16,1. 21,8. 22,5; 9. 27,2-3. 31,5. 33,3-4; 7. 36,1. 37,1. 38,5-6. 40,1. 45,1. 46,1. 49,3. 54,2-3. 64,1. 65,5; 15.

BKM 1,5. 3a,4. 13,4. 14,6. 16,3. 21,4. 22,2. 23,8. 57,13.

CAM 5,14-15. 14,23; 48; 58. 26,8. 29,5. 37,2.

CHS B3. 2,1. 7,2. 9,6-7. 21,1.

CON 3,2.

DBY 1,2; 6; 11; 15-16; 18; 20-21; 33. 2,1-3. 3,3. 5,3-4. 6,4-7; 14; 17-18; 24-25; 27-28; 30-32; 34-35; 37-40; 43-47; 49-58; 60; 63-69; 73; 76; 78; 80; 83; 85; 90; 92; 94; 98-99; 101. 7,1-3; 6-8; 13. 8,1-6. 9,1. 10,1-2; 4; 7; 9-11; 13; 17-18; 23-25. 11,1-2; 4. 12,1-2; 4. 13,1-2. 14,1-3; 6. 16,3; 7. 17,5-6; 10; 12; 15; 22.

DEV   1,24; 32; 57-58; 64.
2,13; 16. 3,7-8; 26; 93. 5,10; 12. 7,1. 11,1.
15,4; 32; 40. 16,17; 30; 55; 63; 80; 84; 87;
92; 172. 17,33; 43; 45; 56; 59; 69; 74; 102.
19,31. 23,6. 24,8; 17; 21; 28; 30. 25,1; 12;
24-25. 32,10. 33,2. 34,10; 19; 51. 35,10.
36,20. 39,12. 40,4; 6. 41,2. 42,12. 47,13.
49,1. 50,5. 51,1; 5. 52,38; 53.

DOR   1,21. 2,6. 3,8; 13.
7,1. 11,1; 4; 10; 14. 12,14. 13,1. 26,4; 52.
27,6. 36,2; 4; 7. 47,9. 55,21. 56,12; 20; 45.
57,1; 3; 12.

HAM   1,1; 8; 13; 19-20;
24; 26; 28-30; 39; 44; 47; W4; W6-8; W13-
14; W19. 2,4-5; 9-10; 13; 15; 18; 20-21; 23-
25. 3,1; 5; 11; 21; 25-27. 6,12; 17. 10,1.
14,2-3; 5-6. 15,1-2; 5. 18,1. 21,6; 8. 23,6;
10-12; 14; 16; 20; 23; 25-26; 28; 33; 35-36;
38; 42; 44-45; 49. 24,1. 26,1. 28,1-2. 35,8.
43,3-4; 6. 44,1; 3. 45,1; 3. 47,3. 49,1. 51,1.
53,2. 56,2. 62,1-2. 66,1. 68,6. 69,4-5; 8;
10; 28; 32; 36; 50. NF9,2; 13; 40; 44.
IoW1,6-7; 13. IoW2,1. IoW6,4; 6; 9; 12;
15-16; 21. IoW7,4; 6-7; 13-14. IoW8,9; 11.
IoW9,1-3; 23.

HEF   2,5.
HRT   34,24.
HUN   1,8. 2,3; 5; 7. 4,5.
6,7; 22. 7,1; 7. 9,4. 11,1. 12,1. 13,1. 19,12-
13; 15; 17; 30. 20,5-6.

KEN   1,1-2; 4. 2,4; 7-8;
10-12; 14-16; 20; 22; 25-26. 3,2-3; 5-6; 8;
12-14; 20-22. 4,2; 6; 9-10; 12-14; 16. 5,2;
11; 16; 30; 39; 41-43; 53; 60; 74-75; 80; 88;
93; 95; 106-108; 111; 119; 122; 127; 143;
147; 152; 162-163; 165; 170; 175-177; 179-
180; 224. 7,7-9; 18; 20; 23; 29. 8,1. 9,1; 4;
6; 10; 12; 22; 25; 28; 36-37. 11,2. 12,1; 3.

LEC   3,12; 15. 10,8.
11,2. 13,1; 6; 10; 15-17; 19-20; 23-24; 34-
35; 37; 40; 44; 47; 50; 52-57; 60-61; 63-64;
66-67; 70. 15,10. 20,2. 21,2. 23,1; 4-5.
24,1. 25,1; 5. 41,2-3.

LIN   1,4; 13; 28-29; 38;
66; 81; 91. 2,1; 5; 14-15; 17; 34; 37; 40; 42.
3,3-4; 8; 27; 37; 43. 4,1; 6; 15; 17; 20; 38;
40; 42-43; 54; 66; 69; 72; 74; 79. 7,1; 3-5;
10; 16; 20; 23; 26; 28; 30; 40-41; 43; 46;
50; 53-54; 56; 58. 8,1-2; 4-5; 8-9; 18; 22;
34; 36. 9,1-2. 10,1. 11,2. 12,8; 19; 21; 37;
42-43; 48; 55-56; 61; 64-67; 91; 93. 13,1-3;
9; 23; 26; 31; 33; 38; 42; 44-45. 14,1; 4; 9;
13; 15; 17-18; 20; 23; 25-26; 29; 31; 39-41;
46-48; 51-52; 59; 63; 65-66; 73-74; 77-80;
82-83; 97-98; 100-101. 15,1. 16,7; 22; 27;
36; 43. 17,1; 3. 18,3-4; 6; 11; 16; 22; 24-
25. 22,7; 10; 16; 22; 24; 26; 29; 31; 35. 23,1.
24,1; 3; 6; 14-15; 20; 24-25; 27; 32; 37-41;
47; 49; 63-64; 66; 72-74; 77; 87; 90; 92; 95;
98-101; 103-105. 25,1-3; 11; 13; 15; 20; 24.
26,1-2; 7-11; 17; 25; 44; 46. 27,1; 5; 7; 23;

34; 39; 41-42; 48; 50; 58; 61. 28,1; 11; 13;
17; 33; 43. 29,1; 6; 8; 20; 26; 29; 33. 30,3;
6; 29. 31,2; 4; 7; 9; 11; 13; 15-18. 34,1-2;
5-6; 8-10; 15. 35,1-2; 4; 6; 11-12; 14-15.
36,3. 37,2; 7. 38,1; 3; 8. 39,1; 3. 40,2; 7-
8; 12; 17. 42,1; 4; 9; 15-16. 43,2. 44,8; 10.
46,3. 47,1; 8. 51,2-6. 55,1. 56,9; 12-13; 15-
16; 20. 57,1; 7; 10; 14; 21; 33; 38-39; 45;
55. 58,8. 59,4; 13; 15; 17-18. 61,1; 6-7.
63,4; 10-13; 15; 19. 64,2; 8; 14; 17. 65,3.
67,7; 13; 24. 68,3-4; 22; 34; 39; 42.

MDX   11,1. 14,1. 22,1.
24,1.

NTH   1,8-10. 3,1. 4,7-9;
18; 20-21; 23; 29; 33-34. 6,3; 5-6; 8; 10a;
13. 6a,2; 6; 10. 8,8; 10-11. 9,1; 3; 6. 11,1-
2. 16,1. 18,3-4; 13; 71; 77; 84; 96. 19,1.
23,2. 30,6; 8-9; 12-13; 16. 32,1. 35,1e,i;
3a; 10; 12; 16; 23. 36,3. 39,5. 40,6. 41,2.
42,3. 48,12. 49,1. 54,2. 55,3-4. 56,1; 27;
40; 48-50. 58,1. 60,5.

NTT   B19. 1,2; 7; 15; 21;
23; 27; 32; 34-35; 39-40; 43; 45; 51-52; 54;
56; 58-59; 61; 63. 2,2; 4; 9. 3,1; 3. 4,1; 3; "
5-7. 5,1; 3-4; 7-8; 11; 13; 15. 6,1-3; 12-13.
7,2. 8,1. 9,2-3; 8; 12; 14-15; 17; 19-20; 22;
26; 28-32; 36-37; 39; 43; 45-46; 50-52; 55-
57; 59-60; 62; 64-67; 70; 72; 74; 76-77; 79-
84; 88; 90; 95-97; 100; 102; 104; 107-108;
110-111; 115-116; 118; 122; 126; 129-131.
10,1; 3; 5; 7-11; 15-18; 20; 24-25; 29; 31;
34; 43; 46-47; 49-51; 53; 55-61; 64-65.
11,1-3; 5; 7-9; 12; 14; 18-19; 22; 25-26; 29-
33. 12,8; 10; 12; 16-17; 19-20. 13,1-2; 4;
6-9; 11. 14,1; 3-5. 15,1; 4-5; 8-9. 16,6-7.
17,1-3; 7-13; 15-18. 18,1; 3; 5; 7. 19,1.
20,1-2; 8. 21,2. 22,1-2. 23,1-2. 24,1. 25,1.
27,1-2. 28,1. 30,4-5; 8-9; 13; 15; 21; 34;
47; 51.

OXF   2,1. 3,1-2. 4,1.
6,1b; 4-5; 7-9; 15. 7,1; 13; 45-47; 49; 57;
59. 9,2. 13,1. 15,1. 17,1; 8. 18,2. 20,5.
23,1-2. 24,5. 27,4. 28,1-2; 5-7; 9-11; 20-
22; 25-26; 28. 29,5-6; 10; 12; 20. 32,1.
33,2. 35,6; 10; 17; 21; 24; 31. 44,1. 55,2.
57,1. 58,18; 20-21; 26; 30; 38. 59,6; 12; 14;
18; 20; 25.

RUT   R5-6; 8-11; 14; 16-
17; 19-21.

SHR   4,20,4-5. 6,30. 7,4.
SOM   1,10. 2,12. 3,1-2.
5,3-4; 14; 23; 26; 31; 43; 48-54; 59; 61-62;
67. 6,9; 16. 8,5; 9; 13; 21; 27; 33-34. 9,3.
13,1. 19,1; 7; 16; 38; 41; 51; 53; 79-81; 86.
21,1-2; 12; 23-27; 42; 98. 22,20; 26. 24,4-
5; 13; 16-19; 21; 24. 25,3; 10; 12-13; 16; 29;
32; 37-38; 55. 26,2; 6. 35,6. 36,6. 37,10;
12. 45,3.

STS   1,1-2; 7-8; 12; 17;
19; 24; 29-30. 2,3; 10; 20. 4,1; 4-5; 7. 5,1.
7,1; 3; 5; 7-8; 10; 13-15; 17-18. 8,4; 13; 15;

32. 9,1. 10,3; 5; 7-8. 11,25; 52; 56. 12,1; 15; 24; 29; 31.

SRY   1,2-3; 13. 2,1-2; 4-6. 4,1. 5,1a; 7-8; 21. 8,9; 12; 28-30. 10,1. 11,1. 16,1. 18,2-4. 19,1; 3-7; 10; 16-17; 20; 23; 29; 31; 36-37; 46. 21,3. 22,2; 5. 25,2-3. 27,1-2. 29,1. 30,1-2. 32,2. 35,2. 36,5-7; 10.

SSX   2,1a. 3,8-9. 5,1-3. 8,1. 8a,1. 9,2-3; 5-9; 11; 13-17; 24; 38-39; 52; 82-83; 91; 96; 104-105; 108-109; 111; 120-122. 10,2-3; 16; 22; 27; 33; 43; 66-67; 108; 117. 11,3; 9; 18; 22; 37; 44-47; 53; 56; 62-63; 66; 68; 78-82; 84; 88-89; 91-92; 103; 110. 12,4-6; 13; 21; 30; 33; 37; 42; 46-47; 51; 54-55. 13,9; 11-12; 19; 22; 28; 30; 34; 38; 43; 56.

WAR   3,1. 4,3. 6,10; 20. 11,3. 12,2-4; 8. 15,4-6. 16,6; 8-10; 12; 16; 32; 46; 51; 54; 59-60. 17,1; 5; 7; 10-11; 17; 21; 29; 31; 33; 37; 42; 44; 55; 57-58; 60-61; 66; 68; 70. 18,3; 5; 11-13. 19,4; 6. 21,1. 22,4-5; 17; 23; 26. 23,3. 24,1. 27,4. 28,17-18. 31,1. 36,1-2. 37,1; 7. 38,2. 39,3-4. 42,3. 44,9-10; 14. 45,1.

WIL   1,1; 4; 16; 18. 2,1; 3. 3,5. 8,3; 6; 8; 11. 12,3. 13,9. 21,2. 24,3; 13; 17-18; 31. 25,1-2. 27,1; 11; 15. 29,6; 8. 37,11. 45,1. 53,1. 56,1. 61,1.

YKS   C23; 32. 1Y17. 1N54; 65; 106. 2,3. 2B1-4; 7; 13. 2W6-7. 2E2; 6; 12; 18; 21; 23; 25; 38. 3Y1; 13. 5N11; 47-48; 53; 58; 62; 67. 5E10; 15; 31; 35; 38; 44; 55; 66. 5W7-8; 12-13; 16-17; 19-20; 32; 34. 6N19; 49; 53-55; 59-60; 66; 103; 113; 116; 119-120; 122; 129; 132; 136-137; 143; 162. 6W1-3. 8N1; 6; 8-9. 8E1. 9W1-2; 5-6; 8; 22-23; 26; 28; 34-40; 42; 44-45; 48-56; 62; 64; 67; 72; 74; 96; 98; 116; 119; 138-139. 10W1-4; 14-15; 19-20; 22-23; 26-27; 29; 34; 37-39; 43. 11E3. 11N4. 12W1. 13W1-3; 8-9; 21; 26; 28; 30-33. 13E1; 4-5; 12. 13N4; 9; 12-14; 17. 14E42; 48. 15E1; 4. 17W1. 19W3. 21E5-6; 11. 21W3; 6. 23N1; 3-4; 9-11; 13; 19; 15-16; 23-26; 28; 31-32; 35. 23E2-5; 11-12; 14-15; 17-18. 24W2; 6-7; 19. 25W8. 26E10. 27W1-2. 28W8; 32-33; 39. 29W1; 3-5; 10; 22. 29E1; 3; 5; 10; 19; 25. 29N1; 6; 8; 12-13.

Same ploughs as   BDF   1,1a; 2a-b; 3;
plough land   5. 2,4-5; 7-8.
3,1-8; 10-15. 4,1-5. 6,1-3. 8,1; 5-9. 9,1. 10,1. 13,1. 15,7. 16,3-9. 17,1-5; 7. 18,1-7. 19,3. 21,3-5; 9; 12-14; 16-17. 23,1-5; 7-10; 12-16; 18-20; 24-30; 32; 36-43; 46-51; 53-54; 56-57. 24,2-4; 6-7; 9; 11; 14; 20-27; 29-30. 25,1-2; 4; 7-12; 15. 26,1. 28,2. 32,3-5; 8-9. 34,1-3. 39,1-2. 40,1. 42,1. 43,1. 44,1-2; 4. 45,1. 46,1-2. 47,1-2; 4. 49,1; 3-4. 51,1-3. 53,1-4; 6; 8-10; 12; 14-16; 18; 23;

26; 28-29; 31-33; 35-36. 54,1; 4. 55,2-7; 9-10; 12-13. 56,2-3. 57,2; 3ii-iv; 6; 8; 13; 15-16; 18; 20-21.

BRK   1,17; 19; 25-26; 31-32; 34; 37; 40. 2,2. 3,1. 4,1. 7,19-21; 25-26; 36; 47. 12,1. 16,3. 17,3; 5; 9. 20,1. 21,6-7; 10; 14; 17; 19. 22,1; 7. 23,1-2. 24,1. 25,1. 26,2. 27,1. 31,6. 35,2; 4. 36,5. 38,1. 41,2. 42,1. 43,1. 44,2. 45,2. 46,2; 4-5. 49,2. 53,1. 54,1; 4. 55,3-4. 57,1. 58,1. 60,1. 61,1-2. 62,1. 63,1; 4. 65,3-4; 7; 12; 17; 19.

BKM   B2. 1,3. 2,1-3. 3a,1-2; 6. 4,2-3; 6-8; 10-13; 15-23; 25-26; 28-29; 32; 35; 41. 5,1; 6-16; 18-19; 21. 6,2. 7,2. 8,1. 9,1. 10,1. 11,1. 12,2-5; 8-12; 16; 20-22; 25; 28-29; 32-35. 13,1. 14,1; 3-5; 7-14; 17-18; 21-24; 30-32; 34-38; 41-46; 48-49. 15,1-2. 16,1-2; 4; 6; 10. 17,1-2; 4-5; 8-9; 11; 15-17; 19-20; 22-28; 30. 18,1; 3. 19,1-7. 21,2-3; 5-6. 22,1. 23,1-17; 19; 22-24; 27; 30; 33. 24,1-3. 25,3. 26,1-2; 4-5; 7-9. 27,1. 29,2-4. 32,1. 34,1. 35,3. 36,1. 37,2. 39,2. 41,1-2; 5. 42,1. 43,1-5; 7. 44,1-5. 45,1. 50,1. 51,3. 52,1-2. 53,1-3; 7-10. 54,1. 55,1. 56,1. 57,1; 4; 6; 8-9; 11-12; 14-18.

CAM   1,1; 3; 8; 14; 18-20. 2,1; 3. 4,1. 5,5; 7-11; 18; 20; 21; 23; 25; 28; 36; 39; 44-55; 59. 6,1. 7,2-3; 9; 11. 8,1. 9,1. 10,1. 11,1-4; 6. 12,1-2. 13,1-2; 4; 6-8. 14,2; 4-5; 7-9;11; 13-17; 19; 21-22; 26; 28-29; 31-34; 36; 40-41; 42; 43; 45-46; 50; 53-54; 56; 59-71; 75-78; 80-81. 15,3-4. 16,1. 17,1-4. 18,1; 5-8. 21,1; 3-4; 7-8. 22,1-4; 6-9. 23,3-5. 24,1. 25,3-4; 6-7; 9. 26,3; 5-6; 9-11; 14; 16-17; 19; 24-26; 30; 32; 36; 40-43; 45-48; 51-53; 56. 27,1. 28,1. 29,1-4; 6-9. 30,1. 31,1; 3; 6. 32,1-3; 6; 12; 14; 16; 20-21; 23; 28; 30; 32; 36; 39; 43. 35,2. 38,2-5. 39,1; 3. 40,1. 41,4; 7-8; 16. 42,1. 44,1.

CHS   A5; 8; 11; 18; 20-21. 1,5; 13. 2,8; 13; 22; 25. 4,1. 5,4; 9; 11. 6,1. 8,2; 9-10; 13-15; 17; 29-30; 33; 35; 37; 40; 45. 9,1-2; 8; 18-19; 23-24. 12,2-3. 14,13. 15,1. 17,5; 12. 18,4. 19,2. 20,3. 22,2. 23,1. 26,3; 12. FD2,1-2; 4-6. FD3,1. FD5,2-3. FD6,1. FD7,1. FD8,1-2. FT1,1-8. FT2,1-10; 12-16. FT3,1-2; 4-5.

CON   1,4. 4,8. 5,2,15; 22; 29. 5,3,9. 5,6,6. 5,7,2. 5,11,3; 5. 5,16,2. 5,19,1. 5,24,18. 5,25,1. 5,26,1. 7,1.

DBY   1,4; 7; 13; 19; 27. 3,4-6. 6,15; 33; 59; 86; 88-89; 91; 95; 97. 7,4. 10,6; 12; 19-20. 14,4; 7-8. 17,1.

DEV   1,3; 11-12; 19; 23; 37; 43; 47; 59; 66; 69; 72. 2,2; 4; 6; 8; 20; 22. 3,6; 22; 24; 27; 29; 51; 62; 78; 85; 91; 94-95; 97; 99. 4,1. 5,2-3; 14. 6,2; 5. 8,1. 10,2. 11,3. 13a,3. 15,3; 6; 12; 15; 18-19; 24-25; 31; 33; 35; 38; 48; 57; 60-61; 66. 16,7; 9; 16; 23; 28; 41; 46; 49; 58-59; 61; 72-73; 91; 97; 101-102; 105-106; 116; 124;

132; 134; 137; 144-147; 154; 156-157; 160; 165-166; 168; 176. 17,3; 6; 8; 18; 24-25; 27; 29-31; 34; 36-37; 47; 50-55; 57; 60; 63; 65-66; 70-72; 78; 86; 95; 106. 19,2; 9; 11-19; 21; 24; 29; 41; 43. 20,7-8; *9*. 21,7-8; 12. 22,2. 23,1; 13; 16; 26. 24,2; 4; 6-11; 13-14; 18; 22; 29; 32. 25,2-3; *4;* 5-8; 11; 14; 16; *20;* 21; 28. 28,7; 9; 13. 29,1-2; 4; 9. 30,2. 32,1; 4-5. 34,4; 7-9; 12; 14-15; 20; 23; 26; 29-31; 33; 35; 38-39; 42-45; 47. 35,1-3; 14; 16; 19; 24. 36,16. 39,13. 40,1-2. *41,1.* 42,3; 11; 14; 17; 19; *21;* 22. 43,3; 5. 44,2. 45,2-3. 46,1. 47,*9;* 10. 48,2; 7. 49,3; 5; 7. 50,2; 4. 51,3; 6; 8; 13; 15-16. 52,1; 4-5; 9; 16-17; 22; 24-25; 27; 29; 31; 37; 40; 44-45; 50; 52.

DOR   1,4; 10-11; 16-17; 19-20; 30. 2,1; 3. 3,2-5; 11; 14; 16; 18. 6,1. 10,3. 11,5; 7; 15. 12,4-5; 9; 15. 13,3-6; 8. 16,1; *2.* 19,2; 4-10; 12-13. 23,1. 26,3; 5; 8-9; 13; 19; 30; 34; 39; 41; 43; 45; 47; 49; 54; 56; 58-59; 62-65; 68; 71. 27,1-2; 4; 9; 11. 28,3; 6. 30,2; 4. 31,1-2. 32,3-5. 33,1; 5-6. 34,1; 9-10; 13-14. 35,1. 36,1; 5; 7; 9-11. 37,7; 9. 39,2. 40,2; 4-8. 41,5. 43,1. 44,1. 47,3; 11. 48,1. 49,1; 4-6; 11; 14. 50,1-3. 52,1-2. 53,1. 54,1; 4-5; 7-14. 55,4; 15; 17; 22; 24; 31; 33; 35; 37; 41-43; 45. 56,7-10; 13; 15; 17-18; 21; 23-24; 32; 36-37; 48; 59; 61-62. 57,4; 8-11; 13; 21. 58,1; 3.

HAM   1,2; 5-6; 12; 16; 25; 32; 40; 43; 46; W5; W9-12; W17-18; W20-21. 2,3; 6; 8; 11; 14; 17. 3,5-9; 13-14; 16-18; 20. 6,3-4; 6-9; 11; 14. 15,3-4. 16,1; 3; 5. 17,2-3. 21,3-4; 7. 22,1. 23,3; 9; 13; 15; 17-19; 21; 24; 27; 29-30; 32; 46-48; 50-52; 55; 61-62; 67. 25,1. 27,1. 28,5-6; 9. 29,3; 8-12; 15. 32,2. 34,1. 35,1; 5. 36,2. 38,1. 39,2-4. 45,2; 5-7. 46,1-2. 50,1. 51,2. 53,1. 55,1. 56,1. 57,2. 60,1. 61,1. 63,1. 65,1. 67,1. 68,2-3; 8. 69,2-3; 9; 12; 17-22; 24; 26; 29; 35; 37-43; 45; 47; 52. NF3,4; 8; 10-13; 16; 34; 37-39; 41; 43; 45. NF10,1-2. IoW1,3; 8-10. IoW3,1. IoW6,1-2; 5; 7-8; 17; 19. IoW7,2-3; 10; 19; 22-23. IoW8,1; 7-8; 12. IoW9,6; 10; 16-19; 24.

HRT   1,1; 7-8; 13-17. 2,1. 3,1. 4,1; 3; 6; 9; 14; 16; 19-20; 23-24. 5,5-6; 9; 13; 15; 21. 6,1. 7,2. 9,6-8. 10,7; 10-12; 14; 20. 15,3; 6; 8; 12. 16,1-3; 8; 10-11. 17,2; 4; 8; 10-15. 19,1-2. 20,1; 5; 7; 10; 12-13. 21,1. 28,6-7. 29,1. 31,6-8. 33,5; 7; 9-11; 13-14. 34,3; 10; 14; 20; 23; 25. 36,2-4; 7-8; 12; 14-15; 18. 37,1; 5-6; 8; 10-11; 13-20. 38,1. 42,6-8; 10. 43,1.

HUN   1,5; 7. 5,1-2. 6,8; 20-21; 23; 25. 8,1-2. 13,5. 17,1. 18,1. 19,24; 28. 20,1. 22,2. 29,5.

KEN   2,13. 3,7; 11; 19. 4,1; 5; 7-8; 11. 5,4; 14; 21; 31-32; 36; 46; 49; 58-59; 62; 68; 70; 77-78; 81-82; 91-92; 96-97; 102; 104; 109; 113-114; 118; 124;

138; 149; 153; 158; 164; 182; 225. 7,2-3; 6; 12-13; 21; 26-28. 9,2-3; 13-14; 20-21; 24; 32; 45; 50. 10,2.

LEC   3,2; 5-6; 16. 6,2. 7,2. 9,3. 10,1; 11; 14-15. 13,5; 7; 18; 25-27; 30; 32; 38-39; 43; 46; 59; 71-73. 16,5. 17,2; 8-9; 31. 19,1. 20,1; 3. 24,3. 25,2; 4. 27,1. 41,1. 42,7.

LIN   1,1-2; 5; 11; 25. 2,3; 16; 18; 21; 25; 29; 31; 33; 36; 41. 3,32; 39; 47-48; 51; 54. 4,8; 13; 18; 26; 33; 37; 39; 44; 47; 58; 81. 7,8-9; 24; 29; 35; 52. 8,11; 35. 10,2. 11,3; 5. 12,17; 20; 31; 34; 39; 41; 47; 70. 13,4; 6; 10; 14; 24; 32; 41. 14,5; 10; 53; 56; 58; 64; 67-70; 72; 75-76; 81; 85; 88. 16,16. 18,1; 5; 10; 13-14; 17; 23; 26-27; 31. 19,1. 20,1. 22,1; 14; 36; 38. 24,10; 17-18; 22; 26; 45; 54; 62; 68; 71; 82; 84; 86. 25,5-6; 9; 17; 23. 26,4; 13; 26; 47-48. 27,9; 22; 35; 47. 28,30; 41-42. 29,9; 11-12; 24-25; 34. 30,4; 9; 31. 32,1; 12. 35,3; 5. 40,4. 42,17. 43,1. 44,2-3; 7. 47,2; 7; 9. 48,1; 8. 56,8; 11; 14; 18. 57,2; 13; 18; 22. 58,2; 5. 61,4. 63,6-7; 14; 22-23. 64,4. 67,19; 26. 68,1; 15-16; 18-20; 23; 27; 31; 40; 45.

MDX   2,3. 3,1-2; 4-6; 23-26; 28-30. 4,2; 4-5; 7; 9-11. 6,1. 7,1; 5; 7. 8,1-2. 9,2-3; 6; 8. 10,2. 11,2-3. 13,1. 15,1. 16,1. 17,1. 19,1. 25,1.

NTH   1,1; 8; 20-21; 23; 25; 27-28; 31. 2,1-3; 5-6; 10. 4,3; 6; 11; 14-17; 19; 22; 24-28; 32. 5,3-4. 6,1; 9; 12; 14; 16. 6a,5; 12; 14-15; 20; 24; 28; 31; 33. 7,1. 8,1-2; 4-7; 13. 9,2; 4-5. 10,1-2. 11,3-6. 12,3-4. 14,1-2; 5. 17,2-3. 18,5; 12; 15-16; 18; 21; 23-25; 27; 32; 35; 41-45; 47; 49; 53; 58; 60-62; 66-70; 72-73; 75-76; 78; 82-83; 85; 87; 90; 92-93; 97-99. 20,1. 21,2-3. 22,2; 4-5. 23,1; 7; 13; 17. 24,1. 25,1-3. 26,9; 11. 27,1. 28,2-3. 29,1. 30,1; 3; 10; 14. 35,1a-d,f; 2; 3b-f; 4; 6-8; 13-15; 17-18; 19c,f-g; 21-22; 26. 36,1-2. 39,1-2; 4; 6-7; 13-14; 16-17. 40,2-4. 41,4-5; 8-9. 42,1. 43,1-2; 4-5; 9-10. 44,1b-c; 2. 45,1; 4; 6-9. 46,3-7. 47,2. 48,1-11; 14-17. 51,1. 54,1. 55,1; 5. 56,7; 12; 15-20e,h-i; 23-26; 29-33; 37; 39; 41-43; 45-47; 51; 55; 58-61; 66. 57,1-2; 4. 59,1-2; 4. 60,1; 3.

NTT   1,1; 3-5; 11; 20; 36-38; 41-42; 53. 2,3; 6. 5,6; 14. 6,9. 7,6. 9,6; 10; 18; 40; 44; 49; 75; 85; 98-99; 103; 106; 119; 121; 125; 127. 10,4; 13-14; 19. 11,20; 27-28. 12,1; 9; 18. 14,7. 15,2. 16,2; 8; 11. 17,4-5; 14. 18,6. 20,5-7. 21,1. 26,1. 30,1; 10; 12.

OXF   6,6; 14. 7,2; 9-10; 12; 15; 20; 25; 29; 31-32; 34-35; 37; 40; 48; 51; 53; 60; 62-64. 8,1; 4. 9,1; 4; 6; 8. 14,1-4. 15,2-3. 16,2. 17,1-3; 6-7. 19,1. 20,6. 22,1-2. 24,1; 4. 26,1. 27,1-2; 6-8. 28,3; 15; 18-19; 27; 29. 29,2; 7; 9; 11; 13-15; 18-19.

32,2. 33,1. 35,1-3; 5; 8-9; 12-13; 16; 25-
26; 28-29. 38,1. 39,1-2. 40,1; 3. 41,2. 47,1.
48,1. 51,1. 52,1. 54,1. 55,1. 58,1-3; 9; 16-
17; 23; 27-29; 31-32; 35-36. 59,3-5; 8-10;
21-22; 24; 29.

RUT ´R7; 13.

SHR 1,5. 4,1,3. 4,3,38.
4,14,26; 28. 4,17,1. 4,19,9; 11-12. 4,20,2;
27. 4,21,7; 11; 15-16. 4,23,2; 8. 4,25,2; 6.
4,26,4. 4,27,6; 8; 10; 12-13; 22-23; 28; 35.
6,2; 5; 9; 11; 15-16. 7,1; 4; 6.

SOM 1,2; 4-5; 18; 22-24;
35. 5,2; 8-9; 12-13; 15; 17; 19; 21-22; 24;
27-28; 30; 32; 33; 35-36; 42; 46; 55-58; 66;
68-70. 6,7; 14. 7,3; 7-8; 10-11; 14. 8,1; 3;
7; 12; 26. 9,2; 6. 10,3; 5. 12,1. 15,1. 16,5;
7. 17,1; 3; 8. 18,4. 19,9; 12; 23; 25-27; 30;
33; 36; 39; 42; 44; 46-47; 49; 52; 57; 62;
66-67; 69-71; 73-76; 82; 84. 20,2. 21,3-8;
14-15; 17; 21-22; 29; 32-35; 38; 41; 43-45;
47; 51; 54-55; 63; 74-75; 82; 84; 89-90; 92;
96. 22,4; 6; 17; 21-22; 25; 28. 23,1. 24,7-
8; 10; 12; 20; 22; 25-28; 32-37. 25,4; 8; 11;
21-22; 24-25; 27; 30-31; 33-34; 42-43; 45;
48. 26,3; 8. 27,1. 28,1. 29,1. 30,2. 31,1.
32,3; 8. 35,3-4; 10; 13; 15; 17; 19-21. 36,1-
3; 8; 12-13. 37,3-4; 7-8; 11. 39,1-2. 41,3.
42,1-3. 44,1-2. 45,1-2; 5; 7-9; 11-13; 15-
18. 46,4-12; 15; 17; 19; 22; 25. 47,10-11;
13-14; 18; 20; 23.

STS 1,7; 9; 11; 26. 2,13;
15; 17. 3,1. 4,9. 5,2. 7,2; 4. 8,10-11; 27.
10,6. 11,1; 14-16; 30; 35-36; 41; 44; 51; 60-
63; 68. 12,7; 9; 12-14; 18; 21; 26. 13,3; 7.
15,1-2. 16,3. 17,6-7; 10; 14.

SRY 1,6; 11-12; 14-15.
4,2. 5,3; 9-10. 6,2. 8,3; 6; 14; 17; 22. 12,1.
15,1. 19,11-12; 15; 19. 21,4. 22,3. 28,3.
29,2. 31,1. 33,1. 36,1; 9.

SSX 2,2-3; 5. 3,6-7.
9,10; 19; 22-23; 26; 34-35; 60; 103; 106-
107; 110; 123; 125. 10,6; 8; 14; 24; 45-46;
51; 53-56; 59-60; 62; 64; 72-74; 83; 86; 91;
96-97; 104-105; 113-116; 118. 11,4-6; 8;
11; 13; 15; 19-21; 24; 26; 28-29; 31; 48; 51-
52; 55; 59; 61; 64-65; 67; 69-74; 76-77; 83;
85-87; 93-96; 100; 106; 108-109; 111. 12,7-
8; 10; 14; 18-20; 22; 26; 34; 38; 44. 13,1;
5; 8; 15-16; 20; 25; 29; 35; 46; 50; 53-54.
14,1-2.

WAR 2,2. 3,2-3; 6. 4,6.
5,1. 6,1; 6; 11; 17. 7,1. 10,1. 11,2; 5. 12,5.
13,1. 16,11; 17; 22; 25; 28; 34; 39-40; 42;
45; 47; 57; 61. 17,8; 12; 14-15; 18; 20; 23;
25-27; 32; 34-35; 39-40; 49; 51-52; 59; 62-
65. 18,1-2; 4. 19,2. 22,3; 10; 12; 14; 20-22;
28. 23,1-2; 4. 24,2. 25,1. 28,2; 5; 7; 10; 13;
16; 19. 29,4. 31,8-9; 12. 32,1. 37,2. 39,2.
40,1-2. 43,1-2. 44,3-4; 6; 8; 11.

WIL 1,1-2; 5; 8-9; 11;
13-14; 20; 23j. 2,4; 7; 11-12. 3,1-4. 4,1-2;

4. 5,1-2; 4-5; 7. 6,2. 7,10; 16. 8,1; 4-5; 12.
10,4-5. 11,1. 12,1-2; 4; 6. 13,1; 5; 8; 10-
13; 17; 20. 14,2. 16,2-4; 6-7. 17,1. 18,1-2.
19,2. 20,1-2. 21,3. 22,2; 5. 23,7; 10. 24,4-
5; 7-12; 15; 19-21; 23-24; 26-29; 32; 34; 36;
38-39. 25,3-4; 11-12; 14-15; 17; 22-24.
26,2; 4-6; 9-12; 15; 18; 20. 27,2-3; 5; 7; 9;
12-14; 16; 18; 23-26. 28,5; 10; 12-13. 29,1-
2; 5; 7. 30,3-5. 32,1; 3-4; 8-14. 34,1. 35,1.
36,2. 37,2; 5; 7; 12-13; 15. 38,1. 39,2. 40,1.
41,3; 5; 7-8; 10. 42,1; 4-7; 10. 43,1. 44,1.
45,3. 47,1. 48,1; 3; 5-6; 9-12. 50,2; 5. 52,1.
53,2. 56,4. 58,1-2. 59,2. 63,1. 64,1. 66,1;
3; 5-8. 67,2-8; 10-16; 32-33; 39-41; 48; 51;
53; 56; 61; 66; 68; 72; 76; 80-81; 86-87; 94-
98. 68,3-4; 6; 8-11; 15; 20-22; 24; 27; 29.

YKS 1Y5. 1N92; 105.
1W39. 2B14. 2N23. 2W1. 2E7; 27; 41.
3Y10, 5N1; 27. 5E7; 36. 5W6; 8; 33. 6N8;
20; 27-28; 52; 56; 101-102; 121; 134-135;
138; 146. 8N3; 5. 8E2. 9W17; 19; 24; 27-
28; 43; 46; 57; 59; 61; 65-66; 79; 81; 94-95;
97; 117; 121; 125; 140-141. 10W10-13; 30;
32. 11E1. 11N1; 17. 11W3-4. 13W7; 10;
12-13; 16; 18-19; 25; 29; 36. 13N19.
14E17; 22; 30; 44; 47; 51. 16E1. 16N1-2.
16W1. 18W3. 21E2-3; 7. 21W2; 5. 22W4.
23N27; 29; 36. 23E10; 19. 24W10; 16.
24E2. 25W6. 28W7; 28; 34. 29W9; 18; 28.
29N5.

Less than before   HEF 29,11.
More ploughs   BDF 1,1c; 4. 2,1-3; 6; 9.
possible   4,7. 5,1-2. 7,1. 8,2-
3. 11,1. 12,1. 15,1-2; 5-6. 16,1-2. 19,1.
20,1. 21,6; 15. 22,1. 23,11; 17; 21-22. 24,1;
5; 10; 13; 15-19; 28. 25,5; 13-14. 26,2-3.
28,1. 29,1. 30,1. 31,1. 32,1-2; 10-11; 13;
16. 33,1-2. 41,1-2. 48,1. 49,2. 51,1. 52,1.
53,5; 7; 11; 13; 20-21; 30. 54,2-3. 55,1; 11.
57,3v.

BKM B1. 1,1-2; 4; 6-7.
2,1. 3,2. 3a,5. 4,1; 4-5; 14; 27; 30-31; 33-
34; 36-40. 5,2-3; 5; 17; 20. 6,1. 7,1. 8,2-
3. 12,1; 6-7; 9; 17; 24; 30-31; 36-37. 13,2-
3. 14,2; 16; 25-29; 33; 39-40. 16,5; 7-9.
17,6-7; 10; 12; 18. 18,2. 20,1. 21,1; 7-8.
23,18; 20; 26; 29; 31-32. 24,1. 25,1. 26,3;
8. 27,2. 28,2-3. 29,1. 31,1. 35,1-2. 36,2.
37,1. 38,1. 39,1. 40,1. 41,3-4; 6-7. 43,6;
8-11. 46,1. 47,1. 48,1. 49,1. 51,1-2. 56,3.
57,2-3; 7; 10; 13; 17.

CAM 1,2; 4-7; 9; 11-12;
17. 2,2; 4. 3,1; 3-4; 6. 5,1; 3-4; 6; 12; 29;
31; 34; 38; 41; 42; 57; 60-63. 7,4; 8; 10.
9,2-3. 12,4. 13,9; 11. 14,1; 27; 44; 49; 55;
73-74. 15,1-2. 18,3. 20,1. 21,5. 26,21; 23;
27; 31; 49. 28,2. 29,10. 30,2. 31,2; 7. 32,4-
5; 7-8; 10; 22-25; 31; 33-35; 37-38; 40.
35,1. 38,1. 39,2. 41,1; 3; 9; 12-13. 43,1.
44,2.

CHS 16,2.

ESS   6,2. 9,7. 18,16; 43. 20,1. 24,21; 24; 38. 27,4. 28,14. 30,27; 34. 37,18; 20.

GLS   11,5-6.

HEF   1,3; 5; 18; 48. 2,4-6; 11; 13; 23-24; 40; 44. 5,2. 8,5; 8. 9,8; 12; 18. 10,6; 25; 50; 55-57; 59-61; 63; 66; 69-70; 73. 14,8. 15,2; 10. 16,1. 18,1. 19,9. 20,1-2. 21,1; 4. 22,3. 23,5. 24,2; 4; 7. 25,3; 8. 27,1. 31,3-5.

HRT   1,1-6; 9-12; 18. 2,2-3. 4,4-5; 7-8; 10-13; 15; 17-18; 22. 5,1; 4; 8; 14; 16-18; 20; 23-24; 26. 7,1. 8,1-3. 9,1; 4-5; 9-10. 10,1-6; 8-9; 15-16; 18-19. 11,1. 12,1. 13,1-5. 14,1-2. 15,1-2; 4-5; 10. 16,4-6; 9. 17,1; 3. 20,2; 8-9; 11. 21,2. 22,1-2. 23,2-4. 24,1; 3. 25,1-2. 26,1. 27,1. 28,3-5; 8. 30,1-2. 31,1. 32,1-2. 33,2-3; 8; 12; 15; 17-18; 20. 34,1; 4-5; 7; 11-13; 15-16; 18-19; 21-22. 35,1-3. 36,7; 11; 13; 16; 19. 37,4; 21-23. 38,2. 41,1-2. 42,1-2; 9; 11. 42a,1. 44,1.

LEC   3,4-5.

MDX   2,1-2. 3,3; 7; 12-14; 16-22. 4,1; 3; 8; 12. 5,1. 7,3-4; 6; 8. 8,3-6. 9,1; 4; 7. 10,1. 11,4. 12,1-2. 14,2. 18,1-2. 20,1. 21,1.

NTH   17,1. 23,16.
RUT   R1-2; 17.
SHR   1,4; 8. 2,1. 3b,2. 3c,2-4; 8-9; 13-14. 3d,1-3. 3f,2-3. 3g,3-5; 8. 4,1,1-2; 4-7; 11; 14; 17-18; 22-23; 25-32. 4,2,1. 4,3,1-3; 5-7; 9-11; 13-15; 17; 19-21; 23-25; 27-31; 44-46; 52; 54; 56; 58; 63-69. 4,4,3; 10; 12-14; 16; 18-20; 23; 25. 4,5,1; 4; 6; 8-11; 13. 4,6,2. 4,7,1-5. 4,8,1-2; 4-5; 7-10; 13. 4,9,2-3. 4,10,1. 4,11,1; 5; 7-8. 4,13,1. 4,14,18. 4,19,1.

STS   11,48.
SFK   1,1. 4,31. 6,143; 148; 172. 7,6. 8,11. 16,2. 26,12a. 34,15.
WOR   1,1c-d; 2; 5. 2,85. 3,1-3. 11,2. 12,2. 14,2. 15,3. 16,1. 18,1-2. 19,1-3; 5-10; 12-14. 20,2-4; 6. 21,1; 3. 23,2; 4; 7-9; 12. 26,1; 3; 9-10; 12; 17.

PLOUGH iron (ferrum)
Render of   BDF   8,1. 24,13.
              BKM   12,3; 7. 17,4. 24,1. 26,3. 29,3.
See also: Pasture; Plough share; Woodland.

PLOUGH share (vomer; soccus)
Render of   CAM   5,9; 20; 53. 14,2. 17,1. 18,7. 26,16. 29,10.
              GLS   39,12. 68,4.
              HAM   1,W6. IoW7,16. IoW8,2.
              HEF   1,7; 41.
              HRT   33,9.
See also: Burgess; House; Marsh; Pasture; Plough iron; Port.

PLOUGHING
Land for   LIN   12,11. 44,11.
Land which cannot be ploughed   CHS   G3.
Land recently ploughed   HEF   31,2.
Service   GLS   1,24. 19,2.
            WOR   8,5-7.
See also: Cultivation; Freeman; Land; Man; Ox; Road; Smallholder; Stranger; Villager.

PLOUGHLAND
(terra de aratura)   ESS   1,3.
Strip of (cultura terrae)   LIN   CN4.
                              SRY   14,1.

PLOUGHLAND (terra x carucis) (land for x ploughs) Comparative information:-
less 1086 than   BDF   1,1c. 4,4; 7. 5,1-2.
number of hides/   6,3. 8,6. 9,1. 16,2;
carucates/sulungs in   8-9. 17,1; 5; 7.
1086 (or TRE if no   21,1-3; 5; 17. 22,1.
1086 detail)   23,7; 11; 34-35; 50-51; 57. 24,22; 24; 28. 25,1; 6-7; 9. 27,1. 32,4. 38,2. 39,1. 47,4. 48,1. 52,2. 53,1; 11-12; 36. 55,2; 4; 11. 56,2-4. 57,3iii-iv.

BRK   1,11; 33; 41. 2,2. 3,2. 5,1. 7,3-4; 9; 11; 13-14; 16; 18; 22-26; 35; 38; 46-47. 10,2. 20,1. 21,2; 9-12; 14-15; 19. 22,6-7; 9; 11. 23,1; 3. 26,2. 27,1-3. 28,1-2. 31,5. 33,5; 7-8. 35,1. 36,4-6. 38,2. 41,1; 3-4. 42,1. 44,2; 5. 45,2. 46,2. 54,2-3. 55,1; 3-4. 59,1. 64,1. 65,2-3.

BKM   1,3-5. 2,1; 3. 3a,2. 4,2; 5; 7; 18; 21; 26-27; 32-39; 42. 5,2-3; 6; 9; 11-12; 15-17; 21. 6,2. 7,2. 10,1. 12,1-3; 9; 14-18; 20-21; 25-26; 30; 34. 13,1. 14,2-3; 8; 10-12; 19-21; 24; 30; 33-34; 36; 43; 45. 15,1. 16,4; 6-8. 17,2; 5; 7; 11; 13; 15; 18. 18,1-2. 19,4-5. 21,3; 5. 22,1-2. 23,1; 4; 10; 15-16; 26-28. 24,1-2. 25,3. 26,9. 28,2. 29,1-3. 30,1. 38,1. 39,2. 42,1. 43,1; 4-5; 7-8. 44,3-5. 45,1. 47,1. 50,1. 51,1-2. 53,2-3; 6; 9. 56,3. 57,2; 9; 14; 16-17.

CAM   1,9. 3,3-6. 5,41-42. 7,7-8; 10. 9,2-3. 13,10. 14,56; 59; 75. 18,5. 21,7-8. 23,3-4; 6. 25,5. 26,18; 47; 49. 32,4; 16; 19; 23; 27; 33-40; 43-44. 40,1. 41,7; 12-13; 15.

CHS   2,8. 12,3. 27,3. FD5,3.

DBY   1,1; 4; 18; 22. 2,3. 3,5. 4,1. 6,13; 19; 86; 90. 12,1. 14,9-10. B1.

DOR   1,9; 12; 14-15; 17; 19-20; 22; 26-28; 31. 2,1. 3,2-3; 6-8; 14-16. 5,1. 6,1; 3-4. 9,1. 10,6. 11,1-2; 5; 7; 10; 15. 12,1-5; 9-11; 15. 13,1-5. 15,1. 17,2. 19,3; 7-9; 12-13. 20,1-2. 21,1. 23,1. 26,1-3; 5-11; 14; 16-22; 25-26; 28-38; 40; 43-51; 54-55; 60; 68. 27,2; 4-8. 28,2; 5. 29,1. 30,3-4. 31,1-2. 32,1-2; 5. 34,2-3; 5-12; 15.

35,1. 36,2-7; 10-11. 37,2; 4; 9-11. 38,1-2. 39,1. 40,2-4; 6; 9. 41,5. 43,1. 44,1. 46,1-2. 47,1-5; 7; 9-10; 12. 48,1. 49,1-5; 9-11; 14-16. 50,2; 4. 51,1. 52,1. 53,1-2. 54,1; 3; 5; 9; 12. 55,2; 4; 16-17; 19-20; 22; 29-30; 33; 41-43. 56,1-2; 7-8; 10; 12-15; 17; 27-29; 31-33; 37-38; 40; 42; 47-48; 55; 57; 59; 61-62. 57,1-4; 10-13; 17. 58,1-3.

GLS   W12.

HAM   2,1-2; 7; 10; 14; 19; 21; 23. 3,8; 11; 25-27. 6,4; 6; 12; 16. 16,4-5. 21,2; 5; 9. 23,1; 3; 10; 12; 35; 39; 44; 46; 48; 50; 53; 55; 57-58. 27,1-2. 28,1-2; 5-6. 29,12; 15-16. 32,2. 34,1. 36,1. 43,1. 44,1. 45,8. 47,3. 55,2. 60,1. 68,10. 69,3; 19; 21-22; 28; 34. NF10,5. IoW6,19. IoW9,1; 3.

HRT   5,2; 6; 9. 8,1. 9,2-4; 6-7. 14,1. 15,3; 5; 8; 12. 20,7. 21,2. 23,1. 25,2. 28,7. 31,3. 32,2. 33,1-2; 8. 34,3; 14-15. 36,4; 11. 37,5; 11; 15. 39,1. 42,6-7.

HUN   2,3; 5-6. 6,14; 16. 7,7. 8,3-4. 9,4. 19,4; 6-7; 23.

KEN   5,108. 9,4.

LEC   3,7-9; 12; 15. 4,1. 6,2. 7,2. 8,2. 10,8-9; 11-13. 13,2-4; 6-7; 10; 12-13; 15-21; 23-33; 35-37; 39-46; 48-67; 69-73. 15,10; 16. 16,5. 17,1; 15. 19,1. 20,2-3. 21,2. 23,1-2; 4-5. 25,3-5. 41,1-2. 42,7.

LIN   1,1-4; 14; 26-29; 31; 34. 2,40-41. 4,77; 79. 7,7; 45-46; 49-50; 54. 8,10; 18; 32. 9,1-2. 11,1-2; 7. 12,60; 63-64; 67; 73; 83-84; 92. 13,4; 6; 10; 14-15; 35-36. 14,98. 16,49. 18,30. 19,1. 21,1. 22,16. 24,3; 20; 38-39; 47; 73; 76; 97; 99; 101; 104-105. 26,26-27; 29; 34; 50. 29,33. 30,23; 26. 31,11; 13-18. 32,24-25. 33,2. 34,25. 35,17. 37,7. 44,18. 45,4. 48,14-15. 56,5-6; 9-10; 14-16. 57,26; 36; 51. 58,8. 59,3; 19. 61,6-7. 63,8; 16; 18-20; 22-23. 65,1-4. 67,1; 3; 25. 68,4.

MDX   2,1-3. 3,1-3; 6-8; 13; 15-16; 18-22; 28; 30. 4,1-4; 6-12. 5,1-2. 6,1. 7,1-8. 8,1; 3-4; 6. 9,1-2; 4-9. 10,1-2. 11,1-4. 12,1-2. 14,2. 15,1-2. 16,1. 17,1. 18,1-2. 19,1. 25,1-2.

NTH   1,10; 25. 4,32-33. 18,81. 39,4-5.

NTT   3,1. 9,75; 85. 10,33; 62.

OXF   1,7b. 3,1. 6,1b; 2-3; 5; 12; 14. '7,2-3; 9; 11; 15; 19; 23-24; 29; 31; 35; 39-40; 48-49; 51; 57; 60. 9,3; 7-9a. 12,1. 15,1-2. 16,1. 17,2; 5-6. 20,2; 6. 23,1-2. 27,5. 28,2; 4; 7; 9-10; 14; 16; 19; 21; 24-25; 28. 29,1; 4; 6; 11-12; 21-22. 30,1. 32,1. 34,1-2. 35,1; 4; 13; 16-17; 20; 22; 31. 36,1. 39,2. 42,1. 44,1. 52,1. 55,2. 58,1; 3; 5; 15-16; 18; 20; 23-24; 26-27; 32; 35. 59,1-3; 9; 16-19; 26.

SOM   1,18; 33. 3,2. 4,1.

5,1-2; 4; 14; 22; 24; 26-28; 42-43; 49-52; 55; 60; 62; 69. 6,2; 17. 7,5-7; 9; 13. 8,13; 24; 29; 32. 9,6. 13,1. 18,4. 19,1; 5; 26; 28; 45; 52-53; 55; 60; 64; 69; 74-75; 86-87. 20,1. 21,20; 22; 55. 24,18; 30-31; 37. 25,30; 54-55. 26,2; 5. 28,1. 37,12. 39,2. 44,3. 45,1; 6-7; 14; 18. 46,10. 47,14; 17; 19; 21; 23.

STS   1,29; 47. 2,2. 7,7-8; 13; 18. 11,45. 12,30.

SRY   1,2-4. 2,4. 5,1d; 7; 13; 21; 23; 27. 6,4. 8,6; 12; 20; 28; 30. 10,1. 12,1. 13,1. 19,16. 21,3. 22,1; 5. 30,2. 33,1.

SSX   2,1a; 5; 8. 3,3; 7-9. 5,2. 6,1. 8,1. 8a,1. 10,2-3; 8; 12; 15-16; 19; 24; 29; 33; 42-43; 46; 48; 74; 82; 86; 88-89; 91; 94; 118. 11,3; 5; 8-9; 11; 14; 16; 24; 28; 32; 48-52; 56; 62-63; 65-69; 71-76; 78-81; 83-87; 89; 92; 102-104; 106-110; 112. 12,7-9; 11-16; 18-21; 23; 26-27; 33-34; 41-42; 49; 51. 13,8; 29; 39; 43. 14,2.

WAR   3,7. 4,1; 4; 6. 6,13. 15,5. 16,18-19; 58; 60; 62; 66. 17,5; 7-8; 14; 23; 33; 37; 44; 47. 18,5. 19,4; 6. 20,1. 22,22. 23,1. 28,12-13. 30,1. 32,1. 34,1. 39,4. 42,3. 44,12.

WIL   1,6; 9; 12-14; 20-22; 23a,c,g,j. 2,1-5; 7-12. 3,1-5. 4,1-2. 5,1; 3-4; 7. 6,2. 7,1-4; 6; 8-12; 14-16. 8,1-2; 8-9; 11-13. 10,2-3; 5. 11,1. 12,3-6. 13,1-5; 7-14; 16; 18-19. 14,1-2. 15,2. 16,1-4; 6-7. 17,1. 18,1-2. 19,1-2. 20,1-5. 21,1-2. 22,4; 6. 23,1-2; 4-5; 7-9. 24,1-6; 8; 10-13; 18-19; 21; 23-25; 28; 31; 35; 37; 41-42. 25,2-4; 8; 11-12; 15; 18-20; 24; 26-27. 26,1-5; 8-14; 16-19; 21. 27,1-3; 6-14; 16; 18-20; 22; 24. 28,3-5; 7-11. 29,2-7; 9. 30,1; 3-6. 32,1-4; 7-9; 11; 13; 17. 33,1. 34,1. 36,1-2. 37,2; 4-8; 10; 12-13. 38,1. 39,2. 40,1. 41,1; 3; 5; 8. 42,1-2; 5-6; 9-10. 43,1-2. 48,1-3; 5; 7-12. 49,1-2. 50,2-5. 51,1. 52,1. 53,1. 54,1. 55,1. 56,1-2; 4. 57,1. 58,2. 59,1. 60,1; 63,1. 66,2-4; 7. 67,2-3; 5-10; 13-18; 21-23; 25; 36-39; 42-44; 46; 49; 60-63; 67; 69-70; 73-74; 77; 79; 84-86; 89-91; 94-95; 97-98. 68,2; 4; 6; 11-12; 14-15; 18; 22; 24-26; 29.

YKS   C22-26; 28; 30-34. 1Y1-5; 7-19. 1N5; 7-31; 33-42; 44-48; 50-60; 62-82; 84-85; 87; 89-96; 98-137. 1E1; 3-4; 6-12; 14-25; 28-34; 36-37; 40-42; 44-60. 1W1-26; 29-39; 42-52; 54-55. 2,1-2. 2B1; 3-6; 8-19. 2N2-6; 14; 19-27. 2W1-9; 12. 2E1-2; 4-9; 11-12; 14-19; 21-23; 27; 29-30; 36; 38; 41. 3Y1-2; 4-5; 8-18. 4N1-3. 4E1-2. 5N1; 4; 6-30; 32; 45-48; 50; 52-54; 58-62; 65-67; 73; 75. 5E1; 3-5; 7-8; 10-11; 13-15; 18-21; 23; 27; 29-32; 34-36; 38-40; 42-44; 55; 65-66; 68; 72. 5W1; 3; 6-7; 10-13; 15-18; 20-30; 32; 36; 38. 6N1; 4; 16; 19-20; 22-37; 39; 42-50; 52-68; 70; 72; 75-88;

90-103; 105-110; 113; 116; 118-132; 134-141; 143-152; 161-162. 6W1-5. 6E1. 7E1. 8N1-2; 4; 6-9; 11-19; 21-23. 9W1-5; 7-18; 20-22; 25; 27-29; 31-35; 39-40; 44-46; 52; 54-57; 59-74; 76-87; 89-90; 92-101; 107-108; 115-116; 119-144. 10W1-2; 5-6; 8-17; 19-20; 22-32; 34-35; 37; 39-43. 11E1-5. 11N1; 3-7; 9; 14-18; 24. 11W1-4. 12W1. 13W1-28; 30-38. 13E1-2; 4-7; 9-16. 13N1-5; 7-19. 14E1-2; 4-5; 8; 11; 15-16; 24; 27; 32; 42; 48; 54. 15E1-6; 8-17. 16E1-5. 16N1-2. 16W1-6. 17W1. 18W2-3. 19W2-3. 20E1-4. 21E1-10; 12. 21W1-3; 5-6; 8-14. 22W1-2. 23N1-21; 23-36. 23E1-19. 24W1-2; 4-7; 9-16; 18-21. 24E1. 25W3; 5; 24; 27. 27W1-2. 28W1; 5-29; 31-40. 29W1-7; 9-13; 15-22; 24-38. 29E1-15; 17-30. 29N1-13. SN,CtA45.

more 1086 than BDF 1,1a; 2-3. 2,1; 4-7; number of hides/ 9. 3,3-8; 10-13; 15-carucates/sulungs in 17. 4,1-2; 6. 6,2. 1086 (or TRE if no 8,1-3; 7-8. 10,1. 1086 detail) 11,1. 12,1. 13,1. 15,2-5; 7. 16,1; 3-5; 7. 17,2-4. 18,1-2; 4-6. 19,1; 3. 20,1. 21,4; 8; 16. 23,1-3; 6; 8-10; 13-17; 19; 21-24; 26-27; 30; 32; 36-41; 44-46; 48; 54-55. 24,3-5; 8-10; 13-21; 23; 25-27; 30. 25,2-5; 11; 14-15. 26,2-3. 28,1-2. 29,1. 30,1. 31,1. 32,2-3; 5-6; 8-11; 13; 15. 33,2. 34,1-3. 35,1. 36,1. 37,1. 40,3. 41,2. 42,1. 44,1; 4. 46,1-2. 47,1-2. 48,2. 49,1-4. 51,1; 3. 53,2-8; 13-17; 20; 24-25; 27; 29; 31; 33; 35. 54,2; 4. 55,3; 6; 9. 56,6-7. 57,4; 6-7; 10-13; 15-19.

BRK 1,2-10; 12; 15; 18-19; 21; 24-32; 34-40; 43-45; 47. 2,1; 3. 3,1; 3. 4,1. 7,1-2; 8; 12; 15; 19-21; 27-28; 30-34; 36; 40; 42-45. 8,1. 9,1. 11,1. 13,1. 15,2. 16,1-2. 17,1; 3; 5-8; 10-11. 18,1-2. 20,2-3. 21,1; 3; 5-8; 13; 16-18; 20; 22. 22,1-3; 5. 24,1. 25,1. 26,1; 3. 28,3. 29,1. 31,6. 33,3-4; 6. 34,1-4. 35,2-3; 5. 36,1-2. 37,1. 38,1; 3-6. 39,1. 40,1. 41,5-6. 43,1. 44,3-4. 45,1. 46,1; 3-6. 48,1. 49,2. 50,1. 51,1. 52,1. 53,1. 54,1; 4. 55,2. 58,1-2. 60,1. 61,1-2. 62,1. 63,1-5. 64,2. 65,1; 4-5; 7; 11-13; 15-17; 19.

BKM 1,2; 6-7. 2,2. 3,1-2. 3a,1; 4-6. 4,4; 6; 10-13; 15; 17; 20; 22-23; 28-29; 41. 5,4-5; 7; 10; 14; 18; 20. 6,1. 7,1. 8,1-3. 12,4; 7-8; 10; 27; 29; 36-38. 13,2. 14,4-6; 9; 13; 15-17; 25-26; 32; 35; 38; 40-42; 46-47; 49. 15,2. 16,1-2; 10. 17,3-4; 9-10; 16-17; 20; 22; 26-29. 19,1-3; 6. 20,1. 21,1-2. 23,12; 14; 18-19; 22; 25; 29; 31-32. 24,3. 25,1-2. 26,1-3; 10-11. 27,1. 28,3. 29,4. 31,1. 33,1. 36,1-3. 37,1. 39,1. 40,1. 41,1-4; 6-7. 43,2; 6. 44,1-2. 46,1. 48,1. 49,1. 51,3. 52,1-2. 53,1; 4-5; 7. 54,1. 55,1. 56,1-2. 57,1; 5-7; 10; 13; 18.

CAM 1,1-8; 11-12; 14; 17-20. 2,1-4. 4,1. 5,1; 3-15; 18-20; 23; 25;

28-29; 31; 34; 36-38; 44-48; 50-54; 57; 59-63. 6,1. 7,2-5; 9; 11. 8,1. 9,1. 10,1. 11,1; 3-4. 12,1; 3-4. 13,1-2; 4; 6-9; 11-12. 14,1-3; 5-11; 13-17; 20-24; 26-34; 36; 39-44; 46; 48-51; 53; 55; 58; 61-74; 77-78; 80-81. 15,1-4. 16,1. 17,1-5. 18,1-3; 6-8. 19,1-2; 4. 20,1. 21,1; 3; 5-6. 22,1; 3-4; 6-8; 10. 23,1-2. 24,1. 25,1; 3-4; 7-8. 26,3; 5; 9-10; 17; 19; 21-24; 26-35; 37-45; 48; 51-53; 55. 28,1-2. 29,1-4; 6-10. 30,1-3. 31,1-4; 7. 32,1-3; 5-8; 10-15; 18; 20-23; 26; 30-31. 33,1. 35,1-2. 36,1. 37,1-2. 38,1-3. 39,1-2. 41,1; 3-5; 9-10. 42,1. 44,1-2.

CHS B3-5; 8-9. A2-5; 7; 9-10; 12-14; 16-22. 1,1-4; 6-10; 12-21; 23; 25-28; 30-36. 2,1-7; 9-12; 14-20; 24-25; 27-31. 3,1-11. 4,1-2. 5,1-14. 6,1. 7,1-4. 8,1-4; 7-12; 14-19; 21-45. 9,1-2; 4-20; 22; 24-25; 28-29. 10,4. 11,1-8. 12,2; 4-8. 13,1-5; 7. 14,1-2; 4-13. 17,1-4; 6-9; 11. 18,1-6. 19,1; 3. 20,1; 3-6; 8-12. 21,1. 22,1-2. 23,1-3. 24,1-3; 5-6; 8-9. 25,1-3. 26,1-4; 6-12. 27,1-2; 4. FD1,1. FD2,1; 4. FD5,1. FD7,2. FD8,1. FT3,1. R1,3.

CON 1,2-12; 14-19. 2,1-11. 3,1-6. 4,1-20; 23-27; 29. 5,1,1-18; 20-22. 5,2,1-33. 5,3,1-28. 5,4,1-20. 5,5,1-22. 5,6,1-10. 5,7,1-13. 5,8,1-10. 5,9,1-4. 5,10,1. 5,11,1-7. 5,12,1-3. 5,13,1-12. 5,14,1-6. 5,15,1-16. 5,16,1-2. 5,17,1-4. 5,18,1. 5,19,1. 5,20,1-2. 5,21,1. 5,22,1. 5,23,1-5. 5,24,1-5; 7-23; 25. 5,25,1-5. 5,26,1-4. 6,1. 7,1.

DBY 1,5; 9-11; 13; 16; 19-20; 24; 26; 38. 3,1; 3-4. 5,1-2; 4-5. 6,1; 14; 24-25; 27; 29-30; 35; 38-39; 41; 43-44; 46-47; 50; 52-53; 56; 60; 63-65; 76; 78; 88-89; 91-92; 94-97; 99. 7,1; 3; 13. 8,1-6. 9,1; 4. 10,1-2; 4-8; 10-14; 19-21; 23; 27. 11,2-5. 12,3-4. 13,1. 14,2; 5. 16,3-8. 17,1-2; 4-6; 8-10; 12; 15; 18-19; 22. B3.

DEV 1,3-6; 8-13; 15-72. 2,2-24. 3,4-31; 33-70; 72-99. 4,1. 5,1-9; 11-14. 6,1-5; 7-12. 7,1-4. 8,1. 10,1-2. 11,1-3. 12,1. 13,1. 13a,2-3. 14,1-4. 15,2-15; 17-79. 16,3-176. 17,3-107. 18,1. 19,2-31; 33; 35-46. 20,1-17. 21,1-4; 6-21. 22,1-2. 23,1-4; 6-26. 24,1-32. 25,1-28. 26,1. 27,1. 28,1-16. 29,1-9. 30,1-3. 31,1-4. 32,1-10. 33,1-2. 34,1-16; 18-55; 57. 35,1-5; 7-30. 36,1-26. 37,1. 38,1-2. 39,1-21. 40,1-7. 41,1-2. 42,1-24. 43,1-5. 44,1-2. 45,2-3. 46,1-2. 47,1-14. 48,1-12. 49,1-3; 5-7. 50,1-2; 4-5. 51,1-16. 52,1-29; 31-38; 40-53.

DOR 1,7-8; 18; 21; 23-25. 2,3-4; 6. 3,5; 9-10; 13. 8,1-3; 6. 10,2-3; 5. 11,4; 6; 16-17. 12,14; 16. 13,6-7. 16,1. 19,2; 4; 6; 10. 22,1. 24,2; 5. 26,4; 23; 39; 58-59; 61-65; 69. 27,10. 28,1; 4; 7. 32,3-4. 35,1; 6. 34,1; 4; 14. 37,7; 13-14. 40,1; 8. 41,1. 45,1. 49,12. 54,7; 13-14. 55,25; 31;

35-36; 40; 46. 56,3-5; 18-19; 44; 46; 51; 58; 64; 66. 57,8-9; 20.

GLS   W11.

HAM   1,1; 3-6; 8; 12-16; 18-20; 24-26; 28-30; 32; 35-36; 39-40; 42; 45-46; W2-4; W6-21. 2,3-5; 8-9; 11; 16; 18; 20; 22; 24-25. 3,1-3; 5-7; 9-10; 12-13; 16; 18-22. 5,1. 6,3; 5; 8-9; 11; 13-15; 17. 7,1. 9,1. 10,1. 11,1. 13,1. 14,1-6. 15,1; 3-5. 16,1; 3; 6. 17,2-3. 18,1-3. 19,1. 20,1. 21,1; 6-7. 22,1. 23,4-9; 11; 13-14; 17-29; 32; 34; 36; 38; 40-42; 45; 47; 49; 51-52; 56; 59; 68. 24,1. 25,1. 26,1. 28,7-8. 29,1-8; 10-11; 13-14; 16. 30,1. 31,1. 32,1. 33,1. 35,1-4; 6-9. 37,1. 38,1. 39,1-3; 5. 40,1. 41,1. 42,1. 43,4-6. 44,3-4. 45,1; 3-6. 46,1. 47,2. 48,1. 49,1. 50,1. 51,1. 52,1. 53,1-2. 54,1. 55,1. 56,1-3. 57,2. 58,1. 60,2. 61,1. 62,1-2. 64,1. 65,1. 66,1. 67,1. 68,1-3; 5-6. 69,1-2; 5; 8-9; 11-18; 20; 23-24; 27; 29; 31-32; 35; 37-38; 40-43; 45-48; 50; 52-54. NF1,1. NF2,1-3. NF3,2; 4; 8-16. NF4,1. NF5,1. NF8,1. NF9,2-7; 9-11; 13; 21; 24-32; 34; 36-38; 40-41; 43-45. NF10,1-3. IoW1,1-5; 7-10; 12-15. IoW2,1. IoW3,1. IoW5,1. IoW6,1; 3-6; 8-9; 12; 15-17; 22. IoW7,1-8; 10-15; 17-21; 23. IoW8,1; 3-12. IoW9,2; 5-6; 8; 10-12; 16-20; 22-24.

HEF   1,64-65. 6,1; 8. 7,1-2; 4. 9,13. 10,38; 43; 52; 62; 65; 72. 14,9. 24,3; 6. 25,7; 9. 29,15. 30,1-2.

HRT   1,1-18. 2,1-3; 5. 3,1. 4,2-20; 22-25. 5,3-4; 7-8; 10; 13-24; 26. 6,1. 7,1-3. 8,2-3. 9,5; 8-10. 10,2-12; 14-16; 18-20. 11,1. 12,1. 13,3; 5. 14,2. 15,1-2; 10-11; 13. 16,1-7; 9-12. 17,1-3; 5-9; 11-13; 15. 19,1-2. 20,1-5; 8-13. 21,1. 22,1-2. 23,2-4. 24,1-3. 25,1. 26,1. 27,1. 28,1; 3-6; 8. 29,1. 30,1-2. 31,1; 5-8. 32,1. 33,3; 5-7; 9-12; 14-18; 20. 34,1-2; 4-7; 9-12; 16-22; 24-25. 35,1-3. 36,1-3; 5-9; 12; 14-18. 37,2; 4; 6-9; 12-14; 16-23. 38,1-2. 41,1-2. 42,1-3; 5; 8-14. 42a,1. 43,1. 44.1.

HUN   1,1-3; 5-7; 9-10. 2,1-2; 8-9. 4,2-3. 5,1. 6,1-5; 7-13; 15; 20; 23-26. 7,1-6. 8,1-2. 9,1-3. 10,1. 11,1-2. 13,1-3. 14,1. 16,1. 17,1. 19,1-3; 5; 8; 12; 14-15; 19-22; 29-32. 20,1-3; 5-8. 21,1. 22,1-2. 23,1. 24,1. 25,1-2. 28,1. 29,1; 3; 5-6.

KEN   1,1-2; 4. 2,4; 7-17; 19-20; 22-23; 25-26; 31-33; 41-43. 3,2-8; 11-14; 16; 19-22. 4,1-2; 5-14; 16. 5,2; 4; 10-11; 13-19; 21; 30-33; 36; 39; 41-43; 46-47; 49; 51-54; 58-60; 62-64; 66-68; 70-83; 86; 88-89; 91; 93; 95-98; 102; 104-105; 109; 111-112; 114-115; 118-124; 126-129; 138-139; 141-142; 144-149; 151-156; 159; 162-168; 170-172; 175-177; 179-180; 208; 220; 224-225. 6,1. 7,2-3; 5-9; 12; 15; 17-21; 23; 26-29. 8,1. 9,1; 3; 5-6; 10-14; 16-17; 19-

22; 24-25; 28-32; 37; 41-42; 45-50. 10,2. 11,1-2. 12,1; 3-4.

LEC   3,2. 5,1-2. 7,1. 10,1; 10. 11,1. 13,1-2; 5; 8; 11; 22. 15,9; 12-13. 17,10. 20,1. 22,1. 23,3; 6. 25,1-2. 39,2. 41,3. 42,8.

LIN   1,5; 10-12; 15; 35; 38-39; 65-66; 80-81; 90-91; 106. 2,1-25; 27-28; 37-38; 42. 3,1-11; 13-14; 16-17; 19-21; 23; 27-28; 30-33; 35-37; 39-42; 47-48; 50-54. 4,2; 5; 7-8; 10-23; 26-28; 30-54; 56-69; 71-75; 78. 5,1; 3. 7,8; 11; 14; 16; 18-29; 40; 53; 57-58. 8,2; 9; 16-17; 19-20; 22-23; 27; 29-31. 12,1-2; 4; 7-10; 14-15; 17; 19-21; 23-40; 42-45; 51; 57; 68-71; 81-82; 85; 87-88; 93; 96. 13,1-3; 5; 8-9; 13; 17-19; 21; 23-24; 26; 28-33; 38-39; 41-44. 14,1-6; 8-18; 23-24; 26; 29-35; 38-40; 43-46; 49; 51; 54; 58-60; 62; 64-65; 80-81; 84-86; 92; 101. 15,1-2. 16,1-14; 16; 18-20; 22-24; 27-28; 30; 33; 35-36; 38-41; 43-45; 50. 17,1-2. 18,3; 7-10; 20; 22; 24; 31-32. 20,2. 22,1; 3-8; 10-12; 14; 18-19; 21-26; 28-29; 31-36; 38. 23,1. 24,1; 7; 10-11; 13-15; 17-18; 21; 24; 26; 37; 41-44; 54-59; 61-62; 64; 66-72; 86-90; 93; 95; 100; 102-103. 25,1-3; 5-14; 17-22; 25. 26,1; 4-5; 7-11; 14-18; 20-21; 23-25; 33; 35; 37; 39-45; 47-49; 53-54. 27,1-10; 12; 14-15; 19-27; 29-33; 43; 48; 50; 56; 59-61; 63-64. 28,1-2; 7; 11-13; 15-16; 19-21; 23-25; 27-31; 33; 35-39; 43. 29,1-5; 7; 9; 11; 14-15; 22; 29; 32. 30,1-2; 5-21; 27; 33; 36. 31,2; 4-5; 10. 32,1-9; 12; 19-23; 26; 28-29; 31. 34,1-23; 27. 35,1-2; 4; 6-10; 16. 36,1-3. 37,3-5. 38,1; 3; 5-6; 10-12; 14. 39,1-2. 40,1-10; 12; 15-18; 21-23; 25-26. 41,1-2. 42,7; 10; 18. 43,1; 3; 6. 44,1-2; 4-5; 7-12; 15-16. 45,1-3. 46,1; 3-4. 47,1-10. 48,1-2; 4-5; 9-13. 49,2; 4-6. 50,1. 51,12. 54,1. 55,1-3. 56,2; 8; 11-13; 17-18; 22-23. 57,1-3; 6-8; 15-16; 18-19; 21; 23; 27-30; 32-34; 41-42; 46-47; 53. 58,1-2; 4; 6-7. 59,20. 61,9. 63,1-2; 5; 7; 10. 64,9-10; 14; 18-19. 66,1-2. 67,7-8; 24. 68,5; 8; 13-14; 26-27; 30-33; 39-46; 48.

MDX   3,4; 23-24. 4,5. 20,1. 24,1.

NTH   1,1; 2a-f; 3-4; 7-9; 11-13a,d; 14; 15a,l; 16-21; 23-24; 26-32. 2,1-8; 10-12. 3,1. 4,3-30; 34; 36. 5,1-4. 6,1-5; 7-10a,c; 11-17. 6a,2; 4-6; 10-16; 20; 22-29; 31-33. 7,1-2. 8,1-2; 4-10; 13. 9,1; 4-6. 10,1-2. 11,1; 3-6. 12,1-4. 13,1. 14,1-6. 16,1. 17,2-3. 18,1-7; 9-80; 82-93; 95-99. 19,1-2. 20,1. 21,1-21. 22,1-9. 23,1-19. 24,1. 25,1-3. 26,1-11. 27,1. 28,1-3. 29,1. 30,1-6; 8; 10-17. 31,1. 32,1. 33,1. 34,1. 35,1a-f,i; 2; 3a-f; 4-10; 12-18; 19a-g; 21-25. 36,1-2; 4. 38,1. 39,1-2; 6-18. 40,1-6. 41,1-6; 8-10. 42,1-3. 43,1-11. 44,1a-c; 2. 45,1-9. 46,1-7. 47,1a-c; 2. 48,1-12; 14-17.

49,1. 50,1. 51,1. 52,1. 53,1. 54,1-3. 55,1-6. 56,1; 7-8; 12; 15-19; 20a-f,h-j; 21-27; 29-43; 45-52; 56; 57h; 58-61; 64-66. 57,1-4. 58,1-2. 59,2-4. 60,1-5.
NTT   1,1-7; 9-18; 20-21; 23; 27-29; 31-32; 34-43; 51-56; 58-59; 61-63. 2,1-4; 6-10. 3,2-4. 4,1-3; 5-8. 5,1; 3-16; 18. 6,1-15. 7,1-6. 8,1-2. 9,1-8; 10-20; 22-24; 26-46; 49-57; 59-62; 64-67; 69-74; 76-84; 88-89; 95-103; 106-111; 113-119; 121-131. 10,1-5; 7-10; 13-14; 16; 18; 20; 22; 25; 29-30; 34; 38; 46; 50; 55-61; 64-65. 11,1-12; 14; 18-20; 22-33. 12,1-2; 4; 7-9; 11-13; 15-20; 23. 13,1-2; 4; 6-11; 13. 14,1-5; 7-8. 15,1-2; 4; 8. 16,1-11. 17,1-5; 7-18. 18,1-7. 19,1. 20,1-3; 5-8. 21,1-3. 22,1-2. 23,1-2. 24,1-3. 25,1-2. 26,1. 27,1-2. 28,1-2. 30,1-15; 19-25; 36-41; 43; 45-49; 54-56.
OXF   1,9. 2,1. 3,2. 6,6-9; 13; 15; 17. 7,1; 5-6; 8; 12; 20-22; 25-27; 30; 32; 34; 36-37; 41; 44-47; 50; 52-53; 56; 58-59. 8,2-4. 9,1; 5; 10. 10,1. 13,1. 14,1; 4. 15,3; 5. 17,3. 18,1-2. 19,1. 20,1; 3; 5; 7-10. 22,1. 24,1; 4. 26,1. 27,1-3; 7; 10. 28,1; 3; 13; 15; 17-18; 23; 26. 29,2-3; 5; 7-9; 15-16; 18-19; 23. 31,1. 32,2. 33,1. 35,2-3; 6-11; 18-19; 25-26; 28. 37,1. 38,1-2. 39,1. 40,1; 3. 41,1. 43,1-2. 45,2-3. 46,1. 47,1. 49,1. 50,1. 51,1. 53,1-2. 54,1. 55,1. 56,1-4. 58,2; 4; 7-8; 10; 12; 25; 30-31; 36-37. 59,5-6; 10-15; 20; 25; 27-28.
RUT   R1-2; 5-17; 19-21.
SHR   1,5. 3e,1. 3f,4-5. 4,1,5-6; 8; 12; 33. 4,3,32-41; 43; 47; 59; 71. 4,4,2; 9; 20. 4,5,3; 6. 4,9,4. 4,11,4; 9-10; 14; 17-19. 4,12,1. 4,14,1-5; 7-17; 19-29. 4,15,1-3. 4,16,2. 4,17,1-3. 4,18,1-3. 4,19,2-13. 4,20,1-3; 5-9; 12-27. 4,21,1-6; 8-19. 4,22,1-3. 4,23,1-5; 8-13; 15-18. 4,24,1-4. 4,25,1-4; 6-7. 4,26,3-7. 4,27,1-4; 6; 8-13; 15; 17-35. 4,28,1-3; 6. 5,1-7; 9. 6,1-2; 5-27; 29-31. 7,1; 3-6. 8,1-2. 9,1-2.
SOM   1,6; 11-17; 19; 21; 23; 25-30; 34. 2,1; 9-11. 5,3; 5-8; 11-13; 16-17; 19; 21; 23; 30; 32-36; 39-41; 45; 47; 53; 57-59; 61; 63-65; 68; 70. 6,1; 3-9; 11-15. 7,2; 4; 10-12. 8,1-2; 4-9; 11-12; 14; 16-17; 20-22; 27-28; 33-35. 9,2; 7. 10,1-2; 4-5. 11,1. 12,1. 16,2-4; 7-8; 13. 17,1-4; 7. 18,1-3. 19,4; 7; 9; 11-16; 20-22; 29-30; 34-35; 38-43; 57-58; 63; 66-67; 70; 76-78; 80; 83; 85. 20,2-3. 21,1-17; 19; 21; 23-37; 39-53; 56-79; 81-87; 89-93; 95-96; 98. 22,1-2; 4-22; 25-26. 23,1. 24,1-5; 7-9; 11-17; 19; 21-29; 32-36. 25,1-29; 31-44; 46-47; 49-53; 55. 26,8. 27,1-3. 29,1. 30,1-2. 31,1-5. 32,1-8. 33,1. 35,1-8; 10-15; 18-22. 36,2; 4; 7; 10; 13. 37,2-9. 38,1. 39,1; 3. 41,1-3. 42,1. 43,1. 44,1-2. 45,2-3; 8-13; 15. 46,1; 3-9; 11-15; 17-18; 21-23; 25. 47,1; 4-9; 11-13; 15-16; 18; 20; 24.

STS   1,1-2; 4; 6-13; 16-28; 30-36; 38-46. 2,1; 5; 15-16. 3,1. 4,1-8; 10. 5,1-2. 6,1. 7,1-6; 9-10; 17. 8,1-15; 17-28; 30; 32. 10,3-6; 8-9. 11,1-2; 4-6; 8-32; 34-44; 47; 49-50; 52-60; 62-63; 65-68. 12,1-3; 5-23; 26; 29. 13,1-8. 14,1-2. 15,1. 16,1. 17,2-3; 8-16; 18-21.
SRY   1,5; 8; 11-14. 2,1-3; 5-6. 4,1-2. 5,1a,c; 2-3; 5; 8; 11; 22. 6,3; 5. 7,1. 8,1-3; 9; 13-14; 17; 21-22; 25; 29. 11,1. 14,1. 15,1-2. 16,1. 17,1; 4. 18,2-3. 19,1-8; 10-12; 15; 17; 19-20; 23-24; 26; 29; 31-32; 35-39; 44-48. 20,1-2. 21,4; 6-7. 24,1. 25,1-3. 26,1. 27,1-3. 29,1-2. 30,1. 31,1. 32,2. 34,1. 35,2. 36,1; 5-10.
SSX   1,2. 2,2; 9. 3,2. 4,1. 5,1; 3. 7,1. 9,1-11; 14-19; 21-24; 26; 29-30; 34-35; 37-39; 52; 55; 60; 82-83; 96; 99; 103-111; 120-123; 125. 10,7; 10; 18; 20-22; 26-28; 30-32; 35-39; 45; 49-53; 56; 59-68; 76; 78; 81; 83; 90; 92-93; 95-97; 99-106; 108-117. 11,4; 6-7; 10; 12-13; 18-21; 23; 25-26; 29-31; 37; 40; 44; 54-55; 59; 70; 93-94; 96; 98-100; 111; 113. 12,3-6; 22; 30-32; 36-37; 39-40; 43-44; 47-48; 54-55. 13,1; 5-7; 9-15; 17; 19-20; 22-23; 25; 27-28; 30; 33-35; 38; 42; 46-50; 53; 56. 14,1.
WAR   1,1; 6-7. 2,1-3. 3,1-3; 5-6. 4,2-3. 5,1. 6,1-8; 10-12. 14-20. 7,1. 8,1. 9,1. 11,1-5. 12,1-11.́ 13,1. 14,2-6. 15,1-4; 6. 16,1-3; 5-9; 11-17; 20-26; 28-31; 33; 35-48; 52; 54; 57; 59; 61; 63. 17,1-3; 6; 9; 12-13; 15; 17-22; 25; 27-29; 32; 34-36; 38-40; 43; 49-50; 52-54; 56-57; 59; 61-62; 64; 66-70. 18,1; 6-9; 11; 13-15. 19,1-3; 5. 22,1-7; 9-10; 12-13; 15-17; 19; 21; 23-26. 23,2. 24,1-2. 25,1. 26,1. 27,1-6. 28,1; 3; 6-11; 15-17; 19. 29,1-5. 30,2. 31,1-8; 10-11. 33,1. 35,1. 36,1-2. 37,1-6. 38,1-2. 39,1-3. 40,1-2. 41,1-2. 42,1. 43,1-2. 44,2-11; 14.
WIL   1,10-11; 16-19; 23h. 2,6. 5,6. 6,1. 8,3-6; 10. 11,2. 12,2. 13,20. 15,1. 19,4. 20,6. 21,3. 22,1; 3. 23,10. 24,13; 17; 20; 22; 26; 29-30; 33-34; 38. 25,5; 17; 22-23; 25. 26,15; 20. 27,5; 15; 17; 25-27. 28,2. 29,1; 8. 30,7. 32,5-6; 10; 12; 14-15. 37,1; 3; 11; 15. 39,1. 41,2; 7; 10. 42,4; 8. 45,1; 3. 46,1. 47,1. 48,6. 50,1. 53,2. 56,6. 58,1. 64,1. 66,5-6. 67,1; 28; 32; 35; 41; 45; 48; 50-51; 56; 59; 65; 68; 80; 83; 87. 68,3; 7-9; 17; 19-20; 27.
WOR   21,2.
YKS   1N61. 2E20. 3Y3. 5E56; 71. 5W2; 8-9; 19; 33; 35. 6N1; 111. 9W19; 23; 36; 38; 42; 48; 50-51; 109. 10W4; 7; 33; 36; 38. 14E1-2; 6-7; 11; 20; 37; 49; 53. 18W1. 19W1. 21E7. 22W4. 25W30. 28W3. SN,CtA45.
same 1086 as
number of hides/
carucates/sulungs in

BDF   1,3; 5. 2,2-3; 8. 3,1-2; 14. 4,3; 5; 8. 6,1. 7,1. 8,5; 9. 13,2.

See also: Harbour; Market; Ship.

PORTER (portarius)

	DEV	51,1.
	GLS	*1,59-60*.
	HAM	68,7-8.
	KEN	*C1*.
	SOM	19,38.
	SFK	14,167.

POSSESSION

Based on

dying declaration of holder	BDF	17,5.
predecessor ploughing land	BRK	1,37.

Delivered of land as a
manor · · · · · · · · · · · · · LIN 57,56.

Given

because land held by free men	SFK	77,4.
dwelling, of	SFK	38,3.
free men, of	SFK	16,34.
King's seal, by	HRT	1,9.
	NFK	58,3.
	WOR	*2,72*.
	YKS	C2.

King's seal, by,
after dis-possession · · LIN CK10.

King and his
deliverer, through · · BDF 17,1.

land, of	BDF	24,14.
	SFK	8,63. 39,3.

when land holder
went overseas in
King's service · · · · MDX 25,2.

unknown by whom
or how given

	ESS	24,4.
	HUN	6,17.
	NTT	30,22.

Not given

by King's
commissioner · · · · · HAM 69,16.

to land holder's
predecessor · · · · · · CAM 19,4.

Held

without writ	ESS	6,9.
	HUN	D1.
wrongfully	SRY	25,1.

King's evidence
needed to prove · · · HAM 69,16.

Obtained through
King

	BDF	17,2.
	ESS	43,1.

Regained after
disseisin · · · · · · · · DOR 34,8.

Re-possession

on breach of agreement	LIN	CK48.
following judgment	SFK	21,95.

on land holder
becoming a monk

	SFK	14,68.
	WOR	2,27.

ordered by King · · · · SOM *22,19*.

Retained against

King's right · · · · · · · OXF 29,13.

Taken of

free man	NFK	8,138.
	SFK	26,15. 32,16.

free man because of
patronage · · · · · · · · NFK 15,11.

Freeman in King's
despite · · · · · · · · · · NFK 1,195.

land

	DEV	34,34.
	ESS	79,1.
	LEC	19,6.
	LIN	CK49.
	SFK	8,55.

land of another

	NTT	20,7.
	YKS	CW17.

land without proof
of right · · · · · · · · · · CHS C10.

land by force · · · · · · KEN P20. 1,3.

land by or for King

	GLS	16,1.
	NFK	58,3.
	SFK	25,1.

land of outlaw · · · · · NFK 9,49.

land – payment for · · CHS C11.

land without King's
writ · · · · · · · · · · · · SRY 5,25-26.

man · · · · · · · · · · · · NFK 10,61.

Not witnessed · · · · · SRY 19,27. 23,1. 25,2.

by Wapentake	LIN	CK55.
by writ or officer	ESS	6,9.
	LIN	CS19.

See also: Claim; Death duty; Deliverer; Forfeiture;
Gift; Installer; Land; Ownership; Patron;
Relinquishment; Restoration; Surrender; Writ.

POSTPONEMENT (respectus)

Land held through

	CAM	5,21.
	SFK	21,45.

POTTER (potarius;
figulus)

	GLS	53,10.
	WIL	1,16.

POTTERY (ollaria;
potaria) · · · · · · · · · · OXF 7,22.

POUND (libra) · · · · · Passim.

POWER (potestas) – See Authority.

PRAYERS given
daily for King and all
Christians · · · · · · · · SFK 14,167.

See also: Mass; Psalms.

PREBEND
(prebenda)

	KEN	M1-2; 4-8; 10; 13-
		14; 18; 20-22. *1,3*.
	NTT	5,1.
	SSX	9,11. 11,8; 81.

See also: Clothing; Common; Supplies.

PREBENDARY
(prebendarius) · · · · · YKS 2W2.

King's · · · · · · · · · · · BDF ·56,9.

Payments from
city/borough for

	ESS	B6.
	NFK	1,61; 70.
	SFK	1,122g.

See also: Almswoman; Canon; Common;

Purveyor.

PREDECESSOR (antecessor)

Of 1086 chief lord/landholder	BDF	16,3. 17,2; 4. 23,2. 24,14. 25,7. 28,1. 31,1. 32,14. 40,3. 46,1.
	BRK	1,37. 31,4.
	CAM	*14,35. 18,3; 6. 19,4. 20,1; 26,9. 28,2. 29,1; 4; 6; 11. 35,1; 2.*
	DBY	B16.
	ESS	1,24-25; 71. 9,14. 10,3. 20,36; 56. 23,30. 30,3. 33,6. 34,2; 6; 10; 27-28. 35,7; 11; 13. 49,6. 90,64-65; 67-68; 85-86. B3b,e-f,t.
	GLS	31,2. 32,9. 34,8.
	HAM	2,1; 10. 23,3; 16. 33,1. 43,6. 69,16.
	HEF	1,65.
	HRT	1,6. 19,1. 21,1.
	HUN	D13.
	KEN	M18.
	LEC	14,23.
	LIN	C21. CS11, 18; 25; 27-29; 32; 34; 36-37. CN8; 18. CW5; 11; 15. CK16; 31; 35-36; 38; 44; 46; 63; 65; 67-69.
	NFK	1,57; 106; 120-121; 192; 195; 205; 208; 218; 221; 226; 239; 241. 2,1. 4,39; 53; 56. 6,7. 7,3-4; 9; 20-21. 8,8; 18; 29; 31; 33; 49; 51; 66-67; 137. 9,1; 14-15; 30; 79; 87; 99-100; 179-180; 184; 187-191; 193-194; 196-198; 200; 204; 211; 227-228; 232. 10,20; 50; 352-53; 61; 76; 93. 12,17; 34; 38; 45. 13,10; 19; 22. *15,28.* 19,36; 40. 20,7; 17; 29; 31; 36. 21,8; 14. 23,14; *16.* 24,6-7. 25,15; 25. 27,1. 28,1. 29,7-8. 31,11. 34,4; 6. 35,8; 15-16. 36,5. 44,1. 48,2; 4-6. 49,5. 50,13. 56,6. 65,16. 66,1-5; 7-9; 11-13; 16-17; 39; 44; 47-49; 66; 68; 71-72; 84-85; 87; 90; 94; 100; 106-107.
	OXF	B9.
	SHR	4,3,8; 71.
	SFK	1,14. 2,5-6; 9; 17-18; 20. 3,28; 56; 86; 89; 94-95; 98-102. 4,2; 6; 9; 13; 15; 36; 42. 5,4. 6,2-4; 8; 11; 33; 38-39; 45-47; 49; 57; 79; 82; 92; 97; 112; 159; 177; 210-211; 216-218; 227; 251; 263; 299; 301-302; 318. 7,1; 5; 13; 15-17; 19; 24-26; 30; 56; 58-60; 64-67; 71; 75; 79; 136-137; 140; 143-146; 148. 8,4; 8; 32; 35; 42; 46; 55; 59; 63. 15,4. 16,1; 8; 14-16; 20-23; 25-26; 29-30; 33; 38; 41. 19,9. 21,30; 45; 58; 83; 86. 25,18; 25; 35; 37; 51; 60; 75; 78; 103; 105; 107; 111. 26,4; 8; 12d-13. 28,2; 6. 29,1; 8. 30,2. 31,2; 15; 19; 43; 45-47. 32,1; 28. 33,1-4. 34,2-3; 12; 15. 35,2; 7. 36,5. 38,6; 11. 39,12. 41,11; 18. 43,1; 5. 44,2. 45,1. 48,1. 51,1-2. 52,1; 9. 53,1-

3; 6. 59,1. 64,1. 66,3; 11. 67,1-5; 10-11; 15; 19. 68,5. 73,1. 75,2-3; 5. 76,1-2; 4-5; 7; 13; 16; 18; 21-22. 77,2; 4.

	SRY	5,6. 8,18. 19,28.
	WOR	26,16.
	YKS	5E27. CE14. CW1; 36.
identified by name	BDF	17,2; 4. 23,2.
	BRK	1,37.
	CAM	*14,35. 18,3; 6. 20,1. 29,1; 11.*
	DBY	B16.
	ESS	23,30. 90,64; 85. B3b,e-f,t.
	GLS	31,2. 32,9. 34,8
	HAM	2,1; 10. 69,16.
	HEF	1,65.
	HRT	1,6. 19,1. 21,1.
	HUN	D13.
	LEC	14,23.
	LIN	C21. CS25; 27; 29; 34; 36. CW5; 15. CK16; 31; 35-36; 38; 44; 63; 65; 67.
	NFK	1,57; 120-121; 195; 205; 218; 226. 4,39; 53. 6,7. 7,4; 9. 8,137. 9,14-15; 30; 183; 228. 10,20; 53. 12,17. 20,1; 31. 21,8. *23,16.* 24,6. 25,25. 29,7-8. 35,8; 16. 44,1. 66,84; 94; 100.
	SHR	4,3,8; 71.
	SFK	2,5-6; 9. 3,95. 4,15; 36. 5,4. 6,2-3; 8; 57; 79; 82; 92; 97; 112; 159; 177; 210; 216; 227. 7,13; 19; 24-25; 56; 58-59; 64-66. 8,4; 8; 35; 42; 46-47; 55; 59; 63. 15,4. 16,8; 14; 16; 20-23; 25-26; 29-30; 33; 38; 41. 25,25; 35; 37; 51; 75; 78. 26,12d-13. 28,2. 29,1; 8. 31,43; 45-46. 32,1. 34,3. 35,2. 36,5. 38,6; 11. 39,12. 41,11. 43,1. 51,1. 52,1. 53,1. 64,1. 67,1-2; 5; 10-11; 15. 75,5. 76,2; 4-5; 21. 77,2-4.
	SRY	19,28.
	WOR	26,16.
	YKS	CE14. CW1; 36.
free men not belonging to Goatherd, being Land	NFK	1,120. 9,184.
	HAM	33,1.
not belonging to	BRK	58,2.
	CAM	19,4. 29,4.
	ESS	90,65.
	GLS	50,4.
	HUN	D13.
	LIN	CS19. CK31.
	NFK	8,31.
	YKS	5E27. CE14.
not given to successor	ESS	34,2.
seized by successor	ESS	34,2.
taken by successor although predecessor not entitled	ESS	34,28.

Total holding given
by King to successor BDF 28,1.
Transfer of land by
claimant's predecessor
to holder's
predecessor LIN CK63.
Without customary
due or patronage ESS 90,68.
See also: Claim; King Edward.
PRE-EMPTION – see Marten skins; Sale; Sell.
PREMISES
(occupatum) HRT B8.
PREMIUM
(gersuma) ESS 1,2-4; 19; 24. B6.
HEF 1,39; 47.
KEN 3,18.
NFK 1,11; 61; 67; 71; 85;
93-94; 133; 135; 139; 143; 150; 152; 163;
182; 185-186; 192-194; 197-199; 203.
OXF 1,12.
SFK 1,75-76; 90; 103.
9,1.
WAR B4.
See also: Gift.
PRESENTATION (presentatio)
Fish, of CAM 5,45; 48-50; 52; 56-
57. 7,11. 9,2.
32,38.
HUN 19,29.
to King CAM 1,1.
value of CAM 5,45; 47; 56-57.
7,11.
Fishery, of CAM 5,55.
PRIEST (presbiter) BDF 1,2b. 2,4. 4,4. 13,1.
14. 22,2. 23,25; 39; 55. 28,2. 40,1-2. 57,4;
19.
BRK B6-7. 1,1; 3; 7-8;
10; 14; 24; 33-34. 3,1. 7,8; 22; 29. 8,1. 15,1.
20,1. 38,6. 63,2.
BKM 2,1. 12,20. 17,22.
23,21. 57,5.
CAM B7. 1,9. 5,40.
14,16; 21; 29; 36. 18,1; 8. 26,26; 29. 29,10.
30,3. 31,3. 32,23. 41,6; 9.
CHS B3; 8-9. 1,1; 8; 22.
2,1; 25. 5,10. 8,7; 16; 30. 9,6; 17; 25. 12,2.
13,3. 14,3; 10. 17,7. 18,1. 19,1. 24,3; 5.
27,3. FT1,8. FT2,2; 7. FT3,5. R1,17; 21.
R5,6. R6,4.
CON 1,6. 4,28. 5,14,2.
5,24,18. 5,25,5.
DBY 1,9; 11; 13-14; 16;
19-20; 27; 29; 37. 2,1; 3. 4,1. 5,4. 6,6; 24-
25; 27; 30; 34; 39-40; 43; 54; 57; 66-67; 69;
95; 97-98. 7,13. 8,1; 3; 5. 9,1; 4. 10,1; 4;
9-10; 26. 12,2. 17,11; 15. B11-12.
DEV 1,4; 18; 33. 3,7.
13a,1-3. 15,7. 16,51; 129; 135. 24,26.
25,19. 34,17; 50. 42,14; 23. 45,2. 51,6; 15-
16.
DOR 1,31. 13,5. 24,1-4.

28,5. 56,7; 31.
ESS 1,10; 13; 24. 3,11.
4,11; 14. 5,8. 10,2. 17,1. 19,1. 20,4; 7; 13;
17; 77. 22,6-8. 23,3-4. 24,5. 25,4; 15. 26,2.
27,3. 29,2. 30,15; 24. 32,16. 33,6-7. 34,9;
28; 37. 35,3. 36,2. 40,2-3. 41,3. 42,3. 53,1.
68,8. 70,3. 82,1. B3a; 7.
GLS G4. W4. 1,1; 18;
20; 22; 37; 50; 53; 65. 3,4-5; 7. 4,1. 7,1.
9,1. 12,1; 3-7. 23,2. 26. 27,1. 28,1. 30,1-
2. 34,8. 38,4. 39,6; 8; 12; 17-19. 41,1-2.
49,1. 50,2-3. 55,1. 56,1-2. 60,5. 63,1; 3.
66,5-6. 67,1. 68,10. 72,2. 78,15.
HAM 1,1; 7; 37; 44. 2,9;
20. 3,5; 7. 5,1. 5a,1. 17,1-2. 23,51; 64.
45,1. 64. 69,8. S2. IoW1,7. IoW9,1.
HEF A1. 1,1; 6-8; 10a,c;
39; 56; 62. 2,12; 24-26; 29-30; 49; 51. 7,4;
9. 8,9-10. 10,27; 47-48; 50; 61; 64. 13,2.
19,2-3; 6; 10. 23,4;9. 29,2; 9; 11.
HRT 1,2; 6; 18. 2,2. 4,2;
16-17; 22. 5,8; 20. 7,2. 8,1. 9,1; 10. 10,7;
9. 11,1. 13,5. 15,1. 16,9. 17,3; 8; 11-12; 15.
20,7. 21,2. 23,2-4. 25,2. 26,1. 28,4; 8. 30,1.
31,6. 32,1. 33,9; 17-18. 34,19; 21; 24. 36,7.
37,3; 7; 11; 14; 21. 42,2; 9-11. 42a,1. 43,1.
44,1.
HUN 1,1-2; 5; 8; 10. 2,2;
4-5. 4,2. 5,1. 6,1-7; 9; 11-13; 24; 26. 7,1-
6. 9,1. 10,1. 11,1-2. 13,1. 18,1. 19,8-9; 31.
20,1-3; 5-6; 8. 21,1. 22,1. 23,1. 24,1. 29,1.
D1; 6; 12.
KEN 2,25. 4,4. 5,124;
172; 214. 7,8. 9,2-
3; 6; 39.
LEC 1,3. 3,1. 6,3; 6. 8,1;
4-5. 9,3. 10,1; 9. 11,1. 12,2. 13,1; 4-5; 17-
18; 40; 44; 56-57; 60; 65; 72. 14,6; 23; 31.
15,4-5. 16,9. 17,19; 30. 19,1; 17. 29,3; 10.
36,1. 40,12; 16-17; 24; 32; 41. 41,2.
LIN C2-5; 14; 16. S6.
1,4-7; 9; 18; 26; 49; 65; 102. 2,16; 18. 4,1;
26; 39; 44; 69. 7,1; 18; 30; 32; 40; 43; 46;
54-55; 58. 8,1. 9,1. 12,7; 14; 21; 29; 43; 47-
49; 65; 67; 75. 13,1; 34; 37. 14,18; 23; 47;
89. 15,1. 16,47; 50. 17,1-2. 18,7; 28-29.
22,7; 30. 24,1; 5; 10; 12-13; 24; 37-38; 40;
66; 78; 102-104. 25,19. 26,14; 53. 27,34;
53. 30,22; 27. 31,3; 11; 15-17. 32,11; 32-
34. 34,1-2; 12. 35,1; 14. 36,1. 37,2. 39,1;
3. 40,17. 42,1; 16. 43,1; 6. 44,8-9. 53. 54.
56,9; 14; 18; 23. 57,17-18; 21; 24; 28; 30;
34; 37-38. 58,1-2. 61,1. 62,2. 64,1; 6; 14-
15; 17-18. 68,3; 25; 28; 31; 38; 42; 46-47.
CS19. CN16.
MDX 2,1-2. 4,6-7; 12.
7,4-5. 8,6. 9,7; 9. 10,1-2. 11,3. 12,1. 13,1.
19,1. 21,1. 24,1.
NFK 1,64; 66; 195-196.
4,45. 8,78. 10,32-33. 14,29; 37. 31,6. 44.
45.

CHS	B3.
HEF	2,21.
LIN	13,40.
SHR	4,3,14.
SOM	*46,6.*

Wife of	LIN	C14.
	SFK	47,3.

Woman and priest
holding land NFK 46,1.
See also: Alms; Church; Claim; Croft; Dwelling;
Escort; free man; Give up; Inheritance;
Jurisdiction; Man; Mass; Ordeal; Outlaw;
Patronage; Patronage, sub; Plea; Seizure.

PRIEST'S land	HUN	D6.
	NTT	20,4.

PRODUCE (mercedes)

Of land	HEF	1,4.

PROFIT (lucrum; proficuum)
From land wrongfully

taken	BRK	7,28.
	HAM	3,9.
	OXF	1,11.

Land held on
condition of making
profit for King SFK 1,103.
See also: Income.

PROTECTION (tuitio; defensio; protectio)
Land holder
putting himself/
land under

another's	BRK	3,2.
	HAM	69,40.
	SRY	8,8. 23,1.

turning to another
for HRT 19,1.
Man commended to
another's by King's
writ BDF 17,5.
See also: Enclosure; Protector; Queen.

PROTECTOR
(protector; defensor;

tutor)	ESS	90,48.
Bishop claimed as	KEN	D8.
King claimed as	NFK	19,2.
by woman	NFK	1,124.

Man claiming his lord

as	ESS	90,78.
	HRT	20,2.
	SFK	21,95.

Not produced	ESS	90,77.
Sheriff claimed as	HRT	37,19.

See also: Cite.
PROVE (deratiocinare)

A claim	ESS	30,30.
	HAM	1,21. 53,2.
	KEN	*2,43.* 4,16.
	NFK	19,2.
	SFK	21,17; 19; 45-46;
		49-50; 52. 25,52;
		60.
	WIL	24,14; 19.

WOR	2,24; 63.

before Bishop	NFK	*15,22.*
	SFK	21,17.

before 4 Counties	WAR	3,4.
	WOR	10,12.

before King's

barons	DEV	2,2.
	WOR	10,12.

in Hundred and

County	KEN	*1,3.*
to free man	NFK	17,63. 25,15.
to Freeman	NFK	15,10; 13.
By Englishmen	WIL	24,19.

By evidence of men
present at making of
agreement SFK 1,103.
Land to be free SFK 77,4.
Men willing to, by
any means NFK 9,49.
SFK 1,77.
See also: Adjudge; Claim; Combat; Hundred;
Ordeal; Plea; Queen; Thaneland.

PROVISIONS (victus) – See Supplies.
PSALMS (psalterium)
Sung for King NFK 45,1.
See also: Prayers; Mass.
PUNISHMENT
Burning of house HEF A4.
Vengeance by
relatives HEF A4.
See also: Crime/offence.
PURCHASE

Church/house, of	HEF	C2.
	HRT	B7.
	HUN	D1.
	YKS	C11.

Land, of	BDF	56,2-3.
	CAM	35,2.
	DOR	27,9-10. 35,1.
	GLS	1,63.
	HAM	2,17. 6,5. 69,12-13.
		NF9,42.
	HEF	1,44. 29,1.
	HRT	4,1.
	KEN	4,16.
	LEC	13,63. 23,4.
	LIN	22,26. 51,12.
		CK39.
	NFK	10,23; 25; 30.
		12,34.
	NTH	41,3.
	SOM	28,2. *45,14.*
	SFK	16,3.
	SRY	8,29.
	WAR	6,5. 7,1. 17,60.
		44,11.
	WOR	9,1e; 4. 11,2. 23,1.
		26,17.
	YKS	CN4. CW22.

with Archbishop's
own money LIN CK10.

with church's
goods/money   CON   *3,7.*
              WOR   *11,2.*
with King's
permission   WAR   17,56. 21,1.
              WOR   *11,2.*
from King   HAM   69,4.
              HRT   19,1.
from King with
land holder's
consent   HRT   33,18.
witnessed by
Wapentake   LIN   CK10.
Price greater than
dues received from
land   ESS   23,2.
Purchase price of
land   HEF   1,44.
              HRT   19,1. 42,6.
              LIN   CS5. CK39.

              NFK   17,22.
              WOR   11,2.
              YKS   CN4.
mill   CAM   14,35.
See also: Holding; Purchase and sale; Re-purchase;
Residence; Sale; Sheriff; Ship; Tenure.
PURCHASE and sale
Of:-
   Freeman   NFK   1,7; 57; 195.
   horse   SSX   12,1.
   man   SSX   12,1.
   oxen   SSX   12,1.
See also: Rape (administrative unit); Timber.
PURVEYOR (prebendarius)
King's   WIL   67,74.
See also: Prebendary.
PUT land outside
manor-holder could
not   HRT   15,6.
See also: Transferability.

Q

QUARRY
(quadraria)   OXF   13,1.
   SSX   11,10; 20. 14,2.

Millstones, for
(molaria)   NTT   17,16.
   SSX   11,78.

Stone, for (fossa
lapidum)   SRY   11,1.

QUARTER (ferlang;
ferdingus)   GLS   12,10.
   HAM   NF10,4. IoW1,8.
   NTT   14,5.
   SSX   9,47; 107.

Borough, of   HUN   B1; 7; 9-12.

See also: Farthing; Furlong (ferlingus).

QUEEN Edith

Death of   SFK   37,2.

Gift of land by after
1066   BKM   56,1.

QUEEN Matilda

Lifetime of   DOR   *1,16.*

QUEEN

Administration
(ministerium) of
property of   DEV   C2.

Claim proved before   HAM   53,2.
   WAR   3,4.

Gift to (gersuma;
donum)   NFK   1,61.
   NTH   B36.

   OXF   1,12.
   WAR   B4.

Hand of, land holder
putting herself in with
land –   SRY   31,1.

Land held from   BRK   1,47. 65,5; 16-17.
   BKM   5,1-2. 14,13.
   DEV   1,71. 23,6.
   DOR   1,22-29. 54,8.
   HAM   10,1. 23,7. 69,6; 26.
   HRT   18,1.
   KEN   13,1.
   LIN   68,30-31.
   MDX   9,1.
   SOM   5,46.
   SFK   6,112. 54,3. 77,1.
   WOR   18,2.

Land holder rendering
service to   BRK   21,20.

Payments to
   gold, of   BDF   1,2a; 3.
   sheriff, by   WOR   C2.

Work (opus) of,
payment of gold for   BDF   1,1a.

See also: Alms; Chamberlain; Claim; free man;
Freeman; Gift; Gold embroidery; Grange; Grant;
Holding; Jurisdiction; Jurisdiction, full; Man;
Market; Marriage; Mass; Patronage; Sheriff;
Thane; Third/two thirds part; Wardship; Wool.

QUIT (adquietare; quietus) – See Clear; Exempt.

R

RADKNIGHT (radchenister) – See Riding man.
RADMAN (radmannus) – See Rider.
RAM (aries) BDF 24,5. 33,1.
Render of NFK 31,6.
  as woodland dues BDF 33,1.
RANCH (hardwica; wica) – See Dairy; Dairy
farm.
RANSOM – See Pledge.
RAPE (rapum) (Administrative unit)
Land
  in another SSX 2,2. 5,2. 8,1; 3.
    9,120. 10,2-3; 18-19; 22; 27; 30-32; 35-37;
    49; 51; 56; 61-64; 66; 86-87; 89; 91; 93; 95-
    103; 108. 11,37; 56-57; 65-66; 71-73. 12,1-
    4; 6-8; 10-11; 20-21; 26; 33; 36; 43-44; 46;
    48-49. 13,1-3; 10-12; 15-16; 28; 30; 38; 48;
    53; 57.
  outside SSX 5,2. 8,3; 15. 9,122;
    125; 127. 10,49; 62-64; 96-100; 101-104;
    106-110; 114; 116. 12,18. 13,16.
  not taxed in SSX 8,16.
Purchase and sale
within SSX 12,1.
See also: Villager.
RAPE (raptum) – See Crime/offence; Violation of
women.
REALM (regio)
Land belonging to SFK 1,1; 120.
Manor belonging to NFK 4,1.
  SFK 31,44.
See also: Throne.
REAPING (metere; secare)
Men not reaping CHS R6,2.
Service GLS 19,2.
  for 1 day in lord's WOR 8,7; 9b; 10a; 11; 14;
    meadow 17; 23.
  from burgesses HEF C3.
    WOR 19,12.
  from free men CHS R2,2.
    WOR 8,9b.
  from thanes'
    harvester for 1 day CHS R1,40a.
See also: Scything.·
REARGUARD (redrewarde) – See Army.
REBELLION of
Ralph Wader CAM 19,4.
See also: Forfeiture.
RECALL (revocare) – See Cite.
RECORDED
(inbreviatus; haberi) BDF 12,1.
  CAM 5,12. 25,10.
  DOR 12,13.
  GLS 1,43; 56.
  HAM 69,48.

  WIL 1,5. 25,9.
Claim to free man put
in writing NFK 66,61-62.
Grant recorded SOM 2,9
Nothing recorded HEF 10,72.
  NTT 12,21.
See also: Domesday survey; Meadow; Plough;
Village.
RECOVERY of land ESS 1,3. 3,9.
  WIL 48,12.
  WOR 26,16.
  by sheriff's grant NFK 1,64.
See also: King's hand; Restoration; Return.
REDEMPTION – See Forfeiture; Pledge.
REED (juncus) CAM 5,51.
REEVE (prepositus) BDF 57,3iii.
  BRK B1. 7,14.
  CHS C18; 21. 2,5-7; 19.
    6,1.
  DEV 1,4.
  DOR 35,1. 56,26.
  ESS 1,18. 52,2. 83. 86.
    90,76.
  GLS G1-4. W2. 1,14; 16;
    47-49; 54. 16,1.
    39,12. 63,1.
  HAM 1,21; 23; 47. 3,3.
  HEF C2. 1,3; 7-8; 10a;
    11; 16; 33; 39-42; 44. 2,12; 30; 46; 49. 7,1.
    8,7. 9,19. 10,5; 29-30; 33; 48; 50; 56.
    19,10. 24,11. 29,2; 11.
  HRT 9,4. 33,17.
  KEN C8. 1,3. 2,27.
  LIN T1.
  NFK 10,58. 17,22.
    66,79.
  NTH B33. 1,9.
  SHR 1,7. 4,1,4; 10; 14;
    31. 4,8,16. 4,20,6.
    6,11-12.
  SOM 24,24. 25,29. 35,1.
  STS 1,8.
  SFK 1,7; 103. 4,15.
    14,129; 167. 25,3.
    74,4; 7.
  SRY 1,9.
  WIL 3,2-3. 8,12.
  WOR 1, 1a; 2. 2,4; 47-48;
    79; 84. 9,6c. 19,6.
  under-reeve NFK 9,167.
Acquiring value of
land ESS 90,74.
Adding resources/free
men to manor/

197

Exempt from
everything | LIN | C11.
House sited on | NTT | B8.
King having toll/
forfeiture from | LIN | C4.
Land tribute (gablum)
from, in and outside
city wall | LIN | C4; 8.
Owned/occupied by
  Bishop | LIN | C11.
  burgess | HAM | 32,1.
   | LIN | T1.
  Freeman | LIN | S4.
  lawman | LIN | S5.
Paying nothing to
King | GLS | G4.
Purchased | GLS | *G1-4.*
Rent from/paying | GLS | G4.
   | LIN | C4.

See also: Borough; Castle; Claim; Jurisdiction, full;
Plot; Revenue; Town; Wall.

RESIDENT (casatus)
of manor | SFK | 9,3.

RESOURCES, classes of – See Alder grove; Ash
wood; Assart; Beehive; Box wood; Bramble
thicket; Brushwood; Church; Copse; Dairy; Dairy
farm; Dam; Dependency; Dwelling; Dyke;
Enclosure; Eyrie; Fair; Fence; Ferry; Field; Fir
wood; Fishery; Fishing; Fishpond; Fold; Forest;
Forge; Fuel; Garden; Grange; Grazing; Guildhall;
Hall; Harbour; Heathland; House; Hunting;
Inland; Kitchen; Landing place; Livestock;
Lodging; Market; Marsh; Marshland; Meadow;
Mere; Mill; Mine; Mint; Moor; Open land;
Orchard; Outlier; Oven; Park; Pasturage; Pasture;
Pasture land; Plot; Plough; Ploughland; Pool; Port;
Pottery; Profit; Quarry; Reed; Reeveland;
Residence; River; Salt house; Scrub; Settled land;
Sheepfold; Ship; Site; Smithy; Spinney; Stock;
Thaneland; Timber; Turf land; Underwood; Vine;
Vineyard; Wall; Warland; Warren; Waste; Water
meadow; Waterway; Weir; Willow bed; Wood;
Woodland; Wool house.

RESOURCES, nil – See Land; Lordship; Village.

RESTORATION of
land/property | ESS | 1,1.
   | YKS | C9.
By holder with goods
to Abbey | WIL | 14,1.
By judgment | CON | 4,21.
By King | BDF | 56,6.
   | BRK | 41,6.
   | CHS | B7.
   | DOR | 19,14.
   | HEF | 2,12; 26; 31-33; 37;
   | | 48; 50.
   | WOR | 3,3.

See also: Possession; Recovery; Relinquishment;
Return; Surrender.

RETENTION of
land despite King's

right | OXF | 29,13.
RETURN (breve; responsus)
Abbey, of | NFK | 13,1. 23,9.
King, of | CAM | 1,13.
   | WOR | X3.
King's treasury, to | NFK | 66,64.
Land entered in that of
another County | WOR | X2.
Land holder, of | NFK | 66,81.
No one to make | GLS | 28,7. 75,2.
   | SFK | 2,8.
None | HEF | 2,57.
   | SSX | 10,82.

See also: Domesday survey; Recorded.

RETURN of land (reddere; revertere)
By King to
  Englishman | LIN | 68,37.
  former holder | HAM | 6,12. 44,1.
   | SFK | 7,70.
Ordered by King | SHR | 3d,7.

See also: Monk; Recovery; Re-purchase;
Restoration; Tenure.

RETURN (redditus) – See Payment.

REVENUE (firma)
Borough/city
  held at/of (firma
  burgi) | BRK | B8.
   | CHS | C19; 21-22.
   | GLS | G4. B1.
   | HUN | B17.
   | KEN | 2,2.
   | LIN | S16.
   | SHR | 4,1,37.
   | SFK | 1,122g.
  lordship, of | SOM | 1,30.
  reduced | SFK | 1,122g.
  toll, of | CHS | FT2,19.
County
  pleas, of | SHR | 4,1,37.
  revenue paid in
  another | WOR | X3.
Customary dues, of | WOR | 2,4.
Day/night, of
  half (½) day | BDF | 1,1a; 2a; 3.
   | HAM | 1,17; 27.
  one day | HAM | 1,43-44.
   | SSX | 13,1.
  two days | NFK | 14,35.
  three days | CAM | 1,1-2.
  eight days hay to
  Archbishop | BKM | 2,1.
  quarter (¼) night | HEF | 1,1.
  half (½) night | DOR | 1,5-6.
   | GLS | 1,13.
   | SHR | 4,1,12.
  three quarters (¾)
  night | SOM | 1,10.
  one night | DEV | *1,19-21.*
   | DOR | B1-3. 1,2-4.
   | GLS | 1,9; 11.
   | SOM | 1,1-6; 8-9.

	HEF	1,5; 10b; 47; 57; 61; 71; 75. 2,37. 28,2.
	HRT	1,13. 15,8.
	HUN	D5.
	KEN	1,1. *2,15; 18-19. 3,5; 21.* 5,49-50; 84-85; 89; 99-100; 102; 122; 128; 154; 160; 175; 183; 196; 209. 7,22. 13,1.
	LEC	1,2; 5; 9-10.
	MDX	9,1.
	NFK	1,209. 8,98. 20,10. 64,1-2; 9. 66,64.
	NTH	1,3-4; 14.
	OXF	1,9. 59,1-2.
	SHR	3d,5. 4,1,1; 6; 19. 4,4,8. 4,6,5. 4,25,4. 4,26,7. 4,27,3; 30. 6,31.
	SOM	*1,28. 2,1. 45,15. 46,3. 47,1.*
	SFK	4,1. 5,1. 6,96. 7,49; 71. 16,26; 37; 41. 21,3; 16. 25,57. 58,1. 67,3.
	SRY	1,9. 5,1a; 3; 28. 8,27. 19,21.
	SSX	2,1a. 3,2; 9. 5,2. 6,1. 10,57. 13,5; 9.
	WAR	1,6. 44,6.
	WIL	1,3; 5. 3,1. 25,1; 15; 21.
	WOR	1,1b; 2. 2,3; 30.
held at harshly and wretchedly	BKM	17,16.
held at yearly revenue to be agreed	LIN	CK48.
not belonging to	BRK	1,12-13.
	DOR	1,21.
	GLS	1,54.
part of	HEF	10,11.
	OXF	6,1a; 2-3; 5.
placed in/at attached/added to	GLS	1,5; 60; 62. 2,8.
	HEF	16,3-4.
	NFK	1,217. 20,7.
	SFK	1,103.
put outside	BRK	43,1.
	GLS	1,8; 13.
transferred to that of another place	SRY	5,3.
	WOR	1,1b.
wrongfully included in	HEF	1,70.
Lordship, land part of	DOR	26,64.
	SOM	1,9; 11.
	WIL	13,2. 45,2.
Manor		
at revenue for 3 years	SFK	9,1.
given to reeve at	SFK	25,3.
held wrongfully in revenue of another		

County paid to another	GLS	1,63.
County paying less than granted for	WOR	1,5-6.
	NFK	20,10.
	SFK	25,57. 67,3.
so high as to ruin men holding it	SFK	9,1. 67,3.
Manor/village, of	DEV	*3,8.*
	GLS	41,5.
	SHR	4,1,37. 4,27,5.
	SOM	1,20. 19,*33;* 35.
Mill at	CAM	15,2. 17,2.
Outlier in	ESS	1,28.
Payment		
excessive	WIL	7,1.
more paid 1086 than TRE	SFK	1,60.
not given/paid	GLS	75,1.
	NFK	1,209.
	SOM	1,17.
not paid but holder lived off land	GLS	1,61.
paid at will of payer	WOR	*9,1e.*
payments to revenue	DEV	*1,70.*
	GLS	1,11-13; 16.
	SFK	1,60; 73; 110-111.
unable to bear	HAM	1,16. 2,11; 15. IoW2,1.
	NFK	8,98.
	SFK	21,3. 25,3.
	SSX	3,9. 13,5.
Rendered in corn/honey/malt	CAM	1,1-2.
Salt houses etc, at Sheriff	WOR	1,3a-b.
revenue of	HEF	1,1.
	LIN	T1.
	NTH	B37.
	WOR	C3.
too high for sheriff to bear	CAM	22,6.
Site (haga), at	BRK	1,2.
Value of	NTH	B36.
	SSX	13,1.
Villagers holding land at	DEV	*25,28.*
Wales		
North Wales, of	CHS	G1.
Welsh district, of	SHR	4,3,42.
White (firma alba)	HAM	1,W10.
Wich at	CHS	S1,7. S2,1. S3,1.
Woodland in	HAM	1,27.

See also: Castle; Corn; Dwelling; Fishery; Forester; free man; Freeman; Hawk; Honey; Lease; Malt; Manor; Plea; Pledge; Reeve; Salt worker; Separated; Sheriff; Taken away; Tenure; Third part; Villager; Wheat.

REVERSION – See Tenure.

RIDER (radman)   CHS   B4; 9. A8; 18. 1,1;

5; 15; 21-22; 26; 34. 2,3; 5-6; 13; 27; 31.
3,4; 9-11. 5,1-4; 11-14. 7,3. 8,3; 6; 8; 11-
15; 22-23; 26-27; 29-30; 32; 41-42; 44-45.
9,'10; 17; 22-24. 11,3. 12,2-3. 13,1; 4-5.
14,5-6; 12-13. 17,4. 18,1; 4; 6. 19,2. 20,2-
3; 11-12. 21,1. 22,2. 23,3. 24,3-4; 6-7.
26,1-3. 27,4. FD2,2; 4; 6. FD3,2. FD5,1;
3. FD7,1. FD8,2. FT2,11; 17. R1,43; 45.
R6,4-5.

| | HEF | 1,10a; 39-40. 2,7; |

26; 28; 30-33; 49; 51-52. 7,1. 9,6; 19. 16,4.
19,4. 24,9. 29,8. 31,4.

| | SHR | 2,1. 3c,2-3; 8. 3f,2; |

6. 3g,5; 9. 4,1,1-2; 8; 14; 36. 4,3,1; 4; 7;
26; 30-31; 44-45; 51; 63-64; 66; 70. 4,4,3;
5; 12; 16; 19-20; 22. 4,5,4; 9-10; 13-15.
4,7,1; 3. 4,8,4-5; 7; 9; 11; 15. 4,9,1-2.
4,10,3. 4,11,2; 11; 13. 4,13,1. 4,14,1; 7; 10.
4,15,1-3. 4,19,1; 12. 4,20,3; 7-8; 15-16; 18.
4,21,1; 5; 11-12. 4,23,5; 12. 4,26,3-4; 6.
4,27,9; 12-13; 15; 18; 20-21; 24; 33. 5,1; 4;
9. 6,1-2; 9; 11; 13; 30; 33. 7,3-4. 9,2.

| | WOR | 2,29; 38; 45; 48; 68. |

3,1. 8,9g; 10a; 21; 26a-b. 9,2-3; 5b; 6a. 10,5;
10. 14,1. 15,1; 4; 6; 9. 18,5. 19,7. 21,4.

Agricultural services of	WOR	8,10a.
Put outside manor	HEF	1,39.
Rendering cattle as dues	SHR	4,20,8.

See also: Man.

RIDING (treding)	LIN	Passim
	YKS	Passim
Decision on claims against claimant	LIN	CS8; 12; 14; 18-19; 25; 27; 36.
for claimant	LIN	CS10; 16-17; 29. CW17; 68.
Evidence by	LIN	CS9; 11; 13; 15; 20-21; 40. CN8; 27. CK1; 67; 69-70.
	YKS	CW39.
Unaware of facts	LIN	CN18.

See also: Man; Wapentake.
RIDING horse (palefridus) – See Horse.

| RIDING man (radchenistre) | BRK | 7,23. |
| | GLS | 1,15; 21; 24-25; 28; |

36; 43; 47; 53; 59-60. 2,1; 4; 10. 3,1; 4-5;
7. 4,1. 7,1-2. 10,3. 19,2. 24,3. 28,1. 34,3;
8. 38,3. 39,6; 8; 12. 41,2. 45,1. 49,1. 60,1.
66,6.

| | HAM | 1,8; 28; 30. |
| | HEF | 1,4; 6-7; 10a; 11-12; |

16; 26. 9,5; 7; 10. 10,24; 32; 34; 44; 49-50;
58. 19,8. 27,1. 29,4; 11.

	WOR	1,1c; 2. 2,84.
Agricultural services of	GLS	1,24. 19,2.
Defined as free man	GLS	19,2.

| Serving lord | HEF | 29,4. |

See also: Man.
RIGHT

To land doubted if no service done	LIN	31,3.
Ownership by	HAM	44,1.
Person without	SRY	22,4.

RIGHT, customary (consuetudo)

| In land | HAM | 33,1. |
| In woodland | SRY | 4,1. |

See also: Customary due.
RIVER

Burgesses fishing rights in	NTT	B6.
living beyond	CHS	FD5,2.
Obstruction to navigation of	NTT	B20.
Waters of comprised in holding	CHS	FT1,1. FT2,1.

ROAD

Boundary, as	STS	11,38.
Digging in	KEN	C6.
Dyke, making near	NTT	B20.
House on	KEN	C2.
King's	KEN	C6.
	NTT	B20.
	YKS	C37.
King's public	KEN	D12. C2.
Narrowing of	KEN	C6.
Obstruction to	KEN	D12; 23.
Offences on	KEN	D14. C6-7.
Pigsty (sudis), near to	KEN	C6.
Ploughing near	NTT	B20.
Posts on	KEN	C6.

See also: Crime/offence.
ROBBERY (latrocinium; revelach) – See
Crime/offence.
ROBBERY, highway (foristel) – See
Crime/offence; Customary due.

ROBE maker (parmentarius)	SFK	14,167.
ROD/ROOD (virga)	DOR	11,6; 17. 30,2.
	HUN	14,1.
	NFK	8,6; 131. 9,142.

13,16. 24,3. 48,2.
66,75.

| | SFK | 1,67. 7,36; 110. |

38,14. 52,7.

| | SRY | 19,20. |
| | YKS | 10W29. |

See also: Iron.
ROE deer (capreolus) – See Deer.
ROUEN pence – See Money.
RUIN/impoverishment – See free man; Revenue;
Value.
RURAL work – See Agricultural work.
RUSTIC (rusticus) – See Countryman.
RYE (siligo)

| Rendered by mill | SHR | 4,17,3. |
| Sester of | SHR | 4,17,3. |

S

Worker/boiler
(salinarius)   BKM 1,3.
              DEV 1,26. 11,1. 15,23.
                   34,11. 36,9.
              DOR 8,6. 12,13. 26,67.
                   57,14.
              WOR 1,1a.
paying revenue DEV 15,23.
rendering salt to
manor in another
County   BKM 1,3.
See also: Burgess; Cart; Earl; Fish; Horse; House;
Salt house; Third penny.
SALT house (salina) CHS 2,2. S1,1; 7. S2,1.
                          S3,2.
                     CON 5,1,3.
                     DEV 1,23-24; 71. 2,4;
18. 7,3-4. 10,1. 12,1. 15,44; 46; 65-66.
16,157. 17,69; 105. 19,10. 21,20. 35,20; 27.
36,10. 39,19-20.
                     DOR 26,15; 61.
                     ESS 1,27; 31. 3,5; 7.
4,2-3. 5,10-11. 9,8; 14. 11,8. 18,43. 20,19;
57; 62. 24,64. 27,16. 28,17. 30,18. 32,38;
45. 33,16; 23. 34,36. 35,9; 11. 39,7; 9.
41,12. 66,1.
                     GLS 1,13. 34,8. 39,6.
                          61,2.
                     HAM 1,10; 19. 3,27. 6,4.
10,1. 15,4. 18,1. 21,1. 28,2. 68,5. NF5,1.
NF9,2. IoW6,14.
                     KEN P19. 1,3-4. 2,11;
13-14; 18; 21-22; 35; 43. 3,7; 14; 17. 5,115;
122; 124; 128; 141; 145; 147; 175. 7,8-9.
9,10.
                     LIN 1,34; 77; 85. 2,6;
30. 3,6; 16; 47. 4,24; 42. 7,34; 36. 8,11.
11,6. 12,19; 38; 59-62; 64; 70-71; 75-76; 89-
90. 13,7; 33. 14,1; 97. 18,9. 22,25-26.
24,74-75. 25,7; 12. 27,16. 28,41. 29,20.
30,9. 32,1. 37,6. 38,14. 44,6; 14. 56,1; 22.
57,44. 61,5. CN22.
                     NFK 1,88; 94; 132-133;
147; 152; 201-203; 212; 217. 2,4. 4,26; 44.
5,2. 7,2. 8,13; 21; 24; 47; 107. 9,90-93. 10,2; 30.
13,12; 14. 14,4-5. 15,4; 6. 17,1; 61; 63.
19,4; 36-37. 21,9. 22,1; 16; 19. 23,4-5; 11.
29,3-4. 31,22; 31-32. 34,1-2; 4. 35,1. 38,14.
51,3. 55,1. 64,1. 65,8-9. 66,17; 55.
                     OXF 1,6.
                     SFK 1,32; 58; 118. 3,77;
82. 4,14. 6,143. 7,6; 106. 27,10. 32,6. 33,6-
7. 36,2. 39,17. 68,1. 69,1.
                     SSX 5,1. 6,1. 9,1; 3;
6-7; 23. 10,2-3; 27; 30; 34; 36-37; 67-68;
77; 83; 86; 93. 11,43; 59; 63; 69. 12,4. 13,9-
10; 19-20; 28-29; 38; 43-46.
                     WOR 1,2; 3a-b. 2,56. 4,1.
8,12-13. 12,1. 14,2. 15,13. 19,12-14. 23,8.
26,6; 10-11; 16-17.
three quarters (¾)

(3 parts)   NFK 9,92.
two thirds (⅔) (2
parts)   NFK 8,48.
half (½)   CHS 17,5.
                      ESS 27,17.
                      LIN 12,58; 60. 25,7.
                      NFK 1,15; 72; 132; 155;
202-204; 217. 2,4; 26. 4,44-45. 5,2. 7,2.
8,21-22; 24; 26-27; 30. 9,88; 90-91. 10,73;
82. 12,6. 13,13. 17,10. 19,3. 21,10. 23,12.
29,1. 31,31-32. 65,8-9.
one third (⅓) (1
part)   KEN 9,10.
                      NFK 9,2. 13,14.
one quarter (¼)   NFK 1,202. 5,1. 20,8.
                           64,4.
                      SSX 10,36-37.
one twelfth (1/12)   NFK 51,4.
Belonging to village
elsewhere   LIN 27,16. 44,6; 14.
Boundaries of –
penalties within   CHS S1,5.
Comparative information
less 1086 than TRE   ESS 5,11. 20,57.
                      NFK 1,133. 8,13. 10,2.
                           23,11.
                      SFK 33,6. 68,1.
more 1086 than
TRE   ESS 27,16-17.
                      NFK 8,21. 15,4.
Customs of   CHS S1,2-6. S2,1. S3,1.
Derelict/disused
(vasta)   CHS 1,1. 17,5.
Droitwich, at
appurtenant to
manor/village
elsewhere   GLS 1,24-27.
                      HEF 1,40-41. 2,18; 20;
                           26-28.
                      OXF 1,6.
                      SHR 4,1,25-26.
                      WOR 1,1c. 2,7; 77-78.
                           5,1. 10,10. 14,1.
                           26,8. 28,1.
rendering salt to
manor/village
elsewhere   GLS 1,47-48. 18,1. 50,1.
                      HEF 1,4. 2,34.
                      OXF 58,4.
                      WAR 35,1.
                      WOR 1,1a; 5. 2,48; 68;
                           79; 84. 9,1a. 15,9.
                           26,2; 13; 15. 27,1.
Dues, without (sine   HAM 1,27. IoW1,7.
censu)   IoW5,1.
Earl's, exempt from
toll   CHS S1,1; 3.
Exempt   CHS 8,16.
King's   ESS 1,31.
King/Earl, divided
between   CHS S1,1; 3. S2,1.

Lordship, in	NFK	1,203.
	SSX	10,77.
	WOR	1,3b.
Northwich, at –		
appurtenant to		
manor/village		
elsewhere	CHS	FD5,2.
Rendering salt	DEV	15,66.
	GLS	1,13. 34,8. 39,6.
		61,2.
	KEN	7,9.
	WAR	28,16. 40,2.
	WOR	3,3. 17,1. 18,3; 6.
		20,6. 22,1. 24,1.
enough for a year	CHS	S1,1.
hall, to	CHS	1,1.
Serving hall	CHS	1,8.
Thane holding		
exempt from boiling		
render	CHS	S3,2.
Timber for	WOR	1,1a. 2,15. 8,12.
Wich, at –		
appurtenant to		
manor/village	CHS	1,1; 8. 8,16. 17,5.
elsewhere		S1,1.

See also: Claim; Revenue; Salt; Sheriff; Third part; Wich.

SALT pan (salina) – See Salt house.
SALT worker (salinarius) – See Salt.
SALTERN (salina) – See Salt house.

SCOT tax (scotum)		
payment by Hundred	NFK	1,71. 22,1.
SCOTLAND –		
William Percy's		
return from	YKS	C10.
SCRIBE (scriba)	GLS	G4.
SCRUB/scrubland		
(boscus; frutectum)	DOR	1,2.
	ESS	B4.
	HRT	10,9. 28,4.

SCRUBWOOD – See Underwood.

SCULLION		
(scutularius)	DOR	57,22.
SCYTHING (falcare)	GLS	19,2.

See also: Reaping.

SEA		
Crossing of	ESS	3,11. 6,11.
	HAM	53,2.
	HRT	37,19.
	MDX	25,2.
	OXF	1,6.
Flooding property	LIN	57,36.
Guarding of	SSX	12,1.
Land		
extending to	SFK	14,162.
taken away by	SFK	6,84.
Port	SFK	33,6.
Service	KEN	2,43. 5,178.
	LIN	57,43.
	WOR	2,21.

See also: Army; Battle; Expedition; Harbour; Port;

Ship; Weir.

SEAL (sigillum)		
Bishop's, land held by	LIN	4,1.
King's	DOR	19,14.
	HAM	69,30; 33.
	HUN	D1.
	NFK	14,16.
	OXF	1,13.
	SFK	6,79. 14,37.
	SRY	5,28.
	YKS	CW39.
seen	BRK	21,22.
	LIN	CK10.
not seen	BRK	7,38. 21,22.
	HAM	1,42. 35,2. 69,16.
	HUN	D20.
	NFK	10,28.
shown	GLS	59,1.
Not seen	HUN	D21.
	SRY	21,3.

See also: Possession; Writ.
SECURITY – See Pledge.

SEEK lord where he		
would, Freeman		
could 1086	LIN	S4.

See also: Transferability.

SEISIN (saisitio) – See Deliverer; Dispossession; Installer; Patron; Possession.

SEIZURE (saisire; invadere)		
Land, of	DEV	34,5.
	LIN	CN19.
priest, by	LIN	C14. 62,2.
marshalls, by	YKS	CW17.
Land and priest's wife		
whilst in King's		
possession	LIN	C14.

See also: Annexation; Dispossession; Taken away.

SELL land		
free man		
could	ESS	20,61. 24,22. 40,9.
	NFK	15,7-8.
	SFK	8,46. 14,139.
		25,32. 26,1. 27,3.
		34,2. 41,10. 55,1.
could not	SFK	5,2. 6,59-60. 8,45.
		16,4. 26,1; 4. 34,2.
		40,1. 53,1.
could without		
permission	NFK	1,217.
	SFK	16,10. 25,30; 42.
		41,11. 43,3.
could not without		
permission	NFK	29,7.
	SFK	8,46.
could within		
jurisdiction of		
Abbey	SFK	8,45.
could not whilst in		
the jurisdiction	SFK	34,3.
could after first		
offering to lord	NFK	35,16.

free woman could not SFK 54,2.
Freeman
  could BDF 23,39; 45; 49; 54.
48,2. 51,3. 53,21;
24; 26.
                BKM 1,3. 17,10.
                CAM 1,23. 3,4. 5,29; 33.
14,27; 30. 15,4. 17,4. 21,4; 6. 23,4. 25,10.
26,16; 18; 32; 44–45; 47–48. 31,2–4; 6. 32,5;
8; 16; 19–20; 30–32; 36. 41,10.
                ESS 35,13–14.
                HRT 1,9; 15. 4,25. 15,2.
17,10. 19,1. 20,7. 25,2. 33,19. 34,15; 17.
36,11. 37,16. 41,1. 43,1.
                NFK 23,11.
                SFK 14,120.
  could not CAM 5,33. 26,16; 49; 51–
53. 32,36.
                HRT 23,3.
                NFK 13,21.
                SFK *16,6. 21,13-14; 29.*
25,39; 42. 28,2.
31,42. *32,30.*
  could without
  permission CAM 14,55.
                HRT 1,8.
                NFK 13,21.
                SFK 2,7.
  could not without
  permission CAM 5,5; 61. 32,2.
                HRT 7,2. 36,11.
                MDX 7,4. 11,4.
                SFK 21,12.
  could with the
  jurisdiction HRT 42a,1.
  could, but not CAM 26,48–49. 32,27;
  jurisdiction 37.
                HRT 33,17. 42a,1.
  could but
  jurisdiction
  remained in another
  manor ESS 57,5.
  could not outside
  Abbey HRT 10,13.
  could where he
  would MDX 7,8.
  could to whom he BDF 17,2. 21,7; 17.
  would 23,12; 27; 50; 53;
55; 57. 24,24. 25,9. 33,1. 34,1. 48,1. 55,1.
57,3iii.
                CAM 13,9–10. 14,56.
  so bound to
  monastery he could
  not sell nor forfeit
  outside it NFK 17,9.
Land holder
  could BDF 2,6; 8. 3,10. 15,7.
16,5. 21,9; 15. 23,19; 29; 32; 35–36; 42–43;
46; 51. 24,25. 28,2. 31,1. 32,9. 34,2. 40,1–
2. 46,1–2. 49,2. 53,7; 9; 15; 17; 19; 23; 25;

27–28; 31; 35–36. 54,4. 55,2. 56,5; 8.
57,3iv–v; 12.
                BKM 3a,5. 4,4–9; 11; 13;
15; 19; 21–22; 24–26; 28; 31–32; 34–38; 40–
42. 5,1–4; 6; 10–19; 21. 6,2. 7,2. 12,1–4; 6–
18; 20–29; 31–38. 13,2. 14,1–3; 6; 8–9; 14–
20; 25–28; 31–37; 40–49. 15,1–2. 16,1–3; 7–
8. 17,1; 3–9; 11–15; 18–21; 23–25; 28–31.
18,2–3. 19,4–7. 21,2; 8. 22,1. 23,2–6; 9–11;
13; 15; 17; 20–33. 24,1–3. 25,1; 3. 26,1–3;
5–8; 10–11. 27,1. 28,1–3. 29,1; 4. 30,1.
31,1. 32,1. 33,1. 34,1. 36,1–3. 37,1–2. 39,1–
2. 41,1–2; 4–7. 43,2–6; 10. 44,1–5. 45,1.
46,1. 47,1. 48,1. 49,1. 50,1. 51,1–3. 53,1–
7; 10. 57,1–5; 7–9; 11–12; 14–17.
                CAM 3,6. 5,33. 13,3; 6–7.
14,28; 40; 47; 53–54; 57. 15,2. 21,5; 8. 22,7;
10. 26,17; 28–29. 30,2. 31,5. 32,24; 35; 39;
43–44. 33,1. 34,1. 35,1. 38,4. 39,2. 40,1.
41,9; 11–13; 15–16. 43,1.
                ESS 23,32. 40,9.
                HRT 1,11–14. 2,2; 4–5.
4,1; 3–7; 9–20; 23–24. 5,3–5; 7–11; 13–23;
25–26. 6,1. 7,1–3. 9,9. 15,5; 7–8. 16,3–6; 8;
10–12. 17,1–4; 6–9; 11–14. 18,1. 19,2. 20,1–
5; 7–13. 22,2. 23,1–2. 24,1; 3. 25,2. 26,1.
28,1; 3; 5; 7. 29,1. 30,1; 3. 31,1–3; 5; 7–8.
32,2. 33,1–6; 8–20. 34,1–5; 7–12; 14; 18–25.
35,1–3. 36,1–3; 5; 8–9; 12; 16–17; 19. 37,1–
6; 8; 10–13; 15; 17–20. 38,1–2. 41,2. 42,1–
2; 5–9; 12; 15. 42a,1. 44,1.
                MDX 9,3; 6. 15,2. 18,2.
21,1. 22,1. 25,1–2.
                NFK 9,100. 13,19.
15,10.
                SFK 38,2.
  could not CAM 5,2. 26,13; 20; 50.
30,3. 32,37.
                HRT 4,8. 10,17. 16,1.
17,15. 28,5. 33,1;
17.
                MDX 3,6.
                SFK 6,19; 22. 14,132.
31,40.
  could without
  permission BKM 16,7. 17,26. 53,9.
                CAM *38,2.*
                HRT 1,6. 4,8.
  could not without
  permission BKM 6,1. 19,1. 21,4; 6.
23,18.
                ESS 10,3.
                HRT 5,2; 6. 20,6. 30,2.
33,7. 34,7. 36,8.
37,7; 9.
                MDX 9,5–6.
                SFK 8,46. 12,6. 67,1.
  could, but not
  depart with land WAR 16,7.
  could not as land
  always alms lands
  of King and

predecessors HRT 17,15.
could, but not
jurisdiction CAM 26,17. 32,28.
could after first
offering to lord NFK 29,10.
could not outside
manor/village HRT 1,16. 36,4.
could where he
would CAM 32,37.
could to whom he BDF 2,4. 3,8; 17. 13,2.
would 15,2; 6. 17,4. 18,
2-4. 21,2. 23,48; 52. 24,2-3; 5; 7; 18; 30.
25,1-3; 7-8. 28,1. 32,1-3. 50,1. 52,2.
53,10; 13; 34. 55,5. 56,7. 57,1; 10; 21.
BKM 4,30. 5,7. 14,10-12.
17,22; 27. 18,3. 25,2. 26,4. 43,9; 11.
CAM 26,47.
HRT 21,2.
MDX 10,1. 11,3. 14,1-2.
15,1. 17,1. 18,1.
19,1. 20,1. 25,3.
WOR 26,17.
Land holder so free he
could sell where he
would with full
jurisdiction ESS 30,15.
Land holder could not
sell or separate from
Abbey CAM 32,37; 39. 40,1.
HRT 2,3.
See also: Dispose; Do; Give up; Go away; Go
where he would; Grant and sell; Jurisdiction;
Jurisdiction, full; Leave; Put; Remove; Seek;
Separated; Turn; Withdraw.
SEPARATED
free man could not be
from manor with land GLS 1,2.
Land could not be
from
    Abbey BDF 8,6.
BKM 2,3.
CAM 5,29. 18,3. 32,23;
37.
DOR 11,13.
HRT 2,1-2. 10,6; 10; 12.
SOM 2,8. 7,15. 8,16; 20;
32; 39; 41. 10,6.
25,7-8.
WIL 2,12. 7,3-4. 58,2.
    Bishop SOM 6,6.
    church SOM 2,8.
WIL 2,12.
    lord DEV 15,49.
    manor SHR 4,8,3.
SOM 2,5. 19,40. 21,90.
    manor's revenue SOM 1,20. 19,33.
Land holder could not
be from
    Abbey CON 4,6-11; 12; 13-17;
22.
DEV 5,1.

DOR 8,5. 12,16. 49,10;
17. 55,21.
SOM 2,11. 5,10-12; 43;
50. 6,4. 7,11. 8,2; 4-5; 11; 17-20; 24-25;
27-30; 33-34; 37. 9,3; 6. 10,2. 21,54-55; 98.
25,7. 37,9.
WIL 5,6. 7,1; 8; 10-11.
16. 8,2-3; 6-7; 11-12. 10,2-3. 12,3; 6. 13,3;
9; 13. 15,1-2. 16,1. 25,6. 30,2. 41,8.
Abbey with land DOR 13,8.
SOM 6,4.
Abbey's service DOR 12,16.
Bishop/Bishopric DOR 2,4.
SOM 2,7. 6,1. 22,20.
WIL 2,7; 10-11. 3,1; 4.
25,2.
Bishop with land SOM 22,20.
King's service DOR 47,9.
land DEV 25,27.
lord DEV 3,94. 17,33. 20,13;
15. 24,21.
DOR 1,16. 57,19.
lord with land DEV 1,63. 15,33.
lord of manor DEV 1,63. 15,39; 41.
SOM 1,21; 25. 25,9.
manor BDF 54,3.
CON 1,1.
DEV 24,22.
GLS 3,1.
HEF 1,4.
SOM 1,28. 3,1. 21,90.
22,5; 21. 25,55.
Land holder could be
from lord with land DEV 42,4.
Monk could not be
from Abbey SOM 8,26.
See also: Dispose; Do; Give up; Go away; Go
where he would; Grant and sell; Land; Leave; Put;
Remove; Seek; Sell; Turn; Withdraw.
SEPARATION – See Marriage.
SERF (servus) – See Slave.
SERGEANT (serviens) – See Servant.
SERVANT (serviens) CAM 5,58.
CHS 3,8.
ESS 23,42.
LIN CS40.
NTH 6a,19.
SHR 4,4,25. 7,4.
STS 12,17.
WIL 12,4.
WOR 10,16.
Abbot's NFK 14,32.
Count's HRT 15,1.
SFK 2,8.
Earl's CHS 26,5. FT1,3.
NFK 14,32.
French LEC 13,63.
King's DEV 51.
DOR 57.
ESS 1,16a. 6,9. 86,2.
HEF 1,2; 4.

property, for | ESS | B5.
Land
  exempt/free from | GLS | 1,24; 38. 10,1. 11,4.
  | HEF | 7,2.
  not rendering | OXF | 58,11-12.
Not performed | BDF | 56,2-3.
Not received | CAM | 13,8.
Not rendered | NFK | 65,17.
Overseas | BKM | 38,1.
  | MDX | 25,2.
Thane rendering like
villager | CHS | R1,40a.
Water, by | BRK | B1.
See also: Burgess; House; Separated; Town.
SESTER (sextarium) – See Barley; Flour; Honey;
Oats; Rye; Salt; Wheat; Wine.
SETTLED land (hospitata)
Newly settled | LIN | C22.
  | SSX | 13,52.
Payments for | HEF | 10,43-44.
SETTLER (hospes) | HEF | 10,47.
  | SHR | 4,23,17. 4,25,3. 4,27,27.
Having nothing | CHS | 2,9.
SHAMBLES (macellum) – See Market.
SHEAF of corn (garba) – See Corn.
SHEEP (ovis) | CAM | 1,16. 29,12.
  | CON | *1,1-6; 8-12; 14-17. 2,1-6; 8-11. 3,1-5. 4,1-2; 5-16; 18-19; 22; 23-28. 5,1,1-13; 22. 5,2,2-3; 5-7; 10-11; 15-19; 21-22; 24-25. 5,3,3-14; 16-24; 26-28. 5,4,1; 5; 7; 11-16; 18. 5,5,2-10; 12; 15-18; 20. 5,6,1-10. 5,7,2-4; 6-12. 5,8,1-4; 6; 9-10. 5,9,1-2; 4. 5,10,1. 5,11,1-6. 5,12,1-3. 5,13,1-2; 5; 8-9; 11. 5,14,1-2; 4. 5,15,1-6. 5,16,1-2. 5,17,1; 3-4. 5,19,1. 5,20,1-2. 5,21,1. 5,23,1-3; 5. 5,24,3-4; 8-10; 12; 15; 18; 21-25. 5,25,1-3; 5. 5,26,1-4. 7,1.*
  | DEV | *1,3-5; 7-12; 14-20; 23-41; 43-47; 49-51; 54-72. 2,2; 4-8; 11-12; 14-24. 3,4-9; 12-14; 16-26; 28; 30-31; 33; 36-38; 40; 43-49; 51; 53-54; 56; 58-67; 69; 73-80; 84; 86; 89-93; 95; 97; 99. 4,1. 5,1-8; 11-14. 6,1-5; 7-12. 7,1-4. 8,1. 10,1-2. 11,1-2. 12,1. 13a,2-3. 15,2-6; 8-14; 17-18; 21; 23-27; 30; 33-35; 37-45; 47-49; 51; 56-58; 61; 63-67; 70-71; 74-77; 79. 16,3-9; 11-15; 17-29; 31-37; 39-40; 43-52; 55-59; 63; 65-74; 76; 78; 80; 82-88; 90; 92-97; 99; 102; 104-114; 117-123; 125-126; 128-133; 135-138; 140-145; 148; 150; 152; 154-155; 157-158; 160; 162-167; 170-171; 173; 175-176. 17,3-9; 12-17; 20-23; 26-36; 41-44; 46; 48-51; 53-57; 59-61; 63-69; 71; 73; 76; 78-81; 83; 86; 88-89; 91-92; 95; 97; 100; 102-103; 106-107. 18,1. 19,2; 4-21; 23-31; 33; 35; 37-41; 44; 46. 20,1; 3-5; 10-15; 17. 21,1-4; 7-10; 14-16; 18-21. 22,1. 23,1-7; 9-12; 14-16; 18; 20-26. 24,2-3; 5-10; 14; 17; 19; 21-23; 26-28; 32. 25,1-2; 4-5; 7; 9; 11;*

13-16; 20; 22-25. 27,1. 28,1-13; 15-16. 31,1-2. 32,2-7; 10. 33,1-2. 34,1-2; 4; 6; 8; 10; 12; 14-16; 18-20; 22-31; 33; 35; 38-41; 43-44; 46; 48-51; 55. 35,1-5; 8-10; 12-15; 20-23. 36,3-4; 7; 10; 15-17; 20; 23-26. 37,1. 38,1. 40,2; 4-5; 7. 41,2. 42,1-4; 6-10; 12-14; 16-19; 21-24. 43,2. 45,2. 46,1-2. 47,3; 5-8; 11-12. 48,1; 3-5; 7-8; 10. 49,2. 50,1; 5. 51,1-3; 5-7; 9-16. 52,1; 4-5; 10-14; 16-20; 22-25; 27; 29; 31-33; 35-38; 41-45.
  | DOR | *1,1-21; 24; 26-28. 11,1-6; 10-15; 17. 12,1-5; 7-10; 12; 16. 13,1-6; 8. 16,1. 36,1-7; 9-10. 41,1-2; 5; 9. 48,1-2. 55,1-9; 11; 15-17; 19-22; 24; 27-29; 31; 33-36; 38; 40; 42. 58,2.*
  | ESS | 1,1-4; 9; 11-13; 19; 24-29. 2,1-9. 3,1-2; 8-10; 12-15. 4,1-2; 5-6; 8-9; 11-12; 14-15; 17. 5,1-5; 7; 9-12. 6,1-2; 4-5; 8; 11-12; 14-15. 7,1. 8,1-11. 9,1-2; 7-8; 11-14. 10,1-5. 11,2-3; 6-8. 13,1-2. 14,2-3; 5-6. 15,1-2. 16,1. 17,1. 18,1-5; 14; 22; 25; 28; 36-41. 20,1-2; 6; 9; 15; 19-23; 25-26; 28; 34; 36-40; 43-46; 48; 52-53; 55-57; 59; 63-69; 71-72; 74; 77-78; 80. 22,3-15; 19-20. 23,2; 5; 11; 15; 32; 38-40. 24,1-3; 7-10; 15-26; 28-37; 42; 44-46; 48-49; 53-54; 59-60; 62; 64-66. 25,1-3; 5-8; 10-11; 15-25. 26,1; 3; 5. 27,1-4; 10-11; 13-14. 28,5; 9; 11; 13; 16-17. 29,2-5. 30,1; 4-5; 16-19; 22; 27; 33; 45-46; 50. 31,1. 32,1-4; 6; 8-9; 12-26; 28; 30; 32-35; 38-39; 41-45. 33,1; 3-4; 6-8; 11-17; 19-20; 22-23. 34,1; 4-13; 15; 18-22; 27; 29; 33-37. 35,1-6; 8-12. 36,1; 3; 11-12. 37,1-4; 7; 9-11; 13; 15-16. 38,1-4; 6-8. 39,1; 4-5; 7-8. 40,3-4; 6; 8. 41,2; 5; 9-10; 12. 42,1-3; 6-9. 44,1-3. 45,1. 46,1-2. 47,1-3. 48,1-2. 49,4-5. 51,2. 52,1-2. 53,1-2. 54,1-2. 55,1. 56,1. 57,1-6. 58,1. 60,1-3. 61,1-2. 65,1. 67,1-2. 68,2-4; 7. 69,2. 71,2; 4. 76,1. 81,1. 84,2.*
  | GLS | *1,59-60.*
  | HEF | 1,1; 49.
  | HRT | *8,1-3.* 31,8.
  | HUN | *4,1-4.* 20,6.
  | KEN | 5,15; 105; 110; 124.
  | NFK | 1,1-3; 15-17; 19; 29-30; 32; 40; 42; 52; 57; 59; 69; 71-73; 77-78; 81-82; 85-89; 92; 94; 105; 123; 132-133; 135-136; 138-141; 144; 147; 150-152; 185-186; 192; 194; 197-203; 205; 208-212; 215-217; 228; 231; 237-238. 2,2; 4. 3,1. 4,1-2; 17; 26; 30-31; 38-39; 42; 47; 52. 5,1-4; 6. 6,1-3; 6. 7,1-3; 15-16; 18. 8,1-3; 6-7; 16; 21-22; 30; 33-35; 46-47; 55; 62-64; 91-92; 98-100; 102-103; 105; 107-110; 115; 119; 122; 132. 9,1-2; 6-9; 11-12; 46; 59; 63; 70-71; 73-78; 80-81; 83-84; 87-88; 94-95; 98-99; 104; 233. 10,1-6; 8-11; 16; 20-22; 25; 30; 33; 57; 76. 11,1. 12,1; 17; 20; 27; 30; 32; 42. 13,2-7; 9-10; 12-16; 19; 23-24.*

14,1-2; 4-6; 8; 11; 13-16; 18; 23; 25-26; 35; 40-41. 15,1-5; 7-10; 16-17; 24. 16,1; 4-5. 17,1-3; 8; 16-17; 19; 35; 51; 54; 64. 18,1. 19,1; 4; 11-13; 15; 17; 22-23; 32; 36. 20,1; 6-8; 14; 23-24; 26-27; 35-36. 21,2-7; 9-10; 14; 16; 19; 21; 23-27; 29; 32-33; 37. 22,1; 3-6; 16; 23. 23,1-5; 7; 11-13; 16-17. 24,5; 7. 25,1; 16-17. 26,1-3; 5. 27,1. 28,1-2. 29,1-3; 5; 10. 30,3; 5. 31,1-2; 5-8; 16-17; 20-22; 24-25; 31; 33-35; 37-38; 41-43. 32,1-2; 4-5; 7. 33,1-2; 6. 34,1-5; 7-9; 15; 17-18; 20. 35,6; 9-10; 15-16. 36,5-7. 38,1-2. 39,1-2. 40,1. 42,1. 46,1. 48,2-3. 49,1-2; 4; 6. 50,1; 4-6; 8-9; 11. 51,3; 5-6; 8; 10. 52,2; 4. 54,1. 55,1. 57,1. 58,2. 59,1. 60,1. 61,1. 66,5.

SOM *1,1-12; 15-24; 26-30; 32; 34. 2,1; 6-7; 11-12. 3,1-2. 4,1. 5,1-6; 8-9; 11-16; 18; 22-24; 26; 28; 31-37; 39-51; 53-58; 62-63; 65-67; 69-70. 6,1-4; 6-13. 7,3-11; 13. 8,1-7; 9-11; 14; 16-18; 20-21; 23-31; 33-34. 9,3-4; 6-8. 10,1-3; 5. 11,1. 12,1. 14,1. 15,1. 16,1; 5; 8; 12. 17,1; 5-6; 8. 18,1-2. 19,1-13; 15-16; 17; 20-21; 23-25; 26; 27; 28-35; 38-39; 41; 43-47; 49-60; 62; 64; 68; 70; 75-77; 79-82; 84-86. 20,1. 21,1-3; 5-8; 12; 14; 19; 22; 25; 27; 29; 32; 37-38; 41-42; 44-45; 47; 49-50; 56; 58-60; 62; 64; 70-72; 78-79; 81-82; 85; 89; 93-96; 98. 22,1-3; 6; 8; 10-15; 17; 19; 21; 24; 26-28. 23,1. 24,1; 3-4; 10; 13; 15-22; 25-30; 33-34. 25,1; 5; 7-13; 16; 21-22; 24; 26-27; 29-31; 33-34; 37-41; 43; 49-51; 53-56. 27,1-3. 28,1-2. 29,1. 30,1-2. 31,1; 3. 32,1-4; 8. 34,1. 35,3-6; 10-12; 16-20; 23. 36,1-3; 5; 7-13. 37,1-3; 5-8; 10-12. 39,2-3. 40,1-2. 41,1-3. 42,1. 44,1; 3. 45,1; 4-9; 11; 13; 18. 46,1; 4-6; 8-9; 16; 22-23. 47,2-4; 7-8; 11; 13-14; 16; 18-24.*

SFK 1,2; 8; 14; 16; 23; 32-33; 35; 44-53; 55-56; 75; 88; 90; 96-98; 100-102; 107; 110-111; 115; 118-121; 122b. 2,6. 3,1; 9-10; 34; 46; 56; 61; 67; 69; 74; 88; 94; 98. 4,1; 10; 13; 18-20; 24; 30; 35; 38; 42. 5,1; 3; 5. 6,1-3; 11; 26; 28; 42-44; 48; 62; 80-81; 83; 85; 90; 92-93; 110; 112; 129-130; 143; 148; 165; 172; 187; 191-192; 201; 215; 223; 251; 260-261; 272; 303-309; 312. 7,1; 3-5; 7; 13-15; 18-19; 42; 47; 56; 58; 60-61; 64; 71; 73; 75-76; 98; 147. 8,1; 7; 11; 13; 31; 33-35; 46-47; 49; 55; 81. 9,1-3. 12,1; 3-7. 13,2. 14,1-10; 18-21; 23-25; 32; 38-39; 42; 45; 47-54; 69-70; 72-77; 102-103; 106; 108-109; 117-119; 129; 139; 163-164. 15,1-3; 5. 16,2; 10-12; 16-17; 20-21; 26; 29-30; 40-41. 17,1. 18,1; 4. 19,16. 20,1. 21,1; 3; 5-7; 10-11; 15-16; 26; 28; 38-40; 42-43; 45; 47; 53-55; 58; 80; 83; 95. 23,2. 24,1. 25,1-7; 11-12; 19; 34; 46-47; 49; 52-53; 55; 61; 63; 76; 78-81; 84-85; 105. 26,3-4; 6; 8-10; 12a-c; 13-16. 27,3-7; 9-11; 13.

28,1a-b; 3; 6-7. 29,1; 11-12. 30,1. 31,3; 8; 20; 40-42; 50-51; 53; 56; 60. 32,1; 3-4; 6; 16; 19; 21. 33,1-4; 6-9; 13. 34,1-3; 5-9; 12-13; 15. 35,1-2; 5-6. 36,1-2; 4. 37,1; 4-6. 38,1; 4; 6; 8; 16; 22. 39,3; 6-7; 12; 16-17. 40,2-4; 6. 41,1-2; 7; 10; 14-15; 17. 42,1. 43,2-5. 44,1-3. 45,2. 46,1; 3-4; 7. 47,2-3. 48,1. 49,1. 51,1. 52,1; 5. 53,1-3; 5-6. 54,1-3. 55,1. 58,1. 59,1-2. 60,1. 62,4. 64,1; 3. 65,1. 66,1-4; 6. 67,3; 11; 15; 19; 23; 27-28; 31; 33. 68,1. 70,1. 71,1. 76,4-5.

	WIL	*34,1.*
	WOR	*1,1c.*
half (½)	NFK	8,99.
Flock	LIN	24,21.
Render of	HEF	1,56.
with lambs	HEF	1,1; 6; 8; 55.
	SOM	1,4. 3,1. 19,17; 23-25; 27; 29.

See also: Crime/offence; Customary due; Fleece; Lamb; Marsh; Pasture; Ram; Wether.

| SHEEPFOLD (ovile) | GLS | 60,1. |
| | HUN | 20,6. |

Cheese from
See also: Fold.

| SHEPHERD (bercarius) | SSX | 12,5. |

SHERIFF (vicecomes)	BDF	1,1a; 2a; 3. 17,7. 23,25. 57,1; 3.
	BRK	B11. 1,10; 26-27; 32; 37; 42. 21,15; 17; 22; 57.
	BKM	1,3. 4,5. 17,20. 19,3. 44,1.
	CAM	B11. 3,5. 5,16. 21,9. 22,6. 32,35; 38; 43. 33,1.
	DEV	C2. 1,5; *36-38; 40. 2,24.* 16. *17,38.* 52,33.
	DOR	B1; 3-4. 42. 49,15-16.
	ESS	1,23; 27-28. 10,5. 83,1.
	GLS	G4. W8; 15. B1. 1,2; 8; 10-13; *59-60.* 2,10. 3,7. 34,8; 12. 53. 56,2.
	HAM	1,30; 42; W3. 6,10. 12,1. 30,1. 47,1. 69,4; 33.
	HEF	C3. 1,1; 7; 31; 38; 70. 8,1. 10,19; 66.
	HRT	B11. 1,6; 8-9; 12-13; 18-19. 4,1; 6; 9; 23. 5,4; 10-11; 14. 9,10. 17,4. 25,2. 28,1; 7. 31,7. 32. 34,6; 8; 18; 25. 36,8; 9; 11; 13. 37,1; 14; 17; 19. 38,2. 42,13.
	HUN	B10. 19. 19,25. D20.
	KEN	C1. 1,1-3. 2,16; 31.

6,1-5; 7-13. 7,2-4. 8,1. 10,1-2. 11,1-3.
12,1. 13,1. 13a,2. 14,1-2. 15,3-6; 8-20; 22-
27; 30-43; 45-51; 53-62; 64; 66-67; 70-76;
78-79. 16,3-9; 11-24; 26-38; 40-41; 43; *44;*
45-53; 55; 57-61; 63-78; 80; 83-97; 99-123;
125-133; 135-148; 150; 152-160; 162-166;
168-171; 173; 175-176. 17,3-8; 10; 12-17;
19-22; 26-34; 36-39; 41-43; 45-53; 55; 58-
61; 63-69; 72-76; 78-81; 83; 88; 95; 97; 100;
102-103; 105-106. 18,1. 19,2; 4-21; 23-31;
33; 35; 37-42; 44-46. 20,1; 3-5; 10-17.
21,1-4; 6-8; 12-14; 16; 19-21. 22,1-2. 23,1-
22; 26. 24,3-5; 7-10; 12-14; 17; 19; 21; 23;
25-28; 30; 32. 25,1-7; 9; 11-17; 20-24; 27.
26,1. 27,1. 28,1-11; 13; 15-16. 29,1-6; 8-
9. 30,1-3. 31,1-2; 4. 32,1-8; 10. 33,1-2.
34,1-2; 4; 6-10; 12; *13;* 14-16; 18-19; 22-
31; 33-36; 38-40; 42-44; 47-52; 55-56. 35,1-
5; 7; 9-10; 12-15; 18; 20-21; 25-26; 29-30.
36,1; 3-4; 6; 8; 10; 12-14; 16-20; 24; 26.
37,1. 38,1-2. 39,1-21. 40,1; 4; 6-7. 41,2.
42,1-4; 6-10; 12-13; 15; *16;* 17-18; 20-24.
43,1-3; 5. 44,1-2. 45,2. 46,2. 47,3; 5-9; 11-
14. 48,2-8; 10. 49,1-2; 5-7. 50,1-3; 5. 51,1-
5; 7-16. 52,1-2; 4-6; 10-14; 16-29; 31-45;
50-53.

               DOR   1,1-21; 23-24; 26-
28; 30. 2,1-4; 6. 3,1-11; 13; 16-18. 4,1. 5,1-
2. 6,1; 3-4. 8,1-5. 9,1. 10,1; 3; 6. 11,1-7;
9-17. 12,1-5; 7-12; 14. 13,1-6; 8. 14,1.
16,1. 17,1-2. 19,1-2; 4; 8-10; 12-14. 20,1-
2. 21,1. 22,1. 23,1. 24,4-5. 25,1. 26,1; 3-
4; 14; 18-20; 22-24; 26; 28; 32; 35-37; 39;
42-46; 49-50; 52; 58-59; 61-65; 67; 70-71.
27,1; 3-5; 7; 9-11. 28,1-4. 30,1; 4. 31,1-2.
32,1; 33,1-2; 5. 34,1-2; 5-13; 15. 35,1. 36,2-
7; 9-11. 37,1-2; 11-12. 38,1-2. 39,1-2.
40,1-4; 6-9. 41,1-2; 4. 42,1. 43,1. 45,1.
46,2. 47,1-7; 9. 48,2. 49,4-6; 8-12; 15-16.
50,1; 3-4. 51,1. 53,1-2. 54,3; 5-6; 8-11.
55,1-2; 4-6; 8-9; 11; 16-17; 19-20; 22; 24;
27; 29-31; 33; 38; 40-42. 56,1-2; 7-9; 12;
14-17; 21; 23; 28-29; 31-33; 35-36; 38; 44-
45; 48; 53-54; 57-60; 64. 57,1; 3-4; 10-13;
15. 58,1-2.

               ESS   1,1-4; 8-13; 19; 22-
24; 26-30. 2,1-8. 3,1-3; 5-11; 13; 15-16.
4,1-2; 4-6; 8-11; 13-15; 17-18. 5,1-5; 7-12.
6,2; 5; 8-9; 11-12; 14-15. 7,1. 8,1-3; 6-11.
9,1-2; 5; 7-9; 11-14. 10,1-5. 11,2-4; 6-8.
12,1. 13,1-2. 14,2-7. 15,1-2. 16,1. 17,1.
18,1-3; 5; 8; 11; 14-15; 18; 21a-22; 24; 29-
30; 36-43; 45. 19,1. 20,1-3; 6-9; 12-13; 15-
16; 18-23; 25-28; 30-34; 36-41; 43-52; 54-
59; 62-72; 74-79. 21,2; 4; 6; 10. 22,3-9; 11-
18; 20; 22. 23,1-4; 6-10; 13; 15-17; 26; 28-
31; 36; 38-41; 43. 24,1-10; 13; 16-17; 19-
20; 24-31; 35; 42; 44-46; 48-49; 53-54; 57-
58; 60-61; 64-66. 25,1-8; 11-12; 14-16; 18-
26. 26,1-2; 5. 27,1-6; 8; 10-17. 28,1-3; 5-
6; 8-9; 11-13; 15-18. 29,1-5. 30,1-11; 14;

16-25; 27-35; 37; 39-40; 44-46; 50-51. 31,1.
32,1-9; 12-19; 21-26; 28; 30; 35-36; 38-45.
33,1; 3-7; 11-20; 22-23. 34,1; 4-8; 10-13;
15-16; 18-21; 23-24; 26-27; 32-34; 36-37.
35,1-2; 4-6; 8-13. 36,1-4; 6; 8-12. 37,1-4;
7; 9-12; 14-17; 20. 38,2; 4-8. 39,1-5; 7-9.
40,1-4; 6; 8-9. 41,2-3; 5-7; 9-10; 12. 42,1-
9. 43,1; 3-6. 44,1-4. 45,1. 46,1-3. 47,1-3.
48,1-2. 49,1. 51,2. 52,1-3. 53,1-2. 54,2.
55,1. 57,3-5. 58,1. 59,1. 60,2-3. 61,1-2.
64,1. 65,1. 66,1-2. 67,1. 68,2; 4; 7. 69,2.
71,2; 4. 72,2-3. 74,1. 76,1. 77,1. 78,1. 80,1.
81,1. 83,1. 84,1-2. 86,1. 90,7; 15; 20; 22-
23; 25-26; 30; 35-36; 47; 50-51; 53; 57-58;
63; 65. B1; 7.

               GLS   W9; 15. 1,1-7; 9-
15; 17; 20-22; 24-30; 33-37; 41; 47-51; 54;
58-62; 65-67. 2,3; 5; 8-13. 3,1-5; 7. 4,1.
5,1-2. 6,1-2; 4-9. 7,1. 8,1. 10,1-10; 12-13.
11,1-12; 14. 12,1-2; 4-6; 8-9. 13,1. 14,1.
15,1. 16,1. 18,1. 19,1-2. 20,1. 21,1. 22,1.
23,1-2. 26,1-4. 27,1. 28,1; 4. 29,1. 30,1-3.
31,1; 7-11. 32,1-7; 11; 13. 33,1. 34,1; 4-9;
11. 35,1. 36,1-3. 38,1-2; 4. 39,1-2; 4-9; 12-
21. 40,1. 41,1-5. 42,1-3. 43,1-2. 44,1. 45,1-
3; 5. 46,1-3. 47,1. 48,1-2. 49,1. 50,1-3.
52,1; 3-7. 53,1-3; 5; 8-11. 54,1-2. 55,1.
56,1-2. 57,1. 58,1; 4. 59,1. 60,1-5; 7. 61,1-
2. 62,1; 3-6. 63,1-4. 64,2-3. 66,1; 3-6. 67,1;
3-7. 68,1-5; 7; 9-10; 12. 69,1-3; 6-7. 70,1-
2. 72,1-3. 73,1-2. 74,1. 75,1-2. 78,1-3; 5;
7-13; 15-16.

               HAM 1,1-3; 8-10; 15-20;
22-30; 39-43; 45-47; W3-4; W9-12; W14-
15; W19; W21. 2,1-2; 4-6; 8-11; 13-15; 20;
22-25. 3,1-9; 11; 13-14; 16; 18; 20-21; 24.
5,1. 6,1-9; 11-17. 7,1. 9,2. 10,1. 13,1.
14,2-4; 6. 15,1-3. 16,1-6. 17,1-3. 18,1-3.
19,1. 20,1. 21,1-3; 5-7. 22,1. 23,1; 4-8; 10-
14; 16-20; 22-23; 25; 27-32; 36; 38-40; 42;
44; 47; 49-53; 57; 59-62. 24,1. 25,1. 26,1.
27,2. 28,2; 6-7. 29,1-3; 5-8; 11-16. 30,1.
31,1. 32,1-2; 4. 34,1. 35,1; 3-9. 36,1-2.
37,1-2. 38,1. 39,2-4. 40,1. 42,1. 43,1. 44,1;
3-4. 45,3; 5. 46,1. 47,3. 49,1. 50,1-2. 51,1.
52,1. 54,1. 56,1-2. 57,2. 58,1. 60,1. 61,1.
63,1. 66,1. 67,1. 68,1-3; 5-6; 9-10. 69,1-2;
4-6; 14; 32; 36; 40-44; 48. NF3,8-9; 12.
NF9,36-37; 40; 44. NF10,1. IoW1,1-5; 7-
10; 12-13. IoW2,1. IoW6,1; 4; 6; 11; 14;
21. IoW7,6; 17-18; 21; 23. IoW8,3-4; 6; 8.
IoW9,2-3; 6; 24.

               HEF   1,1-2; 4-8; 10a,c;
17-18; 20-21; 23; 26-28; 30-31; 34; 40-42;
44; 46; 48; 53; 56; 61-62. 2,8; 12; 14; 17-18;
20-21; 24-25; 29-31; 39; 42; 48-49; 57-58.
5,1-2. 6,2. 7,1; 4; 6; 8-9. 8,1-3; 5; 8; 10.
9,1-3; 5-6; 9-10; 17; 19. 10,1; 4-6; 8-9; 11;
14-16; 19-21; 27-30; 32-33; 35-36; 40; 44;
46-52; 54; 57; 59-60; 63-64; 66-71; 74. 11,1.
12,2. 14,1-4; 10; 12. 15,5-8; 10. 16,1-4.

17,1-2. 18,1. 19,5-6; 8-10. 20,1. 21,1; 4-5.
22,1; 4-5; 7. 23,1; 4-5. 24,1; 8; 10. 25,2.
26,1. 27,1. 29,1-3; 8-9; 11; 13. 31,4; 6.
34,1. 35,1. 36,1.

HRT 1,1-6; 9-10; 18. 3,1.
4,2-3; 5-6; 8-12; 14; 16-20; 23-24. 5,1; 4;
8; 13-14; 17-18; 20; 23-24; 26. 7,1-3. 8,1-
3. 9,4; 10. 10,1; 3-4; 6-11; 15-16; 19. 11,1.
12,1. 13,1-5. 14,1-2. 15,1; 3; 5; 10-12.
16,2; 4; 7-10. 17,1-4; 8; 10; 12-13; 15. 19,1-
2. 20,2; 7-8; 11; 13. 22,1-2. 23,3-4. 24,1;
3. 25,2. 26,1. 27,1. 28,4-5; 7-8. 29,1. 30,1.
31,1; 3; 6-7. 32,1-2. 33,5; 9-10; 12-13; 17-
18. 34,4-5; 10; 12-13; 16; 20; 24. 35,1-3.
36,3-4; 7; 11; 14; 16; 19. 37,5-6; 8; 11; 14;
16; 20-22. 38,1-2. 41,1. 42,1-2; 6-7; 10.
42a,1. 43,1. 44,1.

HUN *4,1-4.*

KEN M6. 1,1-4. 2,3-5;
7-12; 14-16; 19-21; 23; 25-26; 29; 31; 35-
37; 41. 3,2-6; 11-16; 18-21. 4,1-3; 6; 8-13;
16. 5,1-8; 12-14; 17-20; 23-26; 28-30; 32-
34; 36; 38-49; 51-60; 63; 65; 67-70; 72-78;
80-83; 85-87; 89; 91; 93-96; 98-106; 109;
115-120; 123; 128-129; 134; 142; 146; 149;
152-153; 155; 159; 162-164; 167-168; 170;
172; 176; 191; 195; 206; 217; 225. 6,1. 7,2;
9; 14; 19. 8,1. 9,1; 4; 6; 12; 22; 31; 37; 42;
45; 47-50. 10,1-2. 11,1-2. 12,1; 3. 13,1.

LEC 1,1a-b; 10. 2,1; 3;
5-6. 3,6; 8; 11-12; 14. 4,1. 6,1; 5. 7,2. 9,3;
5. 10,1; 3; 7; 10. 12,1. 13,1; 4-5; 12; 15-23;
26-28; 35; 37; 39-41; 50-51; 53-58; 61; 63-
66; 69-70; 72. 14,1; 5-6; 9-10; 14; 16. 15,2-
5; 8; 10-15. 16,1; 3; 5-9. 17,9; 12; 18. 18,3-
4. 19,5; 13; 15. 20,1-2; 4. 21,1-2. 24,1; 3.
25,1; 5. 28,1-2. 29,3; 5-6; 10. 31,1. 37,1.
38,1. 40,1; 10; 15-17; 32. 41,3. 42,1; 3.
43,1; 6; 9-11. 44,3-4; 6-10; 12.

MDX 2,1. 3,14. 4,3; 5-9;
12. 5,1. 7,4-5. 8,4-5. 9,2; 4; 7-9. 10,1. 11,1;
3. 13,1. 18,1-2. 19,1. 20,1. 21,1. 22,1.
24,1. 25,1.

NFK 1,1-3; 15-17; 19; 21;
23; 42; 57; 70-73; 77-78; 81-82; 85-89; 92;
94; 105; 128; 135-138; 140; 142; 145-147;
150-152; 169; 175; 182-183; 185-186; 191-
194; 197-198; 202; 209-212; 215-216; 218-
219; 228; 231; 237-238. 2,2; 4. 4,1-3; 6; 9;
15; 26; 29; 31; 38-39; 47; 49; 52. 5,2; 4; 6.
6,1-4; 6. 7,1-3; 18. 8,1-3; 6-7; 14; 16; 18;
21-22; 24; 27-30; 34-35; 37; 40; 44; 46-47;
50; 55; 61-63; 65-66; 68; 91; 95; 98-100;
102-103; 105; 107; 109-110; 115; 119-122;
130; 132. 9,1-2; 6-12; 24; 60; 70-77; 80-81;
83-84; 87; 94-95; 98; 100; 102; 139; 168-
169; 178; 221; 233. 10,1-2; 4-8; 10-11; 15-
16; 20-22; 28; 30; 38; 56; 76. 11,1-2. 12,1;
17; 27; 30; 32; 42. 13,2-5; 7; 9-10; 12; 14-
16; 19; 23-24. 14,1-2; 5-6; 11; 13; 16; 21;
23; 37; 39-40. 15,1-2; 4-5; 7-12; 16-17; 24-

25; *28.* 16,1; 4-5. 17,2; 16-18; 25; 35; 53.
18,1. 19,4; 11; 13; 15; 17-18; 24; 32; 36.
20,1; 6-10; 14; 23; 26; 34-36. 21,2-7; 9-10;
14; 16-17; 19; 21; 24-25; 27; 29; 34. 22,1;
4-6; 10; 16; 23. 23,1-3; 5; 11-13; 16-17.
24,6-7. 25,1; 7; 21. 27,1. 28,1-2. 29,2-8;
10. 31,1; 5; 7-8; 10; 12; 17; 20-22; 24-25;
34-35; 37-38; 41-44. 32,1-2; 4. 33,1-2; 6.
34,1-4; 7-11; 13; 15; 17-18; 20. 35,1-3; 6;
10. 36,6-7. 37,1; 3. 38,1-2. 39,1. 40,1.
41,1. 42,1. 43,1. 46,1. 48,2. 49,1-2; 4-7.
50,1; 4-6; 8; 12. 51,1; 3; 8. 52,1. 55,1. 58,2.
66,30. 64.

NTH 1,1; 4; 6; 8; 13a; 26;
30. 2,2; 6-7; 12. 3,1. 4,1-4; 7; 9; 11-12; 14-
17; 24; 27; 30-34; 36. 5,2-4. 6,1-4; 6; 8;
10a; 11-12; 15. 6a,1-2; 4-5; 11; 13; 22-23;
25; 28-29; 33. 8,13. 9,5-6. 11,4-6. 12,3.
14,2-3; 6. 15,1. 16,1. 18,1; 3-5; 7; 9-11; 15;
17; 19; 23; 27; 34; 36-37; 44; 46-48; 52-53;
57-60; 62; 69; 71; 75-76; 79-80; 83; 85-86;
88; 90; 92-93; 95-97. 19,1-2. 21,1-2; 5-6.
22,1; 3-5; 9. 23,2; 4-5; 8-9; 11; 13-14; 17-
18. 24,1. 25,1-3. 26,1-6; 8; 11. 27,1. 28,1-
2. 30,9; 14-15. 31,1. 32,1. 33,1. 34,1.
35,1a; 3a; 4; 6; 8-10; 12; 16; 19a; 21-24; 26.
36,2. 39,2; 5-9; 11; 13; 16-18. 40,2; 4. 41,1;
4-6. 42,1; 3. 43,1-2; 4-6; 8-9; 11. 45,1-2;
4-9. 46,1; 3-4; 7. 47,1a; 2. 48,3-9; 11-12;
14. 49,1. 52,1. 53,1. 54,1-3. 55,4. 56,1; 7-
8; 15-16; 18; 21; 23; 25; 27; 36; 38-39; 47;
49; 51; 65-66. 57,1-2. 58,1. 59,3. 60,1; 4.

NTT 10,1; 16; 39. 11,10.
12,1; 16; 18. 30,47.

OXF 1,1; 3; 5-7a; 8-9.
2,1. 3,1-2. 4,1. 5,1. 6,1c; 4-5; 8-13; 15-17.
7,1-4; 6-7; 9-11; 14; 17-18; 20; 22; 24-27;
29; 32; 36-37; 39-40; 45-47; 49; 51; 53; 56;
58-61. 8,2-4. 9,1-2; 6-7; 9a-b. 10,1. 11,1.
12,1. 13,1. 14,6. 15,2-3. 16,1. 17,1-7. 18,1-
2. 19,1. 20,1-3; 5. 22,1. 23,1-2. 24,1; 3-5.
26,1. 27,1-4; 6-8; 10. 28,1-4; 6-7; 9-15; 17-
23; 25-26; 29. 29,1-8; 10-12; 14; 16; 18-19;
21-22. 30,1. 31,1. 32,1-2. 33,1-2. 34,1-2.
35,1-4; 6-11; 13; 16; 18; 20-22; 24-26; 29;
31; 34. 36,1. 38,1-2. 39,1; 3. 40,1; 3. 41,1-
2. 42,1. 43,1-2. 44,1. 45,1-3. 46,1. 47,1.
48,1. 50,1. 53,1-2. 54,1. 55,1-2. 56,1; 3-4.
57,1. 58,1; 3-5; 7-8; 12; 15-16; 18; 21-25;
27; 30; 33; 35-36; 38. 59,1-3; 6; 8-10; 12-
14; 17-18; 20; 22-27.

SHR 1,5-7. 2,1-2. 3b,2-
3. 3c,2-4; 6-8; 10-11. 3g,4. 4,1,5-6; 16; 18-
20; 24; 26; 29-32; 36. 4,3,1-9; 11; 13-18; 20-
21; 24; 26-31; 44-45; 48; 54-56; 60-61; 63-
71. 4,4,1; 3-4; 10-15; 18; 20. 4,5,4; 6; 9-
10; 12. 4,6,5. 4,7,3. 4,8,1; 4-7; 11-13; 15-
16. 4,9,1-2; 4. 4,10,1; 3. 4,11,1; 3-8; 12;
19. 4,13,1. 4,14,3-5; 8; 11-12; 16; 25; 28.
4,16,2. 4,17,3. 4,19,6; 9-10; 12-13. 4,20,2-
3; 5-8; 14-17; 24. 4,21,2-3; 5-12; 14; 16; 19.

4,22,2-3. 4,23,1; 3; 5-6; 8-10; 12; 14; 16-
18. 4,24,2. 4,25,1; 6. 4,26,3-4. 4,27,1-2; 6;
8; 10; 19; 22-24; 26; 29; 35. 5,1-2; 8. 6,1-
2; 6-9; 11-12; 15; 33. 7,1; 3-6. 9,2.

SOM 1,1-7; 9-14; 16-30;
32-33; *35*. 2,1; 6-9; *10*; 11-12. 3,1-2. 4,1.
5,1; 3-9; 11-18; 20; 22-27; 29-34; 36-37; 39-
54; 56-59; 61-64; 66-70. 6,1-17. 7,2-9; 11;
13-15. 8,1-2; 4-7; 9-11; 13-18; 20-34. 9,1-
4; 6-7. 10,1-5. 11,1. 12,1. 13,1. 15,1. 16,1-
2; 5; 8. 17,1-4; 6-8. 18,1-4. 19,1-2; 4-11;
13; 15-16; 19-21; 23-35; 38-41; 43-54; 56-
57; 59-66; 68; *69*; 71-72; 75; 77; 79-82; 85-
87. 20,1; 3. 21,1-4; 6; 8; 12; 14-15; 17; 19;
23; 26-27; 29; 37; 39; 41; 43; 47; 49-50; 54-
56; 58-60; 63; 70-74; 76-77; 80-83; 85; 89-
90; 93-94; 96; 98. 22,1-4; 8; 10-15; 19-22;
25-26. 23,1. 24,1; 3-4; 8-9; 11-29; 31; 33-
35. 25,1; 3-5; 7-14; 16; 18; 24-27; 29-31;
33-34; 36; 38-39; 41; 43-47; 49-55. 26,1; 3-
6; 8. 27,1-2. 28,1-2. 30,1-2. 31,1-4. 32,1-
5; 8. 33,1-2. 34,1. 35,1-6; 8-13; 16-20; 22-
23. 36,2; 5; 7; 9-11; 13. 37,1-6; 8-10. 38,1.
39,2-3. 40,1-2. 41,1-3. 42,1-2. 43,1. 44,1-
3. 45,3-5; 7-13; 15; 17-18. 46,1; 4; 8; 12;
15-16; 18-22. 47,2-3; 5-6; 9; 12-14; 16-21.

STS 1,1; 6-7; 9; 11-12;
19-20; 24; 27; 29; 32. 2,1; 10; 16; 20. 6,1.
7,1-2; 13-15; 17. 8,4-5; 7-12; 14-15; 17; 24;
26-27; 32. 9,1. 10,4; 9. 11,2; 6; 8-9; 11; 14-
16; 24; 27-29; 31; 33; 35; 37-39; 43-44; 48;
50; 52; 54; 56; 58; 60-62; 65-66. 12,1; 6-8;
10-11; 14-15; 20; 22; 24; 30-31. 14,1-2.
17,7.

SFK 1,1-2; 8-9; 12; 23;
32-35; 47; 49; 51; 75; 88; 90; 96-98; 100-
102; 110-111; 115; 119-121. 2,1; 6-7; 10;
13. 3,1; 3; 9-10; 34; 46; 56; 67; 72; 88; 94.
4,10; 14; 18-20; 22; 24; 30; 35; 38. 5,1; 3-
4. 6,1-2; 30; 42-43; 57; 62; 80; 83; 85; 112;
187; 191-192; 213; 222-223; 260; 271; 303.
7,1; 6-7; 10-11; 13; 18; 47; 56; 60; 67; 71;
75; 98; 136. 8,1; 11; 31; 34-35; 44-49; 55-
56. 9,3. 11,4. 12,1; 3-4; 6. 13,2; 6. 14,1-
10; 13-14; 16; 18-21; 23-24; 26-27; 32; 36;
38; 42; 45; 47-54; *59*; 68-70; 72-76; 78-79;
82-83; 88; 90; 102-103; 106; 108-109; 113-
114; 120. 15,1-3; 5. 16,10-11; 40. 17,1.
18,1; 4. 19,16. 20,1. 21,1; 3; 5-7; 10-11;
15-16; 26; 38-40; 42-43; 47; 53-54; 80; 95.
23,2-3. 24,1. 25,1-10; 19-20; 33-34; 47; 52-
53; 55; 66; 78-80; 84. 26,3; 8-10; 12a-b; 13-
15. 27,3-6; 9; 13. 28,1a-b; 3; 7. 29,11-12.
31,3; 20; 40-42; 50; 53; 60. 32,3-4; 6; 14;
19; 21. 33,1; 3-4; 6-7; 9-10; 12-13. 34,1-3;
5-6; 8; 12. 35,1-2; 5-6. 36,1-2. 37,1; 4-5.
38,1. 39,5-6; 17. 40,2-3; 6. 41,1-2; 7; 10;
15; 17. 42,1-2. 43,1-3; 6. 44,1-4. 46,1-4.
47,3. 48,1. 49,1. 52,5. 53,1; 3; 5-6. 54,1-
3. 55,1. 60,1. 61,2. 64,1; 3. 65,1. 66,1; 3-
4; 6; 10. 67,15. 68,1. 69,1. 70,1. 76,4-5.

SRY 1,3; 6; 8; 11-15.
2,2-3; 5-6. 3,1. 4,1. 5,1a,f; 4; 6; 8; 15; 19-
23; 27. 6,1-2; 5. 7,1. 8,3-4; 9; 17; 22-23;
28; 30. 11,1. 14,1. 15,1-2. 16,1. 17,1. 18,2-
4. 19,1-3; 5; 7-9; 12; 14-17; 19-21; 23; 27;
31-32; 35-39; 44-47. 21,4; 6. 22,1; 4-5.
25,2-3. 26,1. 27,1-2. 28,1. 29,1. 30,1.
32,1-2. 33,1. 35,2. 36,1; 4-6.

SSX 1,1-2. 3,3-4; 7. 5,2.
6,1-2. 7,2. 8,1. 9,14; 96; 120. 10,11; 13; 26;
29-30; 32; 34; 41; 43; 53; 87; 91; 117. 11,3;
6; 8-14; 18-25; 27; 29-31; 35-37; 39-41; 46;
49; 55; 61; 63; 67-68; 78; 81; 91-92; 108-
109; 111-112. 12,3-5; 7; 9; 11; 13; 16; 30;
36; 39; 42. 13,9; 11; 13; 19-20; 23; 25; 29-
31; 34-35; 38. 14,1-2.

WAR 1,1-4; 6-7. 2,1-3.
3,1; 6. 4,2; 5. 5,1. 6,2-8; 10-12; 14-20. 9,1.
10,1. 11,1-4. 12,1; 3-5; 8-10. 13,1. 14,1.
15,2; 5-6. 16,1-2; 5-16; 18; 20; 22-23; 26;
29-32; 35-37; 41; 44; 50; 54; 56-57; 61-62;
64; 66. 17,1; 5; 13; 16; 21-23; 25-26; 29; 31;
33; 37; 44; 47; 52; 54; 56-60; 62; 64; 66-67;
69-70. 18,2-6; 14. 19,3-4. 20,1. 21,1. 22,2;
4-5; 7-8; 11-12; 14-17; 19-27. 23,1; 3. 24,1.
26,1. 27,1-3; 6. 28,1; 6-7; 11; 13-19. 29,1;
3. 30,1. 31,1-3; 5-7; 9-12. 32,1. 33,1. 34,1.
35,1. 37,2-7. 38,1-2. 39,1-3. 40,1-2. 42,1;
3. 43,1-2. 44,3; 6; 10-11; 14. 45,1.

WIL 1,1-22. 2,1-10; 12.
3,1-3. 4,1-3. 5,1-2; 6-7. 6,2. 7,1-4; 6; 8-12;
14-16. 8,1-13. 10,1-5. 11,1. 12,1; 4-6. 13,1-
2; 7-9; 11; 13; 17. 14,1-2. 15,1-2. 16,1-4;
6. 17,1. 18,1-2. 19,1. 20,1-3; 6. 21,1; 3.
22,1-6. 23,1; 5; 7-10. 24,1-2; 4; 7; 10-13;
15; 17-19; 22-25; 27-28; 31-33; 37-38; 40-
41. 25,1-2; 8; 19; 22; 24; 26. 26,1-7; 9; 11-
14; 16-19. 27,1-3; 8-9; 11-15; 17-20; 23-
26. 28,1-3; 7; 9-13. 29,1-2; 5; 9. 30,2; 5-7.
31,1. 32,1-4; 7-8; 10; 12; 15. 34,1. 36,1-2.
37,1-2; 5; 7-8; 11; 15. 38,1. 39,1-2. 40,1.
41,1-2; 5-9. 42,1-2; 4; 6; 8-10. 43,1-2.
45,1; 3. 47,1. 48,1; 3-5; 7-12. 49,2-3. 50,2;
4. 51,1. 52,1. 53,1-2. 54,1. 55,1. 56,1-2;
4. 58,1. 59,1-2. 63,1. 64,1. 65,1. 66,3; 6.
67,1-2; 5-9; 14; 16-17; 19; 32; 37-39; 44;
60-64; 72-73; 77; 80; 86; 94; 98. 68,3-4; 7-
11; 16; 18-21; 25-26; 29.

WOR 1,1a,c; 2. 2,2-5; 9;
15; 17-23; 25-26; 28; 31; 38-39; 41-43; 45-
48; 53-54; 58-66; 68; 72-73; 75-79; 81-85.
3,1-3. 8,1-4; 7-9a,c,e,g; 10,a-d; 11; 14-17;
19-20; 22-24; 26a. 9,1a-b,d; 3-5b. 10,3; 5;
7-9; 11-12; 14. 11,1-2. 13,1. 14,1-2. 15,1-
2; 4; 8-12. 16,1-4. 17,1. 18,1; 3-4. 19,1-2;
4-6; 8; 10-14. 20,2-3; 5. 23,2-3; 6; 8-11.
24,1. 26,1-2; 6-7; 13; 15-17. 28,1.

Breaking holiday,
penalty   CHS   B1.
Burgess, being   SFK   25,52.
Comparative information

less 1086 than TRE ESS 1,11-12; 22; 24; 27-
28. 2,1-3; 8. 3,2; 5; 8; 10; 15. 4,1; 4-6; 8-
9; 13-15; 17. 5,7; 9. 6,12. 7,1. 8,2-3; 6-8;
10-11. 9,1; 5; 7; 12-13. 10,3-5. 12,1. 13,2.
14,2. 16,1. 17,1. 18,3; 11; 14; 29-30; 41.
19,1. 20,1; 3; 6; 9; 13; 15; 19-22; 25-26; 33;
36-41; 43; 52; 54-55; 57-58; 62-63; 65-70;
74-75. 21,6; 10. 22,3-5; 8-9; 13-14; 16-18;
22. 23,1-2; 6-8; 10; 13; 16; 28; 30-31; 38;
40-41. 24,1; 4; 6; 8-10; 16; 19; 24-25; 28;
30; 35; 42; 45; 49; 54; 60-61; 64; 66. 25,1-
6; 12; 14; 16; 18; 21-22. 26,1-2; 5. 27,1; 3-
6; 10-12; 14-15. 28,2-3; 5; 8-9; 13; 15.
29,2-5. 30,3-5; 9; 11; 14; 18-21; 23-25; 31;
33; 35; 40; 44; 46; 50. 31,1. 32,1; 3-6; 9;
14; 16-19; 21; 23; 26; 28; 35; 38-39; 42; 44.
33,1; 3-5; 7; 11-13; 17; 19-20; 22-23. 34,4-
7; 10-11; 13; 15; 20-21; 23; 26-27; 32; 34;
36. 35,4-5; 11. 36,2; 9-12. 37,1; 3; 7; 9; 15;
17; 20. 39,1-5; 8. 40,1-2; 9. 41,3; 12. 42,2-
3; 7-9. 43,1; 4; 6. 44,1-4. 45,1. 46,1; 3.
47,1-3. 48,1. 51,2. 52,2-3. 53,1. 54,2. 57,3;
5. 61,1-2. 64,1. 67,1. 68,7. 71,2. 74,1.
90,7; 23; 25; 47; 51; 56; 58; 63; 65.
　　　　　　NFK 1,1; 21; 57; 71; 85;
87; 89; 92; 94; 105; 128; 135; 140; 147; 169;
175; 194; 209; 211-212; 216; 218; 228; 231.
2,4. 4,2; 9; 26; 38-39; 47; 49; 52. 5,6. 6,4;
6. 7,18. 8,21-22; 30; 34; 55; 62; 68; 98-99;
107; 109; 119. 9,6; 9; 12; 70-71; 75; 84; 87;
95; 102; 221; 233. 10,1; 4-6; 10-11; 15-16;
21; 30. 12,1; 27. 13,3; 12; 24. 14,6; 37.
15,1; 4; 7; 9. 17,35. 19,11; 18; 24. 20,1;
10; 34-36. 21,2; 4-5; 9; 16; 24; 27. 23,1; 3;
11; 16. 29,8; 10. 31,1; 5; 8; 17; 34-35; 38;
41; 44. 33,1-2. 34,2; 17. 35,1. 41,1. 42,1.
43,1. 46,1. 49,1; 7. 50,1; 4-5; 8. 52,1. 55,1.
　　　　　　SFK 1,1; 23; 32-33; 75;
97; 100; 102; 110-111; 119-120. 2,1; 6-7;
13. 3,1; 3; 34; 46. 5,1; 4. 6,1-2; 43; 85; 112;
191; 222-223. 7,6; 71. 8,11; 35; 44; 46; 48-
49; 56. 12,1. 14,1; 21; 42; 45; 48; 50; 69;
72; 74-75; 102. 15,1; 5. 16,40. 21,1; 3; *15;*
16; 26; 39; 43; 53-54; 80; 95. 26,12a-b; 13-
14. 27,3-4; 6. 28,1b; 3. 31,40-42; *60.* 32,3;
21. 33,1; 3-4; 9; 12-13. 34,1; 3. 35,6. 36,1-
2. 37,5. 39,17. 40,2; 6. 41,7; 17. 43,2-3.
46,3. 54,2. 55,1. 66,1; 4. 69,1. 70,1. 76,4.
more 1086 than ESS 1,2-3; 13; 19; 26.
TRE　　　　　3,6-7. 4,18. 5,1; 4.
7,1. 9,9; 14. 18,36-37. 20,2; 36. 24,26; 53.
25,11; 25. 27,16. 28,17. 30,2; 16; 32; 34; 45.
32,25; 30; 45. 35,6; 13. 37,12; 16. 38,6.
60,2. 66,1. 77,1. 80,1. 83,1. 84,1-2. 90,22.
B7.
　　　　　　NFK 1,19; 71; 192. 6,3.
8,121. 15,9. 24,7.
34,4. 49,2. 50,6.
　　　　　　SFK 1,98. 6,83. 14,5; 49;
52; 73. 17,1. 32,14.
49,1.

Female (ancilla)　　CHS A15. 2,6. 20,5.
FT2,8. R1,43.
　　　　　　DEV 51,4.
　　　　　　DOR 34,11.
　　　　　　GLS W9. 1,15; 24-27;
30; 34-35; 37; 58-60. 2,8. 3,1; 4. 4,1. 6,1.
11,2-4; 10-11. 18,1. 21,1. 28,1; 4. 34,4-5;
7-8. 35,1. 39,4-6. 45,1. 46,1. 48,2. 50,3.
52,6. 53,8. 61,1-2. 62,3; 5-6. 63,3. 66,1;
3-4. 68,7-8. 72,1. 78,8-9.
　　　　　　HEF 1,2; 6-10a; 17-18;
21; 26; 40-42; 44; 46; 48; 60. 2,4; 11-12; 14;
16-17; 19-20; 33; 35; 39; 42; 44-46; 49; 51;
57. 8,1; 7. 10,20-21; 34; 44; 58. 14,1; 8.
16,4. 21,1. 22,1. 29,2; 11.
　　　　　　KEN 5,7.
　　　　　　LEC 2,1; 3. 3,6. 9,1; 3.
10,4. 13,1; 51; 53; 58; 69. 25,1. 37,1. 40,16.
43,1; 6. 44,13.
　　　　　　NTH 1,6; 11. 4,9; 17; 26.
6,7; 17. 11,6. 18,17. 23,9; 13. 35,10; 12;
19a. 39,2; 5; 17-18. 41,4. 43,1; 4-6. 47,1a.
49,1. 56,8; 27; 46. 57,1-2.
　　　　　　NTT 12,1; 18.
　　　　　　SHR 3b,2. 3g,4. 4,1,16;
20; 23; 25; 27-28; 30-31. 4,3,16; 21; 26; 30-
31; 48. 4,6,5. 4,8,7; 13. 4,21,14; 16. 4,22,3.
4,27,2. 6,33. 7,4-6.
　　　　　　STS 10,3.
　　　　　　WAR 1,1-4. 3,3. 11,1.
16,33; 46; 52.
17,55; 63. 18,2-3.
31,1; 6. 40,1-2.
　　　　　　WOR 1,1a; 2. 2,2; 15; 17-
18; 21; 23; 25-26; 31; 42. 2,46-47; 62-66;
68; 72-73; 75-76; 78-79; 81-84. 8,1-2; 7-
9a,c,e,g; 10a; 14; 16; 18; 23. 14,1-2. 19,1.
23,2. 24,1. 26,2; 6. 27,1. 28,1.
Made free　　　　GLS 38,2.
Not paying tax　　BRK 30,1.
SMALLHOLDER　BDF 1,1a,c; 2-4. 2,1-6;
(bordarius)　　　　9. 3,1-5; 7-8; 10-
12; 15-16. 4,1-3. 5,2; 6,3. 7,1. 8,1-3; 5; 7-
8. 9,1. 10,1. 11,1. 12,1. 13,1. 15,2; 4-7.
16,1-3; 5-8. 17,1-2; 4-5. 18,1-4; 6. 19,1.
20,1. 21,1-2; 4; 6; 12; 14-17. 22,1. 23,1; 3-
7; 9-10; 12-15; 17-18; 20-30; 32-34; 41; 46-
50; 57. 24,1; 3-11; 13-24; 27. 25,1; 4; 7; 9-
11; 13. 26,1-3. 28,1-2. 29,1. 30,1. 31,1.
32,1-6; 8-13; 16. 33,1-2. 34,1-3. 35,1.
36,1. 39,1. 40,2. 41,1-2. 42,1. 44,2. 45,1.
46,1-2. 47,1-2; 4. 48,1-2. 49,1; 4. 50,1.
51,1-2. 52,1. 53,2-12; 14-17; 20-22; 24-26;
29-33. 54,1-3. 55,1-9; 13. 56,3; 5. 57,5-6;
11-12; 16.
　　　　　　BRK 1,1-2; 15-41; 43-47.
2,1. 3,1; 3. 6,1. 7,1-4; 6-25; 27-30; 32-37.
8,1. 10,1. 14,1. 15,1-2. 16,1-2. 17,1-3; 5-6.
18,1-2. 20,3. 21,1-6; 14-22. 22,1-12. 23,1-
2. 24,1. 25,1. 26,1-2. 27,1. 28,1; 3. 29,1.
30,1. 31,1-2; 6. 33,1-2; 6-8. 34,1; 3-4. 35,1-

11-15; 17-19. 20,1-4. 22,1. 23,1; 4-6. 24,1.
25,1-5. 27,1. 28,1-5. 29,1-3; 5-8; 10-11;
13; 15-16; 18-19. 30,1. 31,1. 33,1. 35,1.
36,1-2. 37,1-2. 38,1. 40,2; 8-9; 12-13; 15-
19; 22-27; 32-34; 36. 41,2-3. 42,1; 6-8; 10.
43,1-3; 5-6; 8-11. 44,1-4; 6-13.

LIN   1,1; 4-7; 9-11; 14;
17-19; 21; 23; 25-26; 28; 32; 35; 38; 40-41;
46-47; 55; 62-63; 66; 71; 77-82; 84; 86; 88;
90-91; 93; 96; 100-106. 2,1-2; 5-6; 8-11; 16-
18; 20; 23; 29; 32-35; 38; 42. 3,3-4; 6-7;
11; 13-15; 22; 31; 33; 35-39; 41-42; 47-48;
50-52. 4,2; 5-6; 8; 11; 13-17; 23; 26; 31-
32; 38-39; 42-46; 53-57; 59; 61; 63; 65-67;
69; 73-74; 76-80. 6,1. 7,3-5; 7-8; 19-20; 24;
27-28; 30; 32; 36; 38-40; 43; 46; 48-49; 51-
52; 54; 58. 8,1; 3; 5; 9; 11; 13; 16-17; 20;
22-23; 28; 31; 34-36; 39. 9,1. 10,1; 3. 11,2-
4; 9; 14-15; 17; 19-21; 24-25; 30; 32; 34-
36; 38-39; 42-44; 47-56; 58-60; 62; 64-65;
70-72; 74-78; 91; 93; 95-96. 13,1-3; 5-10;
12; 14-17; 19; 21-24; 26; 28; 30-31; 34-39;
41-42; 44-45. 14,1; 3; 9; 15-17; 22-23; 25-
26; 34; 39; 41; 43-46; 48-49; 51; 53-55; 58-
59; 63; 66-68; 70-71; 77; 79-82; 86-90; 95-
101. 15,1-2. 16,4; 8-10; 12-13; 18-19; 23;
27; 33; 35; 39; 41; 44; 47; 50. 17,1-2. 18,5-
7; 9-11; 13; 15; 17; 19-20; 27; 29; 31-32.
19,1. 21,1. 22,1; 3; 5; 8; 12; 16-17; 24; 29;
35-36. 24,1; 3; 6-7; 10; 12-14; 17; 20; 25;
27; 32-33; 36; 38; 40; 43-50; 56-57; 62-63;
70; 72-74; 77-78; 80-86; 88-93; 95-97; 99;
101-103; 105. 25,1; 3; 5-9; 11; 13-14; 17;
21; 24-25. 26,1-2; 4-5; 8; 10-11; 13-14; 22;
25; 30-36; 38; 40-44; 47-49; 53. 27,2-3; 5;
7; 12-15; 37; 39; 45; 47-48; 50-51; 53-54;
56-59. 28,5; 7; 13; 15-17; 21-22; 24; 29; 38.
29,5; 7-9; 11; 14; 16; 18; 22; 28; 30; 32; 34.
30,3; 9; 20; 22-24; 27-28; 30-32; 36-37.
31,1-2; 4-7; 9; 11-18. 32,1-2; 4; 6-7; 9; 11;
17; 19; 21; 24-27; 29; 31-32; 34. 33,1. 34,1-
2; 7-8; 13-15; 21; 24; 27. 35,1; 4; 11; 14-
16. 36,1-3. 37,1-2; 5; 7. 38,1; 3-4; 14. 39,1.
40,1-2; 4-5; 10; 12; 23. 42,1-3; 15-16. 43,1-
3. 44,2; 5; 7; 10-11. 45,2. 46,1-2. 47,1-3;
5; 8. 48,4-7; 10-11; 13-15. 49,1-2. 50,1.
51,2; 10; 12. 52,1. 53,1-2. 54,1. 55,1-3.
56,5-7; 9; 11; 13-14; 18; 20-21. 57,3; 5; 7;
10-11; 14-15; 18; 21; 24; 27-28; 30-32; 37-
39; 41; 44-45; 47-48; 50; 54; 56. 58,1-2; 5-
8. 59,1-2; 7-8; 11; 14-15; 17. 60,1. 61,1; 5-
7. 63,5-7; 12-13; 15. 64,1-3; 5-9; 14-15; 17-
19. 65,3-4. 67,5; 9; 12-14; 17-18; 20; 26.
68,1-4; 13; 15; 18; 24-25; 27; 31; 34-35; 38;
44; 46; 48.

MDX   2,1. 3,2-4; 6-8; 12;
14; 16-17; 20; 23; 30. 4,3; 5-6; 8-9; 12. 5,1.
6,1. 7,4-8. 8,5. 9,1-3; 6; 8-9. 10,1-2. 11,1-
4. 12,1-2. 13,1. 14,1. 15,1. 16,1. 17,1.
18,1-2. 20,1. 22,1. 24,1.

NFK   1,1-3; 5; 11-21; 28-

33; 40-42; 48; 50-53; 55-57; 59; 61; 65; 70-
74; 77-79; 81; 83-96; 100; 104-106; 108;
110-111; 114; 119; 123-124; 127-128; 131;
134-136; 138-140; 143-152; 155-156; 159-
162; 169-171; 174-177; 182-183; 185-188;
190-195; 197-200; 202; 205-206; 208-213;
215-219; 222-224; 228; 230-233; 235; 237-
241. 2,1-5; 7; 10-11. 3,1-2. 4,1-3; 5-9; 11;
14-20; 22-23; 26; 28; 30-31; 33; 35; 37-42;
44-47; 49-53; 55-56. 5,1-4; 6. 6,1-7. 7,1-
11; 13-21. 8,1-3; 6-8; 10-16; 18; 20-35; 37-
38; 40-44; 46-48; 50-64; 66-70; 72; 77-85;
87-95; 98-100; 102-103; 105; 107-119; 121-
127; 130-133; 135-136. 9,1-3; 5-7; 9; 11-
12; 15-16; 19; 24-26; 29-33; 42; 46-48; 50-
54; 56; 60; 63-64; 68; 70-74; 76-78; 80-88;
91; 93-96; 98-100; 102-107; 109; 112-113;
115-117; 119; 123-124; 126-127; 129-132;
136-138; 140-147; 149-151; 153-155; 157;
159-162; 165; 167-170; 173-182; 186; 188;
190-192; 194; 196-198; 200-201; 203; 208-
209; 212-214; 216-218; 221; 224-225; 228-
229; 232-234. 10,1-10; 12; 15-16; 18-25; 30;
32-33; 35-40; 42; 46-47; 50-51; 55-58; 60;
65; 67-69; 72-74; 76; 78; 80-83; 87; 91-93.
10a,1. 11,1-2; 4-5. 12,1; 4; 6; 8-9; 11; 14;
16-18; 24; 27; 30; 32-34; 36-37; 40; 42.
13,2-3; 5-7; 9-17; 19; 24. 14,1-3; 5-12; 14-
19; 23-27; 29-31; 35-42. 15,1-11; 13-19; 23-
28. 16,1-6. 17,1; 3-9; 11-14; 16-20; 23-30;
32-33; 35-44; 46-47; 51-56; 59; 61-65. 18,1.
19,1; 3-5; 7; 9-13; 15-25; 27; 29; 31-37.
20,1-2; 4-10; 13-15; 17-21; 23-29; 31-36.
21,2-5; 7-10; 14; 16-18; 21; 23-34. 22,1; 3-
6; 11-13; 15-19; 23. 23,1-16; 18. 24,1; 5-7.
25,1-3; 5-7; 9-12; 15; 17-19; 21; 23-27.
26,1-6. 27,1. 28,1-2. 29,1; 3-10. 30,1-6.
31,1-8; 10-12; 15-17; 20-22; 24-27; 31; 33-
35; 37-39; 41-45. 32,1; 3-5; 7. 33,1-2; 6.
34,1-4; 7-20. 35,1-3; 6-7; 10; 12-18. 36,1-
2; 5-7. 37,1-3. 38,1-2; 4. 39,1-2. 40,1. 41,1.
42,1.-43,1-2. 44,1. 46,1. 47,2; 4; 6. 48,1-
6; 8. 49,1-3; 5-6; 9. 50,1; 4-11. 51,1-8; 10.
52,1-4. 55,2. 56,2; 4; 6-7. 57,1-3. 58,1-3.
59,1. 60,1. 61,1-4. 62,1-2. 63,1. 65,1-2; 8;
14-15; 17. 66,2; 9; 14; 16; 18; 21-23; 25;
29-30; 35; 37-38; 40; 43; 49; 53; 58; 60; 64;
66-69; 79; 81; 87; 89; 95-97; 107.

NTH   1,1-2a,g; 3-4; 6; 8-
13a,d; 14-15a; 16-21; 23-27; 29-32. 2,1-5;
7-8; 10-12. 3,1. 4,1-5; 7-15; 17-18; 20-21;
23-34; 36. 5,1-4. 6,1-8; 10a,c; 12-13; 15-
16. 6a,1; 4-6; 10-11; 13-14; 19-25; 27-30;
32-33. 7,1-2. 8,1-5; 13. 9,1; 4-6. 10,1-3.
11,1-6. 12,1-4. 13,1. 14,1-6. 15,1. 16,1.
17,2-4. 18,1; 3-7; 9-11; 13; 15; 19; 21; 23-
32; 34-35; 37; 42-50; 53; 55-58; 61-62; 64-
68; 70; 72; 76-80; 82; 85; 87-89; 92-93; 96;
98. 19,1-2. 20,1. 21,1-6. 22,1-2; 4-5; 8-9.
23,2-4; 6-9; 11-12; 16-18. 25,1-3. 26,1-11.
27,1. 28,1; 3. 29,1. 30,6; 9-10; 12-16. 31,1.

38-40; 42-47; 49-50; 53-55; 64; 66; 69-70;
80; 90; 95; 103. 22,2. 23,1-3. 24,1. 25,1-7;
9-12; 16; 19-21; 27; 29; 31-34; 39-44; 46-
48; 51-53; 55-57; 59; 61; 63-67; 71-72; 75-
76; 78-86; 98-99; 101; 107; 111. 26,1-5; 8-
10; 12a-d; 13-16. 27,1-7; 9-11; 13. 28,1a-b;
2-4; 6-7. 29,1; 3; 7; 11-13. 30,1; 3. 31,3;
5; 9; 15; 20; 25; 27-28; 40-51; 53; 56; 60.
32,1; 3-6; 9; 14-16; 19; 21; 27; 29. 33,1-10;
12-13. 34,1-3; 5-10; 12-13; 15; 18. 35,1-3;
5-6. 36,1-2; 4; 6-9; 11-12. 37,1; 5. 38,1-2;
4-6; 8; 11; 16; 22. 39,1; 5-10; 12; 16-17.
40,2-4; 6. 41,1-4; 7; 10-11; 14-15; 17. 42,1.
43,1-7. 44,1-4. 45,2-3. 46,1-5; 7-9. 47,1-3.
48,1. 49,1. 50,1. 51,1. 52,1-2; 5; 9; 11.
53,1-3; 5-7. 54,1-3. 55,1. 56,1. 57,1. 58,1.
59,1-2. 60,1. 61,1-2. 62,1; 4-5. 64,1; 3.
65,1. 66,1-4; 6-8; 10; 17. 67,1-4; 8-10; 15-
17; 19-21; 27; 30-31; 33. 68,1; 3; 5. 69,1-
3. 70,1. 71,1-2. 72,1. 74,1. 75,4-5. 76,2-5;
7; 23. 77,1-2; 4.

SRY 1,2-14. 2,1; 3-6.
3,1. 4,1-2. 5,4-6; 10-11; 13; 15; 17; 19-23;
26-27. 6,1; 3; 5. 8,4; 9; 12; 14-15; 17-22; 25;
27-30. 9,1. 11,1. 13,1. 14,1. 15,1-2. 16,1.
17,1-2; 4. 18,2-3. 19,1-4; 6-12; 14; 17; 19-
24; 29; 34-39; 41; 44-47. 20,1-2. 21,3-7.
22,5. 25,1; 3. 26,1. 27,3. 28,1. 30,1-2.
31,1. 32,1-2. 33,1. 36,1; 3-6; 8-9.

SSX 1,1-2. 2,1a-f; 2-3;
5-10. 3,1-9. 5,1-2. 6,1-4. 7,1-2. 8,1; 3; 7;
16. 9,1-2; 4; 120-123; 126; 130. 10,2-8; 14-
16; 18-19; 22; 24-27; 29-37; 41-43; 46-49;
52-53; 57-61; 64-66; 68; 71-72; 75-76; 78-
81; 83; 86-89; 91; 93; 96; 109; 111-113; 115-
118. 11,3-46. 12,3-16; 18-23; 26-28; 30-37;
39-44; 46-51; 54. 13,1; 3-17; 19-20; 22-23;
25-50; 53-54; 56-57. 14,1-2.

WAR 1,1-9. 2,1; 3. 3,1-3;
6-7. 4,1-3; 5-6. 5,1. 6,1-8; 11-12; 14-20.
7,1. 8,1. 9,1. 10,1. 11,1-4. 12,1-6; 8-10.
13,1. 14,1-3; 5-6. 15,1-2; 4-6. 16,1-3; 5-18;
20-26; 29-40; 42; 44-48; 50-54; 56-63; 66.
17,1-2; 5-10; 14-16; 21-23; 25-32; 34-35;
37-39; 41-42; 44-45; 49-52; 55-67; 69-70.
18,1-6; 8-14. 19,1-2; 4; 6. 20,1. 22,1-9; 11-
19; 21-23; 25-26. 23,2-4. 24,1. 25,1. 26,1.
27,1-6. 28,1; 3-10; 12-14; 16-19. 29,1; 3-4.
30,1-2. 31,1-6; 9-11. 32,1. 33,1. 34,1.
35,1-2. 36,1-2. 37,1-7; 9. 38,1-2. 39,1-4.
40,1-2. 41,1-2. 42,1; 3. 43,1-2. 44,1; 3; 5-
8; 10-12; 14; 16. 45,1.

WIL 1,1; 3; 5-6; 8-9; 12-
14; 16-23a,h. 2,1-3; 6-7; 9-10; 12. 3,1-5.
4,1-3. 5,1-7. 6,1-2. 7,1; 4; 6-12; 14-16. 8,1;
3; 11-13. 10,3-5. 11,1-2. 12,2-6. 13,1; 3-6;
8-14; 16-17; 19-20. 14,1-2. 15,1-2. 16,6-7.
17,1. 18,1-2. 19,2. 20,1-2; 4-5. 22,1; 4-6.
23,2-3; 5; 8-10. 24,1-3; 6-7; 10-12; 19-21;
24; 26-28; 34-36; 38; 40. 25,1-5; 8; 22-23;
25-27. 26,1-3; 5-6; 9-15; 17-18; 20-22.

27,1; 3; 5-13; 18-20; 23-26. 28,1; 3; 5; 7-9;
11-12. 29,1-2; 5-9. 30,1-2; 4-7. 31,1. 32,1-
6; 8-9; 12-13; 15; 17. 33,1. 34,1. 36,1. 37,1-
2; 5-10. 38,1. 39,2. 40,1. 41,4-10. 42,1-5;
8; 10. 43,2. 44,1. 45,3. 47,1-2. 48,1; 5; 8-
9; 12. 49,1-3. 50,2; 4-5. 51,1. 53,1-2. 54,1.
55,1. 56,1-6. 58,1. 59,1-2. 62,1. 63,1. 65,1.
66,1-2; 5-7. 67,1-2; 5; 11; 14-16; 28; 31-
34; 36-40; 43; 48; 54; 56-57; 61-65; 68; 71;
73; 77; 80-81; 86; 89-90; 92; 94; 98; 100.
68,1; 11; 14-16; 18-20; 22; 24-25; 27; 30;
32.

WOR 1,1a,c; 2; 5-6. 2,2-
3; 5-15; 17-29; 31-35; 38-41; 45-48; 52; 54-
68; 70-73; 75-76; 78-79; 81-85. 3,1-3. 8,2-
9a,c,e-g; 10,a-d; 11-12; 14-15; 17-19; 21-
23; 26a,c. 9,1a-b,d; 2-3; 5a-c; 6b-c. 10,1;
3; 5-6; 9-12; 14-16. 11,1-2. 12,2. 13,1.
14,1-2. 15,1-6; 8-13. 16,1-4. 17,1. 18,1-4.
19,1-14. 20,1-6. 21,3. 23,1-6; 8-13. 24,1.
25,1. 26,1-17. 27,1. 28,1.

YKS C23; 30; 32. 1Y1; 3;
5-6; 10; 12-13; 15-17. 1N38; 65. 1W25. ·
2,1-3. 2B1; 3-4; 18. 2N23. 2W1; 4; 6-9; 11-
12. 2E1; 18-19; 21; 23; 30-31; 38-39; 41.
3Y1; 4-6; 9. 4N1. 4E1. 5N22; 54; 67. 5E5;
7-8; 15; 24; 34; 36; 44. 5W8-13; 15-21; 30;
32-34. 6N1-2; 13; 19; 21; 24-25; 46; 49-50;
52-53; 56-58; 65-66; 92; 101-104; 109; 112-
113; 116-118; 120-123; 125; 129; 131; 135-
138; 146; 152. 6W2-3; 6. 7E1. 8N7-9. 8E1-
4. 9W1-3; 5-6; 8-9; 12; 17; 19; 24-28; 32-
40; 42; 44-56; 58-61; 63-69; 72; 76-77; 79;
81-82; 94-99; 115; 119; 138-140. 10W1-5;
10-13; 15-17; 19-20; 23; 26; 29-32; 34; 37-
39; 43. 11E2-3. 11W4. 12W1-2; 4; 7-8; 10-
13; 16-17; 19; 22; 27. 13W1; 3; 7-9; 13; 16;
26; 28; 30-33; 35-36. 13E5; 13. 13N5; 13;
17. 15E1-2; 4-7; 9; 11; 13-15; 17; 19; 21-
22; 27-28; 33-34; 37-40; 43-46; 48. 18W1.
19W1; 3. 20W3. 21E1; 3. 22E1-2; 5; 9-11.
22W6. 23W2-4. 23N8; 17. 23E2; 6; 14.
24W2; 6-7; 10; 20. 24E2. 25W1; 3; 6; 8; 12;
15-17; 19; 28. 27W1-2. 28W1; 9; 11; 14;
29; 31; 39. 29W1; 3-4; 6-7; 9-10; 25. 29E1;
15; 25; 30. 29N1; 3; 5-6; 12.

half (½)   NFK   1,11; 197; 202.
4,37. 8,14. 9,49; 93; 115; 143-144. 10,18-
19; 46; 63. 17,18. 19,29; 37. 23,8. 24,7.
32,3. 35,13. 48,4; 8. 49,7. 66,85.

SFK   1,92. 6,159; 165;
265. 7,19; 30; 54. 12,7. 13,5. 14,12; 43; 95.
21,71; 91. 53,5.

Being man of another NFK   20,20.
Belonging to manor/   NFK   4,31. 9,51; 87.
village elsewhere   10,30.

NTT   20,4.
SFK   7,80.
Comparative information
  less 1086 than TRE ESS   1,15; 30. 3,8; 10.
4,17. 5,1. 6,12.

	HUN	10,1.
	NTH	1,6-7. 7,1.
	SHR	4,3,3; 23. 4,6,2. 4,19,12. 4,20,6; 15. 7,4.
	SOM	8,1.
	SFK	6,110. 7,37; 76. 55,1.
	WAR	16,24.
	WOR	9,6b. 15,10. 16,1. 19,1. 20,4. 23,10. 26,8.
	YKS	9W53.
Executed for robbery	ESS	1,3.
King's	SRY	25,2.
Paying nothing	NTH	1,7.
Service, exempt on making horseshoes for King	HEF	C8.
SMITHY (ferraria)	LIN	7,1.
	WIL	26,14.
Working for the hall	SRY	8,18.

See also: Forge.

SOKE (soca) – See Jurisdiction.

SOKEMAN (socmanus) – See Freeman.

SOLDIER (solidarius) NFK   31,37.

SOLDIER (miles) YKS   2,1. 2B1; 3; 9; 18. 2E1; 26; 28; 36; 39. 6N134; 136-138. 10W1; 3. 13W36. 14E11; 31; 34; 48. 21E10.

See also: Man-at-arms.

SON (filius)   BDF   2,6-7. 15,7. 21. 22,1. 23,41. 24,2; 6-7; 9. 25,2; 5; 7. 26,1. 29,1. 38. 43. 44. 45. 48.

BRK   B1; 3; 7; 9. 1,1; 42. 7,24; 38. 10,1. 22. 27. 28. 30. 31. 32. 40. 48. 49. 51. 55. 64. 65,6; 20.

BKM   B3; 5; 9. 1,7. 4,16; 25; 31. 5,9; 20. 12,1; 14; 27-29; 31-35; 38. 14,3; 5; 7-8; 10; 26; 28-29; 33; 37; 41; 44; 46. 17. 18,2. 19,3; 6-7. 23,31. 29. 33. 34. 35. 41,1; 4; 6. 47,1. 49,1. 53,6. 57,7; 17.

CAM   13,11. 17,4. 19. 24. 25. 25,5; 10. 26,35-36; 39. 30,1-2. 32,10; 12; 18; 20; 24. 35. 36.

CHS   B13. 2. 9. 12. 16,2. 24. FD4. FD5. FD5,3. FD6. FT3,1-2.

CON   *2,5.*

DBY   2,1. 6,99. 10. 15. 17,20. B6. S5.

DEV   1,11. *3,32. 15,10; 42. 16,44; 50; 115; 155. 17,3. 19,12; 16; 19;* 35; *39;43. 24,21.* 26. 30. *34,12; 14.* 36. 37. 42.

DOR   1,22. 2,6. 3,6. *11,5. 12,14.* 13,*1;* 4. 19,11. 23,1. 30. 33. 36,*3;* 8. 37,13. 54,8; 11; 13. 55. 56,36. 57,15.

ESS   1,2; 4; 11; 13; 27. 3,5. 4,2; 15; 18. 11,1. 15,1. 18,1; 4-6; 8; 10; 20; 34; 36. 20,6. 23. 24,4; 11; 23; 25; 29; 31; 35; 43; 49; 53; 55; 59; 64. 27,2; 16-17. 30,23. 34,26; 30. 40. 40,1. 41. 58. 61.

63. 73. 74. 76. 78. 83,1. 90,12; 15; 18; 35; 49; 75. 85. 88,2. B1; 3a; 3p; 7.

GLS   S1; 4. W18-19. 1,11; 13; 22; 39; 47; 53. 2,8. 3,1-2; 7. 6,1. 16,1. 19,2. 31,5. 32. 35. 35,2. 37. 39,21. 48,3. 52. 54. 55. 56. 61. 67. 69,7. 75. 78,5; 11; 16.

HAM   1,35. 3,5. 10. 6,13. 9,1. 28. 30. 38. 46. 47. 48. 50. 51. 54. 59. 68,2-3; 10. 69,9; 13; 16-17; 21; 29; 39; 51. NF9,1; 36-37. S2-3. IoW1,5-7; 11. IoW6. IoW7. IoW8. IoW9,2.

HEF   1,1; 3-5; 7; 10c; 12; 28-29; 38; 48; 51; 53; 58; 63. 10,1. 15. 16. 17. 19,8. 22,7. 23. 24. 25. 25,3. 26. 29,1. 31, 31,7. 34,2.

HRT   4,6. 5,6. 10,9. 15,7. 17,1-2. 19,1. 20,6; 9. 21, 1-2. 31. 34,4. 36,19. 37,9; 40. 42a,1.

HUN   B10. 6,17. 15. 16,1. 22,2. 23. 25,1. 27. 28. 28,1. 29,5. D8-9; 20.

KEN   D10. M3; 16; 19; 22. P19. 2,29. 33; 38. 5,3; 6; 10; 24-25; 31; 33; 44; 51-52; 54; 61; 71; 78; 90; 93; 97; 103-105; 108; 119; 124-125; 128; 130; 135; 138; 149; 156; 158-159; 171; 200; 202; 205-206; 209; 216; 225. 7,19. 9,29; 35; 48. 11. 13,1.

LEC   1,2. 3,15. 13,41; 53. 16,9. 22. 29,3; 18. 43,9.

LIN   C2-4; 9; 13-14; 16; 20; 25. S3. T5. 1,23. 2,40. 3,4. 13,10. 24,53; 66. 25. 28. 29. 39,4. 57,12. 62. 68,45. CS3; 21-22; 30. CN8; 17; 19; 24; 30. CW3. CK10; 21; 27; 66.

MDX   3,10-11. 9,1. 11. 13. 16. 19. 25.1.

NFK   1,3; 11; 57; 61-62; 64; 69; 221. 229. 4,8. 8,29. 9,6; 8-9; 11-12; 24; 32; 45; 73; 80; 82-83; 85; 95; 100; 118; 120; 135; 150; 174; 196-197; 231. 10,21; 43. 12,45. 15,14. 19,8. 20,23. 21. 22,11. 27,2. 29. 30,1. 31,11-12; 17; 44. 35. 39. 42. 46. 50. 50,9. 57. 65,2; 9. 66,44; 51; 71; 75; 84; 99.

NTH   B16; 29. 1,4. 2,2-3. 4,29; 32; 36. 18,1; 67. 36. 36,4. 41,5. 42.

NTT   B3; 12. S5. 2,4. 3,1. 13. 22. 27. 28. 30,38.

OXF   B9. 1,6. 6,12. 7,45. 9,6. 21. 29,16. 36,1. 45. 47. 50. 58,4-5; 8.

RUT   R14.

SHR   3c,14. 3d,7. 4,4. 4,5. 4,9. 4,22.

T

229

in Hundred/

Wapentake	DBY	10,12.
	HUN	D14.
	NFK	23,4.
in 2 Hundreds	SFK	25,3.
tax never paid	SSX	9,60; 81.
Kept back	DEV	*15,14.*
	GLS	31,7.

Land

cleared of (adquietare)	HRT	1,5. 16,1.
from which King has never had his tax	DOR	*55,28. 58,3.*
put for tax	HAM	23,25.
tax on paid by other land	SHR	4,3,15.
which did not/has never paid tax	BRK	1,2-3; 9; 22. 21,6. 31,3. 33,1. 44,1. 58,3.
	CAM	5,58.
	CHS	FT2,18. FT3,1-6.
	CON	2,6. 4,1-4; 12; 22; 24-25. 5,6,6; 10. 5,14,2.
	DEV	2,11. 6,13. 23,5.
	DOR	1,2-6; 21. 2,1-2; 4-6. 3,1; 10-11. 8,1; 3. 26,40. 27,7. 34,8. *55,16.*
	ESS	32,29.
	GLS	2,4. 3,5. 16,1. 22,1. 78,10.
	HAM	1,7; 16; 29; 42; 45;

W1. 6,1; 10; 17. 11,1. 16,6. 29,9. 55,1. NF9,23. IoW6,21.

	HEF	2,57. 10,41. 24,3.
	KEN	7,20. 9,39.
	OXF	9,7. 14,1. 24,6. 28,5; 28. 35,33. 55,1. 58,12-13.
	SHR	4,20,4. 5,8.
	SOM	1,1-10; 20. 2,1. 6,1.

8,1; 5; 20. 9,1. 10,5. 11,1. 19,7; 13. 46,1. 47,9.

	SRY	1,2-3; 14-15. 5,1a; 18. 6,4. 10,1. 19,16; 18. 21,3.
	SSX	3,10. 5,5. 9,14; 20;

27; 33; 35; 37-59; 85-102; 113-119; 125. 10,61-64; 97-103; 106-110; 114; 116. 11,59-60; 64; 70; 94. 12,6; 11; 14; 20; 24-25; 30; 36; 41; 45; 47-48; 53. 13,1; 10-11; 16; 21; 48.

	WIL	1,1-5; 7; 23a. 19,2.
	WOR	8,1; 8; 11; 13; 18; 22.
which did not pay last tax	ESS	32,29.
which did not pay tax 1086	BRK	1,7; 9-10; 19; 23; 34-36. 15,1.

	CHS	9,17.
	CON	*4,3.*
	DOR	*36,8.*
	GLS	5,1; 4. 19,2. 32,8; 10. 37,1. 39,6. 58,3.
	HAM	1,1; 4-5; 19-20; 32-

33; 35-36; 40; W11-12; W20. 6,1. 23,56. 43,5. 68,7. 69,31; 33. NF2,1. NF9,2. IoW1,7.

	HEF	1,38. 2,12. 6,5-6.

7,6. 9,2. 10,10; 46; 51; 62-63. 12,2. 14,2. 24,7. 29,3; 5; 12; 20. 31,7.

	KEN	*2,41.*
	OXF	7,55. 35,22. 58,11.
	SHR	3c,4-7; 9. 4,4,8; 12; 21-22. 4,5,12.
	SFK	1,122b.
	SRY	1,12. 5,1a,h. 36,10.
	SSX	10,96. 11,89. 12,3; 7; 18. 13,9.
	WIL	25,23.
	WOR	2,77. 3,3. 8,25. 9,6a. *10,1; 5.* 11,1.
which never paid except to Abbey without tax	CON	4,22.
	DBY	1,12; 28.
	LIN	T2. 1,9. 13,1. 56,4.
	YKS	9W43; 64.

Land holder

not wishing to give tax	HAM	2,20.
who never paid	CON	4,28.

Lord receiving tax from tenant, but not

himself paying	SSX	13,9.
Meadow without	LIN	1,9. 8,33.
Men not paying 1086	HEF	1,49; 53.
Not met (adquietare)	HRT	1,5.

Not paid

by assent of King's Edward and William	GLS	7,1.
because land held by Monastery	HAM	29,9.
because land in King's revenue	BRK	21,6.
because land in lordship	HEF	8,2.
from land in King's lordship	HEF	10,41.
King, to	DOR	*1,20.*
	ESS	23,42.
King, to – reason unknown	HAM	29,9.
Not received by King	DEV	19,6.
	DOR	34,6.

Paid

before 1066 but not after	WIL	32,17.
King's use, for	GLS	39,20.

villager   CHS   R1,40a.
Forfeiture/death duty
divided between
Abbey and Earl   LIN   CW11.
Forfeiture, land and
money shared King/
Earl and wife/heirs   DBY   S4.
                            NTT   S4.
Free (liber/francus
tainus)   CHS   12,2.
                            DOR   1,30. 40,7. 50,3.
                                   56,7.
                            ESS   27,17.
                            SHR   4,3,10. 4,5,3; 14.
                                   4,16,2. 4,27,18.
                            STS   11,9; 49; 54–55; 57;
                                   61.
                            WAR   16,5; 20.
free man, being/
serving as-   CHS   2,20.
                            NFK   12,32.
                            OXF   1,7b.
                            SHR   6,3.
                            STS   11,39–40; 50.
                            SFK   37,6.
Given to another   LIN   35,12.
                            OXF   1,7b.
Hall, having   NTT   9,20; 26; 50; 69.
Land
   for use of   DOR   *11,12.*
                            SOM   *9,6.*
   held freely by   DEV   1,15; 32; 46; 49.
     3,22; 26. 15,14–31; 40; 47; 52. 16,5. 17,14.
     20,7. 34,10. 35,22. 36,23; 25. 39,15. 40,5.
     42,4; 10; 21. 51,5.
                            DOR   26,8; 15–16; 21–22.
                                   47,10. 55,6; 32.
                            ESS   30,4.
                            LEC   40,17; 23. 43,2.
                            NTH   18,38. 23,12.
                                   58,61.
                            OXF   27,10. 30,1. 59,1.
                            SOM   25,46. 36,7. 37,6.
                                   45,3. 46,14.
                            STS   12,24.
                            WAR   16,60. 18,11. 41,1.
                                   44,1; 8.
   held on lease by   DOR   55,23.
   held where he did
     not live   KEN   5,198.
Lordship, in   OXF   1,76.
Lordship thane of
King Edward   NFK   12,16.
Man/thane of
   Abbot   BKM   12,12.
   Earl   BDF   24,14.
                            BKM   4,37. 5,10. 43,4.
                            HEF   10,39; 58. 23,6.
                            SFK   8,33.
                            WOR   1,1c–d. 15,2; 4.
                                   19,6.

Earl Harold   BKM   43,11.
                            GLS   1,60; 62. 68,2.
                            HEF   10,28; 51. 22,1.
                            HRT   15,1. 17,3; 13.
                                   20,13. 24,3. 34,24.
King   BDF - 25,14. 57,16.
                            DBY   17.
                            DEV   52.
                            DOR   56.
                            ESS   20,12. 24,10; 15–
                                   16. 25,1; 5. 27,2.
                                   34,6.
                            GLS   78.
                            HAM   69. IoW9.
                            HRT   42.
                            HUN   29.
                            LIN   CK11.
                            NFK   20,23.
                            NTT   30.
                            SOM   47.
                            STS   17.
                            SFK   3,88. 25,63. 32,6.
                            WIL   67.
                            YKS   29W. 29E. 29N.
King Edward   BDF   1,1b. 3,16. 4,1; 3.
     15,2; 4–6. 16,1. 18,1–2. 19,1. 21,1–2; 6; 9.
     22,1. 23,1; 3; 5–6; 11–12; 15; 18–19; 22; 33;
     38. 24,15–16; 18. 25,12. 26,1–3. 27,1. 28,1.
     29,1. 30,1. 32,1; 3–6; 8; 10; 12–13; 15. 33,1.
     41,2. 45,1. 46,2. 47,2. 48,1. 53,1; 6; 11; 13.
     55,6; 13. 57,6; 16.
                            BKM   1,7. 4,2; 4; 23; 29;
     32; 36; 38. 5,3; 5; 9; 15; 18. 12,3; 24. 13,3.
     14,2–3; 7; 9; 16–17; 21–23; 31–32; 34; 36; 42.
     15,1. 16,1; 3–7. 17,17; 19; 27. 18,2–3. 19,1;
     4. 21,1. 22,1. 23,3–4; 29; 32. 26,4; 8. 28,1.
     29,3. 35,1–2. 39,2. 42,1. 43,2; 5; 7; 10.
     47,1. 48,1. 50,1.
                            CAM   13,11. 15,1; 3.
     17,4. 18,1; 8. 20,1. *21,5.* 23,1; 5–6. 24,1.
     26,42; 47. 29,1–3; 5; 7–10. 31,2. 33,1. 34,1.
     42,1.
                            ESS   4,11. 12,1. 20,1.
                                   24,1–2; 25. 34,9.
                            GLS   1,58; 61. 6,5. 39,6–
                                   7; 16. 42,1.
                            HEF   1,41.
                            HRT   4,3; 5. 9,9. 15,3.
     17,15. 20,2; 7. 21,1. 22,1. 28,4; 8. 29,1.
     31,1; 5–7. 33,2. 34,16; 21–22. 36,14; 18–19.
     40,1. 42,1–2; 5.
                            KEN   5,198.
                            MDX   4,11. 7,6. 8,4–6.
                                   10,1–2. 19,1. 21,1.
                            NFK   1,175. 20,2.
                            STS   12,10.
                            SFK   4,10. 7,71. 8,32;
                                   46. 16,40. 25,61.
                                   28,1. 34,6. 35,1.
                                   39,16. 41,10. 46,1.
                            WOR   9,1e. 15,3. 20,6.

	LIN	C27.
	NFK	1,61; 66; 70.
	NTT	S1.
	OXF	B1.
	SHR	C12.
	STS	B12.
	SSX	11,1. 12,1.
	WIL	B5.
	WOR	C2.
Borough payments, half King's share given to another	STS	B12. 11,7.
Borough and Half Hundred divided Queen/Earl	SFK	1,122a.
Customary dues and works of the jurisdiction, of	DBY	S6.
	NTT	S6.
Forfeiture/death duty, of, divided between Abbey/Earl	LIN	CW9-11.
Freeman, of, divided between Abbey/King	ESS	17,2.
Hundred, of forfeitures of divided King/ Abbey	ESS	17,2.
jurisdiction of divided King/Earl	NFK	1,67.
payments of divided King/Earl	NFK	1,44.
revenue of	CHS	S2,1.
Jurisdiction, of divided King/Chief lord	ESS	17,2.
Land, of in King's revenue	DOR	1,2.
Manor's value, of divided King/Chief lord	DBY	6,88.
Mill, of divided King/Earl	HUN	B17.
	NFK	1,70.
Salt houses/wich, from, income of	CHS	S1,1. S2,1. S3,1.
Tribute, of divided King/Earl	HUN	B18.
Waterway, of income divided King/Earl	SRY	5,28.

See also: Third part; Third penny.
THRAVE (trabs) – See Corn.
THRONE (regnum)

Land belonging to	DEV	*1,1.*

See also: King William; Realm.
TIMBER (timber) – See Marten skins.
TIMBER (lignum)

Cartload (caretedis), of	WIL	13,10; 18.
	WOR	2,48. 8,12.
Houses, for repair of	WOR	2,31.

Payments for	HEF	1,39.
Purchase of	HEF	1,10a.
Salt house, for	WOR	1,1a. 2,15. 8,12.

See also: Wood; Woodland.

TITHE (decima)	BRK	1,7.
	BKM	2,1.
	DOR	24,1.
	GLS	1,56; 60.
	HAM	1,19; W4. 17,1. IoW1,7.
	HEF	1,1-3; 6-9; 39-40; 43; 45; 47-48. 10,50.
	KEN	1,3.
	LIN	CK24; 37; 56; 62.
	SSX	6,1.
	WIL	1,19.
	WOR	*8,13.*
Acres of	HAM	1,19.
King's	WOR	8,13.
King's land, of	HAM	3,16.
King's payments, of	HAM	IoW4,1.
Land holder could dispose where he would	DBY	B16.
Manor, of	HAM	1,19; W4. 5a,1.
	HEF	1,2-3; 7; 9; 40; 43; 45.
Village/villagers, of	HAM	1,19; 25. 3,16.
	HEF	1,47. 10,50.

See also: Alms.
TITLE deeds (cartae)

Church, gift of manor to, by	SFK	25,1.
Claim to property through	KEN	*5,149.*
Evidence of	SFK	14,37.
	WOR	10,10.
Land delivered by	LIN	CS13.
Produced	DEV	2,2.

See also: Altar; Seal; Writ.
TOFT (tofta) – See Plot.

TOLL (theloneum)	BDF	1,2a.
	BKM	1,1.
	CAM	1,5.
	CHS	FT1,1. FT2,1.
	DBY	B1.
	HAM	1,43; 45. IoW1,7.
	HRT	10,5. 15,1.
	KEN	D5. C1. P9. 1,3.
	LIN	S1; 4. T1.
	NTT	9,74.
	OXF	B1.
	SRY	2,3. 6,1.
	SSX	10,1. 11,2. 12,1.
	WOR	8,1.
Bread, on	LIN	CN1-2.
Exemption from	KEN	D5.
Fine for non-payment	CHS	C18.
Fish, on	LIN	CN1-2.
King's	LIN	C4.

	STS	11,48.
New	LIN	CS39. CN1; 14.
Skins, of	LIN	CN1-2.

See also: Borough; Burgess; Cart; Claim; Fishing net; House; Market; Revenue; Salt; Salt house; Ship; Shore; Site; Stranger; Third penny; Town.

TOWN (villa; port)	BRK	1,1.
	DEV	*17,1.*
	GLS	G2. S1. 4,1.
	HRT	10,5. 15,1.
	KEN	D4-5; 7. 2,1.
	LIN	S7. 1,9.
	NFK	1,61; 63.
	NTH	6,1.
	OXF	B4.
	SOM	1,1. 8,1.
	STS	4,1. 7,5.
	SFK	1,97. 3,55. 14,167. 38,3.
	SRY	1,1b.
	WIL	23,7. 24,9.
	WOR	10,1.
Arable land, none outside town	LIN	1,9.
Burning of	KEN	D7.
Customary dues of	CAM	B10.
Enlargement by taking in arable land	SFK	14,167.
Evidence by men of	SRY	5,28.
Hides, never assessed in	BDF	B.
Jurisdiction, having its own	SFK	1,97.
Land outside	LIN	S14. T2.
Payments of	GLS	S1.
	HRT	10,5.
	SFK	14,167.
Residence of lying in another County	LIN	S9.
with land outside town	LIN	S7-8.
Service answering for every service of King	DOR	B3-4.
on expedition by	BDF	B.
Small (suburbium)	LIN	T2.
Tolls of	HRT	10,5.
Tradespeople of	SFK	14,167.

See also: Borough; City; Meadow; Service; Third part; Third penny; Wall.

| TRACT of land (divisio) | SFK | 14,162. |

See also: Territory.

| TRADING – men living by | STS | 10,1. |

See also: Merchant; Town.

TRANSFERABILITY of property and/or persons – See Dispose; Do; Give up; Go away; Go where he would; Grant; Grant and sell; Leave; Put; Remove; Seek; Sell; Separated; Turn; Withdraw.

TREASURER (thesaurarius)	DOR	*1,21.*
	HAM	56.
TREASURY, King's Payments accounted for in returns to	NFK	66,64.
TREE (arbor) Obstruction of road by felling	KEN	D12.
Taking branches/ foliage	KEN	D12.

See also: Crime/offence; Wood; Woodland.

TRIAL (judicium) Dispute between Bishop and Abbot, of	WOR	*App V H.*
Dispute settled without	SFK	27,7.
Offered by whatever mode be adjudged	NFK	34,17.

See also: Combat; Judicial enquiry; Ordeal; Plea.

TRIBUTARY (censor)	DBY	1,37. 6,38. 9,4; 6. 10,5-6; 9. 14,3.
	DOR	16,1. 33,4.
	LIN	2,36. 30,26. 35,2. 59,13. 63,10. 68,1; 25.
	NTT	10,3.
	YKS	C33. 1Y10; 14. 2B5; 11; 19. 2W3. 2E16. 8N7; 9-10. 15E17. 29E28.
More 1086 than TRE	ESS	7,1.

See also: Tribute payer.

TRIBUTE (census; gablum) Burgesses, paid by	GLS	*G1-4. B1.*
	KEN	C1. *2,16.* 7,4.
	SHR	C1.
	SSX	10,1.
	YKS	1Y11.
Burgesses, received by	KEN	C3.
Countryman, paid by	KEN	8,1.
Dwelling, paid by	HAM	1,28.
	WIL	M1.
Exemption from	BRK	1,1.
Fine for non-payment	CHS	C12.
free man added to tribute elsewhere	NFK	1,239.
paying in Hundred	NFK	66,81.
not paying	SFK	1,121.
put at	NFK	1,131. 10,69.
in tribute of King's manor/elsewhere	NFK	8,5. 66,102.
in tribute of manor	NFK	1,45-46; 239.
in tribute of manor/village elsewhere	NFK	66,98.
Freeman at tribute	NFK	1,216.
not paying	NFK	1,7.

in tribute of manor/village	NFK	1,216. 31,22.
House, paid by	BRK	B7.
	KEN	*C2.*
	OXF	28,8.
	WIL	M1.
House, not paid by	OXF	28,8.
Hundred, of	NFK	1,75.
Land		
added to tribute elsewhere	NFK	65,10.
held at tribute from Abbot	KEN	*7,14.*
Manor/village/land		
at tribute	KEN	3,3.
	NFK	1,124. 66,84.
in tribute of manor/village	NFK	1,135; 239. 9,167.
elsewhere		65,10. 66,98.
in tribute of King's manor elsewhere	NFK	66,102.
Payment of	BRK	B1; 7.
	HAM	1,28. 11,1. S1.
	HEF	1,38.
	KEN	C1; 3. 3,3; 10.
		5,118. 8,1. 13,1.
	LIN	S1.
	NFK	1,80; 179.
	OXF	B1. 1,5.
	SOM	1,2.
	SRY	2,1. 19,28.
	SSX	10,1. 12,1; 13.
	WIL	M1.
not paid	NFK	1,127. 9,167.
	SFK	1,122g.
herring, in	SSX	12,13.
pigs, in	SSX	12,42. 13,1.
Retained by land holder	BDF	32,1.
Site, paid by	BRK	B1.

Village, in	NFK	1,113.
Villager		
paying	DOR	*47,7.*
paying outside city with smallholders	KEN	*7,4.*
paying to land holder's men	SRY	19,28.

See also: Archbishop; Forfeiture; Land tribute; Third/two thirds part; Wages.

TRIBUTE payer (gablator)	SOM	1,2.

See also: Tributary.

TRUCE (treuua)		
King's	KEN	D4.
Season of	KEN	D4.

See also: Crime/offence; Holy days; Peace.

TURF land (torvelande)	LIN	4,42. 12,20.

TURN (vertere)		
Land holder		
could where he would	DOR	4,1.
	KEN	5,149.
	SRY	8,8; 10; 23-24.
		36,2.
could where he would with land	GLS	1,16.
	SRY	8,11. 19,27.
	WAR	3,4.
could not to another lord	HAM	33,1.
could not with land elsewhere	WOR	2,1; 78.
did to another lord of his own accord	WIL	25,21.
wife of, turned with land by force TRE	HRT	16,1.

See also: Dispose; Do; Give up; Go away; Go where he would; Grant and sell; Leave; Put; Remove; Seek; Sell; Separated; Withdraw.

U

UNCLE (avunculus) HAM 69,38. NF9,44.
                   HEF 19,3.
                   KEN D10.
                   LIN CS22.
                   NFK 1,144; 185. 8,31.
                        38,3.
                   OXF 35,25.
                   SFK 33,10.
                   WOR 26,16.
See also: Relations.
UNCULTIVATED land – See Land.
UNDERWOOD (silva minuta; nemusculus) – See Wood.
UNJUSTLY (injuste)
Land so lost   HAM 67,1.
See also: Wrongful.
URBAN affairs – See Borough; Bridge; Burgess; Burning; Citizen; City; Ditch; Dwelling; Guild; Guildhall; Holiday; House; Kitchen; Market; Merchant; Mint; Moneyer; Narrative; Plot; Poll tax; Port; Quarter; Residence; Revenue; Site; Third part; Third penny; Third/two thirds part; Town; Wall.

USE (opus)
Land claimed for
claimant's use   NTH 2,3.
Land held for use   ESS 3,7.
                     LIN 65,5. CS19.
                     YKS CE18; 29. CW7; 9-
                          10; 17; 24; 26-27;
                          32; 38-39.
See also: Abbot; Adjudgment; Jurisdiction, full; King; Monk; Work.
USHER (hostiarius)   CAM *39,3.*
                     DEV *5,9.* 51,2; *6-12.*
                     LEC 20. 43,9.
                     NTT 29.
                     SOM *2,8. 6,7. 8,26.* 46,6-
                          7; *9-11.*
                     WIL 68,18-19.
USURPED land
(terra intercepta)   DBY 16,1.

239

V

VACANT land (terra
vacua)   DEV *3,76.*
     KEN 5,204.
But cultivated   LIN 57,57.
See also: Village; Waste.
VALET
(berchenister)   HAM 69,28; 48.
VALUATION – See Assessment; Value.
VALUE, face (ad numerum) – See Money.
VALUE of manor/village/land
Assessment
  by English   ESS 9,7.
     WIL 1,10-12. 26,5.
  by English and
  French   ESS 23,2.
  by English and
  French reeve   KEN 1,1.
  by French   ESS 9,7.
  by men   WIL 7,1.
  by men of County   GLS 28,7.
  by men of Hundred   ESS 7,1.
     SFK 7,121.
  inability to make   KEN D7.
  not assessed as
  included in head
  manor   WOR *1,1.*
  paid with difficulty   NFK 23,6.
     SFK 2,5-6. 8,51.
  unable to be borne   HAM 2,11. 3,11.
     SSX 2,2; 5; 8.
"At most"   LIN 18,18.
Could not be fully
paid   SFK 34,3.
Could scarcely be paid SFK 31,47.
Manor undervalued   HEF 1,10b.
Nil 1086   ESS 89,2.
     NFK 1,80. 26,2.
     OXF 25,1.
     SFK 76,22.
     SSX 9,25.
     WAR 17,53.
     YKS 9W144.
Nil TRE   STS 1,25.
     SSX 9,25.
Nil because nothing
there   NFK 1,80.
Not given but land
assessed   NFK 29,9.
     SFK 6,105.
Not known because
  not in revenue TRE HEF 1,2.
  sheriff paid what he
  wished   GLS 1,10.
Payment of fixed sum

despite actual value   HAM IoW1,11.
Reduced because
  of confusion of land WIL 7,1.
  could not be paid   NFK 9,147; 151.
  despoiled of
  livestock   KEN 11,1.
  holding diminished HAM 55,2.
  manor destroyed   GLS 1,38.
Sub-holding, of   SFK 14,54.
Value
  when peace in the
  land   KEN 7,8.
  with and without
  woodland   WOR *18,3.*
Yearly value   ESS 79,1.
See also: Church; Cow; free man; Freeman;
Herring; Hundred; Jurisdiction; Man; Market;
Payment; Reeve; Village; Villager; Woodland.
VALUE of manor/village/land – Comparative
information
  value less 1086 than BDF 1,5. 2,1-2; 4-9.
    TRE   3,7-9; 13-17. 4,3;
    6-8. 5,1-2. 6,2-3. 7,1. 8,1-3; 6. 10,1. 11,1.
    12,1. 15,1-7. 16,1-4; 7-9. 17,5-6. 18,1-2;
    4-5. 20,1. 21,2-4; 7-8; 11-15; 17. 22,1-2.
    23,7-8; 13-14; 16-18; 20-23; 25-26; 30; 34-
    35; 40-42; 44; 46; 52; 56-57. 24,1-5; 7-9;
    13-15; 17-19; 22-24; 26; 28-30. 25,2; 5-10;
    12-15. 26,1-3. 27,1. 29,1. 30,1. 31,1. 32,1-
    4; 6-7; 15-16. 33,1-2. 34,1-3. 38,2. 40,1-
    3. 41,1-2. 43,1. 44,1-4. 46,1-2. 47,1; 3-4.
    48,1-2. 49,2-4. 50,1. 52,1-2. 53,1-7; 10-
    15; 17-18; 20-21; 23-28; 30-32; 36. 54,1-4.
    55,1-2; 4; 8; 10-13. 56,5-7. 57,1-3iii,vi; 4;
    7; 11-12; 15-16; 21.
    BRK   1,3-4; 6; 12; 14-16;
    20-22; 24; 28-29; 36; 40; 47. 3,1. 5,1. 7,4-
    5; 8; 10-11; 15; 21-22; 29-30; 32-33; 35-36;
    38; 43-47. 8,1. 9,1. 10,1. 11,1. 14,1. 15,1.
    16,1. 17,5; 7; 12-13. 21,1-3; 5; 11-16; 18-
    19; 22. 22,1-7; 10-12. 23,1-2. 24,1. 26,1-2.
    27,1. 28,1-3. 29,1. 30,1. 31,1. 32,1. 33,1;
    4-7. 34,2-4. 35,2-4. 37,1. 38,2-4. 39,1.
    40,2. 41,1; 3. 43,1. 44,2. 46,2-3; 6-7. 49,1.
    54,2. 55,1; 3. 56,1. 58,2. 59,1. 63,2. 64,1.
    65,1-2; 5-6; 12-13; 16-17; 19-21.
    BKM   B2. 1,7. 3a,2; 6.
    4,1; 4; 6-9; 15; 17; 19; 21-23; 26; 28; 30-31;
    33-34; 39-43. 5,1-2; 6; 8; 10; 12; 14-15; 17-
    19; 21. 6,1. 7,1-2. 10,1. 12,2; 6-8; 12; 16;
    20; 23-26; 35-38. 13,1-4. 14,3; 6-7; 10-12;
    14; 16-17; 20; 26; 31; 33-34; 36-37; 39-43;
    45-48. 15,1. 16,1; 8-9. 17,2-6; 8; 10; 12-
    13; 17; 19; 22-23; 26-28; 31. 18,2-3. 19,3;

6. 20,1. 21,1-3; 5. 22,1. 23,2-6; 8; 12; 19-20; 23; 25-27; 31. 24,1-3. 25,2. 26,3-4; 7-9; 11. 27,1-2. 28,3. 29,4. 30,1. 31,1. 35,1-2. 36,1-2. 37,1-2. 39,2. 40,1. 41,1; 3-4; 6-7. 43,1; 4-5; 10. 44,4-5. 45,1. 47,1. 48,1. 50,1. 51,1-3. 53,1-3; 5; 7; 9-10. 56,1; 3. 57,2; 4-5; 7; 11-14.

CAM 1,6; 8; 11-12; 20. 2,2-3. 3,1-6. 4,1. 5,1; 3-4; 12-13; 20; 23; 25; 28; 31; 34; 36; 38-39; 41-42; 44; 46; 48; 50-55; 57; 59-63. 6,3. 7,2-5; 8-11. 8,1. 9,1-3. 10,1. 11,1; 3-4. 12,2; 4. 13,1; 4; 6; 8-9; 11. 14,11; 19-24; 26; 28-33; 36; 39; 41-45; 49; 53-56; 58; 60; 67-69; 73; 78. 15,1-4. 17,3-4. 18,7. 19,1; 4. 20,1-2. 21,5; 7-9. 22,1; 7; 9-10. 23,1; 3-6. 24,1. 25,10. 26,10; 15-20; 23-25; 27; 30-32; 34-36; 42-43; 45; 48-49. 27,1. 28,1-2. 29,3. 30,1-3. 31,1-4; 7. 32,4-8; 10-11; 14; 19-25; 27-28; 30-40; 43. 33,1. 35,2. 36,1. 37,2. 38,1-5. 39,1-2. 40,1. 41,9-13; 15-16. 43,1. 44,1-2.

CHS B4-5; 8. A3; 5-7; 10; 12; 16-17. 1,1; 3-5; 7; 14; 21-23; 25-26; 31; 34. 2,1-2; 4-7; 9; 13; 18; 20; 23-24; 27; 29-30. 3,4-5; 7-9. 5,2-3; 5-7; 10; 12-13. 7,2; 4. 8,3-4; 7-10; 15-18; 21-23; 25-26; 28; 31-32; 34; 36; 38; 40; 42; 44-45. 9,3-4; 10; 16; 20; 23. 10,1; 3. 13,2; 4-5. 14,3-7; 11. 17,2-3; 5-7. 18,1. 20,4. 23,1-2. 24,5-6. 25,2. 26,1-2; 6; 8. 27,1; 4.

CON 1,1; 4; 6; 19. 2,11. 4,2; 8-11; 13-15. 5,1,13-22. 5,2,1; 4-6; 9-14; 16-18; 24-26; 28; 30-33. 5,3,1; 3; 5-6; 8-28. 5,4,1-2; 4-7; 10; 12-16; 18-19. 5,5,1-6; 9-11; 13-20; 22. 5,6,2-3; 6-8. 5,7,1; 10; 13. 5,8,1-3; 5-6; 8; 10. 5,9,1. 5,10,1. 5,11,1-3; 5; 7. 5,12,1-3. 5,13,1-12. 5,14,2-6. 5,15,1-6. 5,16,1-2. 5,17,1-4. 5,18,1. 5,20,1-2. 5,22,1. 5,23,1-5. 5,24,1-5; 7-16; 19; 21; 24-25. 5,25,1-3; 5. 6,1.

DBY 1,19-20; 25; 29; 32; 36. 2,3. 3,1; 4. 4,1. 5,1; 3-5. 6,5-7; 13; 16; 18; 20-23; 25; 28; 30; 33; 35-38; 40; 43-47; 49-50; 52-66; 68; 76; 80; 82; 84; 86; 88-89; 91-92; 94-96; 99; 101. 7,2-6; 9. 8,4. 9,1-4; 6. 10,1; 5-7; 9-13; 17-22; 24-25. 11,1-3; 5. 12,3; 5; 13,1-2. 14,1; 4; 7-11. 15,1. 16,1; 5-6; 8. 17,2-4; 8-10; 18-20.

DEV 1,50. 3,9; 12; 18-19; 22; 24-25; 27; 42; 52; 63-64; 68-70; 79-81; 86-88; 90-91. 5,1. 15,17-18; 22; 26-27; 29-30; 34; 37-39; 44-45; 47; 50-52; 54; 56-57; 62; 64-65; 67-76; 79. 16,5; 8; 16; 32; 40; 58; 66; 76-77; 83; 92; 97; 102; 119. 17,4-5; 7; 9-10; 14-18; 33; 35; 38-41; 61-62; 75; 84; 94; 107. 18,1. 19,3-4; 46. 20,15. 23,5; 10; 21. 24,24. 25,1. 26,1. 28,1; 3; 6. 31,2. 32,8; 10. 34,4-5; 7; 48. 35,4-6; 20. 36,1; 7; 13-14; 18-19; 24. 37,1. 38,1. 39,4-5; 11. 40,5. 42,2; 4; 6; 16. 47,2. 49,2; 6. 51,8; 14. 52,9; 11-14; 16-17; 24.

DOR 1,26-27. 3,15. 4,1. 8,1; 4. 10,1; 6; 14. 16,2. 20,2. 26,18; 23-24; 28-29; 33; 50-51; 70. 28,1-2. 29,1. 34,4. 35,1. 36,2-4; 7. 38,1. 39,1. 40,1. 42,1. 47,1. 53,1. 54,12. 55,1; 3; 5; 8; 10-11; 13; 25; 29-30; 33-34; 38; 41. 56,1; 14; 16; 32; 64. 57,13.

ESS 1,2-3; 6-7; 15-16a; 25; 27. 3,2-3; 9; 14-15. 4,4; 8; 11; 17. 5,1. 6,4. 8,8. 9,8; 11. 10,1; 5. 14,4. 17,1. 18,2-3; 5; 7; 11; 19-20; 30; 33; 36; 44. 20,2; 9-10; 21; 39-40; 56-57; 59; 61-63; 68. 22,24. 23,33. 24,3; 16; 44. 25,23. 26,1-2. 27,4; 6; 10; 14; 17. 28,5-6. 30,19-20; 46; 48; 51. 32,28; 30; 40; 42. 33,3-4; 9; 22. 34,2; 6; 15-16; 24; 26-27; 33. 35,1. 37,1-2; 20. 39,4; 7-10. 40,1; 3; 9. 41,3-4; 11-12. 42,4; 8. 44,3. 46,2-3. 47,2. 60,3. 62,3. 66,1. 68,6; 8. 69,2-3. 70,1-2. 71,3. 80,1. 89,2. 90,4-5; 12; 27-28; 65. B3b,p.

GLS 1,16; 22; 27-29; 33-38; 41; 43; 45; 67. 2,1; 7; 9-10; 12-13. 3,2; 5; 7. 5,1-2. 6,2-4. 7,1. 10,12. 11,1-3; 11. 13,1. 14,2. 15,1. 19,2. 21,1. 27,1. 28,1; 4. 29,1. 30,1-3. 31,4; 7-8; 11-12. 32,1-2; 4-8; 11; 13. 34,1-10; 13. 35,1; 36,2-3. 38,2-5. 39,15; 17; 19; 21. 40,1. 41,1. 44,1. 45,1; 3; 5-6. 46,1-2. 48,1-2. 52,1; 3-4. 53,1; 6; 9; 11. 56,2. 58,1-2; 4. 62,3-6. 63,1-3. 64,1. 65,1. 66,1; 5. 67,1; 5; 7. 68,4-5; 7-10. 69,1. 70,1-2. 72,2-3. 73,1-3. 74,1. 75,1. 76,1. 78,4; 8; 11-13; 15.

HAM 1,7; 17; 21; 24-31; 40; W3-4; W9-11; W13-18; W21. 2,9-10; 15-16; 18-19. 3,5-8; 19; 25. 6,8-9. 7,1. 8,1. 9,1. 10,1. 13,1. 16,7. 18,1-3. 21,2-4. 22,1. 23,2-3; 12; 24; 41; 45-46; 48; 51; 53-54; 59-60; 65. 28,3; 5-7. 29,1-3; 6-7; 11; 13-16. 30,1. 31,1. 33,1. 34,1. 35,2. 37,1. 38,1. 39,1; 3-4. 43,1; 4. 44,1; 4. 45,1-2; 5-6; 8-9. 49,1. 50,2. 51,1. 55,2. 56,3. 57,2. 58,1. 59,1. 60,1. 61,1. 64,1. 66,1. 67,1. 68,3; 7; 10-11. 69,1; 6; 11; 13-14; 16-17; 22-24; 26-30; 32-34; 36; 39-40; 48; 51; 54. NF3,3; 8-9; 11-13; 15-16. NF4,1. NF5,1. NF8,2. NF9,2; 11; 13; 36-39. NF10,1. IoW1,2-3; 6. IoW3,1. IoW6,12; 22. IoW7,1-2; 10-12; 14; 17; 20. IoW8,1; 3-5; 8-9. IoW9,4-5; 8; 11-12.

HEF 1,15; 31; 33; 71. 2,12; 16; 42; 51. 6,6. 7,2-3; 5; 8. 8,8; 10. 9,19. 10,5-6; 8; 12; 30-31; 41; 44; 67-69. 11,2. 12,1. 14,3; 8-9. 15,6; 10. 19,2-3; 6-10. 20,1-2. 22,5; 8. 23,1; 5. 24,7; 9-10. 25,1. 27,1. 29,3-4; 11; 15. 30,1. 31,4-5. 33,1. 34,2. 36,2.

HRT 1,6; 10; 12-15; 17-18. 2,1-3. 3,1. 4,2-5; 8; 11-20; 22-25. 5,1; 3-6; 8-11; 13-14; 16-21; 23-26. 6,1. 7,1-3. 8,1. 9,1-5; 7-10. 10,1; 4-7; 9; 11-12; 14; 16-18. 11,1. 12,1. 13,1-5. 14,1-2. 15,1-7;

10-12. 16,1; 4-8; 10-11. 17,1; 3-4; 6; 8; 10-
12; 14-15. 18,1. 19,1-2. 20,1-11; 13. 21,1-
2. 22,1-2. 23,1-4. 24,1; 3. 25,1-2. 26,1.
27,1. 28,1; 3-8. 29,1. 30,1-2. 31,1; 3. 32,1.
33,1-4; 6; 8; 11-15; 17-18; 20. 34,1; 3-4; 7;
10-19; 21-22; 24-25. 35,3. 36,2-5; 7-8; 11-
15; 19. 37,1-5; 8-15; 17; 22-23. 38,2. 41,2.
42,1-2; 6-10.

　　　　　HUN　1,1; 5; 9. 2,4-6. 4,1.
6,1; 4-5; 7; 14; 16-17; 20; 22; 26. 7,1; 3.
8,4. 9,2. 16,1. 19,1-2; 4; 6-7; 11; 19; 23-
29; 31-32. 20,6-7. 21,1. 24,1. 25,1-2. 29,3.

　　　　　KEN　M2-4; 7; 10-11; 13;
15-16; 18; 20-24. C1. 2,34; 39. 3,2. 5,4; 15;
21; 27-28; 37; 46-47; 51; 56; 59; 64; 79; 81;
121; 123; 135-136; 152; 157-160; 168; 176;
185; 187; 191-195; 197; 200; 203; 207; 215.
7,1; 15; 19; 21. 9,22; 24; 30; 36; 41-42.
11,1. 12,4. 13,1.

　　　　　LEC　3,7. 5,2. 7,1-2.
8,2-3. 9,5. 17,11. 18,1. 23,6. 34,1-2. 39,2.
41,1.

　　　　　LIN　1,6; 26; 31; 34.
2,17; 20; 27-28; 33; 42. 3,5; 7-9; 20; 36; 39-
40; 42-43; 48. 4,3; 8; 15-16; 54; 73; 75; 77-
78. 7,1; 8; 16-20; 26; 28; 32; 36; 51-52; 57.
8,7; 9; 14-15; 17; 19-20; 22-23; 27-28. 11,3.
12,1; 3-4; 7-8; 13-14; 37; 51; 53; 59; 80; 88.
13,10; 22; 30; 33-34. 14,5; 11; 14; 20; 22;
29-31; 38; 40; 43-44; 62; 65; 89; 92; 95.
16,2; 4-5; 8-9; 22; 27-28; 30; 33; 39; 44;
46. 18,4; 6; 12; 17-18; 20; 24. 20,1. 21,1.
22,8; 25-26; 33. 24,5; 10; 14; 24; 59; 68;
73; 82-83. 25,5; 8; 13; 25. 26,3; 11; 27; 44.
27,3; 7; 14; 27; 45; 55. 28,5; 7-8; 14; 17;
33. 29,11; 18; 27-28. 30,1; 6-7; 9; 12; 17-
18; 20; 22; 27-30; 33. 31,3; 10. 32,13; 15;
19; 26; 28. 34,3-5; 8; 12. 35,1; 4; 6; 9; 11;
14; 16. 36,1. 38,1; 14. 39,1; 3. 40,1; 4-5;
15. 41,1. 44,1; 4; 10-11. 45,2; 4. 46,1-3.
47,1; 4-6; 10. 48,1-2; 8; 10; 13-14. 49,1-2;
5. 50,1. 51,1; 3-4; 7; 10. 52,2. 55,1; 3. 56,8;
19. 57,5; 10; 14; 19; 27; 41; 48; 56. 58,6.
59,1-3; 5; 9; 11; 16; 18. 60,1. 61,5; 8. 63,2;
5-6; 10; 12; 15; 21; 25. 64,18. 68,8; 19; 21;
38; 42-44; 46; 48.

　　　　　MDX　2,1-3. 3,1-9; 12-14;
17-21; 23; 26-28; 30. 4,1-3; 5-6. 5,1. 6,1.
7,1-2; 4-8. 8,1-6. 9,1-4; 6-7. 10,1-2. 11,2-
4. 12,1-2. 13,1. 14,1-2. 15,1-2. 16,1. 17,1.
18,1-2. 19,1. 25,1-3.

　　　　　NFK　1,57; 73; 78; 113;
141; 211. 4,16; 18; 37; 47. 8,18; 78; 89; 102;
114. 9,1; 11-12; 29; 84; 117-118; 120; 137-
140. 10,11; 21; 24; 49; 63; 69-70; 79-80; 88.
13,6-7; 13; 21-22. 14,14; 21. 15,11-12; 19-
20; 25. 16,1; 5. 17,18; 37. 19,8; 17. 20,2;
8; 16; 31. 21,2-3; 7; 10; 14; 18; 22. 22,9.
23,1; 9; 12; 17-18. 24,1-4. 25,1; 15; 19; 24.
26,2. 30,1. 31,3; 20-21; 39. 35,4-5; 18.

38,2. 42,1. 43,1-3. 47,3. 49,6-8. 52,4. 60,1.
66,27-28; 30; 87; 97; 100.

　　　　　NTH　1,10. 2,4; 7. 5,4.
6a,26. 18,12; 40; 64-65; 96. 21,5. 26,1-3.
30,8; 17. 35,2. 39,12; 18. 43,2; 4; 11.

　　　　　NTT　1,60-61. 2,1-3; 6.
3,2; 4. 4,1-3; 5; 7-8. 5,3; 5-6; 11; 13. 6,1;
6; 8-13; 15. 7,1; 3; 5. 8,2. 9,2-3; 5; 12; 16;
19-20; 31; 33; 36-37; 39-41; 43-45; 50-51;
53-55; 57; 59-60; 64-66; 69-70; 74; 79; 84;
88-89; 92; 94; 98; 101; 104-105; 120; 122;
131. 10,2-3; 5; 16; 28-29; 31; 33; 35; 39;
49; 53-55; 57; 66. 11,6; 8; 11; 24. 12,1; 11-
12; 19; 23. 13,1; 6-9; 12. 14,3; 8. 15,1; 3-
6. 16,2-7; 9; 11-12. 17,1-4; 7-9; 12-16.
18,4-6. 20,3; 5; 7-8. 21,1-2. 22,1. 23,1.
26,1. 28,3. 29,1. 30,1-2; 4; 7; 12-14; 19-20;
22-24; 27; 30-32; 35-36; 38-40; 45-48; 51-
52; 54.

　　　　　OXF　1,9. 6,4. 7,5-7; 9;
17; 19-20; 28; 30-31; 36; 38; 59; 61; 63. 9,3;
9a. 11,2. 14,5. 17,5. 18,1-2. 20,2. 24,2-3.
25,1. 27,5. 28,13-14; 24. 35,20; 26. 43,1-2.
45,1. 46,1. 49,1. 53,2. 56,1; 3. 58,6; 14-
15; 36. 59,11; 17.

　　　　　SHR　2,1-2. 3c,2-5; 7-9;
13. 3f,1; 4. 3g,3-4; 6; 10. 4,1,8; 22; 24-25;
27-28; 30-32. 4,3,1-3; 6-7; 9-10; 13; 15; 17;
19; 21; 24; 27-31; 45; 47; 53; 56; 58-59; 63-
64; 67-70. 4,4,1-4; 11-13; 17-18; 20-21.
4,5,1; 3-4; 9-10; 15. 4,7,2-5. 4,8,1-2; 5; 9-
10; 13-14. 4,9,2-3. 4,10,2-4. 4,11,4-7; 10;
12-13; 17; 19. 4,14,1; 7-11; 13-18; 22-23;
25; 27. 4,15,1-3. 4,16,2. 4,17,2-3. 4,19,1;
4-8; 13. 4,20,2-3; 5-6; 8; 14; 24. 4,21,1; 3-
5; 7; 9; 11-12; 19. 4,22,1-3. 4,23,1; 4; 6; 8-
9; 11; 17-18. 4,25,6-7. 4,26,3-4; 6. 4,27,3;
11-12; 17-20; 25-26; 32; 34. 5,1; 3; 8-9.
6,1; 6; 8-9; 13; 19; 21. 7,3. 9,1-2.

　　　　　SOM　1,27. 5,4; 10-11; 16;
24; 27; 34; 53. 6,15. 8,20. 17,2. 18,3. 19,2;
5; 28-29; 48; 54-55; 57; 64-65; 67; 78.
21,15; 28; 78-79; 86-88; 92. 22,9-10; 12; 19;
23. 23,1. 24,1; 9. 25,5; 36. 26,5. 33,1.
36,9-11. 37,8; 10. 43,1. 46,6; 17-18; 21; 23-
24. 47,4; 6-7; 14; 19; 23.

　　　　　STS　2,1. 4,2-4; 6; 10.
8,2-3.

　　　　　SFK　1,12; 15-16; 54; 69;
71; 73; 77-78; 110; 122g. 3,67-68; 96; 100-
101; 104. 4,2; 4; 6; 11; 14; 38. 6,11; 42; 46;
80; 88; 98; 109-110; 112; 119; 129; 171-172;
175; 177; 216; 227; 238; 254; 260; 262; 276;
283; 305-306. 7,13; 54-55; 58; 60; 71; 75;
133. 8,4-9; 11-14; 20; 22; 27; 31-32; 35; 44;
46-47; 50-51; 56-57; 59; 66-67; 70. 12,2.
14,26; 63; 70; 115. 15,1. 16,2-3; 6; 8; 14-
16; 18; 20; 22; 25-26; 30; 32; 38; 41; 46.
18,1; 3. 19,7; 13-14; 17. 21,26; 45; 62; 95.
25,55; 63; 69. 26,12b; 15-16. 27,10; 13.
29,1; 11-12. 30,1. 31,15; 18; 27; 44-47; 49.

32,3; 5; 19. 34,12-13; 15; 17. 35,3. 36,2; 4; 6-11; 13-14. 38,5-6. 39,3; 7-10; 12. 40,3-4. 41,11; 15. 43,5. 46,3. 47,2-3. 50,1. 52,6. 53,1. 54,3. 55,1. 58,1. 62,5. 66,1; 4; 6. 67,3; 5-6; 10; 15; 17; 20; 27; 33. 68,1. 69,2. 70,1. 71,1. 76,22.

SRY   1,1a; 6; 9-10; 15. 3,1. 4,1-2. 5,5; 8; 16; 19; 21; 23. 6,1. 8,3-4; 6; 8-9; 17; 21-22; 26; 28-30. 15,1. 17,1. 18,1. 19,1; 5; 12-13; 16; 21; 23-24; 34; 36; 47. 20,1. 21,4; 6-7. 22,5. 25,1-2. 26,1. 28,1. 29,1-2. 32,1-2. 35,2. 36,4.

SSX   1,2. 3,1. 6,1; 3. 8,1. 9,1; 4; 18-19; 23-25; 31; 33-34; 37; 77; 99-101; 109; 111; 113-114; 119-120; 122. 10,4-7; 9; 12; 18-22; 25-27; 29-38; 42; 46; 48; 51-52; 64; 66; 68-69; 75-76; 78; 80-81; 86-90; 93; 99-101; 103-105; 108-109; 111-113; 116; 118. 11,1-4; 7; 10; 12-14; 33; 56; 62; 75-76; 85-86; 88; 92; 103; 106-107; 109; 113-115. 12,3-6; 30; 32-33; 36-37; 39; 41; 48-50. 13,3; 6; 10; 12; 14-15; 17; 23; 26-27; 30; 38.

WAR   6,3-4; 13; 18. 8,1. 11,4. 12,6; 8; 10. 15,1; 6. 16,5; 13; 31; 33; 36-37; 43; 53; 58; 60. 17,3; 6; 25; 36; 45; 47-48; 53. 19,2-3. 22,27. 24,2. 25,1. 28,4; 6; 9; 11-13; 15; 18-19. 29,2. 30,2. 41,1. 42,1.

WIL   2,6. 8,5. 21,1. 23,8; 10. 25,8; 21; 25. 26,7; 9; 12; 15; 19. 27,1; 4; 8. 28,1-2; 9. 30,1; 6-7. 31,1. 32,2; 6; 10; 15. 35,1. 48,4. 56,1. 60,1. 66,3. 67,6; 15; 100. 68,28.

WOR   1,1c-d; 2. 2,2; 4; 9-10; 15; 21-22; 25-26; 47; 52; 59-61; 72-73; 76; 78-79; 82-83. 3,1-2. 5,1. 8,4; 16-17; 19-20; 23-24; 26c. 9,1a; 2-3; 5a; 6b. 10,5; 7-8; 10; 14-15. 11,2. 12,2. 14,1. 15,2; 9; 12. 16,1. 18,2-6. 19,2; 6-7; 9-10; 13-14. 20,3-6. 21,2-3. 23,1-13. 25,1. 26,1-7; 9-12; 15-17. 27,1.

YKS   C22; 26; 28. 1Y1; 3-7; 10; 12-16; 18-19. 1N38; 54; 65-66; 93-94; 105. 1W25; 30; 39. 2,1-2. 2B3-4; 6-7; 9; 11; 13; 15. 2N2; 14; 20-22; 24-25. 2W1-2; 4; 6; 8; 12. 2E1-2; 5-6; 8; 12; 14. 3Y1; 4; 9-11. 4N1-3. 4E1. 5N1; 17-19; 22; 27-29; 45; 48; 50; 53; 58-60; 63; 65-66. 5E5; 7; 11; 15; 17-18; 21; 29-30; 32; 34; 36; 38-39; 42; 66. 5W1; 6-9; 11; 13-22; 30; 32-34; 38. 6N2-3; 21; 24-25; 29; 31; 34-36; 46-47; 49-50; 59; 63-66; 69; 92; 102; 112-113; 117-119; 125; 131; 136; 138-140; 143; 146-147; 150; 152. 6W5-6. 7E1-2. 8N8-10. 8W1. 9W2-3; 7-12; 15-17; 24-25; 32; 34-35; 37; 39-40; 42; 44; 46-47; 49-52; 54-70; 72; 75-77; 87; 94; 96-99; 115; 117; 119-121; 138; 140-141; 144. 10W1-2; 4-5; 8; 10-17; 20-32; 34; 37-38; 41. 11E1-3. 11N17. 11W2-4. 13W2; 7; 9-12; 18-21; 26-28; 30; 32; 34-

13E1-2; 7; 12; 14-16. 13N5; 10; 13; 15; 18-19. 14E1-2; 4; 6-8; 10-13; 15-17; 19; 21; 24-25; 27; 29; 31-34; 37-40; 43-45; 48; 50-53. 15E1-3; 12. 16E1. 16N2. 16W1; 3; 5. 17W1. 18W2-3. 19W1; 3. 20E4. 21E1-2; 7; 9. 21W2; 6. 22W2-4. 23N5; 9-11; 18; 21; 24; 26-27; 29-30; 36. 23E5; 8; 12; 14. 24W4; 9-12; 20. 25W2-3; 8-17; 19-20; 22; 24; 28-30. 26E1; 8. 27W1-2. 28W1; 6-7; 9-11; 13-14; 28; 31; 33; 35; 37; 39. 29W1; 3-6; 9-10; 14; 24-25; 27-28; 34; 36. 29E25; 30. 29N3; 6; 8; 13.

value more 1086   BDF   2,3. 3,1-6. 4,1-2.
than TRE   17,2. 18,1. 19,1. 21,1; 6. 23,3; 5; 11-12; 15; 19; 24; 29; 37-38; 45. 24,20-21; 25. 25,1; 11. 32,5; 8-9; 13. 39,1-2. 49,1. 51,1-2; 9. 53,16; 29. 57,18.

BRK   B8. 1,2; 5; 7; 9-10; 17-18; 25; 27; 32-35; 37-39; 41. 2,1-3. 3,2. 4,1. 6,1. 7,1-3; 6; 12; 18-20; 23-27; 37. 10,2. 15,2. 17,8-9. 18,2. 20,2. 21,6-9; 20-21. 22,8. 23,3. 25,1. 27,2-3. 31,6. 33,2; 8. 34,1. 36,1; 4. 38,6. 41,2. 44,3-4. 45,1. 46,4. 47,1. 49,2. 50,1. 52,1. 54,1. 61,1-2. 63,4. 65,4; 7.

BKM   B1. 1,1-3; 5-6. 3,1-2. 3a,1; 4. 4,16; 18; 20; 35; 37. 5,3; 8-9. 12,1; 3. 14,5; 27-29; 32; 38. 17,7; 9. 19,1-2. 21,4. 25,3. 28,2. 38,1. 52,1-2. 55,1.

CAM   2,1. 5,5-6; 11; 14-15; 45; 47; 49. 14,2; 7; 13; 27; 46; 48; 59; 61; 63-65; 71; 74; 81. 17,1-2. 18,3. 21,1. 22,6; 8. 25,4-5; 9. 26,6; 14; 46; 51. 29,1-2; 5; 7; 9-10. 32,2; 12. 41,7.

CHS   B3; 10. A15; 20. 1,15; 35. 2,14-15; 17; 19; 21; 25-26; 28. 3,6; 10. 4,1-2. 5,1; 4; 9; 11. 6,1. 7,1; 3. 8,1-2; 6; 11; 14; 29; 33; 35; 37. 9,2; 6-8; 17-19; 25. 10,4. 12,2. 14,1; 10; 13. 16,2. 17,1; 5. 18,6. 19,1-2. 20,1. 24,1; 7; 9. 25,3. 26,3. FD2,6.

CON   2,3-4; 6; 9. 5,1,1-3; 5-6; 8-12. 5,7,2-3; 8; 12. 5,11,4; 6. 5,14,1. 5,24,18.

DBY   1,1; 9; 11; 15-16; 37. 3,2-3. 5,2. 6,12; 14; 27; 85; 93; 97. 7,1; 7-8. 8,5-6. 14,3. 16,2-3; 7. 17,6. B2.

DEV   2,2; 4-5; 12; 14; 21; 23-24. 3,5-7; 10; 20; 22; 38-40; 44-47; 49; 51; 53-54; 56-58; 60; 62; 65-66; 73-74; 76-78; 83; 85; 93-94; 98-99. 5,2-4; 6-8; 12-14. 6,2; 5; 9-12. 13,1. 13a,2. 14,4. 15,3-5; 8; 11; 19; 24-25; 31; 35; 42-43; 46; 48; 58-61; 66. 16,6-7; 9-14; 17-18; 21-22; 24; 28-31; 33-35; 39; 41-43; 45-50; 52-54; 56-57; 60; 63-64; 72; 78-80; 91; 93-95; 100-101; 104-110; 112; 114; 116-117; 121-130; 132-133; 138; 140-148; 150; 153-157; 159; 161-165; 170; 172-173; 176. 17,8; 13; 20; 25-29; 31; 33; 37; 42-45; 47; 58; 73; 76-77; 79-82; 85;

89; 99; 102. 19,2; 5; 7-8; 10; 12; 15-17; 19-
21; 24-25; 28-31; 33; 35; 37-39; 41. 20,16.
21,2-3; 7-10; 12-13; 15-17; 19-21. 22,2.
23,3-4; 6-7; 9; 12-14; 16; 18; 20. 24,2; 5-
6; 9; 13-14; 19; 22-23; 28; 30-32. 25,3-14;
16-17; 24. 27,1. 28,10; 12-13; 15-16. 29,1-
6; 8-9. 30,1-2. 32,1-3; 9. 34,1-2; 6; 8; 10;
12; 14-16; 19-20; 22; 27-30; 32; 35; 39-40;
44; 49; 52; 55. 35,1; 3; 5; 7; 9; 11-18; 23-
27; 29-30. 36,2-4; 6; 8; 17. 39,7-8; 12-13;
19-21. 40,1; 3. 41,2. 42,1; 3; 7; 10-11; 20;
22-23. 43,2-5. 44,1. 46,1-2. 47,3-8; 13.
48,1-2; 4-7; 11. 49,1; 5; 7. 50,1; 5. 51,1-3;
5-7; 10-11; 13. 52,4; 20-21.

DOR   1,14-16; 24. 5,1-2.
6,1. 12,16. 19,2-4; 6-8; 10; 14. 21,1. 22,1.
24,5. 26,1; 6; 21; 46; 49; 54; 66. 27,9-11.
32,2; 5. 33,3-4. 34,5; 9-12. 36,1; 5. 37,2.
40,2; 9. 43,1. 45,1. 47,5-6. 49,1; 9; 11-12;
14-16. 50,4. 52,2. 53,2. 54,6; 8. 55,2; 6;
16-17; 19-20; 22; 24; 31; 35; 42; 45. 56,12;
28-29; 46. 57,3; 8-9; 12; 21.

ESS   1,2-4; 8-13; 17; 19;
21; 25; 29. 2,2-9. 3,1; 6-8; 16. 4,1-3; 9. 5,2;
4-5; 11-12. 6,1-2; 5-9; 11-12; 14-15. 7,1.
8,2. 9,2; 7; 12. 10,2-5. 11,2; 4; 6-7. 12,1.
13,1. 14,2-3; 6-7. 15,1. 18,1-2; 4-6; 13; 15;
17-18; 21a-24; 26-29; 35-39; 41; 45. 20,1;
5; 7-8; 13; 17; 19; 23-27; 29-30; 32; 34-38;
41; 43; 45-46; 48-52; 54-56; 58; 64; 66-67;
72; 74-75; 77-80. 21,1-2; 4-6; 8; 11. 22,2-
3; 6-7; 9-13; 15-16; 19-20; 23. 23,1-8; 10-
13; 15; 28; 30-31; 38; 40-41; 43. 24,2; 7;
15; 18-21; 23-33; 41-42; 45-48; 53-54; 57;
59-61; 64-66. 25,3-6; 10-12; 14-22; 24-25.
26,3-4. 27,2-3; 11; 13. 28,8; 11-17. 29,1-2;
4. 30,1-7; 9-11; 14; 16-18; 22; 27-43; 45.
31,1. 32,6; 8-9; 12-13; 15-16; 18-19; 21-22;
24; 27; 32-33; 38-38a; 41; 45. 33,1-3; 5-7;
10-13; 15-20. 34,1; 4; 7-10; 18; 20-23; 25;
29; 32; 34-35. 35,2-6; 8-14. 36,1; 3; 5-8;
11-12. 37,3-4; 7; 9-12; 14-16. 38,1-8. 39,3.
40,4; 6. 41,5; 7; 9. 42,3; 7; 9. 43,1-6. 44,1;
4. 45,1. 46,1. 48,1-2. 49,1; 3. 51,1. 52,1.
53,1. 54,1. 55,1. 56,1. 57,5-6. 63,2. 65,1.
66,2. 67,1-2. 71,1; 4. 72,2. 74,1. 76,1. 78,1.
83,1. 86,1. 89,3. 90,7; 10; 17; 20; 22; 26;
29-30; 35-36; 47; 50-58; 63; 70; 73; 87. B7.
GLS   •1,1-2; 7; 17; 20; 65.
2,4-5; 8; 11. 3,1; 3. 4,1. 8,1. 9,1. 10,1-9;
11. 11,4; 10. 12,1-7. 16,1. 20,1. 24,1. 31,2.
36,1. 37,1-3; 5. 39,1; 8; 12; 18. 41,3-4.
42,1. 46,3. 47,1. 49,1. 50,2. 53,5; 7-8.
54,1. 55,1. 60,1-2. 66,6. 67,4. 68,2-3; 12.
72,1. 75,3. 78,1; 3.

HAM   1,12; 20. 2,1; 3-6; 8;
10-11; 13-14; 21-22. 3,1-6; 8; 11; 14-16; 20-
21; 24. 4,1. 5,1. 6,1; 3; 12-17. 14,2-5. 15,1-
3. 16,1. 17,1-2. 18,1. 20,1. 21,1; 6. 23,4-
8; 15; 20; 25-27; 29; 34; 36-37; 39-40; 42;
44; 47; 50; 55-58; 61-62; 64; 66. 28,1. 29,8;

10. 32,2; 4. 35,3-4; 6. 39,2. 40,1. 42,1.
44,2. 45,3. 46,2. 47,3. 51,2. 53,1-2. 54,1.
56,1. 62,1-2. 65,1. 68,5. 69,2; 4; 35; 37-
38; 50; 53. NF9,41; 44-45. NF10,2.
IoW1,5. IoW2,1. IoW6,3; 5-6; 9; 15.
IoW7,3-5; 7; 13; 21; 23. IoW9,2-3; 13; 16;
18; 21.

HEF   1,4-6; 11; 16; 21-23;
26-28; 30; 32. 2,4-6; 11; 14; 26; 34-36; 45-
46; 48; 57-58. 8,2-3; 5-6. 9,4-7; 10-11.
10,9; 11; 14; 21; 23-26; 33; 36; 45; 47; 51;
53-54; 56-62; 66; 70-71; 73-75. 14,1-2; 4-
6; 12. 16,3-4. 17,1. 18,1. 19,1; 4-5. 21,1-
4; 7. 22,7. 23,6. 24,1-2; 8; 11. 25,3; 8-9.
26,2. 29,1-2; 8-10; 19. 34,1.
HRT   1,3; 19. 4,1. 5,2.
8,3. 10,2-3; 10; 15; 19. 31,6-8. 37,6. 41,1.
HUN   1,2. 2,3. 4,3-4. 6,3;
13. 7,5. 11,1. 13,1. 17,1. 20,8-9. 23,1.
26,1. 28,1.

KEN   M5-6; 8-9; 14; 19.
R1. P9; 13. 1,1-2; 4. 2,3; 5-23; 25-32; 35;
37; 41-43. 3,1; 3-8; 10-21. 4,1-15. 5,2-3;
5-6; 8-9; 12-14; 17-20; 22-25; 29-30; 32; 35-
36; 39; 43-45; 48-49; 52-55; 58; 67-71; 73-
74; 76; 85-86; 88-90; 92-98; 100; 109; 111;
113-115; 118-119; 124; 127-129; 131; 134;
137; 139-143; 146; 153; 155; 162; 164-165;
170-172; 174-175; 178-180; 199; 201-202;
206; 210; 212; 216; 219; 224. 6,1. 7,1; 4-5;
7-10; 12; 17-18; 20; 23-25; 27-29. 8,1. 9,4;
6; 10; 12-13; 16; 19; 25; 28; 31; 45-50; 54.
10.1-2. 12,1; 3.

LEC   1,1c; 2; 5-9; 12. 2,1;
4-6. 3,5-6; 8-9; 12-16. 5,1; 3. 6,2; 5. 9,1-
3. 10,1-17. 11,1. 12,2. 13,3-13; 15-22; 24-
27; 30; 34-48; 50-52; 54-56; 59-60; 62-67;
69-73. 14,1-3; 5-7; 9-14; 18; 20-23; 26-27;
29; 31-33. 15,1-5; 8-11; 16. 16,1-9. 17,1-5;
7-10; 12-13; 15-16; 18-26; 28; 30; 32-33.
19,13-15. 21,1. 22,1. 23,1-2; 4-5. 24,1; 3.
25,1-5. 27,1-3. 28,1; 3-5. 29,3-6; 10; 13-
15; 18-19. 30,1. 32,2. 33,1. 35,1. 36,2.
39,1. 40,1; 3; 6-10; 12-23; 26-27; 29; 31;
41. 42,1-3; 8. 44,3-11; 13.

LIN   S9; 19. T2. 1,1; 4;
9; 28; 35; 38; 65; 81; 91. 2,3; 6; 11; 16; 21;
29; 34; 36; 40. 3,1-4; 6; 16; 27; 32; 35; 53.
4,2; 5; 7; 9-10; 14; 17; 23; 26; 31; 34; 36;
38-40; 43; 50; 53; 59; 65; 67; 70; 74; 81.
7,14-15; 23-24; 30; 38; 40; 43; 53-54; 56;
59. 8,1; 8. 10,1. 12,17-21; 29; 43; 47-49;
52; 57; 60; 91; 96. 13,1; 17; 21; 38; 44-45.
14,1; 9; 12; 15-18; 20; 23-25; 28; 32-34; 39;
41; 45-46; 58-59; 63; 66; 84; 87; 93; 97.
15,1. 16,3; 12; 14; 18; 43; 47. 17,2. 18,1;
7; 13; 15; 25; 29; 31-32. 19,1. 22,3; 7; 16;
24; 28; 30-32; 35. 24,1; 20; 22; 25; 32; 36-
37; 54; 70; 72; 74; 76; 80. 25,1; 9; 15; 19.
26,1-2; 4; 7-8; 10; 14; 17; 20; 23; 25-26;
33; 36; 48-50. 27,1; 5; 10; 22; 24-26; 30;

33-34; 37-38; 41-44; 47; 50; 59. 28,1-3; 11;
16; 19-20; 29; 35; 37-38. 29,1; 9; 22. 30,32.
31,1; 7; 11; 15-18. 32,1; 3; 11; 21; 32. 33,1.
34,1-2; 6; 24. 35,3; 13; 15. 36,2. 37,1-2.
38,3; 8; 10. 40,9; 17. 42,1; 13; 16. 43,1; 5.
44,2; 7; 9; 16. 45,1. 47,8. 48,4. 56,1; 5; 9;
11-12; 14; 17. 57,1; 13; 15; 18; 22; 29-30;
37; 45; 47; 50. 58,2. 59,4; 13; 19. 61,4; 6.
62,1. 64,1; 15. 66,1-2. 67,1; 9-10; 19. 68,1;
5; 27; 35; 47.

MDX 3,15-16; 24-25.
24,1.

NFK 1,1; 5-6; 11; 19-20;
23; 28; 31-32; 42; 45; 52; 57; 59; 61; 67; 70-
72; 74; 77-78; 81-82; 85-88; 90; 93-94; 105;
122; 124; 128; 131; 133; 136; 139; 143-147;
150-152; 174; 179; 182-183; 185-187; 191-
194; 197-203; 206; 208-210; 212; 216; 219;
230; 237-238. 2,2-4; 7; 12. 4,1-3; 6-7; 14;
26; 29-31; 35; 39-40; 52-53. 5,1; 3-4; 6. 6,2-
3; 5. 7,3-4; 7; 9-12; 15-19. 8,1; 4; 7-8; 12-
13; 15-16; 22; 30; 33-34; 36; 38-39; 47-48;
58-60; 62; 64; 67-70; 72; 77; 81; 83-84; 87;
90-92; 94; 98-99; 101; 103; 105; 108-110;
112; 115; 121-122; 131-132; 134. 9,2-3; 6-
9; 18; 23-24; 27-28; 31-33; 42; 45; 47; 50;
52; 60; 63; 74; 76; 78; 80-81; 83; 86-88; 94-
95; 98; 100; 102; 104-105; 129; 136; 142-
156; 159; 161-162; 165; 168-169; 174-179;
182; 198-199; 226; 234. 10,1-6; 8-10; 13;
15; 20; 22-23; 25-26; 28; 30; 34; 36; 38-40;
44; 46; 55-58; 60; 62; 65; 67-68; 72-73; 77;
81-82; 84-87; 90-91; 93. 11,1-2; 5. 12,1; 4;
6; 16-17; 20; 27; 30; 32-34; 42. 13,15-16;
19; 24. 14,2; 9; 11-12; 14-15; 17-18; 23-24;
31; 35; 37; 39-41. 15,4; 8; 16-17; 24; 28.
17,2-3; 5; 8; 10-15; 17; 23; 26-28; 32; 43;
53; 63-64. 18,1. 19,1; 3-4; 9; 11-13; 15; 20-
22; 24-25; 27; 32; 36-37. 20,1; 5-9; 14; 18;
24-27; 30; 32; 34-36. 21,4; 6-7; 9; 13; 19;
23-24; 26-28; 30; 32. 23,2-3; 6-8; 11; 16.
24,5-7. 25,1-3; 5; 10-13; 16-18; 20-21; 25-
28. 26,1-2; 5-6. 27,1-2. 29,6; 8; 11. 30,2;
5. 31,2; 5-8; 10; 12; 15-17; 21-22; 24; 31;
34; 36-37; 41-42; 44-45. 32,3-5; 7. 33,1; 6.
34,4; 9; 12; 16; 18. 35,2; 6-8; 10; 13-15; 17.
36,1; 5-7. 37,1. 41,1. 43,4. 44,1. 46,1.
47,4-5. 48,2; 5-6. 49,1-2. 50,4; 6-7; 9; 11-
12. 51,3-4. 52,2-3. 53,1. 55,2. 57,1. 59,1.
61,2-3. 64,1-6; 8. 66,1; 26; 29; 35; 78; 80;
89; 93; 99; 101.

NTH 1,1; 2g; 3-4; 6-8;
13e; 15l; 16-17; 20; 25-26; 30-32. 2,1-2; 6;
10; 12. 4,1-5; 7-10; 13-18; 20-26; 28; 32-35.
5,3. 6,1-6; 8-13; 15-17. 6a,1-2; 4-8; 10-20;
22-24; 27-33. 8,1; 13. 9,3-6; 10,1-3. 11,2-
5. 14,2-3; 5-6. 18,1-2; 4-5; 7; 9; 11; 13-14;
16-21; 23; 25-37; 41-44; 46-48; 51-58; 62;
66-67; 70-71; 73; 75; 77-90; 92-93; 95. 19,1.
20,1. 21,3. 22,2. 23,2-9; 11-14; 16-18.
24,1. 25,2-3. 26,4-11. 27,1. 28,1-3. 29,1.

30,2-6; 9; 12-15. 31,1. 32,1. 35,4-8; 10; 13;
16-18; 23-24. 36,1-2. 38,1. 39,2; 7-11; 15;
17. 40,1-2; 4; 6. 41,1-5; 9. 42,1-3. 43,1; 3;
5-8. 44,1-2. 45,1; 4-8. 46,1-4; 6-7. 47,1c;
2. 48,3-4; 8-12; 14-15; 17. 51,1. 53,1. 54,3.
55,2-4; 6. 56,7; 12-14; 20-21; 23-27; 34; 37-
38; 45-46; 48; 50-52; 57-59; 61; 64-65.
57,1-2; 4. 58,2. 59,1-4. 60,1-4.

NTT B7. 1,1; 9; 36; 45;
51; 58-59. 2,7. 5,1. 7,6. 9,6; 72-73; 76-77;
90; 95; 100; 106-107; 116; 118-119; 121;
126-127. 10,1; 20; 24; 56; 59; 61; 65. 11,2;
4; 12; 14; 17-18; 20; 26. 12,16. 13,10. 14,5.
15,8. 16,8. 18,1; 3. 19,1. 24,1. 27,1. 30,9;
41.

OXF 1,7a. 2,1. 3,1-2.
5,1. 6,1a-c; 2-3; 5; 7; 9; 12-17. 7,1-4; 8; 10;
12; 15-16; 21; 23; 25-26; 32-34; 37; 40-41;
45-47; 49; 51-53; 64-65. 8,2. 9,1-2; 4; 7;
9b. 10,1. 12,1. 13,1. 14,4. 15,1-3. 16,2.
17,4; 6-8. 20,3; 6. 22,1-2. 23,1-2. 24,5-6.
26,1. 27,1; 3-4; 6-7; 9. 28,1-4; 9; 12; 15;
17-22; 25; 27-29. 29,2-4; 6; 12-13; 15; 17;
19-22. 31,1. 32,2. 34,1-2. 35,3-11; 16; 24;
31; 33. 36,1. 39,1. 40,2-3. 41,1. 45,3. 48,1.
50,1. 54,1. 55,1-2. 56,4. 57,1. 58,1; 5; 7;
9; 16-17; 20-22; 24; 28; 30-32. 59,2-3; 6; 9-
10; 13-15; 18-19; 21; 23-25; 29.

RUT R5-9; 11-13; 15-16;
21.

SHR 1,3; 6; 8. 3b,3; 5.
3c,6; 10; 12. 3d,1-2. 3e,2. 3f,2-3; 5-6. 3g,5;
9. 4,1,1; 3; 7; 9; 14; 16-20; 23; 26; 29. 4,3,4;
8; 11; 14; 16; 18; 22-23; 49; 52; 54-55; 57;
60-61; 65-66; 71. 4,4,15; 19; 23. 4,5,7-8;
12-13. 4,6,1; 3; 6. 4,8,4; 6-7; 11-12; 14-16.
4,10,1-4. 4,11,1-3; 11; 14-15. 4,13,1.
4,14,4-6; 12; 24. 4,17,1. 4,19,2; 9; 12.
4,20,1; 7; 15-17. 4,21,2; 6; 8; 10; 15-16;
18. 4,23,2-3; 10; 12-14. 4,24,2; 4. 4,25,1-
3. 4,27,1-2; 22; 24; 27; 29; 33; 35. 5,2. 6,2;
5; 10-12; 16; 20; 30; 33. 7,1; 4; 6.

SOM 1,26; 28-29. 2,1;
10. 5,3; 8; 14-15; 17; 20-21; 35-36; 41; 49-
51; 54-55; 57-58; 61-62; 68-70. 6,2; 12. 7,5;
7-10. 8,30; 35. 17,6. 19,1; 26-27; 32; 34;
38-42; 44; 47; 51; 53; 66; 69; 73; 77; 80-81.
21,1-2; 4; 8; 18; 23; 29; 54; 61; 70; 72-73;
77; 90; 96. 22,1-2; 15; 21. 24,10; 13; 18;
23. 25,8-9; 12; 14-16; 21-22; 25-26; 29-34;
37-41; 43; 45; 47; 49; 53-55. 32,2-4. 35,10;
22. 36,13. 37,6-7; 10. 39,1-3. 40,1-2. 42,1.
44,1. 45,1-5; 7-8; 10; 12-13; 18. 46,4; 7-
12. 47,3; 5; 10; 20.

STS 1,2; 4; 7-9; 11; 13-
15; 17; 19-22; 24-26; 29. 2,2-3; 8; 15. 4,1;
5. 6,1. 7,13-15; 17-18. 8,1. 9,1. 12,31. 13,9.
15,1-2. 16,1.

SFK 1,1; 3-4; 8; 14; 40;
44; 67; 75-76; 82; 88; 90-91; 96-97; 99; 110-
111; 115; 118-121. 2,4-6; 13; 16-20. 3,1; 3;

8; 10; 46; 55-56; 61; 72-75; 88; 99. 4,1; 13;
15; 18-19; 21; 24; 35-36; 38; 40; 42. 5,1; 3-
7. 6,1-3; 12; 26; 32; 42; 44; 47-48; 58; 60-
62; 75; 81; 83-84; 90; 92; 95; 110; 117; 121;
133; 141; 148; 157; 159; 161-163; 165-166;
170; 174; 177-179; 184; 186-188; 190-192;
194; 209-210; 215; 218; 221-223; 236; 238;
261; 283; 307-308; 311-313; 315. 7,1; 4; 6;
10-11; 40-42; 45; 47-49; 51; 56-58; 61; 64;
67; 73; 75-76; 136. 8,1; 6; 10; 34; 48; 55;
81. 11,4. 12,1; 3-7. 14,1-8; 16-21; 23-25;
27; 32; 35; 38; 45; 48-52; 58-62; 64-65; 67;
69-70; 72-73; 75-76; 78-82; 86; 90; 92; 102-
106; 108-113; 118-119; 139; 167. 15,2-3; 5.
16,12; 14-15; 20-21; 26; 33; 37; 40-41; 43.
17,1. 18,4. 19,2; 10; 14-18. 20,1. 21,1; 3;
5-6; 10-11; 15-16; 26-28; 38; 40; 42; 46; 55;
58; 62; 71-72; 83-84; 86. 22,1. 23,2. 24,1.
25,2-7; 11; 14; 32; 52-53; 56-57; 59; 61; 67;
70; 72-76; 78-83; 85-86; 96-97. 26,3; 6-10;
16. 27,3-7; 13. 28,1a-b; 2-3; 6. 29,7. 31,20;
24; 26-29; 41-42; 60. 32,16; 19; 21. 33,1-
2; 4-6; 9-10; 12-13. 34,1-3; 6-9. 35,1; 5-6.
36,1; 12; 15. 37,5. 38,8; 11; 16; 21. 39,16.
40,1-2. 41,1-2; 7; 10; 14; 17. 42,1. 43,1-3.
44,1; 3-4. 45,2. 46,1; 4. 49,1. 52,1; 5; 11.
53,5-6. 62,1; 4. 64,1. 65,1. 66,1-2; 11. 67,1;
7-9; 11; 19; 28; 31. 69,1. 76,2; 4.

          SRY   1,3; 5; 11; 14. 2,1-
5. 5,1a; 4; 9; 15; 17; 20. 6,2-3; 5. 7,1. 8,1-
2; 12; 14; 18; 25. 11,1. 12,2. 13,1. 14,1.
16,1. 17,4. 18,4. 19,2-4; 11; 14; 19; 26-27;
31; 37-39; 44. 20,2. 21,1-3. 22,1-3. 24,1.
25,2. 27,1; 3. 30,1-2. 31,1. 33,1. 36,3; 5.

          SSX   2,1a; 5; 7-9. 3,2-3;
5-8. 5,1-3. 7,2. 8a,1. 9,2-3; 5-8; 11-17; 22;
27; 29; 60; 66; 72; 74-75; 80; 82-83; 89-90;
94; 96; 103; 107; 115; 117; 121; 123; 125.
10,2-3; 15-16; 43; 45; 54; 58-59; 67; 73; 83;
97; 102; 114; 117. 11,3; 6; 9; 15; 19-21; 23-
24; 27; 30-32; 35; 39; 44-45; 55; 61; 63; 66;
74; 78-79; 81; 104; 108; 110-112. 12,1; 8-
11; 13-16; 18-22; 34; 43-44; 46-47; 54-55.
13,1; 5; 8-9; 11; 19; 28; 33; 39; 43; 46; 50;
53; 56. 14,1.

          WAR   1,1; 6. 2,2-3. 3,1-3;
5; 7. 4,1; 3-6. 5,1. 6,2; 7-8; 10-12; 14; 16-
17; 20. 7,1. 9,1. 10,1. 11,1-3. 12,1-5; 9.
13,1. 14,1-3; 5. 15,2-5. 16,1-3; 8-12; 15-
18; 20-21; 30; 32; 34; 47; 50-52; 54; 57; 59;
61-62; 66. 17,1; 9-10; 13; 18-19; 21-24; 26-
28; 31-33; 37-38; 44; 49; 51-52; 54-65; 67-
70. 18,1-9; 11-12. 19,4. 21,1. 22,1-5; 7; 14;
16-17; 19; 23-26. 23,2-3. 27,1-4. 28,5; 10;
14; 17. 29,1; 3. 30,1. 31,1; 4; 11-12. 33,1.
34,1. 35,1-2. 36,1-2. 37,1-2; 6-9. 38,1-2.
39,1-4. 40,2. 42,3. 43,1-2. 44,1; 3-4; 6-9;
11-12; 14; 16. 45,1.

          WIL   1,14-15; 18-21. 2,1-
2. 3,5. 4,3-4. 5,1. 7,1; 6-9. 8,1; 3; 10. 10,1;
4-5. 12,1; 5. 13,1; 3; 5; 7; 11-14; 20. 14,2.

16,3-4; 6. 19,1. 20,1-3. 21,3. 22,1; 4-5.
23,5. 24,1-5; 10-13; 15-16; 18-28; 30-32;
35-39; 41. 25,2-3; 11-19; 22; 24; 26-28.
26,1-2; 5-6; 10-11; 14; 16-17; 20. 27,3; 11-
16; 21-22; 24-27. 28,3. 29,1-3; 7; 9. 30,2;
4. 32,8; 13; 17. 33,1. 34,1. 36,2. 37,1; 4;
6; 12. 38,1. 41,2; 6; 8. 42,1; 3; 5-7; 9-10.
45,3. 47,1. 48,1-3; 5-12. 49,1-2. 50,4-5.
51,1. 52,1. 53,1-2. 54,1. 55,1. 56,4. 58,1-
2. 59,2. 61,1. 63,1. 65,1. 66,2; 6-8. 67,7;
43; 54; 98. 68,3; 14-16; 24-25; 27; 29.

          WOR   1,1b. 2,5; 18; 28;
32; 34; 38; 45-46; 50; 55; 58; 75; 81. 8,15;
18; 27. 9,4. 10,1; 9; 11. 11,1. 14,2. 15,1; 3-
4; 6; 8; 10; 13. 16,2-3. 18,1. 19,3; 8; 11-12.
20,1. 26,8; 13.

          YKS   C20; 27; 33. 2B2; 8.
2N19. 2W11-12. 2E7. 5N62. 6N8; 13; 19-
20; 28; 32; 51; 53; 55; 58; 60; 109; 116;
120-122; 129; 132; 134-135. 6W3. 8N1; 6-
7. 8E1; 3. 9W5-6; 19; 48; 53. 10W3. 11N4.
12W28. 13W1; 16-17; 33. 13E4-5. 13N4;
9; 12; 17. 21E3; 5-6; 11. 23N1; 4; 16; 32-
33. 23E2-3; 17-18. 24W2; 7. 24E2. 25W1.
29N5; 12.

value same 1086 as   BDF   1,1c; 2b; 4. 3,10-
TRE   11. 4,4-5. 6,1. 8,5;
7-8. 9,1. 13,1-2. 14,1. 16,5-6. 17,1; 4. 18,3;
6-7. 20,2. 21,5; 9; 16. 23,1; 4; 6; 10; 27-28;
31-33; 36; 39; 43; 47; 49-51; 53-55. 24,6; 8;
10; 16; 27. 25,3-4. 28,1-2. 32,10-12. 42,1.
45,1. 47,2. 51,3. 53,8; 19; 33-35. 55,3; 5-
7; 9. 56,1-4; 8. 57,3iv-v; 5-6; 8-10; 13-14;
20.

          BRK   1,1; 8; 11-13; 19;
23; 26; 30-31; 43-44. 7,13-14; 16-18; 28; 31;
39-42. 12,1. 13,1-2. 16,2-3. 17,1; 3-4; 6;
10-11. 18,1. 19,1. 20,1; 3. 21,4; 10; 17.
22,9. 26,3. 31,3; 5. 35,1; 5. 36,2; 6. 38,1;
5-6. 40,1. 41,4-6. 42,1. 43,2. 44,5. 45,2.
46,1. 48,1. 49,3. 51,1. 53,1. 54,3-4. 55,2;
4. 57,1. 58,1. 60,1. 62,1. 63,1; 3; 5. 64,2.
65,3; 8-11; 15.

          BKM   1,4. 2,1-3. 3a,3; 5.
4,2-3; 5; 10-14; 24-25; 27; 29; 32; 36; 38.
5,4-5; 11; 13; 16; 20. 6,2. 8,1-3. 9,1. 11,1.
12,4-5; 9-11; 13-15; 17-18; 21-22; 28-34.
14,1-2; 4; 8-9; 13; 15; 18-19; 21; 23-25; 30;
35; 44; 49. 15,2. 16,2-7; 10. 17,1; 11; 15-
16; 18; 20-21; 24-25; 30. 18,1. 19,4-5; 7.
21,6; 8. 22,2. 23,7; 9-11; 13-18; 21-22; 24;
28-30; 32-33. 25,1. 26,1-2; 5; 10. 28,1.
29,1-3. 32,1. 33,1. 34,1. 35,3. 36,3. 39,1.
41,2; 5. 42,1. 43,2-3; 6-9; 11. 44,1-3. 46,1.
49,1. 53,4; 6; 8. 54,1. 56,2. 57,3; 6; 8-10;
15-18.

          CAM   1,6; 18; 21. 2,4. 5,2;
7-10; 18; 21; 40. 6,1. 7,1; 7. 11,2. 12,1.
13,2-3; 5; 7. 14,1-2; 4-5; 17; 40; 51-52; 57;
62; 66; 70; 72; 75-77. 16,1. 17,5-6. 18,1-2;
5-6; 8. 21,3-4; 6. 22,2-4. 23,2. 25,3; 6-8.

26,1-5; 7; 9; 12; 21-22; 26; 28-29; 33; 37-39; 41; 44; 47; 50; 53; 56. 29,4; 6-8. 31,6. 32,3; 16-18; 23. 34,1. 35,1. 37,1. 39,3. 41,1; 3-4; 8; 14. 42,1.

CHS   B9. A2; 8-9; 11; 13-14. 1,13. 3,3. 5,8; 14. 8,5; 12-13; 19-20; 27; 30; 41; 43. 9,1; 5. 10,2. 11,3. 12,4. 15,1. 17,4. 18,2. 21,1. 23,3. 24,2-3. 26,9. FD5,2.

CON   1,18. 2,1-2; 5; 7-8; 10. 3,1-6. 4,12; 16. 5,1,4. 5,2,2-4; 7; 15; 19; 21-22; 29; 32. 5,3,2-4; 7. 5,4,3; 8-9; 11; 17; 20. 5,5,7-8; 12; 21. 5,6,1; 5; 9-10. 5,7,4-7; 9; 11. 5,8,4; 7; 9. 5,9,2-4. 5,19,1. 5,24,17; 20; 22-23. 5,25,4. 7,1.

DBY   1,18; 33-34. 2,2. 3,5-6. 6,2-4; 17; 29; 32; 34; 39; 42; 51; 69; 73; 83; 90; 98. 7,13. 8,1-3. 10,4; 8; 27. 11,4. 12,1-2; 4. 14,2. 17,1; 5; 11-12; 15; 22.

DEV   1,34. 2,6; 9; 15-17; 20. 3,4; 13-14; 16-17; 19; 21; 26; 28-31; 33; 36-37; 41; 43; 48; 50; 59; 61; 67; 84; 95; 97. 4,1. 6,1; 7. 11,2-3. 12,1. 14,1-3. 15,9-10; 12-16; 20-21; 23; 28; 32-33; 36; 38; 40; 49; 55; 57; 63; 77-78. 16,4; 15; 19-20; 23; 26; 36; 44; 51; 55; 59; 61-62; 65; 67-71; 73-74; 81-90; 96; 98-99; 103; 111; 113-115; 118-120; 131; 134; 136-137; 139; 144; 149; 151-152; 158; 167-168; 171; 175. 17,3; 6; 11-13; 17; 19; 21-24; 30; 32; 34; 36; 46; 48-57; 59-60; 63-72; 74; 78; 83; 86-88; 90-91; 93; 95-98; 100-101; 103-104; 106. 19,6; 9; 11; 13-14; 22-23; 26; 34; 40; 42; 44-45. 20,1; 3-15; 17. 21,4; 6; 14. 22,1. 23,2; 15; 17; 19-20; 22-23; 25. 24,1; 3-4; 7-8; 10; 15; 17; 21; 25-27; 29. 25,2; 15; 18; 20-23; 27. 28,4-5; 7-9; 11. 30,3. 31,1; 4. 32,5; 7. 34,9; 13; 18; 23-26; 31; 33; 36; 38; 41; 43; 50-51; 54. 35,2; 8; 10; 19; 21; 28. 36,5; 10; 12; 15-16; 20-22; 26. 38,2. 39,1-3; 6; 9-10; 14-16; 18. 40,2; 6. 41,1. 42,5; 8; 12; 17-19; 21; 24. 43,1. 44,1-2. 47,11-12. 48,3; 8-10. 49,3. 51,9; 12. 52,5-6; 22-23; 25; 43.

DOR   1,7; 9-13; 17-18; 20-21; 28; 30. 2,1; 4. 3,16. 6,2-3. 7,1. 8,1-2. 10,1; 3. 11,2; 8; 10-11; 15-17. 17,1-2. 19,1; 12; 14. 23,1. 25,1. 26,3-4; 8; 13-14; 19; 26; 32; 36; 40; 43-44; 52; 55-56; 58-60; 62; 64-65; 68; 71. 27,1-2; 4; 6; 8. 28,3-6. 30,1; 3-4. 32,1. 33,1-2. 34,1-2; 6-8; 13-15. 35,1. 36,6; 8-9. 37,1; 4-7; 11. 38,2. 39,2. 40,3-5. 41,1-5. 44,1. 46,1-2. 47,2-4; 9. 48,2. 50,3. 51,1. 52,1. 54,1; 5; 7; 9-10. 55,4; 9; 12; 14; 18; 26; 40. 56,2; 34; 50-51; 53; 58. 57,7; 10-11; 15; 18.

ESS   1,1. 3,10. 4,2-3; 5-6; 10; 14. 5,3; 7-10. 6,13. 8,3; 6-8; 10. 9,1; 9; 13-14. 11,2-3. 14,5. 16,1. 18,14; 21-22; 43. 20,6; 43; 69-71. 21,3. 23,39. 24,17; 22. 25,2; 13. 26,5. 27,7-8; 14; 16. 28,9. 29,3; 5. 30,21; 24; 44; 49. 32,3; 7; 14; 17; 20; 24-26; 28; 34-36; 44-45. 33,6; 13; 21;

23. 34,5; 11-12; 19; 27; 30; 36-37. 35,2. 36,2; 10-11. 37,3. 39,1-2; 4-5; 7-8. 41,2; 6; 10. 42,1-2; 6. 44,3. 45,1. 47,1; 3. 49,3. 51,2. 52,2-3. 54,2. 57,1; 3. 58,1. 59,1. 60,2. 61,2. 62,1. 64,1. 68,3-4. 71,2. 72,3. 77,1. 79,1. 84,2. 90,15; 25; 49. B1.

GLS   1,18; 24-25; 30-31; 40-41; 44; 66. 2,2-3. 3,4; 6. 6,1; 5-9. 7,2. 11,5-9; 12. 12,8. 17,1. 18,1. 19,1. 22,1. 23,1. 25,1. 26,1-2; 4. 31,1; 3; 5-6; 9-10. 32,3. 33,1. 34,11. 37,4. 38,1. 39,2-7; 9-11; 13-14; 16; 20. 42,2-3. 43,1-2. 45,2. 50,3-4. 51,1. 52,2; 5-7. 53,2-4; 10; 12-13. 54,1. 56,1. 57,1. 59,1. 60,3-7. 61,1-2. 63,4. 64,2-3. 65,1. 66,2; 4. 67,3; 6. 68,1; 6; 11. 69,2-8. 77,1. 78,2; 5; 7; 10; 14; 16-17.

HAM   1,1-6; 8; 13-14; 16; 18-19; 46; W5-8; W12; W19-20. 2,2; 7; 12; 20; 23-24. 3,8-9; 12-13; 17-18; 22; 26-27. 6,2; 4-7; 10-11. 9,2. 11,1. 14,1; 6. 15,1; 4-5. 16,2-6. 17,3. 21,5; 7-10. 23,1; 9-11; 13; 16-19; 21-23; 28; 30-32; 43; 49; 52; 63; 67-68. 24,1. 25,1. 26,1. 27,1-2. 28,2; 4; 6; 8. 29,4-5; 9. 32,1. 35,1; 7-9. 36,1-2. 37,2. 41,1. 43,2; 6. 44,3. 45,4. 47,2. 50,1. 54,2. 55,1. 56,2. 57,1. 60,2. 68,2; 6; 8-9. 69,3; 5; 7; 9-10; 12; 15; 18-21; 41-42; 44-47; 49; 52. NF1,1. NF2,1-3. NF3,1-2; 10; 14. NF9,34; 40; 42-43. NF10,3-4. IoW1,1; 4; 6-7; 9-10; 12-15. IoW5,1. IoW6,1-2; 4; 7; 11; 13; 17-21. IoW7,6; 15; 19; 22. IoW8,6; 10-12. IoW9,1; 6-7; 9-10; 15; 17; 20; 23-24.

HEF   1,7; 9; 24; 29; 34; 75. 2,13; 15; 17-21; 26-33; 37-41; 44; 47; 49-50; 52. 5,2. 6,2-6. 7,1; 4; 6; 9. 8,7. 9,2-3; 8; 17. 10,4; 10; 15; 19-20; 22; 27-29; 32; 34-35; 37; 39-40; 48-52; 63-64. 11,1. 12,2. 14,10-11. 15,1-3; 5; 7-9. 16,1-2. 17,2. 19,2. 21,4-6. 22,1-4. 25,2; 8. 26,1. 28,1. 29,5; 12-14. 31,3; 6. 32,1. 35,1. 36,1.

HRT   1,8-11; 16. 2,4-5. 4,6-7; 9-10. 5,7; 12; 15; 22. 7,3. 8,2. 10,8; 13; 20. 15,8-9. 16,2-3; 12. 17,2; 5; 7; 9; 13. 20,12. 24,2. 28,2. 30,3. 31,2; 5. 32,2. 33,5; 7; 9-10; 16; 19. 34,2; 5-6; 8-9; 20; 23. 35,1-2. 36,1; 10; 18. 37,16; 18-21. 38,1. 39,1. 42,4-5; 11-15.

HUN   B20. 1,6-8; 10. 2,1-2; 7-9. 3,1. 4,2. 5,1-2. 6,2; 6; 8-9; 11-12; 15; 18-19; 21; 23-25. 7,2; 4; 6. 8,1-2. 9,1; 3. 10,1. 11,2. 14,1. 15,1. 18,1. 19,3; 5; 8-9; 12-15; 17-18; 20; 30. 20,1-5. 22,1-2. 29,1-2; 5-6.

KEN   M17. P5. 1,3. 2,25; 33. 3,9. 4,16. 5,7; 10-11; 16; 26; 31; 33-34; 38; 40-42; 50; 57; 60; 62-63; 65-66; 72; 75; 77-78; 80; 82-84; 87-91; 95; 99; 110; 112; 120; 122; 126; 132; 138; 144-145; 150-151; 154-156; 161; 163; 166-167; 169-170; 181-183; 186; 196; 204; 208; 214; 218; 220; 225.

7,2-3; 6; 11; 13-14; 16; 22; 26. 9,1-3; 5; 7;
9; 11; 14-15; 18; 20-21; 23; 27; 29; 32-34;
37; 44; 51-53. 11,2.

LEC   2,7. 3,11. 8,1; 5.
11,2-3. 12,1. 13,1; 23; 28-29; 31-33; 53; 57-
58. 14,16-17; 19. 15,6; 12-14. 17,6; 17.
18,4-5. 19,1-7; 9; 11; 17-19. 20,1-4. 28,2.
29,1-2; 7-8; 11-12; 20. 36,1. 37,1-3. 38,1.
40,5; 11; 24-25; 32-36; 40. 41,2-3. 42,4; 6-
7. 43,6; 9-11. 44,12.

LIN   1,5; 29. 2,1; 5; 8-9;
18; 37-38. 3,13; 21-22; 25; 31; 33; 41; 50-
51. 4,1; 4; 11; 13; 28; 41-42; 46; 51; 55-57;
61; 72; 79. 6,1. 7,10; 21-22; 27; 55; 58. 8,4-
6; 11; 13; 31; 33-34; 36; 38-39. 10,4. 11,1-
2; 4-5; 9. 12,9; 40; 42; 55-56; 58; 62; 69;
86; 90; 92. 13,24; 26; 31-32; 39; 41-42.
14,3; 6; 13; 26-27; 60; 64; 79. 16,1; 7; 36;
41; 45; 49. 17,1. 18,3; 11; 27-28. 20,4.
22,1; 10; 22; 29; 34. 23,1. 24,12; 17; 33; 61;
78; 81. 25,2-3; 6-7; 11. 26,5-6; 16; 21-22;
30-31; 35; 37; 40; 43; 45-47; 54. 27,2; 12;
15; 19; 35; 40; 51; 53-54; 56-58; 60-61.
28,13; 25; 32; 42. 29,3-4; 8; 10; 15; 29-30.
30,19; 31; 36. 31,2; 5; 9. 32,4; 6-9; 12; 17;
24; 27; 29; 31. 33,2. 34,7; 9; 27. 36,3-4.
37,6. 38,12. 40,2; 6-7; 10; 12; 20; 23; 26.
42,2; 7; 9; 14; 17. 44,5; 8- 45,3. 46,4. 47,2-
3; 7. 48,5; 11-12; 15. 49,4. 51,4; 12. 52,1.
53,1-2. 56,6-7. 57,6-7; 11-12; 23-24; 28; 33;
38; 43-44; 46; 54-55. 58,1. 59,7; 15; 17; 20.
61,1; 9. 62,1. 63,1; 7. 67,7-8; 12-13; 20;
23-24; 26. 68,2; 4; 13; 15-18; 22-26; 30-32;
34; 39-40; 45.

MDX   1,1. 3,11; 22. 4,4.
5,2. 7,3. 9,5; 8-9. 11,1. 20,1. 21,1. 22,1.
23,1. 25,2.

NFK   1,21; 46-49; 52; 62;
98; 140; 142; 204; 216-217. 2,6. 3,1. 4,5;
17; 19-20; 24; 33; 37; 41-43; 49-50. 5,2. 6,1.
7,5-6; 8; 13-14; 18. 8,2-3; 6; 8; 16; 44; 54-
55; 63; 65-66; 93; 95-97; 111; 113; 123-128;
130. 9,9; 14; 16-17; 19-22; 25; 29-30; 46;
48-49; 53-54; 59; 68; 70-73; 99; 119; 157;
160; 163-164; 166-167; 170-173; 228; 230.
10,16; 19; 32-33; 35; 52; 64; 71; 73-75; 78;
81; 83; 87; 92. 11,3. 13,1-5; 9; 12-14. 14,1;
13; 20; 25. 15,1; 2; 4; 5; 7; 9; 13-14; 23;
26-27. 16,6. 17,1; 16; 25; 35; 54; 56. 19,10;
13; 18-19; 28-29. 20,11; 15; 19; 23; 34.
21,3; 5; 14; 16-17; 21; 24-25; 29; 37. 23,4.
25,4; 6-7; 22-23. 26,3. 28,1-2. 29,3; 7.
30,3-4. 31,1; 5; 22; 29; 33; 38. 32,1. 33,2.
34,5-8; 10-11; 17; 19. 35,1; 3; 7; 9; 16.
36,2. 37,3. 38,3-4. 39,1-2. 40,1. 47,2. 48,3.
50,1; 8. 51,5-6; 8. 55,1. 56,1-4; 7. 58,1; 3.
61,1. 63,1. 64,7; 9. 65,8. 66,41; 55; 64; 82-
83; 91.

NTH   1,9; 11-12; 14; 18-
19; 29; 31-32. 2,3; 5; 11. 3,1. 4,11-12; 30-
31; 36. 5,1. 6,7. 7,1-2. 8,2-12. 9,1-2. 11,6.

13,1. 14,1. 18,4; 6; 10; 15; 24; 38; 45; 49-
50; 59-61; 63; 69; 72; 76. 22,1; 3-9. 23,1;
10; 15; 19. 25,1. 30,1; 11; 16. 33,1. 35,9;
12; 21-22; 26. 36,3-4. 39,1; 5-6; 14; 16.
40,3. 41,7; 10. 43,9-10. 45,2; 9. 46,5. 48,1-
2; 5-6. 49,1. 50,1. 52,1. 54,1-2. 55,1; 5.
56,1; 6; 8; 10-11; 15-18; 22; 28-29; 31; 36;
39-42; 47; 49; 66. 60,5.

NTT   B19. 2,4; 9. 3,1; 3.
5,7; 10. 6,5. 7,2. 8,1. 9,1; 10-11; 15; 17-
18; 22; 26; 28; 32; 46; 52; 62; 78; 80; 82; 96-
97; 102-103; 108; 110-111; 113-115; 125;
128-129. 10,4; 15; 17-18; 22; 25; 27; 34;
40; 46-47; 51; 58; 64. 11,1; 9-10; 22; 25; 33.
12,18. 13,2; 11; 13. 15,7; 9. 16,1. 18,7.
20,1; 6. 22,2. 24,2. 25,1. 30,3; 5-6; 34; 37;
50.

OXF   B5. 1,7b-8. 4,1.
6,6; 8. 7,11; 13-14; 18; 22; 24; 27; 29; 35;
39; 43-44; 48; 50; 54; 56-58; 60; 62. 8,1; 3-
4. 9,5-6; 8; 10. 14,1-3; 6. 15,4. 16,1. 17,1-
3. 19,1. 20,1; 4-5; 7-10. 21,1. 24,1; 4. 27,2;
8; 10. 28,6-7; 10-11; 16; 23; 26. 29,1; 5; 7-
11; 14; 16; 18; 23. 30,1. 32,1; 3. 33,1-2.
34,3. 35,1-2; 12-14; 17-19; 21-23; 25; 27-
30; 32; 34. 37,1. 38,1-2. 39,3. 40,1. 41,2.
42,1. 44,1. 45,2. 47,1. 51,1. 52,1. 53,1.
58,2-4; 8; 10-12; 18-19; 23; 25-27; 29; 33;
35; 37-38. 59,1; 4-5; 8; 12; 16; 20; 22; 26-
28.

RUT   R10; 14; 18.
SHR   1,4-5; 7. 3a,1.
3c,11. 3d,3. 3g,7; 11. 3h,1. 4,1,2; 21. 4,3,5;
12; 20; 26; 44; 48; 50-51. 4,4,5-6; 8; 14; 22;
24. 4,5,6; 11. 4,6,2. 4,7,1. 4,9,1. 4,11,2; 8;
16; 18. 4,14,2-3; 26; 28. 4,19,10-11.
4,20,13. 4,21,14. 4,23,5; 9; 16. 4,24,1.
4,27,6; 10; 13-15; 21; 23; 28. 6,25.

SOM   1,28-29; 32; 34-35.
2,11-12. 3,1-2. 4,1. 5,1; 9; 12-13; 18; 22-
23; 25-26; 28; 30-33; 37-48; 52; 59-60; 63-
67. 7,2-4; 6; 12; 15. 8,3-4; 7; 14-15; 18; 21-
22. 9,1; 4. 13,1. 14,1. 15,1. 17,1; 3-4; 7.
18,1-2. 19,7; 10; 13-14; 19-20; 24-25; 30-
31; 33; 35-37; 45-46; 50; 52; 56; 61-63; 72;
74-75; 79; 85; 87. 20,1. 21,6-7; 10-14; 17;
19-22; 24-25; 27; 31; 33-34; 36-37; 39-40;
45; 47; 49; 53; 55; 60; 68; 74-76; 80; 82; 85;
89; 91; 93-95. 22,4-6; 8; 13; 18; 20-21; 25;
28. 24,2-3; 5; 8; 14; 16; 26; 28; 30-31; 33-
37. 25,1; 3-4; 6; 9; 11; 13; 17; 19; 23; 28;
42; 46; 48; 50-52; 55-56. 26,5-6. 27,1-3.
28,1. 30,1-2. 31,1; 3-5. 32,1; 5. 34,1. 35,1-
2; 4-7; 9; 12-14; 20. 36,3-5; 7. 37,2; 5; 9;
11-12. 38,1. 41,1; 3. 44,2. 45,9; 11; 14-15.
46,5; 13-16; 19-20; 22; 25. 47,8-9; 11-12;
21.

STS   1,3; 10; 12; 27-28;
30-32. 2,5-7; 11; 16; 19-20. 3,1. 4,7. 8,4.
12,1; 6-15; 17-30.

SFK   1,23; 36; 44-51; 53;

58-63; 107; 110-112. 2,7; 9-10. 3,9; 17; 56; 98. 4,10; 13; 16; 18-20; 22-23; 26; 30; 37; 39; 42. 6,28; 30; 32; 46; 49; 64-65; 82-83; 85-86; 90; 93; 96; 100; 128-130; 135; 155-156; 172; 176; 183-184; 189; 211; 213-215; 239; 245; 247; 251; 260; 264; 271-272; 277; 282; 291-292; 299; 303-304; 309; 317-318. 7,7-8; 15; 18; 29-30; 37; 60; 67; 71; 75-76; 121. 8,2-4; 7; 17; 21; 33; 36-37; 45; 49; 81. 9,1. 11,4. 13,2. 14,1; 3; 9; 11-16; 21-22; 28-29; 31; 36-37; 42; 47; 53-55; 66; 68; 71-72; 74-75; 77; 83-85; 87-89; 91; 93-100; 114; 117; 121; 129-132; 134; 137; 164; 166. 16,3; 6-7; 10-11; 16-17; 19-20; 26-27; 29; 40-41. 19,1; 16-17; 19; 21. 21,1; 7; 38-39; 47; 53-54; 79-81; 83; 90-91; 99-100. 25,1; 9-10; 27; 31; 34; 79; 84. 26,11-12c; 13. 27,9; 11. 28,1b; 4; 7. 29,10; 14. 31,3; 7-8; 25; 32; *40;* 43; 48; 50-51; 53. 32,1; 4; 9; 14; 16; 30. 33,2-3; 6-10; 12-13. 34,5. 35,2; 7. 37,1; 6. 38,4; 11. 39,6. 40,6. 43,4; 6. 44,2. 46,2; 7. 48,1. 52,3. 54,1-2. 57,1. 59,2. 60,1. 62,2. 64,3. 66,1-4; 10. 67,10-11; 14-15; 19; 21; 29-30. 69,3. 76,21. 77,4.

SRY 1,2; 4; 8; 12-14. 2,6. 5,2-3; 6-7; 10-11; 13-14; 22; 26-27. 6,4. 8,7; 10-11; 13; 15; 19-20; 23-24. 9,1. 12,1. 15,2. 17,3. 18,2-3. 19,6-10; 15; 17; 20; 22; 29-30; 32-33; 39; 41; 45-46; 48. 21,2. 22,4. 23,1. 25,3. 27,2. 34,1. 36,1; 6-7; 9-10.

SSX 1,1. 2,2-3; 6. 3,4; 9. 4,1. 6,2; 4. 7,1. 8,3. 9,9-10; 21; 26; 30; 35-36; 38-51; 61-65; 67-71; 73; 76; 84-88; 91-93; 95; 97-98; 102; 104-106; 108; 110; 112; 116; 118; 124; 129-130. 10,10-11; 14; 17; 24; 41; 47; 53; 55-57; 60-63; 65; 70-71; 91-92; 94; 96; 110; 115. 11,5; 8; 11; 16-18; 22; 26; 28-30; 36-38; 40-41; 46-54; 57-60; 64-65; 67-68; 70-73; 77; 80; 82; 84; 87; 89-91; 93-102; 105; 115. 12,7; 12; 23; 25-27; 29; 31; 40; 42; 51-53; 56. 13,2; 4; 7; 13; 16; 20-22; 25; 29; 31-32; 34-37; 40-42; 44-45; 47-49; 51; 54. 14,2.

WAR 1,7. 2,1. 3,6. 4,2. 6,5-6; 8; 15; 19. 12,2. 14,6. 16,6-7; 14; 29; 35; 38-42; 44-46; 48; 56; 63. 17,2; 4-5; 7-8; 11-12; 14-17; 20; 29-30; 34-35; 39-43; 46; 50; 66. 18,10; 13-16. 19,1; 5-6. 20,1. 22,6; 12; 15; 18; 21-22; 28. 23,1; 4. 26,1. 27,5-6. 28,1-3; 7-8; 16. 31,2-3; 5-10. 32,1. 37,3-5. 40,1. 41,2. 44,5.

WIL 1,17; 23j. 2,3. 5,2-3; 5-6. 6,1. 7,12; 15. 8,2; 4; 11. 11,1. 12,3-4. 13,4. 16,2; 7. 18,2. 20,5. 21,2. 22,6. 23,1. 24,7; 29; 33-34. 25,4-6. 26,3-4; 18; 22-23. 27,2; 7; 9-10; 17-20; 23. 28,7-8; 10-13. 29,6; 8. 30,3; 5. 32,1; 3-5; 9; 12; 16. 36,1. 37,2; 5; 7-11; 15. 39,2. 40,1. 41,1; 3; 5; 7; 9-10. 42,2; 8. 43,1-2. 44,1. 45,1. 47,2.

49,3. 50,2. 56,2-3. 59,1. 62,1. 64,1. 66,1; 5. 67,23; 28; 38. 68,2; 13; 19-20; 22; 30; 32.

WOR 2,6; 8; 11-14; 16-17; 19-20; 23-24; 27; 29-31; 33; 35; 39-40; 42-43; 53-54; 57; 62-68; 70-71; 77; 79; 84. 3,3. 9,1c; 4. 10,3; 5-6; 12-13; 16. 15,5; 7; 11. 16,4. 17,1. 19,1; 4-5. 20,2. 22,1. 24,1. 26,14. 28,1.

YKS C30; 32. 1Y17. 2B1. 2W3. 3Y13. 5N11; 47; 67. 5E1; 27; 31; 35; 44; 65. 5W31. 6N12; 15; 27; 52; 54; 56-57; 101; 103-104; 162. 6W1-2. 8N4-5. 8E2. 9W1; 22-23; 26-28; 33; 36; 38; 43; 45; 74; 95; 139. 10W19; 39. 11N1. 13W13; 15; 31; 36. 13E13. 13N14; 22. 14E30; 36; 46-47. 21W5. 22W5. 23N15. 23E6; 10-11; 15; 19. 24W6; 16. 25W18. 28W8; 32; 38. 29N1.

less TRE than when acquired/received/found/later

BDF 2,3. 3,3; 6. 7,1. 17,2; 4; 7. 19,1. 23,29; 38. 25,11. 32,9. 35,1. 51,2. 53,16. 57,5.

BRK B8. 1,10; 32. 3,2. 4,1. 7,1; 6; 37.

BKM 1,7. 4,20. 12,1; 24; 31. 14,32-33. 16,5. 17,9; 12; 26. 28,2. 29,4. 57,1.

CAM 5,15; 47. 14,2; 7; 35; 48; 59; 61; 65; 74. 17,1. 22,6. 29,10. 30,1. 41,15.

CHS 3,1; 6. 7,3. 8,6. 9,7. 22,2.

ESS 1,9; 11-13; 30. 15,1. 20,19; 23; 25-27. 21,8. 22,7; 9. 23,10-12; 28. 24,19; 25; 29. 25,4. 28,11. 30,29. 32,12-13. 34,10; 20. 36,10. 37,14. 40,4. 46,1-2. 49,1. 81,1. 90,55; 58.

HAM 3,21; 24. 6,1; 3; 12. 14,3-5. 15,3. 19,1. 20,1. 23,1; 5; 15. 32,2. 35,3-4. 39,2. 44,1. 52,1. 53,1. NF9,44. IoW1,5. IoW7,5.

HEF 2,14; 46. 10,58-60. 29,2.

HRT B11. 8,3. 10,20. 41,1.

KEN 1,4. 2,5; 9-10; 26-27. 3,6. 5,43; 45; 48; 101; 109; 127; 131; 175. 6,1. 7,7. 10,2. 11,2.

MDX 3,15-16; 24. 22,1. 25,1.

NFK 1,71; 77; 94; 105; 122; 124; 128; 133; 135; 139; 143-145; 147; 150-152; 174; 179; 182-183; 185; 192-194; 197-203; 209; 212; 216; 219. 2,4. 4,1-2; 29; 31; 47. 7,9. 8,16; 58; 98-99; 121; 132. 9,1; 18; 23; 26; 87-88; 94; 159; 196. 10,5; 20; 90-91. 11,5. 12,1; 32. 19,32. 20,1; 8; 35. 21,9. 24,5-6. 25,1; 25; 27-28. 26,5. 31,20. 32,5. 35,6. 41,1. 48,2. 55,2. 59,1.

OXF 6,5; 13. 9,1. 15,2.

28,12; 17; 22. 32,2.
54,1. 55,1. 59,11.
SHR 4,3,20; 52. 4,10,1.
4,14,15. 4,18,2. 4,19,12. 4,20,15. 4,25,1.
6,14; 18; 20; 23; 26; 30. 7,3.
SOM *8,13.*
SFK 1,1; 12; 75; 88; 97;
99; 103. 3,3; 10; 46; 55. 6,83. 7,51; 56.
8,48. 25,2-3. 27,7. 31,60. 33,13. 34,3.
42,1. 43,3.
SRY 5,4. 7,1. 19,11.
SSX 9,17. 11,1; 74.
12,8-9; 16; 31.
WAR 1,6. 2,2-3. 12,3.
15,4. 16,34. 17,57.
WOR 10,1.
less 1086 than when BDF 2,1-2; 6-9. 3,15.
acquired/received/ 7,1. 15,1-6. 16,1.
found 17,4. 18,4. 21,11.
23,34-35. 24,1. 25,6; 12. 26,3. 29,1. 31,1.
32,1; 4; 7. 33,1. 35,1. 41,2. 48,2. 50,1.
52,1. 53,1; 5; 11; 13; 23; 27; 30-31. 55,8.
57,1; 3i; 11.
BRK 1,3-4; 6; 14; 22; 28.
5,1. 7,12. 14,1. 21,5; 15; 18. 22,2. 26,1.
28,1-2. 33,1; 5-6. 54,2. 65,19.
BKM 1,7. 4,22-23. 12,24;
31. 14,7; 11; 33-34. 16,5. 17,12; 22; 26-27;
31. 23,8; 20. 28,3. 29,4. 30,1. 40,1. 57,1.
CAM 1,11. 3,3-5. 5,38.
7,2; 10. 10,1. 13,8; 11. 14,11; 35-36; 53;
61; 73. 15,1-2; 4. 19,1. 21,7. 22,1. 23,4.
25,10. 26,16; 31; 49. 29,3. 30,1; 3. 32,4; 7-
8; 11; 21; 24-25; 30-31; 33-35; 37-38; 40;
43. 37,2. 41,10; 12; 15.
CHS 3,1. 22,2.
CON 4,19-20; 23; 25-27.
5,6,4.
DEV *1,25.* 2,11. *3,72.*
28,16.
DOR 28,2.
ESS 1,2; 25-27. 4,11.
14,4. 18,30; 33; 44. 20,39; 57; 61. 27,6; 14.
28,5. 30,19-20; 46. 32,28; 40. 33,22. 34,6;
24; 26; 33. 36,10. 37,20. 39,4; 7-9. 40,9.
41,12. 46,2-3. 60,3. 66,1. 80,1. 81,1. 90,5;
27. B3b,p.
HAM 1,17; 27-30. 3,5;
19. 6,5. 8,1. 9,1. 18,1-2. 19,1. 22,1. 23,1;
48; 51; 65. 28,3. 29,7; 13. 38,1. 39,1; 4.
43,4. 44,1. 45,1; 6; 8-9. 49,1. 64,1. 69,6;
32; 54. NF3,12. NF4,1. NF9,2; 36.
NF10,1. IoW7,8. IoW8,3; 8-9.
HEF 10,59. 20,1.
HRT 1,10; 12. 5,4; 16;
20; 26. 10,9. 13,1-2. 15,1-3; 10-13. 17,6;
10-11. 19,1. 20,1-3; 5-7; 9-11. 23,3. 26,1.
28,1; 4. 30,1. 33,3; 8; 17; 20. 37,23. 42,6;
9.
KEN C1. R1. 2,27; 34.
5,27-28; 37; 59; 79; 159; 195. 6,1. 11,1-2.

13,1.
MDX 8,1. 9,2. 15,2. 18,1.
22,1.
NFK 1,122; 147. 4,29;
47. 9,6; 12; 29; 31. 13,7. 14,14; 21. 15,25.
'19,17. 20,7. 23,9; 17. 31,20-21. 35,4-5.
43,1-3. 47,3. 52,4. 66,87.
NTH 6a,25. 21,1-2; 6.
OXF 9,4. 11,2. 20,2.
59,11.
SHR 4,3,20; 53. 4,5,4.
4,14,8; 15. 7,3.
SOM *1,28. 6,16.* 8,8; *24;*
30. 18,4. 19,11; 16-18; 57-60; 83. 20,3.
21,16; 30; 66; 71. 22,3; 9; *11;* 14; 24; 27.
24,9; 11; 15; 17; 19-20; *27; 29.* 27,1. 31,1.
35,8; 16; 23. 36,1-2; 7; *8.* 37,1; 4. *41,2.*
SFK 1,12. 3,3; 55. 7,51;
55; 58. 8,46-47. 16,14; 20. 29,1. 31,44-49.
34,13. 36,1-2; 4; 7; 11. 41,11. 54,2. 76,22.
SRY 1,10. 4,1-2. 5,16.
19,47. 25,1. 28,1.
36,4.
SSX 1,2. 9,77; 101.
11,92; 106; 116. 12,31-32; 39; 50. 13,1; 4;
23; 26-27; 30; 38.
WAR 15,6.
WIL 2,6. 23,10.
WOR 10,5; 10; 14-15.
15,2. 18,3.
more TRE than BDF 2,2; 4; 6; 9. 3,2; 4-
when acquired/ 5; 7-9; 11; 13-17.
received/found/ 4,3; 6-8. 5,1-2. 6,2-
later 3. 8,1-3; 5-6. 10,1.
11,1. 12,1. 14,1. 15,2-4; 6-7. 16,1-4; 7-9.
17,5-6. 18,1; 5. 20,1. 21,1-7; 9; 11-17.
22,1-2. 23,1; 4-5; 7-8; 10-14; 16-18; 20-23;
25-26; 30; 32; 34; 36-37; 40-43; 46; 48-52;
56-57. 24,1-10; 13-15; 17-30. 25,1-2; 4-5;
7-10; 13-15. 26,1-3. 27,1. 29,1. 30,1. 31,1.
32,1-4; 6-8; 11; 13; 15-16. 33,1-2. 34,1-3.
36,1. 37,1. 38,2. 40,1-3. 41,1-2. 42,1.
43,1. 44,1-4. 45,1. 46,1-2. 47,1-2. 48,1.
49,2-4. 51,1; 3. 52,1-2. 53,1-7; 10; 12-15;
17-18; 20-21; 24-29; 31-33; 35-36. 54,1-4.
55,1-4; 6-7; 9-13. 56,5-7. 57,2; 3i-iii,vi; 4;
6; 11-12; 15-16; 21.
BRK 1,1; 6; 8; 11-12; 15-
16; 20-22; 24; 28-29; 33-40; 47. 2,1. 3,1.
5,1. 7,2; 8; 15; 21-22; 30; 33; 36; 38; 47.
8,1. 9,1. 10,1. 14,1. 15,2. 18,2. 20,2-3.
21,1; 3; 9; 13; 18-19; 22. 22,1; 5-7; 10-11.
23,3. 26,1. 28,1; 3. 29,1. 30,1. 33,1; 3-6.
36,4. 37,1. 38,2-3. 39,1. 41,1; 5. 43,1.
46,3; 6. 48,1. 49,3. 50,1. 55,1; 3-4. 56,1.
57,1. 59,1. 62,1. 63,2. 64,1. 65,1; 4; 19-
20.
BKM B2. 2,1; 3. 3,1-2.
3a,1-2; 4; 6. 4,1; 4-10; 14-17; 19; 21; 26;
28-31; 33-34; 36-43. 5,1-3; 6-21. 6,1. 7,1-
2. 8,1-2. 10,1. 12,2-3; 6-8; 12; 16; 20; 23;

25-26; 28; 32; 35-38. 13,1-4. 14,3-4; 6; 10-12; 14; 16-20; 26-31; 36-37; 39-43; 45-46; 48. 15,1. 16,1; 3; 8-9. 17,2-8; 10; 13; 17; 19; 23; 28. 18,2-3. 19,1-3; 6-7. 20,1. 21,1-5; 7. 23,2-6; 12; 14; 16; 19; 23-27; 30-32. 24,1-3. 25,1-3. 26,4; 7-9; 11. 27,1-2. 29,1-3. 31,1. 35,1-3. 36,1-2. 37,1-2. 39,1-2. 41,1-4; 6-7. 43,1-8; 10-11. 44,3-5. 45,1. 46,1. 47,1. 48,1. 50,1. 51,1-3. 53,1-3; 5; 7-10. 56,1; 3. 57,2; 4-5; 7; 11-14.

CAM 1,12. 2,1-4. 3,1-6. 4,1. 5,1; 3-6; 8; 12-13; 20; 23; 25; 28; 31; 34; 36; 38-39; 41-42; 44-46; 48-55; 57; 59-63. 6,3. 7,2-5; 8-11. 8,1. 9,1-3. 11,1; 3-4. 12,2; 4. 13,1; 4; 6; 8-9; 11. 14,5; 17; 19-24; 26; 28-33; 39-46; 49; 51; 54-56; 58; 60; 66-72; 78. 15,3. 17,3-4. 18,7-8. 19,1; 4. 20,1. 21,1-2; 4-5; 8-9. 22,7; 9-10. 23,1; 3-6. 24,1. 25,5; 10. 26,2; 10; 15-20; 23-27; 30-32; 34-36; 41-43; 45; 48-49; 51. 27,1. 28,1-2. 30,2-3. 31,1-2; 4; 6-7. 32,5-8; 10; 14; 16; 19-25; 27-28; 30; 32; 34-37; 39-40; 43. 35,2. 36,1. 38,1-5. 39,1-3. 40,1. 41,9-11; 13; 16. 42,1. 43,1. 44,1-2.

CHS B9. 1,1; 5; 13-15; 22-23; 26. 2,2-6; 13; 19; 23-24; 27; 29. 3,4-5; 7-10. 4,1-2. 5,1-3; 5-6; 9; 11-13. 7,1. 8,2-3; 7; 15; 17; 22-23; 28; 31; 34; 36. 9,1; 5; 17-18; 20. 10,1; 3. 13,4-5. 14,1; 3-6; 11. 15,1. 17,1; 3-4; 6. 18,2. 23,1-2. 24,3; 5. 25,2-3. R7,1.

ESS 1,25. 16,1. 20,56; 59; 62-63. 23,30. 25,6. 26,1-2. 27,5; 8; 10; 16-17. 28,5; 8; 13-15. 30,28. 32,8-9; 40; 42. 33,4. 34,8. 36,12. 40,3; 8. 41,10; 12. 46,3. 47,2. 80,1. 90,5. B3p.

GLS 1,38.

HAM 1,3; 12; 16; 18-19; 24-26; 29-30; 39-40; W3-5; W9-11; W14-15; W21. 2,1; 5; 8-11; 14-16; 18-19; 21. 3,2; 4; 6-11; 13; 15-16; 18; 20; 25. 4,1. 5,1. 6,4; 6; 8-9; 11; 16-17. 7,1. 8,1. 9,1-2. 10,1. 18,1; 3. 21,2-4; 6-8. 23,3; 6-8; 12-13; 17-20; 24; 28-29; 31-32; 39; 41; 45-47; 49; 52-53; 55; 59. 25,1. 26,1. 27,1-2. 28,2; 5-7; 9. 29,1-4; 6-7; 10-11; 13-16. 30,1. 31,1. 33,1. 34,1. 35,1-2; 7-9. 36,2. 37,1-2. 39,3-4. 41,1. 42,1. 43,1; 4. 44,3-4. 45,1; 3; 5-6; 9. 47,3. 49,1. 50,2. 51,1. 55,1-2. 56,1; 3. 57,2. 58,1. 60,1-2. 61,1. 65,1. 66,1. 67,1. 68,3; 5-7; 10. 69,1-3; 6-7; 11; 13-14; 16; 21; 35; 48; 54. NF3,8-9; 12. NF5,1. NF9,2; 13; 37; 39-40. IoW1,1-3. IoW6,1; 4; 15. IoW7,1; 6; 8; 17; 22. IoW8,1; 3-6.

HEF 2,26; 42; 51. 7,3. 10,8; 48; 56; 68. 14,3; 8-10. 15,10. 19,7-8. 20,1. 21,1; 4. 22,5. 23,6. 25,8. 27,1. 33,1.

HRT 1,3; 6; 10; 12-15; 17-19. 2,1-3. 3,1. 4,1-5; 8; 11-20; 22-25. 5,1; 3; 5-6; 8-11; 13-14; 17-21; 23-26. 6,1. 7,1-3. 8,1. 9,1-5; 7-10. 10,1; 4-11; 14-19.

11,1. 12,1. 13,3-5. 14,1-2. 15,1-2; 4-8; 11-13. 16,1-2; 4-8; 10-11. 17,1-4; 8; 11-12; 14-15. 18,1. 19,1-2. 20,1-2; 4-11; 13. 21,1-2. 22,1-2. 23,1-4. 24,1; 3. 25,1-2. 27,1. 28,3-8. 29,1. 30,1-2. 31,1; 3; 6-7. 32,1-2. 33,1-6; 8-9; 11-15; 18; 20. 34,1; 3-5; 7; 10-19; 21-25. 35,1-3. 36,2-5; 7-8; 11-15; 17; 19. 37,1-18; 20-22. 38,1-2. 41,2. 42,1-2; 6-8. 42a,1. 43,1. 44,1.

KEN 2,3; 11-12; 20; 30; 32; 39; 41-42. 3,1-2; 4. 5,19; 21-26; 30-31; 34; 36; 38; 40-42; 46-47; 49; 51-53; 55-57; 63-64; 71; 75; 81; 83; 88; 94; 96; 99; 104-105; 119-124; 128; 135-136; 139; 141-147; 152; 155; 158-160; 162-163; 165; 167-168; 170-171; 174; 176; 183; 185-187; 191-194; 197; 200-203; 206-208; 210; 212; 214-216; 219-220; 224-225. 7,2-6; 8-9; 12-13; 15; 19-21; 23-29. 8,1. 9,1; 3-6; 12-14; 16; 18; 22; 24-25; 28-31; 36-37; 41-42; 45-50; 53-54. 10,1. 12,1; 3-4. 13,1.

MDX 2,1-3. 3,1-9; 12-14; 17-21; 23; 26; 28; 30. 4,1-3; 5-12. 5,1. 6,1. 7,1-2; 4-8. 8,2-6. 9,1; 3-4; 6-9. 10,1-2. 11,1-4. 12,1-2. 13,1. 14,1-2. 15,1. 16,1. 17,1. 18,1-2. 19,1. 21,1. 24,1. 25,3.

NFK 1,2; 73; 113; 141. 12,30. 17,18. 21,2. 23,6; 9; 12. 24,1; 3-4. 31,31. 49,1. 55,1. 61,2.

NTH 11,5.

OXF 6,1b; 2; 4; 9; 12. 9,3. 20,2. 24,3. 27,5. 35,20. 58,36. 59,21.

SHR 1,7-8. 2,1. 3b,3. 4,3,1-5; 9-11; 13-15; 18-19; 21-23; 27; 45; 47; 53; 58; 63; 67-68; 70-71. 4,4,3-4; 20-21; 23. 4,5,4; 9; 15. 4,6,1. 4,7,2-3. 4,8,1; 4-5; 7; 9; 11; 13. 4,9,1. 4,10,3. 4,11,2; 4-7; 10-12; 19. 4,14,1-2; 4; 6; 13; 22; 24. 4,15,1-3. 4,16,2. 4,17,2-3. 4,19,1-5; 7-8; 13. 4,20,1; 3; 5-6; 8; 14; 17; 24. 4,21,6-8; 11-12; 15; 18. 4,22,2. 4,23,2; 4; 6; 8; 12; 14; 17. 4,24,2-3; 6. 4,26,3-4; 6. 4,27,2; 32; 35. 5,9. 6,1; 5-6; 8-11; 16; 19; 21. 7,1. 9,1-2.

STS 4,3-4; 6. 8,4.
SFK 1,76. 8,46; 50. 16,12. 29,1. 31,42. 35,16. 54,2. 67,6.
SRY 1,5; 9; 11; 14-15. 2,3-5. 3,1. 5,1a; 5; 7-9; 11; 13; 15-17; 19-23; 27. 6,1; 4-5. 8,4; 8; 25. 11,1. 15,1-2. 16,1. 17,1; 3-4. 18,1; 4. 19,1-10; 12-13; 15-16; 20-21; 23-24; 26-27; 29; 31-32; 36-37; 39; 44. 20,1. 21,1-4; 6-7. 22,1-2; 5. 25,2-3. 26,1. 27,1. 29,1-2. 30,1-2. 31,1. 32,1-2. 35,2.
SSX 1,2. 2,1a; 2; 6; 8-9. 3,1-7; 9. 5,2. 6,1; 3-4. 8,1. 9,1-5; 11; 13-15; 18-19; 21-24; 26; 31; 35; 37; 52; 60; 66-67; 82-85; 87; 89-90; 96; 104-107; 111; 120-122. 10,4-7; 9; 12; 14-15; 18-19; 22; 25-27;

32-34; 36; 38; 42-43; 47; 49; 51-54; 56; 60-
61; 64-66. 11,3-4; 6-24; 29-41; 43-46; 48;
53; 56; 62-63; 75-76; 78-81; 85-88; 90-93;
96; 103; 105-114; 116. 12,3-6; 10-11; 13-
15; 18; 22-23; 30; 33; 35-37; 41-42; 46; 48-
50. 13,1; 3; 5-6; 10-15; 17; 19; 29; 43; 49-
50; 53. 14,1-2.

WAR   2,1. 4,1; 6. 6,2-4; 8;
11-12; 14-18. 8,1. 11,1; 4. 12,1; 4-6. 14,1.
15,1. 16,1; 5; 7; 10; 13-14; 20; 32-33; 35-
36; 54. 17,56; 60; 69. 19,4. 31,1.

WOR   3,3. 10,3; 12; 14-
15. 11,2. 15,1-2; 4; 6; 8-9; 11-12. 17,1.
18,3-4. 19,14. 20,2-3; 5. 26,1.

more 1086 than   BDF   3,1-2; 4-5; 11; 13.
when acquired/   4,1-2; 6. 6,2-3. 8,5.
received/found   10,1. 12,1. 14,1.
16,3; 8-9. 18,1; 5. 21,1-2; 5-7; 9; 12; 14-
17. 22,1. 23,1; 3-5; 10-13; 15; 17-20; 22; 24;
29; 32; 36-37; 40-43; 45-46; 48-51. 24,2-3;
5-10; 13-15; 17-18; 20-21; 24-29. 25,1-2;
4; 7; 9; 11. 26,1. 32,3; 5; 8-9; 11; 13; 15-
16. 33,2. 34,2-3. 36,1. 37,1. 39,1-2. 41,1.
42,1. 45,1. 46,1. 47,2. 49,1-4. 51,1-3. 53,3-
4; 6; 9; 12; 14-15; 20-21; 29; 32-33; 35.
54,2-3. 55,3-4; 6-7; 9; 13. 57,6.

BRK   B8. 1,1; 5; 7-8; 10-
12; 17; 24-25; 27; 29; 32-41; 47. 2,1-3. 3,2.
4,1. 6,1. 7,2-3; 8; 15; 18-20; 26; 33; 36-38;
47. 8,1. 9,1. 10,1-2. 15,2. 18,2. 20,2-3.
21,1; 3; 9; 19. 22,1; 6; 11. 23,3. 28,3. 29,1.
30,1. 33,3-4. 36,4. 38,2; 6. 39,1. 41,1-2; 5.
43,1. 46,3; 6. 48,1. 49,3. 50,1. 55,1; 3-4.
57,1. 59,1. 62,1. 63,2. 64,1. 65,1; 4.

BKM   2,1; 3. 3,1-2. 3a,1-
2; 4. 4,5-6; 10; 14-16; 18; 29-31; 35-39. 5,3;
6-7; 9-11; 13-16; 20. 8,1-2. 12,3; 12; 16; 28;
32; 35-37. 13,1; 4. 14,4-6; 18-19; 27-31; 36;
38-41; 43; 45; 48. 16,3. 17,6-7. 19,1-2; 6-
7. 21,3-4; 7. 23,2-3; 14; 16; 23-24; 26; 30-
32. 24,1; 3. 25,1; 3; 29,1-3. 35,2-3. 37,1.
38,1. 39,1-2. 41,1-2; 4. 43,1-4; 6-8; 11.
44,3. 46,1. 51,3. 52,1. 53,3; 8. 55,1.

CAM   1,12. 2,1-4. 3,1; 6.
5,4-6; 8; 11; 14-15; 44-47; 49-53; 57; 59-
60. 7,4; 8; 11. 8,1. 13,6. 14,5; 12; 17; 21-
22; 26-27; 31-33; 40; 44; 46; 48; 51; 55; 59;
63-64; 66; 69-72; 78; 81. 17,3-4. 18,3; 8.
20,1. 21,1; 4-5; 8. 22,6-8. 25,4; 9. 26,2; 6;
14-15; 24; 26; 36; 41-43; 46; 51. 27,1. 28,2.
29,1-2; 5; 7; 9. 31,2; 4; 6-7. 32,2; 5-6; 12;
16; 20; 22; 32; 36; 39. 38,1; 5. 39,3. 40,1.
41,7; 13; 16. 42,1. 44,1-2.

CHS   B9. 1,1; 5; 13-15;
22-23; 26. 2,2-6; 13; 19; 23-24; 27; 29. 3,5-
10. 4,1-2. 5,1-3; 5-6; 9; 11-13. 6,1. 7,1; 3.
8,2-3; 6-7; 15; 17; 22-23; 28; 31; 34; 36.
9,1; 5-8; 17-18; 20. 10,1; 3. 13,4-5. 14,1;
3-6; 11. 15,1. 17,1; 3-4; 6. 18,2. 20,11-12.
23,1-2. 24,3; 5. 25,2-3.

DEV   *1,10; 15;* 17. 2,18-

19. *3,23; 34-35; 55; 89.* 5,5. 6,8. 11,1. *15,2.*
16,3; *27; 166. 19,18.* 23,22. 24,20. 34,21;
46.

DOR   31,2. 47,7.
ESS   1,10; 30. 3,11; 16.
4,1; 17. 6,4. 14,2-3. 15,1. 16,1. 18,21a; 24;
38; 45. 20,24; 36-37; 43; 45; 52; 54-56; 59;
63; 72; 74-75. 22,7; 9; 11-12; 14. 23,2-3; 6-
8; 10; 13; 15; 28; 30. 24,18; 23; 28; 30; 32;
42; 60-61. 25,6; 10-12; 14-16; 18-19. 26,1.
27,8; 10-11; 16-17. 28,8; 13-17. 29,2. 30,1-
4; 7; 9; 16; 18; 27-28; 30-31; 33; 35-40; 45.
32,8-9; 12-13; 16; 18-19; 27; 38; 42; 45.
33,1; 4-6; 12-13; 15. 34,8; 10; 18; 20; 23;
25; 32. 35,3; 6; 8. 36,1; 3; 12. 37,3; 10-12.
38,2; 5; 7-8. 39,3. 40,6; 8. 41,10. 42,7.
43,5-6. 48,2. 53,1. 54,1. 57,6. 65,1. 74,1.
76,1. 90,22; 26; 35-36; 50-52; 55-57; 63.

GLS   B1.
HAM   1,1; 3; 12; 16; 18;
20-21; 24. 2,1; 3-6; 8-11; 13-15; 18-19; 21-
22. 3,1-9;,11; 13-16; 18; 20-21; 24-25. 4,1.
5,1. 6,3-4; 6; 11; 13; 15-17. 9,2. 10,1. 13,1.
14,2. 15,1-3. 16,1. 21,1-2; 6-8. 23,3-8; 12-
13; 17-20; 26-29; 31-32; 34; 36-37; 39-40;
42; 44; 47; 49-50; 52; 55-59; 61; 64; 66.
25,1. 27,2. 28,1-2; 5-7; 9. 29,3-4; 8; 10-11;
15. 32,2; 4. 34,1. 35,1-2; 4; 6-9. 36,2. 37,2.
40,1. 41,1. 42,1. 43,1. 44,2-4. 45,3. 46,2.
47,3. 51,1-2. 53,2. 54,1. 55,1. 56,1; 3.
60,1-2. 62,1-2. 65,1. 68,3; 5-7; 10. 69,1-4;
7; 13-14; 21; 35; 38; 48. NF9,37; 40; 45.
NF10,2. IoW1,1. IoW2,1. IoW6,1; 4; 6;
15. IoW7,5-6; 21-22. IoW8,1; 4; 6.
IoW9,2.

HEF   2,34-36; 45. 7,3.
10,8; 11; 48; 56; 58; 60; 68. 14,1-3; 9-10;
12. 19,8. 21,1; 4. 23,6. 25,8. 27,1. 29,2.
33,1.

HRT   B11. 1,3; 14; 18-19.
2,1; 3. 3,1. 4,1. 5,1-3; 5; 8-9; 14; 17-19; 21;
23; 25. 6,1. 7,2. 9,9. 10,2-3; 5-6; 8; 10-11;
14-16; 19. 11,1. 15,4-5; 8. 16,2; 4-5; 8; 10.
17,1-2; 4; 8; 14. 20,13. 21,2. 22,1-2. 23,4.
24,1; 3. 25,1-2. 28,5; 7-8. 29,1. 31,1; 3; 6-
7. 32,1-2. 33,5-6; 9; 11; 13; 15; 18. 34,4-
5; 7; 10-11; 13; 16; 23-24. 35,1-3. 36,2-4;
7; 12-15; 19. 37,4-6; 8-11; 13-18; 20-22.
38,1-2. 42,2; 7; 10. 42a,1. 43,1.

KEN   1,2; 4. 2,3; 5-7; 9-
13; 15-23; 25; 30-32; 35; 37; 39; 41-43. 3,1;
3-8; 10-21. 4,1-3; 5-15. 5,8; 19-20; 22-26;
29-32; 34-36; 38-49; 51-58; 63; 67-71; 73-
76; 83; 85-86; 88-90; 92-109; 111; 113-115;
118-120; 122-124; 127-129; 131; 136-143;
145-147; 149; 152-153; 155-156; 158; 162-
165; 167-168; 170-172; 174-176; 178-180;
183; 185-186; 191-194; 197; 199-203; 206-
208; 210; 212; 214-216; 219-220; 224-225.
7,1-10; 12-13; 15; 17-21; 23-29. 8,1. 9,1;
3-6; 10; 12-14; 16; 18-19; 22; 24-25; 28-31;

36-37; 41-42; 45-50; 53-54. 10,1-2. 12,1; 3.

LEC   6,1. 33,1.

MDX   2,1-2. 4,2. 5,1. 7,5. 8,4-6. 9,1; 4; 7-9. 10,1-2. 11,1-2. 12,2. 13,1. 14,1. 16,1. 17,1. 18,2. 19,1. 21,1. 24,1.

NFK   1,1-2; 45; 71; 73; 77-78; 94; 136; 143; 150-152; 179; 185-186; 192-194; 197-198; 201-203; 206. 2,1; 7. 4,26; 30-31; 39; 52. 5,1; 3-4. 6,5. 7,3; 7; 10-12; 15-17. 8,7; 15; 34; 36; 48; 59; 105; 121-122; 131; 134. 9,2; 9; 24; 27; 31-33; 47; 76; 87; 94-95; 142-156; 162; 165; 174-176; 196. 10,77. 12,1; 27; 30; 32. 13,15-16; 24. 14,14. 18,1. 19,11-13; 21. 20,27; 34-35. 21,2; 9; 23; 28; 30. 23,6-8; 12; 16. 25,16. 26,2; 5. 27,2. 31,2; 6; 8; 16; 31; 34; 37; 41; 44. 32,3-5; 7. 33,1; 6. 34,4; 18. 35,10. 37,1. 46,1. 49,1-2. 50,6-7. 51,3-4. 55,1. 61,2.

NTH   11,5.

OXF   6,1b; 2-3; 9; 12-13. 7,2-4. 13,1. 15,2-3. 20,3. 22,1. 24,3; 5. 27,5. 28,1-2; 9; 12; 19; 22. 34,2. 35,3; 20. 54,1. 58,36. 59,21.

SHR   1,7-8. 2,1. 3b,3. 4,3,1-5; 9-11; 13-15; 18-19; 21-23; 27; 32-33; 45; 47; 52; 58; 63; 67-68; 70-71. 4,4,3-4; 20-21; 23. 4,5,9; 15. 4,6,1. 4,7,2-3. 4,8,1; 4-5; 7; 9; 11; 13-14. 4,9,1. 4,10,1; 3. 4,11,2; 4-7; 10-12; 19. 4,14,1-2; 4; 6; 13; 22; 24. 4,15,1-3. 4,16,2. 4,17,2-3. 4,18,2. 4,19,1-2; 4-5; 7-8; 12-13. 4,20,1; 3; 5-6; 8; 14-17; 24. 4,21,6-8; 11-12; 15; 18. 4,22,2. 4,23,2; 4; 6; 8; 12; 14; 17. 4,24,2. 4,25,1-3; 6. 4,26,3-4; 6. 4,27,2; 32; 35. 5,9. 6,1-2; 5; 9-11; 14; 16; 18-21; 23; 33. 7,1. 9,1-2.

SOM   2,1; *11. 5,5; 7; 34; 53; 56. 7,13. 8,1; 9-10; 11-12; 16-18; 21; 23-26; 31; 33. 16,2. 17,5; 8. 19,3-4; 6; 8-9; 12; 15; 21; 49; 70-71; 76; 82; 84. 20,2. 21,3; 26; 32; 37-38; 50-51; 56-59; 63-64; 67; 81; 83.* 22,1-2; *16-17; 22; 26.* 24,4; *12; 21-22; 24-25.* 25,1; 7; 10; *18; 24; 27; 35-36;* 49; 55. 26,2; 4; 8. 28,2. 29,1. *30,2.* 32,8. 35,3; *4; 11;* 15; 17-18; 21. 36,2; *12. 37,6.* 44,3. 46,1. *47,5.*

STS   4,3-4; 6. 8,4.

SFK   1,1; 75-76; 88; 115. 2,6. 3,10; 46. 5,5. 6,1; 3. 8,81. 12,3; 5; 7. 16,12. 25,4; 32. 26,3. 27,7. 28,1a-3. 29,1. 31,42; 60. 34,1-3; 6. 35,1. 39,16. 40,2-3. 41,10. 43,1. 76,2; 4.

SRY   1,2-3; 5; 11; 14. 2,1-5. 3,1. 5,1a; 4-5; 7-9; 11; 13; 15; 17; 19-20; 22-23; 27. 6,1; 4-5. 7,1. 8,4; 8; 25. 11,1. 14,1. 15,1-2. 16,1. 17,3-4. 18,4. 19,1-10; 12-16; 20-21; 23-24; 26-27; 29; 31-32; 36-39; 44. 20,1-2. 21,1-3. 22,1-3; 5. 24,1.

25,2-3. 26,1. 27,1. 29,1-2. 30,1-2. 31,1. 35,2.

SSX   2,1a; 2; 5-9. 3,1-9. 5,2-3. 6,4. 8,1. 9,1-9; 11; 13-19; 21-24; 26; 31; 35; 37; 52; 59-60; 66-67; 72; 74-75; 82-85; 87; 89-90; 96; 103-107; 111; 120-123; 125. 10,2-7; 11-12; 14-16; 18-19; 22; 25-27; 34; 36; 38; 42-43; 45; 47; 49; 51-54; 56; 59-61; 65-66. 11,1; 3-4; 6-12; 14-24; 27; 29-41; 43-46; 48; 53; 55; 61-63; 66; 74; 78-81; 85-87; 90-91; 93; 96; 103-105; 108; 110-114. 12,3-6; 8-11; 13-15; 18-23; 33-36; 41-44; 46-48; 54-55. 13,3; 5-6; 8-11; 13-15; 17; 19; 29; 33; 39; 43; 46; 50; 53; 56. 14,1-2.

WAR   2,1. 3,1-3; 5; 7. 4,1; 6. 6,2-4; 8; 11-12; 14-18. 8,1. 11,1; 4. 12,1; 3-6. 14,1-2. 15,4-5. 16,1; 5; 7-15; 20; 32-35; 54. 17,56-57; 60-61; 69. 19,4. 31,1.

WIL   2,1; 5; 7-12. 5,7. 7,3; 11; 14. 8,6-9; 12. 10,2. 25,1. 26,21. 11,2. 15,1; 4; 6; 8; 10-12. 17,1. 19,3; 12; 14. 20,2-3. 26,1.

WOR   3,3. 10,1; 3; 12.

same TRE as when   BDF   2,1; 7-8. 3,1. 4,1-2. acquired/received/   8,7-8. 15,1; 5. found/later   16,5-6. 17,1; 3. 18,4; 6-7. 19,3. 20,2. 23,3; 9; 15; 19; 24; 27-28; 31; 33; 35; 39; 45; 47; 53-55. 24,16. 25,3; 6; 12. 28,1-2. 32,5; 10; 12. 39,1-2. 48,2. 49,1. 50,1. 53,8-9; 11; 19; 23; 30; 34. 55,5; 8. 56,1-4; 8. 57,1; 3iv-v; 8; 10; 13; 20.

BRK   1,3-5; 7; 14; 17; 25-27; 31; 41; 44. 2,2-3. 6,1. 7,3; 12-13; 18-19; 26; 28; 31; 39; 42. 10,2. 12,1. 16,2-3. 21,4-5; 15. 22,2; 9. 28,2. 31,5. 38,6. 41,2. 45,2. 54,2-3.

BKM   2,1-2. 3a,3; 5. 4,2-3; 11-13; 18; 22-25; 27; 32; 35. 5,4-5. 6,2. 8,3. 9,1. 11,1. 12,4-5; 9-11; 14-15; 17-18; 21; 29-30; 33-34. 14,1-2; 5; 7-9; 13; 15; 21-25; 34-35; 38; 44; 49. 15,2. 16,2; 6-7; 10. 17,1; 11; 14; 16; 18; 20-22; 24-25; 27; 29-31. 18,1. 19,4-5. 21,6; 8. 22,2. 23,1; 7-11; 13; 15; 17-18; 20-22; 28; 33. 26,1-2; 5. 28,3. 30,1. 32,1. 33,1. 34,1. 36,3. 38,1. 40,1. 41,5. 42,1. 43,9. 44,1-2. 49,1. 52,1. 53,4; 6. 54,1. 55,1. 56,2. 57,3; 6; 8-10; 15-18.

CAM   1,11; 18. 5,7; 9-11; 14; 18; 21; 40. 6,1. 7,1; 7. 10,2. 11,2. 12,1. 13,2-3; 5; 7. 14,1; 4; 11; 13; 27; 36; 50; 52-53; 57; 62-64; 73; 75-77; 81. 15,1-2; 4. 16,1. 17,2; 5-6. 18,1-3; 5-6. 21,3; 6-7. 22,1-4; 8. 23,2. 25,3-4; 6-9. 26,1; 3-7; 9; 12; 14; 21-22; 28-29; 33; 37-39; 44; 46-47; 50; 53; 56. 29,1-9. 31,3. 32,2-4; 11-13; 17-18; 23; 31; 33; 38. 34,1. 35,1. 37,1-2. 41,1; 3-4; 7-8; 12; 14.

CHS   6,1. 9,6; 8.

ESS   1,2; 10. 3,11; 16.

4,1; 11; 17. 6,4. 14,2–4. 18,21a; 24; 30; 33;
38; 44–45. 20,24; 36–37; 39; 43; 45; 52; 54–
55; 57; 61; 72; 74–75. 22,11–12. 23,2–3; 6–
8; 13; 15. 24,18; 23; 28; 30; 32; 42; 60–61.
25,10–12; 14–16; 18–19. 27,6; 11; 14; 16–17.
29,2. 30,1–4; 7; 9; 16; 18–21; 27; 30–31; 33;
35–40; 45–46. 32,16; 18–19; 27–28; 38; 45.
33,1; 5–6; 12–13; 15; 22. 34,6; 18; 23–26;
32–33. 35,3; 6; 8. 36,1; 3. 37,3; 10–12; 20.
38,2; 5; 7–8. 39,3–4; 7–9. 40,6; 9. 42,7.
43,5–6. 48,2. 53,1. 54,1. 57,6. 60,3. 65,1.
66,1. 74,1. 76,1. 90,22; 26–27; 35–36; 50–
52; 56–57; 63. B3b.

　　　　　HAM 1,1–5; 8; 13–14; 17;
20–21; 27–28; W6; W19. 2,2–4; 6; 10; 13;
20; 22–24. 3,1; 3; 5; 12; 14; 17; 19; 22. 6,5;
10; 13; 15. 13,1. 14,1–2; 6. 15,1–2. 16,1.
18,2. 21,1. 22,1. 23,4; 9; 16; 26–27; 30; 34;
36–38; 40; 42–44; 48; 50–51; 56–58; 61; 64–
66; 68. 24,1. 28,1; 3–4. 29,5; 8–9. 32,1; 4.
35,6. 36,1. 38,1. 39,1. 40,1. 43,2; 6. 44,2.
45,8. 46,2. 47,2. 50,1. 51,2. 53,2. 54,1.
56,2. 57,1. 62,1–2. 64,1. 68,9. 69,4; 32; 38.
NF3,2. NF4,1. NF9,36; 45. NF10,1–3.
IoW1,4; 7. IoW2,1. IoW6,6. IoW7,21.
IoW8,8–9. IoW9,2.

　　　　　HEF 2,15; 17–21; 26–37;
39–40; 45; 47; 49–50. 10,11. 14,1–2; 12.
17,1.

　　　　　HRT 1,8–9; 11; 16. 2,4–5.
4,6; 9–10. 5,2; 4; 7; 12; 15–16; 22. 7,4. 8,2.
10,2–3; 13. 13,1–2. 15,3; 9–10. 16,3; 12.
17,5–7; 9–10; 13. 20,3; 12. 24,2. 26,1. 28,1–
2. 30,3. 31,2; 5; 8. 33,7; 10; 16–17; 19.
34,2; 6; 8–9; 20. 36,1; 10; 18. 37,19; 23.
39,1. 42,4–5; 9; 11–15.

　　　　　KEN 1,1–3. 2,6–8; 13–19;
21–23; 25; 31; 33–35; 37; 43. 3,3; 5; 7–8; 10–
21. 4,1–3; 5–16. 5,20; 27–29; 32–33; 35; 37;
39; 44; 50; 54; 58–60; 62; 65–70; 72–74; 76–
80; 82; 84–87; 89–93; 95; 97–98; 100; 102–
103; 106–108; 110–115; 118; 126; 129–130;
132; 137–138; 140; 149–151; 153–154; 156–
157; 161; 164; 166–167; 169; 172; 178–182;
195–196; 199; 204; 218. 7,1; 10–11; 14; 16–
18; 22. 9,2; 10; 19; 21; 23; 27; 44; 51–52.
11,1.

　　　　　MDX 3,11. 5,2. 8,1. 9,2;
　　　　　　　　　5. 15,2. 20,1.

　　　　　NFK 1,1; 45; 78; 136;
186; 206. 2,1; 7. 4,26; 30; 39; 52. 5,1–4.
6,5. 7,3; 7; 10–12; 15–17. 8,7; 15; 34; 36; 48;
59; 105; 121–122; 131; 134. 9,2; 6; 9; 12;
24; 27; 29; 32–33; 47; 71; 76; 95; 142–156;
162; 165; 174–176. 10,77. 12,27. 13,7; 9;
15–16; 24. 14,14; 21. 15,25. 18,1. 19,11–
13; 17; 21. 20,7; 27; 34. 21,23; 28; 30. 23,7–
8; 16–17. 25,16; 23. 26,2. 27,2. 30,4. 31,2;
6; 8; 16; 21; 34; 37; 41; 44. 32,3–4; 7. 33,1;
6. 34,4; 18. 35,4–5; 10. 37,1. 43,1–3. 46,1.
47,3. 49,2. 50,6–7. 51,3–4; 8. 52,4. 66,87.

　　　　　OXF 6,3. 7,2–4. 11,2.
13,1. 15,3. 20,1; 3–4. 22,1. 24,1; 5. 27,2;
10. 28,1–2; 6; 9; 19. 32,1. 33,1. 34,2. 35,1–
3.

　　　　　SHR 4,8,14. 4,14,8.
　　　　　　　　　4,20,16. 6,2; 25;
　　　　　　　　　33.
　　　　　SFK 1,115. 2,6. 5,5. 6,1;
3; 251. 7,55; 58. 8,47; 81. 12,3; 5; 7. 16,3;
14; 20. 25,4; 32; 34. 26,3. 28,1a–3. 29,1.
31,8; 41; 43–49. 32,9. 33,3. 34,1–2; 5–6; 13.
35,1. 36,1–2; 4; 7; 11. 39,16. 40,2–3. 41,10–
11. 43,1; 6. 46,1. 54,2. 76,2; 4; 22.
　　　　　SRY 1,2–3; 8; 10; 12–13.
2,1–2; 6. 4,1–2. 5,2; 10. 8,23. 14,1. 18,2–3.
19,14; 17; 38; 45–48. 20,2. 22,3–4. 24,1.
25,1. 27,2. 28,1. 36,1; 4.
　　　　　SSX 1,1. 2,3; 5; 7. 3,8.
5,3. 6,2. 7,1. 9,16; 54–55; 59; 61–65; 68–80;
88; 101–103; 112; 123; 125. 10,10–11; 16–
17; 45; 57; 59; 62–63; 115. 11,27; 47; 49–
52; 54–55; 57; 59; 61; 64–68; 70–73; 77; 82;
84; 89; 95; 99; 102; 104. 12,7; 12; 19–21;
29; 32; 34; 39–40; 43–44; 47; 54–56. 13,2;
4; 7–9; 16; 20; 22–23; 25–27; 30; 33–35; 38–
39; 41–42; 46–48; 51; 56.
　　　　　WAR 3,1–3; 5; 7. 4,2.
　　　　　　　　　14,2. 15,5–6. 16,8–
　　　　　　　　　9; 11–12; 15. 17,61.
　　　　　WOR 10,5; 10. 15,10.
　　　　　　　　　19,3–4; 12.
same 1086 as when BDF 1,5. 2,3–5. 3,3; 6–9;
acquired/received/　　　　14; 16–17. 4,3; 7–8.
found　　　　　　　　　　5,1–2. 8,1–3; 6–8.
11,1. 15,7. 16,2; 4–7. 17,1–3; 5–7. 18,6–7.
19,1; 3. 20,1–2. 21,3–4; 13. 22,2. 23,7–9;
14; 16; 21; 23; 25–28; 30–31; 33; 38–39; 47;
52–57. 24,4; 16; 19; 22–23; 30. 25,3; 5; 8;
10; 13–15. 26,2. 27,1. 28,1–2. 30,1. 32,2; 6;
10; 12. 34,1. 38,2. 40,1–3. 43,1. 44,1–4.
46,2. 47,1. 48,1. 52,2. 53,2; 7–8; 10; 16–19;
24–26; 28; 34; 36. 54,1; 4. 55,1–2; 5; 10–
\12. 56,1–8. 57,2; 3ii–vi; 4–5; 8; 10; 12–16;
20–21.
　　　　　BRK 1,15–16; 20–21; 26;
31; 44. 3,1. 7,1; 6; 13; 21–23; 28; 30–31; 39;
42. 12,1. 16,2–3. 21,4; 13; 22. 22,5; 7; 9–10.
31,5. 37,1. 38,3. 45,2. 54,3. 56,1. 65,20.
　　　　　BKM B2. 2,1–2. 3a,3; 5–
6. 4,1–4; 7–9; 11–13; 17; 19–21; 24–28; 32–
34; 40–43. 5,1–2; 4–5; 8; 12; 17–19; 21. 6,1–
2. 7,1–2. 8,3. 9,1. 10,1. 11,1. 12,1–2; 4–11;
14–15; 17–18; 20–23; 25–26; 29–30; 33–34;
38. 13,2–3. 14,1–3; 8–10; 12–17; 20–26; 32;
35; 37; 42; 44; 46; 49. 15,1–2. 16,1–2; 6–
10. 17,1–5; 8–11; 13–14; 16–21; 23–25; 28–
30. 18,1–3. 19,3–5. 20,1. 21,1–2; 5–6; 8.
22,2. 23,1; 4–7; 9–13; 15; 17–19; 21–22; 25;
27–28; 33. 24,2. 25,2. 26,1–2; 4–5; 7–9; 11.
27,1–2. 28,2. 31,1. 32,1. 33,1. 34,1. 35,1.
36,1–3. 37,2. 41,3; 5–7. 42,1. 43,5; 9–10.

See also: Butter.
VIKINGS,
assessment reduced
by reason of   HAM 2,15.
VILL (villa) – See Village.
VILLAGE (villa)   Passim.
Free   CON 4,26-27.
Inhabitants few/
unknown   YKS 1L1.
King's   YKS 2,4.
Land of
  added to by
  unknown means   ESS 18,1.
  appropriated from
  men of   BDF 24,12.
  held in common by
  men of   BDF 23,43.
Nothing recorded   HEF 10,72.
                          NTT 12,21.
Payments of   BKM 4,38.
Places so named   BDF B. 3,14. 17,5; 7.
  18,1. 21,5. 23,43. 24,12. 32,7; 15. 55,10;
  12. 56,2-4. 57,10; 14.
                          BRK 1,7. 7,25. 20,2.
                               35,2. 65,2.
                          BKM 1,3-5. 4,4; 9. 5,15-
  17; 19. 12,13; 15; 17-18; 22; 37-38. 14,29.
  17,8. 18,3. 23,22; 27. 53,4-5; 7.
                          CAM B10. 1,2-6; 9. 3,5.
  5,2; 5; 7; 10; 19; 21-22; 26-27; 31-33; 37;
  56. 14,4; 6; 9-10; 16; 25; 29-31; 37-38; 64;
  70. 17,3. 18,2. 22,5. 26,7; 28; 30; 39; 57.
  29,6. 30,2-3. 31,2. 32,5; 12; 25. 35,2.
                          CHS B3. 9,15. FT1,1.
                               FT2,1. R2,1. Y2-4;
                               7.
                          DBY 3,2. 6,59; 62. 14,6.
                          DEV 1,18; 23. 2,5-8.
                               17,1.
                          DOR B3-4. 3,1. 26,36;
  64. 33,3. 34,6; 8. 37,2. 47,7. 55,39. 57,9;
  16.
                          ESS 5,8. 14,7. 18,23.
  23,34. 25,14. 27,1. 30,12; 15; 46. 33,12; 23.
  34,19. 43,1. 61,1. 90,2.
                          GLS G2. S1. W2; 4-5;
                               19. 1,60. 4,1. 12,8-
                               9. 20,1. 69,6-7.
                          HAM 1,25. 3,6; 16. 15,1.
                               16,1. 17,1. NF8.1.
                          HEF 1,52. 2,21. 6,8. 8,5.
                               14,9; 11. 20,2.
                          HRT 1,10. 5,10-12. 9,3.
  10,5. 15,1. 17,1; 7. 28,3. 34,16-19. 36,10.
  42,4; 11.
                          HUN 20,6.
                          KEN D4-5; 7. M3. 2,1;
                               24. 5,13; 17.
                          LEC 1,3. 2,2; 4. 3,12.
  5,3. 6,4. 10,4. 13,28; 49; 59; 71. 15,11.

16,7. 17,13. 19,9. 25,2. 29,1. 43,4. 44,11;
13.
                          LIN S7-9; 14. T2. 1,9.
  3,56. 12,60. 13,40. 24,61. 26,45; 54. 27,20;
  35. 29,8. 30 33. 39,1. CN4; 22. CW15.
  CK20; 37.
                          MDX 3,2; 13-14; 16; 23.
                               4,1; 4. 9,5.
                          NFK 1,61; 63; 75; 90; 93;
  147. 8,16; 18; 99-100. 9,11. 10,11; 14; 55;
  73. 12,18. 13,5; 8; 10. 20,19. 21,2-3; 13;
  24-25. 31,20. 34,15. 50,1. 66,7; 16; 99.
                          NTH 6,1. 6a,24; 28.
  18,48; 51; 56. 21,4. 26,11. 30,12-13. 35,13.
  40,5. 44,2. 46,5.
                          NTT 20,4.
                          OXF B4. 7,6; 15; 40; 42;
                               47; 55-58. 9,4; 8.
                               35,3; 23.
                          SHR 3b,4. 4,1,3. 4,3,5.
                               4,26,2.
                          SOM 8,1; 28. 19,84.
                          STS 4,1. 7,5. 8,5. 10,7;
                               10. 11,37. 12,13.
                          SFK 1,77; 97; 99; 115.
  3,55. 5,2. 6,83; 90; 93; 129; 191; 260. 7,28;
  37; 40. 13,3. 14,24; 48-52; 59; 62; 77; 108;
  112; 167. 19,13; 17. 21,14; 83; 100. 25,27.
  26,12a-b. 27,3. 33,10; 13. 38,3. 67,31.
                          SRY 1,1b,d-e; 8. 2,3.
                               4,1. 5,19. 6,1.
                               8.11.
                          SSX 12,12; 14; 21; 28;
                               51. 13,29; 32; 37;
                               44.
                          WAR 16,23; 36; 40.·
                               17,24; 31; 59.
                               22,14. 28,7.
                          WIL 1,1-2; 20-21. 7,13.
  23,2; 7. 24,9. 25,9; 21. 29,3-4. 30,5. 32,17.
  67,23-25.
                          WOR 10,1.
                          YKS C27. 1L1-3; 6.
  2E33. 5N22. 5E24. 6N50. 11N16. 13E12.
  20E2. 21E7; 12. CE4-5.
Resources
  none   BRK 49,1. 63,2.
                          HAM NF9,35.
                          HEF 10,72. 14,11.
                          KEN 9,26; 34.
                          NFK 1,80.
                          SRY 1,2.
                          SSX 11,5. 12,11. 13,18.
                          WIL 27,5.
                          WOR 1,1.
  none except as
  specified   BRK 7,16.
                          DOR 54,2.
                          HAM 1,31. 3,23.
                          HEF 1,70. 10,43; 52.
                               15,3.

KEN 5,50.
SRY 5,6.
SSX 10,20. 13,21; 24; 27.
Uninhabited SSX 12,45.
Valuation of included
in that of a person NFK 9,158.
Worked by men from
another village HEF 6,8.
See also: Burgess; Castle; Church; Cow; Fence;
House; Iron; Livestock; Lordship; Man; Manor;
Mill; Pasture; Reeve; Revenue; Sheriff; Stock;
Tithe; Town; Tribute; Woodland.
VILLAGER (villanus) BDF 1,1a,c; 2-5. 2,1-4;
6. 3,1-2; 4-5; 7-8; 10-13. 4,1; 3-7. 5,1-2.
6,2-3. 7,1. 8,1-3; 5; 7-8. 9,1. 10,1. 11,1.
12,1. 13,1. 15,2; 5-7. 16,1-9. 17,4. 18,1-2;
4; 6-7. 19,1. 20,1. 21,1-7; 9; 12-13; 15; 17.
22,1. 23,1; 3-5; 7; 9-15; 17-24; 26-27; 29-
30; 36-42; 45; 48-49; 51. 24,1; 3-6; 8-11;
13-20; 22; 24; 26-27; 29. 25,1-2; 4; 7-11;
13; 15. 26,1-3. 27,1. 28,1. 29,1. 30,1. 31,1.
32,1-2; 4-6; 8; 13; 16. 33,1-2. 34,1-2. 35,1.
36,1. 37,1. 39,1-2. 40,2. 41,1-2. 42,1.
43,1. 45,1. 46,1-2. 47,1-2; 4. 48,1-2. 49,1-
4. 50,1. 51,1-3. 52,1. 53,1; 3-5; 8-15; 17-
18; 20; 28-33. 54,2-4. 55,1-4; 6-7; 9-10.
56,3. 57,1; 3i-v; 6; 16.
BRK 1,1-12; 14-29; 31-
41; 43-47. 2,1-3. 3,1. 4,1. 5,1. 6,1. 7,1-4;
6-7; 10-15; 17-19; 21-28; 30-39; 42; 44-45;
47. 8,1. 9,1. 10,1-2. 11,1. 12,1. 13,1-2.
14,1. 15,1-2. 16,1-3. 17,1; 3-6; 13. 18,2.
19,1. 20,2-3. 21,1; 3-9; 11-12; 14-16; 18;
20-22. 22,1-3; 5; 7-12. 23,1-3. 24,1. 25,1.
26,1-3. 27,1-3. 28,1-2. 29,1. 30,1. 31,2; 5.
32,1. 33,1; 3-8. 34,1-4. 35,1-5. 36,1; 3-4;
6. 37,1. 38,1-3; 5-6. 39,1. 40,1. 41,1-2; 4-
5. 42,1. 43,1-2. 44,1-5. 45,1-3. 46,1-6.
47,1. 49,1-3. 50,1. 51,1. 52,1. 53,1. 54,1-
4. 55,2-3. 56,1. 57,1. 58,1-2. 59,1. 60,1.
61,1-2. 62,1. 63,1-2; 4-5. 64,1. 65,1-7; 10;
15; 17; 19-20; 22.
BKM B1-2. 1,1-7. 2,1-3.
3,1-2. 3a,1-2; 4-5. 4,1-6; 10; 12-16; 18-23;
26; 28-30; 32-36; 38-43. 5,1-3; 5-10; 12-15;
17-21. 6,1-2. 7,1-2. 8,1-3. 9,1. 10,1. 11,1.
12,2-4; 6-9; 11-13; 15; 20; 22; 24-25; 29-
33; 35-37. 13,1-4. 14,1-14; 16-17; 19-32;
34-39; 41-46; 48-49. 15,1-2. 16,1-10. 17,2-
7; 9-11; 15-28; 30-31. 18,1-3. 19,1-4; 6-7.
20,1. 21,1; 3-8. 22,1. 23,1-8; 10-14; 16; 18-
23; 25-26; 28-29; 31-33. 24,1-3. 25,1; 3.
26,2-5; 7-9; 11. 27,1-2. 28,2-3. 29,1-4.
30,1. 31,1. 32,1. 34,1. 35,1-2. 36,1-2. 37,1-
2. 38,1. 39,1-2. 40,1. 41,1-2; 4-6. 42,1.
43,1-11. 44,2-5. 45,1. 46,1. 47,1. 48,1.
49,1. 50,1. 51,1; 3. 52,1-2. 53,1; 3; 5; 7-
10. 55,1. 56,1-2. 57,1-4; 6; 8-9; 13; 15-16.
CAM 1,1-9; 11-12; 17-18.
2,1-2; 4. 3,1; 3-6. 4,1. 5,1; 3-6; 8-15; 18;

20; 23; 25; 28-29; 34; 36; 38-39; 41-42; 44-
55; 57; 59-63. 7,2-5; 8-11. 8,1. 9,1-3. 10,1.
11,1; 4; 6. 12,1; 3-4. 13,6-8; 11. 14,1-2; 5;
7-9; 11; 13-17; 19; 21-23; 26-29; 31; 34; 36;
40; 42; 44-46; 48-49; 53; 55-56; 58-61; 63-
65; 67-70; 72-75; 78; 80-81. 15,1-4. 16,1.
17,1-2; 4. 18,1-3; 5; 7-8. 20,1. 21,1; 3; 5;
8. 22,2-4; 6-10. 23,1; 5-6. 24,1. 25,1; 3; 6-
7; 9. 26,3; 16; 18; 26-27; 31-32; 37; 42; 45-
49; 51; 53. 27,1. 28,1-2. 29,1-5; 7-10. 30,1.
31,2-3; 6-7. 32,1-2; 4-8; 11; 14-16; 20-25;
31-35; 37; 39-40; 43. 35,1-2. 37,1-2. 38,1-
3; 5. 39,2. 40,1. 41,1; 3-4; 7; 12-13; 15-16.
43,1. 44,1-2.
CHS B3-6; 8-9. A2-5; 7-
12; 16-17; 19-21. 1,1; 3-4; 7-8; 13-15; 22-
23; 26; 34-35. 2,1-7; 14; 17; 20; 25-26; 28;
31. 3,1; 4-11. 4,1-2. 5,1; 3; 5-8; 10; 12-14.
7,1-2. 8,1-11; 15-17; 20-21; 25-30; 32-35;
38-39; 42-43; 45. 9,1-2; 4-8; 11; 17-20; 22-
23; 25. 10,1. 12,2; 4. 13,1-2; 4-5. 14,1; 3-
4; 6-7; 9-13. 16,2. 17,1-5; 7; 12. 18,1-2.
19,2. 20,1-4. 21,1. 22,1-2. 23,1-3. 24,1-7;
9. 25,2-3. 26,6-7; 9; 11. 27,3. FD1,1.
FD2,2-3; 5-6. FD3,2. FD5,1-2. FD6,1.
FD7,1-2. FT1,2-9. FT2,2-3; 6; 8-10; 12-13;
15-16. FT3,2-3; 5. R1,40a; 43. R2,2. R5,5-
6. R6,4-5.
CON 1,1-6; 8-12; 14-17.
2,1-11. 3,1-5. 4,1; 3-5; 7-8; 10; 12-20; 24-
27. 5,1,1-13; 17-18; 22. 5,2,1-2; 5-6; 11-
19; 22-25; 28-29. 5,3,1; 3; 5-15; 18-28.
5,4,1; 5-7; 9; 13-16; 20. 5,5,2-7; 9-10; 13;
16; 22. 5,6,1-3; 5; 7-9. 5,7,3; 5-9; 11. 5,8,1-
3. 5,9,1-2. 5,10,1. 5,11,1-2; 4-6. 5,12,1-3.
5,13,1-6; 8-12. 5,14,1-5. 5,15,1-6. 5,16,1.
5,17,3-4. 5,19,1. 5,20,1-2. 5,22,1. 5,23,3;
5. 5,24,1-2; 4; 6; 10; 12-13; 15; 19-23.
5,25,1-5. 5,26,2.
DBY 1,1; 6; 9; 11-16; 18-
21; 25; 27-29; 31-34; 36-38. 2,1-3. 3,1-7.
4,1. 5,1-5. 6,2-7; 12; 14-18; 20; 24-32; 34-
35; 37-40; 42-47; 49-51; 53-70; 73; 76; 78;
80; 82-83; 85-86; 88-92; 94-99; 101. 7,1-9;
13. 8,1-6. 9,1-4; 6. 10,1; 4-5; 7-8; 10-13;
17-25; 27. 11,1-4. 12,1-4. 13,1-2. 14,1-7.
15,1. 16,1-3; 6-8. 17,1-2; 5-6; 8-12; 14-15;
18; 22. B3.
DEV 1,3-21; 23-72. 2,2-
24. 3,4-9; 11; 12-31; 33; 35-62; 64-77; 79-
81; 83; 85-97. 4,1. 5,1-14. 6,1-12. 7,1-4.
8,1. 9,1. 10,1-2. 11,1-3. 12,1. 13,1. 13a,2-
3. 14,1-2. 15,2-5; 8-20; 22-30; 32-52; 54-
68; 70-79. 16,3-5; 7-49; 51-61; 62; 63-89;
92-97; 101-134; 136-146; 148-155; 157-
166; 169; 170-173; 175-176. 17,3-17; 20-24;
27-37; 39; 41-55; 57-76; 78; 80-83; 85-89;
91-107. 18,1. 19,4-8; 10-21; 23-32; 34-44;
46. 20,1; 3-4; 7-8; 10-16. 21,1-4; 6-21.
22,1-2. 23,1-3; 5-7; 9-12; 14-22; 24; 26.
24,1-10; 12-17; 19-25; 27-32. 25,1; 3-16;

18; 20-25; 28. 26,1. 27,1. 28,1-16. 29,2-10.
30,1-3. 31,1-4. 32,1-10. 33,1-2. 34,1-2; 4-
8; 10; 12-32; 38-41; 43; 45-46; 48-52; 55-
57. 35,1-7; 9-22; 26-29. 36,1-2; 4-6; 10-16;
18-21; 23-26. 37,1. 38,1-2. 39,4-21. 40,2;
4-7. 41,1-2. 42,1-18; 20-24. 43,1-5. 44,1-
2. 46,1-2. 47,1; 4-8; 10-14. 48,2-3; 5-11.
49,1-2; 4-7. 50,1; 4. 51,1-3; 5-16. 52,2-4;
6-14; 16-29; 31; 34-36; 38-46; 48-49; 52-53.
      DOR   1,1-17; 19-21; 24;
26-27; 30-31. 2,1-4; 6. 3,1-11; 13; 16-18.
4,1. 5,1. 6,1; 3-4. 8,1-6. 9,1. 10,2-6. 11,1-
7; 10-17. 12,1-4; 6-10; 12; 14. 13,1-4; 6-8.
14,1. 15,1. 16,1-2. 17,2. 19,1-10; 12-14.
20,1-2. 21,1. 22,1. 23,1. 24,4-5. 25,1. 26,1;
3-4; 7-9; 13; 15; 18-20; 24-26; 33-34; 38;
40; 44-46; 49; 52; 54-56; 59-65; 67; 69; 71.
27,1; 3-4; 6-11. 28,1-7. 30,1-4. 31,1-2.
32,1-5. 33,1-2. 34,1-2; 5; 7-15. 35,1. 36,2;
3; 4-6; 8-11. 37,1; 10-14. 38,1-2. 39,1-2.
40,1; 3-4; 8-9. 41,2-5. 42,1. 43,1. 45,1.
46,1-2. 47,2-7; 9. 48,1-2. 49,4-5; 9-10; 12;
15-16. 50,1; 4. 51,1. 52,1. 53,1-2. 54,1-10;
13. 55,4; 6; 9; *10;* 11; 14; 16-20; 22; 24-25;
29; 31; 33-34; 36; 40-41. 56,1-2; 7-9; 13-
14; 17; 21; 28-29; 31-33; 35-38; 44-46; 48;
57-59; 62; 64. 57,1; 6; 9-11; 13-15. 58,1-3.
      ESS   1,1-4; 6; 9; 11-13;
19-24; 26-30. 2,2-8. 3,1-2; 5-9; 11-16. 4,1-
2; 4; 7-9; 14-15; 17-18. 5,1-5; 7; 9-12. 6,1-
3; 5; 8-14. 7,1. 8,2-4; 6-10. 9,1-3; 7-11; 13-
14. 10,1-5. 11,1-3; 6-8. 12,1. 13,1-2. 14,2-
5; 7. 15,1-2. 16,1. 17,1. 18,1-5; 14; 17; 22;
24; 29-30; 33-34; 36-38; 40-41; 43. 19,1.
20,1-2; 5-9; 12-13; 15; 19; 22-27; 32-33; 36-
37; 39; 43-46; 48; 50-52; 57; 63-64; 66; 68-
72; 74-75; 77-80. 21,1-4; 8-10. 22,3-8; 10-
12; 14; 19-20. 23,2-4; 6; 10; 26; 28-32; 38-
41. 24,1-4; 8-10; 15-18; 20-26; 28; 37; 42;
45-46; 49; 53-54; 57; 59-61; 64. 25,1-5; 11-
12; 14-19; 21-26. 26,1-5. 27,2-5; 8; 11; 13-
15; 17. 28,5-6; 8-9; 11-13; 15-17. 29,1-2;
4-5. 30,2-7; 9-11; 14; 16-22; 24; 26-36; 38;
40; 44-46; 50-51. 31,1. 32,1-4; 6-9; 13-14;
16-19; 21-25; 28-30; 32-36; 38-38a; 40-41;
44-45. 33,1; 3-7; 11-16; 18-20; 22-23. 34,4-
14; 18-23; 26; 28; 33; 35-36. 35,1-6; 8-14.
36,1-2; 5-6; 11-12. 37,3-4; 7-12; 16; 20.
38,3-8. 39,1; 3-5; 7-9. 40,1-2; 4-6; 9. 41,3-
4; 7; 9-10; 12. 42,2-4; 7-9. 43,1; 3-5. 44,1-
3. 45,1. 46,1-2. 47,2-3. 48,1-2. 49,1; 3.
50,1. 51,2. 52,1-3. 53,1-2. 54,1. 55,1.
56,1. 57,3; 5. 58,1. 59,1. 61,1-2. 64,1. 65,1.
66,1. 67,1. 71,2. 74,1. 76,1. 77,1. 79,1.
83,1. 84,2. 90,7; 9-10; 22-23; 25; 35-36; 50;
57-58; 65-66. B1.
      GLS   W13. 1,1-3; 5; 7; 9-
18; 20-25; 27-31; 33-37; 40-44; 47-50; 53-
62; 65-67. 2,1-5; 8-13. 3,1-5; 7. 4,1. 5,1-
2. 6,1-2; 4-5; 8-9. 7,1-2. 8,1. 9,1. 10,1-13.
11,1-3; 5-11; 14. 12,1-8. 13,1. 14,1-2.

15,1. 16,1. 18,1. 19,1-2. 20,1. 21,1. 22,1.
23,1-2. 24,1. 26,1-4. 27,1. 28,1; 4. 29,1.
30,1-3. 31,1-3; 5-7; 11. 32,1-2; 4-7; 9-11;
13. 33,1. 34,2-4; 7-8; 10. 35,1. 38,1-5.
39,1-15; 17-19; 21. 40,1. 41,1-3. 42,1-3.
43,2. 44,1. 45,1-3; 5-6. 46,1-3. 47,1. 48,1-
3. 49,1. 50,1-3. 51,1. 52,3-7. 53,1; 3-4; 6;
8-11. 54,1-2. 55,1. 56,1-2. 57,1. 58,1-2; 4.
59,1. 60,1-6. 61,1-2. 62,1; 3-6. 63,1-4.
64,2-3. 66,1; 3-6. 67,1; 3; 5-7. 68,1-5; 7-
10; 12. 69,1; 6-8. 72,1-3. 73,1-3. 74,1.
75,1. 76,1. 78,1; 5; 7-8; 10-17.
      HAM   1,1-6; 8-30; 32; 36-
47; W3-8; W10; W13-17; W19-22. 2,1-17;
19-25. 3,1-27. 4,1. 5,1. 5a,1. 6,1-6; 8-9; 11-
17. 7,1. 8,1. 9,1-2. 10,1. 12,1. 13,1. 14,1-
3; 5. 15,1-5. 16,1-2; 5-6. 17,1;·3. 18,1-3.
20,1. 21,1-3; 6-9. 22,1. 23,3-21; 23-33; 35-
38; 42-47; 49; 51-52; 55; 57-60; 64; 66-67.
24,1. 25,1. 26,1. 27,1. 28,1-4; 6-7. 29,1-3;
5-16. 30,1. 31,1. 32,1-2; 4. 34,1. 35,1-9.
36,1-2. 37,1. 38,1. 39,1-2; 4. 41,1. 42,1.
43,1-6. 44,1-4. 45,1-3; 5; 8. 46,2. 47,3.
49,1. 50,1. 51,1-2. 53,2. 54,1. 55,2. 56,1-
3. 57,2. 58,1. 59,1. 60,2. 61,1. 62,1-2.
63,1. 64,1-2. 65,1. 66,1. 67,1. 68,1; 6-11.
69,1-2; 4-7; 9-17; 21; 23; 26-28; 32; 37-42;
44-45; 47-48; 50-51. NF3,3-4; 9-12; 14-16.
NF4,1. NF5,1. NF8,2. NF9,2; 13; 38-43.
NF10,1-3. IoW1,1-10; 12-13; 15. IoW2,1.
IoW5,1. IoW6,4; 6-7; 9-10; 13-21.
IoW7,4; 6; 8; 10-11; 13; 19. IoW8,3-4; 6;
8-12. IoW9,2; 5; 13-18.
      HEF   1,1-10a,c; 12; 14;
18; 21-24; 28; 39-47; 56; 60. 2,4-6; 8-9; 11-
21; 23-36; 38-42; 44-53; 55-58. 5,1. 6,3-5;
7. 7,5; 9. 8,2; 5-10. 9,2-7; 10-11; 15-16; 18.
10,4-5; 9; 11; 15; 19; 24; 27-34; 41; 44-45;
48-50; 53-58; 60; 63-64; 66-70; 74-75. 12,1-
2. 13,1. 14,2; 4; 6; 8-9. 15,1-2; 5-8. 16,2-
4. 17,1. 18,1. 19,2-3; 5-10. 20,1-2. 21,1; 3;
6-7. 22,7. 23,4. 24,1-2; 4; 7-9; 11. 25,1-3;
8. 26,1-2. 29,2; 5; 8; 11. 31,3-4; 6-7. 33,1.
36,1.
      HRT   1,1-7; 9-11; 13; 17-
18. 2,1-3. 3,1. 4,1-3; 8-17; 19-20; 22; 24-
25. 5,1; 4; 8-9; 13-15; 17-18; 20-21; 23-24;
26. 7,1-2. 8,1-3. 9,1; 4-5; 7; 9-10. 10,1-12;
14-16; 18-20. 11,1. 13,1-5. 14,1-2. 15,1;
3-6; 11-12. 16,2; 4-5; 9-10. 17,1-3; 8; 12-
13; 15. 19,1. 20,1-2; 7-9; 13. 21,1-2. 22,1-
2. 23,2-4. 24,1; 3. 25,1-2. 26,1. 27,1. 28,1;
3-5; 7-8. 29,1. 30,1-2. 31,1; 3; 7. 32,1-2.
33,1-3; 5; 8-9; 11; 15; 17-18. 34,2-5; 7; 10;
12-13; 15-16; 18; 22; 24. 35,1-3. 36,2-3; 7;
11; 13-15; 18-19. 37,1; 6-8; 10-11; 14; 17;
21-23. 38,2. 40,1. 41,1-2. 42,1-2; 6-7; 9.
42a,1. 43,1. 44,1.
      HUN   B21. 1,1-2; 5-8; 10.
2,1-8. 4,1-5. 5,1-2. 6,1-13; 15-16; 18-26.
7,1-7. 8,1-4. 9,1-4. 10,1. 11,1-2. 12,1. 13,1;

3. 14,1. 15,1. 16,1. 17,1. 18,1. 19,1-3; 5-
6; 8; 11-13; 15; 17-20; 23; 27; 29-31. 20,1-
9. 21,1. 22,1-2. 23,1. 24,1. 25,1-2. 26,1.
28,1. 29,1-3; 5.

KEN   M2-5; 8-11; 13-24.
P1-5; 18. 1,1-4. 2,3-36; 39; 41-43. 3,1-9;
11-22. 4,1-14; 16. 5,1-3; 5-9; 11-49; 51-54;
56-60; 63-64; 66-80; 82-87; 89-91; 93; 95-
99; 102-111; 114-115; 118-120; 122-124;
128-131; 134-136; 138; 141-149; 152; 154-
155; 157; 159-166; 168-171; 174-177; 179-
180; 182-183; 185-187; 189; 191-193; 196-
197; 200-202; 206-209; 213; 215-220; 222-
225. 6,1. 7,1-5; 7-9; 12; 15; 17-24; 27-29.
8,1. 9,1-7; 10; 12; 16-19; 22; 24-25; 27-32;
41-42; 44-46; 48-49; 53. 10,1-2. 11,1-2.
12,1; 3-4. 13,1.

LEC   1,1-10; 12. 2,1-7.
3,1-2; 6-9; 11-16. 4,1. 5,1-3. 6,1; 3; 5-6.
7,1-2. 8,3. 9,1; 3; 5. 10,1; 3-4; 6-9; 12; 14-
17. 11,1-2. 12,1-2. 13,1-2; 4-11; 13; 15-23;
25-29; 32; 34-35; 37-41; 44-48; 50-51; 53-
67; 69-71; 73. 14,1-7; 9-21; 23; 27; 29; 31-
33. 15,1-5; 8-16. 16,2-3; 6-9. 17,1-2; 4-7;
9-10; 12-15; 18-20; 22-25; 28-30; 32. 18,1-
5. 19,1-3; 5-7; 11-15; 17-19. 20,1-4. 21,1-
2. 22,1. 23,1; 4. 24,1; 3. 25,1-5. 27,1; 3.
28,1-5. 29,1-3; 5-6; 8; 10; 13; 15-17; 19-
20. 30,1. 31,1. 32,1-2. 33,1. 34,1-2. 35,1.
36,1-2. 37,1. 38,1. 39,1. 40,1; 7; 10-13; 15-
24; 26-27; 29; 31-33; 40-41. 41,1-3. 42,2-
3; 5-9. 43,1-3; 5-6; 8-11. 44,1-4; 6-10; 12.

LIN   1,1-2; 4-8; 10-14;
17-18; 21-22; 25-26; 28-31; 34-35; 38; 41;
45; 55; 63; 65-68; 70-71; 74; 76; 80; 85-86;
88-94; 96; 105-106. 2,1; 3; 5-7; 9; 11-12;
14; 16-22; 25; 27-29; 32-34; 36-42. 3,3-8;
13; 15-16; 20-22; 25; 27-28; 30-33; 35-36;
38-39; 41-44; 47-48; 51-53; 55. 4,2-9; 11;
13-17; 20; 23-24; 26; 28; 30-33; 37-47; 50-
57; 59-62; 65-69; 71-72; 74; 76-79. 5,1-2.
6,1. 7,1; 4; 10; 14; 16-21; 23-24; 26-30; 32-
36; 38-40; 43; 47; 51-54; 56-59. 8,1; 3-9;
11-12; 15-20; 22-23; 28-29; 31-39. 9,1.
10,1-2; 4. 11,1-6; 9. 12,3-4; 7-12; 14; 17-
21; 29; 32; 37; 42-44; 47-53; 55-58; 60-62;
64-65; 67; 70; 75-76; 78-79; 81-84; 86; 88-
93; 96-97. 13,1-10; 17-19; 21-22; 24; 26-35;
38-39; 41-42; 44-45. 14,1; 3; 6; 10-18; 20;
23-26; 28-34; 36; 39; 41-43; 45-50; 52-56;
58-60; 62-69; 71-90; 92-93; 95; 97-101.
15,1. 16,1-5; 9-10; 12; 14; 17-19; 22-24; 27-
28; 32-36; 38; 41; 43-47; 49. 17,1-2. 18,1-
4; 6-7; 11-16; 19; 24-32. 19,1. 20,1. 21,1.
22,1; 3; 5; 7-8; 10; 16; 22; 24-26; 29-32;
34-36. 23,1. 24,1; 5; 10-13; 15; 17; 19-20;
22; 24-27; 32; 36-37; 40; 43; 50-51; 55-58;
61-62; 65-68; 70-76; 78; 80-83; 86; 104.
25,1-3; 5-16; 19-20; 23; 25. 26,1-11; 14;
17; 20; 22-23; 25-28; 30-31; 35-37; 40; 42;
44-46; 48-49; 51; 53-54. 27,1-8; 10; 12-14;

19; 22-27; 30; 33-35; 37-42; 44-45; 47-48;
50-60; 62. 28,1; 3; 8; 11; 13-20; 25; 29; 32-
33; 35; 38; 41-42. 29,1-3; 8-10; 12-18; 20;
22-24; 28-29; 32-34. 30,1; 3; 5-7; 9; 12; 14-
19; 22; 25; 27-29; 31-33; 36-37. 31,1-5; 7-
9; 11; 15-18. 32,1-11; 13; 15-18; 20; 28-34.
33,1. 34,1-10; 12; 19; 23-25; 27. 35,1; 3-6;
9; 11-16. 36,1-4. 37,1-2; 5-7. 38,1; 3-6; 8-
14. 39,3. 40,1-2; 4-7; 10; 14; 20-21; 23; 26.
41,1; 42,1-3; 9-10; 14; 16-17; 19. 43,1-5.
44,1-2; 5; 7-11; 16-17; 19. 45,1-4. 46,1; 3.
47,2; 6-8. 48,1-2; 4-5; 7; 11; 14-15. 49,1-
2; 4. 51,1-3; 7-8; 12. 52,1-2. 53,1-2. 54,1.
55,1-4. 56,2; 5-14; 17-20. 57,1; 5; 7; 10;
12; 14-16; 18-19; 22; 24; 26; 28; 30-31; 33-
34; 37-39; 41-42; 44-48; 50-56. 58,1-2; 6;
8. 59,1-5; 7-9; 11-14; 16-18; 20. 60,1. 61,1;
5-6; 10. 62,2. 63,1-3; 5-7; 10; 12; 15-16;
22. 64,1-2; 8; 15-16; 18-19. 65,3-4. 66,1.
67,1; 5; 7-11; 13-14; 16-17; 19-20; 22-24;
26. 68,1-2; 4-6; 9-11; 13; 17; 19-20; 22-25;
27; 30; 32; 34-35; 38; 40; 42; 46; 48. CN6;
12.

MDX   2,1-3. 3,1-4; 6; 8;
12-18; 20-26; 28; 30. 4,1; 3; 5-12. 5,1-2.
6,1. 7,1-8. 8,1; 3-6. 9,1; 3-4; 6-9. 10,1-2.
11,1-4. 12,1-2. 13,1. 14,1. 15,1. 16,1. 17,1.
18,1-2. 19,1. 20,1. 21,1. 22,1. 23,1. 24,1.
25,1.

NFK   1,1-3; 11; 15-16; 19;
32-33; 40; 50; 52; 55; 57; 59; 71-73; 75-78;
81-82; 85-87; 92; 94; 105; 123; 128; 131-133;
135-144; 146; 149-152; 169; 176; 182; 185-
188; 191-194; 197-198; 200; 202-203; 206;
208-212; 215-219; 228; 230-232; 236-238.
2,1-5; 12. 3,1. 4,1-2; 6-7; 9-11; 14; 16; 18;
21; 26; 29-31; 33; 35; 37-39; 41; 45; 47; 49-
50; 52; 54; 56. 5,1-4; 6. 6,1-6. 7,1-3; 6; 9;
11; 16-18. 8,1-3; 6-7; 9-13; 18; 21-22; 24;
28; 30; 34-35; 37-38; 40; 42; 44; 46; 48; 50;
55; 58-62; 65-68; 86-87; 90-91; 94-100; 105;
107-109; 113; 115; 119-122; 125-127; 130;
132. 9,2-3; 8-9; 11-12; 24-25; 32; 42; 48;
60; 70-73; 76-78; 80; 83-84; 86-88; 94-95;
98-100; 117; 123; 129; 143; 145-147; 149-
150; 155; 157; 169; 174; 199; 202; 218; 234.
10,1-6; 10-11; 15-16; 18-24; 28; 30-31; 33;
35-36; 38-40; 52; 56-58; 65; 73; 76; 80.
10a,1. 11,1-2. 12,1; 3-4; 7; 27; 30; 32; 42.
13,1-7; 9-10; 12-16; 19; 23-24. 14,1-8; 11-
13; 15-16; 18-19; 21-26; 29; 35-41. 15,1-4;
6-13; 15-18; 24; 26-27. 16,1; 3-5. 17,2-8;
10; 13; 16-17; 23; 25-27; 29-30; 33; 35-38;
40-41; 43; 49; 53; 55-56; 61; 64-65. 18,1.
19,1; 4; 8-9; 11; 13; 15; 17-21; 32; 34; 36.
20,1-4; 6-12; 14; 16; 19; 23-24; 26-27; 29;
31; 33-36. 21,2-7; 9-11; 13-14; 16-17; 19;
23-24; 27-31; 35-36. 22,1; 3-6; 8; 10; 13;
16; 22-23. 23,1-3; 5; 11-12; 14-18. 24,6-7.
25,1; 5; 7; 12. 26,1-6. 27,1-2. 28,1. 29,1-
6; 8; 10. 30,1-2; 5. 31,1-2; 5-8; 10; 16-17;

21-22; 24; 28-29; 31; 33-35; 37-39; 41-45.
32,1-2; 4; 7. 33,1-2; 6. 34,1-2; 4; 9; 14-15;
18; 20. 35,4; 6-7; 9; 13-14. 36,1-2; 5-7.
37,1-3. 38,1. 39,2. 40,1. 41,1. 42,1. 43,1;
4. 44,1. 46,1. 47,2; 5. 48,2-3. 49,3-4; 6.
50,1-2; 5-9; 11-12. 51,3; 5-6; 8; 10. 52,4.
53,1. 54,1. 55,1-2. 56,2. 57,1; 3. 58,1-2.
59,1. 60,1. 61,1-2; 4. 64,1. 65,8; 14. 66,22;
25; 29; 37; 50; 64; 69; 81; 95; 97.

NTH 1,1-2a,g; 4; 6-
13a,d; 14-15a; 16-21; 23-27; 30-32. 2,2-8;
10; 12. 3,1. 4,1-5; 7; 9-12; 14; 16-18; 20-24;
26-28; 30-34; 36. 5,1-4. 6,1-8; 10a-c; 11-
13; 15-17. 6a,1-2; 4-6; 10-20; 22-25; 27-30;
33. 7,1-2. 8,1; 3; 13. 9,1-6. 10,1-3. 11,1-6.
12,1-4. 13,1. 14,1-3; 5-6. 15,1. 16,1. 18,1-
7; 9-12; 14-15; 17-19; 21; 27-31; 33-34; 36-
37; 40; 42-44; 46-51; 54; 56-60; 63; 65-67;
69-72; 76; 78; 80-82; 84-88; 90; 92-93; 95-
97. 19,1-2. 20,1. 21,1-4; 6. 22,1-9. 23,1-
6; 8-10; 12-14; 16-18. 24,1. 25,1-3. 26,1-5;
8-10. 27,1. 28,1-3. 30,6; 10; 13-14; 17.
31,1. 32,1. 33,1. 34,1. 35,1a,g,i; 2-3a; 4-
10; 12-13; 16-19a; 21-24; 26. 36,1-4. 38,1.
39,2; 4-18. 40,2-4; 6. 41,1-6; 8-9. 42,1; 3.
43,1-11. 44,1a-c. 45,1-9. 46,1-7. 47,1a; 2.
48,1-6; 8-9; 11-16. 49,1. 50,1. 51,1. 52,1.
53,1. 54,1-3. 55,1-4; 6. 56,1; 7-8; 10; 12;
15-16; 18; 20a,i; 21; 23; 25-27; 29-31; 33;
36-40; 45-51; 57h; 59; 61; 64-66. 57,1-2; 4.
58,1-2. 59,1-4. 60,1-2; 4-5.

NTT B1; 19. 1,1-4; 9; 12;
15; 23; 27; 31-32; 34-45; 51-52; 54-55; 57-
59; 61; 63; 65-66. 2,4-9. 3,1; 3. 4,1; 3; 5-7.
5,1; 3-11; 13; 15-18. 6,1; 5; 9-10; 12-13.
7,1-3; 5-6. 8,1-2. 9,1-3; 5-6; 10; 12; 14-20;
22; 26; 28-29; 31-32; 36-37; 39-40; 43; 45-
46; 49-52; 55-57; 59-60; 62; 64-66; 68; 70-
77; 79-80; 82; 84-90; 92; 94-98; 100; 102-
104; 107-108; 110-111; 114-116; 118; 120-
124; 127; 129-131. 10,1-3; 5-6; 9-10; 15-18;
20; 22; 24-25; 27; 29; 31; 34-36; 39-40; 46-
47; 49-51; 53-59; 61; 65-66. 11,1-2; 4; 6; 8-
10; 12; 14-16; 18; 20; 22; 25-26; 30. 33.
12,1; 11-12; 16; 18-19. 13,1-2; 4; 6; 8-12.
14,1; 3; 5; 7-8. 15,1; 4-5; 7-9. 16,1; 3-7;
11-12. 17,1-4; 7-9; 12-16. 18,1; 3; 5; 7.
19,1. 20,2; 5; 8. 21,1-2. 22,1-2. 23,1. 24,1-
2. 25,1. 26,1. 27,1. 28,1; 3. 29,1-2. 30,4-
6; 8-10; 13-15; 19-23; 25; 31-32; 34; 38-41;
43-45; 47; 50-52; 54.

OXF 1,1-7a; 8-10. 2,1.
3,1-2. 4,1. 5,1. 6,1-15; 17. 7,1-8; 10-14;
17-18; 20; 22; 26; 29-34; 36-40; 43; 45-47;
49-54; 57-65. 8,1-4. 9,1-3; 5-10. 10,1. 11,1.
12,1. 13,1. 14,1; 6. 15,1-5. 16,1. 17,1-4;
8. 18,1-2. 19,1. 20,1-5; 7-9. 21,1. 22,1-2.
23,1-2. 24,1; 3-6. 25,1. 26,1. 27,1-10.
28,1-7; 9-23; 25-26; 29. 29,1-6; 8-14; 18-
21; 23. 30,1. 31,1. 32,1-2. 33,1-2. 34,1-2.
35,1-11; 13; 16-24; 26-28; 30-32. 36,1.

37,1. 38,1-2. 39,1-3. 40,1; 3. 41,1. 42,1.
43,1-2. 44,1. 45,1-3. 47,1. 48,1. 49,1. 50,1.
51,1. 52,1. 53,1-2. 54,1. 55,1-2. 56,1; 3-4.
57,1. 58,1-2; 4; 7-12; 15-16; 18; 20; 22; 24-
25; 30-31; 35-38. 59,1-3; 5-6; 9-12; 14-15;
17-20; 22-23; 25; 27; 29.

RUT R5-17; 19-21.

SHR 1,4-8. 2,1-2. 3b,2-
3. 3c,2-6; 8-9; 11-12; 14. 3d,1-2; 5-6. 3f,2-
5; 7. 3g,3; 6-8; 10-11. 4,1,1-8; 10; 12; 14;
16-32; 36. 4,3,1-2; 4; 6-16; 18; 20-26; 28-
31; 44-46; 48-52; 54-58; 60-61; 63-67; 69-
71. 4,4,2-6; 11-12; 14-16; 18-20; 23. 4,5,1;
3-4; 6-9; 11; 13. 4,6,1-5. 4,7,3-5. 4,8,1; 4-
5; 7; 9-16. 4,9,1-3. 4,10,1; 3. 4,11,2-9; 11;
15-19. 4,13,1. 4,14,1-2; 4-8; 13; 18; 22-23.
4,16,2. 4,18,1-2. 4,19,1-2; 6; 8; 10-13.
4,20,1-3; 5-6; 8; 13-18; 24. 4,21,1-2; 4; 6-
8; 10; 14-16; 19. 4,22,1-3. 4,23,1-2; 4; 6;
12; 14; 16; 18. 4,24,1; 4. 4,25,1; 3; 6-7.
4,26,3-4; 6. 4,27,2; 9; 11; 14; 17; 20-21; 24;
32-34. 5,1; 3-4; 9. 6,1-2; 5-7; 9-11; 13-14;
18; 20-21; 23; 26; 30; 33. 7,1; 3-6. 9,1.

SOM 1,1-30; 32-33; 35.
2,1; 6-12. 3,1-2. 4,1. 5,1-19; 21-27; 30-34;
36-37; 39-45; 47-54; 57-70. 6,1-17. 7,2-3;
5-11; 13; 15. 8,1-9; 11; 13-14; 16-18; 20-
35. 9,1-4; 6-8. 10,1-5. 11,1. 12,1. 13,1.
14,1. 15,1. 16,1-3; 6. 17,1-8. 18,1-3. 19,1-
5; 7-11; 13; 15-16; 18-22; 24; 26-32; 34-41;
43-68; 70; 72-73; 75-76; 78-81; 85-87. 20,1-
3. 21,1-8; 12-15; 17-19; 23-24; 26-28; 33;
36-37; 39-41; 43-45; 47; 49-51; 54; 56; 63;
65-67; 72-79; 81-82; 84-88; 90; 92-94; 96;
98. 22,1-5; 8-15; 17; 19-22; 24-27. 24,1-2;
4-5; 8-11; 13-25; 27-31; 33-34; 37. 25,1; 3;
5-19; 21-23; 25-27; 28; 29-35; 37-40; 41;
43-45; 47; 49-56. 26,1-6; 8. 27,1-3. 28,1-
2. 29,1. 30,1-2. 31,1-4. 32,1-8. 33,1-2.
34,1. 35,1-2; 4-7; 10-13; 16-22. 36,1; 2; 4-
5; 7; 9-11; 13-14. 37,1-2; 4-8; 10-12. 38,1.
39,1-2. 40,1-2. 41,1-2. 42,2. 43,1. 44,1-3.
45,2-6; 9-13; 16. 46,6-12; 15-16; 19; 21-23;
25. 47,1-4; 6; 7; 8; 10-14; 17-21; 23.

STS 1,1-4; 6-32. 2,1-3;
5-8; 10-11; 13-22. 3,1. 4,1-7; 9-10. 5,1-2.
6,1. 7,1-2; 5; 7-8; 13; 15; 17-18. 8,1-6; 8-
15; 17; 19-32. 9,1. 10,3-5; 8-9. 11,1-2; 5-
6; 8-22; 24-52; 54-59; 61-67. 12,1; 4-10;
12-15; 18-31. 13,1-2; 5-8. 14,1-2. 15,1.
16,1-3. 17,1-2; 8-15; 17; 19-20.

SFK 1,1-2; 8; 12; 14; 16;
18; 23; 32-33; 35-39; 44; 47-50; 58; 60; 76;
88; 90; 96-98; 100-102; 110-111; 115; 118-
121. 2,6; 9-10; 13. 3,1; 3-5; 9-10; 14-15; 20;
34; 46; 49; 56; 61; 67-68; 70; 72-74; 76; 79;
93-94; 98-99. 4,1; 11-13; 15-16; 19-20; 24;
30-31; 35; 37-38; 42. 5,1; 3; 7. 6,1-2; 11;
26; 32; 42-43; 62; 69-70; 80; 83; 85-87; 90;
105; 110; 112; 129; 148; 156; 163; 172; 176;
187; 191-192; 204; 222-223; 225; 260; 264;

271-272; 281; 303-306; 308-309. 7,3-4; 6-
8; 10-11; 13-15; 18-21; 23; 38; 42; 45-46;
49; 51; 56; 59-60; 67; 70-71; 75-76; 79; 90;
102; 146. 8,7; 11; 14; 20-21; 33; 35; 37; 42;
45-48; 55-56. 9,2-3. 10,1. 12,3-5. 13,2; 5-
6. 14,1-10; 13-14; 18-20; 23-26; 28; 32; 36;
38; 42; 45; 48-53; 55; 58; 68-70; 73-76; 78;
81; 93; 96; 98; 102-103; 105-109; 119-120;
134-135; 163-164. 15,1-2; 5. 16,2; 10; 20;
25; 30; 37; 40; 44. 17,1. 18,1; 4. 19,2; 16.
20,1. 21,1; 5-6; 10-11; 15-16; 26; 28; 30;
38-39; 42-43; 46-47; 53-55; 80; 95;98. 22,1-
2. 23,1-3. 24,1. 25,1-3; 6-8; 10; 23; 34-37;
42; 52-53; 56-57; 59; 61; 63-64; 66; 75-76;
80; 84-86. 26,3; 6; 9-10; 12a-d; 13-14.
27,3-7; 9-10; 13. 28,1a-b; 3; 7. 29,1; 12.
30,1. 31,3; 6; 8; 20-21; 40-42; 53; 60. 32,3-
6; 16; 21. 33,1; 3-10; 13. 34,1-3; 8; 12-13;
15. 35,1-3; 5-6. 36,1-2; 4; 6. 37,1; 4. 38,1;
6; 16. 39,6; 12; 15-17. 40,3; 6. 41,1-2; 7;
10; 17. 42,2. 43,1-3. 44,1-4. 46,1-6. 47,2.
49,1. 50,1. 51,1-2. 52,1; 5; 9. 53,1; 5. 54,1-
3. 55,1. 58,1. 65,1. 66,6. 67,7; 10-11; 28-
30. 68,1-2. 69,1. 70,1. 71,2. 76,3; 7.

        SRY   1,2-15. 2,1-6. 3,1.
4,1-2. 5,1a-c,f; 2-8; 10-11; 13-16; 19-23;
25-26. 6,1-5. 7,1. 8,1-3; 6-11; 13-14; 17-22;
25-30. 9,1. 10,1. 11,1. 12,1-2. 13,1. 14,1.
15,1-2. 16,1. 17,1; 3-4. 18,2-4. 19,1-17;
19-21; 23-24; 26-27; 29-34; 36-39; 44-48.
20,1-2. 21,1-4; 6-7. 22,1-3; 5. 24,1. 25,1-
3. 26,1. 27,1-3. 28,1. 29,1-2. 30,1-2. 31,1.
32,1-2. 33,1. 34,1. 35,1-2. 36,1; 3-10.

        SSX   1,1-2. 2,1a-f; 2-3;
5-10. 3,1-9. 4,1. 5,1-3. 6,1-4. 7,1-2. 8,1-2;
4-10; 12-13. 8a,1. 9,1-11; 13-24; 26; 28-31;
33-52; 54-63; 68-69; 71-79; 81-83; 85; 87-
89; 91-102; 104-111; 115-116; 118; 120-
124; 127-128; 130-131. 10,2-4; 6; 8; 10-12;
14-17; 19-20; 22; 26-38; 41-43; 45-47; 50-
56; 58-63; 65-67; 69; 73; 78-79; 83; 86-88;
90; 92-100; 102; 104-106; 108-118. 11,3-
25; 27-38; 39-41; 43-59; 61-76; 78-89; 91-
96; 98-100; 102-104; 107-108; 110-111.
12,3-9; 11; 13-16; 18; 20-25; 27-44; 46-52;
54-56. 13,1-16; 19-20; 22-23; 25; 27-36;
38-40; 42-51; 53-56. 14,1-2.

        WAR   1,1-9. 2,1-3. 3,1-3;
5-7. 4,1-4; 6. 5,1. 6,1-8; 10-12; 14-20. 7,1.
8,1. 9,1. 10,1. 11,1-4. 12,1-11. 13,1. 14,1-
6. 15,1-6. 16,1-3; 5-17; 20-48; 50-52; 54;
56-64; 66. 17,1-10; 13-16; 21-30; 32; 34-
35; 37-38; 41; 43-44; 46-47; 49-52; 54; 56-
62; 64; 66-67; 70. 18,1-16. 19,1-4; 6. 20,1.
21,1. 22,1-6; 8-17; 19-27. 23,1-4. 24,1-2.
25,1. 26,1. 27,1-6. 28,1-8; 10-11; 13-19.
29,1-4. 30,1. 31,1-12. 32,1. 33,1. 34,1.
35,2. 36,2. 37,1-9. 38,1-2. 39,1-4. 40,1-2.
41,1-2. 42,1-3. 43,1-2. 44,1-12; 14; 16.
45,1.

        WIL   1,1-22; 23e. 2,1-12.

3,1-5. 4,1-3. 5,2-3; 5-7. 6,2. 7,1-4; 6-11;
14-16. 8,1-13. 10,1-5. 11,1. 12,1-6. 13,1-
2; 4-5; 7-12; 14; 18-20. 14,1-2. 15,1-2.
16,1-3; 6-7. 17,1. 18,1-2. 19,1-2. 20,1-2;
4-6. 21,1-3. 22,1; 4; 6. 23,1; 3; 5-10. 24,1-
2; 4-5; 7; 10; 13; 18-19; 22-25; 27-29; 31;
33-36; 38-39; 41. 25,1-2; 5; 23; 27. 26,1-5;
7; 9-14; 18; 21-22. 27,1-2; 4-5; 7; 9; 11;
13-20; 23-26. 28,1-3; 7; 9; 11-13. 29,1-9.
30,1-2; 4-7. 31,1. 32,1-5; 7; 9; 11-13; 15;
17. 33,1. 34,1. 36,1-2. 37,1-2; 6-8; 11; 15.
38,1. 40,1. 41,1-3; 5-7; 9-10. 42,1-2; 4; 7-
10. 43,1-2. 44,1. 45,1; 3. 47,1. 48,1; 4; 7;
9-11. 49,1-2. 50,1-2. 51,1. 52,1. 55,1.
56,1-2; 4-5. 58,2. 59,1-2. 61,1. 63,1. 64,1.
66,1; 4; 6-7. 67,1-9; 11; 13-14; 16; 28; 32;
34-39; 42-44; 48; 54; 59-63; 72-73; 77; 80;
86; 89; 94-95; 98. 68,3-4; 7; 11-12; 14; 18;
21-22; 24-25; 27; 32.

        WOR   1,1a,d; 2; 5-6. 2,2-
7; 14-25; 27-28; 31-34; 38-39; 41-43; 45-48;
52; 55-57; 59; 61-66; 68; 70-73; 75-79; 81-
85. 3,1; 3. 8,1-9a,c,e-g; 10a,d; 11-12; 14-
16; 18-24; 26a; 27. 9,1a-b; 2-5b; 6b-c. 10,3;
5-14; 16. 11,1-2. 13,1. 14,1-2. 15,6-9; 11-
13. 16,2-3. 17,1. 18,1-2; 4. 19,1-6; 9-13.
20,1; 5-6. 21,3. 23,1-2; 4-6; 8-13. 26,5-8;
10; 13; 15; 17. 28,1.

        YKS   C23; 28; 30; 32-33.
1Y1-7; 10-11; 13; 15-18. 1N38; 54; 65-66;
92-93; 105-106. 1W25; 39. 2,1-3. 2B1; 3-
4; 6-9; 13-14. 2N2; 14; 19; 21-23. 2W1-2;
4; 6-9; 12. 2E1-2; 6-9; 12; 18-23; 25; 27;
30; 32-34; 36; 38-41. 3Y1; 4; 6; 9-11; 13.
4N1-3. 4E2. 5N1; 11; 17-19; 27-29; 45;
47-48; 50; 53-54; 58-64; 66-67; 74; 76. 5E1;
3; 5; 7; 10; 15; 18; 22-24; 29; 31-32; 34-36;
38-39; 42; 44; 55; 65-66. 5W1; 6-14; 16-17;
19-22; 30; 32-34; 38. 6N1-3; 8; 13; 15; 19-
21; 24-25; 27-29; 31-32; 36; 46; 49-60; 64-
66; 92; 101-104; 109; 112-113; 116-125;
129; 131-132; 134-138; 140; 143; 146-147;
152; 161-162. 6W1-3; 5-6. 6E1. 7E1. 8N1;
3-9. 8W1. 8E1-4. 9W1-3; 5-8; 12; 16-17;
19; 24-28; 32-40; 42; 44-52; 54-70; 72; 74;
76; 79-81; 93-99; 104; 115-117; 119; 121;
125; 138-141. 10W1-5; 8; 10-17; 19-20; 22-
23; 26-32; 34; 37-39; 41; 43. 11E1-3. 11N1;
4; 17. 11W3-4. 12W1-2; 9; 15; 18; 23-25;
28. 13W1-2; 7-10; 12-13; 16-18; 20-21; 25-
26; 28-33; 35-37. 13E2; 4-5; 7; 12-16.
13N4; 9; 12-14; 17-19. 15E1-2; 4-9; 11-15;
17; 19-20; 22; 25; 30-34; 37-39; 42-48; 51-
53. 16E1-4; 12. 17E1. 17N1-2. 17W1; 3.
18W1. 19W1; 3. 20W3. 21E1; 3. 22E1-3;
5-7; 9-11. 22W2; 6. 23W2-3; 5. 23N1-5; 7-
11; 13; 15-17; 19-21; 23-33; 35. 23E2-6; 8-
12; 14-15; 17-19. 24W2; 6-7; 10; 12; 16; 19-
20. 24E2. 25W1-2; 6; 8-16; 19-20; 24; 28-
30. 26E1; 8; 10. 27W1-2. 28W1; 6; 8-11;
14; 28-29; 31-35; 37; 39. 29W1; 3-7; 9-10;

14; 18; 22; 24; 28; 36. 29E1; 3; 9; 13-14; 19; 25; 28; 30. 29N1; 3; 6; 8-9; 12-13.

half (½)	CAM	7,9. 14,31. 15,4.18,1. 25,6. 29.8. 41,9.
	DEV	19,43. 34,45.
	GLS	W15. 16,1. 32,1. 41,5. 67,4.
	HRT	19,1.
	LIN	29,3; 15.
	NFK	3,1. 14,22-23. 15,27.
	SHR	2,2. 7,4.
	SFK	7,67.
Abbot's	LIN	8,33.
Added to manor	NFK	9,87.
elsewhere	SFK	1,10.
Attached to land	ESS	1,3.
Belonging/lying in		
Hundred elsewhere	SFK	16,30.
manor/village		
elsewhere	LIN	40,14.
	NFK	9,25; 87. 10,31. 19,34. 21,35.

Comparative information

less 1086 than TRE ESS 1,2; 4; 11; 19; 24; 30. 2,2. 3,1-2; 6; 8-9; 12-15. 4,7; 9; 14; 17-18. 5,4; 11-12. 6,2; 5; 8; 11-12; 14. 8,6; 10. 10,5. 13,2. 15,1. 16,1. 18,3; 14; 24. 20,1-2; 6-7; 12; 22; 25; 32; 36; 39; 52; 57; 63; 66; 68-70; 72. 21,3. 22,4; 6; 10; 20. 23,2; 6; 38-40. 24,4; 8; 15; 17-18; 22; 24; 45; 49; 60; 64. 25,2-3; 11; 17; 22-23; 25. 26,1-5. 27,3; 11; 14. 28,5; 8; 15; 17. 29,5. 30,16; 19; 21; 26-27; 29; 31-34; 36; 45-46. 32,1-2; 6; 13-14; 19; 21; 35; 38-38a; 40-41; 44. 33,1; 4; 14; 19. 34,6; 9; 12; 29; 33. 35,2; 4; 9-11; 13. 36,11. 37,3; 9; 11; 16; 20. 38,4. 39,1; 4-5; 7. 40,1-2; 6; 9. 41,7; 9; 12. 42,3-4. 43,3-5. 44,1-2. 45,1. 46,1-2. 47,2-3. 48,1. 50,1. 51,2. 64,1. 66,1. 71,2. 74,1. 90,7; 25; 50.

NFK 1,1-3; 40; 57; 71-73; 77-78; 105; 128; 133; 135; 137; 182; 192; 194; 210-212; 216; 218; 228; 231. 2,2. 4,1; 26; 35; 41; 47. 6,3. 7,1-2; 18. 9,9; 11-12; 70-71; 80; 94; 202. 10,1; 6; 11; 16; 20; 33. 13,7; 16; 24. 14,21. 15,7; 9; 11; 16. 17,16-17; 23. 19,9; 11. 20,6; 8; 23; 29; 34-35. 21,4; 10; 14; 16; 19; 27; 29. 22,3; 23. 23,2; 16; 18. 26,2-3; 5. 28,1. 29,2; 6; 8. 30,1. 31,1-2; 5-6; 8; 16; 22; 33; 35; 38. 34,4. 35,4. 37,1. 43,1; 4. 48,3. 49,3; 6. 51,5-6. 55,1-2. 58,1.

SFK 1,32-33; 36; 76; 96; 100-102; 115; 121. 3,4; 34. 4,30; 38. 5,1. 6,1; 32; 80; 110; 112; 148; 172; 191; 260; 305; 308. 7,7; 60; 76. 8,20; 35; 46. 9,2-3. 12,5. 14,75; 119. 15,1; 5. 16,40. 18,1. 19,16. 21,16; 43; 47; 53-54; 80; 95. 25,1-2; 34; 63. 26,3; 12b. 27,3-5; 13. 28,1b. 29,12.

31,41-42. 33,1; 4-5; 9. 34,3; 12-13. 35,1; 6. 36,1-2. 37,4. 39,17. 40,3; 6. 41,7. 42,2. 43,2. 44,2; 4. 46,1. 53,1; 5. 54,3. 68,1. 70,1. 76,7.

more 1086 than TRE ESS 1,1; 3; 13; 23; 28-29. 2,3-4; 6. 4,1. 5,1-2. 8,7. 9,2; 7-8; 10; 13-14. 10,4. 11,6. 13,1. 14,2; 5. 18,2; 37-38; 40-41. 20,5; 8-9; 15; 19; 44; 78. 22,3; 8; 14. 24,25; 37; 46; 61. 25,1; 5; 15-16; 18. 28,12; 16. 29,2. 30,2; 27; 35. 31,1. 32,8-9; 18; 24; 28; 45. 33,5; 15; 20; 23. 34,4; 8; 10; 19-20; 23; 36. 35,5-6. 36,5-6; 11-12. 37,7. 40,4. 41,3; 10. 48,2. 53,1. 55,1. 57,5. 58,1. 61,2. 90,10; 22.

NFK 1,50; 52; 81-82; 106; 148; 218. 7,11; 16-17. 9,98. 11,2. 13,19. 14,6; 16; 18. 17,26. 21,2; 7. 27,1. 31,22; 34. 50,5; 12. 54,1.

SFK 1,97-98; 100; 115; 120. 3,3. 4,1; 13; 42. 6,303-304; 306. 7,3. 8,35. 14,74. 17,1. 21,42. 22,1. 25,52. 33,13. 54,2.

none 1086	NFK	1,211. 9,11. 10,6. 13,24.
	SFK	6,172. 8,20. 55,1.
Dwelling in different village from where enumerated/assessed	NFK	4,31.
	SFK	3,49. 6,70.
Dwelling with smallholders under Frenchmen and burgesses	MDX	3,12.
Evidence by	HAM	23,3.
	SFK	25,52.
Fines of	SSX	7,1.
Free	NFK	4,9.
Gift of	HEF	10,48.
Individual holdings of	CAM	5,45; 50; 54-55; 57; 59-61; 63. 8,1.
	HRT	33,17.
	MDX	2,1-2. 3,1; 12; 14;

18. 4,1; 5-8; 11-12. 5,1. 7,2; 4-5; 7. 8,4-6. 9,1; 6-9. 10,1-2. 11,1-2. 12,1-2. 13,1. 17,1. 18,2. 19,1. 20,1. 21,1. 22,1. 24,1. 25,1.

King's	KEN	5,118.
Land held by villagers		
generally	BKM	19,1.
	DBY	2,2.
	ESS	27,9.
	HAM	2,14. 3,12; 17.
	KEN	7,26; 28. 9,7.
	MDX	14,1.
	SRY	8,29. 19,28. 29,2.
	SSX	10,98. 12,3; 14; 16-18; 20; 36; 41; 47.
at a revenue	KEN	5,154.
	MDX	3,17.
Land held like a villager	HAM	3,3; 8.

Men of Abbey serving		
as	WIL	13,9.
Paying manor's value	CHS	2,3.
Plough		
not ploughing	LIN	11,6. 14,11. 68,10-11.
	YKS	9W33. 14E1. 28W35.
without a plough	GLS	38,4.
	YKS	9W25.
Queen's wool,		
collecting	SRY	1,8.
Rape, outside of	SSX	12,56.
Sowing land with		
own seed	HEF	1,7; 10a.
	WOR	8,5-7.
Taken away from		
lord	ESS	32,24.
manor/village	ESS	1,19.
	NFK	1,1.
With nothing	SHR	4,9,4.
Work of, belonging to		
manor/village in		
another County	NTT	21,3.

See also: Alms; Borough; Burgess; Church; Clergy; Customary due; Death duty; Due; Dwelling; Fishery; free man; Grazing; House; Iron; Jurisdiction; Law; Manor; Meadow; Mill; Reeve; Revenue; Sheriff; Site; Tax; Thane; Tithe; Tribute; Waste; Woodland.

VILLAGER'S land		
(terra villanorum)	BRK	1,27; 40. 7,3.
	DEV	*1,70.*
	GLS	59,1. 67,1.
	HAM	2,9; 15. 3,5.
	KEN	5,128. 7,8; 19; *20.*
	LEC	44,1.
	MDX	3,12. 4,4.
	OXF	32,1.
	SOM	6,7-8. 8,24; 26.
	SRY	8,22. 33,1.
	SSX	9,1.
	WIL	1,14. 8,7-9; 12. 12,2. 13,2.
	WOR	2,40; 53; 69. 8,21.
Held in lordship	OXF	29,4.
Tax paid like	CON	4,29.
VILLEIN (villanus) – See Villager.		
VINE (vinea)		
Fruit		
bearing	ESS	34,18; 20. 35,6.
not bearing	ESS	34,18; 20.
Newly planted	HRT	26,1.
	MDX	4,2. 8,5.
See also: Vineyard; Wine.		
VINEDRESSER		
(vinitor)	SRY	21,3.
VINEYARD/vine (vinea)		
Acres of	BDF	21,1.
	DOR	49,11.
	ESS	33,20.

	SOM	1,19.
	WIL	24,33.
Arpents of	BRK	21,7.
	BKM	19,1.
	CAM	5,57.
	DOR	49,12.
	ESS	24,17. 25,5. 28,11. 30,5. 34,18; 20. 35,5-6.
	GLS	31,1.
	HRT	15,1. 26,1. 42a,1.
	KEN	5,67; 72. 7,9.
	MDX	4,2; 5. 5,1. 7,5. 8,5. 21,1.
	SOM	8,1. 9,1.
	SFK	21,16. 25,1. 35,1. 66,1.
	WIL	12,4. 55,1.
Good	WIL	24,1.
Payment for land		
containing	MDX	1,4.
Wine, amount		
produced	ESS	24,17.
Young (novella)	WOR	10,11.
See also: Vine; Wine.		

VIOLATION of/violence to women

free men/men		
receiving fines for	CHS	R2,2. R6,2.
Land exempt from		
fine for	CHS	R1,42.

See also: Crime/offence.

VIRGATE (virgata)	BDF	2,1; 6-7. 3,6; 8-9.

4,1-2; 4; 6-7. 5,2. 6,2-3. 8,4. 9,1. 10,1. 13,1-2. 15,3; 6. 16,3; 5; 7; 9. 17,1; 3-7. 18,4-5. 19,3. 20,2. 21,2-5; 7-8; 11; 17. 22,2. 23,1; 7-10; 13; 22; 26-27; 31; 33-35; 40; 44-45; 50-52; 54-55. 24,3; 8; 13-15; 19; 21-24; 26; 29-30. 25,3-4; 6-7; 9; 11; 14. 26,3. 28,2. 32,4-5; 10; 12-13; 15. 34,1; 3. 35,1-2. 37,1. 38,1-2. 39,1. 40,3. 44,1; 3-4. 46,1-2. 47,2; 4. 48,1. 49,1; 4. 51,3-4. 53,1; 5; 12; 14-17; 19-20; 24-25; 27; 29; 33-34. 54,2; 4. 55,4; 6; 9. 56,1-4; 6-9. 57,1; 3iii,vi; 4-7; 9-15; 17-18.

	BRK	B1. 1,1; 5; 7; 12-13;

24-25; 28; 31-32; 37; 42. 7,27; 36; 40; 42; 44-45. 8,1. 11,1. 17,3; 7; 12-13. 20,3. 21,3; 8; 13; 22. 22,5. 26,1-2. 33,1; 3-4. 34,1. 35,1-3. 38,5. 41,4-5. 44,1. 45,1. 46,2. 48,1. 55,3-4. 58,3. 61,1. 65,4; 13-14; 21.

	BKM	1,1; 3-4; 7. 4,7; 10;

15; 21; 24; 26; 28; 39. 5,4; 6; 10-13; 15-17. 7,2. 12,2; 10; 13; 15-18; 20-21; 23; 25; 27; 30-31; 34; 38. 14,15; 20; 35; 41; 43. 16,1; 7; 10. 17,7; 9-11; 14; 18; 20-22; 26-30. 18,3. 19,1; 3. 21,5. 22,2. 23,4; 16; 18-19; 25; 31. 24,1-2. 25,2. 26,9-11. 28,2. 30,1. 33,1. 34,1. 39,2. 40,1. 43,2; 4-5; 7; 9. 44,2. 51,1; 3. 53,1-4; 6; 9. 57,1; 5; 9; 16.

	CAM	1,6-9; 15-16; 18;

20. 2,2-4. 3,2-5. 5,1-2; 9-11; 16-18; 30-31;

23. IoW8,1; 3-9. IoW9,1; 4; 6-7; 13-16; 22; 24.

HEF 1,1-5; 7-8; 11; 20-21; 36; 39-40; 42-47; 69. 2,3-4; 13; 16; 21; 26-28; 30; 33; 49; 58. 8,9. 9,3; 16. 10,10; 12-13; 21; 31; 49-50; 61-62; 65. 13,1. 14,11. 15,3; 9. 16,2. 19,8. 21,7. 22,1. 23,1; 5. 24,7. 29,4; 15; 18. 30,1. 34,1. 35,1.

HRT 1,2; 6-8; 10; 15-18. 2,5. 4,1; 6; 10; 12; 15-16; 25. 5,6; 9-10; 14; 20-21. 6,1. 7,1-3. 9,3; 7; 10. 10,6; 10; 14; 18-19. 11,1. 14,1. 15,1. 16,2-3; 10; 12. 17,1-2; 4; 11-13. 20,5; 7; 12-13. 21,1. 22,2. 23,1-2. 24,2-3. 25,2. 28,1; 5-7. 29,1. 30,1-2. 31,1-2; 4; 7. 33,1; 3; 6-8; 10; 14-17. 34,3; 6-8; 12-15; 17-19; 25. 35,1-2. 36,1; 3; 5-6; 8-11; 14-15; 17-18. 37,1; 3; 5; 7-8; 10; 12; 14-17; 19; 23. 38,2. 40,1. 41,2. 42,3; 5; 8-9; 13-15.

HUN 1,3. 2,6; 8-9. 3,1. 6,12; 22. 7,7. 9,4. 13,2. 14,1. 19,1; 4-5; 8; 10; 13; 15; 18. 28,1. 29,2; 4. D16.

KEN M17. 2,25. 5,145; 169. 7,25. 9,11; 13; 27-28; 43; 50; 54.

LEC 8,3. 13,13; 46. 17,10; 12-14; 17. 27,4. 40,6.

LIN 12,18. 18,28. 40,4.

MDX 2,1-2. 3,1-2; 6; 8; 12; 14-16; 18; 22. 4,1; 3; 5-9; 11-12. 5,1. 6,1. 7,2; 4-5; 7-8. 8,4-6. 9,1; 6-9. 10,1-2. 11,1-4. 12,1-2. 13,1. 15,1. 16,1. 17,1. 18,2. 19,1. 20,1. 21,1. 22,1. 24,1. 25,1.

NTH 1,2a,c; 3; 6; 11; 13b,d; 15,d-j; 16-18; 22; 25-26; 29; 32. 2,2-3; 5-6; 11-12. 4,1; 3-5; 7-10; 14; 18-20; 22-28. 6,8; 10c; 13-16. 6a,5; 7; 9; 13; 19; 21; 23-25; 28; 30. 8,2-10; 12. 9,1. 10,1. 12,1. 14,4. 15,1. 17,1; 3; 5. 18,1-2; 4; 8-9; 13; 15; 17-20; 25-26; 31; 41; 44-45; 47-49; 57; 59-60; 68-75; 77-78; 80-81; 83-84; 86; 88; 90; 92; 94; 97-98. 21,3-5. 22,3; 8. 23,1-2; 5; 15. 25,2. 26,2-4. 27,1. 28,1. 30,6-7; 13-16; 18. 35,1c-f,h-i; 2-3b; 6-7; 12-14; 17; 19a,c-e,g; 21; 23; 25. 37,1. 39,2-4; 6. 40,1-4; 6. 41,2-3; 5; 7-10. 43,4-5. 44,1b. 45,2; 9. 46,2. 47,1b; 2. 48,2-3; 6-7; 12-16. 51,1. 53,1. 54,2-4. 55,1; 3; 6. 56,10-11; 14; 19; 20b-c,f,h; 25; 28-31; 35; 37-45; 52-54; 56; 57b-d,g; 58-63; 65. 57,3-4. 58,1. 59,2; 4. 60,3; 5.

NTT 1,34. 9,59-60. 11,19. 14,8. 15,3. 16,3. 18,4. 30,9; 45.

OXF B9. 1,1; 5; 7b. 6,1a,c; 9; 11; 13. 7,3; 9; 23; 25; 35; 52-53; 55; 57-58. 14.4. 17,6. 19,1. 20,7; 10. 27,2-3; 7; 10. 28,23. 29,3-4; 18-19. 32,1. 35,3; 13; 16; 20. 39,2. 40,3. 46,1. 50,1. 54,1. 55,2. 58,1; 4; 8; 20; 22; 26; 32; 36-37. 59,9; 11; 15; 18; 24; 27.

SHR C13. 1,9. 3c,8. 3d,3. 3e,1. 4,1,17. 4,3,29; 31; 68. 4,4,2; 9; 17; 21; 24. 4,5,12-14. 4,9,4. 4,10,2. 4,11,13. 4,14,8; 20; 28-29. 4,15,4. 4,17,2. 4,20,20; 23; 26-27. 4,21,10; 17. 4,23,5; 8; 15. 4,24,4. 4,27,6-7; 9; 16; 22-23. 4,28,1; 5. 6,3; 11; 24; 26; 28; 30.

SOM 1,2; 5; 6; 11; 13-14; 21; 26-27; 28; 33. 2,1; 6-8; 12. 3,2. 4,1. 5,1-7; 13; 19; 24; 26; 27; 31; 33-35; 37; 39; 42-44; 47; 48-49; 55; 57; 61; 62; 63; 65; 66-67. 6,8; 10; 13; 15; 18-19. 7,4; 7-8; 10. 8,1-2; 4; 10; 12-13; 17; 22-24; 28; 33; 36. 9,3; 6; 7. 15,1. 16,2; 3-4; 7-8; 13. 17,1; 2; 3; 6; 7. 19,4; 5; 9; 10; 11; 12-13; 14; 15-16; 18-19; 21-22; 25; 29; 35; 38; 40; 55; 59-60; 61; 62; 65-66; 67; 69; 72; 74; 77; 81; 87. 20,2. 21,3-4; 5; 8; 9-11; 14-15; 16; 17; 19-22; 23-24; 26-28; 29-35; 37; 39-40; 41; 43; 44-45; 47; 49-50; 51; 53; 54; 55-56; 58; 60-62; 63; 65-67; 69; 70-71; 73; 74; 75-78; 79; 84; 87-90; 91; 93. 22,2; 3; 4-5; 7; 9; 11; 12-14; 16; 17; 20; 21-22; 24-25; 28. 23,1. 24,1; 3-4; 5-7; 8; 10; 11; 13-16; 18; 20; 24-25; 26; 30; 32; 33; 34-37. 25,1; 3-8; 9; 11; 14; 15; 16; 18; 21-23; 25; 26-29; 30; 31; 33; 34-35; 36; 37-38; 42; 44-45; 47-52; 54; 55; 56. 26,4. 27,2; 3. 28,2. 29,1. 30,1. 31,3; 5. 32,8. 35,1-2; 4; 6; 7; 12; 15; 16; 18-19; 20; 21; 23. 36,2; 4; 5; 7. 37,2; 4; 5; 6; 7; 10-11. 39,2-3. 40,2. 41,1; 2. 42,2. 43,1. 44,2. 45,2; 7; 13; 15. 46,1-2; 4-7; 9; 11-12; 14-15; 17; 21; 23; 25. 47,1; 2-4; 8; 9; 12-13; 14; 15-16; 24-25.

STS 1,36; 38; 40-47. 2,16. 4,6-8. 5,2. 7,3-4; 10; 18. 8,23; 26; 28. 10,4; 8. 11,4-5; 10; 16-17; 34-36; 38-42; 50. 12,12; 19; 22. 13,1; 3-4; 7-8. 17,3; 9; 11-12; 14-15; 17-18; 21.

SFK 7,36. 23,4.

SRY 1,2; 6; 9; 12; 16. 2,1; 6. 3,1. 5,15-17; 20. 8,13; 25. 10,1. 12,1. 17,3. 18,3. 19,11; 17; 23; 29; 31; 37; 39; 42; 44. 21,2. 30,2. 32,1. 35,2. 36,2; 6.

SSX 2,1g; 8-9. 3,2; 5; 7. 8,1; 3-7; 10-15. 9,1-4; 6; 8; 10-15; 17-20; 25; 27-31; 33; 37-47; 56; 58-59; 61-69; 71-73; 75-76; 78-79; 81; 83; 87; 91; 95; 97; 99-102; 109-110; 112-120; 122; 124-125; 127-131. 10,1-2; 10; 20; 27; 31; 50; 63-66; 82; 88; 95; 97; 101-102; 107-108; 110; 115-117. 11,3; 19-21; 26; 50-51; 55; 58; 81; 83; 89-90; 96-99; 101-102; 105. 12,14; 18; 20; 23; 29; 41; 43; 47; 49; 52; 55. 13,5; 9-10; 12; 29; 34; 40-44; 46; 49.

WAR 1,7; 9. 3,7. 4,5. 6,2; 6; 13. 12,2; 6-7. 13,1. 16,2; 20; 28-29; 31; 36; 41; 48-49; 52; 57-58; 61; 64. 17,9; 12; 14; 17-18; 23-24; 27-28; 32-36; 39; 53; 59; 61. 18,9; 11; 15. 22,21; 24. 24,2. 27,6.

28,7-9; 13; 17. 29,2. 32,1. 39,1; 4. 40,1-2.
41,1. 44,9; 12.
        WIL   1,5; 14-15; 17;
23b,f-g. 2,4-5; 11. 3,1; 4. 4,1. 5,1; 4. 6,1.
7,4; 11-12; 15-16. 8,7. 10,1-3. 13,2; 4; 8;
10. 14,2. 15,1. 18,1. 20,4-5. 23,1; 9. 24,10;
14; 17; 19-20; 22; 29; 35; 39. 25,2; 5; 20-
22; 24. 26,13; 15; 19. 27,2-3; 15; 21; 23.
28,5-6; 10. 29,3-7. 30,5. 32,2; 11; 14. 33,1.
34,1. 36,1. 37,2-3; 5-6; 10; 13-15. 39,2.
41,10. 42,4; 9. 43,1-2. 45,2-3. 46,1. 48,5;
8. 49,3. 50,1; 5. 53,1. 56,6. 58,1. 60,1.

66,3-6. 67,3; 13; 18; 21-23; 25; 30; 41; 45-
47; 49; 51; 53; 55-57; 65-66; 68-69; 87-88;
93. 68,3; 7-9; 11; 14; 17; 24; 33.
        WOR   1,1c-d; 2. 2,6; 11;
48; 53; 55; 76. 8,4; 7; 9c,g; 11; 16-17; 21-
22; 26a,c. 9,6c. 15,7. 19,10. 21,4. 23,4.
X1.
              YKS   10W29.
Acreage of   CAM *13,12.*
See also: Meadow; Pasture; Underwood;
Woodland.
VOUCH to warranty – See Cite; Warrant.

W

WAGES (mercedes; solidata)
Land held as　　　　SFK　34,17.
Paid from reeve's
tribute to those doing
King's service　　　BRK　B1.
WAGON load (plaustratum) – See Lead.
WALES
District (finis)　　　SHR　4,1,13; 15. 4,3,42.
King in　　　　　　SRY　5,3.
King of Wales laying
land waste TRE　　HEF　1,49.
March (marcha), of　HEF　9,13. 24,3.
Military service in　　HEF　C10. A8-9.
　　　　　　　　　SHR　C4.
North Wales　　　　CHS　G1-2.
See also: Customs; Hide; Priest; Welshman.
WALL (murus)
Borough/city/town,
of　　　　　　　　HEF　C1; 3; 6.
　　　　　　　　　LEC　3,1.
　　　　　　　　　LIN　C4.
　　　　　　　　　OXF　B4; 9. 28,8. 58,34.
　　　　　　　　　STS　B4.
Dwelling/house
within/without
borough's/city's　　ESS　B3a.
　　　　　　　　　HEF　C3; 6.
　　　　　　　　　LIN　C4.
　　　　　　　　　STS　B4.
Dwelling (mansio
muralis)　　　　　OXF　B5; 9-10.
　exemptions/duties,
　of　　　　　　　OXF　B5; 9.
House below　　　　ESS　B3a.
Land outside
borough/city's　　　LEC　3,1.
Meadow near to　　OXF　28,8.
Mill near to　　　　OXF　58,34.
Property round　　　ESS　B5.
Repair of　　　　　CHS　C21.
　　　　　　　　　OXF　B5; 9-10.
Residence/house
outside city's　　　ESS　B3q.
　　　　　　　　　LIN　C4.
See also: Forfeiture; House; Pasture.
WAPENTAKE
Decisions by, on claims
　for claimant　　　LIN　CS1-2; 4; 6-7; 26;
　　　30-32; 35. CN22; 24. CW7; 19. CK14; 18-
　　　19; 25; 35; 62; 65.
　against claimant　LIN　CS23-25; 27; 30-31;
　　　33; 37. CW6; 8. CK13; 23; 26; 29; 32; 36;
　　　40; 45; 51; 57-59; 63.
Evidence by　　　　DBY　6,99.

　　　　　　　　　LIN　12,59. 22,5. 31,3.
　40,26. 57,18. CS3; 21-22. CN5-6; 9; 21;
　30. CW1-2; 5; 9; 15; 18. CK1-4; 6; 8-9;
　11-12; 16-17; 20-25; 28; 30-31; 34; 37-39;
　41-44; 48; 52-53; 55-56; 61-64.
　　　　　　　　　NTT　20,7.
　　　　　　　　　YKS　CE33. CW17; 24;
　　　　　　　　　　　　31; 38.
　with County　　　LIN　CS30.
　with Riding　　　LIN　CS24-25; 27.
　with concurrence of
　Riding　　　　　LIN　CS21; 23; 38.
Forfeiture/death duty
in, divided between
　Abbey/Earl　　　LIN　CW9; 11.
Unaware of facts　　LIN　12,59. 31,3. CS22.
　　　　　　　　　　　　CK27; 55.
　　　　　　　　　YKS　CW17.
See also: Adjudgment; Customary due; Judgment;
Jurisdiction; Man; Possession; Purchase;
Sheriffdom; Tax; Third penny.
WARD (custodia)
Borough, of　　　　CAM　B1.
　　　　　　　　　LIN　S1-4; 6.
　in another County　LIN　S1.
WARDSHIP (custodia)
Earl's son and land
held by Queen　　　MDX　9.1.
Land of, held by
　dead holder's
　brother　　　　　HAM　69,38.
　relation　　　　　LIN　CK1.
WARLAND　　　　OXF　58,25.
WARNODE　　　　LIN　2,36-37; 42. 51,9-
　　　　　　　　　　　　10. 57,46. CK2; 8;
　　　　　　　　　　　　61.
　meadow, of　　　LIN　CK2; 61.
WARRANTY (warantum)
Failure to give　　　ESS　90,78.
　　　　　　　　　SOM　*22,19.*
　　　　　　　　　SFK　75,1-2.
　　　　　　　　　WAR　44,12.
　　　　　　　　　YKS　1W53.
King claimed to give　ESS　30,22.
Land held without　　HAM　69,11.
　　　　　　　　　SRY　26,1.
See also: Cite; Guarantor; Patron; Protector.
WARREN (warrena)
Hares, for　　　　　LIN　12,44.
WASHER (lavator)　SFK　14,167.
WASTE land (terra vasta)
Cause of waste
　King's Forest　　　STS　7,6.
　King's woodland　　HUN　6,26.

267

laid waste by Irish   DEV   17,41.
laid waste by King's
army   WAR   6,13.
laid waste by Welsh
King   HEF   1,49.
sea flood   LIN   57,36.
Degree of waste
almost/largely/
partly waste   CHS   2,20. R6,4.
                          LIN   26,28.
                          SHR   4,14,19. 4,20,26.
                                 4,27,1.
                          YKS   4N1. 6N2. 11E2.
completely waste   DEV   20,2. 21,5. 52,51.
                          DOR   55,39.
                          STS   12,22.
                          YKS   5E54. 6N1.
Houses and churches
settled on waste land   LIN   C22.
Pasture, used for   DEV   47,7.
Period of waste
before 1066   CHS   A4. 3,1. 12,2. 22,2.
                                 26,11-12.
                          HEF   1,49; 57; 70. 2,4-6;
                                 11; 56. 8,3.
                          SHR   4,1,10-12. 4,2,1.
                                 4,4,16. 4,18,1-2.
                                 6,14; 23; 26.
before and after   CHS   2,8. 3,2. 6,2. 20,11-
1066   12. 27,3. FT1,1-9.
                                 FT2,1-16. FT3,1.
                          HEF   14,1.
                          SHR   4,3,32-33.
before 1066 and in
1086   SHR   4,25,5.
in 1066 and 1086   CHS   11,4.
                          OXF   7,55.
between 1066 and
1086   BKM   4,31.
                          CHS   1,1; 5; 15; 23; 26.
2,2-6; 13; 19; 22-24; 27. 3,9. 4,1. 5,1; 5-6;
9; 11-13. 7,1. 8,2-3; 7; 15; 17; 19-20; 22-
23; 28; 30-31; 34; 36. 9,5; 9; 17-18; 20.
10,1; 3. 13,3-5. 14,1; 3-6; 8-9; 12. 15,1.
16,2. 17,3-4; 6; 8; 12. 18,2-5. 24,3; 5. 25,1.
FD5,2.
                          DEV   3,34; 35. 19,18.
                                 24,20.
                          HEF   19,8.
                          LEC   1,10. 39,2.
                          NTH   1,27.
                          SHR   1,8. 4,3,1-5; 9-11;
13; 19; 21-23; 27; 45; 47; 65; 68; 70. 4,6,1.
4,7,2. 4,8,1; 4-5; 7; 9; 13. 4,11,5-7; 10; 12;
19. 4,14,1; 4; 22; 24. 4,15,1-3. 4,16,2.
4,17,2-3. 4,19,1-2; 4-5; 7-8. 4,21,6-8; 11;
15; 18. 4,22,1. 4,23,2; 4; 6; 8; 12; 17.
4,24,2. 4,25,2-3; 6. 4,26,6. 4,27,2; 32. 5,3;
9. 6,5; 16; 19; 31. 9,1-2.
                          SOM   21,56-58. 46,1.
                                 47,5.

                          SSX   9,11; 14; 18-19; 21;
23; 26; 60; 66-67; 82-83; 85; 105-106; 121.
before 1086   CHS   B3-4; 8. A18-19.
1,2-4; 8; 10-11; 24-25. 2,1; 16; 18; 21; 31.
8,1; 10; 12-13; 27; 29; 44. 9,22. 12,3. 13,1-
2. 14,2; 11. 17,1; 11. 20,4-5. 23,2. 24,6; 9.
25,3. FD4,1. FT3,2-6. R1,36.
                          DEV   16,124. 17,77.
                          HEF   1,17; 35-36. 2,2.
9,4; 11. 10,1; 16; 18; 23; 42. 14,6. 19,4-5.
20,2. 21,7. 22,7. 24,1; 8. 25,3; 6; 9. 26,2.
29,8-9; 19.
                          LEC   1,9. 10,7. 21,2.
                                 31,1.
                          LIN   3,19.
                          NTH   4,18. 6a,28.
                          SHR   3f,7. 3g,8. 4,1,8;
36. 4,3,34; 36; 38. 4,4,25. 4,5,14. 4,6,4.
4,8,2. 4,11,9. 4,18,3. 4,27,7-8. 6,15; 18; 24.
                          SSX   9,126.
                          WOR   1,2. 2,70.
before and/in 1086   CHS   B11. A22. 1,9; 12;
29-31; 33; 36. 9,12-16; 21; 27-29. 11,6-8.
13,6-7. 17,9-10. 19,3. 20,7-9. 24,8. FD1,2.
                          HEF   1,64-67; 73-74. 2,1;
22; 49. 6,1; 10-11. 10,3; 65. 14,7. 22,6.
24,3; 6. 29,6-7; 10; 17-18. 31,1-2.
                          LEC   26,1.
                          NTH   37,1.
                          NTT   5,12.
                          SHR   3d,4; 7. 4,1,33; 35.
4,3,41; 43. 4,4,7. 4,5,2; 5. 4,14,21; 29.
4,19,3. 4,20,11; 19; 21-23; 25. 4,21,13; 17.
4,23,15. 4,24,3. 4,27,5; 18. 4,28,2-3; 6.
5,4-7. 6,17; 22; 27; 29. 8,1-2.
                          STS   8,18.
                          WOR   8,8. 9,6c. 21,1.
                                 23,14.
                          YKS   C35.
in 1086   BDF   8,4. 47,3.
                          BKM   12,27. 26,6. 36,3.
                          CHS   1,1; 16-20; 27; 32.
2,12; 30. 8,21. 11,1-2; 5. 20,10. 26,4; 8; 10.
27,1-2; 4. R5,1.
                          DBY   1,3; 10; 12; 14-15;
24; 30; 35. 4,2. 6,1; 8-11; 19-20; 22-23; 36;
66; 71-72; 74-75; 77; 79; 81-82; 84; 87.
7,10-12. 9,5. 10,3; 14-16. 11,5. 12,5. 14,8-
11. 17,3-4; 7; 16; 21.
                          DEV   20,2. 21,5. 34,37.
                                 36,17. 47,7.
                          DOR   26,2.
                          GLS   W3. 1,13.
                          HAM   6,10. 39,5. IoW1,6.
18; 30; 32; 40; 51. 9,13. 10,38. 29,16. 34,2.
36,2.
                          HUN   19,10; 26. 27,1.
                          LEC   1,3. 14,8; 28; 30;
34. 17,17; 27. 19,8; 10; 16; 20. 23,3. 27,4.
29,9. 35,2. 40,30; 37-38. 42,4. 43,1; 7.

	OXF	34,3.
could without permission	CAM	14,43; 49; 68; 73. 21,1. 26,14. 28,1. 35,1.
could not without permission	CAM	14,1; 34; 36. 26,2; 6; 7; 9. 29,10. 32,1; 29.
	ESS	35,7.
	HEF	10,39. 23,6. 29,19.
could with land	CAM	32,3; 22. 38,2.
	SSX	13,9.
could not with land	HAM	2,21.
	LEC	17,33.
	SOM	19,33.
	STS	11,37.
	SSX	12,4.
could from land without permission	CAM	4,1.
could not from land without permission	ESS	10,5.
	WOR	19,6.
could from lord	CAM	14,33; 41; 43; 45.
	SRY	5,1a.
could not from lord	BRK	7,22.
	CAM	14,4; 16; 82. 19,1. 35,1.
	CHS	26,1.
	HAM	2,15. IoW2,1.
	HEF	10,54.
	SRY	8,12.
	WOR	1,1c. 16,1. 21,2.
could not with land to another lord	HAM	3,1.
could not from head of manor	GLS	1,52.
could not from ecclesiastical body or person	BRK	7,11.
	CAM	5,37.
	DOR	11,1.
	HAM	29,1.
	OXF	9,4.
	SHR	3c,8.
	WIL	2,1; 5.
could not from Abbey without permission	CAM	17,3.
could not with land from Abbey	DOR	13,5.
could not from jurisdiction	ESS	23,34-35; 37.
could not because jurisdiction remained with Abbot	CAM	30,3.
could where/when he would	CAM	2,4. 26,31. 32,12.
could not where he would	HAM	1,13.
could not elsewhere	HAM	1,8; 14.
could with land		

where he would	BDF	23,17.
	SRÝ	5,19.
could where he would with jurisdiction	CAM	38,5.

See also: Dispose; Do; Give up; Go away; Go where he would; Grant and sell; Leave; Put; Remove; Seek; Sell; Turn; Withdraw and sell.

WITHDRAW and/or sell and/or grant land

Freeman could	CAM	44,1.
could not	CAM	41,6.
Land holder could	CAM	14,29. 19,4. 37,2. 38,1.
could not	CAM	1,15.
could where/to whom he would	CAM	14,23; 28. 22,8. 32,6. 38,2.

See also: Dispose; Do; Give up; Go away; Go where he would; Grant and sell; Leave; Put; Remove; Seek; Sell; Turn; Withdraw.

WOMAN (femina)	BRK	65,14; 21.
	BKM	14,18. 24,3. 35,3.
	CHS	C8; 18. R1,42. R2,2. R6,2.
	DEV	23,22. 34,49.
	DOR	3,14. 26,5. 55,4; 9; 18; 23; 37; 39.
	ESS	1,19. 3,1. 5,6. 22,1. 30,43.
	HRT	1,6. 36,10-11.
	KEN	D19. 5,3; 132. 9,43.
	NFK	1,61; 213. 9,196; 198. 10,67. 17,30. 21,14; 19. 66,80.
	SHR	C5.
	SOM	25,8.
	SFK	4,15. 6,93. 14,68. 76,14.
	SRY	1,16. 5,25. 8,8; 16. 31,1.
	SSX	12,1; 38.
	WOR	11,2. 28,1. 34,2.
Abbey, given to	NFK	8,8; 10. 17,24. 26,5.
	SRY	19,35.
Being "man" of another	BDF	53,8.
	BKM	24,1.
	HRT	5,16; 20. 17,4; 6-7; 10; 14. 33,13; 18. 34,14. 36,8. 42,7.
	MDX	20,1.
	SFK	6,93. 25,84.
Daughter given to Abbey with land	BRK	14,1.
	SOM	37,7.
	WIL	13,21. 50,5.
False measure, giving	CHS	C18.
Grant of land to	BRK	1,38.

SRY 1,13. 19,35.
Holding land (except Queens and Countesses)
named woman in BDF 3,5. 10,1. 13,2.
own right 18,5. 23,17. 24,16.
53,8. 54. 55.
BRK B6. 1,8; 12-13.
7,16. 15,2. 31,3. 42,1. 46,5. 52,1. 53,1.
61,2. 65,1; 13-14; 17; 21.
BKM 5,1-2; 7-8. 13,1.
14,13-14; 18. 17,22. 19,3. 24,1; 3. 35,3. 54.
CAM 1,12. 13,1-2; 4; 7.
14,2; 5; 7-9; 11; 13-14; 18-20; 24-25; 27;
31; 35; 37; 44-45; 48; 55; 59-61; 64; 74; 78;
82. 19,2-4. 26,21-22. 38,1. 42.
CHS 2,13. 8,43; 45. 20,5;
7-8; 12. R1,33.
CON 5,1,14. 5,2,6. 5,7,6;
9. 5,9,3.
DBY 1,34. 6,51. 16,6.
DEV 1,50; 63. 3,13-14;
16; 19; 61; 80-81; 92; 95. 10,2. 15,38. 16,40;
92; *128;* 166. 17,19; 92. 19,37; 40; 44; 46.
20,12. 23,2; 9; 25. 24,1-4; 22. 25,1; 7; 11;
20. 28,1; 3. 33,1-2. 34,31; 39; 43. 35,25.
36,7; 15. 37,1. 40,4. 42,12; 15. 52,1; 8; 25;
50-53.
DOR 9,1. 17,1. 26,71.
31,1-2. 37,11. 49,1-2. 50,2. 55a. 57,14.
58,1-3.
ESS 1,19; 30. 3,1. 4,16.
5,1; 6. 18,24. 20,17; 46; 54. 21,2-3; 11-12.
22,1; 5. 23,29. 24,4; 9; 35. 28,13-16. 30,3;
26; 43. 33,4; 6-7; 19-20. 37,5. 47,2. 65,1.
84. 85,1. 90,20. B3a.
GLS 1,63. 24,1. 74,1.
78,7-8.
HAM 1,8; 25; 39; W12.
2,4. 6,12. 23,4. 35,9. 64,1. 69,14; 28; 34-
35. NF9,13. IoW9,11.
HEF 8,8; 10. 9,10; 19.
10,42; 56. 18,1.
19,10.
HRT 1,6; 12. 4,8; 22. 5,6;
16; 19-20; 24. 15,4; 6. 16,2; 7; 10. 17,6; 10;
14. 18,1. 20,6. 32,1-2. 33,7; 13; 18. 34,12;
14. 36,8. 37,21. 42,7. 42a. 43.
HUN 20,3. 28. D2.
KEN 5,60; 62; 69; 78; 97;
151; 191-192; 200; 202; 217; 220-222. 7,24.
LEC 2,7. 14,18. 41.
LIN 18,25. 26,26; 48.
34,1; 3; 8-9; 27. 36,1-2; 5. 42,16. 48,14.
57,43. 59,18. 63,6. 67,27. 68,18; 48.
MDX 17,1. 20,1. 25,1-3.
NFK 1,147; 150. 4,50.
8,24-25; 29; 34-35; 87. 9,11; 31. 10,81.
12,6. 14,21. 21,19-20. 30,5. 31,20-25; 34-
35; 37. 42,1. 51,1; 3. 60.
NTH 4,16. 8,13. 18,51;
85. 27,1. 35,1j; 3g; 7; 10; 22-23; 26. 56,50.
NTT 6,7.

OXF B10. 6,1b; 17. 26,1.
54. 58,21.
SHR C13. 4,3,49; 54.
4,10,4. 4,14,3-4; 6. 4,21,6; 14. 4,25,3; 6.
4,27,6; 26. 6,2; 9; 30-31; 33. 8,1-2.
SOM 1,11; 18; 20; 24.
2,7. 5,16-17; 42. 6,7. 8,24-25. 16,12. 17,4;
7-8. 21,57; 60; 66. 25,8; 48. 28,1. 30,1.
32,1. 35,4. 40,1.
STS 8,21. 11,4; 13; 37;
42. 17,20.
SFK 1,88; 90. 3,69; 91.
6, 57; 62; 91; 213; 222-223; 225; 264. 7,3;
36; 38-39; 75; 103. 8,56. 11,4. 14,117; 138.
15,3. 16,10; 20; 48. 21,25; 50; 70. 25,33;
81; 84. 32,9. 33,1; 12-13. 35,7. 36,11. 39,4.
46,4-5. 52,1; 7. 54,2-3. 67,15; 29. 74,6.
76,14.
SRY 1,16.
SSX 9,26; 58; 84. 10,92;
100; 109. 11,10; 18-19; 69; 72. 12,11; 19;
49; 51. 13,29.
WAR B2. 6,5. 16,14.
17,42; 47. 42. 43,1-
2. 45.
WIL 1,9-10; 20. 4,3. 5,7.
8,10. 13,9. 19,1. 24,7; 24; 27; 41. 26,22.
50,3. 67,25; 48; 83; 86-88; 90. 68,24.
WOR 2,12; 54; 67. 11,2.
19,13. 23,5. 28.
YKS C5; 10. 1N77; 113.
1E42. 5N31; 37. 5E27; 35-36; 53-54. 6N26;
126. 13E5; 12. 15E1-4; 7-10; 12; 14-16.
23N33. 29E7. CE6; 14-15; 40.
un-named woman
in own right BDF 24,16.
BRK 1,6; 8; 38. 42,1.
61,2. 65,13-14.
BKM 12,14.
CAM 32,32. 43.
DBY 6,28.
DEV 3,86-89. 15,41.
16,94; 128; 156. 23,22. *25,20.* 34,49. *42,12.*
44.
DOR 1,14. 2,6. 3,14-15.
8,2-4. 11,6. 13,1; 4. 19,11. 26,5. *36,3.*
37,13. 55. 56,13; 58.
ESS 3,7. 16,1. 18,21;
24. 20,10; 32. 22,8. 33,9; 11. 37,19. 38,6.
39,7; 10. 90,75.
GLS 1,63. 34,12. 39,18.
76.
HAM 1,25. 2,4; 7. 6,16.
NF9,11.
HEF 1,14. 19,6. 34,1.
HRT 1,6. 15,9. 16,1.
34,7. 36,10-11.
44,1.
HUN B10. 29,6.
KEN C4. 5,3. 9,43.
LEC 8,2. 13,37. 17,29.

	LIN	3,32.
	MDX	3,3.
	NFK	1,61; 80; 123; 138;

209; 213. 7,14. 8,8; 16. 9,21; 196; 198.
10,36; 93. 12,21. 17,30. 21,3. 39,2. 66,80.

	OXF	55. 58,17-18. 59,4.
	SOM	1,28; *65*. 6,1; 13;
		14. 46,24-25. 47,1.
	SFK	1,84; 97-98. 6,8; 11;

76-77; 156; 161; 176; 191; 193-195; 199-
201; 216; 229-230; 232; 251; 253; 271. 7,11;
37. 8,21; 31; 79. 14,38. 19,9. 21,66. 29,14.
31,38. 34,13. 38,11. 76,8; 12.

	SRY	1,16. 5,1e; 25-26.
		8,8; 16. 15,1. 19,4-
		5; 34-35. 31,1.
	SSX	12,37.
	WAR	37,9.
	WIL	M15. 3,2-3. 7,1.
		8,6. 24,9. 25,4-5.
		67,80.
together with man	BDF	57,7; 16.
	BKM	4,20.
	DBY	16,6.
	DOR	13,8.
	ESS	23,34. 90,55.
	GLS	39,20.
	HEF	34,2.
	HRT	34,4. 36,19. 42,9.
	HUN	B10. 23,1. 29,5.
	KEN	5,196.
	LEC	21,2.
	LIN	3,32. 13,44. 27,59.
		28,12; 15. 42,16.
		48,4. 59,5. CK1.
	NFK	46,1.
	NTH	18,34.
	SHR	4,14,4; 6. 4,21,6;
		14.
	SOM	*19,72*. *28,1*. 47,15.
	STS	11,23.
	SFK	6,57; 110; 193.
		7,90; 137.
	SRY	8,8.
	WAR	16,10. 22,22. 28,13;
		18.
	WIL	29,5. 38,1.
	WOR	23,5.
	YKS	1N77; 98; 113.

1E10. 1W53. 5E30. 11N4. 13E10-11.
23E18. 29W36. 29E13; 16; 20. CE31; 35.

Old (vetula)	DBY	6,28.
Poor	KEN	5,132.

Property rights
during marriage and
separation   YKS   CE15.
See also: Almswoman; Annexation; Burgess;
Church; Commendation; Cottager;
Crime/offence; Daughter; Dispute; Dower;
Dwelling; English; free man; free woman;
Freeman; Gift; Girl; Holding; House; Jester;

Jurisdiction; Lady of manor; Lease; Marriage;
Narrative; Nun; Ordeal; Patronage; Patronage,
sub; Plea; Protector; Reeve; Relations; Sale;
Sheriff; Slave, female; Stepmother; Taken away;
Theft; Violation of women; Widow; Wife.

WOOD (nemus;	HAM	21,4. 51,1. 69,36.
silva; lucus)	HEF	24,5.
	KEN	P5.
	LEC	2,6. 36,1.
	LIN	51,9.
	SRY	19,12.
	SSX	12,6.
	WIL	1,2; 19. 39,1.
	WOR	23,1. 26,2.
Assessed in pigs	HAM	1,37.
Large	HEF	14,7. ˊ25,9. 29,16.
	SHR	8,1-2.
Little/small	BRK	8,1. 40,2. 44,2.
(silva modica/		65,20.
parva; silvula)	CHS	2,23.
	DOR	3,7; 9.
	GLS	3,7. 30,3.
	HAM	1,39. 28,6. 45,2.
		IoW6,11.
	HEF	9,3; 9. 24,6.
	KEN	2,21; 24. 5,126;
		134; 210. 7,23.
		13,1.
	SHR	4,3,21. 4,19,2.
		4,28,6.
	SOM	1,26. 5,12; 17.
	STS	11,11. 13,4.
	SSX	2,5. 6,3.
	WIL	1,13. 13,11. 24,37.
		27,17.
	WOR	15,5. 23,12. 26,11.
	YKS	5W30. 25W9.
		28W33
rendering nothing	SHR	4,1,4; 11.
Lordship, in	WIL	1,2.
Underwood (silva	CON	2,2; 9. 3,2-3. 4,3;
minuta; nemusculus)		16. 5,4,18. 5,6,2; 8.

5,8,1; 6. 5,10,1. 5,11,2; 4; 6. 5,14,4. 5,20,2.
5,24,17-18. 6,1.

	DBY	1,12-13; 24; 27. 3,1;

3. 6,2-7; 9-10; 13-15; 17; 19; 24; 52; 68; 71-
72; 74; 79. 8,5. 10,4; 22; 27. 13,1. 14,2.
17,12. B2.

	DEV	1,3-5; 11; 13-14; 34;

43. 2,5-7; 11; 13-14; 22-23. 3,4; 76; 78; 81;
83; 86; 98. 5,8. 6,3-4; 8. 7,1. 12,1. 15,*50*;
62; 71; 79. 16,6; *8*; 25; *27*; 35; 37; 39; 41-
42; 65-66; 74; 76; 94; 96; 109; 113; *125*;
136; 144; 149-150; 152; *163*; 169. 17,*21*; 41;
45; 48; 51-52; 55-56; 58-61; *62*; 68; 71; 76-
79; 84; 92; 102; 104. 18,1. 19,7; 11; 14; 20-
21; 29; 31; 38. 20,15. 22,1. 23,9; 19-20; 22-
23; 25. 24,8; 11-12; 17; 19; 25. 25,1; 7; 10;
12; 24-25; *26*. 28,3; *4*; 5; *11*; 13. 30,2-3.
31,1; 3. 33,1-2. 34,19; 21-22; 25-26; 54.

35,3; 5; 7; 11-13; 16; 26-27. 36,2; 6-7; 13. 39,11; 14; 17-18; 21. 40,6-7. 42,8; 14-15; 21. 46,2. 47,6; *13.* 48,5. 49,2. 51,7; 13. 52,*19-20;* 25; 34; 37; 39; 41; 51; 53.
        DOR 1,13. 3,2; 4; 13; 17. *16,2.* 26,45; 70. 36,3. 39,2. 41,1. 46,1. 55,17. 56,54. 57,8.
        HUN 1,5. 2,5; 7-8. 5,1. 6,25. 7,1-4. 9,1. 10,1. 13,4. 15,1. 16,1. 19,2; 5; 14. 22,1. 23,1. 24,1. 25,2.
        KEN *C1.* 5,127; 162. 7,22.
        LIN T2. 1,3; 14; 17-18; 25; 55; 61; 96; 100-102; 104. 2,11; 18; 20-21; 29; 35-36; 38; 41-42. 3,3; 8; 10; 12; 14; 32; 35. 4,2-3; 20; 45; 52; 57; 59; 61; 63; 67; 69. 7,7-8; 10; 24-25; 31-32; 43; 45; 50. 8,3; 5-7; 15; 22; 25-26; 28; 39. 11,9. 12,4; 6; 23; 28-29; 44; 52-53. 13,4; 7; 14-15; 24; 26; 33; 35-36. 14,9; 11; 13; 24-26; 46; 52; 54; 56-58; 63; 65; 75; 81; 87-88; 93; 95. 16,39. 18,4; 15-16; 19; 21-24; 26; 30. 22,10; 14; 18-19; 30; 38. 24,22; 26; 38; 54; 61; 63-65; 72; 76; 81-82; 85; 87; 89; 96-99. 25,16-17; 19-21; 24. 26,8; 13; 22; 26; 36; 40; 43; 50; 52. 27,25; 40; 43; 53-55; 57. 28,17; 23; 25-26; 29. 29,5-6; 27. 30,3; 18-20; 28; 36-37. 31,4; 8; 10; 16; 18. 32,8; 15; 17; 32; 34. 34,8; 12-13; 19-21; 25. 35,1; 4; 12. 38,5. 39,1-2. 40,6; 23. 42,9-10; 16-17; 19. 44,4-5; 10. 45,4. 46,1; 4. 47,9. 48,8; 11-12. 49,1. 51,1; 7; 12. 52,2. 53,1. 55,3. 56,6-8; 10; 16. 57,1; 7; 10-11; 13-14; 16; 18; 21-22; 33; 41; 43; 46; 55. 58,3; 6. 59,4-5; 7-8; 19-20. 61,1; 3-4. 63,2-3. 64,3-4; 6; 16. 65,3-4. 67,1; 4-5; 8-10; 12-13; 25. 68,4; 6; 17; 19; 22; 29; 37. CS24.
        NTH 18,5; 7; 24; 29; 60; 92-93; 97. 56,25.
        NTT B1. 1,3; 58; 61. 5,5. 6,15. 7,2. 8,1. 9,59; 65; 115-116. 10,1; 15; 24; 35; 39-40; 47; 50-51. 11,19; 25. 12,17. 13,1; 4; 6; 8. 15,3; 8-9. 16,1; 7. 18,1; 4. 24,1. 28,3. 30,8; 34; 45; 49.
        OXF 6,1a. 7,23. 15,1. 29,14. 35,22.
        SOM 1,28; 30. 2,7; 11. 4,1. 5,3; 10; 13; 16; 25-26; 30; 35; 37; 42; 44; 46; 48; *54;* 57; 62; 70. 7,3; 5-8; 11; 15. 8,1; 5-7; 11; 18; 20; 23. 10,4. 16,3. 17,4. 19,*2;* 12; 23; 31; 36; 43; 46-47. 20,1. 21,17; 32; 40; 56; 58; 67; 85; 96. *22,17; 19; 28.* 24,21; 30. 25,26; 48. 27,3. 35,21. 36,7. 37,6. 39,2. 42,1. 44,2. 45,7; 9; 17. 46,4-5; 19; 23. 47,19; 23.
        WIL 24,1. 27,24. 32,11. 42,1. 67,10.
        YKS C35. 1N5. 2B1. 2W3-4; 7-8. 3Y1-2. 5N7. 5W4; 6. 6N1-2; 6; 19; 38; 44; 46; 69; 71-72; 92-94; 120; 123; 134; 136; 139-140. 7E2. 8N6. 9W48.

10W15; 20; 23-24; 27; 32; 39; 43. 11E1. 11W1. 13W3-4. 17W1. 21W1. 23N13; 15. 25W10. 28W10-11; 13.
fertile   RUT R19.
little   DBY 1,32; 34. 2,2. 6,30; 42; 60; 80; 91; 94. 7,9. 9,1; 4. 10,18; 21. 17,15-16.
        NTT 1,10.
virgate of   NTT 9,59. 11,19. 15,3. 18,4. 30,45.
See also: Alder; Ashwood; Box wood; Brushwood; Copse; Fence; Fir wood; Fire wood; Fuel; House; Jurisdiction; Spinney; Willow; Woodland.
WOODLAND (silva) BDF 3,6. 14,2. 21,6. 24,5. 32,14. 39,3. 54,2.
        BRK 1,1; 25.
        BKM 4,34. 8,3.
        CHS B3-4; 6; 8. A6; 17; 21. 1,1-3; 7-8; 14; 18-19; 21; 25-28; 31; 33; 36. 2,1; 7-9; 12-15; 18; 20-21; 25-27; 30-31. 3,1. 5,1; 4-5; 8; 11-14. 7,1; 4. 8,1; 3; 11; 13-17; 19; 21; 24-36; 38-42; 44. 9,4-5; 13-14; 16-20; 24; 26; 28. 11,1-3; 5-6. 12,4. 13,2; 4-5. 14,4-10; 13. 16,2. 17,2-4; 6-9; 11-12. 18,1-4; 6. 20,3-4; 11-12. 21,1. 22,1. 24,5; 8-9. 26,1-2; 6-11. 27,1; 3-4. FD1,1. FD2,1; 3-4. FD3,1. FD5,1. FD6,1. FD7,1-2. FD8,2. FT1,2-8. FT2,2; 5; 7-10; 16. FT3,5-6. G3. R1,2; 13; 31; 33-34; 43. R2,1. R4,1. R5,3. R6,1; 4-5.
        CON 1,1-7; 9-12; 16. 2,1; 3-8; 11. 3,1; 5. 4,2; 5; 7; 9-10; 15; 19. 5,1,1-4; 6-10; 12-13; 19. 5,2,1-3; 5; 7; 9-13; 17-20; 22-23; 25-28; 31; 33. 5,3,1; 3-6; 8; 10-15; 17-19; 22-24. 5,4,2-3; 5; 7; 11; 13-14; 16; 19. 5,5,1-4; 6-7; 9; 11; 14-16; 19. 5,6,1; 6-7; 9-10. 5,7,2-3; 6. 5,8,2. 5,11,1; 3; 5. 5,12,1-2. 5,13,1-5; 9; 11-12. 5,14,1. 5,15,3-6. 5,17,1-2. 5,20,1. 5,22,1. 5,23,2-4. 5,24,1-5; 8; 12-16; 19-24. 5,26,3-4.
        DBY 9,3. 17,8.
        DEV 1,3; *4;* 6-10; 12; 16-19; 21; 23-43; 45-48; *49;* 50-72. 2,2; 4; 12; 15-16; 18-19; 21; 24. 3,5-6; 8-9; 12-16; 18-26; 28; 30-31; 36-38; 42-46; 48-49; 52-54; 56; 59-68; 70; 73-75; 77; 79-80; 84; 87; 90-92; 96-97. 4,1. 5,1-8; 10-12. 6,1-2; 5; 7; 9; 11-13. 7,2. 8,1. 9,1. 10,1-2. 11,1-3. 12,1. 13,1. 14,1-2. 15,3; 5; 8-12; 17-18; 20-25; 31; 34; 36-37; 40; 43-44; 46-51; 53; *54;* 56-58; 61-67; 70; 72; 74; 77-78. 16,3-5; 7-24; 26; 29-30; 32-34; 36; *37;* 40; *42;* 43-47; 51-55; 58-59; 61; 63; 67; 69; 71; 73; 75; 77-78; 80; 86-87; 89; 93; 99-100; 102-104; 106-108; 110-111; 115-116; 118; 120-122; 125; 128-131; 133; 137-138; 140-144; 147-148; 153; 157-163; *164;* 165-166; 170; 172-173; 176. 17,3-8; 10-12; 14-17; 20-22; 26; 28-30; 32; 35; 44; 48; *50;* 63; 66; 69-70; 72-73; 75;

69; 70; 72; 74-75; 79. 20,3. 21,1-7; 11-13;
19; 23-24; 26-29; 36-37; 44-45; 47; 49-55;
57; 59-62; 64; 70; 72-77; 81-83; 86-90.
22,1-4; 7-9; 11-15; 17; 19-21; 24-28. 23,1.
24,14-20; 22; 30-31; 37. 25,1; 3-5; 7-10;
12-14; 16-17; 21-24; 27-34; 37-47; 49-56.
26,1-2; 4-5; 8. 27,1-2. 28,1-2. 29,1. 30,1.
31,2; 5. 32,1-4; 6; 8. 33,1-2. 34,1. 35,1; 5-
8; 10-11; *12;* 13-14; 16-20; 22-23. 36,1; 3-
5; 7; 9-12; 14. 37,1; 3; 5-8; 10-11. 38,1.
39,1. 40,1-2. 41,1-3. 42,2. 44,1; 3-5; 8; 12.
46,8; 15-17; 22. 47,5; 7; *9;* 10-12; 16-17;
20-21.

STS 1,1-2; 4; 6-8; 11-25;
27-28; 30-31. 2,1-3; 8-9; 15; 21-22. 3,1.
4,1-3; 5-8; 10. 5,1. 7,2; 13. 8,1-3; 5-6; 8;
10; 13; 15; 17-18; 20-23; 25-27; 29-32. 9,1.
10,5; 8; 10. 11,1; 5-6; 8-9; 12-14; 16-21;
23-39; 41-42; 44-46; 49-52; 54-57; 62; 64-
65. 12,1-2; 10-12; 14; 18; 21-23; 27-29.
13,1-3; 5-7. 14,1-2. 15,1-2. 17,7-14; 17; 19.

SFK 3,59. 6,216. 62,7.
SRY 1,6.
SSX 2,10. 7,2. 9,31.
11,92. 12,6. 13,14;
27; 53.

WAR 1,1-9. 2,2. 3,1; 6.
4,1; 3; 5. 5,1. 6,1; 5-6; 8; 10; 18. 10,1. 11,1-
2. 12,3; 8-9. 14,1; 3. 15,1-2; 4; 6. 16,4; 10;
16; 18-19; 22-24; 26; 42-45; 48; 50-51; 63.
17,1-4; 6-9; 11-16; 49; 52; 54; 69-70. 18,3;
6-7; 13. 19,1. 21,1. 22,6-9; 11; 19; 25-26.
23,2; 4. 26,1. 27,1-6. 28,1-2; 4; 9; 11; 16-
17; 19. 29,3-5. 30,1. 31,5-8. 37,1; 6. 38,1.
39,4. 42,1-2. 43,1. 44,7; 10; 14.

WIL 1,1-12; 14-16; 19-
22. 2,1-8; 11-12. 3,1-5. 4,2. 5,2-3; 5. 6,1-
2. 7,1; 4; 9; 11; 14; 16. 8,2-4; 6-7; 9-13.
10,2-3; 5. 11,1. 12,2-4; 6. 13,2; 6-10; 19.
14,1-2. 15,1-2. 17,1. 19,2; 4; 6. 22,1; 3-5.
23,3; 8; 10. 24,4; 7; 15; 18-19; 22; 25-29;
31; 33; 38-39. 25,1; 5; 7-8; 11-14; 18-20;
22-23; 25; 27. 26,2-4; 7; 11-12; 14; 16-21.
27,1-5; 7; 11; 19; 21-23; 26. 28,1-2; 8; 10;
12-13. 29,1-2; 5. 30,2; 5-7. 31,1. 32,1; 3;
5; 12-13; 16-17. 33,1. 34,1. 36,1-2. 37,2;
11-12; 15. 38,1. 39,1. 40,1. 41,1-2; 5; 8;
10. 42,2-3; 9-10. 44,1. 47,1. 48,4-5; 8; 10-
11. 49,2. 50,1; 4. 53,2. 55,1. 56,4-5. 58,1-
2. 59,1. 61,1. 64,1. 65,1. 66,1. 67,5-7; 9;
16; 32-33; 35; 37; 41; 48; 54; 56; 59; 63-64;
66; 73; 80; 89; 92; 94-96. 68,3-4; 7; 11-12;
20-22; 24; 27-30.

WOR 1,1a-c; 2; 6. 2,2; 5-
9; 15; 17; 22-23; 25-26; 31-36; 38; 48; 52-
54; 56-62; 66-68; 70-72; 77-79; 81-82; 84-
85. 3,1; 3. 8,1; 6-9a,e,g; 11; 14; 16; 19-20;
23; 26a. 9,1a; 2; 5a. 10,4; 10; 13-15. 11,2.
14,2. 15,4; 7; 9; 11-13. 16,1-3. 17,1. 18,1-
4. 19,1-3; 10; 12-14. 20,5. 23,2-3; 5; 9-11;
14. 24,1. 26,1; 3-6; 12-13; 15. 28,1.

	YKS	1Y1-2; 4; 15.
	2N14. 5N65; 67; 76. 5W8. 6W1. 9W108.	
	12W14. 13W12. 23N1; 11; 24. 29W13.	
Arpent of	WIL	68,8.
Authority, none within	HAM	39,4.
Barren/unproductive (infructuosa)	DOR	11,*13;* 16.
	KEN	C1.
	LEC	25,3.
Bovate of	LIN	16,15.
Clearance in (exsartum)	HEF	1,7; 10a. 10,48-49.
Customary dues of/in	BDF	33,1. 48,1.
	BKM	12,30.
	CAM	5,38.
	HUN	7,5. 9,2. 19,8.
none except hunting	HEF	1,3.
Dimensions not stated	HEF	29,16.
Guarding of	HEF	1,44.
Hawk's eyrie, containing	BKM	43,2.
	SHR	3c,5.
Held by more than one holder	WAR	44,7.
Hide of	BDF	39,3.
	DEV	10,2. 34,51.
	ESS	18,1-3; 5-7. 24,1-3; 10; 15. 28,9. 33,3. 83,1. 84,1.
appurtenant to specific hidage	CHS	22,1.
Honey, produce of from	WOR	2,15; 22; 31.
Hunting fit for	DBY	1,30.
produce from	WOR	2,15; 22; 31.
Keeper of	WOR	1,1a.
King held by	WAR	44,7.
lordship, of	CAM	*28,2.*
	HEF	2,11. 8,7.
	STS	11,62.
of	CAM	28,2.
	ESS	1,24.
	HAM	69,4.
	HEF	1,40; 73-74. 2,11. 19,10.
	HUN	6,26.
	SRY	4,1.
	WOR	2,84.
Land put into	HEF	1,40.
reverted to uncultivated because of	HEF	25,6.
	HUN	6,26.
Less 1086 than TRE	ESS	24,10.
Lord's	LEC	1,3.
Lordship, in	HEF	2,11. 8,7.
	SHR	4,3,28.

STS 11,62.
WIL 1,2.

Manor/village
  given away out of ESS 1,11.
  lying in another LIN 16,15.
             SFK 8,55. 52,8.
  to maintain GLS 7,1.
  sufficient for GLS 10,8.
None HAM 29,6.
       NFK 1,50.
       YKS C24.

Pasturage, woodland (pasnagium)
  pigs from (de
  pasnagio) BRK 1,1.
        HAM 1,8; 16-17; 27; 29-
30; 41. 2,1; 3; 5; 10; 15; 20. 3,1-2; 6; 8-9.
6,16. 10,1. 15,3. 20,1. 31,1. 69,32.
        KEN 6,1. 7,1; 12; 28.
8,1. 9,10; 49. 12,3.
        SRY 1,4; 7; 13. 2,3. 3,1.
6,1. 8,18; 20-21; 28; 30. 11,1. 15,1. 18,2-
3. 19,1; 4-6; 19.
        SSX 2,1c-e. 3,3; 5; 9.
5,1-2. 8,1. 9,1; 3. 10,3; 51; 60; 64. 13,10.
        WOR 3,3.
  without pasturage HAM 1,40; W3. 21,3.
29,15. 69,35.
IoW6,11. IoW9,5.
Pasture, woodland DBY 1,1; 8-14; 16; 18-21;
26; 29; 32-33; 35-36. 2,1. 3,1; 5; 7. 4,1-2.
5,1-4. 6,12-13; 18; 22-23; 25; 27-29; 32-33;
35; 38; 40; 43-45; 50-59; 61-64; 66; 68-70;
73; 86; 92; 95-97; 99. 7,1; 3-6. 8,1-4. 9,3;
6. 10,1-2; 4-15; 17; 21-25. 11,1-5. 12,1-5.
13,1-2. 14,1; 3-4; 6-7. 15,1. 16,2. 17,1-2;
4-5; 9; 18-20.
        HAM 1,19.
        HUN 1,1; 7-10. 2,2-4.
4,1-4. 6,1-8; 11-12; 19-20. 9,1. 12,1. 13,1-
3. 14,1. 19,1; 3; 11; 27-30. 20,2-3; 6; 8-9.
25,1-2. 29,1.
        KEN 1,4.
        LIN 1,4; 17; 94-95; 97;
99; 103. 2,18; 37-39. 3,13-15; 33-34; 42.
4,45; 51; 54-55; 59; 61; 63; 73. 7,30; 38-
40; 56. 8,1; 4-5; 8; 17. 9,1. 11,9. 12,91.
13,2-4; 23; 44-45. 14,22; 54-55; 57; 60; 88;
92. 16,17; 23. 17,2. 18,1; 3; 6; 13; 17; 24;
32. 22,16-17; 29; 35. 24,16-20; 25; 31-32;
54; 77; 81; 87. 25,16. 26,20; 48; 51. 27,19;
26; 41; 47; 51. 29,4-5; 8-9; 28. 30,19; 29;
31-32. 31,3-4; 7; 9; 11; 17. 34,12; 23. 35,13-
14. 38,2-4; 10-11; 13. 40,10. 42,1-5; 15.
43,4. 47,8. 48,6. 55,1. 56,2-3; 11; 16-18.
57,45-46. 59,11; 17. 63,5-7; 12-13; 15.
64,1; 18. 67,7. 68,18; 20; 24.
        NTT 1,1-2; 4; 7-9; 11;
15-17; 20-21; 23; 27-28; 35-36; 39-40; 42-
43; 45. 2,4; 9. 4,8. 5,1; 4; 7-10; 13-14; 16.
6,4; 8-9; 13. 9,3; 14; 19-20; 22; 26; 28; 31;
33-34; 36-41; 43-44; 46; 50-51; 53-57; 60;

62; 66; 70; 72; 74; 97; 112-114; 117-119;
121-124; 126-130. 10,3; 20; 29; 31-32; 36;
43; 46. 11,8-10; 12; 18; 20. 12,1; 8-10; 16;
18. 13,9-11. 14,5. 15,1; 4. 16,2; 6; 9; 11.
17,1-5; 7-9; 11-12. 18,3; 5. 21,3. 22,2. 27,3.
30,1-3; 5; 9; 29; 39; 43; 46.
        RUT R5; 7; 12-15; 17;
20.
        STS 7,7. 10,3-4; 7; 9.
11,43. 12,24-26.
        YKS C32. 1Y1; 3-5; 10;
15-16; 19. 1N54-56; 76. 1W25. 2B1; 7.
2N14; 21; 25. 2W1-2; 4; 6-7. 2E1; 17. 3Y4;
10-11. 4N1-2. 4E2. 5N1-3; 9; 11; 18; 46;
49-50; 52-54; 58-59. 5E7; 11; 17; 34-36;
66. 5W1-3; 7-8; 11; 13-14; 16-23; 25; 32-
34. 6N138; 141; 162. 6W2. 6E1. 8N4-5;
8; 22-23. 8W1. 8E5. 9W1-4; 9; 11-12; 14-
17; 24-26; 34-40; 45; 49; 54; 58-60; 63-70;
74-83; 85-87; 89-98; 101-103; 105-107; 109-
130; 133-135; 137-143. 10W1-4; 6; 8; 10-
12; 14; 16-18; 26; 28-31; 35-38; 41. 11E1.
12W1-6; 8-13; 15-17; 19-23; 26-27. 13W2;
5-6; 9; 11; 16-18; 27-28; 30; 33-35; 37.
13E4; 13-14. 13N9; 11-13; 15-17. 14E1;
11; 21; 29; 37; 46. 15E8; 17. 16E1; 3. 16N2.
16W1; 3; 5-6. 18W2-3. 19W1; 3. 21E5; 7;
9. 21W2; 5; 12; 14. 22W2-3. 23N8-9; 18;
26-28; 34. 23E2; 5; 10; 12. 24W1; 7; 15;
18-19. 24E1. 25W2-3; 6; 11-12; 14-20; 28.
28W37. 29W1-7; 9-10; 26.
assessed in pigs SSX 13,9.
unpastured (non
pastilis) DBY 1,28; 30. 5,5.
       NTT 14,8.
       YKS 5N8. 5W5.
virgate of HUN 14,1.
       NTT 9,60.
       YKS 10W29.
without pasture NTH 9,6.
       YKS 23N10.
Payments from
(redditus) BDF 55,6.
       BKM 14,3. 17,4; 17.
       HRT 13,1. 33,17.
in plough-shares BDF 8,1. 24,13.
       BKM 12,3. 17,4. 24,1.
26,3. 29,3.
men living in, by BKM 17,17.
none HEF 2,21; 26-30; 32; 49;
51. 8,5. 10,51.
19,10. 21,7. 22,5.
       KEN 5,146.
       WOR 15,9.
Pig pasture (dena
silvae) SRY 1,9.
Pigs
  woodland for/ BDF 1,1a; 2a-b; 3. 2,1-6;
  assessed in   9. 3,1-2; 4-5; 7-8;
11; 14-15. 4,2-3. 8,1-3; 7. 10,1. 11,1. 12,1.
14,1. 15,2; 6-7. 16,1; 3-4; 8-9. 17,4; 7.

18,1-2. 19,1. 20,1. 21,1; 9; 16. 22,1. 23,1;
3-5; 8; 10-11; 13-24; 26-27; 29; 32; 34-35;
38; 49; 57. 24,2-11; 13-18; 23; 27. 25,1-2;
7; 9; 11-12; 15. 26,1; 3. 28,1. 30,1. 31,1.
32,1; 3-5; 8; 13. 33,1-2. 38,2. 39,1. 40,3.
41,2. 44,1; 4. 46,1. 47,4. 48,1. 49,1-4.
52,2. 53,1-2; 4-6; 8; 10; 13; 15; 29; 31. 54,1-
4. 55,2-3; 6-8; 11-12. 57,3; 16.

BRK   1,2-4; 8; 14-15; 17-
23; 25-26; 28-29; 33; 37; 41; 44-45; 47. 3,1.
4,1. 6,1. 7,12-13; 32; 34-35. 9,1. 10,1.
11,1. 15,1-2. 16,1. 17,1. 21,3-4; 20-21.
22,2-3; 5. 26,1. 27,1. 31,1; 6. 32,1. 34,2.
35,2. 36,6. 37,1. 38,3; 5. 39,1. 41,1. 43,2.
44,1. 45,1. 46,3-6. 48,1. 49,1. 50,1. 51,1.
52,1. 53,1. 54,1. 56,1. 57,1. 58,1. 63,1-2.
65,10; 17.

BKM   1,2-3; 5-7. 2,2-3.
3,1-2. 3a,1-2; 4. 4,5; 10; 12; 14-16; 18-19;
29-33; 35-38; 42. 5,1-3; 8-9; 11-17; 19-21.
6,2. 7,1-2. 12,1; 3-4; 14-18; 28; 30; 34-37.
13,2-4. 14,3-5; 7; 9; 14; 19; 21-23; 25-27;
30; 34-35; 37; 42-45; 49. 15,1. 16,3; 5-6; 9-
10. 17,2; 4-6; 16-18; 22-25; 27-29. 18,3.
19,1-4; 6. 20,1. 21,1; 3-4. 22,1. 23,2-5; 7;
11-12; 14; 16; 26-27. 24,1. 25,3. 26,1-4;
10. 27,1. 29,2-4. 36,1-2. 37,1. 38,1. 39,1.
41,1-3. 42,1. 43,1-2; 5-6; 8. 45,1. 46,1.
48,1. 49,1. 51,1-2. 52,1-2. 53,2-9. 55,1.
56,1-2. 57,7-8; 10-12.

CAM   1,4; 11; 18. 5,1; 4-
6; 15; 38; 45-46; 59; 61; 63. 6,1. 7,11. 10,1.
14,6-7; 11; 13-14; 61-62; 80-81. 16,1. 18,1-
3; 6. 21,1. 25,9. 26,3; 6; 9; 51. 29,1-3; 7-
10. 41,1; 4. 44,1-2.

ESS   1,2-4; 8-13; 19-21;
23-24; 26-30. 2,2-4; 7-8. 3,1-3; 6-8; 10-13;
15. 4,1-3; 6-10; 12; 14-15; 18. 5,1-4; 6-11.
6,5-6; 8-9; 11; 14. 7,1. 8,1-11. 9,1-2; 5-9;
11-12; 14. 10,1-5. 11,1-3; 5-7. 12,1. 13,1.
14,2; 5. 15,1-2. 16,1. 17,1. 18,8-11; 18; 21-
21a; 24-25; 28; 31; 33; 35-43; 45. 19,1.
20,1; 3; 6-8; 12-15; 18-21; 23; 26; 30-34;
36-41; 43-46; 48-60; 62-65; 67-71; 74-75;
77-80. 21,1-4; 6; 8-9; 11. 22,3; 5-9; 11-15;
17-18. 23,1-8; 10-11; 13-16; 19-20; 26; 28-
28-32; 34-36; 38-41; 43. 24,4; 8; 11; 16-17;
20-21; 23; 26; 28; 31; 33; 45-46; 48-49; 53-
54; 57; 59-61; 64; 66-67. 25,1-5; 7; 11-19;
21-23; 25-26. 26,1-5. 27,1-6; 11-18. 28,5-
8; 11; 13-17. 29,2; 4-5. 30,1-5; 7-11; 14; 16;
18; 20-25; 27-36; 38-42; 44-46; 48-50. 31,1.
32,1-2; 4-9; 11; 13-14; 16-17; 19; 21-27; 29-
35; 38-39; 44-45. 33,1; 4-9; 11; 13-16; 18-
20; 22-23. 34,3-4; 6-16; 18-24; 26-30; 32-
34; 36-37. 35,1-9; 11-14. 36,1-7; 9-12.
37,1-7; 9-11; 15-18; 20. 38,1; 3-5; 8. 39,1-
9. 40,1-8. 41,1-4; 6-7; 9; 12. 42,2-4; 6-9.
43,1-2; 4-6. 44,1; 3-4. 45,1. 46,1-2. 47,2-
3. 48,1. 49,1; 3. 50,1. 51,1-2. 52,1; 3. 53,1-
2. 54,1-2. 55,1. 56,1. 57,1; 3; 5. 58,1. 60,1;

3. 61,2. 62,4. 63,2. 64,1. 65,1. 66,1-2.
67,1-2. 68,2; 4-5. 71,2-4. 72,2-3. 74,1.
76,1. 77,1. 78,1. 81,1. 86,1. 87,1. 89,3.
90,5; 10; 15; 17; 22; 25; 29-30; 35-36; 47;
50-51; 53-54; 56-58; 63; 65-66; 68-70.

HAM   1,1-2; 5-6; 9; 11; 15;
19-22; 25-27; 42-44; 46; W14-16. 2,6; 8-9;
11; 15-16; 25. 3,5-10; 12; 16-18; 24-27. 5,1.
6,3-4; 8. 9,2. 11,1. 14,1. 15,1. 16,1. 17,1.
18,1; 3. 21,6-7; 10. 22,1. 23,5-6; 12-14; 17;
20-21; 25-26; 34; 36-38; 40; 42; 49; 52-53;
57. 25,1. 27,1-2. 28,8. 29,5; 7-8; 14. 32,2;
4. 35,1-4. 38,1. 39,1. 42,1. 43,2; 4; 6. 44,3.
47,3. 49,1. 56,2. 58,1. 61,1. 62,1. 63,1.
64,1. 66,1. 68,1; 9. 69,12; 17; 22; 27-29;
32; 39; 51-52. NF9,2; 13; 36-38; 43-44.
NF10,1. IoW1,7-8. IoW2,1. IoW5,1.
IoW6,19. IoW7,6-7; 10. IoW8,9.

HRT   1,2-7; 9-10; 13; 15-
16; 18. 2,1-3. 3,1. 4,2-6; 10-20; 22-25. 5,2-
3; 5; 8-11; 20; 23-24; 26. 7,1. 8,1; 3. 9,1-
10. 10,1-3; 5-6; 8-12; 14-17. 11,1. 12,1.
13,1-3; 5. 14,1-2. 15,1-3; 5; 10-12. 16,2;
9-11. 17,1; 3-4; 8; 10-15. 18,1. 19,2. 20,1-
2; 5; 7; 13. 21,1-2. 22,1-2. 23,3-4. 24,1; 3.
25,1-2. 26,1. 27,1. 28,4; 8. 30,1-2. 31,1; 6-
8. 32,1-2. 33,1-5; 9; 12-20. 34,1-2; 4-5; 10;
12-14; 16; 21-22; 24-25. 35,1. 36,2; 5; 7; 9;
11; 17; 19. 37,8; 20-23. 38,1-2. 41,1-2.
42,1-2; 6-9; 11; 13; 15. 42a,1. 43,1. 44,1.

KEN   1,2-4. 2,3-17; 22-
23; 25-26; 29; 31-33; 41. 3,1-8; 10-13; 20-
21. 4,1-3; 5-9; 11-13. 5,1-3; 5; 8; 12-16; 18-
26; 28-34; 36-42; 44; 46-47; 49; 51; 53; 55-
60; 62-63; 66-83; 85-87; 89-90; 93-103;
106; 115; 118-124; 128-129; 139-145; 149;
155; 159; 163; 165-168; 172; 175; 180; 185;
192; 208-209; 224-225. 7,2-3; 5; 12-13; 17;
19-20; 26-27. 9,16; 22; 24-25; 28-30; 42;
48. 10,1-2. 11,1-2. 12,1.

LEC   13,65.

MDX   2,1-3. 3,1-3; 12-18;
20; 28. 4,1-3; 5; 8-12. 5,1. 6,1. 7,5-8. 8,6.
9,4; 6-9. 10,1-2. 11,1. 12,1. 13,1. 14,2.
15,1-2. 18,2. 20,1. 21,1. 22,1. 24,1. 25,1.

NFK   1,1-3; 15; 19-22; 28;
30; 32; 40; 50; 52-57; 71; 73-74; 77; 81-82;
85-89; 92; 94; 98; 100; 105; 128; 131; 135-
136; 138-139; 143; 146-147; 150-151; 155;
169; 173-174; 179; 182-183; 185-186; 188;
192-195; 197-198; 205; 212; 215-216; 218-
219; 222; 224-226; 228; 231-234; 237-239.
2,4. 3,1. 4,1; 6; 8-9; 15; 18; 21; 29-35; 37-
39; 41; 46; 49-50; 52. 5,6. 6,2; 6-7. 7,1-2;
6; 13; 15-18. 8,1-4; 6-9; 11-12; 35; 40; 44;
46-47; 52; 55; 61-63; 65-70; 82-84; 87; 91;
93; 95-99; 103; 105; 111; 113; 116; 119; 122;
124; 126-127; 132; 134. 9,9; 11-12; 24; 46-
49; 71; 76-77; 80-83; 87-88; 94; 96; 98-101;
104; 119; 124; 126; 129; 132; 145-149; 153;
155; 169; 177-178; 180; 212. 10,1-2; 5-6; 8-

10; 15; 17; 19–21; 24; 28; 32–34; 36; 38–40; 51; 57–58; 60; 63; 65; 67; 72; 76; 78. 10a,1. 11,1. 12,1; 6; 17; 27; 30; 33; 42. 13,14–16; 19; 24. 14,6; 8; 12–13; 16; 18–19; 23–25; 27; 29–30; 35; 37; 41. 15,10–11; 14–18; 24–27; *28.* 17,5; 8; 10–11; 16; 19; 23; 25–28; 35; 37–38; 43; 51; 53; 56; 65. 19,6; 11–13; 15; 18–19; 21–22; 32. 20,5; 7; 9–10; 14; 23–24; 26–29; 32–34; 36. 21,4; 7; 14; 16–17; 19; 21; 24; 27; 29–30; 32–33. 22,1–4; 10–11; 13; 16; 23. 23,1–2; 4–5; 7–8; 11–12; 16–17. 24,1–2; 6–7. 25,2–3; 5–6; 10–12; 21. 26,1–2; 5–6. 28,1–2. 29,3; 6; 8; 10. 30,3; 5. 31,1–2; 5–8; 10; 12; 17; 29; 34–35; 37–39; 43–44. 32,1–2; 4; 7. 33,1–2; 6. 34,1; 5; 8–9; 13–14; 17; 20. 35,4; 6–8; 10; 12; 14–15. 36,2; 6–7. 37,1–3. 38,1. 41,1. 44,1. 46,1. 48,1; 3. 49,3. 50,5–8; 12. 51,5–6; 8; 10. 52,3–4. 54,1. 56,2–4; 7. 57,3. 59,1. 61,1–2. 63,1. 66,24–25; 30; 33; 64; 67; 97.

　　　　　　SHR　1,7–8. 4,3,61. 4,21,7. 6,32.

　　　　　　SFK　1,1; 12; 16; 18; 23; 32–34; 37; 44–53; 55–56; 60; 75–76; 79; 82; 88; 90; 92; 95; 98; 100–101; 107; 110–112; 114; 118; 120–121. 2,6; 10; 13. 3,1; 3–5; 8–11; 13–14; 34; 46; 59; 72; 74; 98; 105. 4,1; 3; 6; 12–13; 18–22; 24; 26; 29–31; 36; 38; 40; 42. 5,1. 6,1; 11; 43; 57–58; 61–62; 68; 76–77; 80–83; 85; 90; 92; 110; 112; 129; 191–194; 209; 211; 213; 216–217; 219; 221–223; 260; 264; 271; 291; 299; 303–309; 311–319. 7,3–4; 6–7; 10; 13–16; 19–20; 23–24; 26–29; 40–42; 47; 49; 51; 54; 64; 67; 73; 146. 8,11; 31; 33–37; 39–40; 42; 46; 48; 55; 81. 9,2–3. 11,4. 12,1. 13,2; 4–6. 14,2–6; 10–11; 13–17; 23–25; 27; 32; 39; 42–43; 47–49; 54–55; 61–62; 65; 72–80; 82; 84–85; 90; 92–96; 102–107; 119–120; 122–124; 126; 128–132; 134; 137–139; 156; 164. 15,1. 16,10; 16; 20; 26; 30; 37; 40; 44. 18,1; 3–4. 19,1–2; 4; 7; 9; 14; 16–17; 21. 21,1; 3; 10–11; 16; 26; 28; 38–40; 42–43; 45–47; 53; 95. 23,3. 24,1. 25,1–7; 27; 32; 42; 46; 52; 54; 57; 61; 84–85; 95. 26,9–10; 12a–b; 14. 27,3; 5; 7; 9. 28,7. 29,1; 11. 30,1. 31,3; 6; 8–9; 20–21; 28; 35–36; 41–43; 45; 50; 53; 56; 60. 32,4; 14; 16; 19. 33,2–10; 13. 34,2–3; 6; 8–9; 12; 15. 35,1–2; 5–6. 36,2. 37,1; 5; 7. 38,4; 6. 39,6; 17. 40,3. 41,1–2; 7; 10–11. 42,2. 43,1; 3–5; 7. 44,1–4. 46,1; 3–5. 47,3, 44,1. 51,1. 52,1; 8–9. 53,3. 5–6. 54,1–2. 55,1. 57,1. 58,1. 62,4–5. 64,1; 3. 66,2–4; 6; 13; 16. 67,7. 68,1; 3; 5. 69,4. 70,1. 75,5. 76,4; 7; 23. 77,3.

　　　　　　SRY　1,2–5; 8–9; 11–12; 14. 2,1–2; 5–6. 3,1. 4,1. 5,1a; 2–3; 8; 10–11; 15; 21; 23; 26–27. 6,3. 7,1. 8,2–3; 6; 9–11; 17; 22; 29. 14,1. 15,2. 18,2. 19,2; 11–12; 15–16; 21; 24; 27; 29; 31–32; 36–37; 39; 44–48. 20,1; 4; 7. 22,5. 24,1. 25,2–3. 27,1–3.

28,1. 29,1. 30,2. 32,1–2. 33,1. 34,1. 36,3–5; 7.

　　　　　　SSX　1,1–2. 2,1a,c; 2–3; 8–9. 3,2; 4. 5,3. 6,2; 4. 8,3; 5–6; 8; 15. 8a,1. 9,2; 5–6; 8; 14–15; 18; 21–24; 26–27; 60; 65; 83–84; 86; 89; 92; 96; 111; 120–123; 125–126; 128; 130. 10,22; 27; 31; 48; 61; 65; 89; 96–97; 100; 102; 105; 111–113; 115; 118. 11,3; 6–10; 12; 14; 16–23; 25; 27; 30; 32; 35; 37; 44; 53–55; 59; 63; 66; 68; 74–76; 78–82; 85; 92–93; 95–96; 104–105; 113. 12,3–8; 14; 16; 27–28; 30–31; 33–34; 36–37; 40–42; 44; 47; 49; 55. 13,1–2; 5; 8–9; 11–13; 19–20; 22; 30; 33–34; 45; 48–50; 54; 56. 14,1–2.

　　　　　　WOR　19,14.

woodland, for　　SHR　2,1. 3b,3. 3c,2–5; 7. fattening　　　　　　3d,1–2. 3f,2. 4,1,36. 4,3,1; 15–16; 18–19; 53; 58–59; 63; 68. 4,4,11–12; 20–24. 4,5,1; 9; 12; 15. 4,7,4–5. 4,8,1; 5; 14–15. 4,9,1–2. 4,10,1. 4,11,1; 4; 11. 4,13,1. 4,14,3–4; 7–8; 11; 26. 4,15,2–3. 4,17,1. 4,18,1–2. 4,19,7; 12–13. 4,20,5; 7; 16. 4,21,1; 8. 4,22,2. 4,23,6; 9; 11–12. 4,24,4. 4,25,6–7. 4,26,3–4. 4,27,5; 11–12; 15; 24–25. 5,1–2. 6,2; 31.

woodland for fewer　ESS　9,5. 14,3–4. 20,6–8; pigs 1086 than TRE　　31. 22,5–6; 13. 23,2–3. 24,20; 45–46; 53. 25,15. 28,5. 30,21; 31; 45; 48. 32,21; 23. 33,7. 34,19. 35,3–4; 7. 38,1. 39,3. 40,1–4. 42,3. 43,1; 5. 44,1. 49,1. 53,1. 57,3. 58,1. 65,1. 90,5; 25; 50–51.

　　　　　　NFK　1,57; 87; 128; 139; 169; 192; 194; 212; 215; 219. 7,16–17. 8,82; 84; 87. 10,5; 10; 15; 38. 13,19. 14,18. 15,16–17; 24; 26. 19,18. 20,29. 21,19. 23,17. 33,2. 66,67.

　　　　　　SFK　1,1; 75–76. 3,10–11. 4,1; 13. 6,11; 43; 80–81; 83; 191–192; 219; 222–223. 7,64; 67. 14,32; 105–106. 16,20; 30. 18,4. 21,26; 28; 39. 25,52; 57; 61. 34,12. 35,5. 46,3. 51,1. 52,8. 53,3. 57,1. 62,5.

woodland for pigs if fruitful　　　KEN　2,10.
woodland for pigs if productive　　HEF　19,8.
woodland for pigs taken away　　　HRT　16,2.
woodland, pigs from without pasture dues　SRY　4,1.
Poor (vilis)　　　　NTH　1,1.
Render of oats from　BDF　24,5.
Ruined (mutilata)　　YKS　4N2.
Sheriff holding　　　WOR　1,1b; 3b.
Timber from, for salt houses　　　　　WOR　1,1a. 2,15.
Unproductive　　　　KEN　C1.
Useless　　　　　　HAM　23,45; 47; 54.
　　　　　　　　　YKS　5W8.

Value
same 1086 as TRE	WAR	16,19.
holding, of, with and without		
woodland	WOR	*18,3.*
when King not hunting there	NTH	56,7.
when stocked/ exploited (onerata)	NTH	1,6. 6,10a. 6a,27. 56,7.
	OXF	2,1. 3,1. 6,6. 7,3. 9,1.
	WAR	1,7. 6,1. 16,4; 16; 18; 42-44. 17,7. 42,1-2. 44,10.
Village lying in	HEF	10,46.
Villagers, of	LEC	1,3.
Virgate of	DEV	47,5.
Waste	ESS	6,2. 24,15. 42,1. 83,1.
Wild	SHR	4,3,34.

See also: Assart; Beast; Building; Claim; Customary due; Defence obligation; Enclosure; Fencing; Fire wood; Forest; Forester; Hen; Honey; Jurisdiction, full; Manor; Pig; Ram; Revenue; Right; Sheriff; Sheriffdom; Taken away; Timber; Wood.

WOOL (lana)
Payments from	OXF	1,7a.
Queen's	GLS	1,7.
	SRY	1,8.

WOOL – house
(lanina) – half (½)	LIN	2,25.

WORK (opus) – See Abbey; Abbot; Agricultural work; Bishop; Burgess; Church; King's use/work; Landholder; Man-at-arms; Meadow; Monk; Queen's work; Sheriff; Thane; Third/two thirds part; Use; Villager.

WORKING land – See Cultivation.

WRECK – See Ship.

WRIT
King's	BDF	12,1. 17,5. 56,5-6.
	BRK	1,38. 7,38. 41,6.
	DOR	19,14.
	HRT	1,9. 36,19.
	HUN	D29.
	NFK	9,42.
	SOM	1,35.
	SFK	6,79. 14,37.
	SRY	5,25-26. 8,30.
	WAR	3,4. 17,56.

	WOR	*2,72.*
	YKS	C1a; 2. CE33.
heard and/or seen	BRK	1,38.
	SFK	33,2.
	YKS	CE33.
not heard/and/or seen	BRK	1,38. 7,38. 41,6.
	CAM	22,6.
	GLS	1,60.
	HAM	35,2.
	LIN	CS13.
	NFK	10,28.
	SRY	6,5. 19,27. 23,1. 28,1.
	YKS	CE34.
giving Abbot full jurisdiction of land and men	SFK	18,4.
King's land comprised in	CAM	1,13.
land holder dispossessed without	BDF	17,1.
ordering possession of free men	SFK	16,34.
King Edward's found in Abbey ordering restoration of land	DOR	19,14.

Land
acquired by false writ	ESS	6,4.
held without	BDF	14,1.
	ESS	6,9.
	HUN	D1.
Not produced to prove ownership	ESS	5,6.
Not seen	HUN	D25.
	LIN	CS19.
	NFK	8,137. 9,104. 66,64.
	SFK	7,55. 31,53.
	SRY	25,2.
Not sent to Hundred to prove King's gift	ESS	1,28.

See also: Grant; Ownership; Peace; Possession; Recorded; Return; Seal; Title deeds.

WRONGFUL (injuste) – See Acquire; Alms; Annexation; Appropriation; Claim; Custom; Dispossession; Fair; Freeman; Land; Manor; Marriage; Mill; Profit; Service, King's; Sheriff; Taken away; Unjustly.

Y

YOKE (jugum)   KEN   D18; 24. M5; 19-
21. 1,3. 2,10; 14-16; 21; 25-26; 30; 38. 3,2;
17; 22. 5,10; 13; 15; 21; 35; 43-44; 50; 52-
54; 62; 65; 83; 90; 93-95; 100-101; 111-112;
117-118; 121; 128; 130; 132-133; 136-137;
140; 145; 148; 150; 152-154; 157; 167; 169;
172; 181; 184; 189; 195-198; 200; 203; 205;
207-208; 211-213; 216; 221; 223; 225. 6,1.
7,1-2; 4; 10; 16-17; 19; 23-24; 27-29. 9,1;
5; 7-9; 11; 14-15; 21; 23; 26; 28; 30; 32-34;
42; 44; 47; 53. 12,1. 13,1.

Word List

Abbas – Abbot
Abbatia – Abbey
Abbatissa – Abbess
Accipere – Acquire
Accipiter – Hawk
Accipitrarius – Falconer
Accommodare – Lend; Lease; Loan
Acra – Acre
Adcensare – Lease
Adjacentia – Appurtenances
Adjutorium – Aid
Adquietare – Meet/settle/clear
  obligations
Adulterium – Adultery
Advocare – Cite
Advocatus – Guarantor; Patron
Afrus – Draught animal
Ager – Field
Agnus – Lamb
Albus – Blanched; White (See
  Money)
Allectus – Herring
Alnetum – Alder grove
Alod – Freehold
Alodiarius – Freeholder
Ambra – Amber (See Salt)
Ancilla – Female slave
Anglicus – Englishman
Anguilla – Eel
Anima – Soul
Animal – Beast; Cattle
Animalia ociosa – Idle cattle
Annona – Corn
Annona grossa – Gross corn
Antecessor – Predecessor
Appendicium – Dependency
Appreciare – Assess
Aqua – Waterway
Arare – Plough

Arbalistarius – Gunner; Bowman;
  Crossbowman
Archidiaconus – Archdeacon
Archiepiscopus – Archbishop
Arcuarius – Archer
Area – Eyrie; Drying place (See
  Salt)
Arma – Arms
Arpenna – Arpent
Arsas et pensatas (libras) – Assayed
  and weighed (See Money)
Artifex – Engineer
Asinus – Ass
Asturco – Goshawk
Aucuparius – Fowler
Auferre – Take away
Augmentum – Increase
Aula – Hall
Aurifaber – Goldsmith
Aurifrisium – Gold
  embroidery/fringe
Avantwarde – Vanguard
Avena – Oats
Avera/Averagium – Cartage
  service
Avunculus – Uncle

Baco – Bacon pig
Balistarius – Gunner; Bowman;
  Crossbowman
Bancus – Stall (See Market)
Baro – Baron
Batsuein – Boatman
Bedellus – Beadle
Bellum – Combat
Bercarius – Shepherd
Berchenister – Valet
Berewica – Outlier
Bertune – Barton

283

Bestia – Beast of the chase
Bestia silvatica – Wild/Woodland beast
Blancus – Blanched; White (See Money)
Blatum – Corn
Bochelanda – Bookland
Bordarius – Smallholder
Bos – Ox
Boscus – Scrubland
Bovarius – Ploughman
Bovatus – Bovate
Brasium – Malt
Breve – Return; Writ
Broca – Water meadow; Marshland
Brocus – Water meadow; Marshland
Bruaria – Heathland
Bullio – Boiling (See Salt)
Burbium – Borough
Burgensis – Burgess
Burgherist – Borough right
Burgus – Borough
Burus – Boor
Buxum – Box wood
Buzecarlus – Boatman

Caballus – Packhorse
Caecus – Blind man
Calcarium – Spur
Calciamentum – Footwear
Calumpnia – Dispute; Claim
Cambitor – Money changer
Camera – Chamber
Camerarius – Chamberlain
Campus – Field
Cancellarius – Chancellor
Candidus – Blanched; White (See Money)
Canis – Dog
Canonicus – Canon
Capella – Chapel
Capellanus – Chaplain

Caper – Goat
Capicerius – Sacristan
Caprarius – Goatherd
Capreolus – Roe deer
Captio – Arrest
Caput hominis – Poll tax
Caput manerii – Head of the manor
Caretedis – Cartload
Carpentarius – Carpenter
Carricare – Load
Carta – Title deed; charter
Caruca – Plough
Carucata – Carucate
Casatus – Resident
Caseus – Cheese
Castellaria – Castlery
Castellatio – Castellany
Castellatus – Castlery
Castellum – Castle
Catallum – Chattel
Cathedra stercoris – Dung stool
Cementarius – Mason
Censor – Tributary
Census – Due; Tribute
Cervisarius – Ale man; Brewer
Cervisia – Ale
Chacepullus – Catchpole
Cherchesoch – Church jurisdiction
Christianitas – Spiritual jurisdiction
Cibum – Food
Cimiterium – Cemetery
Circet – Church dues; Church tax
Civis – Citizen
Civitas – City
Clausura – Fencing
Clericolus – Minor clerk
Clericus – Clerk; Cleric
Cocus – Cook
Cognatus – Kinsman
Colibertus – freedman
Comes – Earl; Count
Comitatus – County
Commendatio – Patronage; Commendation; Assignment

Communitas – Community
Commutatio – Exchange
Compotum, ad – By reckoning
  (See Money)
Concedere – Grant; Assent
Concelatus – Concealed
Concubina – Concubine
Conredium – Allowance
Consanguineus – Kinsman
Constabularius – Constable
Consuetudo – Customary due;
  Customary right; Custom
Consulatus – Earldom
Conuvium – Banquet
Conventio – Agreement
Coquina – Kitchen
Corium – Skin
Coscet – Cottager
Cotarius – cottager
Coterus – cottager
Cotmannus – cottage-man
Crementum – Increase
Crofta – Croft
Cubicularius – Chamberlain
Cultura – Field; Arable holding
Cultura terrae – Strip of
  ploughland
Cuneus – Die (for coining)
Curia – Court
Currus – Cart
Custodia – Bodyguard; Ward (of
  borough); Charge
Custos – Keeper
Custos ecclesiae – Church warden
Cuva – Barrel

Daia – Dairy maid
Dapifer – Steward
Debitum – Debt
Decanus – Dean
Decima – Tithe
Dedicatio – Consecration
Defendere se – Answer for
Defensa – Enclosure

Defensabilis – Fortified (See House)
Defensio – Protection
Defensor – Protector
Deliberare – Hand over (See
  Deliver)
Dena – Pig pasture
Dena silvae – Woodland pig
  pasture
Denarius – Penny
Deratiocinare – Adjudge; Prove
Diaconus – Deacon
Dicra – Dicker
Dies feriatus/festus – Holiday
Dimittere – Give up
Diratiocinare – Adjudge; Prove
Disaisire – Dispossess
Dispensator – Bursar
Divisio – Territory; Tract
Dominica aula – Hall of manor
Dominica firma – Household
  revenue
Dominium – Lordship
Dominus – Lord
Domus – House
Dos – Dower; Dowry
Draparius – Draper
Dreng – Dreng

Ecclesia – Church
Ecclesiola – Small church
Elemosina – Alms
Elemosinarius – Almsman
Emendatio – Fine
Episcopatus – Bishopric
Episcopus – Bishop
Equa – Mare
Equa indomita – Unbroken mare
Equa silvatica – Wild/Forest mare
Equarius – Groom
Eques – Horseman
Equus – Horse
Excambium – Exchange
Exclusa – Dam
Exercitus – Army; Campaign

Exitus – Income
Expeditio – Expedition (military)
Exsartum – Assart
Extraneus – Stranger; Foreign
Exul – Exile; Outlaw

Faber – Smith
Fabrica plumbi – Lead works
Falcare – Scythe
Falda – Fold
Famulus – Household member;
  Servant
Farina – Flour
Fascis – Bundle
Feltrum – Horse cloth
Femina – Woman
Fenum – Hay
Fera silvatica – Woodland beast
Ferdinga – Farthing; Quarter
Feria – Fair
Ferlingus – Furlong; Measure;
  Quarter
Ferraria – Smithy; Forge
Ferrarius – Smith
Ferrum – Iron; Horseshoe
Feudum – Holding
Fideiussor – Surety
Figulus – Potter
Filiolus – Godson
Finis – District (See Welsh);
  Boundary
Firma – Revenue
Firma dominica –
  Lordship/Household revenue
Fluctus aquae –' Tidal waterway
Focus – Fuel
Forensis – Outside (See Service)
Foresta – Forest
Forestarius – Forester
Forgia – Forge
Forinsecus – Outside (See Service)
Forisfactura – Forfeiture; Penalty
Foristel – Highway robbery
Forum – Fair; Market place

Fossa – Dyke
Fossa lapidum – Stone quarry
Fossarius – Ditcher; Dyke builder
Fossatum – Ditch
Francigenus – Frenchman
Francus homo – freeman
Fraxinetum – Ash wood
Frenum – Bridle
Frigesoca – Free jurisdiction (See
  Jurisdiction, free)
Frumentarius – Corn dealer
Frumentum – Corn; Wheat
Frustum terrae – Piece of land
Frutectum – Scrub
Fugitivus – Fugitive
Fumagium – Hearth tax
Furnus – Oven; Furnace
Furtum – Theft

Gablator – Tribute payer
Gablum – Tribute; Land tribute;
  Rent
Gallina – Chicken; Hen
Garba – Sheaf
Geldum – Tax
Gener – Son-in-law
Gersuma – Gift; Premium
Gihalla – Guildhall
Gilda – Tax; Guild
Gort – Weir
Granetarius – Granary keeper
Grangia – Grange
Grava – Copse
Gribrige – Breach of peace
Gurges – Weir

Haberi – Recorded
Haga – Site
Haia – Hedged enclosure
Haia maris – Sea weir
Handsoca – House breaking
Hangewitha – Collusion (with
  thief)
Hardwica – Dairy Farm; Ranch

Harieta – Heriot; Death duty
Harparius – Harper
Heda – Landing place; Hythe
Hega – Close
Heinfara – House breaking
Helvcwecha – Half-week
Herbagium – Grazing
Herciare – Harrow
Herdigelt – Hearth tax
Heres – Heir
Herietum – Heriot; Death duty
Hestha – Loaf
Hevewarda – Bodyguard
Hida – Hide
Hoccus – Hoccus (See Salt)
Homagium – Homage
Homicidium – Homicide
Hominatio – Homage
Honor – Honour
Hortulus – Little garden – (See
  Garden)
Hortus – Garden
Hospes – Settler
Hospitatio – Lodging
Hospitatus – Inhabited; Occupied
Hospitium – Lodging
Hostiarius – Usher
Hundredum – Hundred
Husecarle – Guard

Ignem, ad – Fired (See Money)
Inbreviatus – Recorded
Incaute – Injudiciously
Ingeniator – Artificer
Inhospitatus – Uninhabited;
  Unoccupied
Inimicitia – Enmity
Injuste – Wrongfully
Inland – Inland
Interceptus – Usurped;
  Appropriated
Interpres – Interpreter
Invadere – Seize; Annex
Invenire – Find (of payment)
Inwardus – Escort

Joculator – Jester
Judex – Judge
Judicamentum – Judicial enquiry
Judicium – Judgment; Ordeal; Trial
Jugum – Yoke
Juncus – Reed
Jussum – Command
Juste – By right

Karitas – Allowance

Lacus – Mere
Lagemanus – Lawman
Lampridula – Lamprey
Lana – Wool
Landgablum – Land tribute
Lanina – Wool house
Lardarius – Larderer
Latinarius – Interpreter
Latro – Thief
Latrocinium – Robbery
Lavator – Washer
Legatio – Despatch
Legatus – Commissioner; Officer;
  Messenger
Legrewita – Adultery
Lepus – Hare
Lestus – Lathe
Leta – Leet
Leuca – League
Leuga – Territory
Libera femina – free woman
Liber homo – free man
Libera terra – free land
Liberator – Deliverer
Libertas – Authority
Libra – Pound
Licentia – Permission
Lignum – Timber
Locare – Lease; Let
Locatio – Rent
Loricatus – Mail-clad man
Lorimarius – Lorimer
Loripes – Cripple

Lucrum – Profit
Lucus – Wood

Macellum – Meat market (See Market)
Machinator – Engineer
Mancipius – Pledge
Mancus – Cripple
Maneriolum – Small manor
Manerium – Manor
Mansio – Residence; Dwelling; Place
Mansio muralis – Wall dwelling
Mansio terrae – Measure (piece) of land
Mansura – Dwelling
Mara – Mere
Marca – Mark
Maresc – Marsh
Marescal – Marshal
Mariscus – Marsh
Maritagium – Marriage portion
Marsum – Porpoise
Massa – Lump
Masura – Plot; Dwelling
Masura terrae – Measure (piece) of land
Matricularius – Registrar
Medarius – Mead keeper
Medicus – Doctor
Medietas – Sub-holding (See Holding)
Mel – Honey
Mellitarius – Beekeeper
Membrum – Member
Mensa, terra in – Board land
Mensura – Measure (See Salt)
Mercator – Merchant
Mercatum – Market
Mercedes – Wages; Produce
Mercennarius – Hired man
Messis – Harvest
Messor – Harvester
Meta – Boundary

Metere – Reap
Miles – Man-at-arms; Soldier
Miles probatus – Proven man-at-arms
Mille – Mile
Mineria – Mine
Minister – Officer
Ministerium – Administration
Minuta – Farthing
Misericordia – Mercy
Missaticus – Messenger
Mitta – Measure (See Salt)
Mittere – Dispose
Mittere extra – Put outside
Modium – Measure; Peck
Molaria – Millstone Quarry (See Quarry)
Molendinus – Mill
Monachus – Monk
Monasterium – Monastery
Moneta – Mint
Monetarius – Moneyer
Monialis – Nun
Monitor – Summoner
Mora – Moor
Mulier – Wife; Woman
Multo – Wether
Mutatio – Exchange

Nauta – Sailor
Navis – Ship
Nemus – Wood
Nemusculus – Underwood
Nepos – Nephew
Neptis – Niece
Noverca – Stepmother
Numerum, ad – Face value (See Money)
Nummus – Penny
Nuncius – Emissary
Nutrire – Kennelling (of dogs)

Obolus – Halfpenny
Obsidium – Siege

Occupare – Appropriate
Occupatum – Premises
Ollaria – Pottery
Oneratus – Stocked; Exploited
Opus – Work; Use
Ora – Ora
Ordeum – Barley
Ortus – Garden
Ovile – Sheepfold

Paisso – Fodder
Palefridus – Riding horse
Panifex – Baker
Panis – Loaf
Pannus – Cloth
Paragio, in – Jointly
Parcus – Park
Parens – Family; Relative
Pares – Peers; Co-heirs
Parmentarius – Robe maker
Parochia – Parish
Parochianus – Parishioner
Particula terrae – Parcel of land
Partitio – Division
Pascua – Pasture land
Pasnagium – Pasturage; Pig
  pasturage; Pigs from pasturage;
  Pasture dues
Passagium aquae – Ferry
Pasticius – Entertainment
Pastura – Pasture
Patria – Country; District
Pax – Peace
Pecunia – Livestock; Stock
Pensa – Wey (of cheese)
Pertica – Perch
Pes – Foot (measurement)
Pincerna – Butler
Piscaria – Fishery
Piscator – Fisherman
Piscina – Fishpond; Fishery
Pistor – Baker
Pistrinum – Bake house
Placitare – Enter/undertake plea

Placitum – Plea; Assembly; Suit
Planum – Open land
Plaustratum – Wagon load
Plumba – Bloom (See Iron)
Plumbaria – Lead Mine
Plumbus – Lead vat
Pomerium – Orchard
Porcarius – Pigman
Porcus – Pig
Port – Town
Porta – Town
Portarius – Porter
Portus – Harbour; Market
Potaria – Pottery
Potarius – Potter
Potestas – Authority
Pratum – Meadow
Prebenda – Prebend
Prebendaria – Almswoman
Prebendarius – Prebendary;
  Purveyor
Preceptum – Command
Prefectus – Reeve
Preoccupare – Misappropriate
Prepositus – Reeve
Presbiter – Priest
Presentatio – Presentation
Prestare – Lease
Proficuum – Profit
Protector – Protector
Psalterium – Psalms
Puella – Girl
Pugna – Combat
Pullus – Foal
Puteus – Pit (See Salt)

Quadrans – Farthing
Quadraria – Quarry
Quarentina – Furlong
Quercus – Oak
Querela – Suit; Plea
Quietus – Exempt

Radchenistre – Riding man
Radman – Rider

Raptum – Rape
Rapum – Rape (administrative unit)
Recedere – Withdraw
Recipere – Acquire
Reclamare – Claim
Rectum – Right
Redditus – Payment; Return
Redrewarde – Rearguard
Regio – Realm
Regnum – Throne
Relevamentum – Relief
Relevatio – Relief; Death duty
Relevium – Relief
Relinquere – Relinquish
Requisitio – Petition
Res – Concerns
Respectus – Postponement
Responsus – Return
Rete – Fishing net
Revelach – Robbery
Reveland – Reeveland
Revocare – Cite; Appeal
Rispalia – Brushwood
Runcetum – Bramble thicket
Runcinus – Cob
Rusca – Beehive; Vessel (See Butter)
Rusticus – Countryman

Saca et soca – Full jurisdiction (See Jurisdiction, full)
Sagena – Fishing net
Saisire – Possess
Saisitor – Installer
Sal – Salt
Salictum – Willow bed
Salina – Salt house
Salinarius – Salt worker/boiler
Salmo – Salmon
Sapina – Fir wood
Sartor – Tailor
Scangium – Exchange
Scira – Shire
Scotum – Levy

Scotum de capite – Poll tax
Scriba – Scribe
Scutularius – Scullion
Scyra – Shire
Secare – Reap; Mow
Sedes – Site
Sella – Saddle
Sepes – Enclosure; Fence
Sepultura – Burial fees/rights
Servare – Have charge/custody of; Look after
Serviens – Servant
Servitium – Service
Sextarium – Sester
Sigillum – Seal
Siligo – Rye
Silva – Woodland; Wood
Silva minuta – Wood; Underwood
Silva modica – Small/little wood; Brushwood
Silva parva – Small/little wood
Silva pastilis – Woodland pasture
Silvula – Small/little wood
Soca – Jurisdiction
Soccus – Ploughshare
Sochemanna femina – Freewoman
Socius – Companion; Joint tenant; Associate
Socmannus – Freeman
Soldarius – Mercenary; Soldier
Solidarius – Shilling
Solidata – Wages
Solinus – Sulung
Sorus – Unmewed (See Hawk)
Spinetum – Spinney
Sprevarius – Sparrowhawk
Stabilitio venationis – Game beating
Stabilitura – Stag beat
Stagnum – Pool
Stalrus – Constable
Stica – Stick (See Eels)
Stiremannus – Steersman
Strande – Shore

Submittere se – Seek protection
Suburbanus – Man of suburb (See Suburb)
Suburbium – Borough town; Small town
Sudis – Pigsty
Summa – Packload; Load
Summagium – Cartage service
Summarius – Packhorse
Super – Despite
Superfactum – Encroachment
Sutor – Cobbler

Tabula – Sheet (See Lead)
Tailla – Exaction
Tainlanda – Thaneland
Tainus – Thane
Taurus – Bull
Terminus – Time limit (See Sheriff)
Terra – Land; Estate
Testamentum – Will
Theloneum – Toll
Thesaurarius – Treasurer
Thesaurus – Treasury
Thol et theim – Market rights (See Market)
Tofta – Plot
Torvelande – Turf land
Trabs – Thrave
Tracta – Drag net
Treding – Riding
Treuua – Truce
Trusellus – Bale
Tuitio – Protection
Tutor – Protector

Uncia – Ounce
Ursus – Bear
Utlagus – Outlaw
Utsoca – Outlying jurisdiction (See Jurisdiction, outlying)
Uxor – Wife

Vacarius – Cowman
Vacca – Cow

Vaccaria – Cow pasturage; Dairy
Vacuus – Empty (See Dwelling)
Vadimonium – Pledge
Vas – Beehive; Vessel (domestic)
Vasculum – Measure (See Corn)
Vastus – Waste; Derelict; Destroyed; Unoccupied
Vastare – Oppress
Vavassorius – Vavassor
Vellus – Fleece
Venatio – Hunting
Venator – Hunter; Huntsman
Vertere – Turn
Vestitus – Clothing
Vetula – Old woman
Vicecomes – Sheriff
Vicecomitatus – Sheriffdom
Victus – Supplies
Vicus aquae – Waterfront
Vidua – Widow
Vigilator – Watchman
Villa – Village; Town
Villanus – Villager
Vinitor – Vine dresser
Violentia – Violation
Virga – Rod
Virgata – Virgate; Rod; Rood
Virgultum – Orchard
Vitulus – Calf
Vivarium – Pond; Fishpond
Vocare – Cite
Voluntas – Will; Consent
Vomer – Ploughshare

Walensis – Welshman
Wara – Obligations; Defence obligations
Warda – Custody
Warenna – Warren
Warlanda – Warland
Warnode – Warnode
Warpenna – Guard penny
Wastum – Wasteland
Wica – Dairy; Dairy Farm

CONCORDANCE OF SYSTEMS OF REFERENCE TO THE TWO VOLUMES OF DOMESDAY BOOK

This concordance serves two main purposes. Firstly, to enable readers of the Phillimore Edition of Domesday Book, who are consulting the extensive literature on Domesday, to narrow down the folio references usually quoted to the corresponding Phillimore reference quoted in this Index. It will also enable those readers to follow up any related entries which the Index reveals.

Secondly, it will enable those readers who are using this Index as a guide to their researches in the folios of the Farley or Facsimile Editions, or who are using the Victoria County History translations, to trace references in the Index and to find other folios in which related references may be found.

I. The various systems

The manuscript of the larger volume (here referred to as DB) is divided into numbered chapters, and the chapters into sections, usually marked by large initials and red ink. Farley did not number the sections and later historians, using his edition, have referred to the text of DB by folio numbers, which cannot be closer than an entire page or column. Moreover, several different ways of referring to the same column have been devised. In 1816 Ellis used three separate systems in his indices: (i) on pages i–cvii, 435–518, 537–570; (ii) on pages 1–144; (iii) on pages 145–433 and 519–535. Other systems have since come into use, notably that used by Vinogradoff, here followed. The present edition numbers the sections, the normal practicable form of close reference; but since all discussion of DB for two hundred years has been obliged to refer to folio or column, a comparative table will help to locate references given. The five columns below give Vinogradoff's notation, Ellis's three systems, and that used by Weldon Finn and others. Maitland, Stenton, Darby and others have usually followed Ellis (i).

Vinogradoff	Ellis (i)	Ellis (ii)	Ellis (iii)	Finn
152a	152	152a	152	152ai
152b	152	152a	152.2	152a2
152c	152b	152b	152b	152bi
152d	152b	152b	152b2	152b2

The manuscript of Little Domesday Book (here referred to as LDB) has one column per page but is again divided into numbered chapters and the chapters into sections, usually distinguished by paragraph-marks. Modern users of LDB have referred to its text by folio number, e.g. 152(a) 15 Section III, p. 00.

II. Key to the relation between Vinogradoff's notation of the folios and columns of the MS text of DB and the numbered chapters and sections of the Phillimore edition

KENT (KEN)

1a	D1	- D10
b	D11	- D24
c	D25	- M10
d	M11	- M24
2a	C1	- R1
b	P1	- Landholders
c	1,1	- 1,3
d	1,3	- 1,4
3a	2,1	- 2,7
b	2,7	- 2,11
c	2,12	- 2,16
d	2,16	- 2,22
4a	2,22	- 2,27
b	2,28	- 2,35
c	2,36	- 2,43
d	3,1	- 3,7
5a	3,7	- 3,15
b	3,16	- 3,23
c	4,1	- 4,9
d	4,10	- 4,16
6a	5,1	- 5,8
b	5,9	- 5,18
c	5,18	- 5,25
d	5,25	- 5,34
7a	5,34	- 5,43
b	5,43	- 5,51
c	5,52	- 5,59
d	5,59	- 5,70
8a	5,70	- 5,78
b	5,79	- 5,88
c	5,88	- 5,95
d	5,95	- 5,104
9a	5,104	- 5,115
b	5,115	- 5,124
c	5,124	- 5,128
d	5,129	- 5,138
10a	5,139	- 5,146
b	5,147	- 5,156
c	5,157	- 5,166
d	5,167	- 5,178
11a	5,178	- 5,192
b	5,192	- 5,203
c	5,204	- 5,217
d	5,218	- 6,1
12a	7,1	- 7,8
b	7,8	- 7,17

c	7,18	- 7,23
d	7,23	- 8,1
13a	9,1	- 9,12
b	9,12	- 9,23
c	9,24	- 9,35
d	9,36	- 9,48
14a	9,48	- 10,2
b	11,1	- 12,4
c	13,1	
d	blank	
15a-d	blank	

SUSSEX (SSX)

16a	Landholders	
b	1,1	- 2,1e
c	2,1f	- 2,8
d	2,8	- 3,4
17a	3,4	- 4,1
b	5,1	- 6,1
c	6,1	- 7,2
d	8,1	- 8a,1
18a	9,1	- 9,6
b	9,7	- 9,14
c	9,14	- 9,19
d	9,20	- 9,35
19a	9,35	- 9,55
b	9,56	- 9,74
c	9,75	- 9,91
d	9,91	- 9,109
20a	9,109	- 9,123
b	9,123	- 9,131
c	10,1	- 10,4
d	10,4	- 10,18
21a	10,19	- 10,28
b	10,29	- 10,38
c	10,39	- 10,51
d	10,52	- 10,65
22a	10,65	- 10,80
b	10,80	- 10,93
c	10,93	- 10,105
d	10,106	- 10,118
23a	11,1	- 11,5
b	11,6	- 11,12
c	11,13	- 11,21
d	11,21	- 11,30
24a	11,30	- 11,38
b	11,38	- 11,49

c	11,49	- 11,60
d	11,61	- 11,71
25a	11,71	- 11,81
b	11,82	- 11,92
c	11,93	- 11,105
d	11,106	- 11, 116
26a	12,1	- 12,4
b	12,4	- 12,9
c	12,9	- 12,18
d	12,18	- 12,29
27a	12,29	- 12,37
b	12,37	- 12,44
c	12,44	- 12,53
d	12,54	- 12,56
28a	13,1	- 13,9
b	13,9	- 13,17
c	13,18	- 13,28
d	13,28	- 13,38
29a	13,38	- 13,46
b	13,46	- 13,57
c	14,1	- 14,2
d	blank	

SURREY (SRY)

30a	Landholders	- 1,2
b	1,2	- 1,7
c	1,8	- 1,13
d	1,13	- 2,3
31a	2,3	- 4,1
b	4,1	- 5,3
c	5,3	- 5,11
d	5,11	- 5,22
32a	5,22	- 5,30
b	6,1	- 7,1
c	7,1	- 8,11
d	8,12	- 8,22
33a,b	8,23	- 8,27
c,d	blank	
34a	8,28	- 14,1. 8,22
b	14,1	- 18,1
c	18,2	- 19,4
d	19,4	- 19,15
35a	19,15	- 19,24
b	19,24	- 19,34
c	19,35	- 19,43
d	19,44	- 21,3
36a	21,3	- 22,4. 23,1
b	24,1	- 27,3. 22,5
c	28,1	- 32,2
d	33,1	- 36,10

HAMPSHIRE (HAM)

37a-c	blank	
d	Landholders	
38a	1,1	- 1,8
b	1,8	- 1,16
c	1,17	- 1,21
d	1,22	- 1,28
39a	1,28	- 1,37
b	1,37	- 1,45
c	1,45	- 1W7
d	1,W7	- 1,W20
40a	1,W20	- 2,5
b	2,5	- 2,10
c	2,11	- 2,17
d	2,17	- 2,25
41a	3,1	- 3,5
b	3,5	- 3,8
c	3,8	- 3,14
d	3,14	- 3,24
42ab	4,1. 6,13	- 6,15
cd	6,16	- 6,17
43a	3,24	- 3,27. 5,1-6,5
b	6,5	- 6,12. 7,1
c	8,1	- 13,1
d	13,1	- 15,2
44a	15,2	- 16,7
b	17,1	- 18,3
c	19,1	- 21,5
d	21,6	- 23,3
45a	23,4	- 23,15
b	23,15	- 23,23
c	23,23	- 23,35
d	23,35	- 23,46
46a	23,46	- 23,55
b	23,56	- 23,67
c	23,68	- 28,2
d	28,3	- 29,6
47a	29,6	- 29,16
b	30,1	- 34,1
c	35,1	- 35,9
d	36,1	- 39,5
48a	40,1	- 43,6
b	44,1	- 45,5
c	45,6	- 50,2
d	50,2	- 55,2
49a	55,2	- 60,2
b	61,1	- 67,1
c	68,1	- 68,11
d	69,1	- 69,11
50a	69,12	- 69,22
b	69,23	- 69,33

76a,b	1,31	
c,d	blank	
77a	2,6	- 3,9
b	3,9	- 5,2
c	6,1	- 8,6
d	9,1	- 11,5
78a	11,6	- 12,1
b	12,2	- 13,1
c	13,2	- 18,2
d	19,1	- 19,14
79a	20,1	- 25,1
b	26,1	- 26,21
c	26,22	- 26,40
d	26,41	- 26,61
80a	26,61	- 27,6
b	27,6	- 29,1
c	30,1	- 33,4
d	33,4	- 34,13
81a,b	42,1	
c,d	36,4	- 36,11
82a	34,13	- 36,3. 37,1-7
b	37,8	- 40,7
c	40,8	- 41,5. 43,1- 47,4
d	47,5	- 49,6
83a	49,7	- 50,4. 52,1-2
b	52,2	- 54,14. 51,1
c	55,1	- 55,17
d	55,18	- 55,36
84a	55,37	- 56,9
b	56,10	- 56,32
c	56,32	- 56,55
d	56,56	- 57,8
85a	57,9	- 58,3
b-d	blank	

SOMERSET (SOM)

86a	Landholders	
b	1,1	- 1,5
c	1,6	- 1,10
d	1,11	- 1,20
87a	1,20	- 1,28
b	1,28	- 1,35
c	2,1	- 2,10
d	2,11	- 5,5
88a	5,6	- 5,18
b	5,18	- 5,32
c	5,33	- 5,43
d	5,43	- 5,55
89a	5,56	- 5,70
b	6,1	- 6,8

c	6,9	- 6,17
d	6,18	- 7,15
90a	8,1	- 8,10
b	8,11	- 8,20
c	8,20	- 8,26
d	8,27	- 8,36
91a	8,37	- 10,1
b	10,2	- 16,2
c	16,3	- 17,6
d	17,7	- 19,9
92a	19,10	- 19,24. 19.25
b	19,24	- 19,39
c	19,39	- 19,54. 19,70
d	19,54	- 19,69
93a	19,71	- 20,3
b	21,1	- 21,17
c	21,18	- 21,35
d	21,36	- 21,54
94a	21,54	- 21,75
b	21,76	- 21,94
c	21,95	- 22,13
d	22,13	- 22,28
95a	23,1	- 24,15
b	24,16	- 24,29
c	24,29	- 25,7
d	25,7	- 25,20
96a	25,21	- 25,37
b	25,38	- 25,53
c	25,54	- 27,1
d	27,2	- 31,5
97a	32,1	- 35,2
b	35,3	- 35,18
c	35,19	- 36,7
d	36,7	- 37,5
98a	37,6	- 39,3
b	40,1	- 44,3
c	45,1-2	- 46,1-16
d	46,17	- 47,7
99a	47,7	- 47,23
b	47,24	- 47,25. 45,3-18
c,d	blank	

DEVON (DEV)

100a	C	- Landholders
b	1,1	- 1,11
c	1,11	- 1,23
d	1,23	- 1,35
101a	1,35	- 1,47
b	1,48	- 1,62
c	1,62	- 1,72
d	2,1	- 2,13

102a	2,14	- 3,4
b	3,5	- 3,20
c	3,21	- 3,37
d	3,38	- 3,59
103a	3,59	- 3,76
b	3,77	- 3,94
c	3,95	- 5,5
d	5,5	- 6,4
104a	6,4	- 9,1
b	9,2	- 13a,3
c	14,1	- 15,14
d	15,15	- 15,31
105a	15,32	- 15,44
b	15,44	- 15,58
c	15,59	- 15,74
d	15,75	- 16,7
106a	16,8	- 16,22
b	16,23	- 16,38
c	16,39	- 16,56
d	16,56	- 16,73
107a	16,74	- 16,88
b	16,89	- 16,104
c	16,105	- 16,120
d	16,120	- 16,135
108a	16,136	- 16,149
b	16,150	- 16,166
c	16,167	- 17,5
d	17,5	- 17,17
109a	17,18	- 17,34
b	17,35	- 17,53
c	17,53	- 17,70
d	17,71	- 17,89
110a	17,89	- 17,105
b	17,105	- 19,12
c	19,13	- 19,28
d	19,29	- 19,44
111a	19,44	- 20,14
b	20,14	- 21,11
c	21,12	- 23,2
d	23,2	- 23,15
112a	23,16	- 24,2
b	24,3	- 24,18
c	24,19	- 25,3
d	25,3	- 25,20
113a	25,21	- 28,4
b	28,4	- 29,2
c	29,2	- 31,4
d	32,1	- 34,1
114a	34,2	- 34,17
b	34,18	- 34,32
c	34,33	- 34,49
d	34,49	- 35,5

115a	35,5	- 35,19
b	35,20	- 36,5
c	36,6	- 36,21
d	36,22	- 39,3
116a	39,4	- 39,17
b	39,18	- 41,2
c	42,1	- 42,14
d	42,15	- 43,3
117a	43,3	- 47,5
b	47,5	- 48,8
c	48,8	- 51,2
d	51,2	- 51,16
118a	52,1	- 52,19
b	52,20	- 52,36
c	52,37	- 52,53
d	blank	
119a-d	blank	

CORNWALL (CON)

120a	Landholders	- 1,3
b	1,4	- 1,14
c	1,14	- 2,6
d	2,7	- 2,15. 4,1-6
121a	4,7	- 4,22
b	4,22	- 4,29. 3,1-8
c	3,4	- 3,7. 5,1,1-7
d	5,1,8,	- 5,1,22
122a	5,2,1	- 5,2,18
b	5,2,19	- 5,3,4
c	5,3,5	- 5,3,21
d	5,3,21	- 5,4,10
123a	5,4,11	- 5,4,18. 5,5,1-8
b	5,5,8	- 5,6,2. 5,4,19-20
c	5,6,2	- 5,6,6. 5,6,8- 5,7,8
d	5,7,9	- 5,8,10. 5,6,7
124a	5,9,1	- 5,12,3
b	5,13,1	- 5,14,4
c	5,14,5	- 5,21,1
d	5,21,1	- 5,24,12
125a	5,24,13	- 5,25,5
b	5,25,5	- 7,1
c,d	blank	

MIDDLESEX (MDX)

126a-c	blank	
d	Landholders	
127a	1,1	- 2,2
b	2,3	- 3,4
c	3,4	- 3,12
d	3,13	- 3,19

CONCORDANCE

```

| 128a | 3,20 | - 3,29 |
|---|---|---|
| b | 3,29 | - 4,5 |
| c | 4,5 | - 4,10 |
| d | 4,10 | - 6,1 |
| 129a | 7,1 | - 7,7 |
| b | 7,8 | - 8.5 |
| c | 8,6 | - 9,6 |
| d | 9,6 | - 10,2 |
| 130a | 10,2 | - 12,1 |
| b | 12,1 | - 15,2 |
| c | 15,2 | - 20,1 |
| d | 20,1 | - 25,3 |
| 131a-d | blank | |

**HERTFORDSHIRE (HRT)**

| 132a | B1 | - B11 |
|---|---|---|
| b | Landholders | - 1,2 |
| c | 1,3 | - 1,7 |
| d | 1,7 | - 1,11 |
| 133a | 1,11 | - 1,18 |
| b | 1,18 | - 3,1 |
| c | 4,1 | - 4,8 |
| d | 4,8 | - 4,17 |
| 134a | 4,17 | - 4,25 |
| b | 5,1 | - 5,10 |
| c | 5,10 | - 5,18 |
| d | 5,18 | - 6,1 |
| 135a | 7,1 | - 8,3 |
| b | 9,1 | - 9,10 |
| c | 9,10 | - 10,6 |
| d | 10,6 | - 10,13 |
| 136a | 10,14 | - 10,20 |
| b | 11,1 | - 13,5 |
| c | 14,1 | - 15,5 |
| d | 15,5 | - 16,1 |
| 137a | 16,1 | - 16,11 |
| b | 16,12 | - 17,8 |
| c | 17,8 | - 18,1 |
| d | 19,1 | - 20,7 |
| 138a | 20,7 | - 22,1 |
| b | 22,1 | - 24,1 |
| c | 24,2 | - 26,1 |
| d | 26,1 | - 28,7 |
| 139a | 28,8 | - 31,6 |
| b | 31,6 | - 33,1 |
| c | 33,1 | - 33,8 |
| d | 33,9 | - 33,17 |
| 140a | 33,17 | - 34,5 |
| b | 34,6 | - 34,13 |
| c | 34,13 | - 34,21 |
| d | 34,22 | - 36,1 |

| 141a | 36,2 | - 36,11 |
|---|---|---|
| b | 36,11 | - 36,19 |
| c | 39,19 | - 37,9 |
| d | 37,10 | - 37,19 |
| 142a | 37,19 | - 41,1 |
| b | 41,1 | - 42,11 |
| c | 42,11 | - 42,15 |
| d | 42a,1 | - 44,1 |

**BUCKINGHAMSHIRE (BKM)**

| 143a | B1 | - B13 |
|---|---|---|
| b | Landholders | - 1,1 |
| c | 1,2 | - 1,7 |
| d | 2,1 | - 3a,1 |
| 144a | 3a,2 | - 4,5 |
| b | 4,5 | - 4,15 |
| c | 4,16 | - 4,26 |
| d | 4,27 | - 4,35 |
| 145a | 4,36 | - 4,43 |
| b | 5,1 | - 5,10 |
| c | 5,10 | - 5,19 |
| d | 5,20 | - 8,2 |
| 146a | 8,3 | - 12,5 |
| b | 12,6 | - 12,18 |
| c | 12,19 | - 12,31 |
| d | 12,31 | - 13,2 |
| 147a | 13,3 | - 14,9 |
| b | 14,9 | - 14,20 |
| c | 14,20 | - 14,30 |
| d | 14,30 | - 14,39 |
| 148a | 14,40 | - 14,49 |
| b | 15,1 | - 16,10 |
| c | 17,1 | - 17,10 |
| d | 17,11 | - 17,22 |
| 149a | 17,22 | - 17,31 |
| b | 18,1 | - 19,3 |
| c | 19,4 | - 21,4 |
| d | 21,4 | - 23,3 |
| 150a | 23,3 | - 23,14 |
| b | 23,14 | - 23,28 |
| c | 23,28 | - 25,2 |
| d | 25,3 | - 26,11 |
| 151a | 26,11 | - 29,3 |
| b | 29,4 | - 35,3 |
| c | 36,1 | - 40,1 |
| d | 40,1 | - 43,2 |
| 152a | 43,2 | - 43,11 |
| b | 43,11 | - 47,1 |
| c | 47,1 | - 52,1 |
| d | 52,2 | - 53,10 |
```

153a	54,1	- 57,6
b	57,7	- 57,18
c,d	blank	

OXFORDSHIRE (OXF)

154a	B1	- B9
b	B10	- Landholders
c	1,1	- 1,6
d	1,6	- 1,13
155a	2,1	- 6,1c
b	6,1c	- 6,9
c	6,10	- 7,2
d	7,2	- 7,17
156a	7,17	- 7,33
b	7,33	- 7,49
c	7,50	- 7,65
d	8,1	- 9,10
157a	10,1	- 14,6
b	15,1	- 17,8
c	18,1	- 21,1
d	22,1	- 26,1
158a	27,1	- 28,3
b	28,4	- 28,17
c	28,18	- 29,2
d	29,2	- 29,15
159a	29,16	- 33,2
b	34,1	- 35,10
c	35,10	- 35,26
d	35,26	- 39,3
cd	56,1	- 56,3
160a	39,3	- 45,3
b	46,1	- 55,1
c	55,1	- 55,2. 57,1- 58,14
d	58,15	- 58,34
cd	56,3	- 56,4
161a	58,35	- 59,13
b	59,14	- 59,29
c,d	blank	

GLOUCESTERSHIRE (GLS)

162a	G1	- G4. S. W1-4
b	W5	- W19
c	B1	- Landholders
d	1,1	- 1,10
163a	1,10	- 1,15
b	1,16	- 1,24
c	1,24	- 1,38
d	1,38	- 1,50
164a	1,51	- 1,59
b	1,59	- 1,67
c	2,1	- 2,10
d	2,10	- 3,5

165a	3,5	- 6,2
b	6,2	- 9,1
c	10,1	- 10,13. 11.14
d	10,14	- 12,3
166a	12,3	- 17,1
b	18,1	- 20,1
c	21,1	- 25,1. 27,1- 29,1
d	26,1	- 26,4. 30,1- 31,8
167a	31,9	- 33,1
b	34,1	- 35,2
c	36,1	- 38,5
d	39,1	- 39,15
168a	39,16	- 42,3
b	43,1	- 47,1
c	48,1	- 52,7
d	53,1	- 55,1
169a	56,1	- 60,3
b	60,4	- 63,4
c	64,1	- 67,5
d	67,5	- 68,11
170a	68,12	- 71,1
b	72,1	- 77,1
c	78,1	- 78,16
d	78,16	- 78,17
171a-d	blank	

WORCESTERSHIRE (WOR)

172a	C1	- Landholders
b	1,1a	- 1,3a
c	1,3b	- 2,1
d	2,2	- 2,15
173a	2,15	- 2,28
b	2,29	- 2,45
c	2,45	- 2,59
d	2,60	- 2,70
174a	2,71	- 2,80
b	2,81	- 7,1
c	8,1	- 8,9b
d	8,9c	- 8,14
175a	8,15	- 8,25
b	8,26a	- 9,4
c	9,4	- 10,4
d	10,5	- 10,17
176a	11,1	- 15,3
b	15,4	- 15,14
c	16,1	- 19,2
d	19,2	- 20,3
177a	20,3	- 23,1
b	23,2	- 23,14
c	24,1	- 26,8
d	26,9	- 27,1

178a	28,1	- X3
b-d	blank	

HEREFORDSHIRE (HEF)

179a	C1	- C15
b	A1	- Landholders
c	1,1	- 1,4
d	1,5	- 1,8
180a	1,8	- 1,10c
b	1,11	- 1,32
c	1,33	- 1,41
d	1.42	- 1,48
181a	1,49	- 1,61
b	1,61	- 1,75
c	2,1	- 2,11
d	2,12	- 2,21
182a	2,21	- 2,31
b	2,31	- 2,42
c	2,43	- 2,56
d	2,57	- 6,11
183a	7,1	- 7,9
b	8,1	- 8,8
c	8,9	- 9,10
d	9,10	- 9,19
184a	10,1	- 10,15
b	10,16	- 10,30
c	10,31	- 10,44
d	10,45	- 10,57
185a	10,57	- 10,70
a	10,71	- 13,2
c	14,1	- 15,3
d	15,4	- 17,2
186a	18,1	- 19,8
b	19,8	- 21,6
c	21,7	- 23,6
d	24,1	- 25,2
187a	25,3	- 29,1
b	29,1	- 29,20
c	30,1	- 36,3
d	blank	
188a-d	blank	

CAMBRIDGESHIRE (CAM)

189a	B1	- B14
b	Landholders	- 1,1
c	1,1	- 1,6
d	1,6	- 1,13
190a	1,14	- 1,23
b	2,1	- 3,3
c	3,3	- 5,2
d	5,3	- 5,11

191a	5,11	- 5,22
b	5,22	- 5,32
c	5,33	- 5,42
d	5,43	- 5,50
192a	5,50	- 5,58
b	5,58	- 6,3
c	7,1	- 7,8
d	7,8	- 9,2
193a	9,3	- 11,6
b	12,1	- 13,5
c	13,6	- 13,12
d	14,1	- 14,9
194a	14,9	- 14,19
b	14,19	- 14,27
c	14,28	- 14,38
d	14,39	- 14,48
195a	14,49	- 14,57
b	14,57	- 14,64
c	14,64	- 14,72
d	14,72	- 14,82
196a	15,1	- 17,1
b	17,2	- 18,3
c	18,3	- 19,3
d	19,4	- 21,5
197a	21,5	- 22,5
b	22,6	- 23,2
c	23,2	- 25,5
d	25,5	- 26,5
198a	26,6	- 26,17
b	26,17	- 26,24
c	26,24	- 26,33
d	26,34	- 26,42
199a	26,42	- 26,49
b	26,49	- 28,2
c	28,2	- 29,7
d	29,8	- 31,1
200a	31,1	- 31,7
b	32,1	- 32,8
c	32,8	- 32,16
d	32,17	- 32,23
201a	32,23	- 32,31
b	32,31	- 32,36
c	32,37	- 32,44
d	33,1	- 38,1
202a	38,1	- 40,1
b	41,1	- 41,12
c	41,13	- 44,2
d	blank	

HUNTINGDONSHIRE (HUN)

203a	B1	- B14
b	B15	- B21. Landholders

c	1,1	- 1,10
d	2,1	- 2,9
204a	3,1	- 5,2
b	6,1	- 6,7
c	6,7	- 6,16
d	6,16	- 6,26
205a	6,26	- 7,8
b	8,1	- 9,4
c	10,1	- 13,4
d	13,4	- 18,1
206a	19,1	- 19,11
b	19,12	- 19,23
c	19,23	- 19,32
d	20,1	- 20,7
207a	20,7	- 23,1
b	24,1	- 28,1
c	29,1	- 29,6
d	blank	
208a	D1	- D10
b	D11	- D26
c	D26	- D29
d	blank	

BEDFORDSHIRE (BDF)

209a	B	- Landholders
b	1,1	- 1,2b
c	1,3	- 2,3
d	2,3	- 3,3
210a	3,3	- 3,12
b	3,13	- 4,6
c	4,7	- 7,1
d	8,1	- 8,9
211a	9,1	- 14,1
b	15,1	- 16,2
c	16,2	- 16,9
d	17,1	- 18,1
212a	18,2	- 20,1
b	20,1	- 21,8
c	21,9	- 22,2
d	22,2	- 23,10
213a	23,10	- 23,18
b	23,18	- 23,27
c	23,27	- 23,40
d	23,40	- 23,52
214a	23,52	- 24,6
b	24,6	- 24,17
c	24,17	- 24,27
d	24,27	- 25,6
215a	25,6	- 25,14
b	25,14	- 30,1
c	30,1	- 32,5
d	32,6	- 32,16

216a	33,1	- 37,1
b	38,1	- 42,1
c	43,1	- 47,2
d	47,3	- 50,1
217a	51,1	- 53,4
b	53,4	- 53,14
c	53,15	- 53,28
d	53,29	- 54,3
218a	54,4	- 55,11
b	55,12	- 56,9
c	57,1	- 57,7
d	57,7	- 57,21

NORTHAMPTONSHIRE (NTH)

219a	B1	- B38
b	Landholders	- 1,3
c	1,4	- 1,13a
d	1,13a	- 1,20
220a	1,21	- 1,32
b	2,1	- 3,1
c	4,1	- 4,11
d	4,12	- 4,27
221a	4,28	- 5.3
b	5,4	- 6,10c
c	6,10c	- 6a,6
d	6a,7	- 6a,22
222a	6a,23	- 6a,34
b	7,1	- 9,6
c	9,6	- 12,4
d	13,1	- 17,5
223a	18,1	- 18,15
b	18,15	- 18,34
c	18,34	- 18,53
d	18,54	- 18,71
224a	18,72	- 18,89
b	18,90	- 19,1. 20,1- 21,6
ab	19,2	- 19,3
c	23,1	- 23,15. 24,1
d	23,16	- 23,19. 22,1-9
225a	25,1	- 26,9
b	26,9	- 30,9
c	30,10	- 34,1
d	35,1	- 35,7
226a	35,8	- 35,26
b	35,22	- 38,1
c	39,1	- 39,17
d	39,18	- 41,5
227a	41,6	- 43,5
b	43,5	- 45,5
c	45,5	- 47,2
d	48,1	- 48,17

228a	49,1	- 55,6
b	56,1	- 56,20a
c	56,20a	- 56,31
d	56,32	- 56,46
229a	56,46	- 56,64
b	56,65	- 60,5
c,d	blank	

LEICESTERSHIRE (LEC)

230a	C1	- C18
b	Landholders	- 1,3
c	1,3	- 1,7
d	1,7	- 3,1
231a	3,2	- 4,1
b	5,1	- 8,5
c	9,1	- 10,7
d	10,8	- 12,2
232a	13,1	- 13,15
b	13,16	- 13,29
c	13,30	- 13,46
d	13,47	- 13,63
233a	13,63	- 13,74
b	14,1	- 14,17
c	14,18	- 14,34
d	15,1	- 15,13
234a	15,14	- 16,9
b	17,1	- 17,20
c	17,21	- 18,2
d	18,2	- 19,14
235a	19,15	- 23,2
b	23,2	- 26,1
c	27,1	- 29,3
d	29,4	- 31,1
236a	32,1	- 39,2
b	40,1	- 40,19
c	40,19	- 40,37
d	40,38	- 42,10
237a	43,1	- 43,11
b	44,1	- 44,13
c,d	blank	

WARWICKSHIRE (WAR)

238a	B1	- Landholders
b	1,1	- 1,9
c	2,1	- 3,4
d	4,1	- 6,9
239a	6,10	- 10,1
b	11,1	- 13,1
c	14,1	- 15,6
d	16,1	- 16,14

240a	16,15	- 16,26
b	16,27	- 16,42
c	16,42	- 16,57
d	16,58	- 17,6
241a	17,7	- 17,22
b	17,23	- 17,44
c	17,45	- 17,59
d	17,60	- 17,70
242a	18,1	- 18,14
b	18,14	- 21,1
c	22,1	- 22,17
d	22,17	- 24,2
243a	25,1	- 28,5
b	28,6	- 29,1
c	29,2	- 31,7
d	31,7	- 36,2
244a	37,1	- 39,1
b	39,2	- 43,2
c	44,1	- 44,14. 45,1
d	44,15	- 44,16
245a-d	blank	

STAFFORDSHIRE (STS)

246a	B1	- Landholders
b	1,1	- 1,13
c	1,14	- 1,28
d	1,29	- 1,64
247a	2,1	- 2,16
b	2,16	- 2,22
c	3,1	- 5,2
d	6,1	- 7,18
248a	8,1	- 8,12
b	8,13	- 8,30
c	8,30	- 10,10
d	11,1	- 11,16
249a	11,17	- 11,33
b	11,34	- 11,49
c	11,50	- 11,65
d	11,66	- 12,14
250a	12,15	- 12,28
b	12,29	- 12,31
c	13,1	- 16,1
d	17,1	- 17,21. 16,2-3
251a-d	blank	

SHROPSHIRE (SHR)

252a	C1	- Landholders
b	1,1	- 3a,1
c	3b,1	- 3c,7
d	3c,8	- 3e,2

253a	3f,1	- 3h,1	
b	4,1,1	- 4,1,5	
c	4,1,6	- 4,1,15	
d	4,1,16	- 4,1,26	
254a	4,1,27	- 4,1,37	
b	4,2,1	- 4,3,11	
c	4,3,11	- 4,3,22	
d	4,3,23	- 4,3,36	
255a	4,3,37	- 4,3,53	
b	4,3,53	- 4,3,68	
c	4,3,69	- 4,4,12	
d	4,4,12	- 4,4,25	
256a	4,5,1	- 4,5,15	
b	4,6,1	- 4,8,2	
c	4,8,3	- 4,8,15	
d	4,8,16	- 4,11,4	
257a	4,11,5	- 4,12,1	
b	4,13,1	- 4,14,15	
c	4,14,16	- 4,16,2	
d	4,16,2	- 4,19,5	
258a	4,19,6	- 4,20,7	
b	4,20,8	- 4,20,24	
c	4,20,25	- 4,21,14	
d	4,21,15	- 4,23,8	
259a	4,23,9	- 4,25,2	
b	4,25,3	- 4,27,6	
c	4,27,7	- 4,27,26	
d	4,27,27	- 4,28,6	
260a	5,1	- 6,4	
b	6,5	- 6,19	
c	6,20	- 7,4	
d	7,4	- 9,2	
261a-d	blank		

CHESHIRE (CHS)

262a,b	blank		
c	C1	- C18	
d	C18	- C25	
263a	B1	- B13	
b	A1	- A19	
c	A20	- 1,8. 1,9	
d	1,8	- 1,25	
264a	1,26	- 1,36	
b	2,1	- 2,9	
c	2,10	- 2,26	
d	2,27	- 4,2	
265a	5,1	- 6,2	
b	7,1	- 8,12	
c	8,13	- 8,27	
d	8,28	- 8,42	

266a	8,43	- 9,16	
b	9,17	- 9,29	
c	10,1	- 13,4	
d	13,5	- 16,2	
267a	17,1	- 18,4	
b	18,5	- 21,1	
c	22,1	- 24,9	
d	25,1	- 26,12	
268a	27,1	- 27,4. S3,1-4	
b	S1,1	- S2,4	
c	blank		
d	FD1,1	- FD9,1	
269a	FT1,1	- FT2,8	
b	FT2,9	- FT3,7. G1-3	
c	R1,1	- R1,39	
d	R1,40	- R3,1	
270a	R4,1	- R6,5	
b	R7,1		
c,d	blank		
271a-d	blank		

DERBYSHIRE (DBY)

272a	Landholders		
b	1,1	- 1,12	
c	1,13	- 1,19	
d	1,19	- 1,29	
273a	1,29	- 1,38	
b	2,1	- 3,7	
c	4,1	- 5,5	
d	7,13		
274a	6,1	- 6,12	
b	6,13	- 6,25	
c	6,26	- 6,36	
d	6,37	- 6,48	
275a	6,49	- 6,58	
b	6,58	- 6,68	
c	6,69	- 6,82	
d	6,83	- 6,95	
276a	6,96	- 6,101	
b	7,1	- 7,12	
c	8,1	- 8,6	
d	9,1	- 9,6	
277a	10,1	- 10,10. 10,12	
b	10,10	- 10,11. 10,13-23	
c	10,24	- 11,5	
d	12,1	- 13,2	
278a	14,1	- 15,1	
b	16,1	- 16,8	
c	17,1	- 17,13	
d	17,14	- 17,23	
279a-d	blank		

280a	(Nottingham)	
b	B1	- B16
c	S1	- S6

NOTTINGHAMSHIRE (NTT)

280a	B1	- B20
b	(Derby)	
c	S1	- S6
d	Landholders (also for RUT)	
281a	1,1	- 1,13
b	1,14	- 1,31
c	1,32	- 1,50
d	1,51	- 1,66
282a,b	blank	
c	2,1	- 3,4
d	4,1	- 4,8
283a	5,1	- 5,6
b	5,7	- 5,19
c	blank	
d	6,1	- 6,11
284a	6,11	- 6,15
b	7,1	- 8,2
c	9,1	- 9,15. 9,21
d	9,15	- 9,20. 9,22-28
285a	9,29	- 9,40
b	9,40	- 9,53
c	9,54	- 9,65
d	9,66	- 9,76
286a	9,76	- 9,80. 9,82-93
b	9,94	- 9,106. 9,81
c	9,107	- 9,118
d	9,118	- 9,127
287a	9,128	- 9,132
b	10,1	- 10,15
c	10,15	- 10,28
d	10,29	- 10,46
288a	10,46	- 10,60
b	10,61	- 10,66
c	11,1	- 11,12. 11,13
d	11,12	- 11,25
289a	11,26	- 11,33
b	12,1	- 12,19
c	12,19	- 13,11
d	13,11	- 14,8
290a	15,1	- 15,10
b	16,1	- 16,12
c	17,1	- 17,12
d	17,13	- 17,18
291a	18,1	- 19,1
b	20,1	- 20,8
c	21,1	- 23,2
d	24,1	- 26,1

292a	27,1	- 29,2
b	blank	
c	30,1	- 30,13
d	30,14	- 30,31
293a	30,31	- 30,46
b	30,46	- 30,56

RUTLAND (RUT)

280d	Landholders (with NTT)	
293c	R1	- 12
d	R12	- 20
294a	R21	
b-d	blank	
295a-296d	blank	

YORKSHIRE (YKS)

297a-d	blank	
298a	C1a	- C10
b	C11	- C28
c	C28	- C37
d	C38	- Landholders
299a	1Y1	- 1Y3
b	1Y3	- 1Y7
c	1Y8	- 1Y13
d	1Y14	- 1Y18
300a	1Y18	- 1N20
b	1N21	- 1N61
c	1N62	- 1N94
d	1N95	- 1N132
301a	1N133	- 1E44
b	1E45	- 1W28
c	1W29	- 1W72
d	1W73	- 1L6
302a	1L7	- 1L8
b	2A1	- 2A4
c	2B1	- 2B5
d	2B6	- 2B14
303a	2B15	- 2N7
b	2N8	- 2N25
c	2N26	- 2W5
d	2W6	- 2W13
304a	2E1	- 2E14
b	2E15	- 2E41
c	3Y1	- 3Y7
d	3Y7	- 3Y18
305a	4N1	- 4E2
b	5N1	- 5N12
c	5N13	- 5N27
d	5N28	- 5N48

c	31E1	- 31W3
d	31W4	- 31N8
333a	31N8	- 31N10
b-d	blank	

334a-335d blank

(336a-372d Lincolnshire)

373a	CN1	- CE15
b	CE15	- CE27
c	CE28	- CE33. CW1-4
d	CW5	- CW24
374a	CW25	- CW39
b	CE34	- CE52. CW40-42
c,d	blank	

(375a-37d Lincolnshire)

379a	SN,Y	- SW,Sk. SW,BA1-3
b	SW,BA4	- SW,BA13. SW,Sf1-34
c	SW,Sf35	- Sf37. SW,O. SW,St. SW, Ag1-8
d	SW,Ag9	- SW,Ag16. SW,M. SW, An. SW,Bu1-5
380a	SW,Bu6	- SW,Bu49
b	SW,H1	- SW,Cr5
c	SN,L1	- SN,D4
d	SN,D5	- SN,D21. SN,Ma. SN, B1-6
381a	SN,B7	- SN,B27. SN,Bi. SN,A
b	SN,CtA1	- SN,CtA45
c	SE,He1	- SE,He11. SE,Wel. SE, C. SE,How. SE,Wei1-14
d	SE,Wei5	- SE,Wei7. SE,Sn. SE, Dr. SE,Wa. SE,P. SE, Hu1-6
382a	SE,Hu7	- SE,Hu8. SE,Tu. SE, Bt. SE,Sc. SE,Ac
b	SE,Th1	- SE,Th14. SE,So. SE, Mid. SE,No. SE,Hol-26
c,d	blank	

LINCOLNSHIRE (LIN)

336a	C1	- C11
b	C12	- C21
c	C21	- C33
d	S1	- S16
337a	T1	- T5
b	Landholders	
c	1,1	- 1,7
d	1,8	- 1,15
338a	1,16	- 1,31
b	1.32	- 1,39
c	1,40	- 1,66
d	1,67	- 1,87

339a	1,88	- 1,105
b	1,105	- 1,106
c	2,1	- 2,11
d	2,12	- 2,22
340a	2,23	- 2,35
b	2,35	- 2,42
c	3,1	- 3,11
d	3,12	- 3,26
341a	3,27	- 3,28. 3,30-36
b	3,37	- 3,48. 3,29
c	3,48	- 3,56
d	blank	
342a	4,1	- 4,5. 4,7-11
b	4,11	- 4,25. 4,6
c	4,26	- 4,39
d	4,40	- 4,51
343a	4,51	- 4,63
b	4,63	- 4,75
c	4,75	- 4,81
d	5,1	- 6,1
344a	7,1	- 7,13
b	7,14	- 7,26
c	7,27	- 7,39
d	7,39	- 7,52
345a	7,52	- 7,59
b	blank	
c	8,1	- 8,8
d	8,8	- 8,18
346a	8,18	- 8,32
b	8,33	- 9,2
c	10,1	- 10,4
d	11,1	- 11,9
347a	12,1	- 12,11
b	12,11	- 12,24
c	12,24	- 12,38
d	12,38	- 12,48
348a	12,49	- 12,58
b	12,59	- 12,71
c	12,71	- 12,84
d	12,85	- 12,97
349a	13,1	- 13,9
b	13,9	- 13,21
c	13,22	- 13,33
d	13,34	- 13,45
350a	14,1	- 14,13
b	14,13	- 14,25
c	14,26	- 14,38
d	14,39	- 14,52
351a	14,52	- 14,64
b	14,65	- 14,79
c	14,79	- 14,92
d	14,93	- 15,2

352a	16,1	- 16,14. 16,17
b	16,18	- 16,35. 16,15-16
c	16,36	- 16,50
d	17,1	- 18,6
353a	18,7	- 18,18
b	18,19	- 18,29
c	18,30	- 21,2
d	22,1	- 22,16
354a	22,16	- 22,28. 22,36
b	22,36	- 23,1. 22,29-35
c	24,1	- 24,14. 24,21
d	24,15	- 24,20. 24,22-29
355a	24,30	- 24,44
b	24,45	- 24,62
c	24,62	- 24,77
d	24,77	- 24,90
356a	24,90	- 24,105
b	25,1	- 25,12
c	25,13	- 25,25
d	26,1	- 26,7. 26,9-11. 26,13-15
357a	26,16	- 26,28. 26,8. 26,12
b	26,29	- 26,43
c	26,44	- 26,54
d	27,1	- 27,16
358a	27,17	- 27,32
b	27,33	- 27,44
c	27,45	- 27,57
d	27,58	- 27,64
359a	28,1	- 28,15
b	28,15	- 28,30
c	28,31	- 28,43
d	29,1	- 29,15
360a	29,16	- 29,34
b	30,1	- 30,16
c	30,17	- 30,27
d	30,28	- 30,37
361a	31,1	- 31,10
b	31,11	- 31,18
c	32,1	- 32,4. 32,6-13
d	32,13	- 32,28. 32,5
362a	32,29	- 33,2
b	34,1	- 34,12
c	34,13	- 34,27
d	35,1	- 35,13
363a	35,14	- 36,5
b	37,1	- 37,7
c	38,1	- 38,12
d	38,12	- 39,4

364a	40,1	- 40,15
b	40,15	- 41,2
c	42,1	- 42,15
d	42,15	- 43,6
365a	44,1	- 44,11
b	44,11	- 46,4
c	46,4	- 47,10
d	48,1	- 48,11
366a	48,12	- 50,1
b	51,1	- 51,12
c	52,1	- 55,4
d	56,1	- 56,11
367a	56,11	- 56,23
b	57,1	- 57,14
c	57,14	- 57,26
d	57,27	- 57,40
368a	57,41	- 57,53
b	57,54	- 58,8
c	59,1	- 59,12
d	59,12	- 60,1
369a	61,1	- 62,2
b	63,1	- 63,14
c	63,15	- 63,26. 64,11-14
d	64,1	- 64,10. 64,15
370a	64,15	- 65,5
b	66,1	- 67,11
c	67,11	- 67,27
d	68,1	- 68,15
371a	68,16	- 68,30
b	68,31	- 68,46
c	68,47	- 68,48
d	blank	
372a-d	blank	
(373a-374d Yorkshire)		
375a	CS,1	- CS,15
b	CS,15	- CS,26
c	CS,26	- CS,38
d	CS,38	- CN,13
376a	CN,13	- CN,30
b	CW,1	- CW,13
c	CW,14	- CW,20
d	CK,1	- CK,17
377a	CK,18	- CK,31
b	CK,31	- CK,48
c	CK,48	- CK,64
d	CK,65	- CK,71
378a-d	blank	
(379a-382d Yorkshire)		

III. Key to the relation between the folio notation of the MS. Text of LDB and the Numbered Chapters and Sections of the Present Edition. See section I, above.

ESSEX (ESS)

1a	Landholders			b	18,39	- 18,45
b	1,1	- 1,2		26a	18,45	- 20,2
2a	1,2	- 1,3		b	20,2	- 20,7
b	1,3	- 1,4		27a	20,7	- 20,13
3a	1,4	- 1,8		b	20,13	- 20,19
b	1,9	- 1,11		28a	20,19	- 20,23
4a	1,12	- 1,14		b	20,24	- 20,27
b	1,15	- 1,19		29a	20,28	- 20,34
5a	1,19	- 1,24		b	20,34	- 20,37
b	1,24	- 1,25		30a	20,37	- 20,42
6a	1,25	- 1,27		b	20,43	- 20,46
b	1,27			31a	20,46	- 20,52
7a	1,28	- 1,29		b	20,52	- 20,56
b	1,29	- 1,31		32a	20,56	- 20,62
8a	2,1	- 2,6		b	20,63	- 20,67
b	2,6	- 2,9		33a	20,67	- 20,71
9a	Landholders			b	20,71	- 20,75
b	3,1	- 3,5		34a	20,75	- 20,79
10a	3,6	- 3,9		b	20,79	- 20,80
b	3,9	- 3,13		35a	21,1	- 21,6
11a	3,13	- 4,2		b	21,6	- 21,12
b	4,3	- 4,9		36a	22,1	- 22,5
12a	4,9	- 4,15		b	22,6	- 22,9
b	4,16	- 5,3		37a	22,10	- 22,13
13a	5,3	- 5,8		b	22,13	- 22,18
b5,8	- 5,12			38a	22,19	- 22,24
14a	5,12	- 6,5		b	23,1	- 23,3
b	6,6	- 6,9		39a	23,3	- 23,8
15a	6,9	- 6,15		b	23,8	- 23,16
b	7,1	- 8,1		40a	23,16	- 23,28
16a	8,1	- 8,8		b	23,28	- 23,34
b	8,8	- 8,11		41a	23,34	- 23,40
17a	Landholders			b	23,40	- 23,43
b	9,1	- 9,7		42a	24,1	- 24,5
18a	9,7	- 9,12		b	24,5	- 24,10
b	9,13	- 10,1		43a	24,10	- 24,16
19a	10,2	- 10,5		b	24,17	- 24,20
b	10,5	- 11,3		44a	24,20	- 24,24
20a	11,3	- 11,8		b	24,24	- 24,28
b	12,1	- 14,2		45a	24,28	- 24,33
21a	14,2	- 14,7		b	24,33	- 24,42
b	14,7	- 15,2		46a	24,42	- 24,46
22a	15,2	- 17,2		b	24,46	- 24,53
b	18,1	- 18,5		47a	24,53	- 24,57
23a	18,5	- 18,11		b	24,57	- 24,61
b	18,11	- 18,19		48a	24,61	- 24,66
24a	18,20	- 18,25		b	24,66	- 24,67
b	18,25	- 18,34		49a	25,1	- 25,4
25a	18,34	- 18,38		b	25,4	- 25,10
				50a	25,10	- 25,15
				b	25,15	- 25,19

51a	25,19	- 25,23		79a	36,6	- 36,11
b	25,23	- 25,26		b	36,11	- 37,2
52a	26,1	- 26,4		80a	37,2	- 37,7
b	26,5	- 27,3		b	37,7	- 37,11
53a	27,3	- 27,7		81a	37,11	- 37,17
b	27,8	- 27,13		b	37,17	- 38,1
54a	27,13	- 27,17		82a	38,2	- 38,6
b	27,17	- 28,2		b	38,6	- 39,1
55a	28,3	- 28,8		83a	39,2	- 39,6
b	28,8	- 28,12		b	39,6	- 39,12
56a	28,13	- 28,17		84a	40,1	- 40,4
b	28,17	- 29,2		b	40,4	- 40,9
57a	29,2	- 29,5		85a	40,9	- 41,5
b	30,1	- 30,4		b	41,5	- 41,10
58a	30,4	- 30,7		86a	41,10	- 42,1
b	30,7	- 30,13		b	42,1	- 42,6
59a	30,14	- 30,18		87a	42,7	- 42,9
b	30,18	- 30,22		b	43,1	- 43,5
60a	30,22	- 30,27		88a	43,5	- 44,2
b	30,27	- 30,30		b	44,2	- 45,1
61a	30,30	- 30,34		89a	45,1	- 46,3
b	30,35	- 30,40		b	46,3	- 47,3
62a	30,40	- 30,45		90a	48,1	- 49,1
b	30,45	- 30,49		b	49,1	- 50,1
63a	30,49	- 31,1		91a	51,1	- 52,3
b	32,1	- 32,5		b	52,3	- 54,2
64a	32,6	- 32,9		92a	54,2	- 56,1
b	32,9	- 32,14		b	57,1	- 57,5
65a	32,14	- 32,19		93a	57,5	- 60,2
b	32,19	- 32,23		b	60,2	- 61,2
66a	32,23	- 32,26		94a	61,2	- 64,1
b	32,26	- 32,30		b	64,1	- 66,2
67a	32,30	- 32,36		95a	66,2	- 68,4
b	32,36	- 32,40		b	68,4	- 69,2
68a	32,40	- 32,45		96a	69,3	- 71,3
b	32,45	- 33,2		b	71,4	- 73,1
69a	32,2	- 33,6		97a	73,1	- 77,1
b	33,6	- 33,11		b	77,1	- 81,1
70a	33,11	- 33,13		98a	81,1	- 84,1
b	33,13	- 33,17		b	84,1	- 88,2
71a	33,17	- 33,22		99a	89,1	- 90,4
b	33,22	- 34,2		b	90,5	- 90,14
72a	34,2	- 34,6		100a	90,15	- 90,22
b	34,6	- 34,9		b	90,23	- 90,34
73a	34,9	- 34,13		101a	90,35	- 90,44
b	34,14	- 34,19		b	90,45	- 90,53
74a	34,19	- 34,22		102a	90,53	- 90,63
b	34,22	- 34,27		b	90,64	- 90,73
75a	34,27	- 34,32		103a	90,74	- 90,83
b	34,32	- 34,36		b	90,84	- 90,87
76a	34,36	- 35,2		104a	B1	- B3a
b	35,2	- 35,5		b	B3a	
77a	35,5	- 35,8		105a	B3a	
b	35,9	- 35,12		b	B3a	
78a	35,13	- 36,2		106a	B3a	- B3d
b	36,2	- 36,6		b	B3d	- B3p

107a	B3p	- B6
b	B6	- B7
108a	blank	
b	blank	

NORFOLK (NFK)

109a	Landholders	
b	1,1	- 1,2
110a	1,2	- 1,6
b	1,6	- 1,11
111a	1,11	- 1,16
b	1,16	- 1,19
112a	1,19	- 1,26
b	1,26	- 1,32
113a	1,32	- 1,41
b	1,41	- 1,48
114a	1,48	- 1,52
b	1,52	- 1,57
115a	1,57	
b	1,57	- 1,59
116a	1,59	- 1,61
b	1,61	
117a	1,61	
b	1,61	- 1,64
118a	1,65	- 1,67
b	1,67	- 1,70
119a	1,70	
b	1,71	
120a	1,71	- 1,76
b	1,76	- 1,78
121a	1,78	- 1,82
b	1,82	- 1,86
122a	1,87	- 1,89
b	1,89	- 1,94
123a	1,94	- 1,99
b	1,99	- 1,106
124a	1,106	- 1,116
b	1,116	- 1,122
125a	1,122	- 1,128
b	1,128	- 1,132
126a	1,132	- 1,136
b	1,136	- 1,139
127a	1,139	- 1,143
b	1.143	- 1,146
128a	1,146	- 1,150
b	1,150	- 1,152
129a	1,152	- 1,159
b	1,159	- 1,169
130a	1,169	- 1,176
b	1,176	- 1,182
131a	1,182	- 1,185
b	1,185	- 1,188
132a	1,189	- 1,192
b	1,192	- 1,194
133a	1,194	- 1,196
b	1,196	- 1,198
134a	1,198	- 1,201
b	1,201	- 1,203
135a	1,203	- 1,206
b	1,206	- 1,209
136a	1,209	- 1,210
b	1,210	- 1,212
137a	1,212	- 1,214
b	1,215	- 1,216
138a	1,216	- 1,218
b	1,218	- 1,221
139a	1,221	- 1,226
b	1,226	- 1,228
140a	1,228	- 1,231
b	1,231	- 1,236
141a	1,237	- 1,239
b	1,239	- 1,241
142a	2,1	- 2,4
b	2,4	
143a	2,5	- 2,8
b	2,8	- 3,1
144a	3,1	- 4,2
b	4,2	- 4,9
145a	4,9	- 4,11
b	4,11	- 4,17
146a	4,17	- 4,22
b	4,22	- 4,27
147a	4,28	- 4,31
b	4,31	- 4,34
148a	4,35	- 4,39
b	4,39	- 4,41
149a	4,41	- 4,45
b	4,45	- 4,50
150a	4,50	- 4,53
b	4,53	- 4,56
151a	4,56	- 5,2
b	5.2	- 5,6
152a	5,6	- 6,3
b	6,3	- 6,6
153a	6,6	- 6,7
b	7,1	- 7,3
154a	7,3	- 7,8
b	7,8	- 7,13
155a	7,13	- 7,16
b	7,16	- 7,18
156a	7,18	- 7,21
b	blank	
157a	8,1	- 8,2
b	8,3	- 8,7
158a	8,7	- 8,8
b	8,8	- 8,11
159a	8,11	- 8,13
b	8,14	- 8,17
160a	8,17	- 8,21
b	8,21	- 8,25
161a	8,25	- 8,29

b	17,18	- 17,24	b	29,1	- 29,5
218a	17,24	- 17,31	246a	29,5	- 29,8
b	17,32	- 17,38	b	29,8	- 29,11
219a	17,38	- 17,43	247a	30,1	- 30,4
b	17,44	- 17,52	b	30,4	- 31,1
220a	17,52	- 17,55	248a	31,2	- 31,5
b	17,56	- 17,62	b	31,5	- 31,6
221a	17,62	- 17,65	249a	31,6	- 31,10
b	18,1	- 19,2	b	31,10	- 31,15
222a	19,3	- 19,9	250a	31,15	- 31,17
b	19,9	- 19,11	b	31,17	- 31,22
223a	19,11	- 19,15	251a	31,22	- 31,28
b	19,16	- 19,21	b	31,28	- 31,33
224a	19,21	- 19,25	252a	31,34	- 31,37
b	19,26	- 19,32	b	31,38	- 31,41
225a	19,32	- 19,36	253a	31,41	- 31,44
b	19,36	- 20,1	b	31,44	- 31,45
226a	20,1	- 20,6	254a	32,1	- 32,3
b	20,6	- 20,8	b	32,3	- 32,7
227a	20,8	- 20,10	255a	32,7	- 33,2
b	20,10	- 20,14	b	33,2	- 33,6
228a	20,14	- 20,19	256a	34,1	- 34,3
b	20,19	- 20,24	b	34,3	- 34,6
229a	20,24	- 20,29	257a	34,6	- 34,9
b	20,29	- 20,34	b	34,9	- 34,15
230a	20,35	- 21,2	258a	34,15	- 34,19
b	21,2	- 21,5	b	34,20	- 35,3
231a	21,5	- 21,8	259a	35,3	- 35,8
b	21,8	- 21,13	b	35,8	- 35,13
232a	21,13	- 21,16	260a	35,13	- 35,18
b	21,17	- 21,21	b	35,18	- 36,5
233a	21,22	- 21,25	261a	36,5	- 36,7
b	21,25	- 21,28	b	37,1	- 37,3
234a	21,28	- 21,32	262a	38,1	- 39,1
b	21,32	- 21,37	b	39,1	- 40,1
235a	22,1	- 22,6	263a	41,1	- 43,2
b	22,6	- 22,13	b	43,2	- 45,1
236a	22,13	- 22,21	264a	46,1	- 47,6
b	22,21	- 22,23	b	47,6	- 48,3
237a	23,1	- 23,4	265a	48,3	- 48,8
b	23,4	- 23,8	b	49,1	- 49,5
238a	23,8	- 23,12	266a	49,5	- 49,9
b	23,12	- 23,16	b	50,1	- 50,5
239a	23,16	- 23,18	267a	50,6	- 50,10
b	24,1	- 24,5	b	50,10	- 51,3
240a	24,5	- 24,7	268a	51,3	- 51,8
b	24,7	- 25,1	b	51,8	- 52,3
241a	25,2	- 25,7	269a	52,3	- 54,1
b	25,7	- 25,12	b	54,1	- 56,2
242a	25,12	- 25,17	270a	56,3	- 57,3
b	25,17	- 25,25	b	58,1	- 59,1
243a	25,25	- 26,1	271a	59,1	- 61,1
b	26,1	- 26,3	b	61,1	- 62,2
244a	26,3	- 26,5	272a	62,2	- 64,4
b	26,5	- 27,2	b	64,5	- 65,7
245a	27,2	- 28,2	273a	65,8	- 65,16

328a	6,301	- 6,304		356a	13,3	- 13,7
b	6,305	- 6,308		b	14,1	- 14,3
329a	6,308	- 6,311		357a	14,3	- 14,7
b	6,311	- 6,317		b	14,8	- 14,12
330a	6,317	- 6,319		358a	14,12	- 14,16
b	7,1	- 7,3		b	14,16	- 14,20
331a	7,3	- 7,6		359a	14,21	- 14,24
b	7,6	- 7,10		b	14,24	- 14,28
332a	7,10	- 7,15		360a	14,28	- 14,36
b	7,15			b	14,36	- 14,42
333a	7,16	- 7,20		361a	14,42	- 14,47
b	7,20	- 7,26		b	14,48	- 14,50
334a	7,26	- 7,33		362a	14,50	- 14,53
b	7,33	- 7,37		b	14,53	- 14,59
335a	7,37	- 7,42		363a	14,59	- 14,64
b	7,42	- 7,49		b	14,64	- 14,68
336a	7,49	- 7,56		364a	14,69	- 14,72
b	7,56	- 7,58		b	14,72	- 14,75
337a	7,58	- 7,61		365a	14,75	- 14,77
b	7,61	- 7,65		b	14,78	- 14,81
338a	7,65	- 7,68		366a	14,81	- 14,85
b	7,68	- 7,72		b	14,85	- 14,90
339a	7,72	- 7,75		367a	14,90	- 14,95
b	7,76	- 7,79		b	14,96	- 14,101
340a	7,79	- 7,85		368a	14,102	- 14,106
b	7,85	- 7,92		b	14,106	- 14,110
341a	7,92	- 7,98		369a	14,111	- 14,115
b	7,98	- 7,105		b	14,115	- 14,120
342a	7,105	- 7,111		370a	14,120	- 14,128
b	7,111	- 7,119		b	14,129	- 14,138
343a	7,119	- 7,122		371a	14,138	- 14,153
b	7,122	- 7,133		b	14,154	- 14,166
344a	7,133	- 7,138		372a	14,167. Landholders	
b	7,138	- 7,143		b	15,1	- 15,4
345a	7,143	- 7,148		373a	15,5	- 16,3
b	7,149	- 7,151		b	16,4	- 16,10
346a	8,1	- 8,6		374a	16,10	- 16,14
b	8,6	- 8,9		b	16,14	- 16,17
347a	8,9	- 8,14		375a	16,17	- 16,20
b	8,14	- 8,23		b	16,21	- 16,25
348a	8,23	- 8,32		376a	16,25	- 16,27
b	8,32	- 8,35		b	16,28	- 16,31
349a	8,35	- 8,42		377a	16,32	- 16,35
b	8,42	- 8,46		b	16,36	- 16,40
350a	8,46	- 8,49		378a	16,40	- 16,45
b	8,49	- 8,55		b	16,45	- 17,1
351a	8,55	- 8,56		379a	18,1	- 18,5
b	8,56	- 8,59		b	18,6	- 19,10
352a	8,59	- 8,66		380a	19,11	- 19,16
b	8,66	- 8,78		b	19,16	- 19,18
353a	8,78	- 9,1		381a	19,18	- 20,1
b	9,1	- 9,3		b	21,1	- 21,5
354a	9,3	- 11,2		382a	21,5	- 21,11
b	11,2	- 12,1		b	21,11	- 21,16
355a	12,1	- 12,6		383a	21,16	- 21,25
b	12,6	- 13,3		b	21,25	- 21,29

List of Subscribers

R. V. W. Allsworth
H. F. Austin
Capt. Walter T. Barclay
C. S. Barling
G. R. R. Benwell
John H. Bettinson
John J. Bowater
Harold Lloyd Broadbent
R. Butterfield
F. H. Carter
R. E. Childs
Hugh K. Clark
M. Couchman
Prof. C. R. Dodwell
Ian Downing
Michael A. Faraday
Frederick N. Filby
M. J. Funnell
Michael R. Hickman

Edward Ward Hind
J. R. Horth
Dr. P. Letourmy
O. H. Lucas
D. G. Lynall
D. A. & D. J. Mason
Harley F. Millett
John H. C. Nicholson
Dr. J. A. C. Rouse
John Francis Millar Scholes
Christine Shaw
Dr. and Mrs. A. J. Smith
J. Courtenay Staples
C. L. O. Streeton
B. L. Tee
R. M. Thomas
C. Loring Waldron
M. J. Whitmarsh-Everiss
Douglas Wilson

Society of Australian Genealogists
Bedfordshire County Library
The Queen's University of Belfast
Bermuda Library
Birmingham City Libraries
British Broadcasting Company
British Museum, Dept. of Coins and Medals
Buckinghamshire County Library
London Borough of Camden Public Libraries
Christ Church Library, Oxford
Cleveland County Libraries
Dallas Public Library
Doncaster Central Library
University College Dublin Library
East Sussex County Library
Essex County Library
Fort Wayne and Allen County Public Library
The Society of Genealogists Library
Hampshire County Library
The House of Commons Library
The House of Lords Library
Houston Public Library
Humberside Central Library
States of Jersey Library Service
Keele University Library
Lambeth Reference Library

Lancashire County Library
City of Leeds
Leicester University Library
The London Library
University of London Library
University of New Orleans Library
Newberry Library, Illinois
Norfolk County Library
North Yorkshire County Library
Old Dominion University Library
Ordnance Survey Library
University of Regina Library
The Royal Library, Copenhagen
St Andrew's University Library
St Anne's College, Oxford
Salt Lake City Genealogical Library
Santa Maria Public Library
Sheffield City Libraries
Sheffield University Library
South Glamorgan County Library
Staffordshire County Library
Standard Chartered Bank Ltd.
State Library of South Australia
Toronto Central Library
Washington Memorial Library
University of York Library